Lecture Notes in Computer Science 1247

Edited by G. Goos, J. Hartmanis and J. van Leeuwen

Advisory Board: W. Brauer   D. Gries   J. Stoer

Springer

Berlin
Heidelberg
New York
Barcelona
Budapest
Hong Kong
London
Milan
Paris
Santa Clara
Singapore
Tokyo

John Barnes (Ed.)

Ada 95
Rationale

The Language
The Standard Libraries

 Springer

Series Editors

Gerhard Goos, Karlsruhe University, Germany

Juris Hartmanis, Cornell University, NY, USA

Jan van Leeuwen, Utrecht University, The Netherlands

Volume Editor

John Barnes
John Barnes Informatics
11 Albert Road, Caversham, Reading RG4 7AN, UK
E-mail: jgpb@jbinfo.demon.co.uk

Cataloging-in-Publication data applied for

Die Deutsche Bibliothek - CIP-Einheitsaufnahme

Ada 95 rationale : the language, the standard libraries / John Barnes
(ed.). - Berlin ; Heidelberg ; New York ; Barcelona ; Budapest ; Hong
Kong ; London ; Milan ; Paris ; Santa Clara ; Singapore ; Tokyo :
Springer, 1997
    (Lecture notes in computer science ; Vol. 1247)
    ISBN 3-540-63143-7

CR Subject Classification (1991): D.1-3

ISSN 0302-9743
ISBN 3-540-63143-7 Springer-Verlag Berlin Heidelberg New York

Printed in Germany

Typesetting: Camera-ready by editor
SPIN 10550316   06/3142 – 5 4 3 2 1 0   Printed on acid-free paper

Ada 95
Rationale

The Language

The Standard Libraries

January 1995

Intermetrics, Inc.
733 Concord Ave.
Cambridge, Massachusetts 02138
(617) 661-1840

Foreword

I am delighted to write these words of introduction to this important document which accompanies the new Ada International Standard. It is most satisfying to see the efforts of all those involved with the language revision effort bearing fruit, and I am very confident that Ada 95 will prove to be a worthy successor to Ada 83, extending Ada's Software Engineering advantages to new user communities. With modern features such as Object-Oriented Programming and enhanced interfacing capabilities, Ada 95 will enable the flexible and reliable development of major applications in the coming years.

The new standard, officially ISO/IEC 8652:1995, thus marks an important milestone in Ada's history. Enormous contributions from some of the world's finest software engineers and programming language experts have gone into the revision effort, reflecting both current and anticipated user requirements. I would therefore like to take this opportunity to acknowledge the sterling efforts of all those involved in developing the new standard and in writing this rationale document.

The Ada 95 language revision was prepared by the Ada 9X Design Team based at Intermetrics, Inc., under the direction of William Carlson, Program Manager, and S. Tucker Taft, Technical Director. The Intermetrics team included Robert Duff (Oak Tree Software) and also consultants John Barnes, Ben Brosgol, and Offer Pazy.

A team led by John Goodenough (SEI) prepared the technical requirements specification for the Ada revision, based on preliminary work by the Institute for Defense Analyses under Audrey Hook to analyze the more than 750 revision requests submitted by the Ada community.

The following consultants to the Ada 9X Project contributed to the Specialized Needs Annexes: Ted Baker (SEI, Florida State Univ.), Ken Dritz (Argonne National Laboratory), Anthony Gargaro (Computer Sciences Corp.), John Goodenough (SEI), John McHugh (consultant), and Brian Wichmann (NPL: UK).

This work was regularly reviewed by the Ada 9X Distinguished Reviewers and the members of the ISO Ada 9X Rapporteur Group (XRG): Erhard Ploedereder, Chairman of DRs and XRG (University of Stuttgart: Germany); B. Bardin (Hughes); J. Barnes (consultant: UK); B. Brett (DEC); B. Brosgol (consultant); R. Brukardt (RR Software); N. Cohen (IBM); R. Dewar (NYU); G. Dismukes (Alsys [Telesoft]); A. Evans (consultant); A. Gargaro (Computer Sciences Corp.); M. Gerhardt (ESL); J. Goodenough (SEI); S. Heilbrunner (University of Salzburg: Austria); P. Hilfinger (UC/Berkeley); B. Källberg (CelsiusTech: Sweden); M. Kamrad II (Unisys); J. van Katwijk (Delft University of Technology: The Netherlands); V. Kaufman (Russia); P. Kruchten (Rational); R. Landwehr (CCI: Germany); C. Lester (Portsmouth Polytechnic: UK); L. Månsson (TELIA Research: Sweden); S. Michell (Multiprocessor Toolsmiths: Canada); M. Mills (US Air Force); D. Pogge (US Navy); K. Power (Boeing); O. Roubine (Verdix: France); A. Strohmeier (Swiss Federal Institute of Technology: Switzerland); W. Taylor (consultant: UK); J. Tokar (Tartan); E. Vasilescu (Grumman); J. Vladik (Prospeks s.r.o.: Czech Republic); S. Van Vlierberghe (OFFIS: Belgium).

Early contributors on the Ada 9X Design Team were C. Garrity, R. Hilliard, D. Rosenfeld, L. Shafer, W. White, and M. Woodger. Other valuable feedback influencing the revision process was provided by the Ada 9X Language Precision Team (Odyssey Research Associates), the Ada 9X User/Implementer Teams (AETECH, Tartan, Alsys [Telesoft]), the Ada 9X Implementation Analysis Team (New York University), and the Volunteer Reviewers group under Art Evans (consultant).

The principal authors of this rationale document were John Barnes and Ben Brosgol with valuable contributions from Ken Dritz, Offer Pazy and Brian Wichmann. Many thanks also to

Bill Taylor for providing the material upon which Appendix X is based, and to Tucker Taft and Robert Duff for their comments and review.

Very special thanks go to Virginia Castor, John Solomond and Don Reifer from the Ada Joint Program Office for supporting and sponsoring the Ada 9X Project since its inception, and to Bob Mathis, Convenor of ISO/IEC JTC1/SC22 Working Group 9, for shepherding the revision through the standardization process.

Last but not least, I want to extend my sincerest appreciation to the Ada community at large who have volunteered their time and energy on this project. Without your support we would not have been able to succeed.

Ada 95 is here. It is now up to the users, both those who have appreciated the engineering benefits of Ada 83 and others who may be frustrated with the hazards of their current techniques, to move forward and reap the benefits of this new language.

Christine M. Anderson,
Ada 9X Project Manager

Preface

Modern society is becoming very dependent upon software. Our transport systems, financial systems, medical systems and defense systems all depend to a very large degree upon software. As a consequence the safety of many human lives and much property now depends upon the reliable functioning of software. Moreover, the fall in the cost of hardware has now made possible the development of large software systems.

Ada is a programming language of special value in the development of large programs which must work reliably. This applies to most defense applications (from which background Ada evolved) and extends to many application domains. Indeed over half the Ada programs now being developed are for non-defense applications.

This document describes the rationale for Ada 95, the revised International Standard. Ada 95 increases the flexibility of Ada thus making it applicable to wider domains but retains the inherent reliability for which Ada has become noted. Important aspects of Ada 95 include

- Object Oriented Programming. Ada 95 includes full OOP facilities giving the flexibility of programming by extension which enables programs to be extended and maintained at lower cost.

- Hierarchical Libraries. The library mechanism now takes a hierarchical form which is valuable for the control and decomposition of large programs.

- Protected Objects. The tasking features of Ada are enhanced to incorporate a very efficient mechanism for multitask synchronized access to shared data. This is of special value for hard realtime systems.

These enhancements to Ada make Ada 95 an outstanding language. It adds the flexibility of languages such as C++ to the reliable Software Engineering framework provided and proven by Ada 83 over the past ten years.

Ada 95 is a natural evolution of Ada 83. The enhancements have been made without disturbing the existing investment in Ada 83 programs and programmers. Upward compatibility has been a prime goal and has been achieved within the constraints imposed by other requirements.

This document is in several parts. The first part is an Introduction to Ada 95; it presents a general discussion of the scope and objectives of Ada 95 and its major technical features. The second part contains a more detailed chapter by chapter account of the Core language. The third part covers the various Annexes which address the predefined environment and the needs of specialized application areas. Finally there are three appendices; Appendix X addresses the issue of upward compatibility with Ada 83 and shows that for normal programs the goal of compatibility has been achieved; Appendix Y summarizes the few changes since the two public drafts of the standard; Appendix Z summarizes the requirements and concludes that they have been met. This document will be of special value to program managers, team leaders and all software professionals with concern for the organized development of software.

Ada 95 deserves the attention of all members of the computing profession. It is a coherent and reliable foundation vehicle for developing the major applications of the next decade.

The Ada 9X Design Team,
January 1995

Contents

Part One   Introduction

Part Two   The Core Language

Part Three   The Annexes

Part Four Appendices

Part One

Introduction to Ada 95

This first part is designed to give the reader a general appreciation of the overall scope and objectives of Ada 95 and its main technical features. The opening chapter describes the background to the development of the requirements leading to the new standard. The two main chapters give a technical view of the language from two different standpoints: one highlights the main new features such as type extension, the hierarchical library and the protected type and contains many illustrative examples; the other gives a complete overview of the whole language. The reader is recommended to read this first part before attempting to read the Ada 95 Reference Manual.

I Evolution of Ada 95

Ada is a modern programming language suitable for those application areas which benefit from the discipline of organized development, that is, *Software Engineering*; it is a general purpose language with special applicability to real-time and embedded systems. Ada was originally developed by an international design team in response to requirements issued by the United States Department of Defense [DoD 78].

Ada 95 is a revised version of Ada updating the 1983 ANSI Ada standard [ANSI 83] and the equivalent 1987 ISO standard [ISO 87] in accordance with ANSI and ISO procedures. (ANSI is the American National Standards Institute and ISO is the International Standards Organization.) This present document describes the overall Rationale for the revision and includes tutorial information for the new features.

I.1 The Revision Process

Although Ada was originally designed to provide a single flexible yet portable language for real-time embedded systems to meet the needs of the US DoD, its domain of application has expanded to include many other areas, such as large-scale information systems, distributed systems, scientific computation, and systems programming. Furthermore, its user base has expanded to include all major defense agencies of the Western world, the whole of the aerospace community and increasingly many areas in civil and private sectors such as telecommunications, process control and monitoring systems. Indeed, the expansion in the civil sector is such that civil applications now generate the dominant revenues of many vendors.

After some years of use and many implementations, a decision was made in 1988 to undertake a revision to Ada, leading to an updated ANSI/ISO standard. It is normal practice to automatically reconsider such standards every 5 or 10 years and to determine whether they should be abandoned, reaffirmed as they are, or updated. In the case of Ada, an update was deemed appropriate.

To understand the process it should be explained that ANSI, as the US national standards body, originally proposed that Ada become an ISO standard. It is normal practice that ANSI, as the originating body, should sponsor a revised standard as necessary. The US DoD acted as the agent of ANSI in managing the development of the revised standard. Within the US DoD, the Ada Joint Program Office (AJPO) is responsible for Ada and the Ada Board is a federal advisory committee which advises the AJPO.

The revision effort began in January 1988 when the Ada Board was asked to prepare a recommendation to the AJPO on the most appropriate standardization process to use in developing a revised Ada standard, known in the interim as Ada 9X. The recommendation [DoD 88] was delivered in September 1988 to Virginia Castor, the then Director of the Ada Joint Program Office, who subsequently established the Ada 9X Project for conducting the revision of the Ada Standard. Christine M Anderson was appointed Project Manager in October 1988. Close consultation with ISO was important to ensure that the needs of the whole world-wide Ada community (and not just the defense community) were taken into account and to ensure the timely adoption by ISO of the new standard. Accordingly a Memorandum of Understanding was established between the US DoD and ISO [ISO 90].

The Ada 9X program consists of three main phases: the determination of the Requirements for the revised language; the actual Development of the definition of the revised language; and the Transition into use from Ada 83 to Ada 9X.

The output of the Requirements Definition phase was the Ada 9X Requirements document [DoD 90], which specified the revision needs which had to be addressed. The Mapping/Revision phase defined the changes to the standard to meet those requirements; it achieved this in practice of course by defining the new standard.

The scope of the changes was guided by the overall objective of the Ada 9X effort [DoD 89a]:

> *Revise ANSI/MIL-STD-1815A-1983 to reflect current essential requirements with minimum negative impact and maximum positive impact to the Ada community.*

It is probably fair to observe that the changes which were deemed necessary are somewhat greater than might have been foreseen when the project first started in 1988. However, technology and man's understanding do not stand still and the changes now incorporated are very appropriate to the foreseen needs of a modern language for Software Engineering into the 21st Century.

I.2 The Requirements

The development of the requirements was a somewhat iterative process with a number of sub-phases. First, the community of users was invited to submit Revision Requests, secondly, these were sorted and analyzed in order to determine what was really implied by the requests, and finally, a coherent set of requirements was written.

Establishing the level of the requirements needed care. Quite naturally an individual user would often perceive a need in a manner which reflected a symptom of an underlying problem rather than the problem itself. It was very important that the requirements reflected the essence of the problem rather than what might in effect be simply one user's suggested solution to a part of a problem. One reason for this concern was to ensure that better, perhaps deeper and simpler, changes were not excluded by shallow requirements.

In some cases a complete understanding of a requirement could not be established and this led to the introduction of Study Topics. As its name implies a Study Topic described an area where something ought to be done but for some reason the feasibility of a solution was in doubt; perhaps the needs were changing rapidly or there were conflicting needs or implementing technology was unstable or it was simply that we had an incomplete understanding of some basic principles.

The general goal of the revision was thus to satisfy all of the Requirements and to satisfy as many and as much of the Study Topics as possible. Any unsatisfied Study Topics would be set aside for further consideration for a future Ada 0X (that is the next revision due perhaps around 2005).

The requirements document described 41 Requirements and 22 Study Topics. These were divided into a number of chapters which themselves form two broad groups. The first group covered topics of widespread applicability, whereas the second group addressed more specialized topics.

The first group consisted of the need to support International Character Sets (originally identified by several nations in the 1987 ISO standardization process), support for Programming Paradigms (Object Orientation was included in this category), Real-Time requirements, requirements for System Programming (such as Unsigned Integers), and General requirements. This last topic included specific matters such as error detection and general considerations of efficiency, simplicity and consistency; examples of a number of individually minor but irritating aspects of Ada 83 which fall into this category were given in an appendix.

The second, specialized, group consisted of requirements for Parallel Processing, Distributed Processing, Safety-Critical Applications, Information Systems, and Scientific and Mathematical Applications.

The breadth of these specialized requirements raised the specter of a language embracing so many application areas that it would become too costly to implement in its entirety for every architecture. On the other hand, one of the strengths of Ada is its uniformity and the last thing desired was a plethora of uncontrolled subsets. Accordingly, the Requirements document recommended the concept of a Core language plus a small number of Specialized Needs Annexes as a sensible way forward (with emphasis on keeping the number of such annexes very small). All validated compilers would have to implement the Core language and vendors could choose to implement zero, one or more annexes according to the needs of their selected market places.

The Requirements document also included general guidance on the approach to be taken to avoid unnecessary disruption to the Ada community. This covered vital matters such as the ease of implementation, object code efficiency, keeping a balance between change and need, and upward compatibility. It finally stressed that support for reliability, safety and long-term maintainability should continue to take precedence over short-term coding convenience.

Of all these requirements there was strong emphasis on the overriding goal of upward compatibility in order to preserve existing investment by the Ada community as a whole.

I.3 The Main User Needs

The Requirements reflected a number of underlying User Needs which had become apparent over the years since Ada was first defined. Apart from a small number of very specific matters such as the character set issue, the specialized areas and generally tidying up minor inconsistencies, four main areas stood out as needing attention:

- Interfacing. Ada 83 recognizes the importance of being able to interface to external systems by the provision of features such as representation clauses and pragmas. Nevertheless, it was sometimes not easy to interface certain Ada 83 programs to other language systems. A general need was felt for a more flexible approach allowing, for instance, the secure manipulation of references and the passing of procedures as parameters. An example arises when interfacing into GUI's where it is often necessary to pass a procedure as a parameter for call-back.

- Programming by Extension. This is closely allied to reusability. Although Ada's package and generic capability are an excellent foundation, nevertheless experience with the OO paradigm in other languages had shown the advantages of being able to extend a program without any modification to existing proven components. Not only does this save disturbing existing software thus eliminating the risk of introducing errors but it also reduces recompilation costs.

- Program Libraries. The Ada program library brings important benefits by extending the strong typing across the boundaries between separately compiled units. However, the flat nature of the Ada 83 library gave problems of visibility control; for example, it prevented two library packages from sharing a full view of a private type. A common consequence of the flat structure was that packages become large and monolithic. This hindered understanding and increased the cost of recompilation. A more flexible and hierarchical structure was necessary.

- Tasking. The Ada rendezvous paradigm is a useful model for the abstract description of many tasking problems. But experience had shown that a more static monitor-like approach was also desirable for common shared-data access applications. Furthermore, the Ada priority model needed revision in order to enable users to take advantage of the greater understanding of scheduling theory which had emerged since Ada 83 was defined.

The main changes incorporated into Ada 95 reflect the response to the Requirements in meeting these four key needs while at the same time meeting an overriding need for upward compatibility in order to minimize the effort and cost of transition.

I.4 The Approach

In responding to the revision requirements, the Revision team followed the inspiration of Jean Ichbiah (who led the original design team), both in remaining faithful to the principles underlying the original Ada design, and in the approach to the revision process. To quote Dr Ichbiah in his introduction to John Barnes' textbook on Ada [Barnes 82]:

> *Clearly, further progress can only come by a reappraisal of implicit assumptions underlying certain compromises. Here is the major contradiction in any design work. On the one hand, one can only reach an harmonious integration of several features by immersing oneself into the logic of the existing parts; it is only in this way that one can achieve a perfect combination. On the other hand, this perception of perfection, and the implied acceptance of certain unconscious assumptions, will prevent further progress.*

Wherever possible, enhanced functionality in Ada 95 has been achieved by seeking and eliminating such unnecessary assumptions, thereby permitting the generalization of features already in Ada, and the removal of special cases and restrictions. A careful analysis was made of Ada 83, of language study notes prepared during the original design process and of the many Ada Issues and other comments that have since been received. Based on this analysis, and on the Ada community's experience in implementing and using Ada during the past ten years, the team identified limitations that, while they were included to simplify implementations and/or to lower risk when the language was first standardized, are no longer necessary. They also drew upon the wealth of practical experience gained during the 1980's in the use of object-oriented design methods, object-oriented programming languages, and real-time programming made possible by Ada.

The resulting Ada 95 revision is upwardly compatible for virtually all existing Ada 83 applications. Most incompatibilities are restricted to pathological combinations of features that are rarely used in practice. Total upward compatibility would not have allowed the correction of certain errors and certainly would not have allowed the enhancements needed to satisfy many of the requirements. Indeed, as discussed in Appendix A in more detail, no language revision has ever achieved total upward compatibility. The careful attention to this issue in the design of Ada 95 means that the expected transition costs for existing Ada programs are anticipated to be very low indeed.

Following the guidance of the Requirements document, Ada 95 comprises a Core language, which must be implemented in its entirety, plus several Specialized Needs Annexes which provide extended features for specific application areas. These Annexes provide standard definitions for application-specific packages, pragmas, attributes, and capacity and performance characteristics of implementations. The Annexes address the following areas: Systems Programming, Real-Time Systems, Distributed Systems, Information Systems, Numerics, and Safety and Security.

It should be noted that the Core language includes a considerably extended predefined environment covering important functionality such as mathematical functions and string handling. Much of the functionality of this predefined environment and the specialized annexes is already provided by implementations of Ada 83 but in non-standard ways; providing this within the standard will thus increase portability between implementations.

I.5 Using this Document

This document provides a description of the main features of Ada 95 and the rationale for the changes from Ada 83. It follows the inspiration of the rationale for Ada 83 [IBFW 86] by blending exposition with explanation.

It is in four parts, this first part is designed to give the reader a general appreciation for the scope and objectives of Ada 95 and its major features. Chapter II highlights the main changes — primarily the four key areas outlined in I.3. The intent is to provide a technically oriented management overview illustrating, with examples, the prime benefits of Ada 95 with respect to Ada 83. By contrast, Chapter III provides an overview of the whole language in a discursive style and introduces new terminology where appropriate.

The second and third parts take the discussion a step further. The second part covers the Core language per se; it addresses those important features not discussed in this first part and gives more detail of the rationale including alternatives that were considered and rejected. The third part similarly addresses the predefined environment and the various Specialized Needs Annexes.

Finally the fourth part contains three appendices. Appendix X summarizes the incompatibilities thereby giving guidance to existing Ada 83 programmers in order to smooth their transition to Ada 95. Appendix Y summarizes the main differences between the final International Standard (which this edition of the rationale describes) and the previous two drafts, the Draft International Standard [DIS 94] and the Committee Draft [CD 93]. Appendix Z summarizes the original requirements and briefly analyzes how they have been met by Ada 95.

It is generally assumed that the reader is familiar with Ada 83. This first part should be read before approaching the Ada 95 Reference Manual [RM95] which should then be read in parallel with Parts Two and Three. It should also be noted that the general intent of all parts of this document is to address the broad picture. The rationale for minute detail is admirably addressed in the Annotated Ada 95 Reference Manual [AARM] which is a version of [RM95] including embedded non-normative discussion mainly of interest to language experts and compiler writers.

The chapters in this first part have Roman numbers; the chapters in Parts Two and Three have numbers and letters essentially corresponding to the sections and annexes of [RM 95]. The appendices in Part Four are called X, Y and Z to avoid confusion with the annex chapters. All chapters thus have a unique identifier for ease of cross reference.

II Highlights of Ada 95

The brightest highlights of Ada 95 are its inherent reliability and its ability to provide abstraction through the package and private type. These features already exist in Ada 83 and so in a real sense Ada 83 already contains the best of Ada 95. Indeed, Ada 83 is already a very good language. However, time and technology do not stand still, and Ada 95 is designed to meet increased requirements which have arisen from three directions. These are: feedback from the use of existing paradigms; additional market requirements to match evolving hardware capability; and increased fundamental understanding which has introduced new paradigms. As we will see, Ada 95 follows on from the tradition of excellence of Ada 83 and meets these additional requirements in an outstanding manner.

One of the great strengths of Ada 83 is its reliability. The strong typing and related features ensure that programs contain few surprises; most errors are detected at compile time and of those remaining many are detected by runtime constraints. This aspect of Ada considerably reduces the costs and risks of program development compared for example with C or its derivatives such as C++.

However, Ada 83 has proved to be somewhat less flexible than might be desired in some circumstances. For example, it has not always proved straightforward to interface to non-Ada systems. Moreover, the type model coupled with the flat library mechanism can cause significant costs through the need for apparently unnecessary recompilation.

A prime goal of the design of Ada 95 has thus been to give the language a more open and extensible feel without losing the inherent integrity and efficiency of Ada 83. That is to keep the Software Engineering but allow more flexibility.

The additions in Ada 95 which contribute to this more flexible feel are type extension, the hierarchical library and the greater ability to manipulate pointers or references.

As a consequence, Ada 95 incorporates the benefits of Object Oriented languages without incurring the pervasive overheads of languages such as SmallTalk or the insecurity brought by the weak C foundation in the case of C++. Ada 95 remains a very strongly typed language but provides the prime benefits of all key aspects of the Object Oriented paradigm.

Another area of major change in Ada 95 is in the tasking model where the introduction of protected types allows a more efficient implementation of standard problems of shared data access. This brings the benefits of speed provided by low-level primitives such as semaphores without the risks incurred by the use of such unstructured primitives. Moreover, the clearly data-oriented view brought by the protected types fits in naturally with the general spirit of the Object Oriented paradigm.

Other improvements to the tasking model allow a more flexible response to interrupts and other changes of state.

Ada 95 also incorporates numerous other minor changes reflecting feedback from the use of existing features as well as specific new features addressing the needs of specialized applications and communities.

This chapter highlights the major new features of Ada 95 and the consequential benefits as seen by the general Ada user.

II.1 Programming by Extension

The key idea of programming by extension is the ability to declare a new type that refines an existing parent type by inheriting, modifying or adding to both the existing components and the operations of the parent type. A major goal is the reuse of existing reliable software without the need for recompilation and retesting.

Type extension in Ada 95 builds upon the existing Ada 83 concept of a derived type. In Ada 83, a derived type inherited the operations of its parent and could add new operations; however, it was not possible to add new components to the type. The whole mechanism was thus somewhat static. By contrast, in Ada 95 a derived type can also be extended to add new components. As we will see, the mechanism is much more dynamic and allows greater flexibility through late binding and polymorphism.

In Ada 95, record types may be extended on derivation provided that they are marked as tagged. Private types implemented as record types can also be marked as tagged. As the name implies, a tagged type has an associated tag. The word *tag* is familiar from Pascal where it is used to denote what in Ada is known as a discriminant; as we shall see later, the Ada 95 tag is effectively a hidden discriminant identifying the type and so the term is very appropriate.

As a very simple example suppose we wish to manipulate various kinds of geometrical objects which form some sort of hierarchy. All objects will have a position given by their x- and y-coordinates. So we can declare the root of the hierarchy as

```
type Object is tagged
   record
      X_Coord: Float;
      Y_Coord: Float;
   end record;
```

The other types of geometrical objects will be derived (directly or indirectly) from this type. For example we could have

```
type Circle is new Object with
   record
      Radius: Float;
   end record;
```

and the type Circle then has the three components X_Coord, Y_Coord and Radius. It inherits the two coordinates from the type Object and the component Radius is added explicitly.

Sometimes it is convenient to derive a new type without adding any further components. For example

```
type Point is new Object with null record;
```

In this last case we have derived Point from Object but naturally not added any new components. However, since we are dealing with tagged types we have to explicitly add **with null record;** to indicate that we did not want any new components. This has the advantage that it is always clear from a declaration whether a type is tagged or not. Note that **tagged** is of course a new reserved word; Ada 95 has a small number (six) of such new reserved words.

A private type can also be marked as tagged

```
type Shape is tagged private;
```

and the full type declaration must then (ultimately) be a tagged record

```
type Shape is tagged
   record ...
```

or derived from a tagged record such as Object. On the other hand we might wish to make visible the fact that the type Shape is derived from Object and yet keep the additional components hidden. In this case we would write

```
package Hidden_Shape is
   type Shape is new Object with private;      -- client view
   ...
private
   type Shape is new Object with              -- server view
   record
         -- the private components
   end record;
end Hidden_Shape;
```

In this last case it is not necessary for the full declaration of Shape to be derived directly from the type Object. There might be a chain of intermediate derived types (it could be derived from Circle); all that matters is that Shape is ultimately derived from Object.

Just as in Ada 83, derived types inherit the operations which "belong" to the parent type — these are called *primitive operations* in Ada 95. User-written subprograms are classed as primitive operations if they are declared in the same package specification as the type and have the type as parameter or result.

Thus we might have declared a function giving the distance from the origin

```
function Distance(O: in Object) return Float is
begin
   return Sqrt(O.X_Coord**2 + O.Y_Coord**2);
end Distance;
```

The type Circle would then sensibly inherit this function. If however, we were concerned with the area of an object then we might start with

```
function Area(O: in Object) return Float is
begin
   return 0.0;
end Area;
```

which returns zero since a raw object has no area. This would also be inherited by the type Circle but would be inappropriate; it would be more sensible to explicitly declare

```
function Area(C: in Circle) return Float is
begin
   return Pi*C.Radius**2;
end Area;
```

which will override the inherited operation.

It is possible to "convert" a value from the type Circle to Object and vice versa. From circle to object is easy, we simply write

```
O: Object := (1.0, 0.5);
C: Circle := (0.0, 0.0, 12.2);
...
O := Object(C);
```

which effectively ignores the third component. However, conversion in the other direction requires the provision of a value for the extra component and this is done by an extension aggregate thus

```
C := (O with 46.8);
```

where the expression O is extended after **with** by the values of the extra components written just as in a normal aggregate. In this case we only had to give a value for the radius.

We now consider a more practical example which illustrates the use of tagged types to build a system as a hierarchy of types and packages. We will see how this allows the system to be extended without recompilation of the central part of the system. By way of illustration we start by showing the rigid way this had to be programmed in Ada 83 by the use of variants.

Our system represents the processing of alerts (alarms) in a ground mission control station. Alerts are of three levels of priority. Low level alerts are merely logged, medium level alerts cause a person to be assigned to deal with the problem and high level alerts cause an alarm bell to ring if the matter is not dealt with by a specified time. In addition, a message is displayed on various devices according to its priority.

First consider how this might have be done in Ada 83

```
with Calendar;
package Alert_System is

    type Priority is (Low, Medium, High);
    type Device is (Teletype, Console, Big_Screen);

    type Alert(P: Priority) is
        record
            Time_Of_Arrival: Calendar.Time;
            Message: Text;
            case P is
                when Low => null;
                when Medium | High =>
                    Action_Officer: Person;
                    case P is
                        when Low | Medium => null;
                        when High =>
                            Ring_Alarm_At: Calendar.Time;
                    end case;
            end case;
        end record;

    procedure Display(A: in Alert; On: in Device);
    procedure Handle(A: in out Alert);
    procedure Log(A: in Alert);
    procedure Set_Alarm(A: in Alert);

end Alert_System;
```

Each alert is represented as a discriminated record with the priority as the discriminant. Perhaps surprisingly, the structure and processing depend on this discriminant in a quite complex manner. One immediate difficulty is that we are more or less obliged to use nested variants because of the rule that all the components of a record have to have different identifiers. The body of the procedure Handle might be

```
procedure Handle(A: in out Alert) is
begin
    A.Time_Of_Arrival := Calendar.Clock;
    Log(A);
    Display(A, Teletype);
    case A.P is
        when Low => null;  -- nothing special
        when Medium | High =>
```

```
            A.Action_Officer := Assign_Volunteer;
            Display(A, Console);
            case A.P is
               when Low | Medium => null;
               when High =>
                  Display(A, Big_Screen);
                  Set_Alarm(A);
            end case;
      end case;
end Handle;
```

One problem with this approach is that the code is curiously complex due to the nested structure and consequently hard to maintain and error-prone. If we try to avoid the nested case statement then we have to repeat some of the code.

A more serious problem is that if, for example, we need to add a further alert category, perhaps an emergency alert (which would mean adding another value to the type Priority), then the whole system will have to be modified and recompiled. Existing reliable code will then be disturbed with the risk of subsequent errors.

In Ada 95 we can use a series of tagged types with a distinct procedure Handle for each one. This completely eliminates the need for case statements or variants and indeed the type Priority itself is no longer required because it is now inherent in the types themselves (it is implicit in the tag). The package specification now becomes

```
with Calendar;
package New_Alert_System is

   type Device is (Teletype, Console, Big_Screen);

   type Alert is tagged
      record
         Time_Of_Arrival: Calendar.Time;
         Message: Text;
      end record;

   procedure Display(A: in Alert; On: in Device);
   procedure Handle(A: in out Alert);
   procedure Log(A: in Alert);

   type Low_Alert is new Alert with null record;

   type Medium_Alert is new Alert with
      record
         Action_Officer: Person;
      end record;

   -- now override inherited operation
   procedure Handle(MA: in out Medium_Alert);

   type High_Alert is new Medium_Alert with
      record
         Ring_Alarm_At: Calendar.Time;
      end record;

   procedure Handle(HA: in out High_Alert);
   procedure Set_Alarm(HA: in High_Alert);

end New_Alert_System;
```

In this formulation the variant record is replaced with the tagged type Alert and three types derived from it. Note that Ada 95 allows a type to be derived in the same package specification as the parent and to inherit all the primitive operations but we cannot add any new primitive operations to the parent after a type has been derived from it. This is different to Ada 83 where the operations were not derivable until after the end of the package specification. This change allows the related types to be conveniently encapsulated all in the same package.

The type Low_Alert is simply a copy of Alert (note **with null record;**) and could be dispensed with although it maintains equivalence with the Ada 83 version; Low_Alert inherits the procedure Handle from Alert. The type Medium_Alert extends Alert and provides its own procedure Handle thus overriding the inherited version. The type High_Alert further extends Medium_Alert and similarly provides its own procedure Handle. Thus instead of a single procedure Handle containing complex case statements the Ada 95 solution distributes the logic for handling alerts to each specific alert type without any redundancy.

Note that Low_Alert, Medium_Alert and High_Alert all also inherit the procedures Display and Log but without change. Finally, High_Alert adds the procedure Set_Alarm which is not used by the lower alert levels and thus it seems inappropriate to declare it for them.

The package body is as follows

```
package body New_Alert_System is

    procedure Handle(A: in out Alert) is
    begin
        A.Time_Of_Arrival := Calendar.Clock;
        Log(A);
        Display(A, Teletype);
    end Handle;

    procedure Handle(MA: in out Medium_Alert) is
    begin
        Handle(Alert(MA)); -- handle as plain alert
        MA.Action_Officer := Assign_Volunteer;
        Display(MA, Console);
    end Handle;

    procedure Handle(HA: in out High_Alert) is
    begin
        Handle(Medium_Alert(HA)); -- conversion
        Display(HA, Big_Screen);
        Set_Alarm(HA);
    end Handle;

    procedure Display(A: in Alert; On: in Device) is separate;
    procedure Log(A: in Alert) is separate;

    procedure Set_Alarm(HA: in High_Alert) is separate;

end New_Alert_System;
```

Each distinct body for Handle contains just the code relevant to the type and delegates additional processing back to its parent using an explicit type conversion. Note carefully that all type checking is static and so no runtime penalties are incurred with this structure (the variant checks have been avoided).

In the Ada 95 model a new alert level (perhaps Emergency_Alert) can be added without recompilation (and perhaps more importantly, without retesting) of the existing code.

```
with New_Alert_System;
package Emergency_Alert_System is
```

```
    type Emergency_Alert is
       new New_Alert_System.Alert with private;

    procedure Handle(EA: in out Emergency_Alert);

    procedure Display(EA: in Emergency_Alert;
                      On: in New_Alert_System.Device);

    procedure Log(EA: in Emergency_Alert);

  private
     . . .
  end Emergency_Alert_System;
```

In the Ada 83 model extensive recompilation would have been necessary since the variant records would have required redefinition. Thus we see that Ada 95 truly provides Programming by Extension.

II.2　Class Wide Programming

The facilities we have seen so far have allowed us to define a new type as an extension of an existing one. We have introduced the different kinds of alerts as distinct but related types. What we also need is a means to manipulate *any* kind of alert and to process it accordingly. We do this through the introduction of the notion of class-wide types.

With each tagged type T there is an associated type T'Class. This type comprises the union of all the types in the tree of derived types rooted at T. The values of T'Class are thus the values of T and all its derived types. Moreover a value of any type derived from T can be implicitly converted to the type T'Class.

Thus in the case of the type Alert the tree of types is as shown in Figure II-1.

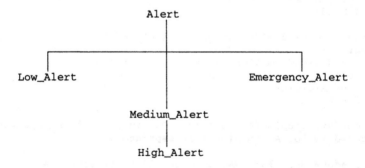

Figure II-1: A Tree of Types

A value of any of the alert types can be implicitly converted to Alert'Class. Note carefully that Medium_Alert'Class is not the same as Alert'Class; the former consists just of Medium_Alert and High_Alert.

Each value of a class-wide type has a tag which identifies its particular type from other types in the tree of types at runtime. It is the existence of this tag which gives rise to the term tagged types.

The type T'Class is treated as an unconstrained type; this is because we cannot possibly know how much space could be required by any value of a class-wide type because the type might be extended. As a consequence, although we can declare an object of a class-wide type we must initialize it and it is then constrained by the tag.

However, we can declare an access type referring to a class-wide type in which case the access could designate any value of the class-wide type from time to time. The use of access types is therefore a key factor in class-wide programming. Moreover, a parameter of a procedure can also be of a class-wide type. There is a strong analogy between class-wide types and other unconstrained types such as array types.

We can now continue our example by considering how we might buffer up a series of alerts and process them in sequence. The whole essence of the problem is that such a central routine cannot know of the individual types because we need it to work (without recompilation) even if we extend the system by adding a new alert type to it.

The central routine could thus take a class-wide value as its parameter so we might have

```
procedure Process_Alerts(AC: in out Alert'Class) is
   ...
begin
   ...
   Handle(AC);  -- dispatch according to tag
   ...
end Process_Alerts;
```

In this case we do not know which procedure Handle to call until runtime because we do not know which specific type the alert belongs to. However, AC is of a class-wide type and so its value includes a tag indicating the specific type of the value. The choice of Handle is then determined by the value of this tag; the parameter is then implicitly converted to the appropriate specific alert type before being passed to the appropriate procedure Handle.

This runtime choice of procedure is called *dispatching* and is key to the flexibility of class-wide programming.

Before being processed, the alerts might be held on a heterogeneous queue using an access type

```
type Alert_Ptr is access Alert'Class;
```

and the central routine could manipulate the alerts directly from such a queue

```
procedure Process_Alerts is
   Next_Alert: Alert_Ptr;
begin
   ...
   Next_Alert := -- get next alert
   ...
   Handle(Next_Alert.all);   -- dispatch to appropriate Handle
   ...
end Process_Alerts;
```

In this case, the value of the object referred to by Next_Alert is of a class-wide type and so includes a tag indicating the specific type. The parameter Next_Alert.all is thus dereferenced, the value of the tag gives the choice of Handle and the parameter is then implicitly converted as before and then passed to the chosen procedure Handle.

Dispatching may be implemented as a simple indirect jump through a table of subprograms indexed by the primitive operations such as Handle. This is generally much more efficient than the alternative of variant records and case statements, with their attendant variant checks.

II.3 Abstract Types and Subprograms

The final topic to be introduced in this brief introduction to the Object Oriented features of Ada 95 is the concept of abstract tagged types and abstract subprograms. These are marked as abstract in their declaration. The purpose of an abstract type is to provide a common foundation upon which useful types can be built by derivation. An abstract subprogram is a sort of place holder for an operation to be provided (it does not have a body).

An abstract tagged type can have abstract primitive subprograms and these dispatch. An abstract type on its own is of little use because we cannot declare an object of an abstract type.

Upon derivation from an abstract type we can provide actual subprograms for the abstract subprograms of the parent type (and it is in this sense that we said they were place holders). If all the abstract subprograms are replaced by proper subprograms then the type need not be declared as abstract and we can then declare objects of the type in the usual way. (The rules ensure that dispatching always works.)

Returning now to our example of processing alerts we could reformulate this so that the root type Alert was just an abstract type and then build the specific types upon this. This would enable us to program and compile all the general infrastructure routines for processing all alerts such as Process_Alerts in the previous section without any concern at all for the individual alerts and indeed before deciding what they should contain.

The baseline package could then simply become

```
package Base_Alert_System is

    type Alert is abstract tagged null record;
    procedure Handle(A: in out Alert) is abstract;

end Base_Alert_System;
```

in which we declare the type Alert as a tagged null record with just the procedure Handle as an abstract subprogram; this does not have a body. (Note the abbreviated form for a null record declaration which saves us having to write **record null; end record;**)

We can now develop our alert infrastructure and then later add the normal alert system containing the three levels of alerts thus

```
with Calendar;
with Base_Alert_System;
package Normal_Alert_System is

    type Device is (Teletype, Console, Big_Screen);

    type Low_Alert is new Base_Alert_System.Alert with
        record
            Time_Of_Arrival: Calendar.Time;
            Message: Text;
        end record;

    -- now provide actual subprogram for abstract one
    procedure Handle(LA: in out Low_Alert);

    procedure Display(LA: in Low_Alert; On: in Device);
    procedure Log(LA: in Low_Alert);

    type Medium_Alert is new Low_Alert with
        record
            Action_Officer: Person;
        end record;
```

```
procedure Handle(MA: in out Medium_Alert);

type High_Alert is new Medium_Alert with
   record
      Ring_Alarm_At: Calendar.Time;
   end record;

procedure Handle(HA: in out High_Alert);
procedure Set_Alarm(HA: in High_Alert);

end Normal_Alert_System;
```

In this revised formulation we must provide a procedure `Handle` for `Low_Alert` to meet the promise of the abstract type. The procedures `Display` and `Log` now take a parameter of `Low_Alert` and the type `Medium_Alert` is more naturally derived from `Low_Alert`.

Note carefully that we did not make `Display` and `Log` abstract subprograms in the package `Base_Alert_System`. There was no need; it is only `Handle` that is required by the general infrastructure such as the procedure `Process_Alerts` and to add the others would weaken the abstraction and clutter the base level.

Corresponding changes are required to the package body; the procedure `Handle` previously applying to `Alert` now applies to `Low_Alert` and in the procedure `Handle` for `Medium_Alert` we need to change the type conversion in the call to the "parent" `Handle` which is of course now the procedure `Handle` for `Low_Alert`. The two procedures thus become

```
procedure Handle(LA: in out Low_Alert) is
begin
   LA.Time_Of_Arrival := Calendar.Clock;
   Log(LA);
   Display(LA, Teletype);
end Handle;

procedure Handle(MA: in out Medium_Alert) is
begin
   Handle(Low_Alert(MA)); -- handle as low alert
   MA.Action_Officer := Assign_Volunteer;
   Display(MA, Console);
end Handle;
```

When we now add our `Emergency_Alert` we can choose to derive this from the baseline `Alert` as before or perhaps from some other point in the tree picking up the existing facilities of one of the other levels.

II.4 Summary of Type Extension

The key points we have seen are as follows.

Ada 95 introduces the notion of tagged types. Only record (and private) types can be tagged. Values of tagged types carry a tag with them. The tag indicates the specific type. A tagged type can be extended on derivation with additional components.

Primitive operations of a type are inherited on derivation. The primitive operations are those implicitly declared, plus, in the case of a type declared in a package specification, all subprograms with a parameter or result of that type also declared in the package specification. Primitive operations can be overridden on derivation and further ones added.

A tagged type can be declared as abstract and can have abstract primitive subprograms. An abstract subprogram does not have a body but one can be provided on derivation. An abstract type provides a foundation for building specific types with some common protocol.

`T'Class` denotes the class-wide type rooted at `T`. Implicit conversion is allowed to values of `T'Class`. Objects and parameters of `T'Class` are treated as unconstrained. An appropriate access type can designate any value of `T'Class`.

Calling a primitive operation with an actual parameter of a class-wide type results in dispatching: that is the runtime selection of the operation according to the tag. This is often called late binding — a key property of Object Oriented languages.

Another term commonly encountered is polymorphism. Class-wide types are said to be polymorphic because their values are of different "shapes" (from the Greek *poly*, many, and *morphe*, form). Polymorphism is another property of Object Oriented languages.

One of the main advantages of type extension is that it can be done without recompiling and retesting an existing stable system. This is perhaps the most important overall characteristic of Object Oriented languages.

II.5 Dynamic Selection

In the previous section we mentioned late binding; this simply means that the procedure to be called is identified late in the compile-link-run process. All procedure calls were bound early in Ada 83 and this was one reason why the language felt so static; even the generic mechanism only deferred binding to instantiation which is still essentially a compile time process.

There were a number of reasons for taking such a static approach in Ada 83. There was concern for the implementation cost of dynamic binding, it was also clear that the presence of dynamic binding would reduce the provability of programs, and moreover it was felt that the introduction of generics where subprograms could be passed as parameters would cater for practical situations where formal procedure parameters were used in other languages.

However, the absence of dynamic binding in Ada 83 has been unfortunate. It is now realized that implementation costs are trivial and not necessarily pervasive; provability is not a relevant argument because we now know that in any safety-critical software where mathematical provability is a real issue, we only use a small subset of the language. And furthermore, the generic mechanism has proved not to be a sufficiently flexible alternative anyway.

We have seen how dispatching in Ada 95 is one mechanism for late binding. Another is provided by the manipulation of subprogram values through an extension of access types.

In Ada 95 an access type can refer to a subprogram; an access-to-subprogram value can be created by the `Access` attribute and a subprogram can be called indirectly by dereferencing such an access value. Thus we can write

```
type Trig_Function is access function(F: Float) return Float;
T: Trig_Function;
X, Theta: Float;
```

and `T` can then "point to" functions such as `Sin`, `Cos` and `Tan`. We can then assign an appropriate access-to-subprogram value to `T` by for example

```
T := Sin'Access;
```

and later indirectly call the subprogram currently referred to by `T` as expected

```
X := T(Theta);
```

which is really an abbreviation for

```
X := T.all(Theta);
```

Just as with many other uses of access types the `.all` is not usually required but it would be necessary if there were no parameters.

The access to subprogram mechanism can be used to program general dynamic selection and to pass subprograms as parameters. It allows program call-back to be implemented in a natural and efficient manner.

There are a number of rules which ensure that access to subprogram values cannot be misused. Conformance matching ensures that the subprogram always has the correct number and type of parameters and there are rules about accessibility that ensure that a subprogram is not called out of context. Flexibility is thus gained without loss of integrity.

Simple classic numerical algorithms can now be implemented in Ada 95 in the same way as in languages such as Fortran but with complete security. Thus an integration routine might have the following specification

```ada
type Integrand is access function(X: Float) return Float;

function Integrate(F: Integrand; From, To: Float;
                   Accuracy: Float := 1.0E-7) return Float;
```

and we might then write

```ada
Area := Integrate(Log'Access, 1.0, 2.0);
```

which will compute the area under the curve for $\log(x)$ from 1.0 to 2.0. Within the body of the function Integrate there will be calls of the actual subprogram passed as a parameter; this is a simple form of call-back.

A common paradigm within the process industry is to implement sequencing control through successive calls of a number of interpreter actions. A sequence compiler might interactively build an array of such actions which are then obeyed. Thus we might have

```ada
type Action is access procedure;
Action_Sequence: array(1 .. N) of Action;

... -- build the array

   -- and then obey it
for I in Action_Sequence'Range loop
   Action_Sequence(I).all;
end loop;
```

It is of course possible for a record (possibly private) to contain components whose types are access to subprogram types. Consider the following example of a package which provides facilities associated with the actions obtained when we press keys on our keyboard or perhaps click our mouse on a window button.

```ada
package Push_Buttons is

   type Button is private;

   type Button_Response is access procedure(B: in out Button);

   function Create(...) return Button;

   procedure Push(B: in out Button);

   procedure Set_Response(B: in out Button;
                          R: in Button_Response);
```

```
   procedure Default_Response(B: in out Button);

   ...

private
   type Button is
      record
         Response: Button_Response := Default_Response'Access;
         ...     -- other aspects of the button
      end record;
end Push_Buttons;
```

A button is represented as a private record containing a number of components describing properties of the button (position on screen for example). One component is an access to a procedure which is the action to be executed when the button is pushed. Note carefully that the button value is passed to this procedure as a parameter so that the procedure can obtain access to the other components of the record describing the button. The procedure Create fills in these other components and other functions (not shown) provide access to them. The procedure Push invokes the action of clicking the mouse and an appropriate default procedure is provided which warns the user if the button has not been set. The body might be as follows

```
package body Push_Buttons is

   procedure Push(B: in out Button) is
   begin
      B.Response(B);   -- indirect call
   end Push;

   procedure Set_Response(B: in out Button;
                          R: in Button_Response) is
   begin
      B.Response := R;   -- set procedure value in record
   end Set_Response;

   procedure Default_Response(B: in out Button) is
   begin
      Put("Button not set");
      Monitor.Beep;
   end Default_Response;

   ...

end Push_Buttons;
```

We can now set the specific actions we want when a button is pushed. Thus we might want some emergency action to take place when a big red button is pushed.

```
Big_Red_Button: Button;

procedure Emergency(B: in out Button) is
begin
   -- call fire brigade etc
end Emergency;

...

Set_Response(Big_Red_Button, Emergency'Access);
```

...

```
Push(Big_Red_Button);
```

The reader will realize that the access to subprogram mechanism coupled with the inheritance and dispatching facilities described earlier enable very flexible yet secure dynamic structures to be programmed.

II.6 Other Access Types

We have just seen how access types in Ada 95 have been extended to provide a means of manipulating subprogram values. Access types have also been extended to provide more flexible access to objects.

In Ada 83, access values could only refer to objects dynamically created through the allocator mechanism (using **new**). It was not possible to access objects declared in the normal way. This approach was inherited from Pascal which had similar restrictions and was a reaction against the very flexible approach adopted by Algol 68 and C which can give rise to dangerous dangling references.

However, the ability to manipulate pointers is very valuable provided the risks can be overcome. The view taken by Ada 83 has proved unnecessarily inflexible, especially when interfacing to external systems possibly written in other languages.

In Ada 95 we can declare a general access type such as

```
type Int_Ptr is access all Integer;
```

and we can then assign the "address" of any variable of type `Integer` to a variable of type `Int_Ptr` provided that the designated variable is marked as aliased. So we can write

```
IP: Int_Ptr;
I: aliased Integer;
...
IP := I'Access;
```

and we can then read and update the variable `I` through the access variable `IP`. Note once more the use of `'Access`. Note also that **aliased** is another new reserved word.

As with access to subprogram values there are rules that (at compile time) ensure that dangling references cannot arise.

A variation is that we can restrict the access to be read-only by replacing **all** in the type definition by **constant**. This allows read-only access to any variable and also to a constant thus

```
type Const_Int_Ptr is access constant Integer;
CIP: Const_Int_Ptr;
I: aliased Integer;
C: aliased constant Integer := 1815;
```

followed by

```
CIP := I'Access;  -- access to a variable, or
CIP := C'Access;  -- access to a constant
```

The type accessed by a general access type can of course be any type such as an array or record. We can thus build chains from records statically declared. Note that we can also use an allocator to generate general access values. Our chain could thus include a mixture of records from both storage mechanisms.

Finally note that the accessed object could be a component of a composite type. Thus we could point into the middle of a record (provided the component is marked as aliased). In a fast implementation of Conway's Game of Life a cell might contain access values directly referencing the component of its eight neighbors containing the counter saying whether the cell is alive or dead.

```
type Ref_Count is access constant Integer range 0 .. 1;
type Ref_Count_Array is array (Integer range <>) of Ref_Count;

type Cell is
   record
      Life_Count: aliased Integer range 0 .. 1;
      Total_Neighbor_Count: Integer range 0 .. 8;
      Neighbor_Count: Ref_Count_Array(1 .. 8);
      ...
   end record;
```

We can now link the cells together according to our model by statements such as

```
This_Cell.Neighbor_Count(1) := Cell_To_The_North.Life_Count'Access;
```

and then the heart of the computation which computes the sum of the life counts in the neighbors might be

```
C.Total_Neighbor_Count := 0;
for I in C.Neighbor_Count'Range loop
   C.Total_Neighbor_Count :=
        C.Total_Neighbor_Count + C.Neighbor_Count(I).all;
end loop;
```

Observe that we have given the type Ref_Count and the component Life_Count the same static subtypes so that they can be checked at compile time; this is not essential but avoids a run-time check that would otherwise be required if they did not statically match.

General access types can also be used to program static ragged arrays as for example a table of messages of different lengths. The key to this is that the accessed type can be unconstrained (such as String) and thus we can have an array of pointers to strings of different lengths. In Ada 83 we would have had to allocate all the strings dynamically using an allocator.

In conclusion we have seen how the access types of Ada 83 have been considerably enhanced in Ada 95 to allow much more flexible programming which is especially important in open systems while nevertheless retaining the inherent security missing in languages such as C and C++.

II.7 Hierarchical Libraries

One of the great strengths of Ada is the library package where the distinct specification and body decouple the user interface to a package (the specification) from its implementation (the body). This enables the details of the implementation and the clients to be recompiled separately without interference provided the specification remains stable.

However, although this works well for smallish programs it has proved cumbersome when programs become large or complex. There are two aspects of the problem: the coarse control of visibility of private types and the inability to extend without recompilation.

There are occasions when we wish to write two logically distinct packages which nevertheless share a private type. We could not do this in Ada 83. We either had to make the type not private so that both packages could see it with the unfortunate consequence that all the client packages could also see the type; this broke the abstraction. Or, on the other hand, if we wished to keep the abstraction, then we had to merge the two packages together and this resulted in a large monolithic package with increased recompilation costs. (We discount as naughty the use of tricks such as Unchecked_Conversion to get at the details of private types.)

The other aspect of the difficulty arose when we wished to extend an existing system by adding more facilities to it. If we add to a package specification then naturally we have to recompile it but moreover we also have to recompile all existing clients even if the additions have no impact upon them.

In Ada 95 these and other similar problems are solved by the introduction of a hierarchical library structure containing child packages and child subprograms. There are two kinds of children: public children and private children. We will just consider public children for the moment; private children are discussed in the next section.

Consider first the familiar example of a package for the manipulation of complex numbers. It might contain the private type itself plus the four standard operations and also subprograms to construct and decompose a complex number taking a cartesian view. Thus we might have

```
package Complex_Numbers is

    type Complex is private;
    function "+" (Left, Right: Complex) return Complex;
    ... -- similarly "-", "*" and "/"

    function Cartesian_To_Complex(Real, Imag: Float) return Complex;
    function Real_Part(X: Complex) return Float;
    function Imag_Part(X: Complex) return Float;

private
    ...
end Complex_Numbers;
```

We have deliberately not shown the completion of the private type since it is immaterial how it is implemented. Although this package gives the user a cartesian view of the type, nevertheless it certainly does not have to be implemented that way.

Some time later we might need to additionally provide a polar view by the provision of subprograms which construct and decompose a complex number from and to its polar coordinates. In Ada 83 we could only do this by adding to the existing package and this forced us to recompile all the existing clients.

In Ada 95, however, we can add a child package as follows

```
package Complex_Numbers.Polar is

    function Polar_To_Complex(R, Theta: Float) return Complex;
    function "abs" (Right: Complex) return Float;
    function Arg(X: Complex) return Float;

end Complex_Numbers.Polar;
```

and within the body of this package we can access the private type Complex itself.

Note the notation, a package having the name P.Q is a child package of its parent package P. We can think of the child package as being declared inside the declarative region of its parent but after the end of the specification of its parent; most of the visibility rules stem from this model. In other words the declarative region defined by the parent (which is primarily both the specification and body of the parent) also includes the space occupied by the text of the children; but it is important to realize that the children are inside that region and do not just extend it. Observe that the child does not need a with clause for the parent and that the entities of the parent are directly visible without a use clause.

In just the same way, library packages in Ada 95 can be thought of as being declared in the declarative region of the package Standard and after the end of its specification. Note that a child subprogram is not a primitive operation of a type declared in its parent's specification because the child is not declared in the specification but after it.

The important special visibility rule is that the private part (if any) and the body of the child have visibility of the private part of their parent. (They naturally also have visibility of the visible part.) However, the visible part of a (public) child package does not have visibility of the private part of its parent; if it did it would allow renaming and hence the export of the hidden private details to any client; this would break the abstraction of the private type (this rule does not apply to private children as explained later).

The body of the child package for our complex number example could simply be

```
package body Complex_Numbers.Polar is

    -- bodies of Polar_To_Complex etc

end Complex_Numbers.Polar;
```

In order to access the procedures of the child package the client must have a with clause for the child package. However this also implicitly provides a with clause for the parent as well thereby saving us the burden of having to write one separately. Thus we might have

```
with Complex_Numbers.Polar;
package Client is
    ...
```

and then within Client we can access the various subprograms in the usual way by writing Complex_Numbers.Real_Part or Complex_Numbers.Polar.Arg and so on.

Direct visibility can be obtained by use clauses as expected. However, a use clause for the child does not imply one for the parent; but, because of the model that the child is in the declarative region of the parent, a use clause for the parent makes the child name itself directly visible. So writing

```
with Complex_Numbers.Polar; use Complex_Numbers;
```

now allows us to refer to the subprograms as Real_Part and Polar.Arg respectively.

We could of course have added

```
use Complex_Numbers.Polar;
```

and we would then be able to refer to the subprogram Polar.Arg as just Arg.

Child packages thus neatly solve both the problem of sharing a private type over several compilation units and the problem of extending a package without recompiling the clients. They thus provide another form of programming by extension.

A package may of course have several children. In fact with hindsight it might have been more logical to have developed our complex number package as three packages: a parent containing the private type and the four arithmetic operations and then two child packages, one giving the cartesian view and the other giving the polar view of the type. At a later date we could add yet another package providing perhaps the trigonometric functions on complex numbers and again this can be done without recompiling what has already been written and thus without the risk of introducing errors.

The extension mechanism provided by child packages fits neatly together with that provided by tagged types. Thus a child package might itself have a private part and then within that part we might derive and extend a private type from the parent package. This is illustrated by the following example which relates to the processing of widgets in a window system.

```
package XTK is
    type Widget is tagged private;
```

```
      type Widget_Access is access Widget'Class;
      ...
  private
      type Widget is tagged
         record
            Parent: Widget_Access;
            ...
         end record;
  end XTK;

  -- now extend the Widget

  package XTK.Color is
      type Colored_Widget is new Widget with private;
      ...
  private
      type Colored_Widget is new Widget with
         record
            Color: ...
         end record;
  end XTK.Color;
```

An interesting point with this construction is that clients at the parent level (those just withing XTK) only see the external properties common to all widgets, although by class-wide programming using Widget_Access, they may be manipulating colored widgets. However, a client of XTK.Color also has access to the external properties of colored widgets because we have made the extended type visible (although still private of course). It should be noted that in fact the private part of XTK.Color does not actually access the private part of XTK although it has visibility of it. But of course the body of XTK.Color undoubtedly will and that is why we need a child package.

Another example is provided by the alert system discussed in II.1. It would probably be better if the additional package concerning emergency alerts was actually a child of the main package thus

```
  package New_Alert_System.Emergency is
      type Emergency_Alert is new Alert with private;
      ...
  end New_Alert_System.Emergency;
```

The advantages are manifold. The commonality of naming makes it clear that the child is indeed just a part of the total system; this is emphasized by not needing a with clause for the parent and that the entities in the parent are immediately visible. In addition, although not required in this example, any private mechanisms in the private part of the parent would be visible to the child. The alternative structure in II.3 where the baseline used an abstract type could also be rearranged.

The benefit of just the commonality of naming is very important since it prevents the inadvertent interference between different parts of subsystems. This is used to good advantage in the arrangement of the Ada 95 predefined library as will be seen in II.13.

Finally, it is very important to realize that the child mechanism is hierarchical. Children may have children to any level so we can build a complete tree providing decomposition of facilities in a natural manner. A child may have a private part and this is then visible from its children but not its parent.

With regard to siblings a child can obviously only have visibility of a previously compiled sibling anyway. And then the normal rules apply: a child can only see the visible part of its siblings.

A parent body may access (via with clauses) and thus depend upon its children and grandchildren. A child body automatically depends upon its parent (and grandparent) and needs no with clause for them. A child body can depend upon its siblings (again via with clauses).

II.8 Private Child Units

In the previous section we introduced the concept of hierarchical child packages and showed how these allowed extension and continued privacy of private types without recompilation. However, the whole idea was based on the provision of additional facilities for the client. The specifications of the additional packages were all visible to the client.

In the development of large subsystems it often happens that we would like to decompose the system for implementation reasons but without giving any additional visibility to clients.

Ada 83 had a problem in this area which we have not yet addressed. In Ada 83 the only means at our disposal for the decomposition of a body was the subunit. However, although a subunit could be recompiled without affecting other subunits at the same level, any change to the top level body (which of course includes the stubs of the subunits) required all subunits to be recompiled.

Ada 95 also solves this problem by the provision of a form of child unit that is totally private to its parent. In order to illustrate this idea consider the following outline of an operating system.

```
package OS is
   -- parent package defines types used throughout the system
   type File_Descriptor is private;
   ...
private
   type File_Descriptor is new Integer;
end OS;

package OS.Exceptions is
   -- exceptions used throughout the system
   File_Descriptor_Error,
   File_Name_Error,
   Permission_Error: exception;
end OS.Exceptions;

with OS.Exceptions;
package OS.File_Manager is
   type File_Mode is (Read_Only, Write_Only, Read_Write);
   function Open(File_Name: String; Mode: File_Mode)
      return File_Descriptor;

   procedure Close(File: in File_Descriptor);
   ...
end OS.File_Manager;

procedure OS.Interpret(Command: String);

private package OS.Internals is
   ...
end OS.Internals;

private package OS.Internals_Debug is
   ...
end OS.Internals_Debug;
```

In this example the parent package contains the types used throughout the system. There are then three public child units, the package OS.Exceptions containing various exceptions, the package OS.File_Manager which provides file open/close routines (note the explicit with clause for its sibling OS.Exceptions) and a procedure OS.Interpret which interprets a command line passed as a parameter. (Incidentally this illustrates that a child unit can be a subprogram as well as a package. It can actually be any library unit and that includes a generic declaration and a generic instantiation.) Finally we have two private child packages called OS.Internals and OS.Internals_Debug.

A private child (distinguished by starting with the word **private**) can be declared at any point in the child hierarchy. The visibility rules for private children are similar to those for public children but there are two extra rules.

The first extra rule is that a private child is only visible within the subtree of the hierarchy whose root is its parent. And moreover within that tree it is not visible to the specifications of any public siblings (although it is visible to their bodies).

In our example, since the private child is a direct child of the package OS, the package OS.Internals is visible to the bodies of OS itself, of OS.File_Manager and of OS.Interpret (OS.Exceptions has no body anyway) and it is also visible to both body and specification of OS.Internals_Debug. But it is not visible outside OS and a client package certainly cannot access OS.Internals at all.

The other extra rule is that the visible part of the private child can access the private part of its parent. This is quite safe because it cannot export information about a private type to a client because it is not itself visible. Nor can it export information indirectly via its public siblings because, as mentioned above, it is not visible to the visible parts of their specifications but only to their private parts and bodies.

We can now safely implement our system in the package OS.Internals and we can create a subtree for the convenience of development and extensibility. We would then have a third level in the hierarchy containing packages such as OS.Internals.Devices, OS.Internals.Access_Rights and so on.

It might be helpful just to summarize the various visibility rules which are actually quite simple and mostly follow from the model of the child being located after the end of the specification of its parent but inside the parent's declarative region. (We use "to with" for brevity.)

- A specification never needs to with its parent; it may with a sibling except that a public child specification may not with a private sibling; it may not with its own child (it has not been compiled yet!).

- A body never needs to with its parent; it may with a sibling (private or not); it may with its own child (and grandchild...).

- The entities of the parent are accessible by simple name within a child; a use clause is not required.

- The context clause of the parent also applies to a child.

- A private child is never visible outside the tree rooted at its parent. And within that tree it is not visible to the specifications of public siblings.

- The private part and body of any child can access the private part of its parent (and grandparent...).

- In addition the visible part of a private child can also access the private part of its parent (and grandparent...).

- A with clause for a child automatically implies with clauses for all its ancestors.

- A use clause for a library unit makes the child units accessible by simple name (this only applies to child units for which there is also a with clause).

These rules may seem a bit complex but actually stem from just a few considerations of consistency. Questions regarding access to children of sibling units and other remote relatives follow by analogy with an external client viewing the appropriate subtree.

We conclude our discussion of hierarchical libraries by considering their interaction with generics. Genericity is also an important tool in the construction of subsystems and it is essential that it be usable with the child concept.

Any parent unit may have generic children but a generic parent can only have generic children. If the parent unit is not generic then a generic child may be instantiated in the usual way at any point where it is visible.

On the other hand, if the parent unit is itself generic, then a generic child can be instantiated outside the parent hierarchy provided the parent is first instantiated and the child is mentioned in a with clause; the instantiation of the child then refers to the instantiation of the parent. Note that although the original generic hierarchy consists of library units, the instantiations need not be library units.

As a simple example, we might wish to make the package Complex_Numbers of the previous section generic with respect to the underlying floating point type. We would write

```
generic
   type Float_Type is digits <>;
package Complex_Numbers is
   ...
end Complex_Numbers;

generic
package Complex_Numbers.Polar is
   ...
end Complex_Numbers.Polar;
```

and then the instantiations might be

```
with Complex_Numbers;
package Real_Complex_Numbers is new Complex_Numbers(Real);

with Complex_Numbers.Polar;
package Real_Complex_Numbers.Real_Polar is
                         new Real_Complex_Numbers.Polar;
```

We thus have to instantiate the generic hierarchy (or as much of it as we want) unit by unit. This avoids a number of problems that would arise with a more liberal approach but enables complete subsystems to be built in a generic manner. In the above example we chose to make the instantiated packages into a corresponding hierarchy but as mentioned they could equally have been instantiated as local packages with unrelated names. But an important point is that the instantiation of the child refers to the instantiation of the parent and not to the generic parent. This ensures that the instantiation of the child has visibility of the correct instantiation of the parent.

The reader will now appreciate that the hierarchical library system of Ada 95 provides a very powerful and convenient tool for the development of large systems from component subsystems. This is of particular value in developing bindings to systems such as POSIX in a very elegantly organized manner.

II.9 Protected Types

The rendezvous model of Ada 83 provided an advanced high level approach to task synchronization which avoided the methodological difficulties encountered by the use of low-level primitives such as semaphores and signals. As is well-known, such low-level primitives suffer from similar problems as gotos; it is obvious what they do and they are trivial to implement but in practice easy to misuse and can lead to programs which are difficult to maintain.

Unfortunately the rendezvous has not proved entirely satisfactory. It required additional tasks to manage shared data and this often led to poor performance. Moreover, in some situations, awkward race conditions arose essentially because of abstraction inversion. And from a methodological viewpoint the rendezvous is clearly control oriented and thus out-of-line with a modern object oriented approach.

In Ada 95 we introduce the concept of a protected type which encapsulates and provides synchronized access to the private data of objects of the type without the introduction of an additional task. Protected types are very similar in spirit to the shared objects of the Orca language developed by Bal, Kaashoek and Tanenbaum of Amsterdam [Bal 92].

A protected type has a distinct specification and body in a similar style to a package or task. The specification provides the access protocol and the body provides the implementation details. We can also have a single protected object by analogy with a single task.

As a simple example consider the following

```
protected Variable is
   function Read return Item;
   procedure Write(New_Value: Item);
private
   Data: Item;
end Variable;

protected body Variable is

   function Read return Item is
   begin
      return Data;
   end Read;

   procedure Write(New_Value: Item) is
   begin
      Data := New_Value;
   end Write;

end Variable;
```

The protected object Variable provides controlled access to the private variable Data of some type Item. The function Read enables us to read the current value whereas the procedure Write enables us to update the value. Calls use the familiar dotted notation.

```
X := Variable.Read;
...
Variable.Write(New_Value => Y);
```

Within a protected body we can have a number of subprograms and the implementation is such that (like a monitor) calls of the subprograms are mutually exclusive and thus cannot interfere with each other. A procedure in the protected body can access the private data in an arbitrary manner whereas a function is only allowed read access to the private data. The implementation is consequently permitted to perform the useful optimization of allowing multiple calls of functions at the same time.

By analogy with entries in tasks, a protected type may also have entries. The action of an entry call is provided by an entry body which has a barrier condition which must be true before the entry body can be executed. There is a strong parallel between an accept statement with a guard in a task body and an entry body with a barrier in a protected body, although, as we shall see in a moment, the timing of the evaluation of barriers is quite different to that of guards.

A good illustration of the use of barriers is given by a protected type implementing the classic bounded buffer. Consider

```
protected type Bounded_Buffer is
    entry Put(X: in Item);
    entry Get(X: out Item);
private
    A: Item_Array(1 .. Max);
    I, J: Integer range 1 .. Max := 1;
    Count: Integer range 0 .. Max := 0;
end Bounded_Buffer;

protected body Bounded_Buffer is

    entry Put(X: in Item) when Count < Max is
    begin
        A(I) := X;
        I := I mod Max + 1; Count := Count + 1;
    end Put;

    entry Get(X: out Item) when Count > 0 is
    begin
        X := A(J);
        J := J mod Max + 1; Count := Count - 1;
    end Get;

end Bounded_Buffer;
```

This provides a cyclic bounded buffer holding up to Max values of the type Item with access through the entries Put and Get. We can declare an object of the protected type and access it as expected

```
My_Buffer: Bounded_Buffer;
...
My_Buffer.Put(X);
```

The behavior of the protected type is controlled by the barriers. When an entry is called its barrier is evaluated; if the barrier is false then the call is queued in much the same way that calls on entries in tasks are queued. When My_Buffer is declared, the buffer is empty and so the barrier for Put is true whereas the barrier for Get is false. So initially only a call of Put can be executed and a task issuing a call of Get will be queued.

At the end of the execution of an entry body (or a procedure body) of the protected object all barriers which have queued tasks are reevaluated thus possibly permitting the processing of an entry call which had been queued on a false barrier. So at the end of the first call of Put, if a call of Get had been queued, then the barrier is reevaluated thus permitting a waiting call of Get to be serviced at once.

It is important to realize that there is no task associated with the buffer itself; the evaluation of barriers is effectively performed by the runtime system. Barriers are evaluated when an entry is first called and when something happens which could sensibly change the state of a barrier with a waiting task.

Thus barriers are only reevaluated at the end of an entry or procedure body and not at the end of a protected function call because a function call cannot change the state of the protected object and so is not expected to change the values of barriers. These rules ensure that a protected object can be implemented efficiently.

Note that a barrier *could* refer to a global variable; such a variable might get changed other than through a call of a protected procedure or entry — it could be changed by another task or even by a call of a protected function; such changes will thus not be acted upon promptly. The programmer needs to be aware of this and should not use global variables in barriers without due consideration.

It must be understood that the barrier protection mechanism is superimposed upon the natural mutual exclusion of the protected construct thus giving two distinct levels of protection. At the end of a protected call, already queued entries (whose barriers are now true) take precedence over other calls contending for the protected object. On the other hand, a new entry call cannot even evaluate its barrier if the protected object is busy with another call until that call (and any processible queued calls) have finished.

This has the following important consequence: if the state of a protected resource changes and there is a task waiting for the new state, then this task will gain access to the resource and be guaranteed that the state of the resource when it gets it is the same as when the decision to release the task was made. Unsatisfactory polling and race conditions are completely avoided.

Protected objects are very similar to monitors in general concept; they are passive constructions with synchronization provided by the language runtime system. However, they have a great advantage over monitors in that the protocols are described by barrier conditions (which are fairly easy to prove correct) rather than the low-level and unstructured signals internal to monitors as found in Modula.

In other words protected objects have the essential advantages of the high level guards of the rendezvous model but without the overhead of an active task.

Protected types enable very efficient implementations of various semaphore and similar paradigms. For example a counting semaphore might be implemented as follows

```
protected type Counting_Semaphore(Start_Count: Integer := 1) is
   entry Secure;
   procedure Release;
   function Count return Integer;
private
   Current_Count: Integer := Start_Count;
end Counting_Semaphore;

protected body Counting_Semaphore is

   entry Secure when Current_Count > 0 is
   begin
      Current_Count := Current_Count - 1;
   end Secure;

   procedure Release is
   begin
      Current_Count := Current_Count + 1;
   end Release;

   function Count return Integer is
   begin
      return Current_Count;
   end Count;

end Counting_Semaphore;
```

This implements the general form of Dijkstra's semaphore. It illustrates the use of all three forms of protected operations: a function, a procedure and an entry. The entry Secure and the procedure `Release` correspond to the P and V operations (from the Dutch Passeren and Vrijmaken) and the function `Count` gives the current value of the semaphore. This example also illustrates that a protected type can have a discriminant which is here used to provide the initial value of the semaphore or in other words the number of items of the resource being guarded by the semaphore.

It is important to note that a task type may also have a discriminant in Ada 95 and this can similarly be used to initialize a task. This can for example be used to tell a task who it is (perhaps from among an array of tasks) without introducing a special entry just for that purpose.

Our final example introduces the ability to requeue a call on another entry. It sometimes happens that a service needs to be provided in two parts and that the calling task has to be suspended after the first part until conditions are such that the second part can be done. Two entry calls are then necessary but attempts to program this in Ada 83 usually run into difficulties; race conditions can arise in the interval between the calls and there is often unnecessary visibility of the internal protocol.

The example is of a broadcast signal. Tasks wait for some event and then when it occurs all the waiting tasks are released and the event reset. The difficulty is to prevent tasks that call the wait operation after the event has occurred, but before the signal can be reset, from getting through. In other words, we must reset the signal in preference to letting new tasks through. The requeue statement allows us to program such preference control. An implementation is

```
protected Event is
   entry Wait;
   entry Signal;
private
   entry Reset;
   Occurred: Boolean := False;
end Event;

protected body Event is

   entry Wait when Occurred is
   begin
      null;                    -- note null body
   end Wait;

   entry Signal when True is   -- barrier is always true
   begin
      if Wait'Count > 0 then
         Occurred := True;
         requeue Reset;
      end if;
   end Signal;

   entry Reset when Wait'Count = 0 is
   begin
      Occurred := False;
   end Reset;

end Event;
```

Tasks indicate that they wish to wait for the event by the call

```
Event.Wait;
```

and the happening of the event is notified by some task calling

```
Event.Signal;
```

whereupon all the waiting tasks are allowed to proceed and the event is reset so that future calls of Wait work properly.

The Boolean variable Occurred is normally false and is only true while tasks are being released. The entry Wait has no body but just exists so that calling tasks can suspend themselves on its queue while waiting for Occurred to become true.

The entry Signal is interesting. It has a permanently true barrier and so is always processed. If there are no tasks on the queue of Wait (that is no tasks are waiting), then there is nothing to do and so it exits. On the other hand if there are tasks waiting then it must release them in such a way that no further tasks can get on the queue but then regain control so that it can reset the flag. It does this by requeuing itself on the entry Reset after setting Occurred to true to indicate that the event has occurred.

The semantics of requeue are such that this completes the action of Signal. However, remember that at the end of the body of a protected entry or procedure the barriers are reevaluated for those entries which have tasks queued. In this case there are indeed tasks on the queue for Wait and there is also a task on the queue for Reset (the task that called Signal in the first place); the barrier for Wait is now true but of course the barrier for Reset is false since there are still tasks on the queue for Wait. A waiting task is thus allowed to execute the body of Wait (being null this does nothing) and the task thus proceeds and then the barrier evaluation repeats. The same process continues until all the waiting tasks have gone when finally the barrier of Reset also becomes true. The original task which called signal now executes the body of Reset thus resetting Occurred to false so that the system is once more in its initial state. The protected object as a whole is now finally left since there are no waiting tasks on any of the barriers.

Note carefully that if any tasks had tried to call Wait or Signal while the whole process was in progress then they would not have been able to do so because the protected object as a whole was busy. This illustrates the two levels of protection and is the underlying reason why a race condition does not arise.

Another consequence of the two levels is that it still all works properly even in the face of such difficulties as timed and conditional calls and aborts. The reader may recall, for example, that by contrast, the Count attribute for entries in tasks cannot be relied upon in the face of timed entry calls.

A minor point to note is that the entry Reset is declared in the private part of the protected type and thus cannot be called from outside. Ada 95 also allows a task to have a private part containing private entries.

The above example has been used for illustration only. The astute reader will have observed that the condition is not strictly needed inside Signal; without it the caller will simply always requeue and then immediately be processed if there are no waiting tasks. But the condition clarifies the description. Indeed, the very astute reader might care to note that we can actually program this example in Ada 95 without using requeue at all. A more realistic classic example is the disk scheduler where a caller is requeued if the head is currently over the wrong track.

In this section we have outlined the main features of protected types. There are a number of detailed aspects that we have not covered. The general intent, however, should be clear. Protected types provide a data-oriented approach to synchronization which couples the high-level conditions (the barriers) with the efficiency of monitors. Furthermore the requeue statement provides a means of programming preference control and thus enables race conditions to be avoided.

It must be remembered, of course, that the existing task model remains; the rendezvous will continue to be a necessary approach in many circumstances of a general nature (such as for directly passing messages). But the protected object provides a better paradigm for most data-oriented situations.

II.10 Task Scheduling and Timing

A criticism of Ada 83 has been that its scheduling rules are unsatisfactory especially with regard to the rendezvous. First-in-first-out queuing on entries and the arbitrary selection from several open alternatives in a select statement lead to conflict with the normal preemptive priority rules. For example, priority inversion occurs when a high priority task is on an entry queue behind a lower priority task.

Furthermore, mode changes may require the ability to dynamically change priorities and this conflicts with the simple static model of Ada 83. In addition, advances in the design of scheduling techniques based on Rate Monotonic Scheduling prescribe a variety of techniques to be used in different circumstances according to the arrival pattern of events; see [Sha 90a] and [Klein 93].

Ada 95 allows much more freedom in the choice of priority and scheduling rules. However, because this is a specialized area (and may not be appropriate on some host architectures), the details are contained in the Real-Time Systems annex to which the reader is referred for more details.

Timing is another important aspect of scheduling and the delay statement of Ada 83 has not proved adequate in all circumstances.

For example, an attempt to wait until a specific time by a sequence such as

```
Next_Time: Time;
...
Next_Time := time_to_be_woken_up;
delay Next_Time - Clock;
```

which is intended to stop the task until the time given by the variable Next_Time, is not foolproof. The problem is that there is a race condition. Between calling the function Clock and issuing the delay statement, it is possible for the task to be preempted by a higher priority task. The result is that when the delay is finally issued, the Duration value will be inappropriate and the task will be delayed for too long.

This difficulty is overcome in Ada 95 by the introduction of a complementary delay until statement which takes a Time (rather than a Duration) as its argument. We can then simply write

```
delay until Next_Time;
```

and all will be well.

The final new tasking facility to be introduced in this section is the ability to perform an asynchronous transfer of control. This enables an activity to be abandoned if some condition arises (such as running out of time) and an alternative sequence of statements to be executed instead. This gives the capability of performing mode changes.

This could of course be programmed in Ada 83 by the introduction of an agent task and the use of the abort statement but this was a heavy solution not at all appropriate for most applications needing a mode change.

Asynchronous transfer of control is achieved by a new form of select statement which comprises two parts: an abortable part and a triggering alternative. As a simple example consider

```
select
    delay 5.0;                      -- triggering alternative
    Put_Line("Calculation did not complete");
then abort
    Invert_Giant_Matrix(M);   -- abortable part
end select;
```

The general idea is that if the statements between then abort and end select do not complete before the expiry of the delay then they are abandoned and the statements following the delay executed instead. Thus if we cannot invert our large matrix in five seconds we give up and print a message.

The statement that triggers the abandonment can alternatively be an entry call instead of a delay statement. If the call returns before the computation is complete then again the computation is abandoned and any statements following the entry call are executed instead. On the other hand if the computation completes before the entry call, then the entry call is itself abandoned.

The entry call can, of course, be to a task or to a protected object as described in the previous section. Indeed, Ada 95 allows an entry call to be to a protected object or to a task in all contexts.

Other refinements to the Ada tasking model include a better description of the behavior of the abort statement and a more useful approach to shared variables by the introduction of a number of pragmas.

II.11 Generic Parameters

The generic facility in Ada 83 has proved very useful for developing reusable software particularly with regard to its type parameterization capability. However, there were a few anomalies which have been rectified in Ada 95. In addition a number of further parameter models have been added to match the object oriented facilities.

In Ada 83 the so-called contract model was broken because of the lack of distinction between constrained and unconstrained formal parameters. Thus if we had

```
generic
   type T is private;
package P is ...

package body P is
   X: T;
...
```

then in Ada 83 we could instantiate this with a type such as Integer which was fine. However we could also supply an unconstrained type such as String and this failed because when we came to declare the object T we found that there were no constraints and we could not declare an object as an unconstrained array. The problem was that the error was not detected through a mismatch in the instantiation mechanism but as an error in the body itself. But the whole essence of the contract model is that if the actual parameter satisfies the requirements of the formal then any body which matches the formal specification will work. The poor user might not have had access to the source of the body but nevertheless found errors reported in it despite the instantiation apparently working.

This serious violation of the contract model is repaired in Ada 95. The parameter matching rules for the example above no longer accept an unconstrained type such as String but require a type such as Integer or a constrained type or a record type with default discriminants (these are collectively known as definite types in Ada 95).

If we wish to write a generic package that will indeed accept an unconstrained type then we have to use a new form of notation as follows

```
generic
   type T(<>) is private;
package P ...
```

In this case we are not allowed to declare an (uninitialized) object of type T in the body; we can only use T in ways which do not require a constrained type. The actual parameter can now be any unconstrained type such as String; it could, of course, also be a constrained type.

Other new parameter models are useful for combining genericity with type extension and for writing class-wide generic packages. The formal declaration

```
type T is tagged private;
```

requires that the actual type be tagged.

We can also write

type T **is new** S;

or

type T **is new** S **with private**;

In both cases the actual type must be S or derived directly or indirectly from S. If we add **with private** then both S and the actual type must be tagged. (Remember the rule that all tagged types have **tagged** or **with** in their declaration.)

In all these cases we can also follow the formal type name with (<>) to indicate that the actual may be unconstrained (strictly, indefinite to use the terminology introduced above). Furthermore if we follow **is** by **abstract** then the actual type can also be abstract (but it need not be).

The last new kind of formal generic parameter is the formal generic package. This greatly simplifies the composition of generic packages. It allows one package to be used as a parameter to another so that a hierarchy of facilities can be created.

Examples are inevitably a bit long but consider first the following two packages in Ada 83. The first defines a private type for complex numbers and the basic operations upon them. The second builds on the first and provides various vector operations on complex numbers. The whole system is generic with respect to the underlying floating point type used for the complex numbers.

```
generic
    type Float_Type is digits <>;
package Generic_Complex_Numbers is

    type Complex is private;

    function "+" (Left, Right: Complex) return Complex;
    function "-" (Left, Right: Complex) return Complex;

    -- etc

end Generic_Complex_Numbers;

generic
    type Float_Type is digits <>;
    type Complex is private;

    with function "+" (Left, Right: Complex) return Complex is <>;
    with function "-" (Left, Right: Complex) return Complex is <>;

    -- and so on

package Generic_Complex_Vectors is

    -- types and operations on vectors

end Generic_Complex_Vectors;
```

and we can then instantiate these two packages by for example

```
package Long_Complex is
    new Generic_Complex_Numbers(Long_Float);

use Long_Complex;
```

```
package Long_Complex_Vectors is
   new Generic_Complex_Vectors(Long_Float, Complex);
```

In this Ada 83 formulation we had to pass the type Complex and all its operations exported from Complex_Numbers back into the vector package as distinct formal parameters so that we could use them in that package. The burden was somewhat reduced by using the default mechanism for the operations but this incurred the slight risk that the user might have redefined one of them with incorrect properties (it also forced us to write a use clause or lots of renamings).

This burden is completely alleviated in Ada 95 by the ability to declare generic formal packages. In the generic formal part we can write

```
with package P is new Q(<>);
```

and then the actual parameter corresponding to P must be any package which has been obtained by instantiating Q which must itself be a generic package.

Returning to our example, in Ada 95, having written Generic_Complex_Numbers as before, we can now write

```
with Generic_Complex_Numbers;
generic
   with package Complex_Numbers is
      new Generic_Complex_Numbers (<>);
package Generic_Complex_Vectors is

   -- as before

end Generic_Complex_Vectors;
```

where the actual package must be any instantiation of Generic_Complex_Numbers. Hence our previous instantiations can now be simplified and we can write

```
package Long_Complex is
   new Generic_Complex_Numbers(Long_Float);

package Long_Complex_Vectors is
   new Generic_Complex_Vectors(Long_Complex);
```

The key point is that we no longer have to import (explicitly or implicitly) the type and operators exported by the instantiation of Generic_Complex_Numbers. Hence the parameter list of Generic_Complex_Vectors is reduced to merely the one parameter which is the package Long_Complex obtained by the instantiation of Generic_Complex_Numbers. We no longer even have to pass the underlying type Long_Float.

Although this example has been couched in terms of a numerical application, the general approach is applicable to many examples of building a hierarchy of generic packages.

II.12 Other Improvements

We have now covered most of the major improvements which give Ada 95 so much extra power over Ada 83. But the discussion has not been complete; we have omitted important facilities such as the introduction of controlled types giving initialization, finalization and user defined assignment and the use of access discriminants to give the functionality of multiple inheritance.

There are also a number of minor changes which remove various irritations and which together make Ada 95 a major improvement within existing paradigms. We will now briefly mention the more notable of these improvements.

The attribute `T'Base` can now be used as a type mark. So if `Float_Type` is a generic formal parameter we can then declare

```
Local: Float_Type'Base;
```

and any constraints imposed by the actual parameter will not then apply to the working variable `Local`. This is important for certain numeric algorithms where we wish to be unconstrained in intermediate computations.

The underlying model for the numeric types is slightly changed by the introduction of fictitious types *root_integer* and *root_real*. This brings a number of simplifications and improvements regarding implicit type conversions and one is the removal of the notorious irritation that

```
for I in -1 .. 100 loop
```

was not allowed in Ada 83. It is allowed in Ada 95.

The rule distinguishing basic declarative items from later declarative items has been removed (this essentially said that little declarations cannot follow big declarations and was intended to prevent little ones getting lost visually but it backfired). As a consequence declarations can now be in any order. This often helps with the placing of representation clauses.

Another irritation in Ada 83 was the problem of use clauses and operators. There was a dilemma between, on the one hand, disallowing a use clause and then having to use prefix notation for operators or introduce a lot of renaming or, on the other hand, allowing a use clause so that infixed operators could be used but then allowing visibility of everything and running the risk that package name prefixes might be omitted with a consequent serious loss of readability. Many organizations have imposed a complete ban on use clauses and burdened themselves with lots of renaming. This is solved in Ada 95 by the introduction of a use type clause. If we have a package `Complex_Numbers` which declares a type `Complex` and various operators `"+"`, `"-"` and so on, we can write

```
with Complex_Numbers; use type Complex_Numbers.Complex;
```

and then within our package we can use the operators belonging to the type `Complex` in infix notation. Other identifiers in `Complex_Numbers` will still have to use the full dotted notation so we can see from which package they come. Predefined operators such as `"="` are also made directly visible by an appropriate use type clause.

Concerning `"="` the rules regarding its redefinition are now completely relaxed. It may be redefined for any type at all and need not necessarily return a result of type `Boolean`. The only remaining rule in this area is that if the redefined `"="` does return a result of type `Boolean` then a corresponding `"/="` is also implicitly declared. On the other hand, `"/="` may itself be redefined only if its result is not type `Boolean`.

The rules regarding static expressions are improved and allow further sensible expressions to be treated as static. A static expression may now contain membership tests, attributes, conversions and so on. Moreover, an expression which looks static but occurs in a context not demanding a static expression will be evaluated statically; this was surprisingly not the case in Ada 83 — an expression such as `2 + 3` was only required to be evaluated at compile time if it occurred in a context demanding a static expression. Note also that rounding of odd halves is now defined as away from zero so `Integer(1.5)` is now 2.

A small change which will be welcomed is that a subprogram body may now be provided by renaming. This avoids tediously writing code which merely calls another subprogram. Renaming is now also allowed for generic units and a library unit may now be renamed as a library unit; these facilities will be found to be particularly useful with child units.

Another change which will bring a sigh of relief is that **out** parameters can now be read. They are treated just like a variable that happens not to be explicitly initialized; this change will save the introduction of many local variables and much frustration. A related change is that the restriction that it was not possible to declare a subprogram with **out** parameters of a limited type is also lifted.

Some restrictions regarding arrays are also relaxed. It is now possible to deduce the bounds of a variable (as well as a constant) from an appropriate initial value, such as in

```
S: String := Get_Message;   -- a function call
```

which avoids having to write the tedious

```
Message: constant String := Get_Message;
S: String(Message'Range) := Message;
```

It is also possible to use a named aggregate with an "others" component as an initial value or in an assignment. Sliding is now permitted for subprogram parameters and function results in return statements which are treated like assignment with regard to array bound matching.

There are also improvements in the treatment of discriminants. A private type can now have a discriminated type with defaults as its full type thus

```
package P is
    type T is private;
private
    type T(N: Natural := 1) is
    . . .
end P;
```

Infuriatingly this was not allowed in Ada 83 although the corresponding problem with matching generic parameters was eliminated many years ago.

An important improvement in exception handlers is the ability to access information regarding the occurrence of an exception. This is done by declaring a "choice parameter" in the handler and we can then use that to get hold of, for example, the exception name for debugging purposes. We can write

```
when Event: others =>
    Put_Line("Unexpected exception: " & Exception_Name(Event));
```

where the function Exception_Name returns the name of the exception as a string (such as "Constraint_Error"). Other functions provide further useful diagnostic information regarding the cause of the exception.

An important improvement which will be a great relief to systems programmers is that the language now includes support for unsigned integer types (modular types). This provides shift and logical operations as well as modular arithmetic operations and thus enables unsigned integer values to be manipulated as sequences of bits.

Another improvement worth mentioning in this brief summary concerns library package bodies. In Ada 83 a package body was optional if it was not required by the language (for providing subprogram bodies for example). However, this rule, which was meant to be a helpful convenience, seriously misfired sometimes when a library package was recompiled and bodies which just did initialization could get inadvertently lost without any warning. In Ada 95, a library package is only allowed to have a body if it is required by language rules; the pragma Elaborate_Body is one way of indicating that a body is required.

Finally, in order to meet the needs of the international community, the type Character has been changed to the full 8-bit ISO set (Latin-1) and the type Wide_Character representing the 16-bit ISO Basic Multilingual Plane has been added. The type Wide_String is also defined by analogy.

II.13 The Predefined Library

There are many additional predefined packages in the standard library which has been restructured in order to take advantage of the facilities offered by the hierarchical library. As mentioned above, root library packages behave as children of Standard. There are just three such predefined child packages of Standard, namely System, Interfaces and Ada and these in turn have a number of child packages. Those of System are concerned with intrinsic language capability such as the control of storage. Those of Interfaces concern the interfaces to other languages. The remaining more general predefined packages are children of the package Ada.

An important reason for the new structure is that it avoids potential name conflicts with packages written by the user; thus only the names Ada and Interfaces could conflict with existing Ada 83 code. Without this structure the risk of conflict would have been high especially given the many new predefined packages in Ada 95.

The existing packages such as Calendar, Unchecked_Conversion and Text_IO are now child packages of Ada. Compatibility with Ada 83 is achieved by the use of library unit renaming (itself a new feature in Ada 95) thus

```
with Ada.Text_IO;
package Text_IO renames Ada.Text_IO;
```

We will now briefly summarize the more notable packages in the predefined library in order to give the reader an appreciation of the breadth of standard facilities provided.

The package Ada itself is simply

```
package Ada is
    pragma Pure(Ada);    -- as white as driven snow!
end Ada;
```

where the pragma indicates that Ada has no variable state; (this concept is important for sharing in distributed systems).

Input-output is provided by the existing packages Ada.Text_IO, Ada.Sequential_IO, Ada.Direct_IO and Ada.IO_Exceptions plus a number of new packages. The package Ada.Wide_Text_IO is identical to Text_IO except that it handles the types Wide_Character and Wide_String. General stream input-output is provided by Ada.Streams and Ada.Streams.Stream_IO; these enable heterogeneous files of arbitrary types to be manipulated (remember that Direct_IO and Sequential_IO manipulate files whose items are all of the same type). The package Ada.Text_IO.Text_Streams gives access to the stream associated with Text_IO; this allows mixed binary and text input-output and the use of the standard files with streams.

There are also nongeneric versions of the packages Text_IO.Integer_IO and Text_IO.Float_IO for the predefined types such as Integer and Float. Their names are Ada.Integer_Text_IO and Ada.Float_Text_IO and so on for other predefined types; there are also corresponding wide versions. These nongeneric packages will be found useful for training and overcome the need to teach genericity on day one of every Ada course.

The package Ada.Characters.Handling provides classification and conversion functions for characters. Examples are Is_Letter which returns an appropriate Boolean value and To_Wide_Character which converts a character to the corresponding wide character. The package Ada.Characters.Latin_1 contains named constants in a similar style to Standard.ASCII which is now obsolescent.

General string handling is provided by the package Ada.Strings. Three different forms of string are handled by packages Strings.Fixed, Strings.Bounded and Strings.Unbounded. In addition, packages such as Strings.Wide_Fixed perform similar operations on wide strings.

Extensive mathematical facilities are provided by the package Ada.Numerics. This parent package is just

```
package Ada.Numerics is
   pragma Pure(Numerics);
   Argument_Error: exception;
   Pi: constant := 3.14159_26535_ ... ;
   e: constant := 2.71828_18284_ ... ;
end Ada.Numerics;
```

and includes the generic child package Ada.Numerics.Generic_Elementary_Functions which is similar to the corresponding standard ISO/IEC 11430:1994 for Ada 83 [ISO 94a]. There are also nongeneric versions such as Ada.Numerics.Elementary_Functions for the predefined types Float and so on. Facilities for manipulating complex types and complex elementary functions are provided by other child packages defined in the Numerics annex.

The package Ada.Numerics.Float_Random enables the user to produce streams of pseudo-random floating point numbers with ease. There is also a generic package Ada.Numerics.Discrete_Random which provides for streams of discrete values (both integer and enumeration types).

The package Ada.Exceptions defines facilities for manipulating exception occurrences such as the function Exception_Name mentioned above.

The package System has child packages System.Storage_Elements and System.Storage_Pools which are concerned with storage allocation.

The package Interfaces has child packages Interfaces.C, Interfaces.COBOL and Interfaces.Fortran which provide facilities for interfacing to programs in those languages. It also contains declarations of hardware supported numeric types. Implementations are encouraged to add further child packages for interfacing to other languages.

II.14 The Specialized Needs Annexes

There are six Specialized Needs annexes. In this summary we cannot go into detail but their content covers the following topics:

Systems Programming

> This covers a number of low-level features such as in-line machine instructions, interrupt handling, shared variable access and task identification. This annex is a prior requirement for the Real-Time Systems annex.

Real-Time Systems

> As mentioned above this annex addresses various scheduling and priority issues including setting priorities dynamically, scheduling algorithms and entry queue protocols. It also includes detailed requirements on the abort statement for single and multiple processor systems and a monotonic time package (as distinct from Calendar which might go backwards because of time-zone or daylight-saving changes).

Distributed Systems

> The core language introduces the idea of a partition whereby one coherent "program" is distributed over a number of partitions each with its own environment task. This annex defines two forms of partitions and inter-partition communication using statically and dynamically bound remote subprogram calls.

Information Systems

> The core language extends fixed point types to include basic support for decimal types. This annex defines a number of packages providing detailed facilities for manipulating decimal values and conversion to external format using picture strings.

Numerics

> This annex addresses the special needs of the numeric community. One significant change is the basis for model numbers. These are no longer described in the core language but in this annex. Moreover, model numbers in 95 are essentially what were called safe numbers in Ada 83 and the old model numbers and the term safe numbers have been abandoned. Having both safe and model numbers did not bring benefit commensurate with the complexity and confusion thereby introduced. This annex also includes packages for manipulating complex numbers.

Safety and Security

> This annex addresses restrictions on the use of the language and requirements of compilation systems for programs to be used in safety-critical and related applications where program security is vital.

II.15 Conclusion

The discussion in this chapter has been designed to give the reader a general feel for the scope of Ada 95 and some of the detail. Although we have not addressed all the many improvements that Ada 95 provides, nevertheless, it will be clear that Ada 95 is an outstanding language.

III   Overview of the Ada Language

The previous chapter introduced the new highlights of Ada 95. In contrast, this chapter gives an overview of the whole Ada language showing the overall framework within which the new features fit and thus also illustrates how Ada 95 is a natural evolutionary enhancement of Ada 83.

Ada is a modern algorithmic language with the usual control structures, and with the ability to define types and subprograms. It also serves the need for modularity, whereby data, types and subprograms can be packaged. It treats modularity in the physical sense as well, with a facility to support separate compilation.

In addition to these aspects, the language supports real-time programming, with facilities to define the invocation, synchronization, and timing of parallel tasks. It also supports systems programming, with facilities that allow access to system-dependent properties, and precise control over the representation of data.

The fact that the limited and predominantly upward compatible enhancements incorported in Ada 95 allow it to support state-of-the-art programming in the nineties and beyond, reconfirms the validity of Ada's underlying principles, and is a proof of the excellent foundation provided by the original design.

III.1 Objects, Types, Classes and Operations

This describes two fundamental concepts of Ada: *types*, which determine a set of values with associated operations, and *objects*, which are instances of those types. Objects hold *values*. *Variables* are objects whose values can be changed; *constants* are objects whose values cannot be changed.

III.1.1 Objects and Their Types

Every object has an associated *type*. The type determines a set of possible values that the object can contain, and the operations that can be applied to it. Users write *declarations* to define new types and objects.

Ada is a block-structured language in which the scope of declarations, including object and type declarations, is *static*. Static scoping means that the visibility of names does not depend on the input data when the program is run, but only on the textual structure of the program. Static properties such as visibility can be changed only by modifying and recompiling the source code.

Objects are created when the executing program enters the scope where they are declared (*elaboration*); they are deleted when the execution leaves that scope (*finalization*). In addition, *allocators* are executable operations that create objects dynamically. An allocator produces an access value (a value of an *access type*), which provides access to the dynamically created object. An access value is said to *designate* an object. Access objects are only allowed to designate objects of the type specified by the access type. Access types correspond to pointer types or references in other programming languages.

A *type*, together with a (possibly null) *constraint*, forms a *subtype*. User-defined subtypes constrain the values of the subtype to a subset of the values of the type. Subtype constraints are useful for run-time error detection, because they show the programmer's intent. Subtypes also allow an optimizing compiler to make more efficient use of hardware resources, because they give the compiler more information about the behavior of the program.

User-defined types provide a finer classification of objects than the predefined types, and hence greater assurance that operations are applied to only those objects for which the operations are meaningful.

III.1.2 Types, Classes and Views

Types in Ada can be categorized in a number of different ways. There are elementary types, which cannot be decomposed further, and composite types which, as the term implies, are composed of a number of components. The most important form of composite type is the record which comprises a number of named components themselves of arbitrary and possibly different types.

Records in Ada 95 are generalized to be extensible and form the basis for object-oriented programming. Such extensible record types are known as tagged types; values of such types include a tag denoting the type which is used at runtime to distinguish between different types. Record types not marked as tagged may not be extended and correspond to the record types of Ada 83.

New types may be formed by derivation from any existing type which is then known as the parent type. A derived type inherits the components and primitive operations of the parent type. In the case of deriving from a tagged record type, new components can be added thereby extending the type. In all cases new operations can be added and existing operations replaced.

The set of types derived directly or indirectly from a specific type, together with that type form a *derivation class*. The types in a class share certain properties (they all have the components of the common ancestor or root type for example) and this may be exploited in a number of ways. Treating the types in a class interchangeably by taking advantage of such common properties is termed polymorphism.

There are two means of using polymorphism in Ada. *Static polymorphism* is provided through the generic parameter mechanism whereby a generic unit may at compile time be instantiated with any type from a class of types. *Dynamic polymorphism* is provided through the use of so-called class-wide types and the distinction is then made at runtime on the basis of the value of a tag.

A class-wide type is declared implicitly whenever a tagged record type is defined. The set of values of the class-wide type is the union of the sets of values of all the types of the class. Values of class-wide types are distinguished at runtime by the value of the tag giving class-wide programming or dynamic polymorphism. The class-wide type associated with a tagged record type T is denoted by the attribute T'Class. Objects and operations may be defined for such class-wide types in the usual way.

As well as derivation classes, Ada also groups types into a number of predefined classes with common operations. This aids the description of the language and, moreover, the common properties of certain of these predefined classes may be exploited through the generic mechanism.

A broad hierarchical classification of Ada types is illustrated in Figure III-1. The following summary of the various types gives their key properties.

- A type is either an elementary type or a composite type. Elementary types cannot be decomposed further whereas the composite types have an inner structure. The elementary types can be further categorized into the scalar types and access types. The composite types comprise familiar array and record types plus the protected and task types which are concerned with multitasking.

- Scalar types are themselves subdivided into the discrete types and the real types. The discrete types have certain important common properties; for example, they may be used to index array types. The discrete types are the enumeration types and the integer types.

The integer types in turn comprise signed integer types and modular (unsigned) types. The real types comprise the other forms of numeric types.

- An enumeration type defines an ordered set of distinct enumeration literals, for example a list of states or an alphabet of characters. The enumeration types Boolean, Character (the 8-bit ISO standard character set) and Wide_Character (the 16-bit ISO standard character set) are predefined.

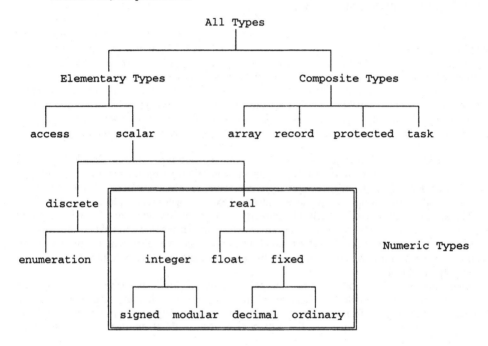

Figure III-1: Ada Type Hierarchy

- The *numeric* types do not exactly fit the hierarchy as presented, but there are certain properties that are common to all numeric types (such as the availability of arithmetic operations), so we have indicated this by a double box surrounding the numeric types. Numeric types provide a means of performing approximate or exact numerical computations. Approximate computations may be performed using either fixed point types with absolute error bounds, or floating point types with relative error bounds. Exact computations may be performed with either integer types, which denote sets of consecutive integers, or with decimal fixed point types. The numeric types Integer, Float and Duration are predefined.

- Access types, the remaining form of elementary type, allow the construction of linked data structures. The value of an access type is, in essence, a pointer to an object of another type, the accessed type. The accessed type may be any type. In particular the accessed type may be a class-wide type thereby allowing the construction of heterogeneous linked data structures. Access types may be used to designate objects created by allocators, declared objects (provided they are marked as aliased) and subprograms.

- Array types allow definitions of composite objects with indexable components all of the same subtype. Array types may be of one or more dimensions. The types of the indexes must be discrete. The array types String and Wide_String are predefined.

- Record types are composite types with named components not necessarily of the same type. Record types may be tagged or untagged. A tagged record type may be extended upon derivation and gives rise to a class-wide type which forms the basis for dynamic polymorphism. A tagged record type may also be marked abstract in which case no objects of the type may be declared; an abstract type may have abstract subprograms (these have no body). Abstract types and subprograms form a foundation from which concrete types may be derived.

- Protected types are composite types that provide synchronized access to their inner components via a number of protected operations. Objects of protected types are passive and do not have a distinct thread of control; the mutual exclusion is provided automatically.

- Task types are composite types which are used to define active units of processing. Each object of a task type has its own thread of control.

Record, protected and task types may be parameterized by special components called *discriminants*. A discriminant may be either of a discrete type or of an access type. A discriminant of a discrete type may be used to control the structure or size of an object. More generally, a discriminant of an access type may be used to parameterize a type with a reference to an object of another type. A discriminant may also be used in the initialization of an object of a protected or task type.

Ada provides a special syntax for defining new types within the various categories as illustrated by the following examples.

```
type Display_Color is    -- an enumeration type
   (Red, Orange, Yellow, Green, Blue, Violet);

type Color_Mask is    -- an array type
   array (Display_Color) of Boolean;

type Money is    -- a decimal fixed type
   delta 0.01 digits 18;

type Payment is    -- a record type
   record
      Amount: Money;
      Due_Date: Date;
      Paid: Boolean;
   end record;

task type Device is    -- a task type
   entry Reset;
end Device;

type Dev is access Device;    -- an access type

protected type Semaphore is    -- a protected type
   procedure Release;
   entry Seize;
private
   Mutex: Boolean := False;
end Semaphore;
```

The following example illustrates a tagged type and type extension. A tagged type declaration takes the form

```
type Animal is tagged
   record
      Species: Species_Name;
      Weight: Grams;
   end record;
```

and we may then declare

```
function Image(A: Animal) return String;
   -- Returns a human-readable identification of an Animal
```

The type Animal could then be extended as follows

```
type Mammal is new Animal with
   record
      Hair_Color: Color_Enum;
   end record;
```

and a corresponding

```
function Image(M: Mammal) return String;
   -- Returns a human-readable identification of a Mammal
```

The type Mammal has all the components of Animal and adds an additional component to describe the color of the mammal's hair. The process of extension and refinement could continue with other types such as Reptile and Primate leading to a tree-structured hierarchy of classes as depicted in Figure III-2.

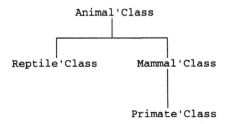

Figure III-2: A Derivation Class Hierarchy

It is important to observe that we have shown the hierarchy in terms of the class-wide types such as Mammal'Class rather than the specific types such as Mammal. This is to emphasize the fact that the type Mammal is not a subtype of Animal; Mammal and Animal are distinct types and values of one type cannot be directly assigned to objects of the other type. However, a value can be converted to an ancestor type (any type if untagged) of the same derivation class by using a type conversion; a value of a descendant tagged type can be formed by using an extension aggregate.

There are a number of other important concepts concerning types regarding the visibility of their components and operations which may be described as providing different *views* of a type.

For example, a *private* type is a type defined in a package whereby the full details of the implementation of the type are only visible inside the body and private part of the package. Private types are of fundamental importance in providing data abstraction.

Furthermore, a *limited* type is a type for which certain operations such as predefined assignment are not available. A type may be inherently *limited* (such as a task type or a protected type or a record type marked explicitly as limited) or it may be that just a certain view is limited. Thus a private type may be declared as limited and the full type as seen by the body need not be limited.

III.1.3 Operations and Overloading

There is a set of operations associated with each type. An operation is associated with a type if it takes parameters of the type, or returns a result of the type. Some operations are implicitly provided when a type is defined; others are explicitly declared by the user.

A set of operations is implicitly provided for each type declaration. Which operations are implicitly provided depends on the type, and may include any of the following

- *Syntactic constructs*, such as assignment, component selection, literals and attributes. These use special syntax specific to the operation.

  For example, an attribute takes the form X'Attr, where X is the name of an entity, and Attr is the name of an attribute of that entity. Thus, Integer'First yields the lower bound of the type Integer.

- *Predefined operators*. These are taken from this set of 21 operator symbols

  - Logical operators: **and or xor**

  - Relational operators: = /= < <= > >=

  - Binary adding operators: + - &

  - Unary adding operators: + -

  - Multiplying operators: * / **mod rem**

  - Highest precedence operators: ** **abs not**

- *Enumeration literals.*

- *Derived operations*, which are inherited by a derived type from its parent type (as explained below).

The *explicitly declared* operations of the type are the *subprograms* that are explicitly declared to take a parameter of the type, or to return a result of the type. There are two kinds of subprograms: *procedures* and *functions*. A procedure defines a sequence of actions; a procedure call is a statement that invokes those actions. A function is like a procedure, but also returns a result; a function call is an expression that produces the result when evaluated. Subprogram calls may be indirect, through an access value.

Procedures may take parameters of mode **in**, which allows reading of the parameters, mode **out**, which allows writing of the parameters, and mode **in out**, which allows both reading and writing of the parameters. In Ada 95, a parameter of mode **out** behaves like a variable and both reading and writing are allowed; however, it is not initialized by the actual parameter. All function parameters are of mode **in**. An **in** parameter may be an *access parameter*. Within the subprogram, an access parameter may be dereferenced to allow reading and writing of the designated object.

The *primitive operations* of a type are the implicitly provided operations of the type, and, for a type immediately declared within a package specification, those subprograms of the type that are also explicitly declared immediately within the same package specification. A derived type *inherits* the primitive operations of its parent type, which may then be overridden.

The name of an explicitly declared subprogram is a *designator*, that is, an identifier or an operator symbol (see the list of operator symbols above). Operators are a syntactic convenience; the operator notation is always equivalent to a function call. For example, X + 1 is equivalent to "+"(X, 1). When defining new types, users can supply their own implementations for any or all of these operators, and use the new operators in expressions in the same way that predefined operators are used.

The benefits of being able to use the operator symbol "+" to refer to the addition function for every numeric type are apparent. The alternative of having to create a unique name for each type's addition function would be cumbersome at best.

The operators are just one example of *overloading*, where a designator (e.g., "+") is used as the name for more than one entity. Another example of overloading occurs whenever a new type is derived from an existing one. The new type inherits operations from the parent type, including the designators by which the operations are named; these designators are overloaded on the old and new types. Finally, the user may introduce overloading simply by defining several subprograms that have the same name. Overloaded subprograms must be distinguishable by their parameter and result types.

The user can also provide new meanings for existing operators. For example, a new meaning of "=" can be provided for all types (only for limited types in Ada 83).

Ada compilers must determine a unique meaning for every designator in a program. The process of making this determination is called *overload resolution*. The compiler uses the context in which the designator is used, including the parameter and result types of subprograms, to perform the overload resolution. If a designator cannot be resolved to a single meaning, then the program is illegal; such ambiguities can be avoided by specifying the types of subexpressions explicitly.

Many attributes are defined by the language. Attributes denote various properties, often defined for various classes of Ada's type hierarchy. In some cases, attributes are *user-specifiable* via an *attribute definition* clause, allowing users to specify a property of an entity that would otherwise be chosen by default. For example, the ability to read and write values of a type from an external medium is provided by the operations T'Read and T'Write. By writing

```
type Matrix is ...
for Matrix'Read use My_Matrix_Reader;
for Matrix'Write use My_Matrix_Writer;
```

the predefined operations are overridden by the user's own subprograms.

III.1.4 Class Wide Types and Dispatching

Associated with each tagged type T is a class-wide type T'Class. Class-wide types have no operations of their own. However, users may define explicit operations on class-wide types. For example

```
procedure Print(A: in Animal'Class);
   -- Print human-readable information about an Animal
```

The procedure Print may be applied to any object within the class of animals described above.

A programmer can define several operations having the same name, even though each operation has a different implementation. The ability to give distinct operations the same name can be used to indicate that these operations have similar, or related, semantics. When the intended operation can be determined at compile time, based on its parameter and result types, overloading of subprogram names is used. For example, the predefined package Text_IO contains many operations called Put, all of which write a value of some type to a file. The implementation of Put is different for different types.

Dispatching provides run-time selection of the proper implementation in situations where the type of an argument to an operation cannot be determined until the program is executed, and in fact might be different each time the operation is invoked.

Ada 95 provides dispatching on the primitive operations of tagged types. When a primitive operation of a tagged type is called with an actual parameter of a class-wide type, the appropriate implementation is chosen based on the tag of the actual value. This choice is made at run time and represents the essence of dynamic polymorphism. (Note that, in some cases, the tag can be determined at compile time; this is simply regarded as an optimization.)

Continuing the example from above, we demonstrate both overloading and dispatching

```
procedure Print(S: in String);
   -- Print a string

procedure Print(A: in Animal'Class) is
   -- Print information on an animal
begin
   Print(Image(A));
end Print;
```

The Print operation is overloaded. One version is defined for String and a second is defined for Animal'Class. The call to Print within the second version resolves at compile time to the version of Print defined on String (because Image returns a String); no dispatching is involved. On the other hand, Image (see example in III.1.2) is indeed a dispatching operation: depending on the tag of A the version of Image associated with Animal or Mammal etc, will be called and this choice is made at runtime.

III.1.5 Abstraction and Static Evaluation

The emphasis on high performance in Ada applications, and the requirement to support interfacing to special hardware devices, mean that Ada programmers must be able to engineer the low-level mapping of algorithms and data structures onto physical hardware. On the other hand, to build large systems, programmers must operate at a high level of abstraction and compose systems from understandable building blocks. The Ada type system and facilities for separate compilation are ideally suited to reconciling these seemingly conflicting requirements.

Ada's support for static checking and evaluation make it a powerful tool, both for the abstract specification of algorithms, and for low-level systems programming and the coding of hardware-dependent algorithms. By *static*, we mean computations whose results can be determined by analyzing the source code without knowing the values of input data or any other environmental parameters that can change between executions of the program.

Ada requires static type checking. The "scope" (applicability or lifetime) of declarations is determined by the source code. Careful attention is given to when the sizes of objects are determined. Some objects' sizes are static, and other objects' sizes are not known until run time, but are fixed when the objects are created. The size of an object is only allowed to change during program execution if the object's size depends on discriminant values, and the discriminants have a default value. Other variable-size data structures can be created using dynamically allocated objects and access types.

Ada supports users who want to express their algorithms at the abstract level and depend on the compiler to choose efficient implementations, as well as users who need to specify implementation details but also want to declare the associated abstractions to the compiler to facilitate checking during both initial development and maintenance.

III.2 Statements, Expressions and Elaboration

Statements are *executed* at run time to cause an action to occur. *Expressions* are *evaluated* at run time to produce a value of some type. *Names* are also evaluated at run time in the general case; names refer to objects (containing values) or to other entities such as subprograms and types. *Declarations* are *elaborated* at run time to produce a new entity with a given name.

Many expressions and subtype constraints are statically known. Indeed, the Ada compiler is required to evaluate certain expressions and subtypes at compile time. For example, it is common that all information about a declaration is known at compile time; in such cases, the run-time elaboration need not actually execute any machine code. The language defines a mechanism that allows Ada compilers to *preelaborate* certain kinds of units; i.e., the actual actions needed to do the elaboration are done once before the program is ever run instead of many times, each time it is run.

III.2.1 Declarative Parts

Several constructs of the language contain a *declarative part* followed by a *sequence of statements*. For example, a procedure body takes the form

```
procedure P(...) is
   I: Integer := 1;   -- this is the declarative part
   ...
begin
   ...                -- this is the statement sequence
   I := I * 2;
   ...
end P;
```

The execution of the procedure body first elaborates all of the declarations given in the declarative part in the order given. It then executes the sequence of statements in the order given (unless a transfer of control causes execution to go somewhere other than to the next statement in the sequence).

The effect of elaborating the declarations is to cause the declared entities to come into existence, and to perform other declaration-specific actions. For example, the elaboration of a variable declaration may initialize the variable to the value of some expression. Often, such expressions are evaluated at compile time. However, if the declarations contain non-static expressions, then the elaboration will need to evaluate those expressions at run-time.

Controlled types allow programmers a means to define what happens to objects at the beginning and end of their lifetimes. For such types, the programmer may define an *initialization* operation, to be automatically invoked when an object of the type is elaborated, and a *finalization* operation to be automatically invoked when the object becomes inaccessible. (Declared objects become inaccessible when their scope is left. Objects created by allocators become inaccessible when Unchecked_Deallocation is called, or when the scope of the access type is left.) Controlled types provide a means to reliably program dynamic data structures, prevent storage leakage, and leave resources in a consistent state.

III.2.2 Assignments and Control Structures

An *assignment statement* causes the value of a variable to be replaced by that of an expression of the same type. Assignment is normally performed by a simple bit copy of the value provided by the expression. However, in the case of nonlimited controlled types, assignment can be redefined by the user.

Case statements and *if statements* allow selection of an enclosed sequence of statements based on the value of an expression. The *loop statement* allows an enclosed sequence of statements to be executed repeatedly, as directed by an *iteration scheme*, or until an *exit statement* is encountered. A *goto statement* transfers control to a place marked with a *label*. Additional control mechanisms associated with multitasking and exception handling are discussed below (see III.4 and III.5).

III.2.3 Expressions

Expressions may appear in many contexts, within both declarations and statements. Expressions are similar to expressions in most programming languages: they may refer to variables, constants and literals, and they may use any of the value-returning operations described in III.1.3. An expression produces a value. Every expression has a type that is known at compile time.

III.3 System Construction

Ada was designed specifically to support the construction of large, complex, software systems. Therefore, it must allow the composition of programs from small, understandable building blocks, while still allowing programmers to engineer the low-level mapping of algorithms and data structures onto physical hardware. Ada provides support for modern software development techniques with the following capabilities

- Packaging, the grouping together of logically related entities into packages.

- Information hiding, where the programmer defines the interface of a program unit for the users of that unit, and separately defines the implementation of the unit.

- Object-oriented programming, where objects can be defined in terms of preexisting objects with possible extension, overload resolution can be used to select operations at compile time, and dispatching can be used to select operations at run time.

- Construction of software systems from large numbers of separately compiled units stored in a library, with full compile-time checking of interfaces between separately compiled units.

- Class-wide programming.

- Construction of mixed language systems, that is programs written in more than one programming language.

The following subsections describe this support in more detail.

III.3.1 Program Units

Ada programs are composed of the following kinds of *program units*

- Subprograms — functions and procedures.

- Packages — groups of logically related entities.

- Generic units — parameterized templates for subprograms and packages.

- Tasks — active entities that may run in parallel with each other.

- Protected objects — passive entities that protect data shared by multiple tasks.

Program units may be nested within each other, in the same way as in other block-structured languages. Furthermore, they may be separately compiled.

As we shall see later, packages at the so-called library level may have child units. Ada has a hierarchical structure both at the external level of compilation and internal to a program unit.

Each program unit may be given in two parts: The *specification* defines the interface between the unit (the "server") and its users ("clients"). The *body* defines the implementation of the unit; users do not depend on the implementation details.

For packages, the specification consists of the *visible part* and the *private part*. The visible part defines the logical interface to the package. The private part defines the physical interface to the package, which is needed to generate efficient code, but has no effect on the logical properties of the entities exported by the package. Thus, the private part may be thought of as part of the implementation of the package, although it is syntactically part of the specification in order to ease the generation of efficient code.

The various parts of a package take the following form

```
-- this is a package specification:
package Example is
   -- this is the visible part
   -- declarations of exported entities appear here
   type Counter is private;
   procedure Reset(C: in out Counter);
   procedure Increment(C: in out Counter);
   --
private
   -- this is the private part
   -- declarations appearing here are not exported
   type Counter is range 0 .. Max;
end Example;

-- this is the corresponding package body:
package body Example is

   -- implementations of exported subprograms appear here
   -- entities that are used only in the implementation
   -- are also declared here
   Zero: constant Counter := 0;
      -- declaration of constant only used in the body

   procedure Reset(C: in out Counter) is
   begin
      C := Zero;
   end Reset;

   procedure Increment(C: in out Counter) is
   begin
      C := C + 1;
   end Increment;

end Example;
```

Tasks and protected objects may also have a private part.

III.3.2 Private Types and Information Hiding

Packages support information hiding in the sense that users of the package cannot depend on the implementation details that appear in the package body. *Private types* provide additional information-hiding capability. By declaring a type and its operations in the visible part of a package specification, the user can create a new abstract data type.

When a type is declared in a package specification, its implementation details may be hidden by declaring the type to be *private*. The implementation details are given later, as a *full type declaration* in the private part of the package.

The user of a private type is not allowed to use information about the full type. Users may declare objects of the private type, use the assignment and equality operations, and use any operations declared as subprograms in the visible part of the package. The private type declaration may allow users to refer to discriminants of the type, or it may keep them hidden. A private type may also be declared as *limited*, in which case even assignment and predefined equality operations are not available (although the programmer may define an equality operation and export it from the package where the type is declared).

In the private part, in the body of the package, and in the appropriate parts of child library units (see III.3.6), the type is not private: all operations of the type may be used in these places. For example, if the full type declaration declares an array type, then outside users of the type are not allowed to index array components, because these implementation details are hidden. However, code in the package body *is* allowed the complete set of array operations, because it can see the full type declaration.

III.3.3 Object Oriented Programming

Modern software development practices call for building programs from reusable parts, and for extending existing systems. Ada supports such practices through object oriented programming features. The basic principle of object oriented programming is to be able to define one part of a program as an extension of another, pre-existing, part. The basic building blocks of object-oriented programming were discussed in III.1.

Abstract data types may be defined in Ada using packages and private types. Types may be extended by adding new packages, deriving from existing types, and adding new operations to derived types. For non-tagged types, such extension is "static" in the sense that the compiler determines which operations apply to which objects according to the typing and overloading rules. For tagged types, however, operation selection is determined at run time, using the tag carried by each such object. This allows easy extension of existing types. To add a new tagged type, the programmer derives from an existing tagged parent type, possibly adding new record components. The programmer may override existing operations with new implementations. Then, all calls to the existing operation will automatically call the new operation in the appropriate cases; there is no need to change or even to recompile such pre-existing code. For tagged types, it is possible to write class-wide operations by defining subprograms that take parameters of a class-wide type. Class-wide programming allows the programmer to avoid redundancy in cases where an operation makes sense for all types in a class, and where the implementation of that operation is essentially the same for all types in the class.

III.3.4 Generic Units

Generic program units allow parameterization of program units. The parameters can be types and subprograms as well as objects. A normal (non-generic) program unit is produced by *instantiating* a generic unit; the normal program unit is said to be an *instance* of the generic unit. An instance of a generic package is a package; an instance of a generic subprogram is a subprogram.

The instance is a copy of the generic unit, with *actual parameters* substituted for *generic formal parameters*. Generic units may be implemented by actually generating new code for each instance, or by sharing the code for multiple instances, and passing information about the parameters at run time.

An example of a generic package is a generic linked list package that works for any element type. The data type of the elements would be passed in as a parameter. The algorithms for manipulating the lists are independent of the actual element type. Instances of the generic package would support linked lists with a particular element type. If the element type is a tagged class-wide type, then heterogeneous lists can be created, containing elements of any type in the class. Generic formal derived types permit generic units to be developed for derivation classes. Generic formal packages allow a generic unit to be parameterized by an instance of another generic package.

III.3.5 Separate Compilation

Ada allows the specifications and bodies of program units to be separately compiled. A separately compiled piece of code is called a *compilation unit*. The Ada compiler provides the same level of compile-time checking across compilation units as it does within a single compilation unit. For example, in a procedure call, the actual parameters must match the types declared for the formal parameters. This rule is checked whether the procedure declaration and the procedure call are in the same compilation unit, or different compilation units.

Ada compilers work within the context of a *program environment*, which contains information about the compilation units in a program. This information is used in part to check rules across compilation unit boundaries. There are rules about order of compilation that ensure that the compiler always has enough information to check all the rules. For example, a specification must be within the environment before all units that have visibility to names declared in that specification can be compiled.

III.3.6 Library Units

A program environment contains information concerning a collection of *library units*. Library units may be packages, subprograms, or generic units.

Package library units may have *child library units*. Thus, an entire hierarchy of library units may be created: the root of each tree is called a *root library unit*; the tree contains the root library unit, plus all of its children and their descendants.

A library unit specification and its body are compilation units; that is, they may be compiled separately.

Visibility among library units is achieved using *context clauses*; a compilation unit can see a particular library unit if it names that library unit in a context clause. Both root library units and child units may be named in a context clause. In addition, the child library units of a parent can see the parent, including the parent's private declarations, and the body of a unit always has visibility into its specification.

Child units may be used to reduce recompilation costs. Apart from dependencies created by context clauses, the immediate children of a given unit may be recompiled in any order. Therefore, if an existing library unit is extended by adding a child unit, the existing unit need not be recompiled; adding a child is accomplished without changing the source code of the parent. More importantly, other units that depend on the existing parent unit will not need to be recompiled.

The root library units are considered to be children of package Standard: context clauses and compilation ordering rules work the same way. Thus, child units are a straightforward generalization of Ada 83 library units.

As an example consider the following

```
package Root is
   -- specification of a root library unit
   ...
end Root;
```

```
package Root.Child is
   -- specification of a child library unit
   ...
end Root.Child;
```

```
package body Root.Child is
   -- body of the child library unit
   ...
end Root.Child;
```

```
private package Root.Local_Definitions is
   -- a private child package specification
   ...
end Root.Local_Definitions;
```

```
package body Root is
   -- body of the root library unit
   ...
end Root;
```

The lines in the above example indicate the separate compilation units; they may be submitted to the compiler separately. Note that the child library units are clearly distinguishable by their expanded names (based on the parent's name). The example also shows a *private child* package — a private child unit is visible only within the hierarchy of units rooted at its parent.

Sometimes, the body of a library unit becomes very large, because it contains one or more nested bodies. In such cases, Ada allows the nested bodies to be separately compiled as *subunits*. The nested body is replaced by a *body stub*. The subunit, which is given separately, must name its parent unit. Visibility within the subunit is as if it had appeared at the place where its body stub occurs. Subunits also support an incremental style of top-down development, because a unit may be compiled with one or more body stubs — allowing the development of those bodies to be deferred.

III.3.7 Program Composition

An executable software system is known in Ada as a *program*. A program is composed of one or more compilation units.

A program may be divided into separate *partitions*, which may represent separate address spaces. Implementations may provide mechanisms for user-defined inter-partition communication. The Distributed Systems annex defines a minimal standard interface for such communication. Partitions are intended to support distributed processing, as explained in the annex. Of course, many programs will not be partitioned; such programs consist of a single partition.

To build a partition, the user identifies a set of library units to be included. The partition consists of those library units, plus other library units depended on by the named units. The Ada implementation automatically constructs this set of units before run time.

Each partition has an *environment task*, which is provided automatically by the Ada implementation. A partition may have a *main subprogram*, which must be a library unit subprogram. The environment task elaborates all of the library units that are part of the partition, and their bodies, in an appropriate order, and then calls the main subprogram, if any. The library units and the main program may create other tasks. Thus, an executing partition may contain a hierarchy of tasks, rooted at the environment task.

III.3.8 Interfacing to Other Languages

Large programs are often composed of parts written in several languages. Ada supports this by allowing inter-language subprogram calls, in both directions, and inter-language variable references, in both directions. The user specifies these interfaces using pragmas.

III.4 Multitasking

Ada tasking provides a structured approach to concurrent processing under the control of an Ada run-time system, which provides services such as scheduling and synchronization. This describes tasks and the methods that are used for synchronizing task execution and for communicating between tasks.

Tasking is intended to support tightly coupled systems in which the communication mechanisms may be implemented in terms of shared memory. Distributed processing, where the processors are loosely coupled, is addressed in the Distributed Systems annex.

III.4.1 Tasks

Tasks are entities whose execution may proceed in parallel. A task has a thread of control. Different tasks proceed independently, except at points where they synchronize.

If there is a sufficient number of processors, then all tasks may execute in parallel. Usually, however, there are more tasks than processors; in this case, the tasks will time-share the existing processors, and the execution of multiple tasks will be interleaved on the same processor.

A task is an object of a task type. There may be more than one object of a given task type. All objects of a given task type have the same entries (interface), and share the same code (body). As a result they all execute the same algorithm. Different task objects of the same type may be parameterized using discriminants. Task types are inherently limited types; assignment and equality operations are forbidden.

Task objects are created in the same ways as other objects: they may be declared by an object declaration, or created dynamically using an allocator. Tasks may be nested within other program units, in the same manner as subprograms and packages.

All tasks created by a given declarative part or allocator are activated in parallel. This means that they can logically start running in parallel with each other. The task that created these tasks waits until they have all finished elaborating their declarative parts; it then continues running in parallel with the tasks it created.

Every task has a *master*, which is the task, subprogram, block statement, or accept statement which contains the declaration of the task object (or an access type designating the task type, in some circumstances). The task is said to *depend* on its master. The task executing the master is called the *parent* task. Before leaving a master, the parent task waits for all dependent tasks. When all of those have been terminated, or are ready to terminate, the parent task proceeds. Tasks may be terminated prematurely with the *abort statement*.

III.4.2 Communication and Synchronization

For multiple tasks to cooperate, there must be mechanisms that allow the tasks to communicate and to synchronize their execution. Synchronization and communication usually go hand-in-hand. Ada tasks synchronize and communicate in the following situations

• Tasks synchronize during activation and termination (as just explained).

• Protected objects provide synchronized access to shared data.

• Rendezvous are used for synchronous communication between a pair of tasks.

• Finally, unprotected access to shared variables is allowed, but requires a disciplined protocol to be followed by the communicating tasks.

This flexibility allows the user to choose the appropriate synchronization and communication mechanisms for the problem at hand. They are depicted in Table III-1.

Ada feature	Synchronization	Communication
Task Creation	(not needed)	Creator initializes discriminants of new task
Task Activation	Creator waits for tasks being activated	Activation failure might be reported
Task Termination	Master waits for children	(none)
Rendezvous	Entry caller and acceptor wait for each other	Entry parameters are passed between the entry caller and the acceptor
Protected Object	Mutual exclusion during data access; queued waiting for entry barriers	Tasks communicate indirectly by reading and writing the components of protected objects
Unprotected Shared Variables	User-defined, low-level synchronization	Reading and writing of shared variables

Table III-1: Summary of Communication and Synchronization

III.4.3 Protected Objects

Protected types are used to synchronize access to shared data. A protected type may contain components in a private part. Moreover, a protected type may also contain functions, procedures, and entries — the *protected operations* of the protected type. The data being shared is declared either as components of the protected type, or as global variables, possibly designated by the components of the protected type. Protected types are inherently limited.

Calls to the protected operations are synchronized as follows. Protected functions provide shared read-only access to the shared data. Multiple tasks may execute protected functions at the same time. Protected procedures and entries provide exclusive read/write access to the shared data. If any task is executing a protected procedure or entry, then no other tasks are allowed to execute any protected operation at the same time; if they try, they must wait.

Protected objects provide a safe and efficient method of synchronizing shared data access. They are safe, because they perform the necessary synchronization operations automatically, and because all synchronizing operations are collected together syntactically. (This is in contrast to lower-level mechanisms such as semaphores, where the user of the shared data must remember to lock and unlock the semaphore.) They are efficient, because their intended implementation is close to the hardware: such as spin-locks in multiprocessor systems.

III.4.4 Protected Operations and Entries

Protected types may export functions, procedures, and entries as described above. Tasks may export entries. All of these operations are called using similar syntax: OBJ.OP(...), where OBJ is the name of the task or protected object, OP is the name of the operation, and (...) represents any actual parameters. Information is passed back and forth using **in, in out, out** parameters. It is the responsibility of the programmer to ensure that operations of protected objects execute for a bounded and short period of time.

A client task which calls an entry of a server task or protected object may be blocked and placed on a queue. When a server task *accepts* the entry call from a client task, we say that the two tasks are in *rendezvous*. At the beginning and the end of the rendezvous, data may be exchanged via parameters. When the rendezvous is over, the two tasks each continue execution in parallel.

Entries of protected objects are controlled by barrier expressions. When a task calls the entry, it can execute the operation immediately if the barrier expression is true; otherwise, the caller is placed on a queue until the barrier has become true. Protected functions and procedures do not have barrier expressions and, therefore, calls on them need not be queued.

From within a rendezvous or the entry body of a protected type it is possible to complete the interaction by requeuing on a further entry; this avoids race conditions which might occur with two quite distinct interactions.

Entries may also be declared in the private part of a task or protected object and thus not visible to external clients. Such entries may be called by internal tasks or by requeuing.

III.4.5 Select Statements

Select statements are used to specify that a task is willing to wait for any of a number of alternative events. Select statements take various forms.

Select statements used by a server task may contain

- One or more *accept alternatives*, which indicate that the task is willing to accept one of several entries; that is, the task waits for another task to call one of those entries.

- An optional *terminate alternative*, which allows a server task to specify that it is willing to terminate if there is no more work to do (i.e., all other tasks that depend on the same master are either terminated or are waiting at terminate alternatives).

Select statements used by a client task may contain

- One *entry call alternative*, which indicates that the task is waiting for an entry to be executed. That is, the task waits either for the server task to accept the entry, or for the protected object barrier to become true.

Both of these forms of select statement can also contain, either

- A *delay alternative*, which allows a task to specify an action to be taken if communication is not started within a given period of time, or

- An *else part*, which allows a task to specify an action to be taken if communication is not immediately possible.

Whichever alternative becomes available first is chosen. Each alternative specifies an action to be executed if and when the alternative is chosen.

The final form of select statement provides for an asynchronous transfer of control; it contains

- A *triggering alternative*, which may be a delay alternative or an entry call followed by a sequence of statements, and

- An *abortable part*, which is aborted if the triggering alternative completes before the abortable part itself completes. Control is then asynchronously transferred from somewhere in the abortable part to the statements of the triggering alternative. If the abortable part completes before being aborted, then the triggering alternative is cancelled and execution continues at the next statement after the select statement.

III.4.6 Timing

Ada provides features for measuring real time. A task may read the clock to find out what time it is. A task may delay for a certain period of time, or until a specific time.

As mentioned above, a delay alternative may be used to provide a time-out for communication or as a triggering event for initiating an asynchronous transfer of control.

III.4.7 Scheduling

Ada separates the concepts of synchronization and scheduling. Synchronization operations determine when tasks must block, and when they are ready to run. Scheduling is the method of allocating processors to ready tasks. The default scheduling policy is defined by the language. The Real-Time Systems annex defines another, priority-based, scheduling policy, based on a dispatching model. Finally, implementations are allowed to add their own policies, which can be specified by pragmas.

III.5 Exception Handling

Most programs need to recover gracefully from errors that occur during execution. Exception handling allows programs to handle such error situations without ceasing to operate.

An *exception* is used to name a particular kind of error situation. Some exceptions are predefined by the language; others may be defined by the user. Exceptions are declared in the same way as other entities

```
Buffer_Full_Error: exception;
```

This exception might be used to represent the situation of a program trying to insert data into a buffer which is already full.

When the exceptional situation happens, the exception is *raised*. Language-defined exceptions are raised for errors in using predefined features of the language. These exceptions correspond to run-time errors in other languages. For example, the language-defined exception `Constraint_Error` is raised when a subtype constraint is violated at run time. User-defined exceptions are raised by the *raise* statement. To continue the `Buffer_Full_Error` example above, the implementation of the buffer data type might contain statements such as

```
if Buffer_Index > Max_Buffer_Size then
    raise Buffer_Full_Error;
end if;
```

Subprograms, package bodies, block statements, task bodies, entry bodies, and accept statements may have *exception handlers*. An exception handler specifies an action that should be performed when a particular exception is raised. When an exception is raised, the execution of the current sequence of statements is abandoned, and control is transferred to the exception handler, if there is one. Thus, the action of the exception handler replaces the rest of the execution of the sequence of statements that caused the error condition. If there is no exception handler in a particular scope, then the exception is propagated to the calling scope. If the exception is propagated all the way out to the scope of the environment task, then execution of the program is abandoned; this is similar to the way in which program execution is abandoned in other languages when run-time errors are detected.

The following example shows a block with two exception handlers

```
begin
    ...
exception
    when Buffer_Full_Error =>
        Reset_Buffer;
    when Error: others =>
        Put_Line("Unexpected exception raised:");
        Put_Line(Ada.Exceptions.Exception_Information(Error));
end;
```

The handlers recognize two situations: if `Buffer_Full_Error` is raised, the buffer is reset. If any other exception is raised, information about that exception is printed. For many applications, it is useful to get such information about an exception when it occurs. A handler may have a choice parameter (`Error` in the example above) of type `Exception_Occurrence`. The predefined function `Exception_Information` takes a parameter of this type and returns a `String`, providing information (including the name) about the exception. These and other related facilities are defined in a child of package `Ada`.

III.6 Low Level Programming

Although the majority of program text can be written in a machine-independent manner, most large software systems contain small portions that need to depend on low-level machine characteristics. Ada allows such dependence, while still allowing the high-level aspects of the algorithms and data structures to be described in an abstract manner. Many of an implementation's machine-specific characteristics are accessible through the package `System`. This defines storage-related types, an `Address` type, and relational and arithmetic operations on addresses.

III.6.1 Pragmas

A *pragma* is used to convey information to the compiler; it is similar to a compiler directive supported by other languages. A pragma begins with the reserved word **pragma**, an identifier which is the name of the pragma, and optionally one or more arguments.

Some pragmas are defined by the language. For example, pragma Inline indicates to the compiler that the code for a subprogram is to be expanded inline at each call whenever possible. Most pragmas apply to a single object, type, or program unit. *Configuration pragmas* are used to specify partition-wide or program-wide options.

Implementations may provide additional pragmas, as long as they do not syntactically conflict with existing ones or use reserved words. Unrecognized pragmas have no effect on a program, but their presence must be signaled with a warning message.

III.6.2 Specifying Representations

Normally, the programmer lets the Ada compiler choose the most efficient way of representing objects. However, Ada also provides *representation clauses*, which allow the user to specify the representation of an individual object, or of all objects of a type. Other representation clauses apply to program units.

The programmer may need to specify that the representation matches the representation used by some hardware or software external to the Ada program, in order to interface to that external entity. Or, the programmer may wish to specify a more efficient representation of certain objects in cases where the compiler does not have enough information to determine the best (most efficient) representation. In either case, data types and objects are first declared in the normal manner, giving their logical properties. Later in the same declarative part, the programmer gives the representation clauses.

In addition to representation clauses, the language defines certain pragmas that control aspects of representation. Implementations may provide additional representation pragmas.

There are predefined attributes that allow users to query aspects of representation. These are useful when the programmer needs to write code that depends upon the representation, although the user might not need to control the representation.

In the absence of representation clauses or pragmas, the compiler is free to choose any representation.

III.6.3 Unprotected Shared Variables

In Ada, variables may be shared among tasks according to the normal visibility rules: if two tasks can see the name of the same variable, then they may use that variable as shared data. However, it is up to the programmer to properly synchronize access to these shared variables. In most cases, data sharing can be achieved more safely with protected objects; unprotected shared variables are primarily used in low-level systems programming. Ada allows the user to specify certain aspects of memory allocation and code generation that may affect synchronization by specifying variables as *volatile* or *atomic*.

III.6.4 Unchecked Programming

Ada provides features for bypassing certain language restrictions. These features are unchecked; it is the programmer's responsibility to make sure that they do not violate the assumptions of the rest of the program. For example, there are mechanisms for manipulating access types that might leave dangling pointers, and there is a mechanism for converting data from one type to another, bypassing the type-checking rules.

The generic function `Unchecked_Deallocation` frees storage allocated by an allocator. It is unchecked in the sense that it can leave dangling pointers.

The generic function `Unchecked_Conversion` converts data from one type to another, bypassing all type-checking rules. The conversion is done simply by reinterpreting the bit pattern as a value of the target type; no conversion actually happens at run time (except possibly bit padding or truncation).

The attribute `P'Unchecked_Access` returns a typed access value to any aliased object of the appropriate type, bypassing the accessibility checking rules (but not the type rules).

III.7 Standard Library

All implementations provide a standard library of various packages. This includes the predefined package `Standard` which defines the predefined types such as `Integer`, and the package `System` which defines various entities relating to the implementation.

The standard library also includes packages `Ada` and `Interfaces`. The package `Ada` includes child packages for computing elementary functions and generating random numbers as well as child packages for string handling and character manipulation. The package `Interfaces` defines facilities for interfacing to other languages.

III.7.1 Input Output

Input-output capabilities are provided in Ada by predefined packages and generic packages.

- *Sequential files* present a logical view of files as sequences of elements. Successive read or write operations to a sequential file result in the transfer of consecutive elements. The generic package `Sequential_IO` may be instantiated for any type to provide operations for creating, opening, closing, deleting, reading and writing sequential files. All elements of a `Sequential_IO` file are of the same type, although if the type is a tagged class-wide type, the elements may have different tags.

- *Direct files* present a logical view of files as indexed sets of elements. The index allows elements to be read or written at any position within a file. The generic package `Direct_IO` provides operations similar to `Sequential_IO`. In addition, `Direct_IO` provides operations for determining the current position and size of a file, and setting the position in the file, in terms of element numbers.

- The `Text_IO` package provides facilities for input and output in a human-readable form.

- A *stream* presents a logical view of a file (or other external medium such as a buffer or network channel) as a sequence of stream elements. Stream input and output are predefined through attributes for all nonlimited types. Users may override these default attributes and the stream operations.

III.8 Application Specific Facilities

Previous sections of this Overview have focused on the Core of the Ada language. Implementations may provide additional features, not by extending the language itself, but by providing specialized packages and implementation-defined pragmas and attributes. In order to encourage uniformity among implementations, without restricting functionality, the *Specialized Needs Annexes* define standards for such additional functionality for specific application areas. Implementations are not required to support all of these features. For example, an implementation specifically targeted to embedded machines might support the application-specific features for Real-Time Systems, but not the application-specific features for Information Systems.

The application areas discussed in the Annexes are

- Systems Programming, including access to machine operations, interrupts, elaboration control, low-level shared variables, and task identification facilities.

- Real-Time Systems, including priorities, queuing and scheduling policies, monotonic time, delay accuracy, immediate abort and a simple tasking model.

- Distributed Systems, including a model for Ada program distribution into partitions and inter-partition communication.

- Information Systems, including detailed support for decimal types and picture formatting.

- Numerics, including a model of real arithmetic plus packages for complex numbers.

- Safety and Security, including pragmas relating to the proof of correctness of programs.

III.9 Summary

The goal of this chapter has been to provide a broad overview of the whole of the Ada language. It also demonstrates that the changes to the language represent a natural extension to the original design of Ada. As a consequence, the incompatibilities between Ada 83 and Ada 95 are minimal. Those of practical significance are described in detail in Appendix X.

Part Two

The Core Language

Part One should have given the reader an overall appreciation of the scope and some of the details of Ada 95. The discussion included some rationale for the main features but did not go into all the details. This second part takes the discussion of the Core language a step further. It covers those important features not discussed in Part One and gives more detail of the rationale including alternatives that were considered and rejected. It is assumed that the reader is familiar with the material in Part One which will be referred to from time to time. It is recommended that this part be read in conjunction with the Ada 95 Reference Manual.

1 Introduction

This second part of the rationale is arranged to generally correspond to the sections in the Ada 95 Reference Manual [RM95]. Thus the discussion on exceptions which is covered in section 11 of [RM95] will be found in Chapter 11 of this part. The only exception to this is that the material covered by sections 3 and 4 of [RM95] is subdivided differently. Chapter 3 of this volume covers types and expressions in general whereas Chapter 4 concentrates on the object oriented features such as type extension and class-wide types.

In a similar way the chapters of the third part correspond to the annexes of [RM 95]; thus chapter C discusses the Systems Programming Annex which is annex C of [RM 95].

Each chapter of this second part starts with a brief summary of the changes, there are then a number of sections addressing the various topics, and finally there is a summary of the requirements addressed by the chapter.

This first chapter briefly covers the following general issues

- The description of Ada 95 uses more defined terms and there is less reliance on informal English.

- The syntax is expanded to bring more rules into the syntax and to increase clarity.

- The categorization of errors is revised and includes the introduction of the concept of bounded errors.

However, before getting down to detail it is appropriate to start with a few words about the approach adopted in the development of Ada 95.

1.1 Overall Approach

Ada 95 is based on a building block approach. Rather than providing a number of new language features to directly solve each identified application problem, the extra capability of Ada 95 is provided by a few primitive language building blocks. In combination, these building blocks enable programmers to solve more application problems efficiently and productively.

Thus in the case of the object oriented area, much of the capability is provided by the interweaving of the properties of type extension, the child libraries and generic packages. Great care has been taken to ensure that the additional building blocks work together in a cohesive and helpful manner. Nevertheless implementation and understandability considerations have sometimes caused some restrictions to be imposed. An example is that type extension of a formal generic parameter is not permitted in a generic body (which would either break the contract model or pose an intolerable pervasive implementation burden).

An area of particular difficulty in tasking is the provision of mutual exclusion (which is done in implementation terms by imposing semaphores and locks at appropriate places). Much of the difficulty with Ada 83 tasking lay in the composition of facilities to provide general paradigms and especially the provision of guarded services. Attempts to solve such problems often resulted in race conditions precisely because the facilities did not compose properly. The only solution was paradigm inversion whereby the high level tasking model was used to provide, in essence, some low-level semaphore which could then be used in a medieval fashion. The introduction of protected types, barriers and the requeue statement with two distinct levels of locking is designed to overcome these difficulties. Together, these building blocks may be used to program natural and efficient solutions to problems involving a myriad of real-time paradigms, including asynchronous communication, efficient mutual exclusion, barrier synchronization, counting semaphores, and broadcast of a signal. To have provided separate features to solve each of these problems would have resulted in a baroque language which would have run into difficulties whenever a problem immediately outside the original goals was encountered.

As mentioned in I.3 (in part one), there are four main areas where it was felt that users needed additional functionality: Interfacing to other systems, Programming by Extension (OOP), Programming in the Large (Program Libraries), and Tasking. Broadly speaking these needs are met in Ada 95 by the following main features and are largely discussed in the chapters indicated.

Interfacing: by new forms of access types, pragmas and interface packages (Chapters 3 and B).

Programming by Extension: by type extension and class-wide types (Chapter 4).

Programming in the Large: by child library units (Chapter 10).

Tasking: by protected objects (Chapter 9).

Chapters 3, 4, 9 and 10 constitute the bulk of this part of the rationale mainly because they contain a number of quite long examples. The changes described in the other chapters are more concerned with supporting detail and less pervasive improvements.

1.2 The Reference Manual

The Ada 83 Reference Manual [RM83] is a remarkable document in that it is one of the few definitions of a programming language that is regularly read by normal programmers. It achieves this by using natural English wherever possible.

A corollary of this success is, however, that it has not proved to be quite so precise as desired by compiler writers. Of course, there are many more programmers than compiler writers and so the importance of the programmer should not be underestimated. However, it is vital that the compiler writer be given as precise a description of the language as is reasonably possible. At the end of the day, provided that the compiler is correct, then any misunderstanding of some subtle point on the part of the programmer will generally give rise to an appropriate message from the compiler. Furthermore, textbooks and other material such as this rationale are available to give pedagogic information to the programmer.

The Ada 95 Reference Manual [RM95] thus continues the tradition of readability and accessibility of the Ada 83 document wherever possible but achieves greater precision by the careful introduction of more specific terminology. Different typography is also used to distinguish normal English words from defined terms and syntax thereby increasing clarity but retaining readability.

In addition to the definitive standard, the Annotated Ada Reference Manual [AARM] is an annotated form containing much additional information aimed largely at compiler writers, language lawyers and others with a need for additional detailed information. This contains such matters as advice for implementers, rationale on fine detail, further awkward examples and so on. Both forms of the reference manual as well as this rationale and other material are available in machine readable form on the sw-eng.falls-church.va.us host in the public/ada9x/rm9x directory.

1.3 Syntax

The syntax is expressed in the same notation as for Ada 83. However, the diligent reader will observe a considerable number of changes to the description of the syntax. Apart from those changes required by the new parts of the language, the changes have been made in order to increase clarity of the exposition.

This increased clarity has been achieved at the cost of introducing rather more new syntax rules than the increased size of the language would suggest. However, the extra clarity achieved brings major benefits not only in understanding the syntax itself but also by some reduction in the need for English text to explain rules which are now expressed by the syntax.

Examples of more notable changes (other than those corresponding to completely new material) are as follows

- The rules for the characters used in the program text have been completely rewritten in a more structured manner. The previous rules were not hierarchical and contained a curious imbalance between upper and lower case letters which is no longer appropriate.

- The category integer is now called numeral. The term integer was somewhat inappropriate for what is simply a syntactic sequence of digits not specifically related to the integer types.

- Reserved words are no longer considered as identifiers. A consequence is that the syntax now explicitly includes those attributes which double as reserved words, namely Delta, Digits, Range and Access (the last being a further such attribute in Ada 95).

- Categories such as defining_identifier are introduced for those occurrences of identifiers which define an entity. Usage occurrences use direct_name or selector_name according to the visibility rules. The term simple_name is no longer used. In Ada 83 the term simple_name was used confusingly for just some usage occurrences.

- The category type_declaration now properly includes both task and protected types. Surprisingly, task type declarations were excluded in Ada 83 probably because of a lack of reconsideration of the rules subsequent to the introduction of task types in around 1980.

- The category type_mark is replaced by subtype_mark because all names of types are now considered to actually denote the first named subtype.

- Scalar and composite constraints are now distinguished.

- A real change is that the category name is broadened to include function_call and type_conversion in accordance with changes to the concept of a name. This causes a number of consequential changes to other definitions such as primary and prefix.

- The one previous category aggregate has now been replaced by some nine syntax rules thereby bringing into the syntax the various distinctions between array and record aggregates and their various rules which were previously expressed by English text.

- The new category handled_sequence_of_statements avoids much repetition in a number of other rules, and clarifies the region of text in which a given handler applies.

- The categories body_stub and renaming_declaration are both broken down into named subcategories for ease of exposition.

• The previous category generic_parameter_declaration which confusingly reused other categories from other contexts is now replaced by some twenty individual categories describing the various classes of generic parameters in a hierarchical manner.

The statistically minded might be interested to observe that Ada 83 is described by 180 rules whereas Ada 95 has about 270. However, the rules introduced for clarity account for about 50 of this increase and so in real terms the syntax for Ada 95 is about one seventh bigger than Ada 83. A major part of this increase is simply due to the introduction of protected types.

1.4 Classification of Errors

The classification of errors in Ada 95 is somewhat different to that in Ada 83. The primary reason for the new classification is to be more realistic and practical regarding the possible consequences of undefined behavior. The effect is often to indicate that the range of possible outcomes of a program execution is less than the Ada 83 rules led one to believe (in practice there is little change).

The most significant new classification is the introduction of the category called bounded errors. The general idea is that the behavior is not fully determined but nevertheless falls within well-defined bounds. Many errors which were previously classed as erroneous (which implied completely undefined behavior) are now simply bounded errors. An obvious example is the consequence of evaluating an uninitialized scalar variable; this could result in the raising of Program_Error or Constraint_Error or the production of a value not in the subtype, see [RM95 4.4, 11.6].

A rather different approach is taken regarding unportable behavior. A program whose behavior depends upon some order of evaluation is no longer classed as incorrect but simply as being not portable. As a consequence the category of error called incorrect order dependences is deleted.

There are also cases where the language has been changed so that a run-time error in Ada 83 is now detected during compilation in Ada 95. Thus static subtype matching is required in some situations as described in 3.9.

The language also allows a compiler to have different modes of operation according to the detection of suspicious situations such as too many warnings. This specifically meets one of the requirements for early detection of errors where possible.

1.5 Requirements Summary

The requirements

  R 2.1-A(1) — Incorporate Approved Commentaries

  R 2.1-A(2) — Review Other Presentation Suggestions

are both addressed by the extra attention given to terminology and by the incorporation of improved text recommended by the Ada Rapporteur Group.

The requirements

  R 2.1-B(1) — Maintain Format of Existing Standard

  R 2.1-C(1) — Machine-Readable Version of the Standard

have also been met as explained in 1.2. Furthermore, the requirement

R 2.2-B(1) — Understandability

is also addressed by the greatly improved terminology as well as by the revisions to the syntax described in 1.3. However, it should be noted that, as expressed in [DoD 90], this particular requirement was perhaps slanted more at certain specific language features rather than clarity of description in general.

In the case of error detection the requirement and study topic

R 2.3-A(2) — Limit Consequences of Erroneous Execution

S 2.3-A(1) — Improve Early Detection of Errors

are addressed by the introduction of the concept of bounded errors and more compilation checking such as static subtype matching.

2 Lexical Elements

There are only a small number of changes in this part of the language but they are important. The following are worth noting

- There are six more reserved words.

- The program text character set is extended.

- The rules regarding pragmas are improved.

2.1 Reserved Words and Identifiers

Ada 95 has six more reserved words which are **abstract, aliased, protected, requeue, tagged**, and **until**. In addition the word "access" is also used as both an attribute and a reserved word.

The introduction of new reserved words poses a potential incompatibility problem. However, the new words are not likely to have been particularly popular as program identifiers and so little problem should arise.

It was suggested by some reviewers that new reserved words should be avoided by the subtle reuse of existing words in various contexts. This might have led to a bizarre and unnatural language for the sake of avoiding very occasional incompatibility. It would certainly have made the language seem strange and unattractive especially to those not familiar with the background to the development. The smooth integration of the new and important features such as type extension and protected types could not have been achieved without the introduction of additional reserved words.

There are some changes to the terminology in order to clarify the exposition. For example, reserved words are no longer formally classed as identifiers; this has some impact on the syntax as mentioned in 1.3. Also the term numeral is introduced in the discussion of literals.

2.2 Program Text

As part of the original agreement between ISO and ANSI to accept ANSI/MIL-STD-1815A as an international standard, ANSI agreed to provide better support for international character sets in the first revision of Ada.

Therefore, Ada 95 uses an 8-bit character set based on ISO-8859, and a 16-bit character set based on ISO-10646. These extended character sets are usable in character and string literals and also in comments.

The text of a program (outside literals) is typically written in the Latin-1 set, ISO-8859-1 and thereby allows accented characters in identifiers.

Moreover, an implementation is allowed to support other character sets provided that it has a mode in which the "standard" sets are supported. This enables national variations to support sets such as those used in Japan. See [RM95 2.1].

In order to promote portability all implementations are required to support a line length of at least 200 characters.

2.3 Pragmas

In order to improve error detection when dealing with implementation defined pragmas, we require that compilers produce a warning when a pragma is unrecognized, and identify as an error a pragma that is misplaced or malformed. In Ada 83, it was permissible for compilers to ignore such pragmas without a warning, which could lead to unexpected behavior.

We have formalized the definition of configuration pragmas to specify options that affect more than a single compilation unit (often an entire program).

There are a number of additional pragmas in Ada 95 which will be mentioned in the course of the discussion.

2.4 Requirements Summary

The requirement and study topic

   R3.1-A(4) — Extended Comment Syntax

   S3.1-A(5) — Extended Identifier Syntax

are both addressed and met by the changes mentioned above. Indeed, recently approved Ada Issues permit Ada 83 compilers to meet these requirements on a voluntary (non-binding) basis.

3 Types and Expressions

This chapter covers a number of changes. Some are essentially functional changes in their own right such as the addition of modular types, but many of the changes are more to provide a better framework for the establishment of the object oriented programming facilities which are described in the next chapter. The main changes are

- The foundation concepts and terminology are improved. The idea of a view is formalized. The concepts of a type and class are clarified. The concept of an object is generalized.

- The rules for derived types and their operations are changed to accommodate type extension.

- Character types are changed to conform to the requirements for 8-bit and wider character sets.

- The numeric model is revised to provide a closer mapping to actual machine architectures; the types *root_integer* and *root_real* are added to aid the description.

- Modular (unsigned integer) and decimal fixed point types are added.

- Discriminants are generalized and the concepts of definite and indefinite subtypes introduced. This is particularly relevant to generic parameter matching.

- The rules for implicit array subtype conversion are liberalized to allow sliding in all contexts except qualification (and, of course, membership tests).

- Array aggregates with **others** are allowed in more contexts.

- Access types are greatly generalized to provide general access types and access to subprogram types.

- The rules for type conversion are extended to cover the new features in the language.

- The rules for staticness are more liberal thereby allowing more expressions to be considered static.

- There are a number of minor improvements such as the removal of the irritating rule regarding the order of declarations.

It be should be noted that the enhanced forms of access types constitute a major extension to the language in their own right. They provide the more flexible interfacing which was highlighted as one of the four main areas of User Need in I.3.

Type extension, class-wide types and polymorphism are discussed in the next chapter.

3.1 Types, Classes, Objects and Views

The term view is widely used in the description to make it easier to separate properties associated with an entity from properties associated with a particular reference to an entity. For example, a type may have two views, one in places where its full declaration is visible, and one where the type is private. Another example occurs in renaming where two subprogram names may denote the same subprogram, but with different formal parameter names associated with these two different views.

We have generalized the term class to include user-defined classes defined by a type and all its direct and indirect derivatives; we call these derivation classes. The concept of language-defined type classes (such as the discrete class or the real class) allowed the description of Ada 83 to be more economical, and easier to understand. This same economy of definition and understanding is valuable for a user-defined type hierarchy forming a class.

There is a strong distinction between specific types and class-wide types. Specific types are those declared by type declarations, and correspond to Ada 83 types. Each specific tagged type T has an associated class-wide type, T'Class. Class-wide types enable class-wide (polymorphic) programming, because a subprogram with a formal parameter of a class-wide type like T'Class accepts actual parameters for any type covered by the class-wide type (that is, T or any of its derivatives). In the implementation of such a subprogram, the operations of the root type (T in this case) are available. It is also possible to write dispatching operations, which automatically dispatch to the appropriate implementation based on the type tag of the actual parameter. A class-wide operation of a tagged class-wide type usually calls one or more dispatching operations of the specific type.

The universal types which existed in Ada 83 remain and act much as class-wide types for the numeric classes. However, there are important differences which are discussed in 3.3.

To simplify and unify the description of the Ada 95 type model, we have adopted the terms elementary and composite for describing the two major categories of Ada types. Elementary types have no internal structure, and are used to represent simple values. Composite types are made up of components and other internal state, and are used to represent more complex values and objects. There are a number of existing Ada 83 rules, and new Ada 95 rules, that are made simpler by expressing them only in terms of elementary and composite types, rather than by enumerating more specific type classes.

There was much confusion in Ada 83 regarding the distinction between types and subtypes. In Ada 95, only subtypes have names. A type declaration such as

type A **is array** (Integer **range** <>) **of** Float;

introduces a first subtype named A. The underlying type has no name. In this case the first subtype is unconstrained. (We now say first subtype rather than first named subtype.) On the other hand a declaration such as

type B **is array** (Integer **range** 1 .. 10) **of** Float;

introduces a first subtype named B which is constrained. Another point is that in Ada 83 a type was also a subtype; this is not the case in Ada 95.

This change of nomenclature has no semantic effect; it is designed to simplify later description. In particular, the term type mark is now replaced by subtype mark since it is always the name of a subtype, and one need never say "type or subtype".

The idea of an object is generalized. The result of a function and of evaluating an aggregate are now considered to be (anonymous) constant objects. One consequence of this is that the result of a function call can be renamed; this is particularly useful for limited types, see 7.3. Some things are not objects, for example named numbers are not objects.

3.1.1 Classification of Operations

We have introduced the term primitive operations to encompass that set of operations that are "tightly bound" to a type, being either explicitly or implicitly declared at the point of the type declaration, and inherited by derivatives of the type. These operations are the closed set that effectively define the semantics of the type. The more general term "operation" of a type is no longer formally used.

Ada 83 used "implicit conversion" to explain how integer literals were usable with any integer type, and how real literals were usable with any real type. For Ada 95, we have adopted a similar mechanism as the basis for class-wide programming. However, rather than using the concept of implicit conversion, the static semantic rules are defined in terms of type resolution between actual parameters and formal parameters. (The implicit conversions still happen but are not part of overload resolution.)

As in Ada 83, if the actual parameter and the formal parameter are of the same type, then the actual matches the formal. However, the type resolution rules also allow certain other combinations. In particular, if a formal parameter is of a class-wide type, then the actual parameter may be of any type in the class. This allows the definition of class-wide operations.

A similar approach is taken with universal types. A formal parameter of a universal type is matched by any type of the corresponding numeric class. Thus the Val attribute (which accepts an operand of type *universal_integer*) can be matched by any integer type. There is a change to the rules for fixed point multiplication and division which now take *universal_fixed* operands as explained in 3.3.1 and can thus be matched by any fixed point type.

In addition to class-wide matching, the type resolution rules cover the use of access parameters (not to be confused with parameters of an access type, see 3.7.1). When a formal is an access parameter, only the designated type of the actual parameter is considered for matching purposes. The actual matches the formal if their designated types are the same, or, in the case of tagged types, one is T while the other is T'Class. In addition, for tagged types, changes of representation are not permitted for derived types, so an actual also matches a formal access parameter if the designated type of the actual is covered by the designated type of the formal.

Access parameters allow operations to be defined that take access values rather than designated objects, while still keeping the operation a primitive operation of the designated type. With tagged types, this allows "dispatching on access types" without requiring the access value to be dereferenced first.

Another important change is that the attribute S'Base may be used as a subtype mark generally, rather than strictly as a prefix for other attributes. S'Base denotes an unconstrained subtype of the type of S and is only allowed for elementary types. It is particularly useful within a generic package that might be instantiated with a constrained numeric subtype, since the temporary variables used to perform a calculation might need to be unconstrained, even if the parameters and final result of an operation must satisfy the constraints of the actual constrained subtype.

For example consider the implementation of Generic_Elementary_Functions. We need to allow the user to instantiate the package with a constrained subtype corresponding to Float_Type, but do not wish the calculations to be constrained. Accordingly the parameters and results of the various functions are of the subtype Float_Type'Base.

One potential problem with allowing the declaration of objects of subtype S'Base is that the first subtype (for example S) may have a size clause that takes advantage of the constraints on S. Objects of subtype S'Base cannot generally be limited by the size specified for S. There are several reasons why this problem is not serious in practice:

- Many compilers already use different sizes for different subtypes of the same type;

- The construct **for** B **in** S'Base'First .. S'Base'Last **loop** ... is already legal in Ada-83 (presuming S is discrete), and is an existing way to effectively create an object (B) of subtype S'Base;

3.1.2 Derived Types

For Ada 95, we have chosen to build upon the Ada 83 derived type mechanism to provide for type extension (single inheritance) and run-time polymorphism, two fundamental features of object-oriented programming. (Derived types were the existing type inheritance mechanism in Ada 83.) If a new inheritance mechanism had been introduced, perhaps based on "package types" or an explicit "class" construct, inheritance based on derived types would still remain as an almost redundant and complicating alternative inheritance mechanism. Choosing to enhance the basic derived type mechanism provides a single robust inheritance mechanism rather than two potentially conflicting and weaker ones.

Rather than introducing an explicit class construct, we have instead chosen to support user-defined classes via a hierarchy of derived types. The (derivation) class rooted at a type T consists of T and all of its direct and indirect derivatives. The existing Ada 83 rules for derived types ensure that all of the types in the class rooted at T have at least the same set of primitive operations as T, because a derivative may override and add operations, but it cannot eliminate an operation inherited from the parent type.

Having a set of operations that are well defined for all types in a class rooted at some type T makes it meaningful to construct class-wide operations that take advantage of this commonality. Much of the power and economy of object-oriented programming comes from the ability to write such class-wide operations easily.

If an operation is explicitly defined on a class-wide type, then it is a class-wide operation via the type resolution rules.

The existing universal types behave very much as class-wide numeric types. In fact we introduce types *root_integer* and *root_real* as the numeric types from which all other numeric types are descended and then the universal types can be considered to be the class-wide types corresponding to these root types.

Ada 83 already had existing operations such as the Val attribute that took an operand of any integer type; in Ada 95 this is described by saying that Val takes an operand of the *universal_integer* type. These are therefore like class-wide operations.

3.2 Character Types

We mentioned in Chapter 2 that the text of an Ada 95 program can be written using more liberal character sets. In this section we consider the support for character types in the executing program.

As part of providing better support for international character sets, the fundamental character set of Ada 95 is changed from the seven-bit ISO 646 standard, to the eight-bit ISO 8859 standard (which includes Latin-1). This means that the type Character in package Standard is now an enumeration type with 256 positions, rather than just 128.

This change is not upward compatible for programs that have arrays indexed by Character, or case statements over Character. However, the benefits of accommodating international character sets were felt to outweigh the costs of this upward incompatibility. See X.2.

To facilitate direct use of character literals and string literals from all languages in the international community, a type Wide_Character is declared in package Standard. The type Wide_Character has 2**16 positions, and starts with the 256 enumeration literals of the type Character.

The predefined library package Ada.Characters has a child package Characters.Handling containing useful classification and conversion functions (such as Is_Letter and To_Lower) and a child package Characters.Latin_1 containing constants for the Latin-1 symbol set.

There is also a string type Wide_String indexed by subtype Positive, with component subtype Wide_Character.

3.3 Numeric Types

The model of numeric types is somewhat different in Ada 95. The overall goal of the change is to give the implementation more freedom for optimizations such as keeping intermediate results and local variables in registers. Most of the change is fine detail that need not concern the normal user and is addressed in the Numerics annex. However, one area that is important in the core language is the somewhat different treatment of universal types and the introduction of the anonymous types *root_integer* and *root_real*.

The essence of the root types is that they can be considered as the types from which all other integer and real types are derived. The base range of *root_integer* is thus System.Min_Int .. System.Max_Int. We will first discuss the integer types and then indicate where the floating types differ.

We have introduced the term base range for the implemented range of a type whereas range refers to the requested range of a particular subtype. Range checks *only* apply to constrained subtypes; overflow checks *always* apply. An important consequence is that we either get the mathematically correct answer or Constraint_Error is raised.

Thus if we write

```
type My_Integer is range -20_000 .. +20_000;
MI: My_Integer;
MIB: My_Integer'Base;
```

then My_Integer'Range will be -20_000 .. +20_000 and all assignments to variables of the subtype My_Integer such as MI will be checked to ensure that the range is not violated; Constraint_Error is raised if the check fails.

On the other hand, the base range of My_Integer is the range of My_Integer'Base and this will be that of the implemented range which might reflect that of a 16-bit word and thus be $-2**15 .. +2**15-1$. No range checks apply to assignments to the variable MIB. However, as an optimization, it might be the case that a particular variable of the subtype My_Integer'Base is held in a register and this could have a wider range than the base range of the subtype. The base range is thus the guaranteed minimum implemented range. Nevertheless overflow checks will always apply and MIB will never have a mathematically incorrect value although the value could be outside the base range. For example, consider

```
X: My_Integer := 18_000;
Y: My_Integer := 15_000;
...
MIB := X + Y;
```

where we will assume that the computation is not all optimized away by a smart compiler!

(Note that no explicit conversion is needed because My_Integer and My_Integer'Base are both subtypes of the same (unnamed) type. Remember that all types are unnamed.)

If MIB is implemented with its base range then an overflow will occur and result in Constraint_Error because the result is outside the base range. If, however, MIB is held in a 32-bit register, then no overflow will occur and MIB will have the mathematically correct result. On the other hand

```
MI := X + Y;
```

will always result in Constraint_Error being raised because of the range check upon the assignment.

In the case of the predefined types such as Integer the same rules apply; the subtype Integer is constrained whereas Integer'Base is not. The base range and range happen to be the same. So the declarations

```
I: Integer;
IB: Integer'Base;
```

have a different effect. Checks will apply to assignments to I but not to assignments to IB (but remember that an implementation is always free to add checks if convenient; they may be automatic).

Another possibility for optimization is that an intermediate expression might be computed with a larger range. This is why the predefined operators such as "+" on the predefined types such as Integer have parameters and result of Integer'Base rather than Integer. There are no range checks on these operations (just overflow checks). Now consider

```
MI := X * Y / 30_000;
```

in which we will assume that the computation is done with the operations of type Integer which has a 16-bit base range on this implementation. If the operations are done from left to right and the operations are performed in 16-bit registers then overflow will occur and Constraint_Error will be raised. On the other hand, the operations might be performed in 32-bit registers in which case overflow will not occur and the correct result will be assigned to MI after successfully performing a range check on the result.

The universal types are types which can be matched by any specific numeric type of their class. We see therefore that the universal types are rather like class-wide types of the respective classes. So *universal_integer* is thus effectively *root_integer*'Class.

The integer literals are, of course, of the type *universal_integer* and so, as in Ada 83, can be implicitly converted to any integer type including the anonymous *root_integer*. An important distinction between universal and tagged class-wide types is that the latter carry a tag and explicit conversion to a specific type is required which is checked at runtime to ensure that the tag is appropriate, see 3.8.

One consequence of treating *universal_integer* as matching any integer type is that the rules for the initial expression in a number declaration are more liberal than they were in Ada 83. The initial expression can be of any integer type whereas in Ada 83 it had to be universal; it still of course has to be static.

Similar remarks apply to real types. In the case of floating point types a range check is only applied if the definition contains a range (this is the same rule as for integer type definitions but they always have **range** anyway). So given

```
type My_Float is digits 7;
type Your_Float is digits 7 range -1.0E-20 .. +1.0E+20;
```

then My_Float is an unconstrained subtype whereas Your_Float is constrained. Range checks will apply on assignments to Your_Float but not to My_Float. The predefined types such as Float are unconstrained; it is considered that their notional definition does not include a range.

Overflow checks apply to floating point computations only if the attribute Machine_Overflows is true as in Ada 83.

By introducing root numeric types, the special Ada 83 rules regarding convertible universal operands are eliminated (only certain simple expressions could be automatically converted in Ada 83). Instead, the distinction between convertible and non-convertible universal operands corresponds directly to the distinction between the universal and specific root numeric types. The operators of the root numeric types return specific root numeric types, and hence their result is not universal (not "implicitly convertible" using Ada 83 terminology). The type resolution rules ensure that these operators accept operands of the universal types, so they may be used on literals and named numbers.

There is an important change to the visibility rules concerning a preference for the root types in the case of an ambiguity. This is discussed in 8.4.

In order to promote precise use of specific hardware the library package Interfaces defines signed integer types corresponding to the hardware supported types with names such as

`Integer_32` and `Integer_16` plus corresponding modular types (see 3.3.2). This package also predefines similar floating types corresponding to the hardware although no names are prescribed.

The description of the real numbers is greatly simplified. The model and safe numbers of Ada 83 have been abandoned because they were not well understood, did not truly provide the portability they sought and obscured the real machine from the specialist. Accordingly the definition of floating point is now in terms of model numbers which roughly correspond to the old safe numbers and are close to the represented numbers. In the case of fixed point the definition is entirely in terms of *small* and the notion of model numbers no longer applies.

To avoid confusion and to improve the correspondence between the real type attributes and the machine attributes, the attributes are completely redefined so that they more closely correspond to the capabilities of the machine.

The description of model numbers is moved to the Numerics annex because of its specialist nature. For more details consult Part Three of this rationale.

We considered removing floating point and fixed point accuracy constraints from the syntax so that delta and digits would only be specified as part of a real type definition. Indeed, AI-571 concluded that reduced accuracy real subtypes should not be represented with reduced accuracy, making their usefulness in the language questionable. However, they are retained (although considered obsolete) for compatibility because of the different format obtained with `Text_IO`.

3.3.1 Operations

The mixed multiplying operators of the Ada 83 universal numeric types are redefined in Ada 95 in terms of the root numeric types.

There were some essentially unnecessary restrictions on the use of literals in fixed point multiplication and division in Ada 83. These operations now take *universal_fixed* as their operands and return *universal_fixed* as the result. However the result must be in a context which provides a specific expected type. As a consequence literals may now be used more freely in fixed point operations and a multiplication or division need not be followed by conversion to a specific type if the context supplies such a type.

So given two fixed point types `Fixed1` and `Fixed2`, we can now write sequences such as

```
X, Y: Fixed1;
Z: Fixed2;
. . .
X := 2.0 * X;
X := Y * Z;
```

which were forbidden in Ada 83. Note that multiple operations as in

```
X := X * Y / Z;
```

remain forbidden since the context does not provide a type (and therefore an accuracy and range) for the intermediate result.

3.3.2 Modular Types

In Ada 95 the integer types are subdivided into signed integer types and modular types. The signed integer types are those with which we are already familiar from Ada 83 such as `Integer` and so on. The modular types are new to Ada 95.

The modular types are unsigned integer types which exhibit cyclic arithmetic. (They thus correspond to the unsigned types of some other languages such as C.) A strong need has been felt for some form of unsigned integer types in Ada and most compiler vendors have provided their

own distinct implementations. This of course has caused an unnecessary lack of portability which
the introduction of modular types in Ada 95 will overcome.

As an example consider unsigned 8-bit arithmetic (that is byte arithmetic). We can declare

```
type Unsigned_Byte is mod 256;   -- or mod 2**8;
```

and then the range of values supported by Unsigned_Byte is 0 .. 255. The normal arithmetic
operations apply but all arithmetic is performed modulo 256 and overflow cannot occur.

The modulus of a modular type need not be a power of two although it often will be. It might,
however, be convenient to use some obscure prime number as the modulus perhaps in the
implementation of hash tables.

The logical operations **and, or, xor** and **not** are also available on modular types; the binary
operations naturally treat the values as bit patterns; the **not** operation subtracts the value from its
maximum. No problems arise with mixing these logical operations with arithmetic operations
because negative values are not involved.

The logical operations will be most useful if the modulus is a power of two; they are well
defined for other moduli but there are some surprising effects. For example DeMorgan's theorem
that

```
not(A and B) = not A or not B
```

does not hold if the modulus is not a power of two.

The package Interfaces defines modular types corresponding to each predefined signed
integer type with names such as Unsigned_16 and Unsigned_32. For these modular types
(which inevitably have a modulus which is a power of two) a number of shift and rotate operations
are also provided.

It is an important principle that conversion between numeric types should not change the
value (other than rounding). Conversion from modular to signed integer types and vice versa is
thus allowed provided the value is in the range of the destination; if it is not then
Constraint_Error is raised.

Thus suppose we had

```
type Signed_Byte is range -128 .. +127;
U: Unsigned_Byte := 150;
S: Signed_Byte := Signed_Byte(U);
```

then Constraint_Error will be raised.

Unchecked conversion can be used to convert patterns out of range. We could neatly write

```
function Convert_Byte is
   new Unchecked_Conversion(Signed_Byte, Unsigned_Byte);
function Convert_Byte is
   new Unchecked_Conversion(Unsigned_Byte, Signed_Byte);
```

providing conversions in both directions and then

```
S := Convert_Byte(U);
```

would result in S having the value -106.

The modular types form a distinct class of types to the signed integer types. There is thus a
distinct form for a generic formal parameter of a modular type namely

```
type T is mod <>;
```

and this cannot be matched by a type such as Integer. Nor indeed can the signed integer form
with **range** <> be matched by a modular type such as Unsigned_32.

The new attribute Modulus applies to a modular type and returns its modulus. This is of particular value with generic parameters.

3.3.3 Decimal Types

Decimal types are used in specialized commercial applications and are dealt with in depth in the Information Systems annex. However, the basic syntax of decimal types is in the core language.

A decimal type is a form of fixed point type. The declaration provides a value of delta as for an ordinary fixed point type (except that in this case it must be a power of 10) and also prescribes the number of significant decimal digits. So we can write

```
type Money is delta 0.01 digits 18;
```

which will cope with values of a typical decimal currency. This allows 2 digits for the cents and 16 for the dollars so that the maximum allowed value is

9,999,999,999,999,999.99

The usual operations apply to decimal types as to other fixed point types. Furthermore the Information Systems annex describes a number of special packages for decimal types including conversion to human readable output using picture strings.

Much as with modular types there is also a special form for a generic parameter of a decimal type which is

```
type T is delta <> digits <>;
```

This cannot be matched by an ordinary fixed point type and similarly the form with just **delta <>** cannot be matched by a decimal type such as Money.

3.4 Composite Types

In Ada 95, the concept of composite types is broadened to include task and protected types. This is partly a presentation issue and partly reflects the generalization of the semantics to allow discriminants on task and protected types as well as on records.

The terms definite and indefinite subtypes are introduced as explained in II.11 when we discussed the generic parameter mechanism. Recall that a definite subtype is one for which an uninitialized object can be declared such as Integer or a constrained array subtype or a record subtype with discriminants with defaults. An indefinite subtype is an unconstrained array subtype or an unconstrained record, protected or task subtype which does not have defaults for the discriminants, or a class-wide subtype or a subtype with unknown discriminants.

As a simple generalization to Ada 83, we have allowed both variables and constants of an indefinite subtype to be declared, so long as an initial value is specified; the object then takes its bounds or discriminants from the initial value. In Ada 83, only initialized constants of such a subtype could be declared. However, the implementation considerations are essentially identical for constants and variables, so eliminating the restriction against variables imposes no extra implementation burden, and simplifies the model.

Here is an example of use

```
if Answer /= Correct_Answer then
   declare
      Image: String := Answer_Enum'Image(Correct_Answer);
   begin
      Set_To_Lower_Case(Image);
```

```
      Put_Line("The correct answer is " & Image & '.');
   end;
end if;
```

Allowing composite variables without a specified constraint to be declared, if initialized, is particularly important for class-wide types and (formal) private types with discriminant part (<>) since such types have an unknown set of discriminants and thus cannot be constrained. For example, in the case of class-wide types, it would otherwise be hard if not impossible to write the procedure Convert in 4.4.3 since we would not be able to declare the temporary variable Temp.

3.4.1 Discriminants

A private type can now be marked as having an unknown number of discriminants thus

```
type T(<>) is private;
```

The main impact of this is that the partial view does not allow uninitialized objects to be declared. If the partial view is also limited then objects cannot be declared at all (since they cannot be initialized). The gives the writer of an abstraction rather more control over the use of the abstraction.

As we have already noted, discriminants are also allowed on task and protected types in Ada 95. (An early draft of Ada 9X also permitted discriminants on arrays and discriminants to be of any nonlimited type. This was, however, felt to be too much of a burden for existing implementations.)

Discriminants are the primary means of parameterizing a type in Ada, and therefore we have tried to make them as general as possible within transition constraints. Task and protected types in particular benefit from discriminants acting as more general type parameters.

In Ada 83, an instance of a task type had to go through an initial rendezvous to get parameters to control its execution. In Ada 95, the parameters may be supplied as discriminant values at the task object declaration, eliminating the need for the extra rendezvous. Variables introduced in the declarative part of the task body can also depend on the task type discriminants, as can the expression defining the initial priority of the task via a Priority pragma. See 9.6 for some detailed examples.

In addition to allowing discrete types as discriminants as in Ada 83, we now also permit discriminants to be of an access type. There are two quite distinct situations. A discriminant can be of a named access type or it can be an access discriminant in which case the type is anonymous. Thus we can declare

```
type R1(D: access T) is ...
type AT is access T;
type R2(D: AT) is ...
```

and then the discriminant of R1 is an access discriminant whereas the discriminant of R2 is a discriminant of a named access type. A similar nomenclature applies to subprogram parameters which can be access parameters (without a type name) or simply parameters of a named access type (which was allowed in Ada 83).

Access discriminants provide several important capabilities. Because they impose minimal accessibility checking restrictions, an access discriminant may be initialized to refer to an enclosing object, or to refer to another object of at least the same lifetime as the object containing the discriminant. Access discriminants can only be applied to limited types. Note also that a task and a protected object can have access discriminants.

When an object might be on multiple linked lists, it is typical that one link points to the next link. However, it is also essential to be able to gain access to the object enclosing the link as well.

With access discriminants, this reference from a component that is a link on a chain, to the enclosing object, can be initialized as part of the default initialization of the link component. This is discussed further in 4.6.3. For a fuller discussion on how access discriminants avoid accessibility problems see 3.7.1. Further examples of the use of access discriminants will be found in 7.4 and 9.6.

Finally, a derived type may specify a new set of discriminants. For untagged types, these new discriminants are not considered an extension of the original type, but rather act as renamings or constraints on the original discriminants. As such, these discriminants must be used to specify the value of one of the original discriminants of the parent type. The new discriminant is tightly linked to the parent's discriminant it specifies, since on conversion from the parent type, the new discriminant takes its value from that discriminant (presuming `Constraint_Error` is not raised). The implementation model is that the new discriminants occupy the space of the old. The new type could actually have less discriminants than the old. The following are possible

```
type S1(I: Integer) is ...;
type S2(I: Integer; J: Integer) is ...;

type T1(N: Integer) is new S1(N);
type T2(N: Integer) is new S2(N, 37);
type T3(N: Integer) is new S2(N, N);
```

The last case is interesting because the new discriminant is mapped onto both the old ones. A conversion from type S2 to T3 checks that both discriminants of the S2 value are the same. A practical use of new discriminants for non-tagged types is so that we can make use of an existing type for the full type corresponding to a private type with discriminants.

```
type T(D: DT) is private;
private
   type T(D: DT) is new S(D);
```

In the case of a tagged type, we can either inherit all the discriminants or provide a completely new set. In the latter case the parent must be constrained and the new discriminants can (but need not) be used to supply the constraints.

Thus a type extension can have more discriminants than its parent, which is not true in the untagged case.

3.5 Array Types

A very minor change is that an index specification of an anonymous array type in an initialized declaration can also take the unconstrained form

```
V: array (Integer range <>) of Float :=
                          (3 .. 5 => 1.0, 6 | 7 => 2.0);
```

in which case the bounds are deduced from the initial expression.

3.5.1 Array Aggregates

Ada 83 had a rule that determined where a named array aggregate with an **others** choice was permitted; see [RM83 4.3.2(6)]. There were a related set of rules that governed where implicit array subtype conversion ("sliding") was permitted for an array value; see [RM83 3.2.1(16) and 5.2.1(1)]. These rules were constructed to ensure that named array aggregates with others and array sliding were not both permitted in the same context. However, the lack of array sliding in certain contexts could result in the unanticipated raising of `Constraint_Error` because the bounds did not match the applicable constraint.

For Ada 95, we have relaxed the restrictions on both array sliding and named array aggregates with others, so that both are permitted in all contexts where an array aggregate with just an others choice was legal in Ada 83. This corresponds to all situations where an expression of the array type was permitted, and there was an applicable index constraint; see [RM83 4.3.2(4-8)]. This ensures that sliding takes place as necessary to avoid `Constraint_Error`, and simplifies the rules on array aggregates with an others choice.

The original Ada 83 restrictions were related to the possible ambiguity between determining the bounds of an aggregate and sliding. In Ada 95, this ambiguity is resolved by stipulating that sliding never takes place on an array aggregate with an others choice. The applicable index constraint determines the bounds of the aggregate.

As an example consider

```
type Vector is array (Integer range <>) of Float;
V: Vector(1 .. 5) := (3 .. 5 => 1.0, 6 | 7 => 2.0);
```

which shows a named aggregate being assigned to V. The bounds of the named aggregate are 3 and 7 and the assignment causes the aggregate to slide with the net result that the components V(1) .. V(3) have the value 1.0 and V(4) and V(5) have the value 2.0.

On the other hand writing

```
V := (3 .. 5 => 1.0, others => 2.0);
```

has a rather different effect. It was not allowed in Ada 83 but in Ada 95 has the effect of setting V(3) .. V(5) to 1.0 and V(1) and V(2) to 2.0. The point is that the bounds of the aggregate are taken from the context and there is no sliding. Aggregates with **others** never slide.

Similarly no sliding occurs in

```
V := (1.0, 1.0, 1.0, others => 2.0);
```

and this results in setting V(1) .. V(3) to 1.0 and V(4) and V(5) to 2.0.

3.5.2 Concatenation

The rules for concatenate (we now use this more familiar term rather than catenate) are changed so that it works usefully in the case of arrays with a constrained first subtype.

In Ada 83 the following raised `Constraint_Error`, while in Ada 95 it produces the desired result

```
    X: array (1..10) of Integer;
begin
    X := X(6..10) & X(1..5);
```

In Ada 83, the bounds of the result of the concatenate were 6 .. 15, which caused `Constraint_Error` to be raised since 15 is greater than the upper bound of the index subtype. In Ada 95, the lower bound of the result (in this constrained case) is the lower bound of the index subtype so the bounds of the result are 1 .. 10, as required.

3.6 Record Types

A record type may be specified as tagged or limited (or both) in its definition. This makes record types consistent with private types, and allows a tagged record type to be declared limited even if none of its components are limited. This is important because only limited types can be extended with components that are limited.

A derived type is a record extension if it includes a record extension part, which has the same syntax as a normal record type definition preceded by the reserved word **with**. For example

```
type Labelled_Window(Length : Natural) is new Window with
   record
      Label: String(1..Length);
   end record;
```

Record extension is the fundamental type extension (type inheritance) mechanism in Ada 95. A private extension must be defined in terms of a record extension. The new discriminants in a discriminant extension are normally used to control the new components defined in the record extension part (as illustrated in the above example).

Record extension is a natural evolution of the Ada 83 concept of derived types. From an implementation perspective, it is relatively straightforward, since the new components may all be simply added at the end of the record, after the components inherited from the parent type.

We considered having other kinds of type extension, including enumeration type extension, task type extension, and protected type extension. However, none of these seemed clearly as useful as record extension, and all introduced additional implementation complexities. In any case, the automatic assignment of tags to type extensions lessens the need for enumeration types, and the added flexibility associated with access to subprogram and dispatching operations makes it less critical to allow task types to be extended.

Type extension of protected objects was another interesting possibility. However, certain implementation approaches do not easily support extension of the set of protected operations, or the changing of the barrier expressions. With some regret therefore it was decided that the benefit of extending protected types was not worth the considerable implementation burden. This is an obvious topic for review at the next revision of Ada.

Type extension is only permitted if the parent type is tagged. Originally we considered allowing any record or private type to be extended, but this introduced additional complexity, particularly inside generics. Furthermore, extending an untagged type breaks the general model that a class-wide type can faithfully represent any value in the class. An object of an untagged class-wide type would not have any provision for holding a value of a type extension, since it would lack a run-time type tag to describe the value.

3.6.1 Record Aggregates

Record aggregates are only permitted for a type extension if both the extension part and the parent part are fully visible. This corresponds to the principle that if part of a type is private, then it must be assumed to have an unknown set of components in that part. In other words we can only use an aggregate where we can view all the components.

However, extension aggregates can be used provided only that the components in the extension part are visible; we do not need a full view of the type of the ancestor expression. Typically we can provide an expression for the ancestor part. Thus suppose we have

```
type T is tagged private;
...
T_Obj: T := ...;
type NT is new T with
   record
      I, J: Integer;
   end record;
```

then we can write an extension aggregate such as

```
(T_Obj with I => 10, J => 20)
```

A variation is that we can also simply give the subtype name as the ancestor part thus

```
(T with I => 10, J => 20)
```

which is essentially equivalent to declaring a temporary default initialized object of the type and then using it as the ancestor expression (this includes calling `Initialize` in the case of a controlled type, see 7.4). This is allowed even if the ancestor type is abstract and thereby permits the creation of aggregates for types derived from abstract types.

3.6.2 Abstract Types and Subprograms

As we have already discussed in II.3, a tagged type may be declared as abstract by the appearance of **abstract** in its declaration. A subprogram which is a primitive operation of an abstract tagged type may be specified as abstract. An abstract subprogram has no body, and cannot be called directly or indirectly. A dispatching call will always call some subprogram body that overrides the abstract one because it is not possible to create an object of an abstract type.

If a type is derived from an abstract type and not declared as abstract then any inherited abstract subprograms must be overridden with proper subprograms. Note, of course, that an abstract type need not have any abstract subprograms.

The interaction between abstract types and private types is interesting. It will usually be the case that both views are abstract or not abstract. However, it is possible for a partial view to be abstract and the full view not to be abstract thus

```
package P is
   type T is abstract tagged private;
private
   type T is tagged ...;
end P;
```

In this case, objects of the type can only be declared for the full view and abstract primitive operations cannot be declared at all. This is because an abstract operation in the visible part would still apply in the private part and would thus be abstract for the nonabstract view.

It is of course not possible for the full view to be abstract and the partial view not to be abstract. This is quite similar to the rules for limitedness. A partial view can be limited and a full view not limited but not vice versa; the key point is that the partial view cannot promise more properties than the full view (the truth) actually has.

Of more interest is private extension where again the partial view could be declared abstract and the full view not abstract. An inherited abstract subprogram would need to be overridden. If this were done in the private part then the partial view of the subprogram would still be abstract although the full view would be of the overriding subprogram and thus not abstract. Thus

```
package P is
   type T is abstract tagged null record;
   procedure Op(X: T) is abstract;
end P;

with P;
package NP is
   type NT is abstract new P.T with private;
private
   type NT is new T with ...;
   procedure Op(X: T);   -- overrides
end NP;
```

The overriding is essential since otherwise we might dispatch to an abstract operation.

Another point is that an abstract type is not allowed to have an invisible abstract operation since otherwise it could not be overridden. The following difficulty is thus avoided.

```
package P is
   type T is abstract ...;
   procedure Nasty(X: T'Class);
private
   procedure Op(X: T) is abstract;   -- illegal
end P;

package body P is
   procedure Nasty(X: T'Class) is
   begin
       Op(X);
   end Nasty;
end P;

with P;
package Q is
   type NT is new P.T with ...;   -- not abstract
   -- cannot see Op in order to override it
end Q;
```

The problem is that we must override Op since by declaring an object of type NT we can then dispatch to Op by calling the procedure Nasty.

The overall motivation for the rules is to ensure that it is never possible to dispatch to a nonexistent subprogram body.

A rather different problem arises when we extend a type which is not abstract but which has a function with a controlling result. The old function cannot be used as the inherited version because it cannot provide values for the type extension when returning the result (parameters are not a problem because they only involve conversion towards the root). As a consequence the type must be declared as abstract unless we provide a new function.

A related restriction is that a function with a controlling result cannot be declared as a private operation since otherwise a similar difficulty to that discussed above would arise on type extension. If extension were performed using the partial view then the function would become abstract for the extended type and yet, being private, could not be overridden.

Observe also that since we do not require every abstract subprogram to be explicit, it is possible for a generic package specification to define an abstract record extension of a formal tagged type without knowing exactly which functions with controlling results exist for the actual type.

Finally, note that it is possible to have an abstract operation of a nontagged type. This is fairly useless since dispatching is not possible and static calls are illegal. However, it would be harder to formulate the rules to avoid this largely because an operation can be primitive of both a tagged and nontagged type (although not of two tagged types, see 4.5).

3.7 Access Types

As we have already seen in II.5 and II.6, access types in Ada 95 have been generalized so that they may be used to designate subprograms and also declared objects.

A new attribute designator, Access, has been defined for creating an access value designating a subprogram or object specified in the prefix. For example:

```
A := Object'Access;      -- point to a declared object
B := Subprogram'Access; -- point to a subprogram
```

Full type checking is performed as part of interpreting the Access attribute. An additional accessibility check is performed to ensure that the lifetime of the designated subprogram or object will not end before that of the access type, eliminating the possibility of dangling references.

Although these two extensions to access types share some common terminology and concepts the details are rather different and so we will now discuss them separately in the following sections.

3.7.1 Access to General Objects

Access types that may designate declared objects are called general access types, as distinguished from pool-specific access types, which correspond to those which were provided by Ada 83.

There are two steps to the use of general access types

- Objects that are to be designated by access values must be aliased. This can be done by using the reserved word **aliased** in their declaration. This serves various purposes. It documents the fact that an object is to be designated by an access value. It forces the object to be properly aligned in memory and informs the compiler that the representation of the object should correspond to that used for objects created by an allocator. In addition, the optimizer is informed that this object is likely to be accessible via one or more access values, and therefore its value might change as a result of an update via an access value.

- The attributes Access and Unchecked_Access, when applied to an object, return an access value that designates the object. Unless the subtype is tagged or has unconstrained discriminants, the subtype of the object must statically match the designated subtype of the access type. The access values which are formed by the Access attribute must obey certain accessibility restrictions, which are generally checked at compile time (at runtime in the case of access parameters). They cannot be used to create access values of a type whose lifetime is longer than the lifetime of the designated object; this prevents an access value from being stored in a global and then leaving the region where the designated object is declared. The access values that are formed by the Unchecked_Access attribute are not subject to such restrictions. It is the responsibility of the programmer who uses such unchecked access values to avoid dangling references.

General access types have the reserved word **all** or **constant** in their definition. We originally considered allowing any (object) access type to designate a declared object (as opposed to an allocated object), but this would have forced all access types to be represented as full addresses. By distinguishing general access types from pool-specific access types, we preserve the possibility of optimizing the representation of a pool-specific access type, by taking advantage of its limited storage-pool size.

A value of a general access type declared with the reserved word **all** can only designate variables (not constants), and may be used to read and update the designated object. If the reserved word **constant** is used, then access values may designate constants, as well as variables. An object designated by an access-to-constant value may not be updated via the access value. An allocator for an access-to-constant type requires an initial value and might generally reserve storage in a read-only part of the address space.

There are two important cases where a view is deemed to be aliased (and thus Access can be applied) even though the word **aliased** does not appear. One is that a parameter of a tagged type is considered to be aliased (see 6.1.2) and the other is where an inner component refers to the current instance of an outer limited type (see 4.6.3).

There is a restriction concerning discriminated records which ensures that we cannot apply the Access attribute to a component that might disappear. This is similar to the rule for renaming which prevents the renaming of a component of an unconstrained variable whose existence depends upon a discriminant.

Indirect access to declared objects is useful for avoiding dynamic allocation, while still allowing objects to be inserted into linked data structures. This is particularly useful for systems requiring link-time elaboration of large tables, which may use levels of indirection in their representation. Such access types are also convenient for returning a reference to a large global object from a function, allowing the object to be updated through the returned reference if desired.

Finally, rather than relying on allocators, it is sometimes appropriate to use a statically allocated array of objects, managed explicitly by the application. However, it may still be more convenient to reference components of the array using access values. By declaring the array components as aliased, the Access attribute may be used to produce an access value designating a particular component.

An interesting example is provided by the following which illustrates the static creation of ragged arrays

```
package Message_Services is
   type Message_Code_Type is range 0..100;

   subtype Message is String;

   function Get_Message(Message_Code: Message_Code_Type)
      return Message;

   pragma Inline(Get_Message);
end Message_Services;

package body Message_Services is
   type Message_Handle is access constant Message;

   Message_0: aliased constant Message := "OK";
   Message_1: aliased constant Message := "Up";
   Message_2: aliased constant Message := "Shutdown";
   Message_3: aliased constant Message := "Shutup";
   ...

   Message_Table: array (Message_Code_Type) of
      Message_Handle :=
         (0 => Message_0'Access,
          1 => Message_1'Access,
          2 => Message_2'Access,
          3 => Message_3'Access,
          -- etc.
         );

   function Get_Message(Message_Code: Message_Code_Type)
      return Message is
   begin
      return Message_Table(Message_Code).all;
   end Get_Message;
end Message_Services;
```

This example is based on Revision Request 018 and declares a static ragged array. The elements of the array point to strings, the lengths of which may differ. The access values are generated by the Access attribute; no dynamic allocation is needed to create the values.

Access types are used extensively in object-oriented applications. To enable the use of access types with the run-time dispatching provided for the primitive operations of tagged types, Ada 95 includes a new kind of in parameter, called an access parameter. We can thus write

```
procedure P(A: access T);
```

This is to be distinguished from a parameter of a named access type which already existed in Ada 83. A similar distinction arises with access discriminants as we saw in 3.4.1.

An access parameter is matched by an actual operand of any access type with the same designated type. Furthermore, if a subprogram has an access parameter with designated type T, and the subprogram is defined in the same package specification as the type T, then the subprogram is a primitive operation of T, and dispatches on the tag of the object designated by the access parameter. Inside the subprogram, an access parameter is of an anonymous general access type, and must either be dereferenced or explicitly converted on each use, or passed to another operation as an access parameter.

An important property of access parameters is that they can never have a null value. It is not permitted to pass null as an actual parameter (this is checked on the call) and of course being of an anonymous type another such object cannot be declared inside the subprogram. As a consequence within the subprogram there is no need to check for a null value of the type (neither in the program text nor in the compiled code). Note also that since other objects of the type cannot be declared, assignment and equality do not apply to access parameters.

For a tagged type T and an aliased object X of type T, X'Access and **new** T are overloaded on all access to T, on all access to T'Class, and on all other access to class-wide types that cover T. These overloadings on access to class-wide types allow allocators and the Access attribute to be used conveniently when calling class-wide operations, or building heterogeneous linked data structures.

Access parameters and access discriminants are important with respect to accessibility which we will now discuss in more detail. The accessibility rules ensure that a dangling reference can never arise; in general this is determined statically. Suppose we have a library package P containing a globally declared access type and a global variable

```
package P is
   type T is ...;
   type T_Ptr is access all T;
   Global: T_Ptr;
end P;
```

then we must ensure that the variable Global is never assigned an access to a variable that is local. So consider

```
procedure Q is
   X: aliased T;
   Local: T_Ptr := X'Access;    -- illegal
begin
   Global := X'Access;          -- illegal
   ...
   Global := Local;
   ...
end Q;
```

in which we have declared a local variable X and a local access variable. The assignment of X'Access to Global is clearly illegal since on leaving the procedure Q, this would result in Global referring to a non-existent variable. However, because we can freely assign access values, we must not assign X'Access to Local either since although that would be safe in the short term, nevertheless we could later assign Local to Global as shown.

Since we do not wish to impose accessibility checks at run-time on normal access assignment (this would be a heavy burden), we have to impose the restriction that the Access attribute can only be applied to objects with at least the lifetime of the access type. The rules that ensure this are phrased in terms of accessibility levels and the basic rule is that the access attribute can only be applied to an object at a level which is not deeper than that of the access type; this is, of course, known at compile time and so this basic accessibility rule is static. This may seem rather surprising since the concept of lifetime is dynamic and so one might expect the rules to be dynamic. However, it can be shown that in the case of named access types, the static rule is precisely equivalent to the intuitive dynamic rule. The reason for this is that the access attribute can only be applied at places where both the object and the access type are in scope; see [Barnes 95] for a detailed analysis. As discussed below, the situation is quite different for access parameters where the type has no name and the checks then have to be dynamic. (In the case of generic bodies, the rule is also dynamic as discussed in 12.3.)

Similar problems arise with discriminants and parameters of named access types. Thus we could not declare a local record with a component of the type T_Ptr. However, access discriminants and access parameters behave differently.

- The anonymous type is essentially declared inside the object or subprogram itself.

- It is not possible to have other components or objects of the same type (since it is anonymous) and they are treated as constants.

- Records with access discriminants have to be limited.

The net result is that the accessibility problems we encountered above do not arise. Revisiting the above example we can write

```
package P is
   type T is ...;
   type T_Ptr is access all T;
   type Rec(D: access T) is limited
      record
         . . .
      end record;
   Global: T_Ptr;
   Global_Rec: Rec(...);
end P;
```

where we have added the record type Rec with an access discriminant D plus a global record variable of that type. Now consider

```
procedure Q is
   X: aliased T;
   Local_Rec: Rec(D => X'Access);      -- OK
begin
   Global := Local_Rec.D;              -- illegal, type mismatch
   Global := T_Ptr(Local_Rec.D);      -- illegal, accessibility check
   Global_Rec := Local_Rec;           -- illegal, assignment limited type
   . . .
end Q;
```

in which we have declared a local record variable with its access discriminant initialized to access the local variable X. This is now legal and the various attempts to assign the reference to X to a more global variable or component are thwarted for the various reasons shown. The straight assignment of the discriminant fails because of a type mismatch. The attempt to circumvent this problem by converting the access type also fails because of an accessibility check on conversions between access types [RM95 4.6]. And the attempt to assign the whole record fails because it is limited.

Access parameters are particularly important since they are the one case where an accessibility check is dynamic (other than in generic bodies). An access parameter carries with it

an indication of the accessibility level of the actual parameter. Dynamic checks can then be made
when necessary as for example when converting to an external named access type. Consider

```
procedure Main is
    type T is ...;
    type A is access all T;
    Ptr: A := null;
    procedure P(XP: access T) is
    begin
        Ptr := A(XP);      -- conversion with dynamic check
    end P;
    X: aliased T;
begin
    P(X'Access);
end Main;
```

The conversion compares the accessibility level of the object X passed as parameter with that of the
destination type A; they are both the same and so the check passes. Observe that if the destination
type A were declared inside P then the check can be (and is) performed statically. So not all
conversions of access parameters require dynamic checks.

Another possibility is where one access parameter is passed on as an actual parameter to
another access parameter. There are a number of different situations that can arise acording to the
relative positions of the subprograms concerned; the various possibilities are analysed in detail in
[Barnes 95] where it is shown that the implementation technique given in [AARM 3.10.2(22)]
precisely meets the requirements of the rules. The rules themselves are in [RM95 3.10.2 and 4.6].

Without access parameters, the manipulation of access discriminants would be difficult.
Given

```
procedure P(A: access T);
```

then we can satisfactorily make calls such as

```
P(Local_Rec.D);
```

in order to manipulate the data referenced by the discriminant. On the other hand declaring

```
procedure P(A: T_Ptr);
```

would be useless for the manipulation of the discriminant because the necessary type conversion
on the call would inevitably be illegal for reasons of accessibility mentioned above.

As a first example of the use of access discriminants we will consider the case of an iterator
over a set. This is typical of a situation where we want a reference from one object to another.
The iterator contains a means of referring to the set in question and the element within it to be
operated upon next. Consider

```
generic
    type Element is private;
package Sets is
    type Set is limited private;
    ... -- various set operations
    type Iterator(S: access Set) is limited private;
    procedure Start(I: Iterator);
    function Done(I: Iterator) return Boolean;
    procedure Next(I: in out Iterator);
    function Get_Element(I: Iterator) return Element;
    procedure Set_Element(I: in out Iterator; E: Element);
private
```

```ada
   type Node;
   type Ptr is access Node;
   type Node is
      record
          E: Element;
          Next: Ptr;
      end record;
   type Set is new Ptr;     -- implement as singly-linked list

   type Iterator(S: access Set) is
      record
          This: Ptr;
      end record;

end Sets;

package body Sets is
   ... -- bodies of the various set operations

   procedure Start(I: in out Iterator) is
   begin
      I.This := Ptr(I.S.all);
   end Start;

   function Done(I: Iterator) return Boolean is
   begin
      return I.This = null;
   end Done;

   procedure Next(I: in out Iterator) is
   begin
      I.This := I.This.Next;
   end Next;

   function Get_Element(I: Iterator) return Element is
   begin
      return I.This.E;
   end Get_Element;

   procedure Set_Element(I: in out Iterator; E: Element) is
   begin
      I.This.E := E;
   end Set_Element;

end Sets;
```

The subprograms Start, Next and Done enable us to iterate over the elements of the set with the component This of the iterator object accessing the current element; the subprograms Get_Element and Set_Element provide access to the current element. The iterator could then be used to perform any operation on the values of the elements of the set.

As a trivial example the following child function Sets.Count simply counts the number of elements in the set. (Incidentally note that the child has to be generic because its parent is generic.)

```ada
generic
function Sets.Count(S: access Set) return Natural;
   -- Return the number of elements of S.

function Sets.Count(S: access Set) return Natural is
```

```
      I: Iterator(S);
      Result: Natural := 0;
   begin
      Start(I);
      while not Done(I) loop
         Result := Result + 1;
         Next(I);
      end loop;
      return Result;
   end Sets.Count;
```

In the more general case the loop might be

```
      Start(I);
      while not Done(I) loop
         declare
            E: Element := Get_Element(I);   -- get old value
         begin
            ...                             -- do something with it
            Set_Element(I, E);              -- put new value back
            Next(I);
         end;
      end loop;
```

Note that if Iterator.S were a normal component rather than an access discriminant then we would not be able to initialize it at its point of declaration and moreover we could not make it point to Sets.Count.S without using Unchecked_Access.

Finally note that the procedure Start could be eliminated by declaring the type Iterator as

```
   type Iterator(S: access Set) is
      record
         This: Ptr := Ptr(S.all);
      end record;
```

and this would have the advantage of preventing errors caused by forgetting to call Start.

3.7.2 Access to Subprograms

Ada 95 provides access-to-subprogram types. A value of such a type can designate any subprogram matching the profile in the type declaration, whose lifetime does not end before that of the access type. By providing access-to-subprogram types, Ada 95 provides efficient means to

*   dynamically select and invoke a subprogram with appropriate arguments,

*   store references to subprograms in data structures,

*   parameterize subprograms with other subprograms (at run-time).

Access-to-subprogram values are created by the Access attribute. Compile-time accessibility rules ensure that a subprogram designated by an access value cannot be called after its enclosing scope has exited. This ensures that up-level references from within the subprogram will be meaningful when the subprogram is ultimately called via the access value. It also allows implementations to create and dereference these access-to-subprogram values very efficiently, since they can be a single address, or an address plus a "static link".

For Subprogram'Access, the designated subprogram must have formal parameter and result subtypes and a calling convention that statically match those of the access type. This allows the compiler to emit the correct constraint checks, and use the correct parameter passing conventions when calling via an access-to-subprogram value, without knowing statically which subprogram is being called. We call this subtype conformance.

Overload resolution of the Access attribute applied to an overloaded subprogram name represents a new situation in Ada. In Ada 83, the prefix of an attribute was required to be resolvable without context. However, for the Access attribute to be useful on overloaded subprograms, it was necessary to allow the Access attribute to use context to resolve the prefix. Therefore, if the prefix of Access is overloaded, then context is used to determine the specific access-to-subprogram type, and then the parameter and result type profile associated with that access type is used to resolve the prefix.

Indirect access to a subprogram is extremely useful for table-driven programming, using, for example, a state machine model. It is also useful for installing call-backs in a separate subsystem (like the X window system). Finally, it often provides an alternative to generic instantiation, allowing a non-generic parameter to be a pointer to a subprogram, such as for applying an operation to every element of a list, or integrating a function using a numerical integration algorithm.

A number of examples of the use of access to subprogram types will be found in II.5. However a very important use is to provide much better ways of interfacing to programs written in other languages. This is done in conjunction with the pragma Import (essentially replacing Interface) and new pragmas Export and Convention. For details see Part Three.

It should be noted that there is no equivalent to access discriminants or access parameters for access to subprogram types. Apart from any aesthetic consideration of writing such an in situ definition, the key reason concerns the implementation problems associated with keeping track of the environment of such a "subprogram value". As a consequence we cannot, for example, use the access to a local procedure as a parameter of a more globally declared procedure. Such values would in any case not be safely assignable into a global.

The accessibility restrictions mean that access to subprogram values do not provide a mechanism to solve the general iterator problem where the essence is usually to apply some inner procedure over every element of a set with the inner procedure having access to more global variables. One alternative approach is to use access discriminants as discussed in 3.7.1; another, perhaps better, approach is to use type extension as illustrated in 4.4.4.

Generic formal subprograms remain the most general means of parameterizing an algorithm by an arbitrary externally specified subprogram. Moreover they are often necessary anyway. For example, consider a typical mathematical problem such as integration briefly mentioned in II.5. In practice the integration function would inevitably be generic with respect to the floating point type. So a more realistic specification would be

```
generic
   type Float_Type is digits <>;
package Generic_Integration is
   type Integrand is
                     access function(X: Float_Type) return Float_Type;

   function Integrate(F: Integrand; From, To: Float_Type;
              Accuracy: Float_Type := 10.0*Float_Type'Model_Epsilon)
                                             return Float_Type;
end Generic_Integration;
```

Suppose now that we wish to integrate a function whose value depends upon non-local variables and that therefore has to be declared at an inner level. All that has to be done is to instantiate the generic at the same inner level and then no accessibility problems arise. So

```
with Generic_Integration;
procedure Try_Estimate(External_Data: Data_Type;
                              Lower, Upper: Float;
                              Answer: out Float) is
   -- external data set by other means

   function Residue(X: Float) return Float is
      Result: Float;
   begin
      -- compute function value dependent upon external data
      return Result;
   end Residue;

   package Float_Integration is
         new Generic_Integration(Float_Type => Float);
   use Float_Integration;

begin
   ...
   Answer := Integrate(Residue'Access, Lower, Upper);

end Try_Estimate;
```

The key point is that the instantiated access type Integrand is at the same level as the local function Residue and therefore the Access attribute can be applied. This technique can of course be used even when there are no generic parameters.

3.8 Type Conversion

Because Ada 95 supports type extension and has more flexible access types, the possibilities and needs for type conversion become much more extensive than in Ada 83. In Ada 83, type conversion involved only a possible representation change and a possible constraint check. If the conversion succeeded, no components were lost or added, and the conversion was always reversible. There were only three kinds of conversions, between derived types, between numeric types and between array types. Note in particular that there were no conversions between access types (except for the case where the type itself was derived from another access type).

Conversions in Ada 95 are classified as view conversions and value conversions. The general idea is that a view conversion doesn't really perform a conversion but just provides a different view of the object.

View conversions arise in two situations, where the operand is an object of a tagged type, and where the conversion is used as an actual parameter corresponding to a formal in out or out parameter. Other conversions are value conversions. Another way of looking at the difference is that view conversions are for situations where an object is being converted whereas a value conversion can apply to an expression.

The use of a view conversion as a parameter existed in Ada 83; for example where a conversion of an object of say type Integer was used as an actual parameter corresponding to a formal in out parameter of type Float. Such view conversions cause a real change of representation in both directions and indeed view conversions of nontagged types are always reversible.

View conversions of tagged types are different; no change of representation ever occurs; we merely get a different view seeing different properties of the same object. And view conversions of tagged types are generally not reversible because of the possibility of type extension.

For tagged specific types there is an important rule that conversion can only be towards the root type. Conversion of a specific type away from the root type is not possible because additional components will generally be required. Such additional components can be provided by an extension aggregate. As we saw in the example of type `Object` and its extension `Circle` from II.1 we can write

```
Object(C)
```

as an acceptable conversion towards the root but must write

```
C: Circle;
O: Object;
...
C := (O with Radius => 12.0);
```

to perform the operation away from the root. (In an early draft of Ada 9X a form of conversion was used for such an extension but it was felt to be confusing and overcomplicate the rules for conversion; it also had generic contract problems.) Note that we have used the named notation for the additional components (in this case only one). Another important point is that the ancestor expression (before **with**) need not be the immediate ancestor of the target type but can be any ancestor. See also 3.6.1.

The same principle applies in the case of conversions from a tagged class-wide type to a specific type; conversion is only allowed if the tag of the current value of the class-wide object is such that conversion is not away from the root. This is not known statically and so a tag check verifies that the type identified by the tag of the operand matches that of the target type, or is a derivative of it. `Constraint_Error` is raised if this check fails.

Conversion from a specific type to a class wide type is always allowed implicitly (that is no conversion need be explicitly stated); of course the specific type must be in the class concerned. We could not convert a `Low_Alert` to `Medium_Alert'Class`; any attempt would be detected at compile time.

Conversion from one class-wide type to another is also possible. The classes obviously have to have a common ancestor and it may be necessary to check the tag at runtime. If the source class is the same as or a subclass of the target class then clearly no check is necessary.

We will consider the conversion of tagged types in more detail when we discuss redispatching in the next chapter (see 4.5).

Conversion between access types was not possible in Ada 83 (unless one was derived from another); each access type was considered unrelated (even if the accessed types were the same). Another issue was that access values need not necessarily be held as addresses but could be indexes into the relevant pool.

However, the introduction of general access types and access parameters means that the conversion between access types is very necessary.

Conversion from pool specific types to general access types and between general access types is therefore permitted provided the accessed types are the same or are suitably related. But we cannot convert from an access to constant type to an access to variable type because we might thereby obtain write access to a constant. In general a conversion may involve constraint and accessibility checks.

Conversions are particularly useful for programming with access types designating tagged types. Essentially, an access type conversion is permitted if access values of the target type may "safely" designate the object designated by the operand access value; or in other words providing the new view is acceptable for the designated object. Thus a conversion from an access to class-wide type to an access to specific type will require a dynamic check to ensure that the designated object is of the specific type (or derived from it). Generally, conversions between access types to tagged types follow exactly the same rules and involve the same checks as conversions between the designated types. Both conversions effectively give new views of the object concerned.

Conversions between access types (in general) may require accessibility checks to ensure that the new value could not give rise to a dangling reference. It is possible to convert between any general access types (including anonymous access types used as access parameters and discriminants) provided the designated types are the same. An example of access type conversion where an accessibility check is required occurs in 3.7.1. Conversions between access types may also require constraint checks to ensure that any constraints on the accessed subtype are satisfied.

As explained above we have generalized implicit subtype conversions on arrays ("sliding") to apply in more circumstances. These new rules should minimize the times when an unexpected Constraint_Error arises when the length of the array value is appropriate, but the upper and lower bounds do not match the applicable index constraint. In effect, we are treating the bounds as properties of array objects rather than of array values. Array values have a length for each dimension, but the bounds may be freely readjusted to fit the context.

Note also that array conversions require that the component subtypes statically match in Ada 95 whereas the check was dynamic in Ada 83. This is a minor incompatibility but avoids unnecessary runtime checks.

3.9 Staticness

In Ada 83, static expressions were limited to predefined operators applied to static operands, to static attributes or to static qualified expressions. For Ada 95, we have extended the rules so that a static expression can also include items such as membership tests and attributes with static constituents. See [RM95 4.9] for details.

By allowing more constructs in static expressions, the programmer has more freedom in contexts where static values are required. In addition, we ensure more uniformity in what expressions are evaluated at compile-time. Some Ada 83 compilers were aggressive in evaluating compile-time known expressions, while others only evaluated those expressions that were "officially" static. By shifting the definition of static to more closely correspond to compile-time-known, uniformity of efficiency is enhanced.

In addition to generalizing the rules for static expressions, we also require that all static evaluation be performed exactly. Although many compilers already perform all compile-time arithmetic with arbitrary precision, this rule will provide more predictability for the value of a static expression. Note that the exact static value must still be converted to a machine manipulable representation when combined in an expression with non-static values.

Static strings are also introduced for use as parameters of pragmas. There are no other contexts in the standard which require static strings.

Staticness is also relevant in other situations such as subtype conformance (see 6.2). This kind of conformance is required between the parameter and result specifications given in an access to subprogram type definition, and the specification of a potential designated subprogram. Subtype conformance is based on a static match between the subtypes of corresponding parameters and the result, if any. This is necessary because when calling a subprogram via an access to subprogram type, the actual parameters must be prepared and the call must be performed given only the address (and perhaps a static link) for the target subprogram. The way parameters are passed, the constraints that need to be checked, the way the result is returned, and any other calling conventions must be determined completely knowing only the definition of the access-to-subprogram type.

A static subtype match is required for access-to-subprogram matching so that no additional checks on the actual parameters are required when calling indirectly through an access to subprogram type.

There is a general philosophy that static matching is required when two subtypes are involved whereas when only one subtype and a value are involved (as in assignment) then dynamic matching (possibly resulting in Constraint_Error) is applied as it was in Ada 83. Thus static matching is also required in matching the component subtypes in array conversions and matching the subtype indication in deferred constants. This change of philosophy eliminates a number of run-time checks and makes for the earlier detection of errors in such situations.

3.10 Other Improvements

Ada 83 had a restriction that type, subtype, and object declarations were not permitted after bodies (including body stubs) within a declarative part. This restriction has been removed in Ada 95. The original restriction reflected Ada's Pascal heritage, where the ordering restrictions between declarations are even more restrictive. However, in retrospect, the restriction seems somewhat arbitrary, and forces the separation of declarative items that might more naturally be grouped together, particularly in a package body declarative part.

By removing this restriction, it becomes legal to move local variable declarations of a subprogram body to the end of its declarative part. This ensures that such variables are not accessible for up-level references from nested subprograms declared in the same declarative part. By so doing, it makes it easier for a compiler to allocate such variables to hardware registers, rather than having to keep them in memory locations to support possible up-level references.

Having removed this restriction, it is necessary to rely more heavily on the Ada 83 rule [RM83 13.1(5-7)] that the representation for a type is "frozen" by the appearance of a body (including a body stub). This rule precludes the separation of a representation clause from its associated declaration by a body. In Ada 83, this requirement was a ramification of the syntax, since representation clauses were not allowed to follow bodies syntactically. In Ada 95, the requirement becomes more relevant, since representation clauses are syntactically allowed to appear anywhere in a declarative part.

3.11 Requirements Summary

The requirements for international users

> *R3.1-A(1) — Base Character Set*

> *R3.1-A(2) — Extended Graphic Literals*

> *R3.1-A(3) — Extended Character Set Support*

are met by the changes to the type `Character` and the introduction of `Wide_Character` and associated packages as discussed in 3.2.

The study topic and two requirements regarding subprograms

> *S4.1-A(1) — Subprograms as Objects*

> *R4.1-B(1) — Passing Subprograms as Parameters*

> *R4.1-B(2) — Pragma Interface*

are met by access to subprogram types and the pragmas `Import`, `Export` and `Convention` as discussed in 3.7.2.

The requirement

> *R6.1-A(1) — Unsigned Integer Operations*

is met by the modular types described in 3.3.2.

The requirement

> *R6.4-A(1) — Access Values Designating Global Objects*

is met by general access types and the study topic

S6.4-B(1) — Low-Level Pointer Operations

is also addressed by general access types and the attribute Unchecked_Access.
The requirement

R10.1-A(1) — Decimal-Based Types

is met by the decimal types mentioned in 3.3.3. Full support for decimal types is provided by the
Information Systems annex to which the reader is referred for further details.
The requirement

S2.3-A(1) — Improve Early Detection of Errors

is addressed by the introduction of static subtype matching.
The requirement

R2.2-A(1) — Reduce Deterrents to Efficiency

is addressed by the introduction of the concept of base range for numeric types as discussed in 3.3
and by the removal of the restriction on the order of declarations mentioned in 3.10.
The requirement

R2.4-A(1) — Minimize Implementation Dependencies

is addressed by the stipulation that all static expressions are evaluated exactly and that rounding of
odd halves is always away from zero; see 3.9 and II.12.
Finally we have mentioned one of the items listed under the general requirement

R2.2-B(1) — Understandability

which is that the restriction on order of declarations is now removed.

4 Object Oriented Programming

This chapter describes the various ways in which object oriented programming is achieved in Ada 95. The main facilities upon which this is based are

- Record types which are marked as tagged may be extended with additional components on derivation.

- The Class attribute may be applied to a tagged type and denotes the corresponding class-wide type.

- Subprogram calls with formal parameters of a specific type called with actual parameters of a class-wide type are dispatching calls.

- Types and subprograms may be specified as abstract.

- There are various new forms of generic parameter corresponding to derived and tagged types.

These topics were discussed in some detail in Part One and are further discussed in other chapters in this part (see Chapter 3 for types, including abstract types and abstract subprograms, and Chapter 12 for generic parameters). The discussion in this chapter is more idiomatic and concentrates on how the features are used in Ada 95 and briefly contrasts the approach with that of other object oriented languages.

4.1 Background and Concepts

Ada has been traditionally associated with object oriented design [Booch 86], which advocates the design of systems in terms of abstract data types using objects, operations on objects, and their encapsulation as private types within packages. The "ingredients" of object oriented design may be summarized as follows:

Objects. Entities that have structure and state.

Operations. Actions on objects that may access or manipulate that state.

Encapsulation. Some means of defining objects and their operations and providing an abstract interface to them, while hiding their implementation details.

Ada 83 was well suited to supporting the paradigm of object oriented design. Object oriented programming, as that term has evolved over the past decade, builds upon the base of object oriented design, adding two other ingredients: inheritance and polymorphism. While the specific properties of these two facilities vary from one programming language to another, their essential characteristics may be stated as

Inheritance. A means for incrementally building new abstractions from existing ones by "inheriting" their properties — without disturbing the implementation of the original abstraction or the existing clients.

Polymorphism. A means of factoring out the differences among a collection of abstractions, such that programs may be written in terms of their common properties.

Ada 83 has been described as an object based language; it does not have the support for inheritance and polymorphism found in fully object oriented languages (see 4.7). Recognizing this, the Ada 9X Requirements reflect the need to provide improved support for this paradigm through three Study Topics [DoD 90] as follows.

S4.1-A(1) — Subprograms as Objects: Ada 9X should provide:

1   an easily implemented and efficient mechanism for dynamically selecting a subprogram that is to be called with a particular argument list;

2   a means of separating the set of subprograms that can be selected dynamically from the code that makes the selection.

S4.3-A(1) — Reducing the Need for Recompilation: Ada 9X recompilation and related rules should be revised so it is easier for implementations to minimize the need for recompilation and for programs to use program structures that reduce the need for recompilation.

S4.3-B(1) — Programming by Specialization/Extension: Ada 9X shall make it possible to define new declared entities whose properties are adapted from those of existing entities by the addition or modification of properties or operations in such a way that:

•   the original entity's definition and implementation are not modified;

•   the new entity (or instances thereof) can be used anywhere the original one could be, in exactly the same way.

Each of these Study topics can be understood in relation to object oriented programming. S4.1-A(1) seeks the ability to associate operations (subprograms) with objects, and to dynamically select and execute those operations. This is one basis on which to develop run-time polymorphism.

Among the various causes of excessive recompilation addressed by S4.3-A(1) are those arising from the breakage of an existing abstraction for the purpose of extending or otherwise reusing it to build a new abstraction.

The topic S4.3-B(1) implies the essence of object oriented programming as defined above. Alternatively, one might think of this in terms of two programming paradigms

Variant programming. New abstractions may be constructed from existing ones such that the programmer need only specify the differences between the new and old abstractions.

Class-wide programming. Classes of related abstractions may be handled in a unified fashion, such that the programmer may systematically ignore their differences when appropriate.

Finally, it should be mentioned that there are two rather awkward problems to be addressed and solved in designing a compiled language for object oriented programming which retains efficiency and avoids unnecessary run-time decisions.

Dispatching.   The means of indicating in the program text when dispatching and especially
    redispatching is used as opposed to static resolution.

Multiple Inheritance.   The means of inheriting components and operations from two or more
    parent types.

   As will be seen, the solution adopted to these problems in Ada 95 illustrates our concern for
clarity and the advantages of the building block approach.

4.2 General Approach

Ada 95 generalizes the type facilities of Ada 83 in order to provide more powerful mechanisms for
variant and class-wide program development and composition. Derived types in Ada 83 provided
a simple inheritance mechanism: they inherited exactly the structure, operations, and values of
their parent type. This "inheritance" could be augmented with additional operations but not with
additional components. Ada 95 generalizes type derivation to permit type extension as we saw in
II.1.

   A tagged record or private type may be extended with additional components on derivation.
Tagged objects are self-identifying; the tag indicates their specific type. Tagged types provide a
mechanism for single inheritance as found in object oriented programming languages such as
Simula [Birtwistle 73] and Smalltalk [Goldberg 83].

   The following example of type extension is inspired by [Seidewitz 91]. We first declare

```
type Account_With_Interest is tagged
   record
      Identity: Account_Number := None;
      Balance : Money := 0.00;
      Rate    : Interest_Rate := 0.05;
      Interest: Money := 0.00;
   end record;

procedure Accrue_Interest(On_Account: in out Account_With_Interest;
                          Over_Time : in Integer);

procedure Deduct_Charges(From: in out Account_With_Interest);
```

and can then extend it

```
type Free_Checking_Account is new Account_With_Interest with
   record
      Minimum_Balance: Money := 500.00;
      Transactions   : Natural := 0;
   end record;

procedure Deposit(Into   : in out Free_Checking_Account;
                  Amount: in Money);

procedure Withdraw(From   : in out Free_Checking_Account;
                   Amount: in Money);

Insufficient_Funds: exception;    -- raised by Withdraw

procedure Deduct_Charges(From: in out Free_Checking_Account);
```

The type Account_With_Interest is a tagged type. The type Free_Checking_Account is
derived from it, inheriting copies of its components (Identity, Balance, Rate, Interest) and

its operations (`Accrue_Interest` and `Deduct_Charges`). The derived type declaration has a record extension part that adds two additional components (`Minimum_Balance` and `Transactions`) to those inherited from the parent. The type adds some new operations (`Deposit` and `Withdraw`) and also overrides `Deduct_Charges` such that if the `Balance` was above the `Minimum_Balance`, no charges would be deducted. All components of the type, whether inherited or declared as a part of the extension, are equally accessible (unlike "nested" record types).

In Ada 83, the types declared in the visible part of a package had special significance for Ada's abstraction mechanisms. Such operations on user-defined types were first-class in a manner that parallels those of the predefined types. For derived types, these operations, together with the implicitly declared basic operations, were the derivable operations on a type.

With the increased importance of derived types for object oriented programming in Ada 95, the notion of the operations closely related to a type in this manner is generalized. The primitive operations of a type are those that are implicitly provided for the type and, for types immediately declared in a package specification, all subprograms with an operand or result of the type declared anywhere in that package specification. The domain is therefore extended to include the private part (but not the body).

Thus, in Ada 95, the derivable operations of Ada 83 have become "primitive operations" and the restriction of these operations to the visible part of a package has been eliminated. These changes support added capability: primitive operations may be private and a type and its derivatives may be declared in the same declarative region (this property is useful for building related abstractions and was used in the package `New_Alert_System` of Part One).

Primitive operations clarify the notion of an abstract data type for purposes of object oriented programming (inheritance and polymorphism) and genericity. They are distinguished from the other operations of a type in the following ways

Inheritance. Primitive operations are the derivable (inherited) operations.

Polymorphism. Primitive operations are dispatching operations on tagged types.

Genericity. Primitive operations are the ones available within generic templates parameterized by a class.

Ada 83 used the term "class" (see [RM83 3.3]) to characterize collections of related types. The class of a type determines how the type is declared, the types it can be converted to, its predefined operations, and its structure. The class of a generic formal type parameter determines the operations that are available within the generic template. Types within a class have common structure and operations (see III.1.2 for a further description of the class structure of Ada).

Ada 95 formalizes the Ada 83 notion of class. A type and its direct and indirect derivatives, whether or not extended, constitute a derivation class. This definition allows for user-defined classes based on derivation. User-defined classes, like the language-defined classes, support type conversion, may be used to parameterize generic units and, in the case of tagged types, provide class-wide programming.

Explicit conversion is defined among types within a class, as it was in Ada 83 for types related by derivation, except that conversion is not allowed away from the root since additional components may be required. Such transformations require an extension aggregate as described in 3.8.

Thus, continuing the previous example, a value of `Account_With_Interest` can be extended to a value of `Free_Checking_Account` by providing values for the additional components `Minimum_Balance` and `Transactions`.

```
Old_Account: Account_With_Interest;
  ...
New_Account: Free_Checking_Account :=
        (Old_Account with Minimum_Balance => 0.00, Transactions => 0);
```

The Ada 95 rules for conversion between types in a class define the semantics of inherited operations in Ada 95 and are consistent with the semantics of inherited operations in Ada 83. Calling an inherited operation is equivalent to calling the parent's corresponding operation with a conversion of the actual to the parent type. Thus, inherited operations "ignore" the extension part.

User-defined classes may be employed to parameterize generic units. A new kind of generic formal, a generic formal derived type, may be used. This kind of formal is matched by any type in the class rooted at the generic formal's specified ancestor type.

For each tagged type T, there is an associated class-wide type T'Class. The set of values of T'Class is the discriminated union of the sets of values of T and all types derived directly or indirectly from T. Discrimination between the different specific types is with a type tag. This tag, associated with each value of a class-wide type, is the basis for run-time polymorphism in Ada 95. Note that ordinary types are referred to as specific types to distinguish them from class-wide types.

The associated class-wide type T'Class is "dynamic" in the sense of [Abadi 91]. The values of the class-wide type can be thought of as pairs consisting of

• A tag. A type descriptor ranging over the types that are members of the class; and

• A value. The value taken from the specific type with the given tag.

Such tag and value pairs are strongly typed, consistent with the philosophy of Ada. But only the class, and not necessarily the type within that class, will generally be known statically.

Class-wide types have no primitive operations of their own. However, explicit operations may be declared for such types, using T'Class as a subtype mark. Such operations are "class-wide" and can be applied to objects of any specific type within the class as well as to objects of the class-wide type or a descendent class-wide type.

Thus the following functions

```
function Size_In_Bytes(Any_File: File'Class) return Natural;
function Get_File_From_User return File'Class;
```

are class-wide operations and can be applied to all specific types of the class of types derived from the tagged type File. No dispatching is involved; the one same function is called whatever the tag of the actual parameter.

On the other hand, when a primitive operation of a tagged type is called with an operand of the class-wide type, the operation to be executed is selected at run time based on the type tag of the operand. As mentioned before, this run-time selection is called dispatching, so primitive operations of tagged types are called dispatching operations. Dispatching provides a natural form of run-time polymorphism within classes of related (derived) types. This variety of polymorphism is known as "inclusion polymorphism" [Cardelli 85].

actual	formal	
	specific	class-wide
specific	static binding	class-wide op
class-wide	dispatching	class-wide op

Table 4-1: Kinds of Binding

An operand used to control dispatching is called a controlling operand. A primitive operation may have several controlling operands; a primitive function may also have a controlling result. For a further discussion on controlling operands and results see 4.5.

The different kinds of binding corresponding to the various combinations of actual and formal parameters are summarized in Table 4-1.

The following example shows how a type File might be the basis for a class of types relating to the implementation of an Ada library

```
type File is tagged private;
procedure View(F: File);
    -- display file F on screen

type Directory is new File with private;
procedure View(D: Directory);
    -- list directory D

type Ada_File is new File with private;
procedure View(A: Ada_File);
    -- open A with Ada sensitive editor

type Ada_Library is
    new Directory with private;
procedure View(L: Ada_Library);
    -- list library units of L and their status

declare
    A_File: File'Class := Get_File_From_User;
begin
    View(A_File);    -- dispatches according to specific type of file
end;
```

The above example presents a user-defined class of File types. The type File is tagged and hence the primitive operation View is dispatching. View is overridden for each type in the class in order to provide a unique behavior for each type of File. When View is called with a parameter that is of type File'Class, the tag will be used to determine the actual type within the class, and the call will dispatch to the View procedure for that type. On the other hand if View is called with a specific type then the choice of View procedure to be called is determined at compile time.

The hierarchy of types in the above example is illustrated in Figure 4-1.

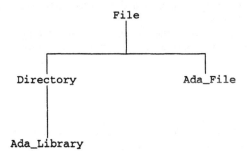

Figure 4-1: The File Hierarchy

An earlier version of Ada 9X introduced class-wide types through the Class attribute for all derivation classes and not just those for tagged types. This was discarded since many reviewers felt that the added flexibility was unwise.

Note also that universal types (for numeric types) behave much as class-wide types although there are differences, see 3.3.

When building an abstraction that is to form the basis of a class of types, it is often convenient not to provide actual subprograms for the root type but just abstract subprograms which can be replaced when inherited. This is only allowed if the root type is declared as abstract; objects of an abstract type cannot exist. This technique enables common class-wide parts of a system to be written without being dependent on the properties of any specific type at all. Dispatching always works because it is known that there can never be any objects of the abstract type and so the abstract subprograms could never be called. This technique is illustrated in II.3.

4.2.1 Benefits of Approach

A number of important practical criteria of concern to both existing and new users were taken into account when designing the object oriented facilities of Ada 95.

Compatibility

Legal Ada 83 programs should remain legal in Ada 95. Ideally, existing Abstract Data Types (ADTs) should be reusable with newly developed ones — the new facilities should not be so radically different from mechanisms of Ada 83 that existing ADTs must be rebuilt before being reused.

Tagged type extension and class-wide types are built upon the Ada 83 model of derived types. Their use is optional, and their presence in the language does not affect Ada 83 programs. Existing ADTs may be combined in some ways with new object oriented abstractions without modification. In other cases, it may be sufficient to add "tagged" to a type declaration, or to make other simple modifications such as changing an access type declaration to designate a class-wide type. Of course, in order to exploit these facilities to the full, it will be necessary to take them into account during the design process.

Consistency

The solution should be conceptually consistent with existing Ada programming models. Intuitions about objects, types, subprograms, generic units, and so on should be preserved.

Ada 95 provides new capabilities in the context of a unified programming model: including types, operations and generic units. Class-wide programming generalizes the classes developed in Ada 83 to user-defined classes.

Efficiency

The solution should offer efficient performance for users of the facility with, ideally, no distributed overhead for non-users.

The introduction of tagged types, and a distinct class-wide type associated with each specific type as the mechanism for dispatch, makes run-time polymorphism optional to programmers (in contrast to languages like Smalltalk), in two senses.

- Programmers can choose whether or not to use object oriented programming, by employing tagged and class-wide types. Types without tags incur no space or time overhead. Only class-wide types allow for class-wide type matching.

- Dispatching occurs only on primitive operations of tagged types and only when an actual operand is of a class-wide type.

Implementability

The solution should be readily implementable within current compiler technology, and provide opportunities for optimizations.

Dispatching may be implemented as an indirect jump through a table of subprograms indexed by the primitive operations. This compares favorably with method look-up in many object oriented languages, and with the alternative of variant records and case statements, with their attendant variant checks, both in implementability and run-time efficiency.

4.3 Class Wide Types and Operations

We have seen that a record or private type marked as tagged may be extended on derivation with additional components. The run-time tag identifies information that allows class-wide operations on the class-wide type to allocate, copy, compare for equality, and perform any other primitive operations on objects of the class-wide type, in accordance with the requirements of the specific type identified by the tag.

The tag is thus important to the inner workings of type extension and class-wide types in Ada 95 and is brought to the fore by using the reserved word **tagged** in the declaration of the type. The concept of a tag is of course not new to programming languages but has a long precedent of use in Pascal (where it is used in the sense of discriminant in Ada) and is discussed by Hoare in [Dahl 72]. More recently the phrase *type tag* has been used by Wirth in connection with type extension [Wirth 88].

The reader might find it helpful to understand the concept of the tag and the dispatching rules by considering the implementation model alluded to at the end of the last section. We emphasize that this is just a *possible* model and does not imply that an implementation has to be done this way. In this model the tag is a pointer to a dispatch table. Each entry in the table points to the body of the subprogram for a primitive operation. Dispatching is performed as an indirect jump through the table using the primitive operation as an index into the table.

As an illustration consider the class of Alert types declared in II.1 in the package New_Alert_System. These types form a tree as illustrated in II.2. Recall that the root type Alert has primitive operations, Display, Handle and Log. These are inherited by Low_Alert without any changes. Medium_Alert inherits them from Alert but overrides Handle. High_Alert inherits from Medium_Alert and again overrides Handle and also adds Set_Alarm. (For simplicity, we will ignore other predefined operations which also have "slots" in the dispatch table; such as assignment, the equality operator and the application of the Size attribute.)

The tags for the various types are illustrated in Figure 4-2. A dispatching call, such as to Handle, is very cheaply implemented. The code simply jumps indirectly to the contents of the table indexed by the fixed offset corresponding to Handle (one word in this example). The base of the table is simply the value of the tag and this is part of the value of the class-wide object. Note moreover that the dispatch table does not contain any class-wide operations (such as Process_Alerts in II.2) since these are not dispatching operations.

In addition to being used as formal parameters to class-wide operations, class-wide types may also be used as the designated type for an access type, and as the type of a declared object. Access types designating a class-wide type are very important, since they allow the creation of heterogeneous linked data structures, such as trees and queues.

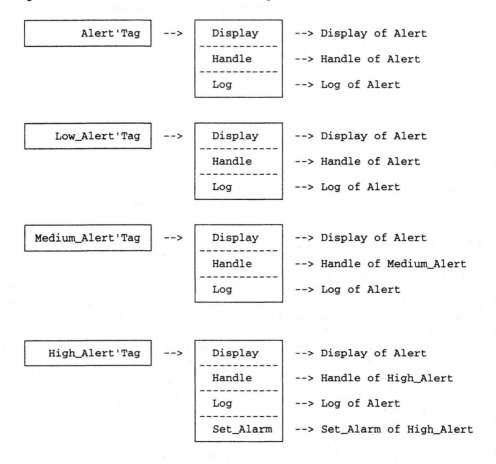

Figure 4-2: Tags and Dispatch Tables

Declared objects of a class-wide type are not as frequently used as are formal parameters and heap objects, but they are useful as intermediates in larger computations. However, because there is no upper bound on the size of types in a class, a declared object of a class-wide type must be explicitly initialized. This determines the size, the tag, and any discriminants for the object, and thereafter neither the tag nor the discriminants may be changed. Of course, it is necessary for all class-wide objects to have a tag so that dispatching works without any unnecessary tests. We have chosen to specify the tag by requiring an explicit initial value.

This indirectly provides a capability somewhat akin to declaration by association using **like** in Eiffel [Meyer 88]. We can thereby ensure, for example, that a locally declared class-wide object has the same tag as an actual parameter.

Note that discriminants of tagged types are not permitted to have defaults; this would have increased the complexity of the language to no great benefit since the tag of an object (specific and class-wide) cannot be changed and the tag is treated as a (hidden) discriminant. It would be inconsistent to allow discriminants to be changed but not tags.

If assignment were allowed to change the tag or the discriminants, then the size of the class-wide object might have to grow, requiring a deallocation and reallocation as part of assignment.

We have avoided introducing operations in Ada 95 that involve this kind of implicit dynamic allocation at run-time. Therefore, an explicit access value with explicit deallocation and reallocation is required if a programmer desires to have the equivalent of an unconstrained object of a class-wide type.

Note that Ada 83 required a similar approach for handling unconstrained arrays and unconstrained discriminated types without defaults for the discriminants. In general, the way unconstrained composite types and their associated bounds or discriminants were handled in Ada 83 is a good model for how class-wide types and their associated type tags are handled in Ada 95.

The predefined equality operators and the membership tests are generalized to apply to class-wide types. Like other predefined operations on such types, the implementation will depend on the particular specific type of the operands. Unlike normal dispatching operations, however, Constraint_Error is not raised if the tags of the operands do not match.

For equality, tag mismatch is treated as inequality. Only if the tags match is a dispatch then performed to the type-specific equality checking operation. This approach allows a program to safely compare two values of a class-wide tagged type for equality, without first checking that their tags match. The fact that no exception is raised in such an equality check is consistent with the other predefined relational operators, as noted in [RM83 4.5.2(12)].

For a membership test such as X **in** S, where X is of a class-wide type, the tag of the value of the simple expression X is checked to see whether it belongs to the subtype mark S. If the subtype mark S identifies a class-wide type, then the membership test determines whether the tag of the value identifies a specific type covered by the class-wide type. If the subtype mark S identifies a specific tagged type, then the membership test determines whether the tag of the value equals the tag of that type. In any case, to be considered a member, the value must satisfy any constraints associated with the subtype mark.

The Tag attribute is defined for querying the tag of a specific type, or of an object of a class-wide type. This allows two class-wide objects to be checked to see whether they have the same tag. It is also possible to compare the tag of a class-wide object with the tag of a specific type; such a comparison is equivalent to a membership test.

Thus (using the alert example from Part One), the test

```
AC in Medium_Alert
```

is identical to

```
AC'Tag = Medium_Alert'Tag
```

but note that the test

```
AC in Medium_Alert'Class
```

has no generally applicable equivalent in terms of explicit user checks on tags because we cannot talk about possible future extensions in terms of tags. It is thus preferable to use membership tests rather than explicit testing of tags in order to ensure that our program is extensible.

The rules for membership tests on class-wide types are constructed so that certain simple type-specific behavior may be performed in a class-wide operation, without the need to declare and define a new primitive operation on all types within the class.

For example, given

```
type Expression_Node is tagged...

type Binary_Operator is new Expression_Node with ...

type Node_Ptr is access Expression_Node'Class;
```

one could define the following operation Display on the access to class-wide type Node_Ptr

```
procedure Display(Expr: Node_Ptr; Prec: Positive := 1) is
   -- display expr, parenthesized if necessary
begin
   if Expr.all in Binary_Operator'Class then
      -- handle the binary operator subclass
      declare
         Binop: constant Bin_Op_Ptr := Bin_Op_Ptr(Expr);
            -- convert parameter to ptr to Binary_Operator
            -- to gain access to its subclass operations
      begin
         if Precedence(Binop) < Prec then
            -- parenthesize if lower precedence
            Put('(');
         end if;
         -- display left, op, right, passing down precedence
         Display(Binop.Left, Precedence(Binop));
         Put(Symbol(Binop));
         Display(Binop.Right, Precedence(Binop));
         if Precedence(Binop) < Prec then
            -- closing parenthesis if necessary
            Put(')');
         end if;
      end;
   else
      -- handle the other kinds of expressions
      ...
   end if;
end Display;
```

An alternative, more "object-oriented" approach would be to define a separate Display primitive operation for each distinct type within the class. See for example [Taft 93].

We conclude this section by discussing a number of important general principles regarding primitive operations and dispatching. It is instructive to map these principles into the implementation model of the tag and dispatch table mentioned above; but remember that this is only a possible model although a very natural one. We can refer to the entries in the dispatch table as "slots".

The first general principle is that dispatching always works without any checking at runtime; in other words that the subprogram referred to by the dispatch table for the tag value can always be safely called. A number of individual rules ensure that this is true. Perhaps the most important is that operations cannot be removed when deriving a new type; they can only be added or replaced. This means that if an operation is primitive for a type then it is necessarily available for all (nonabstract) types in the class rooted at that type. Another vital rule is that we cannot create an object of an abstract type; this prevents dispatching to an abstract subprogram (see 3.6.2). Moreover, as discussed further in 4.5, the tag of an object can never be changed, so the tag of a declared object cannot be changed into the tag corresponding to a type without the appropriate operations.

Another important rule is that type extension is not allowed at a place which is not accessible from the parent type such as within an inner block. This rule ensures that the accessibility of all specific types in a (tagged) class is the same and prevents a value from being assigned to a class wide object and thereby outlive its specific type. A further consequence is that we cannot dispatch to a subprogram which is at an inner level and which might thereby attempt to access non-existent data. Consider

```
package Outer is
   type T is tagged ...;
   procedure P(Object: T);   -- a dispatching operation
   type A is access T'Class;
```

```
      Global: A;
   end Outer;

procedure Dodgy is
   package Inner is
      type NT is new T with ...;   -- an illegal extension
      procedure P(Object: NT);     -- override
   end;

   package body Inner is
      I: Integer := 0;
      procedure P(Object: NT) is
      begin
         I := I + 1;  -- assign to variable local to Inner
      end P;
   end Inner;
begin
   Global := new Inner.NT'( ...);
end Dodgy;

procedure Disaster is
begin
   Dodgy;
   P(Global.all);  -- dispatch to non-existent P
end Disaster;
```

The procedure Dodgy attempts to declare the type NT and then assign an access to an object of the specific type to the class wide access variable Global. If this were allowed then the call of P in the procedure Disaster would attempt to dispatch to the procedure inside Inner and thereby access the variable I which no longer exists. Disallowing extensions at an inner level prevents this sort of difficulty.

Note also that having all the types at the same accessibility level ensures that the "subprogram values" in the dispatch table can be implemented just as simple addresses; no level information is required. There is an analogy with access to subprogram values discussed in 3.7.2.

Another important principle is that the dispatch table is the same for all views of a type; in other words there is just one dispatch table common to both a partial view and a full view. However, it can be the case that some operations are not visible from a partial view. This is discussed further in 7.1.1.

Interestingly, it is also possible to have two operations of the same name (and profile), one visible from one view and the other from another view in such a way that they are never both visible from the same view; in this case they would occupy different slots in the dispatch table. These and related possibilities are also illustrated in detail in 7.1.1.

The freezing rules have an important impact on type extension. The basic idea is that a record extension freezes the parent; the key impact is that further primitive operations cannot then be declared for the parent. However, a private extension does not freeze the parent; freezing is postponed until the later full declaration. See 13.5.1.

Finally, we summarize the rules regarding which operations are primitive. The main rule is that only those operations with an operand or result of the type and declared immediately in the package specification with the type declaration (or type extension) are primitive operations. (This general rule applies to both tagged and other types.) Note that if a type is not declared in a package specification then any operations declared in the same declarative region are not primitive and thus not inherited. Because this might give rise to surprises, especially in the case of tagged types, it is in fact forbidden to call a nonprimitive operation in a dispatching way (that is with a class-wide actual); this eliminates the risk of accidentally declaring a tagged type and then finding that what were presumed to be primitive operations do not dispatch.

Note moreover that, in the case of a type extension, although new primitive operations cannot be added except in a package specification, primitive operations inherited from the parent may be overridden wherever the extension is declared and these overridden versions will of course be inherited by any further extension. Thus new slots can only be created by a type declared or extended in a package specification, but existing slots may be overridden wherever a type extension is declared. Consider

```
package P is
   type T is tagged ...;
   procedure Op1(X: T);      -- primitive of T
end P;

with P; use P;
package Q is
   type NTQ is new T with ...;
   procedure Op1(X: NTQ);    -- overrides inherited Op1 from T
   procedure Op2(X: NTQ);    -- additional primitive of NTQ
end Q;

package body P is
   type NTP is new T with ...;
   procedure Op1(X: NTP);    -- overrides inherited Op1 from T
   procedure Op2(X: NTP);    -- not a primitive of NTP
end P;
```

The type NTQ is declared immediately inside the specification of package Q and thus the operation Op2 is primitive. On the other hand NTP is declared in the body of package P and thus although Op1 overrides the inherited Op1, nevertheless the operation Op2 is not primitive.

These rules are designed to give flexibility with minimum burden. Many type extensions will simply replace existing operations rather than add new ones and it seems a heavy burden to insist that these be in a package specification. Indeed, in the case of the leaves of the tree of types, there is no need to add further primitive operations (if a type is a leaf then any new operation is not inherited by another type and thus there is no need to dispatch); but it is important to be able to override existing operations wherever the type is declared. See the example in 4.4.4.

A minor difference between tagged and nontagged types concerns the parameter modes of overriding operations. In the case of tagged types an overriding operation must have the same parameter modes otherwise dispatching would not work. In the case of nontagged types this does not matter and for compatibility with Ada 83, the modes need not be the same; note that overload resolution ignores parameter modes.

4.4 Examples of Use

This section presents some of the ways in which Ada 95's object oriented programming features may be used and combined with other facilities to address a number of programming paradigms.

An important use of object oriented programming is variant programming. This was amply illustrated by the example of processing alerts in Part One. As we saw, the use of variant records can be both cumbersome and error prone [Wirth 88] whereas the use of type extension is both more flexible and entirely secure.

In this section we give other typical paradigms of use

- An example of different approaches to a standard queue package that can be used as a basis for a wide range of applications.

- An example of a more elaborate heterogeneous doubly linked list abstraction.

- An example showing how alternative implementations can be provided for the same abstraction.

- An example showing how type extension and dispatching can be used to program iterators and similar applications.

4.4.1 Queues

In dealing with the alert example in II.2 we mentioned that the various alerts might be held on a queue ready for processing. Such a queue must have the capability to be heterogeneous because the alerts are of different specific types. This is a common requirement and it is therefore appropriate to develop a package that can be reused for a variety of applications.

However, the strong typing model of Ada 83 made it very difficult to write a common abstraction that could be reused without alteration even through the use of generics. (Only homogeneous structures could be constructed with Ada 83 generic units. Variant records could be used to provide some heterogeneity, but source code changes and possibly extensive recompilation were required to add new variants.)

There are several approaches that can be taken which have a different balance between convenience and efficiency. We will explore a number of these in order to illustrate various considerations and potential pitfalls to be avoided. We will start at the convenient end of the spectrum by considering a package which is generic with respect to the type of data on the queue. The specification might be

```
generic
   type Q_Data(<>) is private;
package Generic_Queues is
   type Queue is limited private;
   function Is_Empty(Q: Queue) return Boolean;
   procedure Add_To_Queue(Q: access Queue; X: in Q_Data);
   function Remove_From_Queue(Q: access Queue) return Q_Data;
   Queue_Empty: exception;
private
   ...
end Generic_Queues;
```

It is important to note that the formal type has an unknown discriminant part. It can then be matched by a specific type or by a class wide type (see 12.5). If we use a specific type then of course the queue is homogeneous but using a class wide type provides a heterogeneous queue. Note also that the exported type Queue is limited private; the implementation will inevitably be in terms of pointers to a chained list and making it limited prevents the user from making a copy which might subsequently become nonsense; we will return to the implementation details in a moment.

Values are added to the queue by calling the procedure Add_To_Queue and removed by calling the function Remove_From_Queue. Making the latter a procedure with profile

```
procedure Remove_From_Queue(Q: access Queue; X: out Q_Data);
```

is rather restrictive because we cannot call the procedure with an uninitialized class-wide object (they are not allowed) and an initialized one will be constrained by its initial value. Such a procedure is therefore only useful if we always know (by some other means) the anticipated specific type of the item being removed. Using a function works because the returned result provides the initial value and thus the constraint.

Incidentally we made the parameter Q of the function an access parameter largely because an in out parameter is not allowed for functions. We could have made it an in parameter but the internal implementation of the queue would then need an extra level of indirection. See 6.1.2 for a fuller discussion on the merits of access versus in out parameters. We also have to choose between declaring a queue directly and making it aliased or creating the queue with an allocator. We choose the latter.

So for the alerts, we can write

```
package Alert_Queues is new Generic_Queues(Q_Data => Alert'Class);
use Alert_Queues;
type Queue_Ptr is access all Queue;
The_Queue: Queue_Ptr := new Queue;
...
MA: Medium_Alert := ...;
...
Add_To_Queue(The_Queue, MA);
```

and a value could be retrieved by

```
Any_Alert: Alert'Class := Remove_From_Queue(The_Queue);
```

where the result provides the constraint for Any_Alert.

Returning to the example in II.2, we could then call the first form of Process_Alerts by

```
Process_Alerts(Any_Alert);
```

and indeed we could directly write

```
Process_Alerts(Remove_From_Queue(The_Queue));
```

It is often preferable to manipulate access values to tagged types rather than tagged type values themselves; partly because this avoids the cost of copying and perhaps more important it overcomes the problem of not knowing the size of the object in the case of a class wide type. So an alternative approach would be to write

```
type Alert_Ptr is access all Alert'Class;
package Alert_Ptr_Queues is new Generic_Queues(Alert_Ptr);
use Alert_Ptr_Queues;
type Queue_Ptr is access all Queue;
The_Queue: Queue_Ptr := new Queue;
...
New_Alert: Alert_Ptr := new Medium_Alert'(...);
...
Add_To_Queue(The_Queue, New_Alert);
```

and then in the body of the second form of Process_Alerts we could have

```
Next_Alert: Alert_Ptr := Remove_From_Queue(The_Queue);
...
Handle(Next_Alert.all);
```

This second formulation is very straightforward since the queue is really homogeneous; all the elements are of the same access type and the heterogeneity comes from the nature of the accessed type.

We now return to consider how the generic package might be implemented. An important point is that since the formal type is indefinite, we cannot declare an uninitialized object of the type or a record with a component of the type. This forces us to use dynamic storage. As a first attempt the private part might be

```
private
   type Data_Ptr is access Q_Data;
   type Node;
   type Node_Ptr is access Node;
   type Node is
      record
         D: Data_Ptr;
         Next: Node_Ptr;
      end record;
   type Queue is
      record
         Head: Node_Ptr;
         Tail: Node_Ptr;
      end record;
end Generic_Queues;
```

This is an obvious approach although slightly cumbersome because of the double levels of indirection. This causes a double allocation whenever a new data item is added; one for the node and one for the data itself. Care is also needed in discarding storage when an item is removed. The details are left to the reader.

A problem with the above approach is the encapsulation of the storage management. Although the generic is very reusable it is somewhat costly because of the storage allocation overheads. Of course if the queue were homogeneous and had a definite parameter without <> then it would be simpler because the values could be stored directly; we are paying for the generality. Insisting that the parameter be definite would not be unreasonable because, as shown above, the client can always pass an access type.

A completely different approach is to arrange things so that the user's type provides the storage for the linking mechanism through type extension; this avoids the overheads of storage management but requires a little more effort on the part of the user. Consider the following

```
package Queues is
   type Queue is limited private;
   type Queue_Element is abstract tagged private;
   type Element_Ptr is access all Queue_Element'Class;
   function Is_Empty(Q: Queue) return Boolean;
   procedure Add_To_Queue(Q: access Queue; E: in Element_Ptr);
   function Remove_From_Queue(Q: access Queue) return Element_Ptr;
   Queue_Error: exception;
private
   type Queue_Element is tagged
      record
         Next: Element_Ptr := null;
      end record;
   type Queue is limited
      record
         Head: Element_Ptr := null;
         Tail: Element_Ptr := null;
      end record;
end Queues;
```

The general idea is that the user extends the type Queue_Element with the data to be queued. The linking is then done through the private component Next of which the user is not aware. The body might be as follows

```
package body Queues is
   function Is_Empty(Q: Queue) return Boolean is
   begin
      return Q.Head = null;
```

```
      end Is_Empty;

      procedure Add_To_Queue(Q: access Queue;
                                E: in Element_Ptr) is
      begin
         if E.Next /= null then
            raise Queue_Error:    -- already on a queue
         end if;
         if Q.Head = null then    -- list was empty
            Q.Head := E;
            Q.Tail := E;
         else
            Q.Tail.Next := E;
            Q.Tail := E;
         end if;
      end Add_To_Queue;

      function Remove_From_Queue(Q: access Queue)
                           return Element_Ptr is
         Result: Element_Ptr;
      begin
         if Is_Empty(Q) then
            raise Queue_Error;
         end if;
         Result := Q.Head;
         Q.Head := Result.Next;
         Result.Next := null;
         return Result;
      end Remove_From_Queue;
   end Queues;
```

Heterogeneous queues can be made because the type Element_Ptr is an access to class wide type. There are a number of ways in which this approach can be used which we will now explore using the alert example.

The first point is that we cannot extend the queue element with a class wide type and so we cannot just make a single extension which directly contains any alert. We could of course just extend with a component of the type Alert_Ptr and then add and remove alerts as follows

```
   type Alert_Element is new Queue_Element with
      record
         The_Ptr: Alert_Ptr;
      end record;
   ...
   type Queue_Ptr is access all Queue;
   The_Queue: Queue_Ptr := new Queue;

   ...
   New_Alert: Alert_Ptr := new Medium_Alert'(...);
   New_Element: Element_Ptr :=
                     new Alert_Element'(Queue_Element with New_Alert);
   Add_To_Queue(The_Queue, New_Element);
   ...
   Next_Alert := Alert_Element(Remove_From_Queue(The_Queue)).The_Ptr;
```

Note the use of the extension aggregate with the subtype name as the ancestor part, see 3.6.1.

We *could* create distinct element types for each alert level although this has its own problems as will soon become apparent. If we write

```
type Low_Element is new Queue_Element with
   record
      LA: Low_Alert;
   end record;

type Medium_Element is new Queue_Element with
   record
      MA: Medium_Alert;
   end record;
...
```

then adding alerts to the queue is relatively straightforward.

```
MA: Medium_Alert := ...;
New_Element: Element_Ptr :=
                  new Medium_Element'(Queue_Element with MA);
Add_To_Queue(The_Queue, New_Element);
```

Removing an alert in this formulation is less straightforward since we have to identify its specific type by interrogating the tag thus

```
Next_Element: Element_Ptr := Remove_From_Queue(The_Queue);
...
if Next_Element'Tag = Low_Element'Tag then
   Process_Alerts(Low_Element(Next_Element).LA);
```

Unfortunately this brings us back to variant programming which we try to avoid. The essence of the difficulty is that we have dispersed the alerts into the different queue elements and lost their commonality. There are two possible different approaches. The best is to plan ahead and ensure that the complete alert hierarchy is developed with the common queue element already in place. Following II.3, we can write

```
with Queues; use Queues;
package Base_Alert_System is
   type Alert is abstract new Queue_Element with null record;
   procedure Handle(A: in out Alert) is abstract;
end Base_Alert_System;
```

and then we develop all the rest of the alert structure as before. Now all alerts themselves have the linking mechanism already in them and can be directly placed on a queue. So we can now simply write

```
New_Alert: Alert_Ptr := new Medium_Alert'(...);
Add_To_Queue(Queue, New_Alert);
...
Next_Alert := Alert_Ptr(Remove_From_Queue(The_Queue));
```

Note that we have to convert the result to the type Alert_Ptr. This conversion requires a runtime check which always passes (because we have only placed alerts on the queue).

An important point to note with this approach is that each element can be on only one queue at a time. An attempt to place an element on a second queue will result in Queue_Error. Note that when an element is removed from a queue, its Next component is set to null so that it can then be placed on another queue. Observe that if we consider the elements as like real objects then they can only be in one place at a time and hence only on one queue at a time; so the restriction should not be unrealistic.

If it is quite impossible to modify an existing hierarchy to incorporate the link in the root (perhaps because we do not have the source), then it is still possible to avoid the variant difficulty when removing elements from the queue. The idea is to add a dispatching operation which can extract the particular alert; we can write

```
with Queues; use Queues;
package Alert_Elements is
   type Data_Element is abstract new Queue_Element with null record;
   type Data_Element_Ptr is access all Data_Element'Class;
   function Extract(D: Data_Element) return Alert'Class is abstract;
end Alert_Elements;
```

By introducing the type Data_Element we provide a place to attach the required dispatching operation. Note of course that Extract only applies to the class rooted at Data_Element and not the class rooted at Queue_Element.

We can now declare the various types such as Low_Element for each alert type as extensions of Data_Element and provide an appropriate function Extract for each such as

```
type Low_Element is new Data_Element with
   record
      LA: Low_Alert;
   end record;

function Extract(D: access Low_Element) return Alert'Class is
begin
   return D.LA;
end Extract;
```

We can add alerts to the queue much as before but removing alerts is now much simpler. Having copied the pointer to the removed element into Next_Element we can then convert to the type Data_Element and then call Extract thus

```
Next_Element: Element_Ptr := Remove_From_Queue(The_Queue);
Any_Alert: Alert'Class := Extract(Data_Element_Ptr(Next_Element));
```

so that dispatching to the appropriate function Extract occurs thereby overcoming the need for variant programming.

Although this mechanism works, it is vulnerable to error if the alert structure is extended. There is a risk that the corresponding extension to the element structure might be forgotten in which case a value of an extended type will not be extracted properly.

We continue this rather long discussion by considering how the original generic queue package could be implemented in terms of the second package. The private part and body might be

```
private
   type Data_Ptr is access Q_Data;
   type Q_Element is new Queues.Queue_Element with
      record
         D: Data_Ptr;
      end record;
   type Queue is new Queues.Queue;
end Generic_Queues;

package body Generic_Queues is
   function Is_Empty(Q: Queue) return Boolean is
   begin
      return Queues.Is_Empty(Queues.Queue(Q));
   end Is_Empty;
```

```
procedure Add_To_Queue(Q: access Queue; X: in Q_Data) is
begin
    Queues.Add_To_Queue(Queues.Queue(Q),
        new Q_Element'(Queues.Queue_Element with new Q_Data'(X)));
end Add_To_Queue;

function Remove_From_Queue(Q: access Queue) return Q_Data is
begin
    if Is_Empty(Q) then
        raise Queue_Empty;
    end if;
    declare
        Q_E_P: Queues.Element_Ptr :=
                        Queues.Remove_From_Queue(Queues.Queue(Q));
        D_P: Data_Ptr := Q_Element(Q_E_P.all).D;
        Result: Q.Data := D_P.all;
    begin
        -- can now discard storage occupied by the queue element
        -- and the data; assuming suitable unchecked conversions
        Free(Q_E_P);  Free(D_P);
        return Result;
    end;
end Remove_From_Queue;
end Generic_Queues;
```

Note that we have to take care not to lose access to the storage so that it can be freed. In particular the result is copied into a local variable; this is allowed despite the type being indefinite because the variable is initialized. Another point is that Is_Empty, Add_To_Queue and Remove_From_Queue can be slightly simplified since Queue is derived from Queues.Queue and therefore inherits subprograms with the same identifiers (although different profiles). For example we could simply write

```
procedure Add_To_Queue(Q: access Queue; X: in Q_Data) is
begin
    Add_To_Queue(Q,
        new Q_Element'(Queues.Queue_Element with new Q_Data'(X)));
end Add_To_Queue;
```

The implementation of the generic queue package involves much copying of the data; nevertheless it provides a clean interface and hides all the problems. However, the lower level package is almost as easy to use if the data is structured correctly. Intermediate designs are also possible; for example a generic package that accepts any definite type. The two subprograms could then both be procedures with in out parameters and less indirection would be required.

We conclude with some general observations. It is much easier to manipulate access values when dealing with class wide data. This is largely because of the difficulties of storing such data. We also note that object oriented programming requires thought especially if variant programming is to be avoided. There is a general difficulty in finding out what is coming which is particularly obvious with input-output; it is easy to write dispatching output operations but generally impossible for input.

4.4.2 Heterogeneous Lists

For the next example we consider doubly-linked lists which are a common programming technique.

The implementation shown below uses tagged types and somewhat similar techniques to the second queue package in the last section although at a lower level of abstraction.

```ada
package Doubly_Linked is

   type Node_Type is tagged limited private;
   type Node_Ptr is access all Node_Type'Class;

   -- define add/remove operations,
   -- assuming head of list is a single Node_Ptr
   procedure Add(Item: Node_Ptr; Head: in out Node_Ptr);
      -- add new node at head of list
   procedure Remove(Item: Node_Ptr; Head: in out Node_Ptr);
      -- remove node from list, update Head if necessary

   -- define functions to iterate forward or backward over list
   function Next(Item: Node_Ptr) return Node_Ptr;
   function Prev(Item: Node_Ptr) return Node_Ptr;
private
   type Node_Type is tagged limited
      record
         Prev: Node_Ptr := null;
         Next: Node_Ptr := null;
         -- other components to be added by extension
      end record;
end Doubly_Linked;
```

This illustrates the specification of a simple doubly linked list abstraction that may be extended with additional components and operations to create useful heterogeneous linked lists. It is similar to the second queue example in that the user extends the type Node_Type to contain the required data and it allows heterogeneous lists because the type Node_Ptr is an access to class wide type and thus allows the various nodes of different specific types to be linked together.

A difference is that the user refers to the list through the parameter Head which is also of the type Node_Ptr. Being doubly linked there is no need to separately maintain a reference to the tail of the list. And indeed it is possible to create variations which deal with circular lists.

The procedure Add places a new item at the start of the list but in contrast to the queue example, the procedure Remove takes the given item from wherever it is in the list. The procedures Next and Prev enable the user to move over the list as required.

The details of the implementation are not shown but should ensure correct behavior when dealing with an empty list and should also guard against adding an item which is already on the list (or another list) or removing something not on the list.

We can now use the Doubly_Linked abstraction to demonstrate programming by extension. We implement a keyed association abstraction using an extension of Doubly_Linked.Node_Type. The generic package Association takes a Key_Type, an equality operation defined on the Key_Type and a hash function defined on the Key_Type. The exported type Element_Type is intended to be further extended with the data to be associated with the key.

```ada
with Doubly_Linked;
generic
   type Key_Type is limited private;
   with function "="(Left, Right: Key_Type) return Boolean is <>;
   with function Hash(Key: Key_Type) return Integer is <>;
package Association is

   type Element_Type is new Doubly_Linked.Node_Type with
      record
```

```
                  Key: Key_Type;
            end record;
      type Element_Ptr is new Doubly_Linked.Node_Ptr;

      function Key(E: Element_Ptr) return Key_Type;

      type Association_Table(Size: Positive) is limited private;
        -- size determines size of hash table

      procedure Enter(Table   : in out Association_Table;
                      Element: in Element_Ptr);

      function Lookup(Table: in Association_Table;
                      Key  : in Key_Type) return Element_Ptr;

      -- other operations on Association_Table (eg, an iterator)...
   private
      type Element_Ptr_Array is array (Integer range <>) of Element_Ptr;
      type Association_Table(Size: Positive) is
         record
            Buckets: Element_Ptr_Array(1 .. Size);
         end record;
   end Association;
```

An Association_Table is a hash table, where each hash value has an associated doubly-linked list of elements. The elements may be of any type derived from Element_Type. The head of each list is of the type Element_Ptr which is itself derived from Node_Ptr (an untagged derived type). All the primitive operations (Add, Remove etc) which apply to Node_Ptr are thus inherited by Element_Ptr. The function Key returns the key component of the object referred to as parameter.

We can now go on to define a symbol table for a simple language with types, objects, and functions using the association structure. The symbol table allows different types of entries for each of types, objects and functions.

```
   with Association;
   package Symbol_Table_Pkg is

      type Identifier is access String;
        -- symbol table key is pointer to string
        -- allowing arbitrary length identifiers
      function Equal(Left, Right: Identifier) return Boolean;
      function Hash(Key: Identifier) return Integer;

      -- instantiate Association to produce symbol table
      package Symbol_Association is
        new Association(Identifier, Equal, Hash);
      subtype Symbol_Table is
        Symbol_Association.Association_Table;

      -- define the three kinds of symbol table elements
      -- using type extension
      type Type_Symbol is new Symbol_Association.Element_Type with
         record
            Category: Type_Category;
            Size    : Natural;
         end record;
      type Type_Ptr is access Type_Symbol;
```

```
        type Object_Symbol is new Symbol_Association.Element_Type with
           record
               Object_Type : Type_Ptr;
               Stack_Offset: Integer;
           end record;

        type Function_Symbol is new Symbol_Association.Element_Type with
           record
               Return_Type  : Type_Ptr;
               Formals      : Symbol_Table(5);    -- very small hash table
               Locals       : Symbol_Table(19);   -- bigger hash table
               Function_Body: Statement_List;
           end record;
     end Symbol_Table_Pkg;
```

A type Symbol_Table is produced by instantiating the generic Association with a key
that is a pointer to a string. Then three extensions of Element_Type are declared, each of which
may be entered into the symbol table. An interesting point is that the elements for the type
Function_Symbol each themselves contain internal symbol tables.

The body of the generic Association package might be as follows

```
package body Association is
     procedure Enter(Table: in out Association_Table;
                     Element: Element_Ptr) is
                        -- enter new element into association table.
        Hash_Index: constant Integer :=
           (Hash(Element.Key) mod Table.Size) + 1;
        use Doubly_Linked;
     begin
        -- add to linked list of appropriate bucket
        Add(Element, Table.Buckets(Hash_Index));
     end Enter;

     function Key(E: Element_Ptr) return Key_Type is
     begin
        return Element_Type(E.all).Key;
     end Key;

     function Lookup(Table: Association_Table;
                     Key: Key_Type) return Element_Ptr is
                        -- look up element in association table.
        Hash_Index: constant Integer :=
           (Hash(Key) mod Table.Size) + 1;
        Ptr: Element_Ptr := Table.Buckets(Hash_Index); -- head of list
        use Doubly_Linked;
     begin
        -- Scan doubly-linked list for element with
        -- matching key.  Return null if none found.
        while Ptr /= null loop
           if Key(Ptr).Key = Key then
              return Ptr;  -- matching element found and returned
           end if;
           Ptr := Next(Ptr);
        end loop;
        return null;  -- no matching element found
     end Lookup;
```

end Association;

The operations Enter and Lookup are implemented in a straightforward manner using the operations of the type Element_Ptr inherited from Node_Ptr.

The function Key is interesting. Note first that since Element_Ptr is derived from Node_Ptr its accessed type is also Node_Type'Class (this is a nontagged derivation and when we derive from an access type the accessed type of the derived type is the same as its parent as in Ada 83). So the expression E.**all** is of the type Node_Type'Class. It is then converted to the specific type Element_Type (this is away from the root and so involves a run-time check which will always succeed in this example) and the component is then selected.

Note that since the type Node_Ptr is visible we could declare an object directly and pass an access to it as parameter to the function Key; this would raise Constraint_Error because the function Key is designed to operate on elements and not on nodes in general. We could overcome this by making the types Element_Type and Element_Ptr private so that the underlying relationship to the type Node_Type is hidden.

4.4.3 Multiple Implementations

A very important aspect of object oriented programming is the ability to provide different implementations of the one abstraction. One can do this to some extent in Ada 83 in that one package could have alternate bodies. But only one implementation can be used in one program.

It is worth noting that the possibility of multiple implementations of an abstraction has been recognized for some time [Guttag 77]. However, when abstraction facilities were incorporated into conventional compiled languages, a single implementation per interface was typically adopted for pragmatic reasons [Dijkstra 72]. This is illustrated by CLU [Liskov 77] and Modula [Wirth 77] as well as Ada 83. It was really C++ [Stroustrup 91] that was the first main-stream systems programming language that recognized that the dynamic binding inherent in having objects identify their own implementation could be provided while preserving performance.

Thus, with a true object oriented language, the common structure of the types and their operations provided by inheritance enable different types to be treated as different realizations of a common abstraction. The tag of an object indicates its implementation and allows a dynamic binding between the client and the appropriate implementation.

We can thus develop different implementations of a single abstraction, such as a family of list types [LaLonde 89], matrices (dense or sparse), or set types, as in the next example.

The specification of an Abstract_Sets package might be

```
-- Given
   subtype Set_Element is Natural;

package Abstract_Sets is

   type Set is abstract tagged private;

   -- empty set
   function Empty return Set is abstract;

   -- build set with 1 element
   function Unit(Element: Set_Element) return Set is abstract;

   -- union of two sets
   function Union(Left, Right: Set) return Set is abstract;

   -- intersection of two sets
```

```
function Intersection(Left, Right: Set) return Set is abstract;

-- remove an element from a set
procedure Take(From: in out Set;
               Element: out Set_Element) is abstract;

Element_Too_Large: exception;
private
   type Set is abstract tagged null record;
end Abstract_Sets;
```

The package provides an abstract specification of sets. The Set type definition is an abstract
tagged private type, whose full type declaration is a null record. It defines a set of primitive
operations on Set that are abstract subprograms. Abstract subprograms do not have bodies and
cannot be called directly. However, as primitive operations, they are inherited. Derivatives of Set
must override these abstract operations to provide their own implementations. Derivatives of Set
can extend the root type with components providing the desired data representation, and can then
implement the primitive operations for that representation.

As an example, one might build an implementation using bit vectors

```
with Abstract_Sets;
package Bit_Vector_Sets is

   type Bit_Set is new Abstract_Sets.Set with private;

   -- Override the abstract operations
   function Empty return Bit_Set;
   function Unit(Element: Set_Element) return Bit_Set;
   function Union(Left, Right: Bit_Set) return Bit_Set;
   function Intersection(Left, Right: Bit_Set) return Bit_Set;
   procedure Take(From: in out Bit_Set;
                  Element: out Set_Element);

private
   Bit_Set_Size: constant := 64;
   type Bit_Vector is
      array (Set_Element range 0 .. Bit_Set_Size-1) of Boolean;
   pragma Pack(Bit_Vector);

   type Bit_Set is new Abstract_Sets.Set with
      record
         Data: Bit_Vector;
      end record;
end Bit_Vector_Sets;

package body Bit_Vector_Sets is

   function Empty return Bit_Set is
   begin
      return (Data => (others => False));
   end;

   function Unit(Element: Set_Element) return Bit_Set is
      S: Bit_Set := Empty;
   begin
      S.Data(Element) := True;
      return S;
```

```
   end;

   function Union(Left, Right: Bit_Set) return Bit_Set is
   begin
      return (Data => Left.Data or Right.Data);
   end;
      ...
end Bit_Vector_Sets;
```

An alternative implementation more appropriate to very sparse sets might be based on using linked records containing the elements present in a set. We could then write a program which contained both forms of sets; we could convert from one representation to any other by using

```
   procedure Convert(From: in Set'Class; To: out Set'Class) is
      Temp: Set'Class := From;
      Elem: Set_Element;
   begin
      -- build up target set, one element at a time
      To := Empty;
      while Temp /= Empty loop
         Take(Temp, Elem);
         To := Union(To, Unit(Elem));
      end loop;
   end Convert;
```

This procedure dispatches onto the appropriate operations according to the specific type of its parameters. Remember that all variables of class-wide types (such as Temp) have to be initialized since class-wide subtypes are indefinite and the tag is given by the tag of the initial value. Note that the equality operators are also dispatching operations so that the expression Temp /= Empty uses the equality operation for the type of From. Furthermore, assignment is also a dispatching operation although this is not often apparent. In this example, however, if the type of From were a linked list then a deep copy would be required otherwise the original value could be damaged when the copy is decomposed. Such a deep copy can be performed by using a controlled type for the inner implementation of the list as explained in 7.4.

Finally, note that the abstract sets package could have been generic

```
generic
   type Set_Element is private;
package Abstract_Sets is ...
```

and this would have added an extra dimension for the possibility of reuse.

4.4.4 Iterators

It is a common requirement to wish to apply some operation over all members of a set. One approach was discussed in 3.7.1 using access discriminants. In this section we show a rather different technique using type extension and dispatching. (We start by assuming the example is not generic and consider the impact of genericity later.)

Consider

```
type Element is ...

package Sets is
   type Set is limited private;
   ... -- various set operations
```

```
   type Iterator is abstract tagged null record;
   procedure Iterate(S: Set; IC: Iterator'Class);
   procedure Action(E: in out Element;
                    I: in out Iterator) is abstract;
private
   type Node;
   type Ptr is access Node;
   type Node is
      record
         E: Element;
         Next: Ptr;
      end record;
   type Set is new Ptr;    -- implement as singly-linked list
end Sets;

package body Sets is
   ... -- bodies of the various set operations

   procedure Iterate(S: Set; IC: Iterator'Class) is
      This: Ptr := Ptr(S);
   begin
      while This /= null loop
         Action(This.E, IC);   -- dispatch
         This := This.Next;
      end loop;
   end Iterate:

end Sets;
```

This introduces an abstract type Iterator which has a primitive subprogram Action. The procedure Iterate loops over the set and calls by dispatching the procedure Action corresponding to the specific type of the object of the Iterator class. The main purpose of the Iterator type therefore is to identify by dispatching the particular Action to be performed.

The simple example of counting the number of elements in a set can now be written as follows.

```
package Sets.Stuff is
   function Count(S: Set) return Natural;
end Sets.Stuff;


package body Sets.Stuff is

   type Count_Iterator is new Iterator with
      record
         Result: Natural := 0;
      end record;

   procedure Action(E: in out Element;
                    I: in out Count_Iterator) is
   begin
      I.Result := I.Result + 1;
   end Action;

   function Count(S: Set) return Natural is
      I: Count_Iterator;
   begin
      Iterate(S, I);
```

```
      return I.Result;
   end Count;
end Sets.Stuff;
```

The type `Count_Iterator` is an extension of the abstract type `Iterator` and the specific procedure `Action` does the counting. The result is accumulated in a component of the type `Count_Iterator` and is thereby made accessible to the procedure `Action`; this component is initialized to zero when the `Count_Iterator` is declared inside the function `Count`.

Observe that the type extension is not immediately within a package specification and so it is not possible to add new primitive operations to it. Nevertheless it is possible to override inherited operations such as `Action` as explained in 4.3. If, for some reason, we wanted to declare additional primitive operations then we would have to introduce an internal package. Note also that we cannot put the type extension inside the function `Count` because this would break the accessibility rules by making the type extension at a deeper level than the parent type as explained in 3.4.

A further point is that if the parent package `Sets` were generic with the type `Element` being a formal parameter as in the example with access discriminants in 3.7.1, then the child package `Sets.Stuff` would also have to be generic. In that case it would be necessary to move the type extension and the overriding operation `Action` into the private part of `Sets.Stuff` for reasons explained in 12.5.

More general actions can be written in a similar manner. Any parameters or results for the action are passed as components in the iterator type. A general procedure to perform some action might be

```
procedure General(S: Set; P: Parameters) is
   I: General_Iterator;
begin
   ...   -- copy parameters into iterator
   Iterate(S, I);
   ...   -- copy any results from iterator back to parameters
end General;
```

and the type `General_Iterator` and the corresponding `Action` procedure take the form

```
type General_Iterator is new Iterator with
   record
      ...  -- components for parameters and workspace
   end record;

procedure Action(E: in out Element;
                 I: in out General_Iterator) is
begin
   E := ...;   -- do something to element using data from iterator
end Action;
```

It is instructive to compare this example with the corresponding example using access discriminants in 3.7.1. Wherever possible similar identifiers have been used to make the analogy easier. The analogy could be made closer by putting the function `Sets.Count` of 3.7.1 inside a package as here.

Perhaps the most striking difference is that the two mechanisms are "inside out" to each other in some sense. A notable thing about the access discriminant approach is that the looping mechanism has to be written out for each action. Using type extension the loop is written out once and the dispatching call of `Action` reaches out to the specific routine required.

The type extension approach has a close similarity to the potential method using an access to subprogram value as a parameter. We would like to write something like

```
   procedure Iterate(S: Set;
                  Action: access procedure(E: in out Element)) is
      This: Ptr := Ptr(S);
   begin
      while This /= null loop
         Action(This.E);
         This := This.Next;
      end loop;
   end Iterate;
```

and then

```
   function Count(S: Set) return Natural is
      Result: Natural := 0;

      procedure Count_Action(E: in out Element) is
      begin
         Result := Result + 1;
      end Count_Action;

   begin
      Iterate(S, Count_Action'Access);
      return Result;
   end Count;
```

but unfortunately we cannot have anonymous access to subprogram parameters as explained in 3.7.2. Declaring a named access type so that the above starts

```
   type Action_Type is access procedure(E: in out Element);
   ...
   procedure Iterate(S: Set; Action: Action_Type) is ...
```

does not work either because then the access to the internal procedure Count_Action is illegal. We have to make the procedure internal so that it can manipulate the variable Result. Note that we would not wish to make Result global because that would not work in multitasking programs. See the further discussion in 3.7.2 which also shows how the difficulties can be overcome with generics.

The reason for disallowing more general access to subprogram values is that they would require extra information regarding the environment of the procedure (in this case giving addressability of the variable Result). The call of the formal procedure and the dispatching call both serve similar purposes; they enable the iterate procedure to call out to the specific action procedure. In both cases extra information is required; the type extension method enables it to be passed in the type itself. The formal procedure method needs it within the underlying implementation and for a number of reasons this is considered too heavy a burden in the general case.

As mentioned earlier, there is a close analogy between the restrictions which ensure that a procedure value is (nearly) always a single address and those which ensure that a dispatching value is always a single address.

4.5 Dispatching and Redispatching

It is important to understand exactly when dispatching (dynamic binding) is used as opposed to the static resolution of binding familiar from Ada 83. The basic principle is that dispatching is used only when a controlling operand is of a class-wide type. In order to facilitate the discussion we will reconsider the New_Alert_System introduced in II.1. The call

```
Handle(A);   -- A of type Alert'Class
```

in the procedure `Process_Alerts` in II.2 is a dispatching call. The value of the tag of `A` is used to determine which procedure `Handle` to call and this is determined at run time.

On the other hand a call such as

```
Handle(Alert(MA));
```

in the procedure `Handle` belonging to the type `Medium_Alert` is not a dispatching call because the type of the operand is the specific type `Alert` as a result of the explicit type conversion.

It is also possible to dispatch on the result of a function when the context of the call determines the tag. Such a result is called a controlling result.

It is an important principle that all controlling operands and results of a call must have the same tag. If they are statically determined then, of course, this is checked at compile time. If they are dynamically determined (for example, variables of a class-wide type) then again the actual values must all have the same tag and of course this check has to be made at run time; `Constraint_Error` is raised if the check fails. In order to avoid confusion a mixed situation whereby some tags are statically determined and some are dynamically determined is not allowed. Thus in the case of the sets example in the previous section, it is illegal to write

```
S: Bit_Set := ...
T: Set'Class := ...
...
S := Union(S, T);   -- illegal
```

even though at run-time it might be the case that the tag of the value of `T` might be `Bit_Set'Tag`. But we could write

```
S := Union(S, Bit_Set(T));
```

and the view conversion will check that `T` is in `Bit_Set'Class` (the tag of `T` does not have to be `Bit_Set'Tag`; it could be of any specific type that can be converted to `Bit_Set`).

A special case arises when the tag is indeterminate. Consider for example the statement

```
To := Empty;
```

in the procedure `Convert`. The parameterless function `Empty` has a controlling result but there is no controlling operand to determine the tag. Consequently the tag is determined from the class-wide parameter `To` which is the destination of the assignment. Of course, the tag of `To` is dynamically determined and this value is used for dispatching on `Empty`. The statement

```
To := Union(To, Unit(Elem));
```

similarly causes dispatching on both `Union` and `Unit` according to the tag of `To`.

Another rule designed to avoid complexity is that it is not legal for a subprogram to have controlling operands or result of different tagged types. Although it is legal to declare two tagged types in the same package, it is not legal to declare a subprogram that has operands or result of both types in that same package. This can, of course, be done outside the package but then the subprogram is not a primitive operation of the types and does not dispatch anyway.

The difficulty with allowing such mixed controlling operands is that it would not be clear how to achieve the various possible combinations of derived operations if both types were derived. If the effect of such mixed operands is required then one type can be replaced by the corresponding class-wide type. See [RM95 3.9.2].

The rules for type conversion (see 3.8) are also designed for clarity. Type conversion is always allowed towards the root of a tree of tagged types and so we can convert a `Medium_Alert` into an `Alert` as in the call

```
Handle(Alert(MA));
```

On the other hand we cannot convert a specific type away from the root (there might be missing components); we have to use an extension aggregate even if there are no extra components. So we can "extend" an Alert into a Low_Alert by

```
LA := (A with null record);
```

where we have to write **null record** because there are no extra components.

We can however convert a value of a class-wide type to a specific type as in

```
MA: Medium_Alert := Medium_Alert(AC);
```

where AC is of the type Alert'Class. In such a case there is a run-time check that the current value of the class-wide parameter AC has a tag that identifies a specific type for which the conversion is possible. Hence it must identify the type Medium_Alert or a type derived from it so that the conversion is not away from the root of the tree. In other words we check that the value of AC is actually in Medium_Alert'Class.

As mentioned in 3.8 some conversions are what is known as view conversions. This means that the underlying object is not changed but we merely get a different view of it.

Almost all conversions of tagged types are view conversions. For example the conversion in

```
Handle(Alert(MA));
```

is a view conversion. The value passed on to the call of Handle (that with parameter of type Alert) is in fact the same value as held in MA but the components relating to the type Medium_Alert are no longer visible. And in fact the tag still relates to the underlying value and this might even be the tag for High_Alert because it could have been view converted all the way down the tree. Remember also that tagged types are passed by reference.

However, if we did an assignment as in

```
MA := Medium_Alert(HA);
```

then the tag of MA would not be changed and would not reflect that of the value in HA. All that happens is that the values of the components appropriate to the type of MA are copied from the object HA. Other components are of course ignored.

Furthermore, if MA were not a locally declared variable but an **out** or **in out** parameter, then again the tag of MA would not be changed. Remember, however, that the tag of MA in this case need not itself be Medium_Alert'Tag since a formal parameter is simply giving a view of the actual parameter and the tag of that could be of any type derived from Medium_Alert. But we do know that both sides of the assignment have the components appropriate to Medium_Alert and so the assignment works.

Note moreover that conversions of tagged types are allowed as the target of an assignment; thus

```
AC: Alert'Class := ...
...
Medium_Alert(AC) := MA;
```

will check that the tag of AC corresponds to Medium_Alert or a type derived from it (or in other words checks that AC in Medium_Alert'Class is true) and then copies just those components corresponding to the Medium_Alert view from the right hand side to the left hand side.

It might help to summarize the golden rules

•   the tag of an object never changes; this applies to both specific and class-wide types,

- conversion can never be away from the root, conversion never changes the tag.

The fact that a view conversion does not change the tag is absolutely vital for the implementation of what is known as redispatching.

There are often situations where one would like "multiple dispatch" either within a class, or between two or more classes. Ingalls cites a number of canonical examples such as displaying various kinds of graphical objects on different kinds of displays, event types and handlers, and unification and pattern matching [Ingalls 86]; he suggests a solution for Smalltalk-80 that is more modular than a single dispatch on one parameter, followed by a case statement on the dynamic type of a second parameter. Multiple dispatch is possible in Ada 95 via class-wide types. We first consider the simple case of redispatching within the same class.

It often happens that after one dispatching operation we apply a further common (and inherited) operation and so need to dispatch once more to an operation of the original type. If the original tag were lost then this would not be possible.

Consider again (from II.1)

```
procedure Handle(MA: in out Medium_Alert) is
begin
   Handle(Alert(MA));                -- handle as plain Alert
   MA.Action_Officer := Assign_Volunteer;
   Display(MA, Console);
end Handle;
```

in which there is a call of the procedure Display. This call is not a dispatching call because the parameter is of a specific type (and indeed there is only one procedure Display which is inherited by all the types).

As written it has been assumed that the display operation is the same for all alerts. However, suppose that in fact it was desired to express the message in different ways according to the level of the alert (in different colors perhaps or flashing).

It would be possible to do this by using the Tag attribute to look at the original value of the tag by writing

```
procedure Display(A: Alert; On: Device) is
   AC: Alert'Class renames Alert'Class(A);
begin
   if AC'Tag = Low_Alert'Tag then
      -- display a low alert
   elsif AC'Tag = Medium_Alert'Tag then
      -- display a medium alert
   else
      -- display a high alert
   end if;
end Display;
```

Note that we could have written

```
AC: Alert'Class := A;
```

rather than the renaming but this would cause an unnecessary assignment. Note moreover that we cannot apply the Tag attribute to an object of a specific type; it would be rather surprising for A'Tag not to be Alert'Tag.

However, using tags in this way inside the body of Display is quite inappropriate since it has reintroduced the rigid nature of variant programming and could not specifically recognize an alert which is a later extension.

The proper approach is to use redispatching. If we need a different display mechanism for the different alert levels then we write distinct procedures for each one (thus overriding the procedure inherited from the root level) and then redispatch in the various procedures Handle as follows

```
procedure Handle(MA: in out Medium_Alert) is
begin
   Handle(Alert(MA));                    -- handle as plain Alert
   MA.Action_Officer := Assign_Volunteer;
   Display(Medium_Alert'Class(MA), Console);   -- redispatch
end Handle;
```

This will work properly and the message will be displayed according to the specific type of the original alert.

Another possibility is that the type Device might not be represented as a simple enumeration, but instead as a record type, with components representing various aspects of the device. A class of device types could be constructed using tagged types and type extension. Each kind of device must implement an Output operation that each kind of alert will use to implement its Display operation. In order to call the appropriate Output procedure two dispatching operations are involved. First, the type of the alert parameter controls the dispatch to the Display procedure, and then within that procedure a dispatch on the Device parameter will select the appropriate Output operation for the device being used as a display. This double dispatching can be accommodated by making Display a class-wide operation of the device class. The Display procedure for Alert then becomes

```
procedure Display(A: Alert; On: Device'Class) is
begin
   . . .
   Output(On);   -- dispatch on On
   . . .
end Display;
```

so that within each Display procedure, a call to Output, with parameter On will dispatch to the appropriate operation for the Device.

Note once more that it would not have been legal for the specification of Display to have been

```
procedure Display(A: Alert; On: Device);
```

since a procedure cannot have controlling operands of more than one tagged type.

4.6　Multiple Inheritance

Some languages permit a derived type, or class, to have more than one parent. These languages are said to support "multiple inheritance". Multiple inheritance is a second-generation object oriented programming mechanism. It originated in MIT's FLAVORS extension to LISP; a precursor to the Common Lisp Object System.

Multiple inheritance poses awkward problems if approached naively, as pointed out by [Budd 91]. There are two conceptual difficulties; what to do if an operation with a given profile belongs to both parents — which, if any, is inherited and how could we distinguish them; and what to do if the same component belongs to both parents from a common ancestor — are there two copies or only one? There are also implementation difficulties associated with these conceptual difficulties.

However, most uses of multiple inheritance fall into one of three idioms each of which can be implemented in Ada 95 using facilities such as access discriminants, generic units and type composition in conjunction with the Ada 95 type extension as will be illustrated in the next few sections.

Given the need to balance the benefits of language defined multiple inheritance with the complexity of the revised language, the potential for distributed overhead caused by multiple inheritance, and the scope of the revision, we chose to support multiple inheritance with a building block approach rather than an extra language construct.

4.6.1 Combining Implementation and Abstraction

The first form of multiple inheritance is, to quote N. Guimaraes of AT&T, "to combine two classes, one that defines the protocol of the component, and another that provides an implementation" [Guimaraes 91]. In languages such as Eiffel and C++, where classes are the only form of module, inheritance is the most common mechanism for combining abstractions. For instance, an Eiffel class `Bounded_Stack[T]`, could be constructed by inheriting from an abstract class `Stack[T]` and a second class `Array[T]`. Class `Array[T]` would then be used to implement the abstract operations not defined by class `Stack[T]`. The programmer must specify the implementation of each such operation, and ideally, the array operations should also be hidden from users of `Bounded_Stack[T]`. The effect of this idiom of multiple inheritance could be achieved in Ada 83 through type composition — inheritance is not required. In Ada, one may implement one type in terms of another, and hide that implementation as a private type.

```
package Bounded is
    type Bounded_Stack(Size: Natural := 0) is private;
    procedure Push(S: in out Bounded_Stack; Element: T);
    procedure Pop(S: in out Bounded_Stack);
    function Top(S: Bounded_Stack) return T;
private
    type T_Array is array (Integer range <>) of T;
    type Bounded_Stack(Size: Natural := 0) is
        record
            Data: T_Array(1..Size);
        end record;
end Bounded;
```

Using the idiom of section 4.4.3 where we discussed the set abstraction, we could derive from a tagged abstract type `Stack`, and implement bounded stacks as arrays. In either case, the operations on `Bounded_Stack` must be explicitly declared, whether being defined or overridden.

4.6.2 Mixin Inheritance

A second idiomatic use of multiple inheritance can be termed mixin inheritance. In mixin inheritance, one of the parent classes cannot have instances of its own and exists only to provide a set of properties for classes inheriting from it. Typically, this abstract, mixin class has been isolated solely for the purpose of combining with other classes. Ada 95 can provide mixin inheritance using tagged type extension (single inheritance) and generic units. The generic template defines the mixin. The type supplied as generic actual parameter determines the parent.

Thus we can write

```
generic
    type S is abstract tagged private;
package P is
    type T is abstract new S with private;
    -- operations on T
private
    type T is abstract new S with
        record
            -- additional components
```

```
    end record;
end P;
```

where the body provides the operations and the specification exports the extended type.

We can then use an instantiation of P to add the operations of T to any existing tagged type and the resulting type will of course still be in the class of the type passed as actual parameter. Note that in this idiom we have specified both the formal type and the exported type as abstract. This enables the supplied actual type to be abstract. We could declare a cascade of types in this manner thereby adding an unbounded sequence of properties to the original type. We would finally make one further extension in order to declare a type which was not abstract.

As a concrete example, the following generic package adds the property of having multiple versions to any tagged type.

```
with OM;   -- Object Manager provides unique object IDs
with VM;   -- Version Manager provides version control
generic
    type Parent is abstract tagged private;
package Versioned is

    -- A versioned object has an ID, which identifies
    -- the set of versions of that object, plus a version
    -- number that, combined with the ID, identifies an
    -- object uniquely.
    type Versioned_Object is abstract new Parent with private;

    -- given an object, return a new version of that object
    procedure Create_New_Version(O    : in  Versioned_Object
                            New_O: out Versioned_Object);
    -- given an object, returns its version number
    function Version_Number(O: Versioned_Object)
                                    return VM.Version_Number;
    -- given an object and a version number, return that
    -- version of the object
    procedure Get_Version(
      ID_From: in  Versioned_Object;
      Version: in  VM.Version_Number;
      Object : out Versioned_Object);

private

    type Versioned_Object is abstract new Parent with
       record
          ID     : OM.Object_ID := OM.Unique_ID;
          Version: VM.Version_Number := VM.Initial_Version;
       end record;

end Versioned;
```

An important variation on this approach allows us to extend a type privately with generic operations that the client cannot see. This relies on the fact that the full type corresponding to a private extension need not be *directly* derived from the given ancestor. Thus the full type corresponding to

```
type Special_Object is new Ancestor with private;
```

need not be directly derived from Ancestor; it could be indirectly derived from Ancestor. We can therefore write

```
private
    package Q is new P(Ancestor);
    type Special_Object is new Q.T with null record;
```

and then the type Special_Object will also have all the components and properties of the type T
in the generic package P. As written, these are, of course, not visible to the client but subprograms
in the visible part of the package in which Special_Object is declared could be implemented in
terms of them. Note also that the type Special_Object is not abstract even though the type Q.T
is abstract.

As another example of mixin inheritance reconsider the second queue package in 4.4.1. We
could make it generic thus

```
generic
    type Data(<>) is abstract tagged private;
package Queues is
    type Queue is limited private;
    type Queue_Element is abstract new Data with private;
    type Element_Ptr is access all Queue_Element'Class;
    function Is_Empty(Q: Queue) return Boolean;
    procedure Add_To_Queue(Q: access Queue; E: in Element_Ptr);
    function Remove_From_Queue(Q: access Queue) return Element_Ptr;
    Queue_Error: exception;
private
```

and then the modified base of the alert system could be

```
with Queues;
package Base_Alert_System is
    type Root_Alert is abstract tagged null record;
    package Alert_Queues is new Queues(Root_Alert);
    subtype Alert_Queue is Alert_Queues.Queue;
    type Alert is
                abstract new Alert_Queues.Queue_Element with null record;
    procedure Handle(A in out Alert) is abstract;
end Base_Alert_System;
```

with the rest of the structure much as before. The major difference is that only alerts can be placed
on an alert queue declared as

```
type Alert_Queue_Ptr is access all Alert_Queue;
The_Queue: Alert_Queue_Ptr := new Alert_Queue;
...
```

whereas previously all queues were quite general. With this formulation there is no risk of placing
an alert on a queue of some other type such as animals. Thus although the queue is heterogeneous,
nevertheless it is constrained to accept only objects of the appropriate class.

This example also illustrates the use of a series of abstract types. We start with Root_Alert
which is abstract and exists in order to characterize the queues; add the queue element property and
thus export Queue_Element which is itself abstract; we then derive the abstract Alert which
forms the true base of the alert system and provides the ability to declare the dispatching operation
Handle. Only then do we develop specific types for the alerts themselves.

Our final example shows how a window system could be constructed and illustrates the
cascade of mixins mentioned above. We start with a basic window and various operations

```
type Basic_Window is tagged limited private;
procedure Display(W: in Basic_Window);
procedure Mouse_Click(W: in out Basic_Window;
```

```
                                Where: in Mouse_Coords);
      ...
```

and then we define a number of mixin generics of the familiar pattern such as

```
generic
   type Some_Window is abstract new Basic_Window with private;
package Label_Mixin is
   type Window_With_Label is abstract new Some_Window with private;
   -- override some operations
   procedure Display(W: in Window_With_Label);

   -- add some new ones
   procedure Set_Label(W: in out Window_With_Label;
                       S: in String);
   function Label(W: Window_With_Label) return String;
private
   type Window_With_Label is abstract new Some_Window with
      record
          Label: String_Quark := Null_Quark;
          -- an X-Windows like unique ID for a string
      end record;
end Label_Mixin;
```

Note that this is slightly different to our previous examples since it can only be applied to the type `Basic_Window` or a type derived from `Basic_Window`.

In the generic body we can implement the overriden and new operations, using any inherited operations as necessary. Thus the new version of `Display` applicable to a `Window_With_Label` might be

```
procedure Display(W: Window_With_Label) is
begin
   Display(Some_Window(W));
   -- display normally using operation of parent type
   if W.Label /= Null_Quark then
      -- now display the label if not null
      Display_On_Screen(XCoord(W), YCoord(W)-5, Value(W.Label));
   end if;
end Display;
```

where the functions `XCoord` and `YCoord` are inherited from `Basic_Window` and give the coordinates for where to display the label.

We might declare a whole series of such packages and then finally write

```
package Frame is
   type My_Window is new Basic_Window with private;
   ...-- exported operations
private
   package Add_Label is new Label_Mixin(Basic_Window);
   package Add_Border is
            new Border_Mixin(Add_Label.Window_With_Label);
   package Add_Menu_Bar is
            new Menu_Bar_Mixin(Add_Border.Window_With_Border);

   type My_Window is
            new Add_Menu_Bar.Window_With_Menu_Bar with null record;
end Frame;
```

Observe that the final declaration has a null extension; it could add further components if required. The various operations exported from the individual mixins can be exported selectively from the package Frame by suitable renamings in the package body.

4.6.3 Multiple Views

Finally, there are uses of multiple inheritance where the derived type or class is truly a derivative of more than one parent and clients of that type want to "view it" as any of its parents. This may be accomplished in Ada 95 using access discriminants which effectively enable us to parameterize one record with another.

An access discriminant can be used to enable a component of a record to obtain the identity of the record in which it is embedded (see 3.4.1). This enables complex chained structures to be created and can provide multiple views of a structure. Consider

```
type Outer is limited private;

private

type Inner(Ptr: access Outer) is limited ...

type Outer is limited
   record
      ...
      Component: Inner(Outer'Access);
      ...
   end record;
```

The Component of type Inner has an access discriminant Ptr which refers back to the enclosing instance of the record Outer. This is because the attribute Access applied to the name of a record type inside its declaration refers to the current instance of the type. This is similar to the way in which the name of a task type refers to the current task inside its own body rather than to the type itself; see [RM83 9.1(4)]. If we now declare an object of the type Outer

```
Obj: Outer;
```

then the self-referential structure created is as shown in Figure 4-3. Note that the structure becomes self-referential automatically. This is not the same as the effect that would be obtained with a record in which an instance might happen to have a component referring to itself as a consequence of an assignment. All instances of the type Outer will refer to themselves; Ptr cannot change because discriminants are constant.

This simple example on its own is of little interest. However, the types Inner and Outer can both be extensions of other types and these other types might themselves be chained structures. For example, the type Inner might be an extension of some type Node containing components which access other objects of the type Node in order to create a tree. Note in particular that Inner could also be

```
type Inner(Ptr: access Outer'Class) is new Node with ...
```

so that heterogeneous chains can be constructed. (Outer has to be tagged in this case.) The important point is that we can navigate over the tree which consists of the components of type Inner linked together but at any point in the tree we can reach to the enclosing Outer record as a whole by the access discriminant Ptr.

It should be noted that an access discriminant is only allowed for a limited type. This avoids copying problems with the self-referring components and dangling references.

We now return to the window example of the previous section and show how access discriminants can be used to effectively mix together two hierarchies.

Suppose that as well as the hierarchy of windows which concern areas on the screen, we also have a hierarchy of monitors.

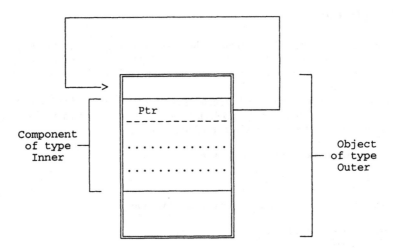

Figure 4-3: A Self-Referential Structure

A monitor is a type which is designed to respond to change; it has a primitive operation Update which is called to perform the response. An object that wishes to be monitored keeps a linked list of monitors and calls their Update operation whenever necessary; the chain may contain many different monitors according to what might need to be updated. If we were doing a complex modelling application concerned with molecular structure then when we change the object we might wish to redraw some representation on the screen, make a record of the previous state, recompute the molecular weight and so on. The various monitors each contain a reference to the monitored object. The type monitored object itself contains a pointer to the start of the chain and is extended with additional information as needed by the application. Thus we have

```
type Monitor;
type Monitor_Ptr is access all Monitor'Class;

type Monitored_Object is abstract tagged limited
   record
      First: Monitor_Ptr;  -- list of monitors
      -- more components to be added by extension
      -- according to the needs of the specific application
   end record;

type Monitored_Object_Ptr is access all Monitored_Object'Class;

type Monitor is abstract tagged limited
   record
      Next: Monitor_Ptr;
      Obj: Monitored_Object_Ptr;
      -- more components to be added by extension
      -- according to the needs of the specific monitor
   end record;
```

```
procedure Update(M: in out Monitor) is abstract;
...
procedure Notify(MO: Monitored_Object'Class) is
   This_Mon: Monitor_Ptr := MO.First;
begin
   while This_Mon /= null loop
      Update(This_Mon.all);    -- dispatch for each monitor
      This_Mon := This_Mon.Next;
   end loop;
end Notify;
```

where Notify is a class wide operation of the type Monitored_Object and calls all the Update operations of the monitors on the chain. If our object representing the molecule has type Molecule then we would write

```
type Monitored_Molecule is new Monitored_Object with
   record
      M: Molecule;
   end record;
...
Proposed_Immortality_Drug: Monitored_Molecule;
```

and then perform all our work on the monitored molecule and from time to time invoke the updates by calling

```
Notify(Proposed_Immortality_Drug);
```

The configuration might be as in Figure 4-4.

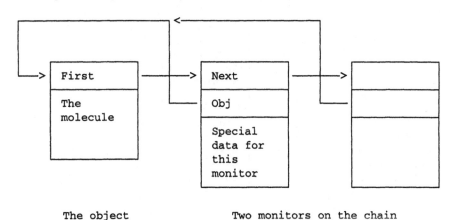

Figure 4-4: A Monitor Chain

Now suppose we want to use one of our windows as part of the updating process so that, for example, the picture of the molecule is displayed within a window rather than directly on the raw screen. In order to do this we need to hang the window display mechanism on the monitor chain so that an appropriate update causes the Display operation to be called. In other words we need to create a Window that can act as a Monitor as well as a Window. First we define a mixin that is a monitor and override its Update operation thus

```
type Monitor_Mixin(Win: access Basic_Window'Class) is
                        new Monitor with null record;
procedure Update(M: in out Monitor_Mixin);
```

The body for this might be

```
procedure Update(M: in out Monitor_Mixin) is
   -- simply redisplay the window
begin
   Display(M.Win.all);   -- this is a dispatching call
end Update;
```

and now we can mix this Monitor_Mixin into any window type by writing

```
type Window_That_Monitors is new My_Window with
   record
      Mon: Monitor_Mixin(Window_That_Monitors'Access);
   end record;
```

where the inner component Mon has a discriminant that refers to the outer type. The monitor component of this can now be linked into the chain as shown in Figure 4-5. Calling Notify on the monitored molecule results in the various procedures Update being called. The Update for the type Monitor_Mixin calls the Display for the type Window_That_Monitors of which it is part and this has access to all the information about the window as well as the information about being a monitor.

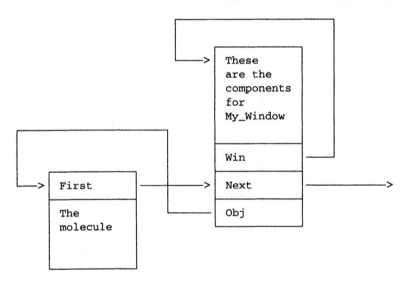

Figure 4-5: The Window-that-Monitors in the Chain

We could of course define a more sophisticated type Monitor_Mixin that did other things as well as simply calling the Display operation of the associated window.

The examples in this and the previous section show that Ada 95 provides support for the construction of effectively arbitrary multiple inheritance hierarchies. This has been achieved without having intrinsic multiple inheritance which could be a pervasive implementation burden on simple single inheritance applications.

4.7 Relationship with Previous Work

Object oriented programming originated with Simula [Birtwistle 73]. Simula was designed to be an almost upward compatible extension of Algol 60, inspired by the application domain of simulation, although it is really a general purpose programming language. The key insights from simulation were that it is useful to think of a complex simulation as being organized around a collection of autonomous, interacting objects, and that the construction of such simulations could be facilitated by abstracting this notion of object into a language construct.

Simula introduced the notion of a class as an abstraction mechanism over objects. A class is a template for creating objects with a common data structure and operations on that data structure. These operations determine the possible behavior of the objects of the class. Operations may be sensitive to the current state of the object, and may update that state by changing the values of the data structure.

A Simula class definition specifies a data structure for the class, the operations on that data, and a body used to initialize objects of the class upon their creation, like the sequence of statements in a package body. The data definition and procedure declarations constitute the class's interface to programmers. The Simula class is somewhere between a data type and a module. Instances of the class may be declared, assigned to variables, and passed as parameters, like values of a typical data type.

Simula introduced a means to define new classes from old ones; a class could "inherit" from another class, deriving its structure and operations from that "parent". The new class could augment or override its inheritance, adding new data and new operations, or replacing one or more of its operations. Data could not be removed.

Smalltalk [Goldberg 83] was influenced by Simula's notion of class and subclassing. While Simula was a compiled language, Smalltalk was interpreted. It was originally intended as an interactive, systems programming language for Alan Kay's Dynabook project.

Smalltalk introduced the "message-passing" style of invoking operations. A message is a request to an object to invoke an operation. The set of messages that an object recognizes and is capable of responding to is called its "protocol" and is determined by the class of the object. When an object is sent a message, a search begins in the class of the object class for a method (operation definition) corresponding to the message. If not found, the search continues in the parent class (superclass), this continues upward in the class hierarchy until either an appropriate method is found or the root of the hierarchy is reached without success, in which case an error is signaled.

The historical fact that some early object oriented languages were interpreted has contributed to the impression that their mechanisms are necessarily too inefficient for real-time or production use. Many object oriented languages (including Simula) also use implicit reference semantics (in which all variables are really pointers), thereby raising the issue of run-time storage management. It was these efficiency considerations that apparently prevented Ada 83 from providing inheritance and polymorphism, given Ada's overriding concerns with run-time efficiency, and type safety [Brosgol 89]. More recently, there have been a number of languages developed that support object oriented programming in a relatively safe, compiled, and efficient style, including Trellis/Owl [Schaffert 86], Eiffel [Meyer 88], Modula-3 [Nelson 91] and C++ [Ellis 90].

The essence of the evolution of OOPLs has thus been to obtain an appropriate balance between compile-time and run-time identification of the operations to be performed. If the identification is at run-time then the operations are usually called methods; alternative terms are virtual functions (C++, Simula) and dispatching operations (the Ada 95 term).

In Smalltalk-80, for example, method invocations have the form

```
receiver Methodname Argstomethod
```

where `receiver` is the name of the target object.

This syntax simplifies dispatch; the dispatch is determined solely by the class of the receiver of the message. Eiffel and C++ also use the "distinguished receiver" approach.

In languages where a function or procedure call syntax is permitted, and where more than one argument of the call may be of the class, the situation is more complex. Trellis/Owl [Schaffert 86]) follows the Smalltalk-80 tradition and arbitrarily designates the first parameter of the call as determining the dispatch. Some languages distinguish this parameter by its appearance as a prefix in the call.

Other possible schemes include

1   All controlled parameters within the class must share the same type tag.

2   The programmer must select a parameter as the controlling one, as a part of the declaration of the parameter's mode.

3   All controlled parameters must share the same code for the operation (their dispatch tables must all point to the same code body for that operation).

4   The most specific type within the class ("nearest ancestor") applicable to all of the parameters is used.

5   The most general type within the class ("furthest ancestor", the root) applicable to all of the parameters is used.

Ada 95 has adopted (1). This is a logical choice, given that the dispatching operations of a type are the primitive operations of that type and are derived from those of the root type with systematic replacement. So, in Ada 95, more than one operand, or even the result, may control the dispatch. For a primitive operation of a type T, the dispatching is controlled by the operands of type T, and the result if it is of type T.

There are a number of other important differences between Ada 95 and other languages; these differences are designed to add clarity (which encourages programmers to write the correct code) and safety (which prevents disaster if they do not).

The first difference is that in Ada 95, an operation is only dispatching when applied to an actual parameter of a class-wide type. In other OOPLs, a dispatch is possible whenever an object reference or pointer is used as the prefix to the operation. In Ada 95 terms, this means that references/pointers in such OOPLs are always treated as though they designate a class-wide type. Ada 95 allows a formal parameter or an access value to have a specific type as its "referent" (this is the default, preserving upward compatibility and safety). Ada 95 also allows an actual parameter or an access value to have a class-wide type as its referent, in which case dispatching is also possible.

A second difference is that, in Ada 95, if a type T is tagged, then all of its primitive operations are dispatching operations; when passed a class-wide operand, they dispatch. In C++, only those particular member functions identified as virtual involve a run-time dispatch. In Ada 95, a (non-dispatching) class-wide operation may be defined by explicitly declaring it with a formal parameter of type T'Class. No dispatch is performed in this case, because the body of a class-wide operation expects its actual parameter to still be class-wide. Note that, as in C++, a run-time dispatch may ultimately occur, when such an operation calls a dispatching operation somewhere within its body. This is illustrated by the procedure Process_Alerts in II.2.

A final and important difference between Ada 95 and some other OOPLs is that dispatching is safe in the sense that a call to a dispatching operation always has a well-defined implementation to dispatch to. In some OOPLs, such as Smalltalk, it is possible to send a message to an object that has no method for handling that message; a run-time error results. In Ada, such errors are always detected at compile time.

When a primitive operation is called with class-wide operands in all controlling positions, a run-time check is made that all of these controlling operands have the same tag value, and the result is defined to return this same tag value. This common tag value is called the controlling tag value for the call, and identifies the specific type whose corresponding primitive operation is used to implement this call.

This requirement that all controlling operands have the same tag value reflects an existing Ada 83 rule for derived types. The type of all operands of a parent type are systematically replaced with the derived type when inheriting a primitive operation. A primitive operation can only be a primitive operation of one tagged type. It is possible but unusual for a primitive operation to also operate on another type within the same class (but it would not be primitive for that other type). Typically, each primitive operation operates only on one type within the class, and may return this same type.

By treating all controlling operands symmetrically, we avoid some of the difficulties and anomalies encountered in other OOPLs with binary operations. For example, taking the intersection of two sets is viewed as a symmetric operation as opposed to thinking of one set as being special (the "receiver"), with the other set being a mere argument.

By allowing the result context to control the dispatch, we allow parameterless functions to be used to represent type-specific literals, like an empty set in a tagged set class. See the discussion on the procedure Convert in 4.5.

There is no need to use run-time dispatch when a controlling operand or result has a statically known specific type. (A mixture of static and dynamically determined tags is not allowed.) In this case, the specific type's implementation of the primitive operation is then called directly (this is effectively a case of "static" binding).

As discussed in 4.3, the canonical implementation model for a type tag is a pointer to a run-time type descriptor, containing pointers to subprogram bodies implementing each of the primitive operations. This implementation model means that the call on a dispatching operation involves only tag-equality checks (if there is more than one controlling operand), and then a call through the appropriate subprogram pointer. The overhead for such a call is bounded, and can be kept to two or three instructions in most cases, ensuring that dispatching operations can be used even in demanding real-time applications. Note that this overhead is typically less than the overhead of using case statements and variant records.

For a tagged type T, even the implicitly provided operations (such as Object'Size and assignment if nonlimited) use dispatching internally when applied to a class-wide operand, to allow for new components that might be added by type extension.

Generally, for each primitive operation of a parent type, a type extension may either inherit the original implementation, or it may override it. For an operation that had an operand of the parent type, if not overridden it becomes an operation with an operand of the type extension, which simply ignores (and does not affect) the extension part of the operand. However, for an operation that returned a result of the parent type, if not overridden, it becomes an abstract operation that has no implementation for the extension. This is because the extension part of the result would not be defined for such an operation.

Abstract operations allow a type to have a specification for an operation but no implementation for it, effectively requiring that each derivative define its own. Such operations have no default implementation, preventing a derivative from mistakenly inheriting a meaningless implementation. Abstract operations correspond to deferred methods or virtual methods in Smalltalk and C++. The corresponding class is called an abstract superclass.

If a tagged type has an abstract primitive operation, then it must be declared as an abstract type, and no objects with a tag identifying that type may be created. This means that a call to an abstract operation will always dispatch to some non-abstract implementation that is defined for some derivative. No run-time check is needed to detect whether an operation is abstract, because no objects with the tag for an abstract type can ever be created.

To conclude, the model of type extension and polymorphism in Ada 95 combines efficiency of implementation, clarity of program text and security in a cohesive manner. It provides the additional flexibility sought in an object oriented language without compromising the security which was the cornerstone of Ada 83.

4.8 Requirements Summary

The three major study topics

S4.1-A(1) — Subprograms as Objects

S4.3-A(1) — Reducing the Need for Recompilation

S4.3-B(1) — Programming by Specialization/Extension

are directly addressed and satisfied by the facilities discussed in this chapter.

5 Statements

There is naturally very little change in this classical area of the language. The only additional statement is the requeue statement and that is addressed in Chapter 9. There are also additional forms of the delay and select statements and these are also discussed in Chapter 9. The mechanism of assignment including user-defined assignment is closely associated with controlled types and these are discussed in 7.4. The return statement is now moved to Chapter 6 where it properly belongs.

6 Subprograms

Perhaps the most important change to subprograms and their use in Ada 95 is the fact that they are more nearly first class types since they may be manipulated as the target of access types. However, this topic is dealt with in Chapter 3 and we concern ourselves here with other relatively minor improvements to subprograms. These are

- Various aspects of the parameter and result mechanism are improved. The notions of by-copy and by-reference parameters are made more formal. Parameters of mode out may now be read. Subprograms may have parameters of mode out for a limited view of a type.

- A parameter may also be of an anonymous access type.

- A subprogram body may now be provided by renaming; this and other changes increases the categories of conformance rules.

- The rules for new overloadings of " = " and " / = " are relaxed.

Other related matters are the calling conventions for interfacing with other languages; these are discussed in Part Three. Abstract subprograms are discussed in Chapter 3.

6.1 Parameter and Result Mechanism

For Ada 95, we define by-copy parameter passing in terms of a subtype conversion and an assignment. This minimizes the number of special rules associated with parameter passing.

For by-reference parameters, the formal parameter is considered a view of the actual.

Certain types are called by-copy types and are always passed by copy. Some other types are called by-reference types and are always passed by reference. For the remaining types the implementation is free to choose either mechanism. Note that the parameter mechanism is independent of the view; thus a private type is always passed by the mechanism appropriate to the full view of the type.

Note that tagged types, task types and protected types are by-reference types.

A similar approach is taken with function results. Certain types are classified as return-by-reference types. Again these include task types and protected types (and most other limited types, see 7.3). In the case of a result returned by reference the function call denotes a constant view of the object denoted by the return expression. In other cases a copy is made. Remember that the result of a function call is treated as an object in Ada 95.

A difference between parameters and results is that tagged types are always by reference as parameters but only returned by reference if limited.

For all modes and both mechanisms of parameters and for results, a subtype conversion is performed if necessary (to provide sliding).

Note in particular that sliding is used for array parameters and results whereas Ada 83 required the more restrictive exact matching of bounds. An array aggregate with **others** is still allowed as a parameter or as a result and with the same meaning although for different reasons. In Ada 83 it was allowed because the matching rules provide the bounds whereas in Ada 95 it is allowed because the rules for **others** in assignment are relaxed but there is the overriding rule that aggregates with **others** never slide.

In Ada 95 it is not erroneous to depend on the parameter passing mechanism (by-reference versus by-copy) for those types that allow both, though it is nonportable. This is an example of reducing totally unpredictable behavior (see 1.3).

6.1.1 Out Parameters

In Ada 83 a formal parameter of mode **out** could not be read, even after being initialized within the procedure. This forced certain algorithms to include a local variable just to accumulate a result and which was then assigned to the **out** parameter. Introducing such a local variable is error prone, because the final assignment may be mistakenly omitted.

Similarly, if an **out** parameter is passed to a second procedure to be filled in, the value returned cannot be checked prior to returning from the first procedure.

For Ada 95, we have removed the restrictions on the use of **out** parameters. Specifying that a formal parameter is of mode **out** indicates that the caller need not initialize it prior to the call. However, within the procedure, once the parameter has been initialized, it may be read and updated like any other variable. As with a normal variable, it is an error to depend on the value of an **out** parameter prior to its being initialized.

The added simplicity and flexibility provided by removing the restrictions on reading an **out** parameter allows many of the special cases associated with **out** parameters to be eliminated, including the restriction regarding their use with limited types.

Safety is preserved by ensuring that a subcomponent does not become "deinitialized" by being passed as an **out** parameter. If any subcomponent of a type passed by copy has default initialization, then the whole object is copied in at the start of the call so that the value of such a subcomponent is not lost as a result of a subprogram call during which no assignment is made to the subcomponent. But in practice records are usually passed by reference anyway.

6.1.2 Access Parameters

A formal **in** parameter may be specified with an access definition. Such a parameter is of a general access type that is totally anonymous (has no nameable subtypes), but is convertible to other general access types with the same designated subtype. Access parameters are valuable because they allow dispatching on access values; they are also convenient for use with access discriminants; see 3.7.1.

Access parameters are often an alternative to **in out** parameters especially for tagged types. Thus suppose we have a tagged type and an access type referring to it and appropriate variables such as

```
type T is tagged
   record ...

type Access_T is access T;

Obj: T;

Obj_Ptr: Access_T := new T'(...);
```

plus subprograms taking parameters thus

```
procedure P(X: in out T);

procedure PA(XA: access T);
```

then within the body of both P and PA we have read and write access to the components of the record. Indeed because of automatic dereferencing the components are referred to in the same way. And since tagged types are all always passed by reference and never by copy, the effect is much the same for many situations. For example dispatching is possible in both cases. However, there are a number of important differences.

In the case of the **in out** parameter, the actual parameter could be Obj or Obj_Ptr.**all** thus

```
P(Obj);   P(Obj_Ptr.all);
```

whereas in the case of the **access** parameter, the actual parameter has to be Obj'Access or Obj_Ptr. Moreover in the former case the variable Obj must be marked as **aliased**

```
Obj: aliased T;
PA(Obj'Access);   PA(Obj_Ptr);
```

Remember also that an actual parameter corresponding to an access parameter cannot be null. Moreover, accessibility checks for access parameters are dynamic and the parameter carries with it an indication of its accessibility.

A vital difference is that a function cannot have an in out parameter and so an access parameter is essential if we need a function. We recall from 4.4.1 that the alternative of a procedure with an out parameter corresponding to the function result is not possible in some cases such as where the result type is class wide and we do not know the anticipated specific type.

Other important considerations occur if we have a sequence of nested calls. Thus suppose we have other procedures Q and QA and that in their bodies we wish to call the procedures P and PA with the parameter passed on. There are four possible combinations of calls to consider. We have

```
procedure Q(X: in out T) is
begin
   P(X);                      -- in out passed on to in out
   ...
   PA(X'Access);              -- in out passed on to access
end Q;

procedure QA(XA: access T) is
begin
   P(XA.all);                 -- access passed on to in out
   ...
   PA(XA);                    -- access passed on to access
end QA;
```

All of these calls are legal. The call of PA from within Q is legal because formal parameters of a tagged type are considered aliased and treated just like an aliased local variable. Hence X'Access is allowed but the accessibility level is that of a variable local to Q. This means that the accessibility level passed to PA indicates that Q.X is local to Q and will not reflect the accessibility level of the original actual parameter passed to Q (and of course that information was not passed to Q anyway).

In the reverse situation where QA calls P no accessibility information is passed on. Moreover, it should be noted that the parameter XA.**all** creates a view of the original parameter and this view is passed on; no local object is created. Thus the information passed on is simply the original "reference" minus the accessibility information.

The uniform cases where Q calls P or QA calls PA are straightforward. The parameter is passed on unchanged, in the first case there is no accessibility information and in the second it is passed on intact.

There is a lot of merit in using access parameters because they pass the correct accessibility level and avoid the risk of an illegal program or unexpectedly raising Program_Error when attempting a conversion to a named access type. For example, assuming T and Access_T are declared at the same level as the procedures and that Q and QA are called with actual parameter Obj or Obj'Access respectively, then it would be illegal to write

```
Obj_Ptr := Access_T(X'Access);
```

inside Q since the static accessibility check fails, whereas it is legal to write the corresponding

```
Obj_Ptr := Access_T(XA);
```

inside QA, and the dynamic accessibility check succeeds.

Furthermore if we also had a procedure

```
procedure RA(XA: access T) is
begin
   ...
   Obj_Ptr := Access_T(XA);
   ...
end RA;
```

in which a similar conversion is performed, then calling RA from Q by

```
RA(X'Access);
```

results in raising Program_Error on the attempted conversion in RA whereas calling RA from QA by

```
RA(XA);
```

works successfully because the original accessibility level is preserved.

However, remember that we can always use Unchecked_Access which avoids the accessibility checks. This would overcome the difficulties in the above examples but of course the use of Unchecked_Access in general can result in dangling references; the responsibility lies with the user to ensure that this does not happen.

For a further discussion on access parameters and a comparison between them and parameters of a named access type see 3.7.1.

6.2 Renaming of Bodies and Conformance

In Ada 95, we allow a subprogram body to be provided by renaming another subprogram. This is a great convenience in those many cases in Ada 83 where the programmer was forced to provide a body which simply called some other existing subprogram. In order that the implementation can be just a jump instruction, the subprogram specification must be "subtype conformant" with the body used to implement it. Subtype conformance is required because the caller sees only the subprogram specification, and therefore has prepared the parameters, performed constraint checks, and followed the parameter passing conventions determined by the specification.

Several different rules existed in Ada 83 governing matching between subprogram specifications. For the purposes of hiding the name of the subprogram, only the types of the formal parameters and the result, if any, were relevant (see [RM83 8.3(15)]). For renaming and generic instantiation, the modes also had to match (see [RM83 8.5(7)] and [RM83 12.3.6(1)]). Between a specification and its body, syntactic equivalence was required ([RM83 6.3.1(5)]).

For Ada 95, in order to support access to subprogram types, and to support the provision of a body by a renaming, an intermediate level of matching is needed. This intermediate level requires static subtype matching, but allows formal parameter names and defaults to differ.

To improve the presentation in Ada 95, the descriptions of these various levels of subprogram matching are gathered into the section on Conformance Rules [RM95 6.3.1]. Each level of matching is given a name and they can be arranged in a strictly ascending order of strength as follows

Type conformance.   This is the matching that controls hiding.

Mode conformance.   This is the matching required for renaming and generic formal subprograms.

Subtype conformance. This is the matching required for access to subprogram types, and for specifying a body via renaming.

Full conformance.   This is the matching required between the declaration and body of a subprogram, and between multiple specifications of a discriminant part.

In addition to centralizing these definitions, we have also relaxed the full conformance rules, in order to make them represent static semantic equivalence, rather than syntactic equivalence. This has the effect of eliminating certain anomalies (such as the non-transitivity of Ada 83 conformance), as well as being more natural for the programmer and easier to implement.

6.3 Overloading of Equality and Inequality Operators

In Ada 83, the "=" operator could be explicitly defined only for limited types (other than via a devious method based on a curious loophole in generic instantiation). This restriction was justified largely on methodological grounds. However, experience with Ada has illustrated several circumstances where it is very natural to provide a user-defined equality operator for nonlimited types. For example, within a three-value logic abstraction, "=" should return either True, False, or Unknown. For vector processing, it is natural to define a component-wise "=" operator for vectors, producing a vector of Boolean values as the result. In such cases, it is also important to be able to explicitly define "/=", since it is not the simple Boolean complement of "=".

In Ada 95, we allow "=" to be treated like any other relational operator. But note that when the result type of a user-defined "=" operator is Standard.Boolean, a complementary definition for "/=" is automatically provided. Explicit definitions for "/=" are also permitted, so long as the result type is not Standard.Boolean. A "/=" operator with a result type of Standard.Boolean may thus become defined only as an implicit side-effect of a definition for "=".

Of course, dispatching can occur on "=". For example in the procedure Convert in 4.4.3, the comparison in

```
while Temp /= Empty loop
```

dispatches. Typically the equality will be predefined but of course it might not be.

6.4 Requirements Summary

Many of the changes in this chapter are consequences of the general requirement

R2.2-C(1) — Minimize Special Case Restrictions

discussed in [DoD 90 A.3]; this lists three examples which have been met by this chapter. They are the ability to redefine "=", the ability to read **out** parameters and the use of sliding (array subtype conversion).

7 Packages

There are a number of important changes to the language addressed in this chapter. Many of these are associated with tagged types such as the addition of private extensions. Another important change is the introduction of controlled types which are implemented using tagged types. In summary the changes are

- A private type may be marked as tagged. The rules regarding private types and discriminants are considerably relaxed.

- Private extensions are introduced in order to allow type extension of tagged types where the extension part is private.

- A deferred constant can be of any type, not just a private type.

- The property of being limited is now separated from that of being private. They are both view properties.

- Controlled types are added. These permit finalization and the user definition of assignment.

An important change regarding library packages is that they can have a body only when one is required; this is discussed in 10.4.

7.1 Private Types and Extensions

To allow for the extension of private types, the modifier tagged may be specified in a private type declaration. A tagged private type must be implemented with a tagged record type, or by deriving from some other tagged type.

We considered allowing a tagged private type to be derived from an untagged type. However, this added potential implementation complexity because the parent type might not have a layout optimized for referencing components added in later extensions. There is a simple work-around; the tagged private type can be implemented as a tagged record type with a single component of the desired parent type.

In Ada 95, we consider a private type to be a composite type outside the scope of its full type declaration. This is primarily a matter of presentation.

Although a private tagged type must be implemented as a tagged type, the reverse is not the case. A private untagged type can be implemented as a tagged or untagged type. In other words if the partial view is tagged then the full view must be tagged; if the partial view is untagged then the full view may or may not be tagged. We thus have to be careful when saying that a type is tagged, strictly we should talk about the view being tagged. The relationship between the full and partial view of a type is discussed further in 7.3 when we also consider limited types.

A good example of the use of a tagged type to implement a private type which is not tagged is given by the type Unbounded_String in the package Ada.Strings.Unbounded. The sample implementation discussed in A.2.6 shows how Unbounded_String is controlled and thus derived from Finalization.Controlled.

We have generalized discriminants so that a derived type declaration may include a discriminant part. Therefore, it is now permissible for a private type with discriminants to be implemented by a derived type declaration. This was not possible in Ada 83.

In addition, a discriminant part may be provided in a task or protected type declaration. As a consequence, a limited private type with discriminants may be implemented as a task or protected type.

Another improvement mentioned in II.12 is that a private type without discriminants may now be implemented as any definite type including a discriminated record type with defaulted discriminants.

A tagged (parent) type may be extended with a private extension part. This allows one type to visibly extend another, while keeping the names and types of the components in the extension part private to the package where the extension is defined.

For a private extension in the visible part, a corresponding record extension must be defined in the private part. Note that the record extension part may be simply

with null record

which uses an abbreviated form of syntax for null records. This abbreviated form was introduced precisely because null extensions are fairly common.

An extension aggregate is only allowed where the full view of the extended type is visible even if the extension part is null. Note that a private extension may always be (view) converted to its parent type. See also 3.6.1 for the case where the ancestor part is abstract.

The interplay between type extension and visibility is illustrated by the following somewhat contrived example

```
package P1 is
    type T is tagged
        record
            A: Type_A;
        end record;
    type T1 is new T with private;
private
    type T1 is new T with
        record
            B: Type_B;
        end record;
end P1;

with P1; use P1;
package P2 is
    type T2 is new T1 with
        record
            C: Type_C;
        end record;
end P2;

with P2; use T2
package body P1 is

    X1: T1;       -- can write X1.B
    X2: T2;       -- cannot write X2.B
    XX: T1 renames T1(X2);
    ...
    XX.B :=       -- changes B component of X2

end P1;
```

The type T has a component A. The type T1 is extended from T with the additional component B but the extension is not visible outside the private part and body of P1. The type T2 is in turn extended from T1 with a further component C. However, although T2 has a component B it is not visible for any view of T2, since the declaration of T2 sees only the partial view of its parent T1. So the B component of T2 is not visible in the package body P1 even though that component of its parent is indeed visible from there. But of course we can do a view conversion of an object of the type T2 and then obtain access to the component B provided we are at a place that has the full view of T1.

It is important that the invisible B component of T2 be invisible for all views since otherwise we would run into a problem if the additional component of T2 were also called B (this is allowed because the existing B component is not visible at the point where the additional component is declared and the potential clash could not be known to the writer of P2). But if there were a view such that all components of T2 were visible (such as perhaps might be expected in the body of P1) then X2.B would be ambiguous.

The important general principle is that the view we get of a type is the view relating to the declaration of it that is visible to us rather than simply where we are looking from.

7.1.1 Private Operations

A tagged type may have primitive operations declared in a private part. These operations will then not be available to all views of the type although nevertheless they will always be in the dispatch table. We noted in 3.6.2 that an abstract type can never have private abstract operations.

A private operation can be overridden even if the overriding operation actually occurs at a place where the private operation is not visible. Consider

```
package P is
   type A is tagged ...;
private
   procedure Op(X: A);
end P;

package P.Child is
   type B is new A with ...;
   procedure Op(X: B);
private
   -- the old Op would have been visible here
end P.Child;
```

The type A has a private dispatching operation Op. The type B is an extension of A and declares an operation Op. This overrides the private inherited operation of the same name despite the fact that the private operation is not visible at the point of the declaration of the new operation. But the key point is that within the private part of the child package, the old Op would have become visible and this is still within the region where it is possible to add primitive operations for B. It is not possible for both operations to be primitive and visible at the same place and it would be impossible for them to share the same slot in the dispatch table. Accordingly the new operation overrides the old. Moreover, they must conform. For a practical example see 13.5.1.

On the other hand if the new operation is declared at a point such that the visibility of the two never clash in this way such as in the following

```
package P is
   type A is tagged ...;
   procedure Curious(X: A'Class);
private
   procedure Op(X: A);   -- first one
end P;
```

```
with P; use P;
package Outside is
   type B is new A with ...;
   procedure Op(X: B);   -- second one
end Outside;
```

then the two operations do not clash and occupy different slots in the dispatch table. Moreover they need not conform since they are quite independent. So in fact B does actually have both operations; it inherits the private one from A and has its own different one. We will dispatch to one or the other according to how a dispatching call is made. The first one is of course a dispatching operation of A'Class whereas the second is a dispatching operation of B'Class. The procedure Curious might be

```
procedure Curious(X: A'Class) is
begin
   Op(X);   -- dispatch to first Op
end Curious;
```

and then

```
Object: B;
...
Curious(Object);
```

will call the inherited hidden operation of B which will apply itself to the part of B inherited from A. This hidden operation is of course just that inherited from A; it cannot be changed and hence can know nothing of the additional components of B.

Note further that we could declare a further type extension from B at a place where the operation of A is also visible. This could be in the private part of a child of P or in a package inner to the body of P. For example

```
with Outside; use Outside;
package P.Child is

private
   type C is new B with ...;

end P.Child;
```

In such a case C inherits both operations from B in the sense that they both occupy slots in the dispatch table. But again the operation acquired indirectly from A is totally invisible; it does not matter that the operation of A is visible at this point; all that matters is that C cannot see the corresponding operation of B. This is another example of the principle mentioned at the end of the previous section that the view we get of a type is the view relating to the declaration of it that is visible to us rather than where we are looking from; or in other words the history of how B got its operations is irrelevant.

7.2 Deferred Constants

In Ada 83, deferred constants were only permitted in the visible part of a package and only if their type was private and was declared in the same visible part [RM83 7.4(4)].

In Ada 95, this restriction is relaxed, so that a deferred constant of any type may be declared immediately within the visible part of a package, provided that the full constant declaration is given in the private part of the package. This eliminates the anomaly that prevented a constant of a composite type with a component of a private type from being declared, if the composite type was declared in the same visible part as the private type.

Another advantage of deferred constants is that in some cases, the initial value depends on attributes of objects or types that are declared in the private part. For example, one might want to export an access to constant value designating a variable in the private part. This prevents the external user from changing the value although the package of course can change the value. This is another example of having two different views of an entity; in this case a constant view and a variable view.

```
type Int_Ptr is access constant Integer;
The_Ptr: constant Int_Ptr;   -- deferred constant
private
Actual_Int: aliased Integer;
  -- is a variable so we do not need an initial value
The_Ptr: constant Int_Ptr := Actual_Int'Access;
-- full definition of deferred constant
```

Note that a deferred constant can also be completed by an Import pragma thereby indicating that the object is external to the Ada program. See Part Three for details.

A small point regarding deferred constants is that they no longer have to be declared with just a subtype mark; a subtype indication including an explicit constraint is allowed. Such a constraint must statically match that in the full constant declaration.

7.3 Limited Types

As in Ada 83, a limited type is one for which assignment is not allowed (user-defined assignment is not allowed either, see 7.4). However, the property of being limited is no longer tied to private types. Any record type can be declared as limited by the inclusion of **limited** in its definition. Thus the type Outer in 6.4.3 is limited. Task and protected types are also limited and a type is limited if it has any components that are limited. Only a limited type can have access discriminants. Finally, a derived type is limited if its parent is limited.

Limited is a sort of view property in that whether a type is limited or not may depend upon from where it is viewed. This is obvious with a limited private type where the full view might not be limited. However, it can occur even in the nonprivate case. Consider

```
package P is
   type T is limited private;
   type A is array (...) of T;
private
   type T is new Integer;
   -- at this point A becomes nonlimited
end P;
```

where the type A starts off being limited because its components are limited. However, after the full declaration of T, its components are no longer limited and so A becomes nonlimited.

Note that in the case of a tagged type, it must have **limited** in its definition (or that of its ancestor) if it has limited components. This prevents a tagged type from the phenomenon of becoming nonlimited. Otherwise one might extend from a limited view with a limited component (such as a task) and then in the full view try to do assignment as in the following variation of the previous example.

```
package P is
   type T is limited private;
   type R is tagged   -- illegal, must have explicit limited
```

```
        record
            X: T;
        end record;
    private
        type T is new Integer;
        -- at this point R would become nonlimited
    end P;

    package Q is
        type T2 is new R with
            record
                A: Some_Task;
            end record;
    end Q;
```

The problem is that the body of P would see a nonlimited view of T and hence assignment would be defined for T'Class and so it would be possible to do an assignment on the type T2 by a dispatching operation in the body of P.

So, in the case of a tagged private type (that is a type for which both partial and full views are tagged), both partial and full views must be limited or not together; it is not possible for the partial view to be limited and the full view not to be limited. On the other hand if the partial view is untagged and limited then the full view can be any combination including tagged and nonlimited. The various possibilities are illustrated in Table 7-1; only those combinations marked as OK are legal.

full view	partial view			
	untagged		tagged	
	limited	nonlimited	limited	nonlimited
untagged limited	O K			
untagged nonlimited	O K	O K		
tagged limited	O K		O K	
tagged nonlimited	O K	O K		O K

Table 7-1: Full and Partial Views

A consequence of the rules is that, in the case of type extension, if the parent type is not limited, then the extension part cannot have any limited components. (Note that the rules regarding actual and formal generic parameters are somewhat different; the actual type corresponding to a formal limited tagged type does not have to be limited. This is because type extension is not permitted in the generic body.)

There was a pathological situation in Ada 83 whereby a function could return a local task (all one could do with it outside was apply the attributes Terminated and Callable); this was a nuisance because all the storage for the local task could not be properly relinquished on the return.

In Ada 95 there is an accessibility check that prevents such difficulties. In essence we are not allowed to return a local object of a limited type (there are some subtle exceptions for which see [RM95 6.5]).

An important consequence of a function result being treated as an object is that it can be renamed. This means that we can "remember" the result of a function even in the case of a limited type. For example, the function Text_IO.Current_Output returns the current default output file. In Ada 83 it was difficult to remember this and then reset the default value back after having used some other file as current output in the meantime; it could be done but only with a contorted use of parameters. In Ada 95 we can write

```
Old_File: File_Type renames Current_Output;
...
Set_Output(Old_File);
```

and the renaming holds onto the object which behaves much as an **in** parameter. But see also Part Three for a more general solution to the problem of remembering a current file.

7.4 Controlled Types

To preserve abstraction, while providing automatic reclamation of resources, Ada 95 provides controlled types that have initialization and finalization operations associated with them. A number of different approaches were considered and rejected during the evolution of Ada 95. The final solution has the merit of allowing user-defined assignment and also solves the problem of returning limited types mentioned in the previous section.

The general principle is that there are three distinct primitive activities concerning the control of objects

- initialization after creation,

- finalization before destruction (includes overwriting),

- adjustment after assignment.

and the user is given the ability to provide appropriate procedures which are called to perform whatever is necessary at various points in the life of an object. These procedures are Initialize, Finalize and Adjust and take the object as an **in out** parameter.

To see how this works, consider

```
declare
   A: T;            -- create A, Initialize(A)
begin
   A := E;          -- Finalize(A), copy value, Adjust(A)
   ...
end;                -- Finalize(A)
```

After A is declared and any normal default initialization carried out, the Initialize procedure is called. On the assignment, Finalize is first called to tidy up the old object about to be overwritten and thus destroyed, the physical copy is then made and finally Adjust is called to do whatever might be required for the new copy. At the end of the block Finalize is called once more before the object is destroyed. Note, of course, that the user does not have to physically write the calls of the three control procedures, they are called automatically by the compiled code.

In the case of a nested structure where inner components might themselves be controlled, the rules are that components are initialized and adjusted before the object as a whole and on finalization everything is done in the reverse order.

There are many other situations where the control procedures are invoked such as when calling allocators, evaluating aggregates and so on; for details the reader should consult [RM95].

In order for a type to be controlled it has to be derived from one of two tagged types declared in the library package Ada.Finalization whose specification is given in [RM95 7.6] and which is repeated here for convenience

```
package Ada.Finalization is

    pragma Preelaborate(Finalization);

    type Controlled is abstract tagged private;

    procedure Initialize(Object: in out Controlled);
    procedure Adjust(Object: in out Controlled);
    procedure Finalize(Object: in out Controlled);

    type Limited_Controlled is abstract tagged limited private;

    procedure Initialize(Object: in out Limited_Controlled);
    procedure Finalize(Object: in out Limited_Controlled);

private
    ...
end Ada.Finalization;
```

There are distinct abstract types for nonlimited and limited types. Naturally enough the Adjust procedure does not exist in the case of limited types because they cannot be copied.

Although the types Controlled and Limited_Controlled are abstract, nevertheless the procedures Initialize, Adjust and Finalize are not abstract. However they all do nothing which will often prove to be appropriate.

A typical declaration of a controlled type might take the form

```
type T is new Controlled with ...
```

and the user would then provide new versions of the controlling procedures as required. Note incidentally that the form of an extension aggregate mentioned in 3.6.1 where the ancestor part is a subtype name is useful for controlled types since we can write

```
X: T := (Controlled with ...);
```

whereas we cannot use an expression as the ancestor part because its type is abstract.

The capabilities provided take a building block approach and give the programmer fine control of resources. In particular they allow the implementor of an abstraction to ensure that proper cleanup is performed prior to the object becoming permanently inaccessible.

The ability to associate automatic finalization actions with an abstraction is extremely important for Ada, given the orientation toward information hiding, coupled with the many ways that a scope may be exited in Ada (exception, exit, return, abort, asynchronous transfer of control, etc). In many cases, the need for finalization is more of a safety or reliability issue than a part of the visible specification of an abstraction. Most users of an abstraction should not need to know whether the abstraction uses finalization.

A related observation concerns the use of controlled types as generic parameters. We can write a package which adds some properties to an arbitrary controlled type in the manner outlined in 4.6.2. Typically we will call the Finalize of the parent as part of the Finalize operation of the new type. Consider

```
generic
    type Parent is abstract new Limited_Controlled with private;
```

```
package P is
   type T is new Parent with private;
   ...
private
   type T is new Parent with
      record
         -- additional components
      end record;
   procedure Finalize(Object: in out T);
end P;

package body P is
   ...
   procedure Finalize(Object: in out T) is
   begin
      ...  -- operations to finalize the additional components
      Finalize(Parent(Object));  -- finalize the parent
   end Finalize;
end P;
```

This will always work even if the implementation of the actual type corresponding to Parent has no overriding Finalize itself since the inherited null version from Limited_Controlled will then be harmlessly called. See also 12.5.

The approach we have adopted enables the implementation difficulties presented by, for example, exceptions to be overcome. Thus suppose an exception is raised in the middle of a sequence of declarations of controlled objects. Only those already elaborated will need to be finalized and some mechanism is required in order to record this. Such a mechanism can conveniently be implemented using links which are components of the private types Controlled and Limited_Controlled; these components are of course quite invisible to the user. Incidentally, this illustrates that an abstract type need not be null.

The following example is of a generic package that defines a sparse array type. The array is extended automatically as new components are assigned into it. Empty_Value is returned on dereferencing a never-assigned component. On scope exit, automatic finalization calls Finalize, which reclaims any storage allocated to the sparse array.

```
with Ada.Finalization; use Ada;
generic
   type Index_Type is (<>);
      -- index type must be some discrete type
   type Element_Type is private;
      -- component type for sparse array
   Empty_Value : in Element_Type;
      -- value to return for never-assigned components
package Sparse_Array_Pkg is
   -- this generic package defines a sparse array type
   type Sparse_Array_Type is
      new Finalization.Limited_Controlled with private;

   procedure Set_Element(Arr: in out Sparse_Array_Type;
                         Index: in Index_Type;
                         Value: in Element_Type);
      -- set value of an element
      -- extend array as necessary

   function Element(Arr: Sparse_Array_Type;
                    Index: Index_Type) return Element_Type;
      -- return element of array
```

```
            -- return Empty_Value if never assigned

      procedure Finalize(Arr: in out Sparse_Array_Type);
            -- reset array to be completely empty

      -- use default Initialize implementation (no action)
      -- no Adjust for limited types
   private
      -- implement using a B-tree-like representation
      type Array_Chunk;
         -- type completed in package body
      type Array_Chunk_Ptr is access Array_Chunk;
      type Sparse_Array_Type is
         new Finalization.Limited_Controlled with
         record
            Number_Of_Levels: Natural := 0;
            Root_Chunk       : Array_Chunk_Ptr;
         end record;
   end Sparse_Array_Pkg;

   package body Sparse_Array_Pkg is
      type Array_Chunk is ...
         -- complete the incomplete type definition
      procedure Set_Element( ...

      function Element(Arr: Sparse_Array_Type;
                       Index: Index_Type) return Element_Type is
      begin
         if Arr.Root_Chunk = null then
            -- entire array is empty
            return Empty_Value;
         else
            -- look up to see if Index appears
            -- in array somewhere
            ...
         end if;
      end Element;

      procedure Finalize(Arr: in out Sparse_Array_Type) is
      begin
         if Arr.Root_Chunk /= null then
            -- release all chunks of array
            ...
            -- reinitialize array back to initial state
            Arr.Root_Chunk := null;
            Arr.Number_Of_Levels := 0;
         end if;
      end Finalize;
   end Sparse_Array_Pkg;
```

Since the sparse array type is derived from a library level tagged type (Ada.Finalization.Limited_Controlled), the generic unit must also be instantiated at the library level. However, an object of the sparse array type defined in the instantiation may be declared in any scope. When that scope is exited, for whatever reason, the storage dynamically allocated to the array will be reclaimed, via an implicit call on Sparse_Array_Type.Finalize.

Such a sparse array type may safely be used by subprograms of a long-running program, without concern for progressive loss of storage. When such subprograms return, the storage will always be reclaimed, whether completed by an exception, return, abort, or asynchronous transfer of control.

Our next example illustrates user-defined assignment. Incidentally, it should be noted that many of the cases where user-defined assignment was felt to be necessary in Ada 83 no longer apply because the ability to redefine "=" has been generalized. Many Ada 83 applications using limited types did so in order to redefine "=" and as a consequence lost predefined assignment. Their need for user-defined assignment was simply to get back the predefined assignment.

An instance where user-defined assignment would be appropriate occurs in the implementation of abstract sets using linked lists where a deep copy is required as mentioned in 4.4.3.

The general idea is that the set is implemented as a record containing one inner component which is controlled; this controlled component is an access to a linked list containing the various elements. Whenever the controlled component is assigned it makes a new copy of the linked list. Note that the type Linked_Set as a whole cannot be controlled because it is derived directly from Abstract_Sets.Set. However, assigning a value of the Linked_Set causes the inner component to be assigned and then invokes the procedure Adjust on the inner component. The implementation might be as follows

```
with Abstract_Sets;
with Ada.Finalization; use Ada.Finalization;
package Linked_Sets is

    type Linked_Set is new Abstract_Sets.Set with private;

    ...  -- the various operations on Linked_Set

private

    type Node;
    type Ptr is access Node;
    type Node is
        record
            Element: Set_Element;
            Next: Ptr;
        end record;

    function Copy(P: Ptr) return Ptr;   -- deep copy

    type Inner is new Controlled with
        record
            The_Set: Ptr;
        end record;

    procedure Adjust(Object: in out Inner);

    type Linked_Set is new Abstract_Sets.Set with
        record
            Component: Inner;
        end record;

end Linked_Sets;

package body Linked_Sets is

    function Copy(P: Ptr) return Ptr is
```

```
begin
   if P = null then
      return null;
   else
      return new Node'(P.Element, Copy(P.Next));
   end if;
end Copy;

procedure Adjust(Object: in out Inner) is
begin
   Object.The_Set := Copy(Object.The_Set);
end Adjust;

   ...

end Linked_Sets;
```

The types Node and Ptr form the usual linked list containing the elements; Node is of course not tagged or controlled. The function Copy performs a deep copy of the list passed as parameter. The type Inner is controlled and contains a single component referring to the linked list. The procedure Adjust for Inner performs a deep copy on this single component. The visible type Linked_Set is then simply a record containing a component of the controlled type Inner. As mentioned above, performing an assignment on the type Linked_Set causes Adjust to be called on its inner component thereby making the deep copy. But none of this is visible to the user of the package Linked_Sets. Observe that we do not need to provide a procedure Initialize and that we have not bothered to provide Finalize although it would be appropriate to do so in order to discard the unused space.

Finally, we show a canonical example of the use of initialization and finalization and access discriminants for the completely safe control of resources. Consider the following:

```
type Handle(Resource: access Some_Thing) is
          new Finalization.Limited_Controlled with null record;

procedure Initialize(H: in out Handle) is
begin
   Lock(H.Resource);
end Initialize;

procedure Finalize(H: in out Handle) is
begin
   Unlock(H.Resource);
end Finalize;

   ...

procedure P(T: access Some_Thing) is
   H: Handle(T);
begin
   ... -- process T safely
end P;
```

The declaration of H inside the procedure P causes Initialize to be called which in turn calls Lock with the object referred to by the handle as parameter. The general idea is that since we know that Finalize will be called no matter how we leave the procedure P (including because of an exception or abort) then we will be assured that the unlock operation will always be done. This is a useful technique for ensuring that typical pairs of operations are performed correctly such as opening and closing files. Note that we have to declare the handle locally because that is where the locking is required and hence an access discriminant has to be used in order to avoid accessibility problems. We have to have a handle in the first place so that its declaration is tied to the vital finalization.

Some examples of the use of finalization with asynchronous transfer of control will be found in 9.4.

7.5 Requirements Summary

The major study topic

S4.2-A(2) — Preservation of Abstraction

is directly addressed and satisfied by the introduction of controlled types as discussed in 7.4.

8   Visibility Rules

This is an area of the language which is largely ignored by the normal programmer except when it produces surprising or frustrating consequences. The changes have thus been directed largely towards making the rules clear and consistent and with more helpful consequences. The changes are

*   The visibility and scope rules are rewritten to make them consistent and clearer. They also incorporate the consequences of the introduction of the hierarchical library.

*   The use type clause is introduced for operators.

*   Renaming is now allowed for subprogram bodies, generic units and library units.

*   There are also a number of minor improvements such as the preference rules for overload resolution.

8.1 Scope and Visibility

This is an area where there is no substitute for a precise description of the rules. Suffice it to say that the rules for Ada 83 were obscure and probably not truly understood by anybody; a consequence was subtle variation between compilers to the detriment of portability. We will not attempt to summarize the 95 rules but refer the reader to [RM95] for the details.

One important change is that character literals are now treated like other literals with regard to visibility. This means that they are always visible although the legality of their use will depend upon the context. So

```
package P is
    type Roman_Digit is ('I', 'V', 'X', 'L', 'C', 'D', 'M');
end P;

with P;
package Q is
 ...
    Five: constant P.Roman_Digit := 'V';
 ...
end Q;
```

is allowed in Ada 95 although in Ada 83 we would have had to write P.'V' or alternatively supplied a use clause for P.

The visibility rules now also take account of the introduction of child packages. Most of the changes are straightforward but there is one interesting interaction with subunits. Consider

```
package P is
 ...
end P;

package P.Q is
```

```
   . . .
end P.Q;

package body P is
   Q: Integer;   -- legal
   procedure Sub is separate;
end P;

with P.Q;        -- illegal
separate(P)
procedure Sub is
   . . .
end Sub;
```

The declaration of Q in the body of P is permitted because the body does not have a with clause for P.Q. But the with clause makes the subunit illegal because it could otherwise see both P.Q the child package and P.Q the variable in the body, and they are not overloadable.

8.2 Use Clauses

As mentioned in Part One the use of operators in Ada 83 caused problems. Many groups of users recognized that the use clause could make programs hard to understand because the origin of identifiers became obscure. Accordingly many organizations banned use clauses. This meant that either operators of user defined types had to be called with prefix notation such as Complex."+"(P, Q) or else had to be locally renamed.

This difficulty also occurred with predefined operators. Thus given an access type T declared in a package P, it was very annoying to find that one could not write

```
with P;
procedure Q is
   X: P.T;
begin
   . . .
   if X /= null then
   . . .
end Q;
```

but had to provide a use clause for P or a renaming for "=" or write the diabolical

```
if P."/="(X, null) then
```

This problem is overcome in Ada 95 by the introduction of the use type clause which just provides visibility of the operators of a type and thereby allows them to be used in the natural infixed form. This ensures that a use package clause is not needed and hence the full name is still required for other identifiers.

The introduction of child units causes some extension to the rules for packages. As explained in Chapter 10, child units are treated like separately compiled but logically nested units. Like nested units, the name of a child mentioned in a with clause becomes directly visible when the logically enclosing parent package is specified in a use clause.

And so, using the example from II.8

```
with OS.File_Manager;
procedure Hello is
   use OS;   -- makes File_Manager directly visible
             -- as well as other declarations in package OS
```

```
    File: File_Descriptor :=
            File_Manager.Open("Hello.Txt", File_Manager.Write_Only);
begin
    File_Manager.Write(File, "Hello world.");
    File_Manager.Close(File);
end Hello;
```

8.3 Renaming

To enhance the usefulness of renaming, the body of a subprogram may be provided by a renaming declaration.

If the subprogram declaration is in a package specification while the subprogram definition via a renaming is in a package body, the renaming must be of a subprogram that has subtype conformance (see 6.2) with the subprogram's declaration. This ensures that the caller of the subprogram will perform the correct constraint checks on the actual parameters, and pass the parameters following the correct calling convention seeing only the subprogram's specification.

A normal subprogram renaming requires only mode conformance. This kind of conformance is too weak for a renaming provided in the body. Given only mode conformance, the caller might perform constraint checks that were too stringent or too lax, and might pass parameters following the wrong calling conventions, putting them in the wrong place on the stack, or in the wrong register.

We considered requiring subtype conformance for all subprogram renaming. However, this introduces upward incompatibilities, particularly given the existing equivalence between generic formal subprogram matching and renaming. Furthermore, it is not always possible to statically match the subtype of a formal parameter of a subprogram, if the subprogram is implicitly declared as part of the type definition. In particular, if the subprogram is derived from a parent type, then the formal parameter subtypes have the constraints that were present on the parent type's subprogram. If the derived type definition itself imposes a constraint, then it is likely that the constraint on the formal parameter of the derived subprogram is actually looser than the constraint on the first subtype of the derived type. This means there is no nameable subtype that has constraints as loose as those on the formal parameter.

In the case of a primitive operation of a tagged type, renaming will cause a new slot in the dispatch table to be created if the renaming is itself primitive (that is in the same package specification as the type). If the original primitive operation is overridden then the renamed view will naturally depend upon whether renaming occurs before or after the overriding. Consider

```
package P is
    type T is tagged ...;
    function Predefined_Equal(X, Y: T) return Boolean renames "=";
    function "="(X, Y: T) return Boolean:  -- overrides
    function User_Defined_Equal(X, Y: T) return Boolean renames "=";
end P;
```

where we have renamed the predefined equality both before and after overriding it. Both renamings create new slots which are then initialized with the current meaning of equality. That for `Predefined_Equal` thus refers to the predefined equal whereas that for `User_Defined_Equal` refers to the overridden version. The consequence is that renaming can be used to hang on to an old primitive operation irrespective of whether that old operation is subsequently overridden. Such a renaming is itself a distinct primitive operation which could later be overridden for any subsequently derived type.

On the other hand a renaming which is not a primitive operation will not create a new slot but will simply refer to the operation at the point of the renaming. Thus if `User_Defined_Equal` is declared in a distinct package Q (after P), then it will not be primitive but will still refer to the overridden operation. This will occur even if the overriding is in the private part and thus not visible to Q. For a further discussion see [AARM 8.5.4].

This ability of renaming to create a new slot may be considered surprising because the general purpose of renaming is simply to create a new name for an existing entity; but there is of course no new entity being created but just a different way of accessing an existing entity.

Another very useful change is the ability to rename a library unit as a library unit. (It was possible to rename a library unit in Ada 83 but only as a local unit.) Library unit renaming is particularly important with the hierarchical library; this is discussed in detail in 10.1.2.

A related change is the ability to rename a generic unit. Curiously enough this was not permitted in Ada 83 although most other entities could be renamed. Thus we can write

```
generic package Enum_IO renames Ada.Text_IO.Enumeration_IO;
```

as mentioned in [RM95 8.5.5].

In order to prevent difficulties with generic children, a child of a generic parent (such a child must be generic) can only be renamed if the renaming occurs *inside* the declarative region of its parent; it could be renamed as a child. This is consistent with the rules regarding the instantiation of such generic child units mentioned in II.8.

8.4 Other Improvements

The overload resolution rules of Ada 83 were confusing and unclear and this section of the reference manual has been completely rewritten.

An important new rule is the preference rule for operators and ranges of root numeric types (see 3.3). Briefly this says that an ambiguity can be resolved by preferring the operator of the root type. This rule coupled with automatic conversion from a universal type removes the need for the special rules in Ada 83 regarding universal convertible operands.

As an example, consider

```
C: constant := 2 + 3;
```

which was allowed in Ada 83 because the expression was required to be universal and so no question of ambiguity arose. It is not ambiguous in Ada 95 either but for different reasons; the expression 2 + 3 is considered to be of type *root_integer* (it could otherwise be Integer or Long_Integer). The *root_integer* is then converted implicitly to *universal_integer* as required for the initial value.

The special rule regarding ranges in loops and for array indexes (which are in the distinct syntactic category discrete_subtype_definition) which result in them by treated as of type Integer if no specific subtype mark is specified is changed in Ada 95. The new rule is that if the range resolves to be of the type *root_integer* then it is taken to be of type Integer.

One outcome of all this is that we can now write

```
for I in -1 .. 100 loop
```

as we have already mentioned in Part One. The interpretation is that -1 resolves to *root_integer* because of the preference rules and then the special rule just mentioned is used so that the range is finally treated as of type Integer.

8.5 Requirements Summary

Many of the changes in this area of the language are aimed at making the language more precise and easier to understand as requested by the general requirement

R2.2-B(1) — Understandability

and we note in particular that the example in [DoD 90 A.2.3] concerning visibility of literals and operations has been addressed and satisfied.

The related requirement

R2.2-C(1) — Minimize Special Case Restrictions

discussed in [DoD 90 A.3.12] contains the example of negative literals in loops which has also been satisfied.

The requirement

R2.2-A(1) — Reduce Deterrents to Efficiency

is addressed by the elimination of the problem of returning task objects explicitly mentioned in the requirement in [DoD 90].

9 Tasking

As explained in Part One, experience with Ada 83 showed that although the innovative rendezvous provided a good overall model for task communication, nevertheless it had not proved adequate for problems of shared data access.

Accordingly, as outlined in Chapter II, this part of the language is considerably enhanced with the major additions being the introduction of protected types, the requeue statement and asynchronous transfer of control. In this chapter we add further examples and discussion to that already given. The main changes to the core language are

*   The protected type is introduced as a new form of program unit with distinct specification and body in a similar style to packages and tasks.

*   The requeue statement is added to provide preference control and thereby overcome various race conditions which could arise in Ada 83.

*   There is a new form of delay statement which allows waiting for an absolute rather than a relative time. This overcomes problems of poor timing which in essence are caused by a race condition with the clock.

*   There is a new form of the select statement which gives asynchronous transfer of control. This can be used to program mode changes.

*   The description of the rules regarding the abort statement is improved.

*   A task (like a protected type) may now have discriminants and a private part.

*   A minor improvement is that entries and representation clauses may now occur in any order in a task specification.

In addition to the above changes there are further packages, pragmas and attributes plus requirements on implementations described in the Systems Programming and Real-Time Systems annexes. These relate to matters such as scheduling and priorities, task identification, shared variable access, accuracy of timing, interrupt handling and the immediacy of the abort statement. For further details on these topics the reader is referred to Part Three.

9.1 Protected Types

In Ada 83, the rendezvous was used for both inter-task communication and for synchronizing access to shared data structures. However, the very generality of the rendezvous means that it has a relatively high overhead. Ada 95 overcomes this problem by introducing a low overhead, data-oriented synchronization mechanism based on the concept of protected objects.

From the client perspective, operating on a protected object is similar to operating on a task object. The operations on a protected object allow two or more tasks to synchronize their manipulations of shared data structures.

From the implementation perspective, a protected object is designed to be a very efficient conditional critical region (see 9.1.3). The protected operations are automatically synchronized to allow only one writer or multiple readers. The protected operations are defined using a syntax similar to a normal subprogram body, with the mutual exclusion of the critical region happening automatically on entry, and being released automatically on exit.

We considered many different approaches to satisfying the needs for fast mutual exclusion, interrupt handling, asynchronous communication, and various other common real-time paradigms. We settled on the protected object construct because it seems to provide a very efficient building block, which is flexible enough to implement essentially any higher-level synchronization mechanism of interest.

Some of the features that make protected objects attractive as a building block are:

Scalability. Protected objects enable the implementation of a synchronization mechanism that scales smoothly from a single processor to a multiprocessor. There is no built-in bias to a monoprocessor or to a multiprocessor.

Adaptability. Additional protected operations may be added to a protected type without the need to modify the existing operations. Approaches that use explicit signals and conditions rather than the conditional barrier approach generally need each operation to be aware of every state of interest, and explicitly signal all possible waiting tasks.

Modularity. All of the operations of a given critical region are identified in the specification of the protected type, and their implementations are encapsulated within the body of the protected type. The directly protected data components are encapsulated within the private part of the protected type, and all of the interesting states are identified explicitly via entry barrier conditions within the body of the protected type.

Efficiency. The size and initialization requirements of a protected object are known at compile time of the client, because all entries and data components are declared in the specification. This enables protected objects to be allocated statically or directly on the stack, rather than via dynamic allocation, and to be initialized in-line. No extra context switches are required to service waiting clients, since the task changing the state may directly execute the entry bodies whose barriers become true. Non-queued locking may be used to implement the mutual exclusion of a protected object because no blocking is permitted during the execution of a protected operation.

Expressiveness. The specification of a protected type makes explicit distinctions between read-only operations (functions), read-write operations (procedures), and possibly blocking operations (entries). This distinction is vital in analyzing a real-time program for correctness, including freedom from deadlock.

Compatibility. The entry call remains the primary mechanism for blocking a task until some condition is satisfied. An entry call on another task is blocked until the corresponding entry in the task is open. An entry call on a protected object is blocked until the corresponding entry barrier is true. An entry call on a task is completed when the rendezvous finishes and an entry call on a protected object is completed when the entry body finishes; possibly with intermediate blockings as part of a requeue in both cases.

From the caller's perspective, an entry call involves a possible initial blocking, one or more intermediate blockings, and then a return. During the entry call, data may be transferred via the parameters. By using the entry call interface for both protected objects and tasks, the existing conditional and timed entry call mechanisms are applicable.

Interrupt Handling. A protected procedure is very well suited to act as an interrupt handler for a
number of reasons; they both typically have a short bounded execution time, do not
arbitrarily block, have a limited context and finally they both have to integrate with the
priority model. The nonblocking critical region matches the needs of an interrupt handler,
as well as the needs of non-interrupt-level code to synchronize with an interrupt handler.
The entry barrier construct allows an interrupt handler to signal a normal task by changing
the state of a component of the protected object and thereby making a barrier true.

Of the many other approaches we considered for supporting data-oriented synchronization,
none could match this set of desirable features.

Like task types, protected types are limited types. Because protected objects are specifically
designed for synchronizing access from concurrent tasks, a formal parameter must always denote
the same protected object as the corresponding actual parameter and so pass by reference is
required (a copy would not preserve the required atomicity).

A protected type may have discriminants, to minimize the need for an explicit initialization
operation, and to control composite components of the protected objects including setting the size
of an entry family. A discriminant can also be used to set the priority and identify an interrupt.

The other data components of a protected object must be declared in the specification of the
type to ensure that the size is known to the compiler when the type is used by a caller. However
these components are only accessible from protected operations defined in the body of the
protected type and thus are declared in the private part of the protected type.

The protected operations may be functions, procedures, or entries. All the entries must be
declared in the protected type specification to ensure that space needed for entry queues is included
when allocating the protected object. Entries which are not required to be visible to external
clients can be declared in the private part. Additional functions and procedures may be declared in
the private part or body of the protected unit, for modularizing the implementation of the
operations declared in the specification.

An example of a counting semaphore implemented as a protected type is given in II.9. This
example illustrates the three kinds of protected operations: functions, procedures, and entries.
Functions provide read-only access (which may be shared) to the components of the protected
object. Procedures provide exclusive read-write access to the components. Entries have an entry
barrier that determines when the operation may be performed. The entry body is performed with
exclusive read-write access to the components, once the barrier becomes true due to the execution
of some other protected operation. It is important to observe that the evaluation of barrier
expressions is also performed with exclusive access to the protected object.

The counting semaphore might be used as follows

```
Max_Users: constant := 10;
-- limit number of simultaneous users of service
User_Semaphore: Counting_Semaphore(Max_Users);

procedure Use_Service(P: Param) is
begin
    -- wait if too many simultaneous users
    User_Semaphore.Acquire;
    begin
        Perform_Service(P);
    exception
        when others =>
            -- always release the semaphore for next user.
            User_Semaphore.Release;
            raise;
    end;
    -- release the semaphore for others
    User_Semaphore.Release;
end Use_Service;
```

This example illustrates that a semaphore can be implemented as a protected object. However, in essence this often constitutes abstraction inversion since it leaves the responsibility for releasing the semaphore in the hands of the user (unless we use a controlled type as illustrated in 7.4). It is precisely to avoid such possibilities that protected types are provided as an intrinsic syntactic form inherent in the language. Semaphores (like the goto statement) are very prone to misuse and should be avoided where possible. However, there are occasions when they are useful and this example shows an implementation.

As mentioned, some of the protected operations declared in the specification may be declared after the reserved word **private**. This makes these operations callable only from within the protected unit. Task types may similarly have a private part, so that certain task entries may be hidden from a direct call from outside the task (they can be called by its sub-tasks or via a requeue statement).

(Alternative structures were also considered and rejected. One was that the private part of a protected unit be visible to the enclosing package. However, this was considered confusing, and felt to be inconsistent with the visibility of the private part of a subpackage. We also considered splitting the protected type (and task) specification into two separate parts, with the private operations and data components declared in a second part included inside the private part of the enclosing package. However, this seemed like an unnecessary extra syntactic complexity, so we finally adopted the simpler suggestion from two Revision Requests (RR-0487, RR-0628) of using private within the specification to demarcate the private operations.)

Each entry declared in the specification of a protected type must have an entry body. An entry body includes a barrier condition following the reserved word **when**; the barrier condition must be true before the remainder of the entry body is executed.

The entry body for an entry family must specify a name for the entry family index, using an iterator notation (**for** I **in** discrete_subtype_definition). We considered a simpler syntax (I: discrete_subtype_definition) but opted for the iterator notation to avoid ambiguity with the formal parameter part.

An entry barrier is not allowed to depend on parameters of the entry, but it may depend on the entry family index, or any other data visible to the entry body. This rule ensures that all callers of the same entry see the same barrier condition, allowing the barrier to be checked without examining individual callers. Without this rule, each caller of a given entry would have to be treated separately, since each might have a different effective barrier value. Rather than entry "queues" one would essentially have a single large "bag" of callers, all of which would have to be checked on each protected object state change.

For flexibility, entry barriers may depend on data global to the protected object. This allows part of the data managed by the protected object to be outside it, if this is necessary due to some other program structure requirements. However, the barriers are only rechecked after completing a protected procedure or entry body, so asynchronous changes to global data have no immediate effect on the eligibility of a caller waiting on an entry queue. For efficiency, implementations may assume that the only meaningful changes to data referenced in an entry barrier of some protected object take place within a protected operation of that protected object.

We considered disallowing references to globals in a barrier expression. However, that would also have disallowed the use of functions (which might reference globals) or the dereferencing of access values. Such a rule was felt to be too complex to implement, and too restrictive when dealing with data types implemented with access types, such as a linked list.

The semantics for protected types are described in terms of mutual exclusion (except that protected functions may execute concurrently). In addition, as the final step of a protected action, the entry queues are serviced before allowing new calls from the outside to be executed. In this context, a protected "action" is the whole sequence of actions from locking to unlocking and thus comprises a series of one or more of:

- a call on a protected subprogram from outside the protected unit,

- the execution of an entry body,

- the addition or removal of a call from an entry queue.

Servicing the entry queues is required if any change has been made that might affect the value of a barrier expression. First, the barriers for the non-empty entry queues must be reevaluated. If at least one such barrier evaluates to true, some eligible caller must be selected, and the corresponding entry body must be executed. The barriers are then reevaluated once more, and this process continues until all non-empty entry queues have a false barrier. The barriers may be evaluated, and the entry bodies executed, by any convenient thread of control. It need not be the thread of the original caller. This flexibility allows for the most efficient implementation, minimizing unnecessary context switches. (For details on how the choice of caller is made see the Real-Time Systems annex.)

While executing a protected operation of some protected object, a task cannot call a potentially blocking operation for any reason, though it may release the mutual exclusive access to the protected object by being requeued. Disallowing blocking while executing a protected operation allows a nonqueued locking mechanism to be used to implement the mutual exclusion. If blocking were allowed, then a queued locking mechanism would be required, since potential callers might attempt to get the lock while the current holder of the lock is blocked. Another advantage is that conditional calls are more meaningful.

In the simplest monoprocessor environment, protected object mutual exclusion can be implemented by simply inhibiting all task preemption. If multiple priorities are supported, then rather than inhibiting all preemption, a ceiling priority may be established for the protected object (see the Ceiling Priorities section of the Real-Time Systems annex). Only tasks at this ceiling priority or below may use the protected object, meaning that tasks at priorities higher than the ceiling may be allowed to preempt the task performing the protected operation while still avoiding the need for a queued lock.

In a multiprocessor environment, spin waiting may be used in conjunction with the ceiling priority mechanism to implement a non-queued protected object lock.

By disallowing blocking within a protected operation and by also using the ceiling priority mechanism, unbounded priority inversion can be avoided. The generality that might be gained by allowing blocking would inevitably result in an increase in implementation complexity, run-time overhead, and unbounded priority inversion.

To simplify composability, protected operations may call other non-blocking protected operations (protected procedures and functions). A direct call on a protected subprogram within the same protected type does not start a new protected action, but is rather considered to be part of the current action. It is considered an error if, through a chain of calls going outside the protected object, a call is made back to the same protected object. The effect is implementation-defined, but will generally result in a deadlock. We considered disallowing all subprogram calls from a protected operation to a subprogram defined outside the protected type, but this seemed unnecessarily constraining, and to severely limit composability.

9.1.1 Summary of Mechanism

Protected types provide a low-level, lightweight, data-oriented synchronization mechanism whose key features are

- A protected object has hidden components; these components are intended to be shared among multiple tasks. The protected operations of the protected object provide synchronized access to the components.

- Protected types have three kinds of protected operations: protected functions, protected procedures, and entries. Protected functions and protected procedures are known as protected subprograms.

- Protected procedures provide exclusive read-write access to the components. Protected functions, since they cannot change the components of the protected object, may be optimized to use a shared read-only lock.

- Protected entries also provide exclusive read-write access to the components, but in addition, they specify a barrier, which is a Boolean expression that generally depends on the components of the protected object. The Run-Time System ensures that the barrier is true before allowing a protected entry call to proceed.

- Each protected object has a conceptual lock associated with it. (This lock may sometimes be an actual one, or can instead be implemented using the ceiling priorities model, see the Real-Time Systems annex). At the start of a protected operation, the calling task seizes the lock. Evaluation of barriers, execution of protected operation bodies, and manipulation of entry queues (see below) are all done while the lock is held. On a multiprocessor, the intended implementation of locks uses busy waiting. (Other, more specialized algorithms, are allowed).

- There is a queue associated with each protected entry. Tasks wait in the queue until the entry's barrier becomes True. If the barrier is already True when the entry call first seizes the lock, then it is executed immediately; the queue is not used. While waiting in the queue, a task does not hold the lock.

- A requeue statement is allowed in an entry body (and an accept statement). The effect of this statement is to return the current caller back to the queue, or to place it on another, compatible, entry queue.

- Ceiling priorities may be associated with protected objects as described in the Real-Time Systems annex. The ceiling rules prevent the priority-inversion phenomenon, and ensure freedom from deadlocks on single-processor systems. For further details see Part Three of this rationale.

9.1.2 Examples of Use

Protected types combine high efficiency with generality and can be used as building blocks to support various common real-time paradigms. In this section we discuss three examples

- An implementation of indivisible counters showing how protected subprograms are used.

- An implementation of persistent signals showing how protected entries are used.

- A generic bounded buffer showing how protected types can be used within a generic package.

A non-generic form of the bounded buffer and an implementation of transient (broadcast) signals will be found in II.9. Examples of the use of the requeue mechanism are shown in 9.2.

We observe that protected types allow Ada 95 to support these and other real-time paradigms with a smaller overall change to the language than the alternative approach where each problem is solved with its own distinct feature.

In the following examples, we refer to the lock as an actual object with lock and release operations. This, of course, is not required, and is simply used for ease of presentation.

The first very simple example shows a counter that is shared among multiple tasks

```
protected Counter is
   procedure Increment(New_Value: out Positive);
private
   Data: Integer := 0;
end Counter;

protected body Counter is
   procedure Increment(New_Value: out Positive) is
   begin
      Data := Data + 1;
      New_Value := Data;
   end Increment;
end Counter;
```

The counter is initialized to zero. A task may increment it by calling the Increment procedure

```
Counter.Increment(New_Value => X);
```

If N tasks do this, each exactly once, they will each get a unique value in the range 1 to N. Note that without the synchronization provided by the protected type, multiple simultaneous executions of Increment might cause unpredictable results. With the protected type, a task that calls Increment will first seize the lock, thus preventing such simultaneous executions.

Since there are no entries in this example, there are no queues. The protected type consists, in essence, of a lock and the component Data.

If we want to define many Counter objects, we would change the above example to declare a protected type instead of a single protected object as follows

```
protected type Counter_Type is
   ... -- same as before
end Counter_Type;

Counter_1, Counter_2: Counter_Type; -- declare two counters

type Many is array (1 .. 1000) of Counter_Type;

X: Many;                            -- declare many counters
```

It is important to note that a lock is associated with each protected object and not with the type as a whole. Thus, each of the objects in the above example has its own lock, and the data in each is protected independently of the others.

This simple example has a short, bounded-time algorithm; all it does is increment the value and assign it to the out parameter. This is typical of the intended use of protected types. Because the locks might be implemented as busy-waits (at least on multiprocessors), it is unwise to write an algorithm that might hold a lock for a long or unknown amount of time. A common approach where extensive processing is required would be to just record the new state, under the protection of the lock, and do the actual processing outside the protected body.

The next example shows a persistent signal. In this example, tasks may wait for an event to occur. When the event occurs, some task whose job it is to notice the event will "signal" that the event has occurred. The signal causes exactly one waiting task to proceed. The signal is persistent in the sense that if there are no tasks waiting when the signal occurs, the signal persists until a task invokes a wait, which then consumes the signal and proceeds immediately. Multiple signals when no tasks are waiting are equivalent to just one signal.

It is interesting to note that persistent signals are isomorphic to binary semaphores; the wait operation corresponds to P, and the signal operation corresponds to V.

```
protected Event is
   entry Wait;           -- wait for the event to occur
   procedure Signal;     -- signal that the event has occurred.
private
   Occurred: Boolean := False;
end Event;

protected body Event is

   entry Wait when Occurred is
   begin
      Occurred := False; -- consume the signal
   end Wait;

   procedure Signal is
   begin
      Occurred := True;   -- set Wait barrier True
   end Signal;

end Event;
```

A task waits for the event by calling

```
Event.Wait;
```

and the signalling task notifies the happening of the event by

```
Event.Signal;
```

whereupon the waiting task will proceed.

There are two possibilities to be considered according to whether the call of Wait or the call of Signal occurs first.

If a call of Wait occurs first, the task will seize the lock, check the barrier, and find it to be False. Therefore, the task will add itself to the entry queue, and release the lock. A subsequent Signal will seize the lock and set the Occurred flag to True. Before releasing the lock, the signalling task will check the Wait entry queue. There is a task in it, and the barrier is now True, so the body of Wait will now be executed, setting the flag to False, and the waiting task released. Before releasing the lock, the process of checking entry queues and barriers is repeated. This time, the Wait barrier is False, so nothing happens; the lock is released, and the signalling task goes on its way.

If, on the other hand, a call of Signal occurs first, then the task will seize the lock, set the flag to True, find nothing in the entry queues, and release the lock. A subsequent Wait will seize the lock, find the barrier to be True already, and proceed immediately with its body. The barrier is now False, so the waiting task will simply release the lock and proceed.

Important things to note are

- Protected subprograms do not have barriers. Protected entries always have barriers. Signal is a protected procedure, because it never needs to block while waiting for the state of the protected type to change; that is, it needs no barrier. Wait is an entry, because it needs to block until the flag is set before proceeding.

- The protected entry queues are not used for tasks waiting for access to the protected data. They are used for tasks waiting for an entry barrier to become true; that is, they are waiting for the state of the protected type to change in order to satisfy some user-specified condition. The lock associated with the protected object synchronizes access to the shared data. The same lock also protects the entry queues themselves; the queues may be considered as part of the shared data.

• Barriers are associated with entry queues, not with individual tasks calling the entries. Therefore, the number of barriers to be evaluated can never be more than the number of entries of the protected object. (Note that the size of an entry family can depend on a discriminant, so the number of entries can vary from object to object of the type.)

• Entry barriers are reevaluated only at well-defined points: in particular, when a call is first made and when a protected procedure or entry associated with that protected object has just finished, but before it has released the lock.

• Protected functions do not change the state of the protected type, and so should not change barrier values. Therefore, entry barriers are not reevaluated when a protected function has just finished.

• The lock stays locked during the actions that happen at the end of a protected procedure or entry (that is, checking the queues for non-empty status, evaluating barriers, removing a task from a queue, and executing the entry body). This means that tasks already on the queues get preference over tasks that are trying to seize the lock.

• Barriers, like protected operation bodies, should contain only short, bounded-time expressions. In typical examples, the barrier simply tests a `Boolean` flag, or checks the number of elements in an entry queue. The programmer has complete control over worst-case waiting times; this worst-case analysis can be done by inspecting the algorithms in the protected bodies, the barriers, and the maximum number of tasks that can be expected to be waiting on each barrier.

• The language does not specify which task executes a particular barrier or entry body. One can think of barriers and entry bodies as being executed by the Run-Time System, not by any particular task. Certain restrictions on what may appear in a barrier or an entry body imply that it does not matter which task does the work. (For example, `Current_Task` cannot be called, see Systems Programming annex.) This is done to ensure that no context switches are required; when one task finishes executing an operation, the task can immediately execute any others that have become ready, without having to switch to the context of the "correct" task.

Our next example is a generic form of a bounded buffer. In this example a protected object provides conditional critical regions, which allow the abstraction to be used safely by multiple tasks.

```
generic
    type Item is private;
    Mbox_Size: in Natural;
package Mailbox_Pkg is

    type Item_Count is range 0 .. Mbox_Size;
    type Item_Index is range 1 .. Mbox_Size;
    type Item_Array is array (Item_Index) of Item;

    protected type Mailbox is
        -- put a data element into the buffer
        entry Send(Elem: Item);
        -- retrieve a data element from the buffer
```

```
    entry Receive(Elem: out Item);
private
    Count     : Item_Count := 0;
    Out_Index: Item_Index := 1;
    In_Index : Item_Index := 1;
    Data      : Item_Array;
end Mailbox;

end Mailbox_Pkg;
```

This example illustrates a generic mailbox abstraction. The protected type has two entries, which insert and retrieve items to and from the mailbox buffer. Like a private type, the data components of the protected type are of no concern outside the body. They are declared in the specification so that a compiler can statically allocate all the space required for an instance of the protected type.

The body of the mailbox package is as follows

```
package body Mailbox_Pkg is
    protected body Mailbox is
        entry Send(Elem: Item) when Count < Mbox_Size is
            -- block until there is room in the mailbox
        begin
            Data(In_Index) := Elem;
            In_Index := In_Index mod Mbox_Size + 1;
            Count := Count + 1;
        end Send;

        entry Receive(Elem: out Item) when Count > 0 is
            -- block until there is something in the mailbox
        begin
            Elem := Data(Out_Index);
            Out_Index := Out_Index mod Mbox_Size + 1;
            Count := Count - 1;
        end Receive;
    end Mailbox;
end Mailbox_Pkg;
```

As we saw in the non-generic example in II.9, Send waits until there is room for a new Item in the mailbox buffer. Receive waits until there is at least one Item in the buffer. The semantics of protected records guarantee that multiple tasks cannot modify the contents of the mailbox simultaneously.

A minor point is that the type Item_Array has to be declared outside the protected type. This is because type declarations are not allowed inside a protected type which generally follows the same rules as records. Allowing types within types would have introduced additional complexity with little benefit. For elegance we have also declared the types Item_Count and Item_Index.

9.1.3 Efficiency of Protected Types

Protected types provide an extremely efficient mechanism; the ability to use the thread of control of one task to execute a protected operation on behalf of another task reduces the overhead of context switching compared with other paradigms. Protected types are thus not only much more efficient than the use of an agent task and associated rendezvous, they are also more efficient than traditional monitors or semaphores in many circumstances.

As an example consider the following very simple protected object which implements a single buffer between a producer and a consumer task.

```
protected Buffer is
    entry Put(X: in Item);
    entry Get(X: out Item);
private
    Data: Item;
    Full: Boolean := False;
end;

protected body Buffer is
    entry Put(X: in Item) when not Full is
    begin
        Data := X;   Full := True;
    end Put;

    entry Get(X: out Item) when Full is
    begin
        X := Data;   Full := False;
    end Get;
end Buffer;
```

This object can contain just a single buffered value of the type Item in the variable Data; the boolean Full indicates whether or not the buffer contains a value. The barriers ensure that reading and writing of the variable is interleaved so that each value is only used once. The buffer is initially empty so that the first call that will be processed will be of Put.

A producer and consumer task might be

```
task body Producer is
begin
    loop
        ... -- generate a value
        Buffer.Put(New_Item);
    end loop;
end Producer;

task body Consumer is
begin
    loop
        Buffer.Get(An_Item);
        ... -- use a value
    end loop;
end Consumer;
```

In order to focus the discussion we will assume that both tasks have the same priority and that a run until blocked scheduling algorithm is used on a single processor. We will also start by giving the processor to the task Consumer.

The task Consumer will issue a call of Get, acquire the lock and then find that the barrier is false thereby causing it to be queued and to release the lock. The Consumer is thus blocked and so a context switch occurs and control passes to the task Producer. This sequence of actions can be symbolically described by

```
Get(An_Item);
    lock
        queue
    unlock
switch context
```

The task Producer issues a first call of Put, acquires the lock, successfully executes the body of Put thereby filling the buffer and setting Full to False. Before releasing the lock, it reevaluates the barriers and checks the queues to see whether a suspended operation can now be performed. It finds that it can and executes the body of the entry Get thereby emptying the buffer and causing the task Consumer to be marked as no longer blocked and thus eligible for processing. Note that the thread of control of the producer has effectively performed the call of Get on behalf of the consumer task; the overhead for doing this is essentially that of a subprogram call and a full context switch is not required. This completes the sequence of protected actions and the lock is released.

However, the task Producer still has the processor and so it cycles around its loop and issues a second call of Put. It acquires the lock again, executes the body of Put thereby filling the buffer again. Before releasing the lock it checks the barriers but of course no task is queued and so nothing else can be done; it therefore releases the lock.

The task Producer still has the processor and so it cycles around its loop and issues yet a third call of Put. It acquires the lock but this time it finds the barrier is false since the buffer is already full. It is therefore queued and releases the lock. The producer task is now blocked and so a context switch occurs and control at last passes to the consumer task. The full sequence of actions performed by the producer while it had the processor are

```
Put(New_Item);
    lock
        Data := New_Item;   Full := True;
        scan: and then on behalf of Consumer
        An_Item := Data;   Full := False;
        set Consumer ready
    unlock
Put(New_Item);
    lock
        Data := New_Item:   Full := True;
        scan: nothing to do
    unlock
Put(New_Item);
    lock
        queue
    unlock
switch context
```

The consumer task now performs a similar cycle of actions before control passes back to the producer and the whole pattern then repeats. The net result is that three calls of Put or Get are performed between each full context switch and that each call of Put or Get involves just one lock operation.

This should be contrasted with the sequence required by the corresponding program using primitive operations such as binary semaphores (mutexes). This could be represented by

```
package Buffer is
    procedure Put(X: in Item);
    procedure Get(X: out Item);
private
    Data: Item;
    Full: Semaphore := busy;
    Empty: Semaphore := free;
end;

package body Buffer is
    procedure Put(X: in Item) is
    begin
        P(Empty);
```

```
      Data := X;
      V(Full);
   end Put;

   procedure Get(X: out Item) is
   begin
      P(Full);
      X := Data;
      V(Empty);
   end Get;
end Buffer;
```

In this case there are two lock operations for each call of Put and Get, one for each associated semaphore action. The behavior is now as follows (assuming once more that the consumer has the processor initially). The first call of Get by the consumer results in the consumer being suspended by P(Full) and a context switch to the producer occurs.

The first call of Put by the producer is successful, the buffer is filled and the operation V(Full) clears the semaphore upon which the consumer is waiting. The second call of Put is however blocked by P(Empty) and so a context switch to the consumer occurs. The consumer is now free to proceed and empties the buffer and performs V(Empty) to clear the semaphore upon which the producer is waiting. The next call of Get by the consumer is blocked by P(Full) and so a context switch back to the producer occurs.

The net result is that a context switch occurs for each call of Put or Get. This contrasts markedly with the behavior of the protected object where a context switch occurs for every three calls of Put or Get.

In conclusion we see that the protected object is much more efficient than a semaphore approach. In this example it as a factor of three better regarding context switches and a factor of two better regarding locks.

Observe that the saving in context switching overhead depends to some degree on the run-until-blocked scheduling and on the producer and consumer being of the same priority. However, the saving on lock and unlock overheads is largely independent of scheduling issues.

The interested reader should also consult [Hilzer 92] which considers the more general bounded buffer and shows that monitors are even worse than semaphores with regard to potential context switches.

9.1.4 Relationship with Previous Work

Protected types are related to two other synchronization primitives: the conditional critical region and the monitor. The protected type has been incorporated in a way that is compatible with Ada's existing task types, entries, procedures and functions.

In 1973, Hoare proposed a synchronization primitive called a conditional critical region [Hoare 73] with the following syntax

```
region V when barrier do
   statements
end;
```

where the barrier is a Boolean expression, and V is a variable. The semantics of the construction may be described as follows [Brinch-Hansen 73]:

> When the sender enters this conditional critical region, the [barrier expression] is evaluated. If the expression is true the sender completes the execution of the critical region ... But if the expression is false, the sender leaves the critical

region temporarily and enters an anonymous queue associated with the shared variable V.

However, Brinch-Hansen pointed out a disadvantage with conditional critical regions [Brinch-Hansen 73]:

Although [conditional critical regions] are simple and well-structured, they do not seem to be adequate for the design of large multiprogramming systems (such as operating systems). The main problem is that the use of critical regions scattered throughout a program makes it difficult to keep track of how a shared variable is used by concurrent processes. It has therefore been recently suggested that one should combine a shared variable and the possible operations on it in a single, syntactic construct called a monitor.

This thus led to the monitor which has a collection of data and subprogram declarations. In Ada terms, the subprograms declared in the visible part of a monitor, and which are therefore visible outside the monitor, are guaranteed to have exclusive access to the data internal to the monitor. The monitor may also have some variables known as condition variables. These condition variables are like semaphores, in that they have Wait and Signal operations. A Wait operation waits for a matching Signal operation. Hoare introduces monitors with somewhat different syntax, but with equivalent semantics [Hoare 74].

The problem with monitors as discussed in [IBFW 86] is that the Signal and Wait operations suffer from the usual difficulties of using semaphores; they can easily be misused and the underlying conditions are not easy to prove correct.

The Ada 83 rendezvous followed CSP [Hoare 78] by providing a dynamic approach to the problem and one which clarified the guarding conditions. However, as we have discussed, the rendezvous has a heavy implementation overhead through the introduction of an intermediary task and can also suffer from race conditions.

Ada 95 protected objects are an amalgam of the best features of conditional critical regions and monitors: they collect all the data and operations together, like monitors, and yet they have barriers, like conditional critical regions. The barriers describe the required state that must exist before an operation can be performed in a clear manner which aids program proof and understanding. Protected objects are very similar to the shared objects of the Orca language developed by Bal, Kaashoek and Tanenbaum [Bal 92].

9.2 The Requeue Statement

Components such as complex servers or user-defined schedulers often need to determine the order and the timing of the service provided by entry or accept bodies based on the values of various controlling items. These items may be local to the server and dependent on its own state, be an attribute of the client or the controlled task, or be global to the system. In addition, these items may often change from the time the entry call is made to the time the selection decision is itself finally made.

For fairly simple cases — that is when the items are known to the caller, do not change from the time of call, and have a relatively small discrete range — the entry family facility of Ada 83 might suffice (see [Wellings 84], [Burger 87], [Burns 87]). However, when those restrictions do not hold, a more powerful mechanism is often needed.

Entry queue selection is sometimes called preference control. Many papers discussing preference control have appeared in the literature [Elrad 88, Wellings 84, Burns 89]. Preference control arises in applications like resource allocation servers, which typically grant satisfiable requests and queue up unsatisfiable requests for later servicing. Wellings, Keefe and Tomlinson [Wellings 84] were unable to find a good way to implement such servers in Ada 83.

An intrinsic provision within a language of the full expressive power to describe the various forms of preference controls would require an elaborate semantic structure and a complex (and potentially large) run-time support system.

Instead, we have chosen to provide a single and simple statement in Ada 95 which allows the programmer to construct the desired control algorithms based on the balance of needs of specific applications. This is the requeue statement and as we saw in Part One, it enables an entry call to be requeued on another or even the same entry.

In order for the server to gain access to the caller's parameters there is no need to resume the caller and to require it to initiate another entry call based on the results of the first; it may simply be moved to another entry queue. An alternate approach that was considered required the caller to first query the state of the server, and then to initiate an entry call with appropriate parameters (presumably using a specific family member index) to reflect the server's state. This approach suffers from the potential of race conditions, since no atomicity is guaranteed between the two calls (another caller may be serviced and the state of the server may be changed), so the validity of the second request which is based on the first, may be lost.

In the case of protected entry calls, exclusive access is maintained throughout the period of examining the parameters and doing the requeue; in the case of accept bodies, the server task controls its own state and since it can refuse to accept any intermediate calls, the atomicity is also maintained.

The requeue statement may be specified as **with abort**. In Ada 83, after a rendezvous had started, there was no way for the caller to cancel the request (or for a time-out to take effect — a time-out request is present only until the acceptor *starts* the service). There was, of course, good reason for this behavior; after the service has commenced, the server is in a temporary state, and removing the caller asynchronously can invalidate its internal data structures. In addition, because of by-reference parameters, the acceptor must maintain its ability to access the caller's data areas (such as the stack). If the caller "disappears", this might result in dangling references and consequent disaster.

However, in some cases, deferring the cancellation of a call is unacceptable, in particular when the time-out value is needed to control the amount of time until the service is completed (as opposed to just started). With the addition of asynchronous transfer of control to Ada 95, the same situation can arise if the caller is "interrupted" and must change its flow of control as soon as possible.

Since there is not a single best approach for all applications, and since no easy work-around exists, the **with abort** is provided to allow the programmer to choose the appropriate mechanism for the application concerned. In general, when cancellation during a requeue is to be allowed, the server will "checkpoint" its data-structures before issuing requeue **with abort**, in such a way that if the caller is removed from the second queue, the server can continue to operate normally. When this is not possible, or when the cancellation during a requeue is not required, a simple requeue will suffice, and will hold the caller until the service is fully completed.

The requeue statement is designed to handle two main situations

•   After an accept statement or entry body begins execution, it may be determined that the request cannot be satisfied immediately. Instead, there is a need to requeue the caller until the request can be handled.

•   Alternatively, part of the request may be handled immediately, but there may be additional steps in the process that need to be performed at a later point.

In both cases, the accept statement or entry body needs to relinquish control so that other callers may be handled or other processing may be performed; the requeue enables the original request to be processed in two or more parts.

The requeue statement allows a caller to be "requeued" on the queue of the same or some other entry. The caller need not be aware of the requeue and indeed the number of steps required to handle a given operation need not be visible outside the task or protected type. The net effect is that the server can be more flexible, while presenting a simple single interface to the client.

As part of the requeue, the parameters are neither respecified nor reevaluated. Instead, the parameters are carried over to the new call directly. If a new parameter list were specifiable, then it might include references to data local to the accept statement or entry body itself. This would cause problems because the accept statement or entry body is completed as a consequence of the requeue and its local variables are thus deallocated. Subtype conformance is thus required between the new target entry (if it has any parameters) and the current entry. This allows the same representation to be used for the new set of parameters whether they are by-copy or by-reference and also eliminates the need to allocate new space to hold the parameters. Note that the only possibility other than passing on exactly the same parameters is that the requeued call requires no parameters at all.

As a first example of requeue, the reader is invited to look once more at the example of the broadcast signal which we first met in II.9 and which we now repeat for convenience.

As in the previous signal example in 9.1.2, tasks wait for an event to occur. However, this is a broadcast signal because when the event is signaled, all waiting tasks are released, not just one. After releasing them, the event reverts to its original state, so tasks can wait again, until another signal. Note also, that unlike the previous example, the event here is not persistent. If no tasks are waiting when the signal arrives, it is lost.

```
protected Event is
    entry Wait;
    entry Signal;
private
    entry Reset;
    Occurred: Boolean := False;
end Event;

protected body Event is

    entry Wait when Occurred is
    begin
        null;              -- note null body
    end Wait;

    entry Signal when True is   -- barrier is always true
    begin
        if Wait'Count > 0 then
            Occurred := True;
            requeue Reset;
        end if;
    end Signal;

    entry Reset when Wait'count = 0 is
    begin
        Occurred := False;
    end Reset;

end Event;
```

The intended use is that tasks wait for the event by calling

```
Event.Wait;
```

and another task notifies them that the event has occurred by calling

```
Event.Signal;
```

and this causes all currently waiting tasks to continue, and the event to be reset, so that future calls to Event.Wait will wait.

The example works as follows. If a task calls Event.Wait, it will first seize the protected object lock. It will check Occurred, find it to be False, add itself to the entry queue, and release the lock. Several tasks might add themselves to the queue in this manner.

Later, the signalling task might call Event.Signal. After seizing the lock, the task will execute the entry body (since its barrier is True). If no tasks are currently waiting, the task exits without updating the flag. Otherwise, it sets the flag to indicate that the event has occurred, and requeues itself on the Reset entry. (Reset is declared in the private part, because it is not intended to be used directly by clients of the protected object.)

Before releasing the lock, the signalling task will check the queues. The barrier for Wait is now True. A task is chosen from the Wait queue, and allowed to proceed. Since the entry body for Wait does nothing, the flag will not change. (See the Real-Time Systems annex for the detailed rules for choosing among the tasks waiting in entry queues.) This sequence of events will be repeated until the entry queue for Wait is empty. When the Wait queue is finally empty (that is Wait'Count equals 0), the barrier of Reset is True, and the Reset body is executed, thereby resetting the flag. The queues are now empty, so the protected object lock is released. Note that implementations can optimize null entry bodies by releasing waiting tasks in one operation, when the barrier is true.

Because the steps described in the last two paragraphs are executed with the protected object locked, any other tasks that try to Wait or Signal on that object during that time will have to wait for the queues to be emptied, as explained above. Furthermore, there are no race conditions because the value of the barrier cannot be changed between the time it is evaluated and the time the corresponding entry body is executed.

The check for now-true barriers happens whenever the state of the protected object might have changed and, of course, before releasing the lock; that is, they happen just after executing the body of a protected procedure or protected entry.

In summary

• A requeue statement is only allowed in an entry body and an accept statement. The target entry may be (possibly the same entry) in the same task or protected object or in a different task or protected object. All combinations are possible.

• Any actual parameters to the original call are passed to the new entry; therefore, the new entry must have the same parameter profile, or else no parameters at all.

In the broadcast example, the requeue statement prevents a race condition that might otherwise occur. For example, if the signalling task were required to call Signal and Reset in sequence, then the releasing of waiting tasks would no longer be atomic. A task that tried to Wait in between the two calls of the signalling task, might have been released as well. It might even be the same task that was already released once by that Signal.

We noted in Part One that this example was for illustration only and could be programmed without using requeue. Here is a possible solution which uses the Count attribute in barriers for both Wait and Signal.

```
protected Event is
   entry Wait;
   entry Signal;
end Event;

protected body Event is
   entry Wait when Signal'Count > 0 is
   begin
      null;
   end Wait;
```

```
entry Signal when Wait'Count = 0 is
begin
   null;
end Signal;
end Event;
```

When the Wait entry is called, the caller will be blocked until some caller is enqueued on the Signal entry queue. When the Signal entry is called, the caller is queued if there are any waiters, then all the tasks on the Wait entry queue are resumed. The signaler is then dequeued and the entry call is complete. If there are no waiters when Signal is called, it returns immediately.

This is an interesting solution. It works because the event of joining a queue is a protected action and results in the evaluation of barriers (just as they are evaluated when a protected procedure or entry body finishes). Note also that there is no protected data (and hence no private part) and that both entry bodies are null); in essence the protected data is the Count attributes and these therefore behave properly. In contrast, the Count attributes of task entries are not reliable because the actions of adding and joining task entry queues are not performed in any protected manner.

9.2.1 Preference Control

Many real-time applications require preference control, where the ability to satisfy a request depends on the parameters passed in by the calling task and often also on the internal state of the server. Examples are

•   The server must serve higher-priority requests first, where the priority of the request is passed as an entry parameter.

•   A particular entry call is used to request any of several resources, where some resources might be available, while others are in use. An entry parameter indicates which of the resources the task is requesting.

•   Several copies of a resource may be allocated at once, where the calling task passes in the number of required resources. A specific instance of this situation is a memory allocator, where the resource is a block of storage units. The calling task asks for a particular number of storage units, and must wait until a contiguous portion of memory of at least the right size is available. It might be that a request for 100 storage units can be satisfied, whereas a request for 1000 storage units cannot.

•   The server is controlling a device that might be ready to serve some requests but not others.

We now consider an example of the last situation. We have a disk device with a head that may be moved to different tracks. When a calling task wants to write to the disk at a particular place, the call may proceed immediately if the disk head is already on the right track. Otherwise, the disk manager tells the disk device to move the head. When the disk has moved the head, it generates an interrupt. While waiting for the interrupt, the calling task is blocked.

Preference control can be implemented in Ada 95 using the requeue statement. The entry call proceeds whether it can be immediately satisfied or not. Then the server checks to see whether the request can be immediately satisfied by looking at the parameters. If it can, the request is processed, and the entry returns. If not, the request is requeued to another entry, to wait until conditions change.

The preference control in our example is simple. We can satisfy requests for the current disk track, and queue the others. Since the disk address is passed in as an entry parameter, some calls to the Write entry can proceed, while others cannot.

```
protected Disk_Manager is
    entry Write(Where: Disk_Address; Data: Disk_Buffer);
        -- write data to the disk at the specified address
    entry Read(Where: Disk_Address; Data: out Disk_Buffer);
        -- read data from the disk at the specified address
    procedure Disk_Interrupt;
        -- called when the disk has interrupted, indicating
        -- that the disk head has moved to the correct track
private
    entry Pending_Write(Where: Disk_Address; Data: Disk_Buffer);
    entry Pending_Read(Where: Disk_Address; Data: out Disk_Buffer);

    Current_Disk_Track: Disk_Track_Address := ...;
        -- track where the disk head currently is.
    Operation_Pending: Boolean := False;
        -- is an incomplete Read or Write operation pending?
    Disk_Interrupted: Boolean := False;
        -- has the disk responded to the move command with
        -- an interrupt?
end Disk_Manager;
```

In order to write on the disk, a task calls Disk_Manager.Write, passing the disk address and data as parameters. The Read operation is similar but the full details are omitted. The body of the protected object is as follows

```
protected body Disk_Manager is

    procedure Disk_Interrupt is
    begin
        Disk_Interrupted := True;   -- release pending operations
    end Disk_Interrupt;

    entry Pending_Write(Where: Disk_Address; Data: Disk_Buffer)
        when Disk_Interrupted is
    begin
        Current_Disk_Track := Where.Track;
            -- we know that the disk head is at the right track.
        ... -- write Data to the disk
        Operation_Pending := False;
            -- allow Reads and Writes to proceed
    end Pending_Write;

    entry Write(Where: Disk_Address; Data: Disk_Buffer)
        when not Operation_Pending is
    begin
        if Where.Track = Current_Disk_Track then
            ... -- write Data to the disk
        else
            ... -- tell the disk to move to the right track
            Disk_Interrupted := False;
            Operation_Pending := True;
                -- prevent further Reads and Writes
            requeue Pending_Write; -- wait for the interrupt
        end if;
    end Write;
```

```
entry Pending_Read(Where: Disk_Address; Data: out Disk_Buffer)
   when Disk_Interrupted is
begin
   ... -- similar to Pending_Write
end Pending_Read;

entry Read(Where: Disk_Address; Data: out Disk_Buffer)
   when not Operation_Pending is
begin
   ... -- similar to Write
end Read;

end Disk_Manager;
```

The Write operation checks whether the disk head is already on the right track. If so, it writes the data and returns. If not, it sends a command to the disk telling it to move the head to the right track, and then requeues the caller on Pending_Write. It sets a flag to prevent intervening Write and Read operations. When the disk has completed the move-head command, it interrupts, causing the Disk_Interrupt operation to be invoked. The Disk_Interrupt operation sets the flag that allows the Pending_Write operation to proceed.

We do not specify here how Disk_Interrupt gets called when the interrupt occurs. It might be attached directly to the interrupt, or some other interrupt handler might call it or set a flag in some other protected object that causes Disk_Interrupt to be called.

A real disk manager would be more complicated; it would probably allow multiple pending requests, sorted by track number, the actual reading and writing might be interrupt driven (in addition to the disk head movement), and so on. But this simple version nevertheless illustrates the key features of preference control.

The following points should be noted

- One might think that an obvious way to implement preference control would be to make the entry barrier depend on the parameters of the entry. However, that is not allowed in order to permit efficient implementations and to avoid complex semantics for the user. Because the barriers do not depend on the formal parameters, the value of the barrier is the same for all callers of the same entry. This means that there is only one barrier value per entry, not one per entry call, so evaluation of barriers can be efficient. If the barrier expression can be evaluated in a bounded amount of time, as is usually the case, the programmer can calculate total worst-case barrier evaluation times based on the worst-case barrier evaluation times of each of the entries.

- It is important that the decisions of when to service a request happen inside a protected operation, because these decisions are based on the protected object's local data, which, of course must be protected. The Ada 95 requeue mechanism achieves such protection.

- The example works properly in the presence of abort and asynchronous transfer of control. For example, if a writing task is aborted while it is waiting on the Pending_Write queue, the abort will be deferred until after Pending_Write has been executed. On the other hand, the programmer might wish to allow the task to be aborted earlier. In that case, the requeue statement would take the form

```
requeue Pending_Write with abort;
```

and then the protected body would have to be written in such a way that callers can silently disappear from the Pending_Write queue without disruption. (The barriers would have to depend upon Pending_Write'Count.)

• In Ada 83, an extra "agent" task was required to "hold" the call in examples such as this. In order to correctly handle abort and asynchronous transfer of control, and still handle multiple outstanding requests, the agent tasks had to be created dynamically, as necessary. Such agent tasks were too expensive for many applications, and their timing behavior was rather unpredictable.

• Other methods in Ada 83 required exporting several entries that had to be called in a particular order. This violated information-hiding principles, and caused race conditions, because events could occur between the multiple calls.

The information-hiding objection could be answered by putting the task in a package, and putting the correct pattern of entry calls in a procedure exported from the package, thus enforcing the required protocol. But then, the resulting exported procedure could not be used in timed, conditional, and selective entry calls.

Other solutions to the race problems generally required the requesting task to poll the server, which was inefficient and nondeterministic, in addition to being error-prone.

9.3 Timing

Ada 83 was unhelpful in the area of timing by notionally providing only one clock that could be used directly for delaying a task or timing an operation. Furthermore, the Ada 83 delay statement required a duration, rather than a wakeup time, making it difficult for a task to wake up at perfectly regular intervals as explained in II.10.

In Ada 95, the delay statement is augmented by a delay until statement. The delay until statement takes the wakeup time rather than a duration as its argument. Furthermore, the Real-Time Systems annex defines the package Ada.Real_Time which contains an additional time type Real_Time.Time with an accompanying function Real_Time.Clock, which may be used in a delay until statement.

The type Real_Time.Time is intended to represent a real-time clock with potentially finer granularity than the time-of-day clock associated with Calendar.Time. Furthermore, the value returned by Real_Time.Clock is guaranteed to be monotonically non-decreasing, whereas the time-of-day Calendar.Clock may jump forward or backward due to resetting of the time by a human operator (perhaps in response to a change of time-zone or daylight saving).

The following example shows a task that awakens each night at midnight and performs some logging function.

```
task body At_Midnight is
    One_Day : constant Calendar.Day_Duration := 86_400.0;
    Now     : Calendar.Time := Calendar.Clock;
    Midnight: Calendar.Time := Calendar.Time_Of(
        Year    => Calendar.Year(Now),
        Month   => Calendar.Month(Now),
        Day     => Calendar.Day(Now),
        Seconds => 0.0);
            -- truncate current time to most recent midnight
begin
    loop
        Midnight := Midnight + One_Day;
        delay until Midnight;
```

```
        Log_Data;
    end loop;
end At_Midnight;
```

Since the delay until expression specifies an absolute time rather than a time interval, there is no opportunity for preemption during the calculation of the interval, and therefore the delay will expire at precisely the time that is specified.

Note furthermore that since the delay is written in terms of the time-of-day clock in the package Calendar, if the time-of-day clock is changed to daylight saving time (or perhaps the cruise liner moves over a time zone), the delay expiration time might be according to the new setting of the clock (although this is not guaranteed).

As a further example we present a task that polls a device every 10 milliseconds.

```
task body Poll_Device is
    use Ada;
    Poll_Time: Real_Time.Time := time to start polling;
    Period: constant Real_Time.Time_Span :=
                            Real_Time.Milliseconds(10);
begin
    loop
        delay until Poll_Time;
        ... -- Poll the device
        Poll_Time := Poll_Time + Period;
    end loop;
end Poll_Device;
```

In this case the Poll_Device task polls the device every 10 milliseconds starting at the initial value of Poll_Time. The period will not drift, as explained above for the At_Midnight example. We use Real_Time.Time instead of Calendar.Time in this example, because we do not wish to be sensitive to possible changes to the time-of-day clock.

The existing (relative) delay statement only takes a value of the type Duration; the basis for relative delays is not necessarily that of the clock in the package Calendar and should be monotonic. The general idea is that relative delays should not be disturbed by a shift in the time base. A ten minute delay still means just that even if the clock moves forward.

Finally note that in Ada 95 the package Calendar is a child of Ada. For compatibility it is also renamed as Standard.Calendar (all such existing library units in Ada 83 are similarly renamed for compatibility).

9.4 Asynchronous Transfer of Control

Asynchronous transfer of control was identified as an important requirement for Ada 95 (Requirement R5.3-A(1)). In Ada 83, the only way to asynchronously change the execution path of a task was to abort it. However, in many applications, it is desirable that an external event be able to cause a task to begin execution at a new point, without the task as a whole being aborted and restarted.

As an example of asynchronous transfer of control, consider an interactive program where the user may choose to terminate a given operation and begin a new one. This is normally signaled by typing a special key or hitting a special button associated with the controlling input device. The user does not want the entire context of the running program to be lost. Furthermore, for a long-running system, it is important that the resources associated with the interrupted processing be reclaimed. This implies that some mechanism for "cleaning up" be available as part of the asynchronous transfer process. Finally, if the abortable operation is updating some global data structure, it is essential to temporarily defer any asynchronous transfers until after the update is complete.

As was briefly explained in II.10, Ada 95 has a form of select statement with an abortable part and a triggering alternative to support asynchronous transfer of control. We showed a simple example where a computation was abandoned if it could not be completed within a stated period of time.

In essence the triggering statement and the abortable part execute in parallel and whichever finishes first causes the other to be abandoned.

If the triggering statement completes before the abortable part, then the abortable part is abandoned and control passes to the sequence of statements following the triggering statement. On the other hand, if the abortable part completes before the triggering statement then the triggering alternative is abandoned.

The important point is that we only need one thread of control. Waiting for a delay or waiting on an entry queue do not require a separate thread. Moreover, when a task entry is accepted it is the called task which executes the accept statement and even in the case of a protected entry it will often be another task which executes the entry body. So the abortable part can generally continue during the execution of the triggering statement. It is only when the entry call finally returns (or the delay expires) that the abortable part has to be abandoned. For full details of the mechanism see [RM95 9.7.4].

By supporting asynchronous transfer of control as a form of select statement, several useful properties are provided

- The statements that are abortable are clearly bracketed in the abortable part.

- The asynchronous transfer of control is directly tied to the acceptance of an entry call or the expiration of a delay. This allows the transfer to occur without requiring an additional task to explicitly signal the occurrence of the triggering event; this is in contrast to what is possible with abort.

- Nesting of abortable regions (which are potentially "sensitive" to different events) and protecting code in these regions from interruption, is naturally achieved by the select construct and protected types.

- The asynchronous transfer cannot be mistakenly redirected by a local handler, as might happen with a mechanism based on asynchronous exceptions.

Here is an example of a database transaction using asynchronous transfer of control. The database operation may be cancelled by typing a special key on the input device. However, once the transaction has begun (is committed), the operation may not be cancelled.

```
with Ada.Finalization; use Ada;
package Txn_Pkg is
   type Txn_Status is (Incomplete, Failed, Succeeded);
   type Transaction is new Finalization.Limited_Controlled with
      private;
   -- Transaction is a controlled type as discussed in 7.4
   procedure Finalize(Txn: in out Transaction);
   procedure Set_Status(Txn: in out Transaction;
                        Status: Txn_Status);
private
   type Transaction is new Finalization.Limited_Controlled with
      record
         Status: Txn_Status := Incomplete;
         pragma Atomic (Status);
         ... -- More components
      end record;
end Txn_Pkg;
```

```ada
package body Txn_Pkg is

   procedure Finalize(Txn: in out Transaction) is
   begin
      -- Finalization runs with abort and ATC deferred
      if Txn.Status = Succeeded then
         Commit(Txn);
      else
         Rollback(Txn);
      end if;
   end Finalize;

   procedure Set_Status(Txn: in out Transaction);
                        Status: Txn_Status) is
   begin
      Txn.Status := Status;
   end Set_Status;

end Txn_Pkg;
```

The package might be used as in the following

```ada
declare
    Database_Txn: Transaction;
     -- declare a transaction, will commit or abort
     -- during finalization
begin
   select
      -- wait for a cancel key from the input device
      Input_Device.Wait_For_Cancel;
       -- the Status remains Incomplete, so that
       -- the transaction will not commit
   then abort
      -- do the transaction
      Read(Database_Txn, ...);
      Write(Database_Txn, ...);
      ...
      Set_Status(Database_Txn, Succeeded);
      -- set status to ensure the transaction is committed
   exception
      when others =>
         Put_Line("Operation failed with unhandled exception");
         -- set status to cause transaction to be aborted
         Set_Status(Database_Txn, Failed);
   end select;
   -- Finalize on Database_Txn will be called here and,
   -- based on the recorded status, will either commit or
   -- abort the transaction.
end;
```

This illustrates the use of controlled types and asynchronous transfer of control. At the end of the block, the Finalize operation is called and this will uniquely either rollback the transaction or commit to it. Note in particular the use of the pragma Atomic; this is described in the Systems Programming annex. Note also that the Finalization is always performed with abort and ATC deferred so that no unfortunate interactions can occur.

The final example shows how asynchronous transfer of control can be used in a real-time application. Current_Coordinates is periodically updated with a new set of computed coordinates. A user task (not shown) can call Read as needed to get the most recently computed coordinates, which might then be used to control an external device.

```
protected Current_Coordinates is
    procedure Update(New_Val: Coordinates);
        -- used by the computing task only
    function Read return Coordinates;
        -- used by whoever needs the result
private
    Current_Value: Coordinates;
end Current_Coordinates;

protected Controller is
    entry Wait_For_Overrun;
        -- called by the computing task
    procedure Set_Overrun;
        -- called by an executive or interrupt handler
private
    Overrun_Occurred: Boolean := False;
end Controller;
```

The protected object Current_Coordinates provides mutually exclusive access to the most recently calculated coordinates. The protected object Controller provides an entry for detecting overruns, designed to be called in the triggering alternative of an asynchronous select statement as shown below.

The following is the body of the Calculate task, which loops, progressively improving the estimate of the coordinates, until its time allotment expires, or the estimate stabilizes.

```
task body Calculate is
    Problem: Problem_Defn;
begin
    Get_Problem(Problem);
    select
        Controller.Wait_For_Overrun;    -- triggering alternative
    then abort
        declare
            Answer: Coordinates := Initial_Value;
            Temp  : Coordinates;
        begin
            Current_Coordinates.Update(Answer);
            loop   -- loop until estimate stabilizes
                Temp := Answer;
                Track_Computation.Improve_Estimate(Problem, Answer);
                Current_Coordinates.Update(Answer);
                exit when Distance(Answer, Temp) <= Epsilon;
            end loop;
        end;
    end select;
end Calculate;
```

The Calculate task sets the value of the Current_Coordinates initially, and then repeatedly calls Track_Computation.Improve_Estimate, which is presumably a time-consuming procedure that calculates a better estimate of the coordinates. Calculate stops looping when it decides that the estimate has stabilized. However, it may be that Improve_Estimate takes too long, or the system undergoes a mode change that requires the use of the current best estimate. There is presumably an executive or interrupt handler that notices such a situation and calls Controller.Set_Overrun. When that happens, the Calculate task does an asynchronous transfer of control thereby ending the computation loop.

We now show a possible (partial) implementation of the Improve_Estimate subprogram. It depends on some work area that has a dynamic size, that can be allocated, lengthened, and deallocated. Improve_Estimate allocates the work area, and tries to compute the result. However, the computation of the result may fail, requiring a larger work area. Therefore, Improve_Estimate loops until it succeeds or the time expires or some resource is exhausted.

```
with Ada.Finalization; use Ada;
package body Track_Computation is
    -- This package includes a procedure Improve_Estimate for
    -- progressively calculating a better estimate of the coordinates.

    -- buffer is used for a work area to compute new coordinates
    type Buffer_Size is range 0 .. Max;
    type Buffer is ...
    type Buffer_Ptr is access Buffer;

    type Work_Area is new Finalization.Limited_Controlled with
        record
            Buf: Buffer_Ptr;
        end record;

    -- these procedures allocate a work area of a given size,
    -- and reallocate a longer work area
    procedure Allocate_Work_Area(
        Area: in out Work_Area;
        Size: in Buffer_Size) is ...
    procedure Lengthen_Work_Area(
        Area  : in out Work_Area;
        Amount: in Buffer_Size) is ...

    -- this procedure is called automatically on scope exit,
    -- and deallocates the buffer designated by Area.Buf
    procedure Finalize(Area: in out Work_Area) is ...

    procedure Improve_Estimate(
        Problem: in Problem_Defn;
        Answer : in out Coordinates) is
        -- calculate a better estimate, given the old estimate
        Initial_Size: Buffer_Size := Estimate_Size(Problem);
        -- compute expected work area size, based on problem definition
        Work_Buffer: Work_Area;
    begin
        Allocate_Work_Area(Work_Buffer, Initial_Size);
        loop
            begin
                ... -- compute better estimate
                Answer := ...;
                exit; -- computation succeeded
            exception
                when Work_Area_Too_Small =>
                    -- the Problem requires a larger work area
                    Lengthen_Work_Area(Work_Buffer, Size_Increment);
                    -- now loop around to try again
            end;
        end loop;
        -- Work_Buffer is automatically deallocated by
        -- finalization on exit from the scope
    end Improve_Estimate;
```

end Track_Computation;

Since it is important that the work area be deallocated when the asynchronous transfer of control occurs, Work_Area is derived from Finalization.Limited_Controlled so that a Finalize procedure can be defined. This provides automatic clean up on scope exit.

Note that the Calculate task does not (and should not) need to know about the implementation details of Improve_Estimate. Therefore, it is not feasible to put the call on Finalize(Work_Buffer) in Calculate. Furthermore, Allocate_Work_Area might not use a normal Ada allocator. It might be allocating from some static data structure. In any case, it is important to reclaim the resources allocated to the work area when the processing is complete or aborted.

Aborts and asynchronous transfers of control are deferred when a task is performing a protected subprogram or entry call, or during an initialization or finalization operation on an object of a controlled type. The programmer has complete control over the amount of code that should be placed in such abort-deferred regions. Typically, such regions should be kept short.

9.5 The Abort Statement

In Ada 95, it is essential that use of the abort statement, and, more importantly, the asynchronous select statement with its abortable part, not result in corruption of global data structures. In Ada 83, abort was deferred for a calling task while it was engaged in a rendezvous. This allowed the rendezvous to complete normally so that the data structures managed by the accepting task were not left in an indeterminate state just because one of its callers was aborted.

For Ada 95, we have generalized this deferral of abort to include the time during which calls on protected operations are being serviced, and the initialization, assignment and finalization of controlled types (see 7.4). (However, we recall that requeue with abort allows a server to override deferral if desired as explained in 9.2.)

Without deferral of abort, any update of a global data structure becomes extremely unsafe, if not impossible. Ultimately all updates are forced into a two-phase approach, where updates are first performed into unused storage, and then the final commitment of a change involves a single atomic store, typically of a pointer of some sort. Such an approach can be extremely cumbersome, and very inefficient for large data structures. In most cases, it is much simpler and efficient to selectively defer asynchronous transfers or aborts, rather than to allow them at any moment.

In addition to deferring abort, it is important to be able to reclaim resources allocated to constructs being aborted. The support for user-defined initialization and finalization of controlled types provides the primitives necessary to perform appropriate resource reclamation, even in the presence of abort and asynchronous transfers.

Reclaiming local storage resources is of course important. However, releasing resources is even more critical for a program involved in communicating with an external subsystem, such as a remote database or other server. For a short-lived program, running on a conventional time-shared operating system, with no contact with external subsystems, it might be argued that there is no need to provide user-defined finalization that runs even when the task is aborted or is "directed" to execute an asynchronous transfer of control. However, for a long-running program, with limited memory, and which is possibly communicating with external subsystems, it is crucial that relatively local events like an asynchronous transfer not undermine global resource management.

In general, the discussion in [RM95] is unified so that aborting a task and aborting a sequence of statements (as in ATC) are described together.

9.6 Tasking and Discriminants

In Ada 95, we have generalized discriminants so that they are applicable to task types and protected types as well as to records. This allows tasks and protected objects to be parameterized when they are declared.

An example of a protected type with a discriminant is the Counting_Semaphore in II.9. The discriminant indicates the number of items in the resource being guarded by the semaphore.

Discriminants of tasks can be used to set the priority, storage size and size of entry families of individual tasks of a type. In the case of storage size this is done with the new pragma Storage_Size by analogy with the pragma Priority. (Note that an attribute definition clause could only be applied to all tasks of a type; the use of such an attribute definition clause for setting the storage size is now obsolescent.)

Of more importance is the ability to indicate the data associated with a task; this obviates the need for an initial rendezvous with a task and can eliminate or at least reduce any bottleneck in the parallel activation of tasks.

For example, in a numerical application we might have an array of tasks each of which works on some data. In each case the data will be shared with an adjacent task and so can be conveniently accessed through a protected object. The tasks do not therefore need to communicate with each other directly but just with the protected objects. We might write

```ada
subtype Data_Range is Integer range 0 .. 1000;
subtype Task_Range is
      Data_Range range Data_Range'First+1 .. Data_Range'Last-1;

protected type Data_Point is
   procedure Put(New_Value: in Data);
   procedure Get(Current_Value: out Data);
private
   -- the protected data
end;
...
The_Data: array (Data_Range) of Data_Point;

function Next_One return Task_Range;
...
task type Computer(Index: Task_Range := Next_One);

The_Tasks: array (Task_Range) of Computer;
```

where we assume that the data at the end-points of the range is fixed (the boundary conditions) and so no task is associated with these.

Successive calls of the function Next_One deliver the unique values throughout the task range. This guarantees that each task has a unique value of the discriminant Index although this might not correspond to its index position in the array since the components can be initialized in any order. However, they are not permitted to be initialized in parallel and so there is no need for the function Next_One to take any action to prevent parallel calls. Each task can then use its discriminant Index to access the data in the protected objects.

An access discriminant is particularly useful for indicating the data associated with a task. We could write

```ada
type Task_Data is
   record
      ...   -- data for task to work on
   end record;

task type Worker(D: access Task_Data) is
```

```
   . . .
end;
```

and then inside the body of Worker we can get hold of the data via the access discriminant D. The data is associated with a particular task in its declaration

```
Data_For_Joe: aliased Task_Data := ...

Joe: Worker(Data_For_Joe'Access);
```

where we note that the data has to be marked as **aliased**. An advantage of access discriminants is that they are constants and cannot be detached from the task; hence the task and its data are securely bound together. We recall from 3.7.1 that there are consequently no access checks on the use of an access discriminant.

An alternative approach is to embed the task inside the data. We can then use the self-referential technique described in 4.6.3.

```
type Task_And_Data is limited
   record
      ... -- some data
      Jobber: Worker(Task_And_Data'Access);
   end record;
```

We can use similar techniques with protected objects. The data logically protected by a protected object need not be directly inside the protected object. It could be indicated by an access discriminant. For example

```
type Resource is
   record
      Counter: Integer;
      ...
   end record;

protected type Guardian(R: access Resource) is
   procedure Increment;
   ...
end Guardian;

protected body Guardian is
   procedure Increment is
   begin
      R.Counter := R.Counter + 1;
   end Increment;
   ...
end Guardian;
```

and then within the bodies of protected procedures such as Increment we can access the data of type Resource in a safe manner. We declare a particular protected object thus

```
My_Resource: aliased Resource := ...
..
My_Object: Guardian(My_Resource'Access);
...
My_Object.Increment;
```

Clearly this approach can be used with any standard protected object such as the mailbox discussed in 9.1.2.

9.6.1 Interaction with OOP

Tasks and protected objects may appear at first sight to be concerned with aspects of programming quite alien to the concepts associated with object oriented programming such as type extension and dispatching. For example, it is not possible to extend a protected type with additional protected operations (this was considered at conflict with other considerations such as efficiency). However, although indeed an orthogonal part of the language, tasks and protected objects work together with tagged types in a remarkable way. Thus we can create structures with both synchronization and extension properties where protected objects or tasks provide the synchronization aspects and tagged types provide extension aspects.

For example, a task or protected object may be a component of a tagged object or conversely may contain a tagged object internally. A powerful construction is where a task or protected object has a class-wide access discriminant that references a tagged object. In this section we give some examples of the use of access discriminants in this way.

The first example illustrates how a task type can provide a template for a variety of related activities with the details filled in with dispatching calls. (Remember from the discussion in 3.7.1 and 4.4.4 that type extension provides a flexible means of parameterizing a general activity such as the use of an iterator.)

Suppose that we wish to perform a number of activities that have the general pattern of performing some job a certain number of times at intervals with perhaps some initial and final actions as well. We can also make provision for a general purpose exception handling mechanism. A suitable task type might be

```ada
task type T(Job: access Job_Descriptor'Class);

task body T is
begin
    Start(Job);
    for I in 1 .. Iterations(Job) loop
        delay Interval(Job);
        Do_It(Job, I);
    end loop;
    Finish(Job);
exception
    when Event: others =>
        Handle_Failure(Job, Event);
end T;
```

Note carefully that the access discriminant Job is class-wide so that dispatching can occur. The various subprograms Start, Iterations, Interval, Do_It, Finish and Handle_Failure are all dispatching operations of the type Job_Descriptor and might be declared as follows.

```ada
package Base_Job is
    type Job_Descriptor is abstract tagged null record;
    procedure Start(J: access Job_Descriptor);
    function Iterations(J: access Job_Descriptor) return Integer
                                                       is abstract;
    function Interval(J: access Job_Descriptor) return Duration
                                                       is abstract;
    procedure Do_It(J: access Job_Descriptor; I: Integer) is abstract;
    procedure Finish(J: access Job_Descriptor);
    procedure Handle_Failure(J: access Job_Descriptor;
                             E: Exception_Occurrence);
end Base_Job;
```

We have made most of the operations abstract so that the user is forced to provide nonabstract versions but have chosen to make Start and Finish just null since that is an obvious default. A convenient default for Handle_Failure would also seem appropriate.

Observe that the various operations dispatch on an access parameter. It would have been possible for the parameters to be just in parameters but then the actual parameters would have had to be Job.all in the various calls. (If we wanted write access to Job then the parameters would have to be in out or access parameters; see 6.1.2 for a discussion on the merits of one versus the other. Moreover, we might make the parameters of Iterations and Interval of mode in just to emphasize that they are read only operations.)

A demonstration task to output a message ten times with one minute intervals might be produced by writing

```
with Base_Job; use Base_Job;
package Demo_Stuff is
   type Demo is new Job_Descriptor with null record;
   function Iterations(D: access Demo) return Integer;
   function Interval(D: access Demo) return Duration;
   procedure Do_It(D: access Demo; I: Integer);
end;

package body Demo_Stuff is
   function Iterations(D: access Demo) return Integer is
   begin
      return 10;
   end Iterations;

   function Interval(D: access Demo) return Duration is
   begin
      return 60.0;
   end Interval;

   procedure Do_It(D: access Demo; I: Integer) is
   begin
      New_Line; Put("This is number "); Put(I);
   end Do_It;
end Demo_Stuff;
...
The_Demo: Demo;                           -- data for the demo
The_Demo_Task: T(The_Demo'Access);    -- create the task
```

This somewhat pathetic demonstration task always does the same thing since there is actually no data in the type Demo. All the object The_Demo does is indicate through its tag the particular subprograms to be called by dispatching. Thus the type Demo is simply a tag.

A more exciting demonstration might be created by giving the type some components indicating the number of iterations and the interval. The procedure Start might then check that the demonstration would not take too long (five minutes would be quite enough!) and, if necessary, by raising an exception cause the demonstration to be cancelled and a suitable message output. This might be written as

```
package Better_Demo_Stuff is
   type Better_Demo is new Job_Descriptor with
      record
         The_Iterations: Integer;
         The_Interval: Duration;
      end record;
   Silly_Demo: exception;
   ...
```

```
end;

package body Better_Demo_Stuff is
   function Iterations(D: access Better_Demo) return Integer is
   begin
      return D.The_Iterations;
   end Iterations;
   ...
   procedure Start(D: access Better_Demo) is
   begin
      if D.The_Iterations * D.The_Interval > 300.0 then
         Raise_Exception(Silly_Demo'Identity, "Sorry; too long");
      end if;
   end Start;

   procedure Handle_Failure(D: access Better_Demo;
                            E: Exception_Occurrence) is
   begin
      Put_Line("Demonstration not executed because: ");
      Put_Line(Exception_Message(E));
   end Handle_Failure;
end Better_Demo_Stuff;
```

For illustrative purposes we have passed the message to be output using the exception message mechanism discussed in 11.2.

Although our example has been merely a simple demonstration nevertheless the approach could be used to much effect in simulations and related applications. By using type extension, unnecessary repetition of common code is avoided.

The next example illustrates how a class of types plus associated protocols originally developed for a non-tasking environment can be encapsulated as a protected type. Again the key is the use of a class-wide access discriminant.

Suppose we have a queuing protocol defined by

```
type Queue is abstract tagged null record;
function Is_Empty(Q: in Queue) return Boolean is abstract;
function Is_Full(Q: in Queue) return Boolean is abstract;
procedure Add_To_Queue(Q: access Queue;
                       X: Queue_Data) is abstract;
procedure Remove_From_Queue(Q: access Queue;
                            X: out Queue_Data) is abstract;
```

Observe that this describes a whole class of queue types. An existent Queue need only supply bodies for these four operations. Incidentally Is_Empty and Is_Full take in parameters since they do not modify the queue whereas Add_To_Queue and Remove_From_Queue take access parameters because they do modify the queue. This protocol is similar to the generic package in 4.4.1 except that we have assumed that we know the anticipated specific type when removing items from the queue.

A general protection template is provided by

```
protected type PQ(Q: access Queue'Class) is
   entry Put(X: in Queue_Data);
   entry Get(X: out Queue_Data);
end;

protected body PQ is
   entry Put(X: in Queue_Data) when not Is_Full(Q.all) is
```

```
begin
    Add_To_Queue(Q, X);
end Put;

entry Get(X: out Queue_Data) when not Is_Empty(Q.all) is
begin
    Remove_From_Queue(Q, X);
end Get;
end PQ;
```

Interference between operations on a queue is prevented by the natural mechanism of the protected type. Moreover, the functions Is_Empty and Is_Full (originally provided to enable the user of the non-tasking protocol to guard against misuse of the queue) can now be sensibly used as barriers to ensure that a user is automatically prevented from misuse of a queue. Note that the particular queue is identified by the access discriminant.

The user can now define a particular implementation of a queue by type extension such as

```
type My_Queue is new Queue with private;
function Is_Empty(Q: My_Queue) return Boolean;
    . . .
```

and then declare and use a protected queue as follows

```
Raw_Queue: aliased My_Queue;
My_Protected_Queue: PQ(Raw_Queue'Access);
    . . .
My_Protected_Queue.Put(An_Item);
```

The unprotected queue object provides the value of the access discriminant for the protected object. Operations upon the protected queue are performed as expected by normal entry calls.

9.7 Other Improvements

An improvement to the syntax allows entries and representation clauses to be in an arbitrary order in a task specification; previously all entries had to precede all representation clauses.

There are a number of other aspects of the control of tasks that are dealt with in the Systems Programming and the Real-Time Systems annexes. These cover topics such as the identification of tasks, task attributes, the handling of interrupts and the control of priorities. For a discussion on these topics the reader is referred to Part Three of this rationale.

9.8 Requirements Summary

The requirement

> *R2.2-A(1) — Reduce Deterrents to Efficiency*

is very clearly addressed by the introduction of protected objects.
    The requirements

> *R5.1-A(1) — Elapsed Time Measurement*

> *R5.1-B(1) — Precise Periodic Execution*

are met by the introduction of Real_Time.Time and the delay until statement (see 9.3).
The requirement

>*R5.2-A(1) — Alternative Scheduling Algorithms*

is generally addressed by the Real-Time Systems annex and is thus discussed in Part Three. A related aspect is selection from entry queues.
The rather general requirement

>*R5.2-A(2) — Common Real-Time Paradigms*

is met variously by the protected type, the requeue statement, and the asynchronous select in the core language and the facilities for priority control in the Real-Time Systems annex.
The requirements

>*R5.3-A(1) — Asynchronous Transfer of Control*

>*R5.1-C(1) — Detection of Missed Deadlines*

are met by the asynchronous select statement discussed in 9.4.
The requirement for

>*R5.4-A(1) — Non-Blocking Communication*

can be met by the use of a protected record as a mailbox buffer.
The study topic

>*S5.4-B(1) — Asynchronous Multicast*

can be met in various ways using protected objects as building blocks.
The requirements

>*R6.3-A(1) — Interrupt Servicing*

>*R6.3-A(2) — Interrupt Binding*

are of great concern to hard real-time programs. They are addressed in detail by the Systems Programming annex.
The study topic

>*S7.2-A(1) — Managing Large Numbers of Tasks*

is addressed by the introduction of task discriminants; see 9.6.
Finally, it should be noted that the two study topics

>*S7.3-A(1) — Statement Level Parallelism*

>*S7.4-A(1) — Configuration of Parallel Programs*

which relate to vector processing are not directly addressed by any features in the language. However, the rules for the interaction between exceptions and optimization have been relaxed [RM95 11.6] so that implementers should be able to add appropriate pragmas to allow statement level parallelism. Mechanisms for controlling the configuration of parallel programs are clearly outside the scope of the language itself.

10 Program Structure and Compilation Issues

There are a number of important changes in this overall structural area of the language. These include the introduction of the hierarchical library which was discussed in some detail in Part One. In this chapter we provide some more examples and also discuss other topics of a structural nature. The main changes are

- The introduction of the hierarchical library provides decomposition of a library unit with possibly distinct views of the hierarchy for the client and implementor.

- The overall program structure is enhanced by the concept of partitions.

- More control of elaboration order is provided.

- A library package is only permitted to have a body if one is required by language rules.

- The mechanism of the program library is no longer specified so precisely. The main issue is that partitions must be consistent.

- Minor changes include the relaxation of a restriction on subunit names.

In addition to the core language changes which introduce the concept of partitions, the Distributed Systems annex describes the concepts of active and passive partitions plus various packages which provide communication between partitions. These are discussed in detail in Part Three.

10.1 The Hierarchical Library

This topic has already been discussed in Sections II.7 and II.8 of Part One where we saw how the introduction of a hierarchical library with public and private child units overcame a number of problems. We recapitulate some of that discussion here in order to bring further insight into the ways in which the hierarchical library may be used.

In Ada 83, there were a number of situations where relatively small changes result in large numbers of recompilations. For example, it was not possible to define an additional operation for a private type without recompiling the package where the type was declared. This forced all clients of the package to become obsolete and thus also need recompiling, even if they did not use the new operation. Massive recompilations could result from what was fundamentally a very small change.

As we have seen, this is overcome in Ada 95 by allowing a library unit package to be effectively extended with child library units. A child library unit is an independent library unit in that it is not visible unless referenced in a with clause. However, a child library unit may be used to define new operations on types defined in the parent package, because the private part and body of the child unit have visibility onto the private declarations of the parent package.

The name of a child library unit indicates its position in the hierarchy. Its name is an expanded name, with the prefix identifying its parent package. Furthermore, when a child library unit is referenced in a with clause, it "looks like" a unit nested in its parent package. This allows the existing naming and visibility rules of nested units to be carried over directly when using child library units.

If a child library unit is not mentioned in a with clause, it is as if it did not exist at all. Adding a new child library unit never causes any immediate recompilation of existing compilation units. Of course, eventually some number of other library units will come to depend on this child library unit, and then recompiling the child will affect these client units. But by distributing the set of operations across multiple children, the number of clients affected by any single change can be kept to a minimum. Furthermore, the with clause provides explicit and detailed indications of interdependences, helping to document the overall structure of the system.

Separate compilation of program unit specifications and bodies is a powerful facility in Ada. It supports good software engineering practice by separating the abstract interface of the unit from its implementation. Clients of the program unit need only know about its specification — changes to the body do not affect such clients, and do not necessitate a client's recompilation. This separation of interface from implementation also applies to private types. Private types have an interface in the visible part of the package in which they are declared and an implementation in the private part of that package. Declarations in the private part were only visible within that private part and in the package body in Ada 83.

For very complex type definitions, the relationship between private types and packages in Ada 83 introduced an unnecessary coupling between abstractions. Consider, for example, a system that implements two private types, File_Descriptor and Executable_File_Descriptor. The first supports general file operations, and the second supports special file operations for executable files. Thus Executable_File_Descriptor might have a write operation that uses scattering writes to write out an entire executable file very quickly.

In Ada 83, if Executable_File_Descriptor must have access to the implementation of File_Descriptor, perhaps for reasons of performance, then both File_Descriptor and Executable_File_Descriptor must be defined in the same package. Clients of either File_Descriptor or Executable_File_Descriptor will depend on this package. If the definition of Executable_File_Descriptor is changed, all units that depend on the common package must be recompiled, even those that only utilize File_Descriptor. The unnecessary coupling between Executable_File_Descriptor and File_Descriptor forces more recompilations than are logically necessary.

The following example shows how to alleviate this situation using child library units

```
package File_IO is
   type File_Descriptor is private;
   -- Operations on File_Descriptor...
private
   ...
end File_IO;

package File_IO.Executable_IO is
   type Executable_File_Descriptor is private;
   -- Operations on Executable_File_Descriptor...
private
   ...
end File_IO.Executable_IO;
```

As a child of package File_IO, File_IO.Executable_IO can use the full declaration of the private type File_Descriptor in the declaration of the private type Executable_File_Descriptor. Clients of the package File_IO do not require recompilation if a child package changes, and new child units can be added without disturbing existing clients.

Another way of looking at the example above is to observe a distinction between the different clients of a package. The traditional clients of a package use the package's visible definitions as their interface. There are other clients that extend the package's abstractions. These extending clients may add functionality to the original abstraction, or export a different interface, or do both. Extending clients will require details of the original package's implementation. Packages that are extending clients are tightly coupled to the original package in terms of implementation, but their logical coupling may be looser — the extending client may be an alternative to the original for other clients. It should be possible to use either package independently. In Ada 95, one or more child library units can share access to the declarations of their parent's private part — to extend their parent's visible interface or provide an alternate view of it.

The distinction between packages that extend another package and packages that simply use the definitions of another package gives rise to the notion of subsystems. A set of packages that share a set of private types can be viewed as a subsystem or subassembly. This concept is recognized by many design methodologies [Booch 87] and is supported by several implementations in their program library facilities. Subsystems are a useful tool for structured code reuse — very large software systems can be designed and built by decomposing the total system into more manageable-sized pieces that are related, but independent, components.

In summary, child library units provide a combination of compilation independence and hierarchical structuring. This combination results in an extremely flexible building block for constructing subsystems of library units that collectively implement complex abstractions and directly model the structure of the subsystems within the language. As an example, the package OS in II.8 illustrates the use of a hierarchy of library units in implementing a subsystem representing an operating system interface.

10.1.1 Summary of Mechanism

In Ada 95, a library package (or a generic library package) may have child library units. Child library units have the following properties

*   Child units are logically dependent on their parent and have visibility of their parent's visible and private parts.

*   Child library units are named like nested units; with an expanded name consisting of a unique identifier and their parent's name as prefix.

*   A child may be any kind of library unit including a generic unit or instantiation.

*   This structure may be iterated — child units that are packages (or generic packages) may themselves have children, yielding a tree-like hierarchical structure, beginning at a root library unit. Note however that a generic unit may only have generic children.

Child library units may be separately compiled. They may also be separately "withed" by clients. A context clause that names a child unit necessarily names all of the child unit's ancestors as well (with clauses are hence implicit for the ancestors). Within the private part of File_IO.Executable_IO, declarations in the private part of File_IO are visible. Hence the definition of Executable_File_Descriptor can use the full declaration of File_Descriptor.

There are two kinds of child units — private child units and public child units. Private children are those declared using the reserved word **private**.

```
private package File_IO.System_File_IO is
   type System_File_Descriptor is private;
private
   ...
end File_IO.System_File_IO;
```

The visibility rules for private child units are designed such that they cannot be used outside the subsystem defined by their parent. A unit's specification may depend on a private child unit only if the unit is itself private and it is a descendant of the original private child's parent. A unit body may depend on a private child unit if it is a descendant of the private child unit's parent.

Public child packages are intended to provide facilities that are available outside the subsystems defined by their parent packages. In the example, File_IO.Executable_IO is a public child generally available to clients. Private child packages are intended "for internal use" in a larger definition. In the example, File_IO.System_File_IO is meant to be private to the hierarchy of units rooted at File_IO.

Child library units observe the following visibility rules.

- A parent unit's visible definitions are visible everywhere in any child unit, whether the unit is public or private.

- A parent unit's private definitions are visible in the private part of a child unit, whether the child unit is public or private.

- A parent unit's private definitions are visible everywhere in a private child unit, since the child package is never visible outside of the parent.

- The entities in a parent's body are never visible in a child unit.

A principal design consideration for child library units was that it should not be possible for a private view to be violated by indirect means such as renaming. As can be seen this has been achieved since a child unit cannot export a parent unit's private definition by renaming it in the visible part.

Note that for root units, private has the effect of making them invisible to the specifications of public root units. Thus private root units concern the internal implementation of the total system and not its public interface. Moreover, we anticipate that some implementations may provide means for one program library to be referenced from another program library, and in this case the private marking might naturally be used to limit visibility across program libraries. See 10.1.5.

In conclusion, the ability to mark a library unit private is extremely valuable in establishing the same separation between interface and implementation at the subsystem level as is provided in Ada 83 at the individual program unit level. The private library units of a hierarchy, plus the bodies of both the private and public library units of the hierarchy, make up the "implementation" of a subsystem. The "interface" to the subsystem is the declaration of the root package in the hierarchy, plus all of the public descendant child library units.

10.1.2 Context Clauses and Renaming

As in Ada 83, a with clause is used to make other library units visible within a compilation unit. In Ada 95, in order to support the identification of a child library unit, the with clause syntax is augmented to allow the use of an expanded name (the familiar dotted notation) rather than just a single identifier.

Once the child library unit has been identified with its full name in the with clause, normal renaming or use clauses may be used within the compilation unit to shorten the name needed to refer to the child.

In addition to renaming from within a unit, renaming may be used at the library unit level to provide a shorter name for a child library unit, or to hide the hierarchical position of a child unit when appropriate. For example, a library unit may be defined as a child unit to gain special visibility on a parent unit, but this visibility may be irrelevant to most users of the child unit.

Other reasons for library unit renaming are

- Essentially all hierarchical naming systems provide some kind of "alias" capability, because of the advantages of allowing the same entity to appear in multiple places within the hierarchy (such as symbolic links in Unix file systems);

- Helper packages that use unchecked conversion to overcome the restrictions on private types may already exist; through the use of library unit renaming, such helper packages can remain available by their current root library unit names, while moving their actual definition into the appropriate place in the library unit hierarchy reflecting their access patterns;

- It is a common practice to establish standard package renaming conventions throughout a project; without library-level renaming, each unit that withs a package must include a copy of the appropriate renaming declaration for the package; this introduces the possibility of nonconformities, and, if done in the specification, overrides the useful lack of transitivity provided for names introduced by with clauses; the program library manager keeps a central record of the project-wide renaming declarations;

- When integrating independently developed libraries into a single library, the hierarchical name space may be used to avoid collisions, and renaming may be used to selectively "export" units from their local name spaces into the root name space for a given user's library;

- Given a large program library, it may be useful to have a flexible subsystem that includes withs for a certain set of units, and then use renaming to select the particular implementations of those units to be used in the particular subsystem configuration appropriate at a given time;

- Renaming can be used to hide from clients the parent child relationship between two packages. Withing a child via a root-level renaming does not give visibility of the parent.

- Renaming is used in the predefined library so that compatibility is preserved for Ada 83 programs. Thus Ada.Text_IO is renamed as Text_IO as mentioned in II.13.

Some of the capabilities provided by library unit renaming are currently supported by some proprietary program library managers. However, by standardizing these renaming capabilities, very large systems can be built and maintained and rehosted without becoming overly dependent on non-standard program library features.

10.1.3 Children of Generic Packages

As mentioned in II.8, a child may also be generic. However there are a number of important rules to be remembered.

Children of a nongeneric unit may be generic or not but children of a generic unit must always be generic. One of the main problems to be solved in the design of the interaction between genericity and children is the impact of new children on existing instantiations. One possibility would be to say that adding a new child automatically added further corresponding children to all the existing instantiations; this would undoubtedly lead to many surprises and would typically not be what was required since at the time of instantiation the children did not exist and presumably the existing instantiation met the requirements at the time. On the other hand one might decide that existing instantiations did not become extended; however, this would sometimes not be what was wanted either.

Clearly a means is required to enable the user to specify just which units of the hierarchy are to be instantiated. Insisting that all children of a generic unit are themselves generic makes this particularly straightforward and natural; the user just instantiates the units required. The existence of nongeneric children would be a problem because there would not be a natural means to indicate that they were required. One consequence is that it is very common for generic children not to have any generic parameters of their own. See for example the package Sets in 3.7.1.

So a typical pattern is

```
generic
   type T is private;
package Parent is
   ...
end Parent;

generic
package Parent.Child is
   ...
end Parent.Child;
```

Since the child has visibility of the formal parameters of its parent it is necessary that the instantiation of the child also has visibility of the corresponding actual parameter of the instantiation of the parent. There are two situations to be considered, instantiation within the parent hierarchy and instantiation outside the hierarchy.

Instantiation inside the parent hierarchy poses no problem since the instantiation has visibility of the parent's formal parameters in the usual way.

Instantiation outside requires that the actual parameter corresponding to the formal parameter of the parent is correspondingly visible to the instantiation of the child. This is assured by requiring that the child is instantiated using the name of the instance of the parent; a with clause for the generic child is necessary in order for the child to be visible. So we might write

```
with Parent;
package Parent_Instance is new Parent(T => Integer);

with Parent.Child;
package Child_Instance is new Parent_Instance.Child;
```

In a sense the with clause for the child makes the generic child visible in every instantiation of the parent and so we can then instantiate it in the usual way.

Note carefully that the instantiations need not be at the library level. An earlier version of Ada 95 did require all instantiations to be at the library level but this was very restrictive for many applications. Of course if we do make the instantiations at the libraray level then the instantiations can themselves form a child hierarchy. However it will be necessary for the child names to be different to those in the generic hierarchy. So we might have

```
with Parent.Child;
package Parent_Instance.Child_Instance is new Parent_Instance.Child;
```

Finally note that there are no restrictions on the instantiation of a generic child of a non-generic parent.

10.1.4 Examples of Interfaces

Programs may use child library units to implement several different kinds of structures. Some possibilities which will now be illustrated are

* A child package may be used to create specialized interfaces to, or views of, an abstraction. This allows independent abstractions to be combined into larger subsystems. The bit-vector and list-based sets example below illustrates this.

- The interface to a system may be organized into subsystems if it is too large to be conveniently implemented as a single package, or if clients do not often need all of the facilities that the package provides. See the discussion of CAIS-A below.

- A hierarchical organization of library units may be used to permit vendor extensions. The form of such extensions can distinguish clearly by package names which parts are standard, and which parts are vendor extensions.

- Child library units may be used to define an extensible, reusable, library of components. Users are encouraged to extend or modify the components by adding new children. An example of this was shown in II.7 as part of a windowing system.

Our first example could be part of a transaction control system for a database. It shows how to use child library units to structure definitions in order to reduce recompilation.

```
package Transaction_Mgt is
   type Transaction is limited private;
   procedure Start_Transaction(Trans: out Transaction);
   procedure Complete_Transaction(Trans: in  Transaction);
   procedure Abort_Transaction(Trans: in  Transaction);
private
   . . .
end Transaction_Mgt;

package Transaction_Mgt.Auditing is
   type Transaction_Record is private;
   procedure Log(Rec: in Transaction_Record);
private
   . . .
end Transaction_Mgt.Auditing;
```

In the example, some clients require facilities for controlling transactions. Other clients need to be able to log a record of each transaction for auditing purposes. These facilities are logically separate, but transaction records require intimate knowledge of the full structure of a transaction. The solution with child library units is to make a child library unit to support the type Transaction_Record. Each unit may be compiled separately. Changes to Transaction_Mgt.Auditing do not require recompilation of the parent, Transaction_Mgt, nor its clients. But note that withing the child implicitly withs the parent; if this is not desired then, as mentioned above, the child could be renamed thus

```
package Transaction_Auditing renames Transaction_Mgt.Auditing;
```

and then withing Transaction_Auditing will not give visibility of Transaction_Mgt.

The next example illustrates how child library units can be used to add new interfaces to an existing abstraction. This is useful, for example, when conversion functions are needed between types in independently developed abstractions.

Imagine that two packages exist implementing sets, one using bit vectors, and the other linked lists. The bit vector abstraction may not have an iterator in its interface (a means of taking one element from the set), and hence a function cannot be written to convert from the bit vector set to the linked list set. A child package can be added to the bit vector set package that provides an iterator. A new package could then be written to provide the conversion functions, implemented using the iterator interface.

```
package Bit_Vector_Set is

   type Set is private;
```

```ada
   function Union(A, B: Set) return Set;
   function Intersect(A, B: Set) return Set;
   function Unit(E: Element) return Set;
   function Empty return Set;
private
   ...
end Bit_Vector_Set;

package List_Set is
   type Set is private;

   function Union(A, B: Set) return Set;
   function Intersect(A, B: Set) return Set;
   function Unit(E: Element) return Set
   function Empty return Set;

   procedure Take(S: in out Set; E: out Element);
   function Is_Empty(S: Set) return Boolean;
private
   ...
end List_Set;

package Bit_Vector_Set.Iterator is

   procedure Take(S: in out Set; E: out Element);
   function Is_Empty(S: Set) return Boolean;

end Bit_Vector_Set.Iterator;

with List_Set;
with Bit_Vector_Set;
package Set_Conversion is

   function Convert(From: in List_Set.Set)
      return Bit_Vector_Set.Set;
   function Convert(From: in Bit_Vector_Set.Set)
      return List_Set.Set;

end Set_Conversion;
```

The child package Bit_Vector_Set.Iterator adds the two missing subprograms needed in order to iterate over the set. The body of the child package has visibility of the private part of its parent and thus can access the details of the set. This example should be compared with that in 4.4.3 which used class-wide types. Note also that it might be infeasible to modify the body of Bit_Vector_Set anyway since it might have been supplied by a third party in encrypted form (such as object code!).

A larger example is provided by CAIS-A [DoD 89b]; this is an interface that provides operating system services in a portable way. The CAIS has a very large specification, with hundreds of packages. The central type, which is manipulated by much of the system, is called Node_Type. It is a limited private type defined in a package called Cais_Definitions. It is needed throughout the CAIS, but its implementation should be hidden from CAIS application developers. The implementation uses Unchecked_Conversion inside packages that manipulate the type. There are a number of subsystems, the largest of which are for manipulating Nodes, Attributes, and I/O. These subsystems also share common types. These common types are implemented using visible types declared in support packages. Only packages in the subsystem are supposed to depend on these support packages.

Using Unchecked_Conversion has several disadvantages.   First, the replicated type definitions must match exactly, which creates a maintenance problem. Secondly, the compiler must represent each type definition in the same way, which would require a representation clause or good luck. Finally, if the data type is a record, the components may themselves be private types whose definitions may need to be replicated. This propagated need for visibility may cause many or all private type definitions to be replicated in several places.

Child library units could be used to restructure these definitions. The type Node_Type might be defined at the root of the hierarchy.   Packages that contain types and operations for manipulating Nodes, I/O, and Attributes might be child packages of the root library package. The common types would be private, and the support packages would be child packages of the packages that contain the type definitions.

The Ada binding to POSIX [IEEE 92] is another system with many packages and many types. Some of these types are system independent, and some are explicitly system defined. When designing portable programs it is useful to know when programs depend on system defined definitions, to eliminate such dependencies where possible, and to contain them when they are necessary.

The POSIX-Ada binding attempts to preserve the principle of with list portability: users should be able to determine if a program depends on system defined features by examining the names of the packages in its with clauses. At the same time, the system dependent packages often require visibility on the private types of the standard packages, and in Ada 83 this could only be accomplished by nesting them within the standard packages. Since a nested package never appears in a with clause, the visibility needs of such system dependent packages is in conflict with the principle of with list portability. Child library units offer precisely what is needed to resolve this conflict.

10.1.5 Existing Program Libraries

We anticipate that implementations will continue to support library unit references between program libraries. The hierarchical library unit naming may allow these inter-library references to be handled more naturally within the language, for example, by treating the library units of one program library as child units of an empty package within the referencing library. This would provide automatic name-space separation between the two libraries, since the names of the units of the referenced library would all be prefixed by a hypothetical parent package identifier. This approach would eliminate any need for global uniqueness of library unit names when two or more program libraries are (conceptually) combined in this way. It should also be noted that this provides a good use for private top level library units. Marking a top level library unit as private such as

```
private package PP is ...
```

means that it is not visible to the specifications of public units in the library but only to their bodies. Hence it cannot be accessed directly but only as a slave to other units. Considering the whole library as a hypothetical unit such as Your_Lib means that in effect the package becomes

```
private package Your_Lib.PP is ...
```

and then (correctly) cannot be accessed from outside the package Your_Lib.

We have avoided specifying standard mechanisms for such inter-program-library references, as implementations vary widely in what they choose to provide in this area.   However, the universal availability of hierarchical library unit naming will ensure that a program built out of units from multiple libraries will have a natural and portable representation by using a hierarchical naming approach.

10.1.6 Relationship with Previous Work

We conclude our discussion of hierarchical libraries by mentioning three alternative approaches which were considered and rejected:

Voyeurism. (The term "voyeurism" is due to D. Emery.) This allows packages to request visibility on another package's private declarations via some kind of enhanced context clause (such as **with all** X; or **with private** X;)

Friends. This allows packages to specify exactly which other packages may have enhanced visibility.

DAG Inheritance. This allows a more general form of hierarchical organization, where packages can, in effect, "nest" within several other packages, without an explicit indication in the parent. This is called "DAG inheritance", since the dependence graph must be a directed acyclic graph.

The voyeur approach has the unsettling characteristic of making the privacy of types a property of other packages' context clauses, instead of a feature of the package that is declaring the type. This inverts the Ada 83 notion of privacy. With child library units, privacy becomes a feature of package hierarchies, which is a generalization of Ada 83's subunit facility. Although many of the same effects can be achieved with either approach, the mechanisms are fundamentally different, and child library units are consistent with this Ada model.

There are serious problems with the **with private** approach — without additional rules, private declarations may be easily reexported to units that do not have a with private clause for the unit. This could happen, for example, via a renaming declaration or deriving from a private type as in the following example

```
package Closed is
   type T is private;
private
   type T is Full_Implementation;
end Closed;

with private Closed;        -- not Ada 95
package Open is
   type D is new Closed.T;
   -- from full declaration of T
end Open;

with Open;
package Surprise is
   type S is new Open.D;
   -- gets full type declaration of T via D
end Surprise;
```

whereby the package Surprise gets visibility of the full declaration of T via the type D declared in the package Open.

The real difficulty with the **with private** approach is that dependence can subsequently become diffused.

One of the important advantages of using private types in a package is that the compiler ensures that clients of the package do not become dependent on the details of the type's implementation. This makes it much easier to safely maintain and enhance the implementation of the package, even if the set of clients is large. With child units, if a given client needs more operations on a private type, they must identify those operations and declare them in a public child of the package. When the private type's implementation is revised, only the children of the package need be checked and updated as necessary.

The **with private** approach results in a very different scenario. If a client needs additional access to a private type, they need not separately declare operations on that type in some child. Instead they can simply change their **with** to **with private**. This means that the dependence is now open ended rather than being encapsulated in a child. After a period of use, it is clear that there could be sufficiently widespread and diffuse dependence on the implementation of the private type so that any change will be unacceptably expensive to the clients (since the amount of client code can easily exceed the size of the package), thereby totally defeating the original purpose of private types.

The "friends" approach is used in C++. This solution was considered and was rejected because it does not allow for unplanned extension of a package without requiring modification and recompilation of that package, conflicting with the requirement to reduce recompilation. In the X and CAIS-A examples above we discussed situations where unplanned extension is desirable. It is highly advantageous that Ada 95 support it with this same mechanism.

Furthermore, the "friends" approach inverts Ada's usual client/server philosophy. In general it is not possible to tell at the point of a particular declaration where that declaration will be used. For example, the declaration of a type does not specify the type's users, a task declaration does not specify the task's callers, a library unit's declaration does not specify which other units depend on it, and a generic unit's declaration does not specify where the generic will be instantiated. Allowing a package's declaration to specify which other units may extend that package is inconsistent with this model.

Although on the surface the voyeurism and friends concepts appear simple, the issue of transitivity is problematical. In Ada, context clauses are not transitive. Presumably this would also be the case for voyeur context clauses as well. In that case the meaning of the following program becomes unclear.

```
with private X;              -- not Ada 95
package Y is
   . . .
end Y;

with private Y;
with X;
package Q is
   . . .
end Q;
```

Here Q has visibility to Y's private declarations which in turn may refer to X's private declarations. However, Q does not have visibility to X's private declarations through its context clause. Any proposal would have to address in this case whether or not Q has visibility to X.

The DAG inheritance approach has characteristics of both child library units and voyeurism. If there is more than one private type involved, it is possible that a tree structured hierarchy cannot provide the exact visibility needed. However, the DAG approach is complex and its ramifications far-reaching. We concluded that such a solution was too ambitious for the Ada 9X revision.

10.2 Program Structure

In Ada 83, an executable program consisted of a main subprogram and all other library units reachable from this main subprogram. Execution proceeded by elaborating the entire program, running the main subprogram to completion, waiting for all library-level tasks to complete, and then terminating. Although this model for a program was appropriate in some environments, for many programming environments, a much more dynamic and distributed model is preferable.

In Ada 95, a program may be formed from a cooperating set of partitions. The core language simply says that partitions elaborate independently, communicate, and then terminate in some implementation-defined manner. Each partition has its own environment task to act as the thread of control for library-level elaboration, and to act as the master for library-level tasks.

The description in the core language is kept purposefully non-specific to allow for many different approaches to dynamic and distributed program construction. However, the Distributed Systems annex describes additional standard pragmas and attributes which form the basis for a standard, portable approach to distribution.

10.3 Elaboration

Because Ada allows essentially arbitrary code to execute during the elaboration of library units, it is difficult for the user to ensure that no subprogram is called before it is elaborated. Ada 83 required that access before elaboration be detected, and Program_Error raised. This could incur significant overhead at run-time.

Ada 95 addresses both the problem of controlling library unit elaboration order, and the run-time overhead of access-before-elaboration checks.

In Ada 95 the Elaborate pragma is effectively replaced by the transitive Elaborate_All pragma. Elaborate_All on a library unit causes not only the body of that library unit to be elaborated, but also causes the bodies of the library units reachable from that library unit's body to be elaborated. This ensures that any call performed during elaboration on a subprogram defined in the unit to which pragma Elaborate_All applies, will not result in an access-before-elaboration error.

The pragma Elaborate_Body in a package specifies that the body of the package must be elaborated immediately after its declaration. No intervening elaborations are permitted. This allows the compiler to know whether or not any elaboration-time code exists between a visible subprogram declaration and its body. If there is no such elaboration-time code, or it can be proved to not call the subprogram, then there is no opportunity for access-before-elaboration, and the check may be completely eliminated for the subprogram. Without this pragma, the compiler must assume that other library units might be elaborated between the elaboration of the library unit's declaration and its body, meaning that the check in a visible subprogram cannot be removed by the compiler.

Ada 95 also contains two further pragmas concerned with elaboration. The pragma Pure in a package specifies that the package does not have any library-level "state", and may depend only on other pure packages. Pure packages are important for distributed systems.

Finally, the pragma Preelaborate indicates that a unit is to be preelaborated; that is elaborated before other units not so indicated; there are restrictions on the actions of a unit which is preelaborated. A unit marked as Pure is also preelaborated. The general intent is that certain structures can be set up at link-time (before program execution begins) and then perhaps loaded into RAM.

It is good advice to give all library units one of the pragmas Pure, Preelaborate, or Elaborate_Body in that order of preference, wherever possible. This will ensure the benefits of possible check eliminations as mentioned above.

Further support for preelaboration is described in the Systems Programming annex.

10.4 Library Package Bodies

In Ada 83, if a package does not require a body, but has one nevertheless (perhaps to do some initialization), its body can become out-of-date, and be silently omitted from a subsequent build of an executable program. This can lead to mysterious run-time failures due to the lack of the package body. Ada 95 overcomes this difficulty by allowing a library package to have a body only if a body is required by some language rule. An obvious rule requiring a body is that a subprogram specification in a package specification requires a corresponding subprogram body in the package body. Another rule which is more convenient for ensuring that a body is required in cases where we wish to use the body just for initialization is that the pragma Elaborate_Body rather obviously requires a body.

Note that an early version of Ada 95 proposed that a library package always have a body; this was eventually rejected because of the irritating incompatibility problems that would have arisen in moving programs from Ada 83.

10.5 Other Improvements

Child library units take over some of the applications of subunits. However, subunits remain the only way for separately compiling a unit that has visibility to the declarative part of the enclosing unit's body. They are also appropriate for providing bodies for individual units that may be undergoing more active development or maintenance than surrounding units.

To simplify the use of subunits, Ada 95 eliminates the requirement on uniqueness of their simple name within an enclosing library unit. Only the expanded name need be unique. Thus subunits P.Q.T and P.S.T where P is the library package name are allowed in Ada 95 whereas this was forbidden in Ada 83. This is in line with the rules for naming child units.

10.6 Requirements Summary

The requirements includes two study topics

> *S4.3-A(1) — Reducing the Need for Recompilation*

> *S4.3-C(1) — Enhanced Library Support*

which are specifically addressed and well satisfied by the hierarchical library mechanism. In addition the further study topic

> *S4.3-B(1) — Programming by Specialization/Extension*

is also addressed by the hierarchical library in conjunction with type extension.

The requirements

> *R8.1-A(1) — Facilitating Software Distribution*

> *R8.2-A(1) — Dynamic Reconfiguration*

are addressed by the concept of partitions described in 10.2 and elaboration discussed in 10.3. However, this is really the domain of the Distributed Systems annex and the reader is thus referred to Part Three of this rationale for further details.

11 Exceptions

The changes to exception handling from Ada 83 are quite small. The main changes are

- The exception Numeric_Error is now a renaming of Constraint_Error and is also obsolescent.

- The notion of an exception occurrence is introduced. This refers to an instance of raising an exception. The package Ada.Exceptions contains procedures providing additional information regarding an exception occurrence.

- The interaction between exceptions and optimization is clarified.

- A minor improvement is that an accept statement may now directly have an exception handler.

11.1 Numeric Error

Those familiar with the early use of Ada 83 will recall that there was considerable confusion between Numeric_Error and Constraint_Error in a number of corner situations. As a consequence the ARG ruled that implementations should raise Constraint_Error in all situations for which Numeric_Error was originally intended. This was a non-binding interpretation with the intention of making it binding in due course.

Essentially all implementations of Ada 83 now raise Constraint_Error although for historic reasons some programs may contain dormant handlers for Numeric_Error.

The development of Ada 95 provided an opportunity to remove this historic wart once and for all. It was thus proposed that Numeric_Error be completely removed. However, many reviewers pointed out that those programs which had conformed to the advice of AI-387 by consistently writing

```
when Constraint_Error | Numeric_Error =>
```

would then become illegal. Accordingly, in Ada 95, Numeric_Error is simply a renaming of Constraint_Error. Such a change alone would still have made the above illegal because, in Ada 83, all the exceptions in a handler had to be distinct; a supplementary change is thus that an exception may appear more than once in a handler in Ada 95.

Allowing multiple instances of an exception in a given handler has benefits in other areas. It now allows sequences such as

```
when Text_IO.Data_Error | Integer_IO.Data_Error =>
```

where there may be documentation advantages in revealing the potential causes of the exception.

Of course if the user had deliberately relied upon a distinction between Numeric_Error and Constraint_Error then the program will now become incorrect. It may be simply incompatible but may also be inconsistent if the handlers are in different frames. For a more detailed discussion see A-4.5. Despite this possibility it was concluded that the perhaps safer alternative of completely removing Numeric_Error was not appropriate for this revision although it should be reconsidered at the next revision.

11.2 Exception Occurrences

It is important in many programs to be able to recover from all exceptions and to continue processing in some way. All exceptions including unexpected exceptions can be caught by an **others** handler. Unfortunately, however, Ada 83 provided no way of identifying the particular exception and it was thus not possible to log the details or take specific appropriate action.

This is overcome in Ada 95 by the introduction of the concept of an exception occurrence and a number of subprograms to access information regarding the occurrence. The type Exception_Occurrence and the subprograms are declared in the package Ada.Exceptions. The user can then declare a choice parameter in a handler through which the particular occurrence can be identified. For example a fragment of a continuous embedded system might take the form

```
with Ada.Exceptions;
task body Control is
...
begin
   loop
      begin
         ... -- main algorithm
      exception
         when Error: others =>
            -- unhandled exception; log it
            Log("Unknown error in task Control"
                 &
                 Ada.Exceptions.Exception_Information(Error));
            -- reset data structures as necessary
      end;
      -- loop around to restart the task
   end loop;
end Control;
```

The choice parameter Error is a constant of the type Exception_Occurrence. The function Exception_Information returns a printable string describing the exception and details of the cause of the occurrence. The actual details depend on the implementation.

Two other functions in Ada.Exceptions are Exception_Name and Exception_Message. Exception_Name just returns the name of the exception (the expanded name) and Exception_Message returns a one-liner giving further details (it excludes the name). Thus Exception_Name, Exception_Message and Exception_Information provide a hierarchy of strings appropriate to different requirements.

The purpose of the three functions is to provide information suitable for output and subsequent analysis in a standard way. Although the details of the strings will depend upon the implementation nevertheless they should be appropriate for analysis on that system.

Exception occurrences can be saved for later analysis by the two subprograms Save_Occurrence. Note that the type Exception_Occurrence is limited; using subprograms rather than allowing the user to save values through assignment gives better control over the use of storage for saved exception occurrences (which could of course be large since they may contain full trace back information). The procedure Save_Occurrence may truncate the message to 200 characters whereas the function Save_Occurrence (which returns an access value) is not permitted to truncate the message. (Note that 200 corresponds to the minimum size of line length required to be supported, see 2.2.)

An occurrence may be reraised by calling the procedure Reraise_Occurrence. This is precisely equivalent to reraising an exception by a raise statement without an exception name and does not create a new occurrence (thus ensuring that the original cause is not lost). An advantage of `Reraise_Occurrence` is that it can be used to reraise an occurrence that was stored by `Save_Occurrence`.

It is possible to attach a specific message to the raising of an exception by the procedure `Raise_Exception`. The first parameter is a value of the type `Exception_Id` which identifies the exception; this value can be obtained by applying the attribute `Identity` to the identifier of the exception. The second parameter is the message (a string) which can then be retrieved by calling `Exception_Message`. This provides a convenient means of identifying the cause of an exception during program debugging. Consider

```
declare
   O_Rats: exception;
begin
   ...
   Raise_Exception(O_Rats'Identity, "Hard cheese");
   ...
   Raise_Exception(O_Rats'Identity, "Rat poison");
   ...
exception
   when Event: O_Rats =>
      Put("O_Rats raised because of ");
      Put(Exception_Message(Event));
end;
```

Calling `Raise_Exception` raises the exception `O_Rats` with the string attached as the message. The second call of `Put` in the handler will output `Hard cheese` or `Rat poison` according to which occurrence of `O_Rats` was raised. See also the example in 9.6.1.

Note that the system messages do not include the name so user and system messages can be processed in a similar manner without the user having to insert the exception name in the message.

11.3 Exceptions and Optimization

The general objective is to strike a sensible balance between prescribing the language so rigorously that no optimizations are possible (which would make the language uncompetitive) and allowing so much freedom that the language semantics are almost non-existent (which would impact on portability and provability). A progressive approach is required that enables different degrees to be permitted in different circumstances.

Much of the difficulty lies with exceptions and ensuring that they are still raised in the appropriate frame. In particular we have ensured that calls to subprograms in other library units are not disrupted.

For details of the approach taken the reader is referred to [RM95 11.6]. A more detailed discussion of the rationale will be found in [AARM].

11.4 Other Improvements

As mentioned in 1.3, the description of exception handling has been simplified by the introduction of a new syntactic category handled_sequence_of_statements which embraces a sequence of statements plus associated exception handlers and is used for all situations where handlers are allowed.

An incidental minor improvement following from this change to the syntax is that an accept statement can now have a handler without the necessity for an inner block, thus

```
accept E do
    . . .
    . . .
exception
    . . .
end E;
```

A further practical improvement is that the concept of a current error file is introduced. This can conveniently be used to log error messages without cluttering other output. This is discussed in more detail in Part Three.

11.5 Requirements Summary

The specific requirement

> *R 4.5-A(1) — Accessing an Exception Name*

is met by the introduction of exception occurrences.
    The requirement

> *R2.2-C(1) — Minimize Special Case Restrictions*

mentions as an example the curious fact that an accept statement cannot have an exception handler. This has been rectified.

12 Generics

There are a number of important improvements and extensions to the generic model in Ada 95. The extensions are mainly concerned with providing appropriate new parameter mechanisms to match the additional functionality provided by tagged and other new types. In addition problems with flaws in the contract model are cured.

The main changes are

*   A distinct formal notation (<>) is introduced that enables definite and indefinite subtypes to be treated separately. This cures a major flaw in the contract model. The (<>) notation is also used in private types to indicate that they have unknown discriminants.

*   There are new formal notations for modular and decimal types.

*   The rules for access type matching are extended to accommodate the additional forms of access types.

*   There is a new formal notation indicating that the actual type must be derived from a given type. Moreover, in both this case and the existing private formal notation, it is possible to indicate that the type must be tagged.

*   There is a new formal notation for package parameters. The generic actual parameter must be an instantiation of a given generic package.

*   Minor changes are that static subtype matching is now required for array and access types, and that the order of evaluation of generic actual and default parameters is not so rigidly specified.

12.1 The Contract Model

As mentioned in Part One, there are a number of new forms of generic parameter in Ada 95. Some of these are introduced to correspond to new types such as tagged types, modular types and decimal types. In addition there are new forms for derived types in general and for package parameters; these simplify program composition. All these new forms were introduced in Part One and are discussed in detail in the following sections.

As was discussed in II.11, Ada 83 had a serious violation of the contract model because of the lack of distinction between unconstrained and constrained formal parameters.

The exact distinction is between subtypes for which objects can be declared (without giving any constraints directly or from an initialization) and those for which they cannot. The former category covers scalar subtypes such as Integer, constrained array and record subtypes and unconstrained record subtypes which have default discriminants. The term definite is introduced for these subtypes.

Ada 95 cures this flaw in the contract model by requiring that the formal parameter include an unknown discriminant part (<>) if an indefinite subtype is to be allowed as actual parameter. In this case the body cannot use the subtype in a context requiring a definite subtype.

On the other hand the existing notation without (<>) now indicates that the actual parameter must be definite.

The two notations are illustrated by the following example

```
generic
    type Key(<>) is private;
    type Item    is private;
package Keyed_Index is ... end;
```

The subtype String, because it is an unconstrained array subtype, could be associated with Key, but not with Item. Within the generic, Key must not be used to declare a component or uninitialized object.

This is an incompatibility as mentioned in I-4.4 but straightforward to detect and fix. If existing instantiations fail to compile under Ada 95, then the generic unit must be modified to specify that the relevant generic formal allows indefinite subtypes.

This new distinction between definite and indefinite parameters eliminates the primary source of situations in Ada 83 where an otherwise legal instantiation is made illegal by a particular usage pattern of a formal type within the body of the generic unit. In other words this distinction eliminates the major gap in the generic contract model of Ada 83.

Having plugged the major gap in the Ada 83 generic contract model, Ada 95 goes further and ensures that the legality of an instantiation never depends on the parameter usage patterns present in the generic body.

This is achieved in various ways. We have just seen how the addition of further information in the formal parameter enables a satisfactory distinction between usage patterns to be made in the case of definite and indefinite subtypes.

However, it is impracticable to impose all pattern matching requirements through the parameter matching rules. Another approach is to impose certain restrictions in the generic body which in essence assume the "worst" regarding the possible instantiations. An example is that if the generic parameter is nonlimited then all the components in an extension of it also have to be nonlimited. This rule is checked in the instance. For further details of this and other ways in which the contract is ensured see [RM95 12.3]

The general principle is to assume the "best" in the generic specification and then to check the assumptions again at the instantiation, and to assume the "worst" in the body so that legality does not depend upon the instantiation. This of course means that full freedom is not possible in the body but the constraints will not generally be found irksome. A common workaround is to move material from the generic body into the private part.

In conclusion, a tight contract model has several desirable properties. It allows implementations to share generics more easily, it leads to the early detection of programming errors, and it eliminates the need to recheck all existing instantiations when a new body is compiled. Ada 95 strengthens the contract model by requiring that the specification of a generic formal private type indicate whether a corresponding actual may be an unconstrained composite subtype. This simplifies the checking required when a new generic body is compiled, since its legality will not depend on the nature of the existing instantiations.

As pointed out in [DoD 90] in the discussion of Study Topic S4.4-B(2), both tight and loose contract models are desirable, each for its own reasons. This tension has been resolved in Ada 95, by specifying that certain checks in the generic specification are only performed at instantiation time.

Our general goal has been to aim towards the ideal situation whereby within the body of the generic, *all* checks are performed when the generic body is compiled, and these checks fail if *any* possible instantiation could fail the checks. This goal has generally been achieved, (although some errors in the instance are detected at runtime; an example is the use of the Access attribute, see 12.3). Ada 95 thus achieves the prime goals associated with a tight contract model, and yet still provides the flexibility required to use generics to their best advantage.

Improving the contract model eases the problems of code sharing for those implementations that use this technique. However, it should be noted that many of the applications of generics where code sharing seemed important can now be done using other techniques such as access to subprogram parameters and tagged types. Moreover, we have not provided an explicit pragma as suggested by the Requirements to control whether code sharing should be used or not since an implementation can use the pragma Optimize as suggested in [AARM 2.8(27)].

12.2 Numeric Types

Additional formal types are provided corresponding to unsigned integer types (modular types) and to decimal fixed point types as already mention in 3.3.

The modular types form a subclass of the integer types. They have additional operations such as the logical operations that do not apply to all integer types. As a consequence a signed integer type cannot match a formal modular type. On the other hand modular types behave differently to signed integer types with regard to overflow since by definition they wrap around. And so a modular type cannot match a formal signed integer type.

Similarly the decimal types form a subclass of the fixed point types. Again they are a distinct subclass to the ordinary fixed point types and one cannot match the other. The reason is that an implementation is allowed to use a significantly different representation (such as packed decimal) for decimal types as opposed to ordinary fixed types; it would impose unacceptable inefficiencies on implementations using shared generic bodies to accommodate both kinds of actual via one kind of formal.

12.3 Access Types

Access types are considerably extended in Ada 95 as discussed in 3.7. They may access general objects not created by allocators; they may be marked as constant and there are also access to subprogram types. Accordingly, the matching rules for generic access parameters are adapted to allow for the proper matching of these other forms.

For example if the formal type is

```
type A is access constant T;
```

then the actual type must also be a general access type with the modifier **constant**. Similarly, if the formal type is

```
type A is access all T;
```

then the actual type must also be a general access type (with **all** but not **constant**) that has the type T as its accessed type.

In the case of access to subprogram types, the profiles of the formal and actual types have to be mode conformant (see 6.2). This is the same category of conformance as for renaming of subprograms (not renaming bodies) and thus naturally continues the general model that generic parameter matching is renaming.

Note that there are restrictions on the use of the Access attribute in a generic body; these are different for access to subprogram and access to object types. The objective is of course to ensure that an access cannot be created to an entity at an inner level.

In the case of an access to subprogram type, the access attribute is not allowed to be applied to a subprogram in a generic body if the access type is external to the generic unit because of worst case considerations. A possible workaround is to move the declaration of the subprogram P to the private part and to declare a constant in the private part thus

```
P_Access: constant Global_Access_Type := P'Access;
```

and this will then be checked in the instance of the specification.

In the case of access to object types a different approach is taken. The access attribute is allowed in a generic body but the check occurs dynamically if the access type is external to the body. This check is therefore similar to that for anonymous access parameters and Program_Error is raised if it fails.

The different approach relates to the fact that anonymous access types are not allowed for subprogram parameters as discussed in 3.7.2. Also the workaround applicable to access to subprogam types of moving the use of Access to the specification cannot usually be applied in the case of access to object types.

12.4 Derived Types

The class-wide programming features of Ada 95 reduce the need to use generics to deal with different types derived from the same root type. However, class-wide programming does not address the important capability, only provided by generics, of defining a new data structure that is parameterized by one or more component types. It is instructive to note that the object oriented programming languages C++, Eiffel, and Modula-3 all include some sort of generic or template mechanism in their latest incarnations.

A new kind of generic formal parameter is provided for derived types. As mentioned above, we see an important role for generics in the definition of new data structures parameterized by one or more component types. For linked data structures, it is often necessary to take advantage of the structure of the components to efficiently implement the (composite) data structure. By using a generic formal derived type, the implementation of the generic can take advantage of the structure and operations of the ancestor type specified for the formal derived type definition.

In the remainder of this section we consider formal (untagged) derived types; tagged types are considered in the next section.

The new notation is

type T **is new** S;

which indicates that the actual type must be derived directly or indirectly from S.

For a generic formal derived type, the primitive operations available on the type in the generic are determined by the specified ancestor type. Analogous to the rule for formal numeric types, the primitive operations available on an untagged formal derived type use the ancestor operation implementations, even if they have been overridden or hidden for the actual type. This rule is necessary for untagged types, because there is no limitation on the kinds of alterations made to the subtype or mode of the formal parameters when overriding a subprogram inherited by derivation. This contrast strongly with tagged types where the whole essence of the concept is to use replaced operations as described in the next section.

Generic formal derived types permit generic units to be parameterized by a user-defined class — the set of all types derived from the parent type specified in the generic parameter declaration. Within the generic template, the operations of the specified parent type are available. This provides support for user-defined classes that is comparable to that available for language-defined classes, such as discrete, integer, fixed and float.

In a sense therefore the formal parameter notation

type T **is range** <>;

is approximately equivalent to

type T **is new** root_integer;

although we cannot actually write the latter.

One use of generic formal derived types is to parameterize a generic with a record type but without having to introduce a specific notation for formal record types which would be unwieldy.

The following example is a generic package for providing I/O for types in a user-defined rational class.

```
package Rational_Arithmetic is
    -- this package defines a rational number type

    type Rational is private;

    function "+" (Left, Right: Rational) return Rational;
    ...
end Rational_Arithmetic;

with Rational_Arithmetic; use Rational_Arithmetic;
with Text_IO;
generic
    -- this package provides I/O for any type derived from Rational
    type Num is new Rational;
package Rational_IO is
    procedure Get(File: in Text_IO.File_Type;
                  Item: out Num;
                  Width: in Text_IO.Field := 0);

    procedure Put(File: in Text_IO.File_Type;
                  Item: in Num;
                  Fore: in Text_IO.Field;
                  Aft: in Text_IO.Field;
                  Exp: in Text_IO.Field);
end Rational_IO;
```

The generic formal parameter Num will only match Rational and its derivatives. Since Rational and its derivatives all share the primitive operations of the Rational type, those operations are available within Rational_IO for implementing the Get and Put subprograms.

12.5 Tagged Types

Other forms of formal parameters apply to tagged types. Thus

```
type T is tagged private;
```

which simply indicates that the actual type can be any tagged type, and

```
type T is new S with private;
```

which indicates that the actual type can be any extension of the type S (or the type S itself).

This last form is very important. A form of multiple inheritance is obtained by defining a generic package that extends a formal type with additional components and operations (see 4.6.2). Because type extension is only permitted for tagged types, allowing the reserved word tagged in a generic formal private type declaration makes it clear in the parameter specification that extension might be performed. But note that it is possible to declare a type extension (of a parameter) only in the generic specification; it is not allowed in the generic body. However, as illustrated in 4.6.2 this fits in with typical patterns of use.

The above restriction is an interesting example of the best and worst case contract principle. The underlying rule that we must not violate is that a type extension must be accessible from the parent type declaration as discussed in 4.3. It is thus necessary that an extension in any instantiation also satisfies this rule. In the case of the specification we assume the best and allow an extension. At the point of the instantiation the resulting specification is checked to ensure that the extension does not violate the rule. In the case of the body the general contract principle is that the body must work for any instantiation and accordingly it is not permitted to allow an error to be discovered in the body for a particular instantiation. Thus we assume the worst and forbid any extension since the instantiation might be at a deeper level at which an extension would violate the accessibility rule. This restriction may seem a burden but a commonly applicable workaround is simply to move the type extension and its operations to the private part. An example where this would be necessary is discussed in 4.4.4.

For tagged types, the primitive operations use the implementations defined for the actual type, though this is expressed for consistency in terms of the normal dispatching behavior of the operations of the parent type. For a tagged type it is possible to use the overriding definitions, because these overriding operations must be subtype conformant with the inherited one.

A further refinement is that the formal type can be declared as abstract. In such a case the actual type can also be abstract but it need not. If the formal is abstract then no objects can be declared.

The parameter matching rules are designed to ensure that abstract subprograms are never called. If a type is abstract it does not follow that all its primitive subprograms are abstract. Non-dispatching calls are allowed in the generic unit on only those primitive operations of the formal type which are not abstract. In order to ensure that any instantiation still correctly works it is necessary that the corresponding primitive operations of the actual type are also not abstract. Consider again the package P in 7.4.

```
generic
   type Parent is abstract new Limited_Controlled with private;
package P is
   type T is new Parent with private;
   ...
private
   type T is new Parent with
      record
         -- additional components
      end record;
   procedure Finalize(Object: in out T);
end P;
```

then although Limited_Controlled is abstract, its primitive operations such as Finalize are not abstract and thus calls on Finalize are allowed in the body. For this to always work it is essential that the actual type has not replaced the inherited procedure Finalize by an abstract one [RM95 3.9.3]. The following is thus illegal

```
type Nasty is abstract new Limited_Controlled with null record;
procedure Finalize(Object: in out Nasty) is abstract;
...
package Q is new P(Parent => Nasty);   -- illegal
```

Class-wide programming and type extension, in combination with generic units, provides many useful facilities.

Generic units may be parameterized by user-defined classes, allowing abstractions to be built around such classes. In this example, Any_Account will be matched by any type derived from Account_With_Interest. Within the template, the primitive operations of Account_With_Interest are available.

```
generic
   type Account_Type(<>) is new Account_With_Interest with private;
package Set_Of_Accounts is
      procedure Add_New_Account(A: in Account_Type);
      procedure Remove_Account(A: in Account_Type);
```

```
function Balance_Of_Accounts return Money;
... -- other operations (e.g. an iterator)
end Set_Of_Accounts;
```

This generic package could be instantiated with a specific derivative of `Account_With_Interest`, in which case it would be a homogeneous set of such accounts. Alternatively, the generic could be instantiated with a class-wide type like `Account_With_Interest'Class`, in which case it would allow a heterogeneous set of accounts. The notation (<>) specifies that the actual account type may have any number of discriminants, or be a class-wide type (that is, it can be indefinite).

12.6 Package Parameters

The final new kind of generic formal parameter is the formal package. A formal package parameter matches any instance of a specified generic package.

Generic formal packages are appropriate in two different circumstances. In the first circumstance, the generic is defining additional operations, or a new abstraction, in terms of some preexisting abstraction defined by some preexisting generic. This kind of "layering" of functionality can be extremely cumbersome if all of the types and operations defined by the preexisting generic must be imported into the new generic. The generic formal package provides a direct way to import all of the types and operations defined in an instance of the preexisting generic.

In other words, generic formal packages allow generics to be parameterized by other generics, which allows for safer and simpler composition of generic abstractions. In particular it allows for one generic to easily extend the abstraction provided by another generic, without requiring the programmer to enumerate all the operations of the first in the formal part of the second. A simple example of the use of this technique was illustrated by the package `Generic_Complex_Vectors` in II.11.

In more elaborate circumstances, there may need to be several formal packages. It then proves convenient to augment the notation

```
with package P is new Q(<>);
```

which indicates that the actual parameter corresponding to P can be *any* package which has been obtained by instantiating Q by the notation

```
with package R is new Q(P1, P2, ...);
```

which indicates that the actual package corresponding to R must have been instantiated with the given parameters.

Returning to our example of complex numbers, we can now write a package which exports standard mathematical functions operating on complex numbers and which takes two packages as parameters. One package defines the complex numbers (as in II.11) and the other package is the standard package `Generic_Elementary_Functions` which provides mathematical functions on normal real (that is not complex) numbers. We write

```
with Generic_Complex_Numbers;
with Generic_Elementary_Functions;
generic
   with package Complex_Numbers is
      new Generic_Complex_Numbers(<>);
   with package Elementary_Functions is
      new Generic_Elementary_Functions(Complex_Numbers.Float_Type);
package Generic_Complex_Functions is
```

```
use Complex_Numbers;

function Sqrt(X: Complex) return Complex;
function Log  (X: Complex) return Complex;
function Exp  (X: Complex) return Complex;
function Sin  (X: Complex) return Complex;
function Cos  (X: Complex) return Complex;

end Generic_Complex_Functions;
```

The actual packages must be instantiations of Generic_Complex_Numbers and Generic_Elementary_Functions respectively. Note that both forms of formal package are used. Any instantiation of Generic_Complex_Numbers is allowed but the instantiation of Generic_Elementary_Functions must have Complex_Numbers.Float_Type as its actual parameter. This ensures that both packages are instantiated with the same floating type.

Note carefully that we are using the formal exported from the first instantiation as the required parameter for the second instantiation. The formal parameters are only accessible in this way when the default form (<>) is used. Finally, instantiations might be

```
package Long_Complex_Numbers is
    new Generic_Complex_Numbers(Long_Float);

package Long_Elementary_Functions is
    new Generic_Elementary_Functions(Long_Float);

package Long_Complex_Functions is
    new Generic_Complex_Functions
        (Long_Complex_Numbers, Long_Elementary_Functions);
```

A second circumstance where a generic formal package is appropriate is when the same abstraction is implemented in several different ways. For example, the abstraction of a "mapping" from a key type to a value type is very general, and admits to many different implementation approaches. In most cases, a mapping abstraction can be characterized by a key type, a value type, and operations for adding to the mapping, removing from the mapping, and applying the mapping. This represents a "signature" for the mapping abstraction, and any combination of types and operations that satisfy such a signature syntactically and semantically can be considered a mapping.

A generic package can be used to define a signature, and then a given implementation for the signature is established by instantiating the signature. Once the signature is defined, a generic formal package for this signature can be used in a generic formal part as a short-hand for a type and a set of operations.

We can thus define a generic package Mapping that defines the signature of a mapping, and then other generics can be defined with a formal package parameter. The mapping package might be

```
generic
    -- define signature for a Mapping
    type Mapping_Type is limited private;
    type Key is limited private;
    type Value is limited private;
    with procedure Add_Pair(M: in out Mapping_Type;
                            K: in Key;
                            V: in Value);
    with procedure Remove_Pair(M: in out Mapping_Type;
                               K: in Key;
                               V: in Value);
```

```
      with procedure Apply(M: in out Mapping_Type;
                           K: in Key;
                           V: out Value);
   package Mapping is end;
```

We can now define a generic that takes an instance of a Mapping as a parameter; for example

```
   generic
      with package Some_Mapping is new Mapping(<>);
      with procedure Do_Something_With_Value(V: Some_Mapping.Value)
   procedure Do_Something_With_Key(K: Some_Mapping.Key);

   procedure Do_Something_With_Key(K: Some_Mapping.Key) is
      V: Some_Mapping.Value;
   begin
      -- translate key to value, and then do something with value
      Some_Mapping.Apply(K, V);
      Do_Something_With_Value(V);
   end Do_Something_With_Key;
```

The reader will note the tedious repetition of Some_Mapping in the generic unit. This can be avoided since a use clause is permitted in a generic formal part in Ada 95; the specification can thus be written as

```
   generic
      with package Some_Mapping is new Mapping(<>);
      use Some_Mapping;
      with procedure Do_Something_With_Value(V: Value)
   procedure Do_Something_With_Key(K: Key);
```

with similar changes to the generic body.

Another and more mathematical example is provided by the following which defines the signature of a group.

```
   generic
      type Group_Element is private;
      Identity: in Group_Element;
      with function Op(X, Y: Group_Element) return Group_Element
      with function Inverse(X: Group_Element) return Group_Element;
   package Group_Signature is end;
```

The following generic function applies the group operation to the given group element the specified number of times. If the right operand is negative, the inverse of the result is returned; if it is zero, the identity is returned.

```
   generic
      with package Group is new Group_Signature(<>);
      use Group;
   function Power(X: Group_Element; N: Integer) return Group_Element;

   function Power(X: Group_Element; N: Integer) return Group_Element is
      Result: Group_Element := Identity;
   begin
      for I in 1 .. abs N loop
         Result := Op(Result, X);
      end loop;
      if N < 0 then
```

```
      return Inverse(Result);
   else
      return Result;
   end if;
end Power;
```

The following instantiation ensures that the long complex numbers are a group over addition

```
package Long_Complex_Addition_Group is
   new Group_Signature(Group_Element => Long_Complex.Complex,
                       Identity => (0.0, 0.0);
                       Op => Long_Complex."+";
                       Inverse => Long_Complex."-");
```

and then finally we can instantiate the power function for the long complex addition group as follows

```
function Complex_Multiplication is
   new Power(Long_Complex_Addition_Group);
```

Note that we have assumed that the type Complex is not a private type so that the aggregate is available for the identity element.

12.7 Other Improvements

A small change is that the matching of subtypes in array and access types now requires static matching as mentioned in 3.10.

Another minor change is that generic actual parameters are evaluated in an arbitrary order consistent with any dependences whereas in Ada 83 all default parameters were evaluated after all explicit parameters. The relaxation of this ordering requirement brings the rules for generic parameters into line with those for ordinary subprogram parameters.

12.8 Requirements Summary

There were a number of requirements in this area. The study topic

   S4.4-A(1) — Generic Formal Parameters

is satisfied by the provision of extra kinds of generic parameters (for derived types and especially package parameters) to enable better abstraction and composition.

The study topic

   S4.4-B(2) — Tighten the "Contract Model"

has been met by the provision of separate templates for definite and indefinite types and other modifications to the rules as discussed in 12.1.

The requirement

   R4.4-B(1) — Dependence of Instantiations on Bodies

has also been met by the improvements to the contract model.

The requirement

R4.4-C(1) — Generic Code Sharing

is discussed in 12.1 where it is noted that the pragma Optimize can be used to control whether sharing is required or not.

13   Representation Issues

This part of the reference manual has always been a pot-pourri of bits and pieces often neglected by users and implementors alike. However, it is an important area especially for embedded systems where tight control of the implementation is required. The changes in Ada 95 are designed to make the vague control promised by Ada 83 into a reality. The main changes are

- The mechanism for specifying representations such as size and alignment is generalized and their meaning is clarified.

- Additional types and operations are provided for address and offset manipulation.

- The Valid attribute enables a potentially dubious value (such as might be obtained through calling Unchecked_Conversion or interfacing to another language) to be checked for validity.

- Facilities are provided for the more detailed control of heap storage for allocated objects.

- The rules regarding the freezing of representations are properly defined.

- The pragma Restrictions is provided for specifying that only a subset of the language is to be used.

- The concept of streams and various stream attributes are introduced.

By their nature, these features of the language concern fine detail for which the reader is referred to [RM95]. In this chapter we will only discuss the broad principles involved. Note that the material on interfacing to other languages is now described in a separate annex of [RM95]; see Chapter B in Part Three. Note also that although the general concept of streams and the stream attributes are defined in section 13 of [RM95], their main application is for input-output and they are therefore discussed in A-1.4.

13.1 Representation of Data

The first point to note is that the notation has been unified so that the attribute form can be used for setting all specifiable attributes. Thus

```
for X'Address use 8#100#;
```

rather than **for** X **use at** 8#100#, and

```
for R'Alignment use 2;
```

rather than **at mod** 2 in a record representation clause. (The old notations are allowed for compatibility although considered obsolete.)

An important reason for the unified notation is that we wish to allow implementations to define additional user-specifiable attributes in a consistent manner. Furthermore the annexes define many additional attributes as discussed in Part Three.

The `Alignment` attribute can be applied to all first subtypes and objects whereas the mod clause only applied to records in Ada 83. An overall rule is that the `Address` of an object must be an integral multiple of its `Alignment`. In the case of internal objects the user must ensure that this is not violated if one or both attributes are specified. In the case of external objects, the attributes may also be specified but then they are more in the nature of an assertion; again it is assumed that the relationship holds.

It is now possible to specify the order of numbering bits. This is particularly important when using record representation clauses to ensure that we know which way round the bits are numbered. For example

```
for R'Bit_Order use Low_Order_First;
```

where R is a record type indicates that the first bit (bit 0) is the least significant.

There was much confusion in Ada 83 over the `Size` attribute. This is now clarified and the reader is referred to the discussion in [RM95] for details. An important point is that the `Size` attribute may now be set for individual objects rather than just to types as in Ada 83.

13.2 The Package System

The package `System.Storage_Elements` contains additional types and operations to enable addresses and offsets to be manipulated in a standard manner. The comparison operators are defined for the type `Address` in the package `System` itself whereas other facilities are in the child package `System.Storage_Elements`.

This latter package includes a type `Storage_Offset` and operations to add and subtract such values to and from values of type `Address`. Storage offsets are of course relative whereas addresses are absolute (echoes of duration and time) and so adding a storage offset to an address returns an address and so on.

The generic child package `System.Address_To_Access_Conversions` provides the ability to convert neatly between values of the type `Address` and values of a given general access type; this enables "peeking" and "poking" to be done in a consistent manner.

Finally note that the pragmas `System_Name`, `Storage_Unit` and `Memory_Size` are now obsolete. They were not uniformly implemented in Ada 83 and it was not at all clear what they should mean. For example, in most implementations, it does not make sense to change the number of bits in a storage unit, and even if it did, it would not be sufficient to make only the package `System` obsolete; clearly all generated code depends on this value. Consequently we no longer require implementations to support these pragmas. Of course, implementations that already support them with some particular meaning can continue to do so (as implementation defined pragmas) for upward compatibility. On the other hand the corresponding named numbers in package `System` are quite useful as queries and so remain.

13.3 The Valid Attribute

There are occasions when `Unchecked_Conversion` is very valuable although inherently dangerous. The `Valid` attribute enables the programmer to ensure that the result of an unchecked conversion is at least a valid value for the subtype concerned (even if not what the programmer hoped for). Some risks of catastrophe are thereby avoided.

The [RM95 13.9.2] lists the ways in which invalid data could be obtained. As well as unchecked conversion this includes results obtain through interfacing to another language and uninitialized data. Note that `Valid` is only defined for objects of scalar types.

13.4 Storage Pool Management

For Ada 95, we have provided the user with the ability to override the default algorithms for allocating and deallocating heap storage. This is done by the introduction of the concept of a storage pool which provides the storage for objects created by allocators. Every access to object type is associated with some storage pool which is a pool of memory from which the storage for allocated objects is obtained.

The storage pool for an access type may be shared with other access types. In particular, any derivative of an access type shares the same storage pool as the parent access type. More importantly, an implementation might use a common global heap by default. An allocator for an access type allocates storage from the associated storage pool.

The package System.Storage_Pools provides mechanisms for defining a storage pool type as an extension of the abstract type Root_Storage_Pool. We can then associate a storage pool with a particular access type by specifying the Storage_Pool attribute for the access type. Alternatively, a bounded storage pool may be requested by specifying the Storage_Size attribute for an access type, as in Ada 83. In the absence of a specification of either the Storage_Pool or Storage_Size attribute of an access type, the implementation chooses an appropriate storage pool for the type.

Pool-specific access values never point outside of their storage pool (in the absence of unchecked conversion and the like). On the other hand, general access values may be assigned to point to any aliased object of an appropriate type and scope, either through the use of the Access attribute or explicit access type conversion.

The storage pool concept makes explicit the notion of a "heap", and when combined with the ability to specify a Storage_Pool object for an access type, gives the user better control over dynamic allocation.

The use of storage pools is illustrated by the following example which shows how an application can use a special allocator algorithm to meet its precise storage requirements. The storage pool associated with the access type supports mark and release operations, allowing rapid reclamation of all storage allocated from the pool during some phase of processing.

```ada
with System.Storage_Pools;
with System.Storage_Elements; use System;
package Mark_Release_Storage is

    type Mark_Release_Pool(Size: Storage_Elements.Storage_Count) is
        new Storage_Pools.Root_Storage_Pool with private;

    type Pool_Mark is limited private;

    -- now provide the controlled operations
    procedure Initialize(Pool: in out Mark_Release_Pool);

    procedure Finalize(Pool: in out Mark_Release_Pool);

    -- now provide the storage pool operations
    procedure Allocate(
        Pool               : in out Mark_Release_Pool;
        Storage_Address: out Address;
        Size_In_Storage_Elements: in Storage_Elements.Storage_Count;
        Alignment          : in Storage_Elements.Storage_Count);

    procedure Deallocate(
        Pool               : in out Mark_Release_Pool;
        Storage_Address: in Address;
        Size_In_Storage_Elements: in Storage_Elements.Storage_Count;
        Alignment          : in Storage_Elements.Storage_Count);
```

```
function Storage_Size(Pool: Mark_Release_Pool)
   return Storage_Elements.Storage_Count;

   -- additional subprograms for the Mark_Release_Pool
procedure Set_Mark(
   Pool: in Mark_Release_Pool;
   Mark: out Pool_Mark);

   -- marks the current state of the pool for later release
procedure Release_To_Mark(
   Pool: in out Mark_Release_Pool;
   Mark: in Pool_Mark);
   -- frees everything allocated from the Pool since Set_Mark.
   -- all access values designating objects allocated since then
   -- become invalid.

private
   ...
end Mark_Release_Storage;
```

This example demonstrates how a package defines a special type of mark/release storage pool, derived from System.Storage_Pools.Root_Storage_Pool (see [RM95 13.11]).

Note carefully that the procedures Allocate and Deallocate are invoked implicitly by the Ada 95 allocator and Unchecked_Deallocation facilities in much the same way as Initialize, Adjust and Finalize are implicitly called by the run-time system for controlled types (see 7.4). Moreover, the type Root_Storage_Pool is itself a limited controlled type and so the procedures Initialize and Finalize are provided.

This example includes two additional operations on the storage pool type, which the user can use to set a mark and then later release the pool to a marked state, and thereby reclaim all recently allocated storage. The declaration of Mark_Release_Pool indicates that it is also extended with additional private components that would be supplied in the private part.

In order to use the above package we first have to declare a particular pool and then specify it as the pool for the access type concerned. We might write

```
use Mark_Release_Storage;
Big_Pool: Mark_Release_Pool(50_000);

type Some_Type is ...;
type Some_Access is access Some_Type;
for Some_Access'Storage_Pool use Big_Pool;
```

This declares the pool Big_Pool of the type Mark_Release_Pool and then associates it with the access type Some_Access by the representation clause. The discriminant of 50,000 acts as an initialization parameter perhaps indicating the total size of the pool. We can then allocate and use objects in the usual way. We can also use the special mark and release capabilities provided by this particular type of pool.

```
declare
   Mark: Pool_Mark;
   Done: Boolean := False;
begin
   -- set mark prior to commencing the loop
   Set_Mark(Big_Pool, Mark);
   while not Done loop
      -- each iteration allocates a data structure composed of
```

```
      -- objects of Some_Type, which may be discarded
      -- before the next iteration.
      declare
         X, Y : Some_Access;
      begin
         -- algorithm that allocates various objects from
         -- the mark/release storage pool
         X := new Some_Type;
         ...

         Y := new Some_Type;
         ...
         -- release storage each time through the loop
         Release_To_Mark(Big_Pool, Mark);
      exception
         when others =>
            -- release storage then reraise the exception
            Release_To_Mark(Big_Pool, Mark);
            raise;
      end;
   end loop;
end;
```

Note carefully that the assignments such as

```
X := new Some_Type;
```

implicitly call the Allocate procedure thus

```
Mark_Release_Storage.Allocate(Pool => Big_Pool,...);
```

Any calls on Unchecked_Deallocation will similarly result in an implicit call of Deallocate.

13.5 Freezing of Representations

Certain uses of an entity or the type of an entity cause it to be frozen; these are situations where the representation has to be known (and if none has been specified the implementation will then choose a representation by default). These uses were called forcing occurrences in Ada 83 (the name has been changed because not all the situations causing freezing are actual occurrences of the name of the entity). The forcing occurrence rules of Ada 83 did not really achieve their objective; sometimes they were too lax and sometimes too rigid; the freezing rules of Ada 95 are intended to more exactly satisfy the objective of identifying when the representation has to be determined.

The situations causing freezing and the operations not allowed on a frozen entity are described in [RM95 13.14]. There seems little point in repeating the discussion here but one point of difference worth emphasizing is that the loophole in deferred constants in Ada 83 which allowed uninitialized access values is now blocked. The new rules were designed to overcome this and similar problems with the Ada 83 rules.

13.5.1 Freezing and Tagged Types

The freezing rules for tagged types are important. The two main ones are that a record extension freezes the parent and a primitive subprogram cannot be declared for a frozen tagged type — this applies to both new ones and overridden ones. Using the illustrative model of the tag and dispatch table in 4.3 this means that the contents of the dispatch table can be determined as soon as the type is frozen.

A consequence of these freezing rules is that we cannot declare further primitive subprograms for a tagged type after a record extension of it has been defined. This was mentioned in II.1 during the discussion of the alert system when we noted the practical benefit of being able to declare a sequence of derived types in one package.

But note that although a record extension freezes the parent type a private extension does not. In the private case the parent type is frozen at the full type declaration (which will be a record extension anyway). So in the following

```
package P is
   type T is tagged ...;
   type NT is new T with private;
   procedure Op(X: T);
private
   type NT is new T with ...;
end P;
```

the partial declaration of NT does not freeze T and so the further operation Op can be added. This operation is also inherited by NT although it is not visible for the partial view of NT (since its declaration was after that of the partial view); it effectively gets added at the full declaration. So

```
A: NT'Class := ...;
Op(A);
```

is illegal outside P but legal in the body of P.

Note that we can add an operation, OpN for NT before the new operation Op for T thus

```
package P is
   type T is tagged ...;
   type NT is new T with private;
   procedure OpN(X: NT);
   procedure Op(X: T);
private
   type NT is new T with ...;
end P;
```

and in this case, perhaps surprisingly, we have added a new operation for the dispatch table of NT before knowing all about the dispatch table of T (which of course forms the first part of the table for NT). However, the full declaration of NT will freeze T and prevent further operations being added for T.

It is instructive to reconsider the alert system discussed in Part One and to rearrange the declarations to minimize spurious visibility. The details of the various types need not be visible externally (we can imagine that they are initialized by operations in some child package). Moreover, it is only necessary for the procedure Handle to be visible externally since Display, Log and Set_Alarm are only called internally from the procedures Handle. However, in the case of Display it is important that it be a dispatching operation if the redispatching discussed in 4.5 is to be possible. The package could thus be reconstructed as follows

```
with Calendar;
package New_Alert_System is

   type Alert is abstract tagged private;
   procedure Handle(A: in out Alert);

   type Low_Alert is new Alert with private;
   type Medium_Alert is new Alert with private;
```

```
    type High_Alert is new Alert with private;

private

    type Device is (Teletype, Console, Big_Screen);

    type Alert is tagged
       record
          Time_Of_Arrival: Calendar.Time;
          Message: Text;
       end record;

    procedure Display(A: in Alert; On: in Device);   -- also dispatches
    procedure Log(A: in Alert);

    type Low_Alert is new Alert with null record;

    type Medium_Alert is new Alert with
       record
          Action_Officer: Person;
       end record;

    -- now override inherited operations
    procedure Handle(MA: in out Medium_Alert);
    procedure Display(MA: in Medium_Alert; On: in Device);

    type High_Alert is new Medium_Alert with
       record
          Ring_Alarm_At: Calendar.Time;
       end record;

    procedure Handle(HA: in out High_Alert);
    procedure Display(HA: in High_Alert; On: in Device);
    procedure Set_Alarm(HA: in High_Alert);

end New_Alert_System;
```

In this formulation all the alerts are private and the visible part consists of a series of private extensions. If the private extensions froze the parent type Alert then it would not be possible to add the private dispatching operation Display in the private part. The deferral of freezing until the full type declaration is thus important. Note that we have also hidden the fact that the High_Alert is actually derived from Medium_Alert. Remember that the full type declaration only has to have the type given in the private extension as some ancestor and not necessarily as the immediate parent.

We can now add a child package for the emergency alert as suggested in II.7 and this will enable a new Display and Handle to be added.

```
package New_Alert_System.Emergency is
    type Emergency_Alert is new Alert with private;
private
    type Emergency_Alert is new Alert with
       record
          . . .
       end record;

    procedure Handle(EA: in out Emergency_Alert);
    procedure Display(EA: in Emergency_Alert; On: in Device);
```

end New_Alert_System.Emergency;

We could make the procedure Display visible by declaring it in the visible part; it would still override the inherited version even though the inherited version is private as mentioned in 7.1.1.

13.6 The Pragma Restrictions

There are some application areas where it is useful to impose restrictions on the use of certain features of the language. Thus it might be desirable to know that only certain simple uses of tasking are made in a particular program; this might allow the program to be linked with an especially efficient run-time system for use in a hard real time application. Another area where more severe restrictions are relevant is for safety-critical applications where it is required that application programs are written using only simple parts of the language so that they are more amenable to mathematical proof. Restrictions on the use of the language may be imposed by the pragma Restrictions. The possible arguments to this pragma are defined in the Real-Time Systems and Safety and Security annexes [RM95 D7, H3].

13.7 Requirements Summary

The requirement

R6.2-A(1) — Data Interoperability

is partially met by the provision of better control over representations such as the alignment of objects.
　　The study topic

S6.4-B(1) — Low-Level Pointer Operations

is addressed by the attribute Unchecked_Access and address and offset operations in the package System.Address_To_Access_Conversions.
　　The requirement

R4.2-A(1) — Allocation and Reclamation of Storage

is met by the storage pool mechanism described in 13.4.

Part Three

The Annexes

The first two parts should have given the reader a good understanding of the Core of Ada 95. This third part describes the material in the Annexes. This includes the predefined environment which is mandatory, as well as the various specialized annexes themselves. It should be noted as a general principle that the annexes contain no new syntax. They are hence largely a description of various packages, attributes and pragmas.

A Predefined Language Environment

One of the main objectives of Ada 95 is to supply a set of supplemental packages of general utility in order to promote portability and reusability. Several packages are essentially intrinsic to the language (such as Ada.Finalization) and are discussed in Part Two. This chapter explains the main design decisions behind the packages described in Annex A of [RM95]. It should be noted that input-output which appeared in chapter 14 of the Ada 83 reference manual [ANSI 83, ISO 87] now appears in Annex A. This move is designed to emphasize that input-output is just one of many facilities provided by the predefined environment and is not really an intrinsic part of the language.

As mentioned in II.13, the predefined library is structured into three packages, Ada, Interfaces and System which can be thought of as child packages of Standard. The main reason for the restructuring is to avoid contamination of the top level name space and consequent risk of clashes with library units defined by the user.

The package System concerns intrinsic facilities associated with the target machine and with storage management and is discussed in Chapter 13. The package Interfaces concerns communication with systems in other languages and also the interface to hardware numeric types. All other predefined packages including input-output are children of Ada.

The major additions to the predefined environment compared with Ada 83 are as follows:

- The packages Ada.Characters and Ada.Strings provide general facilities for the manipulation of characters and strings.

- The package Ada.Numerics provides elementary functions and random number generation.

- There are new packages for completely heterogeneous input-output streams.

- The additional mode Append_File is provided for Ada.Sequential_IO and Ada.-Text_IO.

- Improvements to Text_IO include facilities for looking ahead at the next character, for getting the next character (from the keyboard) without buffering or blocking, and to flush an output buffer. In addition the procedure Get now accepts a wider variety of numeric formats.

- The package Ada.Wide_Text_IO provides text input-output based on the types Wide_-Character and Wide_String. Both Text_IO and Wide_Text_IO also have internal packages for modular and decimal input-output.

- The concept of a *current error file* is introduced in Text_IO by analogy with the current output file. Additional subprograms are added to manipulate current input, output and error in a convenient manner.

- The package Ada.Command_Line enables a program to access any arguments of the command which invoked it and to return an exit status.

In order to avoid incompatibility problems, renamings are provided for packages existing in Ada 83 such as

```
with Ada.Text_IO;
package Text_IO renames Ada.Text_IO;
```

These renamings are considered obsolescent and thus liable to be removed at the next revision of the language.

A.1 Character Handling

Ada 95 provides an empty parent package Ada.Characters with two children: a package of character categorization and conversion subprograms, Characters.Handling, and a child package of constants, Characters.Latin_1, corresponding to the values of type Character. The intent is to provide basic character handling facilities, similar in scope to the contents of the standard C library header <ctype.h> [Plauger 92].

The following were the major issues concerning the design of this package:

- Which kinds of classification functions to supply;

- What to provide for Wide_Character handling;

- Whether to have an analogue to the package Standard.ASCII, extended to account for characters in the "upper half" of the character set;

- What to do about localization.

We had considered declaring the character handling subprograms directly in the package Ada.Characters. However, with such an approach there was some concern that an application needing access only to the constants in Characters.Latin_1 would incur a code-space penalty if the subprograms in the parent package were bound into the application. Placing the subprograms in a child package addresses this concern.

A.1.1 Classification Functions

A preliminary design of the character handling package was based heavily on C's <ctype.h>. Although some of the classification functions are directly applicable, such as testing if a character is a digit, or testing if it is a letter, it was soon apparent that the C model was not completely appropriate for Ada 95. The main issue is that Ada 95, unlike C, has Latin-1 as its default standard character type. Thus the <ctype.h> categorization functions such as ispunct(c) and isspace(c) would have no standard meaning in Latin-1. Moreover, <ctype.h> relies on the C approach to locale, which is rather complicated and has not been adopted by Ada 95.

The categorization functions in Characters.Handling are designed to reflect more the properties of Latin-1 than the heritage of <ctype.h>. Most of the categorizations form a hierarchy:

- Each character is either a control or graphic character

- Each graphic character is either an alphanumeric or a special graphic

- Each alphanumeric is either a letter or a decimal digit

- Each letter is either an upper- or lower-case letter

Supplementing these are further categories; for example a basic character (one without diacritical marks), a hexadecimal digit, and an ISO_646 character (whose position is in the range 0..127).

A.1.2 Wide_Character Handling

There is a single classification function for Wide_Character, namely a test if a value is within the Character subset of the type. We had considered providing additional classification functions for Wide_Character, but this would be premature since there is no widespread agreement on how such functions might be defined.

The Characters.Handling package provides a conversion from Wide_Character to Character, and from Wide_String to String, that leaves a Character value unchanged and that replaces a value outside the Character range with a (programmer-specifiable) value inside this range.

A.1.3 Package of Character Names

The Ada 83 package Standard.ASCII declares a set of constants for the control characters (those whose positions are in the range 0 .. 31, and also the character at position 127), the lower-case letters, and some of the other graphic characters. The contents of this package are a rather uneven mixture, and different motivations led to the inclusion of different parts. The constants corresponding to the control characters are needed, since otherwise references to such characters would have to be in terms of Character'Val(number), which is not in the spirit of the language. It is accepted practice to use ASCII.Nul, ASCII.CR, and ASCII.LF in Ada programs.

On the other hand, the inclusion of constants for the lower-case letters is principally a concession to the fact that, in the early 1980's, the input devices used in some environments did not support upper-case characters. To simulate a string literal such as "Abc" the programmer can write "A" & ASCII.LC_B & ASCII.LC_C.

For Ada 95, the issues were what to do about the package Standard.ASCII, and what to do about names of the characters in the "upper half" (those whose positions are in the range 128 .. 255).

Part of the problem surrounding Standard.ASCII is due to the fact that the name "ASCII" now no longer refers to a 7-bit character set, but rather to ISO 8859-1 (Latin-1). Thus perhaps the most consistent approach would be to add to Standard.ASCII the declarations of names for "upper half" characters, and to introduce renamings where relevant in order to be consistent with ISO nomenclature (for example, Reverse_Solidus as a renaming of Back_Slash). However, this would have the significant disadvantage of introducing a large number of declarations into Standard. Even though they would be in an inner package (and thus not pollute the user's namespace), there was concern that such a specialized package would be out of place if included in package Standard.

These considerations led to the declaration of the child package Characters.Latin_1. This package includes names of the control characters from ISO 646 (the same names as in Standard.ASCII), the graphic characters from ISO 646 excepting the upper case letters and the decimal digits, the control characters from ISO 6429, and the graphic characters in the "upper half". The names of the graphics are based on Latin-1; hence Number_Sign for '#', as opposed to Sharp as in Standard.ASCII. Since Characters.Latin_1 is in the predefined environment, it must be supported by all implementations.

Although there is some overlap between Characters.Latin_1 and Standard.ASCII, we expect that new Ada 95 programs will refer to the former, whereas existing Ada 83 code that is being moved intact to Ada 95 will continue to use the latter. In fact, the main reason to retain Standard.ASCII at all is for upward compatibility; removing it from the language would have been a major incompatibility and was not a realistic design alternative. Instead, it is specified as an obsolescent feature and its declaration appears in [RM95 J].

We recognize that names such as Ada.Characters.Latin_1.Nul are notationally rather heavy. However, we expect that users will typically provide renamings (either at the library level or as local declarations) such as

package Latin_1 **renames** Ada.Characters.Latin_1;

and thus in practice the references will be of the more palatable form Latin_1.Nul.

A.1.4 Character Set Localization

Although the language standard dictates Latin-1 as the contents of type Character, an implementation has permission to supply an alternative set specific to the locale or environment. For example, an eastern European implementation may define the type Character based on ISO 8859, Part 2 (Latin-2); a personal computer implementation may define the type Character as the native PC character set. Of course with such adaptations an Ada program might no longer be portable, but in some environments the ability to exploit the characteristics of the local environment is more important than the ability to move a program between different environments. In fact the explicit permission for a validated compiler to perform such localizations is not new in Ada 95 but applies also to Ada 83 based on a non-binding interpretation of ISO/IEC JTC1/SC22 WG9 Ada [ISO WG9 93].

An implication of such localization is that the semantics of the classification and conversion functions in the Characters.Handling package depends on the definition of Character. For example, the result of Is_Letter(Character'Val(16#F7#)) is false for Latin-1 (this character is the division sign) but is true for Latin/Cyrillic.

A.2 String Handling

Many languages support string handling either directly via data types and operations or through standard supplemental library functions. Ada 83 provided the framework for a solution, through discriminated record types and access types, but the absence of a standard set of string handling services has proved a barrier to portability. To solve this problem, Ada 95 includes a set of packages for string handling that need to be supplied by all implementations.

A.2.1 Categories of Strings

We can divide string data structures into three categories based on their flexibility and associated storage management:

*   A *fixed-length string* has a length whose value is established at object creation and is invariant during the object's lifetime. There is no need to use the heap for the storage of a fixed-length string.

*   A *bounded-length string*, also known in the literature as a varying-length string, can change in length during its lifetime, but the maximum length is established no later than when the object is created. Thus a bounded-length string has both a current length which can change, and a maximum length which does not change.

Since the maximum length is known on a per-object basis, a natural implementation is to reserve this maximum amount of storage when the object is created, rather than using the heap.

• An *unbounded-length string*, also known in the literature as a dynamic string, can change in length during its lifetime with no a priori maximum length other than that implied by the range of the index subtype. Unbounded-length strings need to be managed dynamically, either in the general heap or in some region reserved for strings, because of the wide range of possible sizes for any given object.

In practice the storage allocation performed by the compiler may vary from the "natural" method mentioned. For example, if the length of a fixed-length string, or the maximum length of a bounded-length string, exceeds some threshold value then the compiler may choose to place the object on the heap, with automatic reclamation when the object becomes inaccessible. This may be done because of target machine addressing constraints or (for bounded-length strings with a prohibitively large maximum size) as a means to economize on storage usage.

Ada 95 supplies packages for each of these categories, for both the predefined types String and Wide_String. For fixed-length strings the type is the specific type String or Wide_String. For the other two categories, a private type is supplied (see below) since it is important for purposes of data abstraction to avoid exposing the representation. Each of the three packages supplies a set of string-handling subprograms. The bounded- and unbounded-length string packages also supply conversion and selection functions; these are needed because the type is private.

A.2.2 Operations on Strings

Operations on strings fall into several categories. This section summarizes the various operations that are provided, and notes the semantic issues that arise based on whether the strings are fixed-, bounded-, or unbounded-length.

Constructors

Literals are available for fixed-length strings; for bounded- and unbounded-length strings we need conversion functions (String to/from Bounded_String and also to/from Unbounded_String).

The conversion function from String to Bounded_String illustrates a point that comes up in other contexts when constructing a bounded string: suppose the length of the result exceeds the maximum length of the bounded string? We let the user control the behavior through a parameter to the constructor function. The default effect is to raise an exception (Strings.Length_-Error), but the user can also establish truncation of extra characters either on the right or left.

Concatenation is available automatically for fixed-length strings, and explicit overloadings are provided for bounded and unbounded strings. Note that since the operator form for concatenation of bounded length strings does not offer a possibility for the user to control the behavior if the result length exceeds the bounded string type's maximum length, we provide also a set of Append functions taking an explicit parameter dictating truncation versus raising an exception. The operator form will raise an exception if the result length exceeds the type's maximum length.

For bounded and unbounded strings, there is the question of how many overloaded versions to supply for the concatenation functions. For convenience we allow concatenation of a Bounded_-String with either a Character, a String, or another Bounded_String, returning a Bounded_String result, and analogously for Unbounded_String. We decided against allowing the concatenation of two fixed-length strings return a Bounded_String (or an Unbounded_String), since such an overloading would render ambiguous a statement such as

```
B := S1 & S2 & S3;
```

where S1, S2 and S3 are of type String and B is of type Bounded_String.

If it is necessary to convert between a bounded and an unbounded string, this can be done by producing a String as an intermediate result.

Replication operations are also provided to construct string values. For each of the three string categories a "*" operator is supplied with left operand of subtype Natural and right operand either a Character, a String, or (for bounded and unbounded strings) a value of the corresponding string type. The result is of the string type. For example:

```
declare
    Alpha, Beta : Unbounded_String;
begin
    Alpha := 3 * 'A';       -- To_String(Alpha) = "AAA"
    Alpha := 2 * Alpha;     -- To_String(Alpha) = "AAAAAA"
    Beta  := 2 * "Abc";     -- To_String(Beta)  = "AbcAbc"
end;
```

Copying

The issue in copying is what to do when the source and target lengths differ; this is only a concern in the fixed-length case. For bounded strings the ":=" operation always works: the source and target have identical maximum lengths, so assignment simply copies the source to the target. For unbounded strings the ":=" operation does the necessary storage management through Adjust and Finalize operations to allocate needed space for the new value of the target and to reclaim the space previously occupied by the object.

Our model, based on COBOL, is that a fixed-length string comprises significant contents together with padding. The pad characters may appear either on the right or left (or both); this is useful for report output fields. Parameters to the Move procedure allow the programmer to control the effect. When a shorter string is copied to a longer string, pad characters are supplied as filler, and the Justify parameter guides where the source characters are placed. When a longer string is copied to a shorter string, the programmer establishes whether the extra characters are to be dropped from the left or the right, or if an exception should be raised when a non-pad character is dropped.

Selection

Component selection is not an issue for fixed-length strings, since indexing and slicing are directly available. For both bounded and unbounded strings, we supply subprograms to select and replace a single element, and to select and replace a slice.

Ordering relations

For fixed-length strings the predefined ordering and equality operators are appropriate, but for both the bounded and unbounded string types we provide explicit overloadings. Note that if the implementation chooses to represent bounded strings with a maximum-length array and an index for the current length (see A.2.5 for further discussion), then predefined assignment has the desired effect but predefined equality does not, since it would check the "junk" characters in the string beyond the logical length.

The ordering operators return a result based on the values of corresponding characters; Thus for example the string "ZZZ" is less than the string "aa". Anything more sophisticated would have been out of scope and in any event is dependent on local cultural conventions.

Searching and pattern matching

Each of the string handling packages provides subprograms to scan a string for a pattern (Index, Count) or for characters inside or outside specified sets (Index_Non_Blank, Index, and Find_Token). The profiles for each of these subprograms is the same in the three packages, except for the type of the source string (String, Bounded_String, or Unbounded_String).

A design issue was how to arrange that pattern matches be case insensitive, or in general to reflect user-defined character equivalences. Our approach is to supply to each pattern matching function a parameter that specifies a character equivalence. By default the equivalence mapping is the identity relation, but the programmer can override this via an explicit parameter of type Strings.Maps.Character_Mapping.

Although Index_Non_Blank is redundant, it is included since searching for blanks is such a common operation.

Find_Token is at a somewhat higher level than the other subprograms. We have supplied this procedure since it is extremely useful for simple lexical analysis such as parsing a line of interactively supplied input text.

String transformation

As with the searching and pattern matching subprograms, we supply the same functionality for string transformations in each of the three string handling packages.

A common need is to translate a string via a character translation table. The Translate function satisfies this goal. The procedural form of Translate is included for efficiency, to avoid the extra copying that may be required for function returns.

The other string transformation subprograms are Replace_Slice, Insert, Overwrite, Delete, and Trim. These are not necessarily length preserving.

We had considered including a subprogram to replace all occurrences of a pattern with a given string but ultimately decided in the interest of simplicity to leave this out. It can be written in terms of the supplied operations if needed (see the example in A.2.8).

A.2.3 General Design Decisions

Independent of the functionality provided, several fundamental design questions arose: whether to make the packages generic (with respect to character and string type) or specific to the types in Standard; how to organize the packages (hierarchically or as siblings); and whether to define the string-returning operations as functions, procedures, or both.

Generic vs non-generic form of packages

String handling needs to be provided for the predefined String and Wide_String types, and it is also useful for strings of elements from user-supplied character types. For these reasons it seems desirable to have a generic version of the string handling packages, with language-defined instantiations for Character and String and also for Wide_Character and Wide_String. In fact, an earlier version of the packages adopted this approach, but we subsequently decided to provide non-generic forms instead.

There are several reasons for this decision. First, although the specifications for the packages for handling Character and Wide_Character strings might be the same, the implementations would be different. Second, the generic form would be rather complicated, a pedagogical issue for users and a practical issue for implementations.

Structure of packages

In order to minimize the number of language-defined names for immediate children of the root package Ada, the string handling packages form a hierarchy. The ancestor unit, Ada.Strings, declares the types and exceptions common to the other packages. The package Strings.Maps declares the types and related entities for the various data representations needed by the other packages. Strings.Fixed, Strings.Bounded, and Strings.Unbounded provide the entities for fixed-length, bounded-length, and unbounded-length strings, respectively. The package Strings.Maps.Constants declares Character_Set constants corresponding to the character classification functions in the package Characters, as well as Character_Mapping constants that can be used in pattern matching and string transformations. There are analogous packages Strings.Wide_Maps, Strings.Wide_Fixed, Strings.Wide_Bounded, Strings.Wide_-Unbounded, and Strings.Wide_Maps.Constants, for Wide_String handling.

Procedures vs functions

The subprograms that deliver string results can be defined either as functions or as procedures. The functional notation is perhaps more pleasant stylistically but typically involves extra copying. The procedural form, with an in out parameter that is updated "in place", is generally more efficient but can lead to a heavy-looking style.

Our solution is to provide both forms for all three string-handling packages. Although this increases the size of the packages, the benefits are an increase in flexibility for the programmer, and a regularity in the structure of the packages that should make them easier to use.

A.2.4 Strings.Maps

The package Strings.Maps defines the types for representing sets of characters and character-to-character mappings, for the types Character and String. A corresponding package, Strings.Wide_Maps, provides the same functionality for the types Wide_Character and Wide_String.

The type Character_Set represents sets of Character values that are to be passed to the string handling subprograms. We considered several alternative declarations for Character_-Set:

- A visible constrained array-of-Booleans type;

- A visible unconstrained array-of-Booleans type;

- A private type; and

- A private type with unknown discriminants.

A visible constrained array type is the traditional representation of a set of values from a discrete type; in the case of Character it would be:

```
type Character_Set is array (Character) of Boolean;
pragma Pack(Character_Set);
```

However, this has several disadvantages. First, it would differ from the choice of representations for a set of Wide_Character values, in the package Strings.Wide_Maps; in the latter package a constrained array type is not a realistic decision, since an overhead of 2^{16} (64K) bits for each set would be excessive. Second, even 256 bits may be more than is desirable for small sets, and a more compact representation might be useful.

An unconstrained array of Booleans addresses the second issue:

```
type Character_Set is array (Character range <>) of Boolean;
pragma Pack(Character_Set);
```

In this version, an object CS of type Character_Set represents the set comprising each character C in CS'Range such that CS(C) is true; any character outside CS'Range is implicitly regarded as not being in the set, and of course any character C in CS'Range such that CS(C) is false is regarded as not being in the set. Thus, for example, the empty set is represented by a null Character_Set array (as well as by many other Character_Set values).

The unconstrained array approach was used in earlier versions of the string handling packages, since it is more efficient in storage than the constrained array approach. However, we ultimately decided against this approach, for several reasons.

- Similar to the constrained array-of-Booleans approach, it is not always appropriate for Wide_Character sets. In particular, even if a set is small and has a compact representation, taking the complement of the set can yield a value requiring 64K bits.

- The effect of ":=" is unintuitive. Two Character_Set objects could represent the same set, yet since they might have different lengths, assigning one to another could raise Constraint_Error.

- The need to provide an explicit initialization for each Character_Set variable (since the type is unconstrained) is inconvenient.

The private type approach is much more in the spirit of Ada and allows the implementation, rather than requiring the language, to make the choice of representations for Character_Set. Note that a simple private type (i.e., one without unknown discriminants) is not allowed to have an unconstrained type as its full declaration. Thus if we want to allow some flexibility (rather than just imposing a private type interface on what is certain to be a constrained array type declaration as the full type declaration) we should allow the possibility of having the full declaration be an access type whose designated type is an unconstrained array of Booleans. To do this, we need to compromise the goal of having a pure package (since access types are not permitted in a pure package); instead, we simply make the package preelaborable.

A private type with an unknown discriminant part might seem like a more direct way to allow the unconstrained-array-of-Booleans as the full declaration, but it suffers from a major portability flaw. If Set_1 and Set_2 are objects of type Character_Set, and Character_Set is a private type with an unknown discriminant part, then the assignment Set_1 := Set_2; may or may not raise Constraint_Error, depending on what the implementation chooses for the full type declaration.

As a result of these considerations, we have declared Character_Set as a private type, without an unknown discriminant part, and have specified the package as just preelaborable rather than pure in order to allow the implementation to use an access type in the full declaration of Character_Set.

A consequence of declaring Character_Set as private is that constructor functions are needed for composing Character_Set values. We have provided several such functions, each named To_Set. Since it is often convenient to have a set containing a single character, or exactly those characters appearing in some array, we have overloaded To_Set to take either a parameter of type Character or of type Character_Sequence (the latter is in fact just a subtype with the effect of renaming String). It is also useful to compose a set out of one or more character ranges, and hence we have supplied the appropriate additional overloadings of To_Set. In the other direction, it is useful to get a "concrete" representation of a set as either a set of ranges or a character sequence, and hence we have provided the corresponding functions.

Although introducing the name Character_Sequence is not strictly necessary (the name String would be equivalent), the style of having a subtype as effectively a renaming of an existing (sub)type makes the intent explicit.

Other languages that supply string handling functions represent character sets directly as character sequences as opposed to boolean arrays; for example, the functions in the C standard header <strings.h>. This was considered for the Ada 95 packages but rejected in the interest of efficiency.

Another type declared by Strings.Maps is Character_Mapping, which represents a mapping from one Character value to another. For the same reasons underlying the choice of a private type for Character_Set, we have also declared Character_Mapping as private. A typical choice for a full type declaration would be:

```
type Character_Mapping is array (Character) of Character;
```

with the obvious interpretation; if CM is a Character_Mapping and C is a character, then CM(C) is the character to which C maps under the mapping CM.

Character mappings are used in two contexts:

- To define an equivalence function applicable during pattern matches (e.g., allowing the programmer to do searches where the distinction between upper and lower case letters does not matter); and

- To define a translation table used in string transformation subprograms.

As an example of the use of the Character_Mapping type, the constant Lower_Case_Map (declared in Strings.Maps.Constants) maps each letter to the corresponding lower case letter and maps each other character to itself. The following finds the first occurrence of the pattern string "gerbil" in a source string S, independent of case:

```
Index(Source  => S,
      Pattern => "gerbil",
      Going   => Forward,
      Mapping => Strings.Maps.Constants.Lower_Case_Map)
```

A character C matches a pattern character P with respect to the Character_Mapping value Map if Map(C)=P. Thus the user needs to ensure that a pattern string comprises only characters occurring in the range of the mapping. (Passing as a pattern the string "GERBIL" would always fail for the mapping Lower_Case_Map.) An earlier version of the string packages had a more symmetric definition for matching; namely C matched P if Map(C) = Map(P). However, this yielded some counterintuitive effects and has thus been changed.

There is another possible representation for mappings, namely an access value denoting a function whose domain and range are the character type in question. This would be useful where the domain and range are very large sets, and in fact is used in the string handling packages for Wide_Character and Wide_String. To avoid unnecessary differences between the String and Wide_String packages, we have supplied the analogous access-to-subprogram type in Strings.Maps:

```
type Character_Mapping_Function is
   access function (From : in Character) return Character;
```

Each subprogram that takes a Character_Mapping parameter is overloaded with a version that takes a Character_Mapping_Function. In an earlier version of the string handling packages, the access-to-subprogram type was provided for Wide_String handling but not for String handling, since we were striving to make the latter pure. However, since the package has had to compromise purity for other reasons as described above, there was no longer a compelling reason to leave out the character mapping function type.

A.2.5 Bounded-Length Strings

The major decisions for bounded-length strings were (1) whether the type should be private or not, and (2) whether to realize the maximum length as a discriminant or, instead, as a generic formal parameter.

There are two main reasons to declare a type as private as opposed to non-private:

- To hide irrelevant representational decisions, thus allowing implementation flexibility,

- To ensure that the programmer does not violate data consistency or otherwise abuse the intent of the type.

Both of these apply to Bounded_String; hence it is appropriate for the type to be declared as private.

There are two principal ways to represent a varying- (but bounded-) length string, assuming that access types are to be avoided. One is to supply the maximum length as a discriminant constraint, thus allowing different objects of the same type to have different maximum lengths. The other approach is to supply the maximum length at the instantiation of a generic package declaring a bounded string type, implying that objects with different maximum lengths must be of different types. We thus have the following basic approaches:

```
package Discriminated_Bounded_Length is
    type Bounded_String(Max_Length : Positive) is private;
    function Length(Item : Bounded_String) return Natural;
    ...
private
    type Bounded_String(Max_Length : Positive) is
        record
            Length : Natural;
            Data   : String(1 .. Max_Length);
        end record;
end Discriminated_Bounded_Length;
```

and also the alternative:

```
generic
    Max : Positive:
package Generic_Bounded_Length is
    Max_Length : constant Positive := Max;
    subtype Length_Range is Natural range 0 .. Max_Length;

    type Bounded_String is private;

    function Length(Item : Bounded_String)
        return Length_Range;
    ...
```

```
private
   type Bounded_String_Internals(Length : Length_Range := 0) is
      record
         Data : String(1 .. Length);
      end record;
   type Bounded_String is
      record
         Data : Bounded_String_Internals;
      end record;
end Generic_Bounded_Length;
```

Each of these approaches has advantages and disadvantages (the reason for the seeming redundancy in the private part of the generic package will be discussed below). If there is an operation that needs to deal with Bounded_String values with different maximum lengths, then the discriminated type approach is simpler. On the other hand, predefined assignment and equality for discriminated Bounded_String do not have the desired behavior. Assignment makes sense when the maximum lengths of source and target are different, as long as the source's current length is no greater than the target's maximum length, yet predefined ":=" would raise Constraint_Error on the discriminant mismatch. User-defined Adjust and Finalize operations do not solve this problem. It would be possible to avoid the difficulty by declaring the type as limited private, but this would result in a very clumsy programming style.

A variation is to declare a discriminated type with a default value for the Max_Length discriminant. An object declared unconstrained can thus be assigned a value with a different maximum length (and a different length). This approach, however, introduces other problems. First, if the object is allocated rather than declared, then its discriminant is in fact constrained (by its default initial value). Second, declaring an appropriate subtype for the discriminant — that is, establishing an appropriate bound for Max_Length — is difficult. If it is too small then the user might not be able to create needed objects. If it is too large, then there will either be a lot of wasted space or else the implementation may use dynamic storage allocation implicitly.

The solution is to let the user establish the maximum length as a parameter at generic instantiation. Such an approach avoids these complications, but has two main drawbacks. First, the programmer will need to perform as many instantiations as there are different maximum lengths to be supported. Second, operations involving varying-length strings of different maximum lengths cannot be defined as part of the same generic package. However, the programmer can get around the first difficulty by providing a small number of instantiations with sufficient maximum size (for example, max lengths of 20 and 80). Either explicit overloadings or generics with formal package instantiations serve to address the second issue. For these reasons we have adopted the generic approach, rather than the discriminant approach, to specifying the maximum length for a varying-length string.

Note that Bounded_String in the generic package is declared without discriminants. Max_Length is established at the generic instantiation, and the Length field is invisible to the user and is set implicitly as part of the effect of the various operations. An alternative would be to declare the type as follows:

```
type Bounded_String(Length : Length_Range := 0) is private;
```

However, this would allow the user to create constrained instances, which defeats the intent of the package. In order to prevent such abuses it is best to leave the Length component hidden from the user [Eachus 92].

A final point of rationale for the Bounded_String generic: the reason for declaring Max_Length, which is simply a constant reflecting the value supplied at the generic instantiation, is to allow the user to refer to the maximum length without keeping track manually of which values were supplied at which instantiations.

A.2.6 Unbounded-Length Strings

Unbounded-length strings need to be implemented via dynamic storage management. In Ada 83, in the absence of automatic garbage collection it was the programmer's responsibility to reclaim storage through unchecked deallocation. Ada 95's facilities for automatically invoked Adjust and Finalize plug this loophole, since the unbounded string type implementor can arrange that storage be reclaimed implicitly, with no need for the user to perform unchecked deallocation.

The main design issue for unbounded strings was whether to expose the type as derived from Finalization.Controlled. That is, the type could be declared either as

```
type Unbounded_String is private;
```

or

```
type Unbounded_String is new Finalization.Controlled with private;
```

An advantage of the latter approach is that users can further derive from Unbounded_String for richer kinds of data structures, and override the default Finalize and Adjust. However, we have chosen the simpler approach, just making Unbounded_String private. If a more complicated data structure is desired, this can be obtained by including an Unbounded_String as a component.

Besides providing the private type Unbounded_String, the package Strings.Unbounded declares a visible general access type String_Access whose designated type is String. The need for such a type arises often in practice, and so it is appropriate to have it declared in a language-defined package.

The following is a sample implementation of the private part of the package:

```
private
   use Finalization;

   Null_String : aliased String := "";

   type Unbounded_String is new Controlled with
      record
         Reference : String_Access := Null_String'Access;
      end record;

   -- No need for Initialize procedure
   procedure Finalize (Object : in out Unbounded_String);
   procedure Adjust   (Object : in out Unbounded_String);

   Null_Unbounded_String : constant Unbounded_String :=
      (Controlled with Reference => Null_String'Access);

end Ada.Strings.Unbounded;
```

The following skeletal package body illustrates how several of the subprograms might be implemented.

```
with Unchecked_Deallocation;
package body Strings.Unbounded is
   procedure Free is
      new Unchecked_Deallocation(String, String_Access);
```

```ada
function To_Unbounded_String(Source : String)
   return Unbounded_String is
   Result_Ref : constant String_Access :=
                      new String(1 .. Source'Length);
begin
   Result_Ref.all := Source;
   return (Finalization.Controlled with Reference => Result_Ref);
end To_Unbounded_String;

function To_String(Source : Unbounded_String) return String is
begin
   return Item.Reference.all;
      -- Note: Item.Reference is never null
end To_String;

--  In the following subprograms, the Reference component of each
--  Unbounded_String formal parameter is non-null, because of the
--  default initialization implied by the type's declaration

function Length(Source : Unbounded_String) return Natural is
begin
   return Source.Reference.all'Length;
end Length;

function "=" (Left, Right : Unbounded_String) return Boolean is
begin
   return Left.Reference.all = Right.Reference.all;
end "=";

procedure Finalize(Object : in out Unbounded_String) is
begin
   if Object.Reference /= Null_String'Access then
      Free(Object.Reference);
   end if;
end Finalize;

procedure Adjust(Object : in out Unbounded_String);
begin
   --  Copy Object if it is not Null_Unbounded_String
   if Object.Reference /= Null_String'Access then
      Object.Reference := new String'(Object.Reference.all);
   end if;
end Adjust;

function "&" (Left, Right : in Unbounded_String)
            return Unbounded_String is
   Left_Length   : constant Natural := Left.Reference.all'Length;
   Right_Length  : constant Natural := Right.Reference.all'Length;
   Result_Length : constant Natural := Left_Length + Right_Length;
   Result_Ref    : String_Access;
begin
   if Result_Length = 0 then
      return Null_Unbounded_String;
   else
      Result_Ref := new String(1 .. Result_Length);
      Result_Ref.all(1..Left_Length) := Left.Reference.all;
      Result_Ref.all(Left_Length+1..Result_Length) :=
         Right.Reference.all;
```

```
            return (Finalization.Controlled with
                        Reference => Result_Ref);
        end if;
    end "&";
    ...
end Ada.Strings.Unbounded;
```

A.2.7 Wide String Handling

Since the same functionality is needed for Wide_String as for String, there are child packages
of Ada.Strings with analogous contents to those discussed above, but for Wide_Character
and Wide_String. The only difference is that some of the type and subprogram names have been
adapted to reflect their application to Wide_Character.

As a consequence of providing equivalent functionality for the two cases, we have made it
easier for a programmer to modify an application that deals with, say, String data, so that it can
work with Wide_String data.

A.2.8 Examples

The function below, which replaces all occurrences of a pattern in a source string, is intended as an
illustration of the various string handling operations rather than as a recommended style for solving
the problem. A more efficient approach would be to defer creating the result string until after the
pattern matches have been performed, thereby avoiding the overhead of allocating and deallocating
the intermediate string data at each iteration.

```
with Ada.Strings.Maps, Ada.Strings.Unbounded, Ada.Strings.Fixed;
use Ada.Strings;
function Replace_All (Source  : in String;
                      Pattern : in String;
                      By      : in String;
                      Going   : in Direction := Forward;
                      Mapping : in Maps.Character_Mapping :=
                                      Maps.Identity)
                      return String is
    use type Unbounded.Unbounded_String;
    Pattern_Length : constant Natural := Pattern'Length;
    Start          : Natural          := Source'First;
    Result         : Unbounded.Unbounded_String;
    Index          : Natural;
begin
    loop
        Index :=
            Fixed.Index(Source(Start .. Source'Last),
                        Pattern, Going, Mapping);
        if Index/=0 then
            Result := Result & Source(Start .. Index-1) & By;
            Start  := Index + Pattern'Length;
        else
            Result := Result & Source(Start .. Source'Last);
            return Unbounded.To_String(Result);
        end if;
    end loop;
end Replace_All;
```

The following program fragments show how the string handling subprograms may be used to get the effect of several COBOL INSPECT statement forms.

```
COBOL:     INSPECT ALPHA
           TALLYING NUM FOR ALL "Z" BEFORE "A".


Ada 95:    Alpha : String( ... );
           A_Index, Num: Natural;
           ...
           A_Index := Index(Alpha, 'A');
           Num     := Count(Alpha(Alpha'First .. A_Index-1), "Z");


COBOL:     INSPECT ALPHA
           REPLACING ALL "A" BY "G", "B" BY "H"
           BEFORE INITIAL "X".


Ada 95:    Alpha    : String( ... );
           X_Index  : Natural;
           My_Map   : Character_Mapping :=
                        To_Mapping(From => "AB", To=>"GH");
           ...
           X_Index := Index(Alpha, 'X');
           Translate(Source  => Alpha(Alpha'First .. X_Index -1),
                     Mapping => My_Map);
```

A.3 Numerics Packages and Attributes

Ada 95 includes in the predefined environment several child packages of Ada.Numerics, and the language also provides a comprehensive set of representation-oriented, model-oriented, and primitive-function attributes for real types.

The package Ada.Numerics itself defines the named numbers Pi and e, as well as an exception (Argument_Error) shared by several of its children.

The constants Pi and e are defined for the convenience of mathematical applications. The WG9 Numerics Rapporteur Group did not define these constants in the secondary numeric standards for Ada 83 [ISO 94a], primarily because it could not decide whether to define a minimal set (as has now been done in Ada 95) or a much larger set of mathematical and physical constants. Ada 95 implementations are required to provide Pi and e to at least 50 decimal places; this exceeds by a comfortable margin the highest precision available on present-day computers.

The Argument_Error exception is raised when a function in a child of Numerics is given an actual parameter whose value is outside the domain of the corresponding mathematical function.

The child packages of Ada.Numerics are Generic_Elementary_Functions and its non-generic equivalents, Float_Random and Discrete_Random (see A.3.2); Generic_Complex_-Types and its non-generic equivalents (see G.1.1); Generic_Complex_Elementary_-Functions and its non-generic equivalents (see G.1.2).

A.3.1 Elementary Functions

The elementary functions are critical to a wide variety of scientific and engineering applications written in Ada. They have been widely provided in the past as vendor extensions, but the lack of a standardized interface, variations in the use or avoidance of generics, differences in the set of functions provided, and absence of guaranteed accuracy have hindered the portability and the analysis of programs. These impediments are removed by including the elementary functions in the predefined language environment.

The elementary functions are provided in Ada 95 by a generic package, Numerics.-Generic_Elementary_Functions, which is a very slight variation of the generic package, Generic_Elementary_Functions, defined in [ISO 94a] for Ada 83.

In addition, Ada 95 provides non-generic equivalent packages for each of the predefined floating point types, so as to facilitate the writing of scientific applications by programmers whose experience in other languages leads them to select the precision they desire by choosing an appropriate predefined floating point type. The non-generic equivalent packages have names as follows

```
Numerics.Elementary_Functions          -- for Float
Numerics.Long_Elementary_Functions     -- for Long_Float
```

and so on.

These nongeneric equivalents behave just like instances of the generic packages except that they may not be used as actual package parameters as in the example in 12.6.

A vendor may, in fact, provide the non-generic equivalent packages by instantiating the generic, but more likely they will be obtained by hand-tailoring and optimizing the text of the generic package for each of the predefined floating point types, resulting in better performance.

The Argument_Error exception is raised, for example, when the Sqrt function in Numerics.Generic_Elementary_Functions is given a negative actual parameter. In [ISO 94a] and related draft secondary standards for Ada 83, Argument_Error was declared in each generic package as a renaming of an exception of the same name defined in a (non-generic) package called Elementary_Functions_Exceptions; in Ada 95, the children of Numerics do not declare Argument_Error, even as a renaming. In Ada 83, simple applications that declare problem-dependent floating point types might look like this:

```
with Generic_Elementary_Functions;
procedure Application is
    type My_Type is digits ...;
    package My_Elementary_Functions is
        new Generic_Elementary_Functions(My_Type);
    use My_Elementary_Functions;
    X : My_Type;
begin
    ... Sqrt(X) ...
exception
    when Argument_Error =>
    ...
end Application;
```

In Ada 95, they will look almost the same, the essential difference being the addition of context clauses for Ada.Numerics:

```
with Ada.Numerics; use Ada.Numerics;
with Ada.Numerics.Generic_Elementary_Functions;
procedure Application is
    type My_Type is digits ...;
    package My_Elementary_Functions is
        new Generic_Elementary_Functions(My_Type);
    use My_Elementary_Functions;
    X : My_Type;
begin
    ... Sqrt(X) ...
```

```
exception
   when Argument_Error =>
   ...
end Application;
```

The benefit of the Ada 95 approach can be appreciated when one contemplates what happens when a second problem-dependent type and a second instantiation of Numerics.Generic_-Elementary_Functions are added to the application. There are no surprises in Ada 95, where one would write the following:

```
with Ada.Numerics; use Ada.Numerics;
with Ada.Numerics.Generic_Elementary_Functions;
procedure Application is
   type My_Type_1 is digits ...;
   type My_Type_2 is digits ...;
   package My_Elementary_Functions_1 is
      new Generic_Elementary_Functions(My_Type_1);
   package My_Elementary_Functions_2 is
      new Generic_Elementary_Functions(My_Type_2);
   use My_Elementary_Functions_1, My_Elementary_Functions_2;
   X : My_Type_1;
   Y : My_Type_2;
begin
   ... Sqrt(X) ...
   ... Sqrt(Y) ...
exception
   when Argument_Error =>
   ...
end Application;
```

If one were to extend the Ada 83 example with a second problem-dependent type and a second instantiation, one would be surprised to discover that direct visibility of Argument_Error is lost (because both instances declare that name, and the declarations are not overloadable [RM95 8.4(11)]). To regain direct visibility, one would have to add to the application a renaming declaration for Argument_Error.

The functions provided in Numerics.Generic_Elementary_Functions are the standard square root function (Sqrt), the exponential function (Exp), the logarithm function (Log), the forward trigonometric functions (Sin, Cos, Tan, and Arctan), the inverse trigonometric functions (Arcsin, Arccos, Arctan, and Arccot), the forward hyperbolic functions (Sinh, Cosh, Tanh, and Coth), and the inverse hyperbolic functions (Arcsinh, Arccosh, Arctanh, and Arccoth). In addition, an overloading of the exponentiation operator is provided for a pair of floating point operands.

Two overloadings of the Log function are provided. Without a Base parameter, this function computes the natural (or Napierian) logarithm, i.e. the logarithm to the base e, which is the inverse of the exponential function. By specifying the Base parameter, which is the second parameter, one can compute logarithms to an arbitrary base. For example,

```
Log(U)                  -- natural logarithm of U
Log(U, 10.0)            -- common (base 10) logarithm of U
Log(U, 2.0)             -- log of U to the base 2
```

Two overloadings of each of the trigonometric functions are also provided. Without a Cycle parameter, the functions all imply a natural cycle of 2π, which means that angles are measured in radians. By specifying the Cycle parameter, one can measure angles in other units. For example,

```
Sin(U)                        -- sine of U (U measured in radians)
Cos(U, 360.0)                 -- cosine of U (U measured in degrees)
Arctan(U, Cycle => 6400.0) -- angle (in mils) whose tangent is U
Arccot(U, Cycle => 400.0)  -- angle (in grads) whose cotangent is U
```

Cycle is the second parameter of all the trigonometric functions except Arctan and Arccot, for which it is the third. The first two parameters of Arctan are named Y and X, respectively; for Arccot, they are named X and Y. The first parameter of each of the remaining trigonometric functions is named X. A ratio whose arctangent or arccotangent is to be found is specified by giving its numerator and denominator separately, except that the denominator can be omitted, in which case it defaults to 1.0. The separate specification of numerator and denominator, which of course is motivated by the Fortran ATAN2 function, allows infinite ratios (i.e., those having a denominator of zero) to be expressed; these, of course, have a perfectly well-defined and finite arctangent or arccotangent, which lies on one of the axes. Thus,

```
Arctan(U, V)              -- angle (in radians) whose tangent is U/V
Arccot(U, V)              -- angle (in radians) whose cotangent is U/V
Arctan(U)                 -- angle (in radians) whose tangent is U
Arctan(U, V, 360.0)       -- angle (in degrees) whose tangent is U/V)
Arctan(1.0, 0.0, 360.0) -- 90.0 (degrees)
```

The result of Arctan or Arccot is always in the quadrant (or on the axis) containing the point (X, Y), even when the defaultable formal parameter takes its default value; that of Arcsin is always in the quadrant (or on the axis) containing the point (1.0, X), while that of Arccos is always in the quadrant (or on the axis) containing the point (X, 1.0).

Given that the constant Pi is defined in Numerics, one might wonder why the two overloadings of each trigonometric function have not been combined into a single version, with a Cycle parameter having a default value of 2.0*Numerics.Pi. The reason is that computing the functions with natural cycle by using the value of Numerics.Pi cannot provide the accuracy required of implementations conforming to the Numerics Annex, as discussed below. Since Numerics.Pi is necessarily a finite approximation of an irrational (nay, transcendental) value, such an implementation would actually compute the functions for a slightly different cycle, with the result that cumulative "phase shift" errors many cycles from the origin would be intolerable. Even relatively near the origin, the relative error near zeros of the functions would be excessive. An implementation that conforms to the accuracy requirements of the Numerics Annex will use rather different strategies to compute the functions relative to the implicit, natural cycle of 2π as opposed to an explicit cycle given exactly by the user. (In particular, an implementation of the former that simply invokes the latter with a cycle of 2.0*Numerics.Pi will not conform to the Numerics Annex.)

Similar considerations form the basis for providing the natural logarithm function as a separate overloading, with an implicit base, rather than relying on the version with a base parameter and a default value of Numerics.e for that parameter.

In an early draft of Ada 95, the overloading of the exponentiation operator for a pair of floating point operands had parameter names of X and Y, following the style adopted for the other subprograms in Numerics.Generic_Elementary_Functions. It was subsequently deemed important for new overloadings of existing arithmetic operators to follow the precedent of using Left and Right for the names of their parameters, as in Ada 83.

The exponentiation operator is noteworthy in another respect. Instead of delivering 1.0 as one might expect by analogy with 0.0**0, the expression 0.0**0.0 is defined to raise Numerics.Argument_Error. This is because $0.0^{0.0}$ is mathematically undefined, and indeed x^y can approach any value as x and y approach zero, depending on precisely *how* x and y approach zero. If X and Y could both be zero when an application evaluates X**Y, it seems best to require the application to decide in advance what it means and what the result should be. An application can do that by defining its own exponentiation operator, which would

- invoke the one obtained by instantiating the elementary functions package, and

- handle an Argument_Error exception raised by the latter, delivering from the handler the appropriate application-dependent value.

The local exponentiation operator can be inlined, if the extra level of subprogram linkage would be of concern.

The Ada 95 version uses Float_Type'Base as a type mark in declarations; this was not available in Ada 83. Thus the formal parameter types and result types of the functions are of the unconstrained (base) subtype of the generic formal type Float_Type, eliminating the possibility of range violations at the interface. The same feature can be used for local variables in implementations of Numerics.Generic_Elementary_Functions (if it is programmed in Ada) to avoid spurious exceptions caused by range violations on assignments to local variables having the precision of Float_Type. Thus, in contrast to [ISO 94a] there is no need to allow implementations to impose the restriction that the generic actual subtype must be an unconstrained subtype; implementations must allow any floating point subtype as the generic actual subtype, and they must be immune to the potential effects of any range constraint of that subtype.

Implementations in hardware sometimes do not meet the desired accuracy requirements [Tang 91] because the representation of π contained on the hardware chip has insufficient precision. To allow users to choose between fast (but sometimes inaccurate) versions of the elementary functions implemented in hardware and slightly slower versions fully conforming to realistic accuracy requirements, we introduced the concept of a pair of modes, "strict" and "relaxed". No accuracy requirements apply in the relaxed mode, or if the Numerics Annex is not supported. (These modes govern all numeric accuracy issues, not just those connected with the elementary functions.)

The accuracy requirements of the strict mode are not trivial to meet, but neither are they particularly burdensome; their feasibility has been demonstrated in a public-domain implementation using table-driven techniques. However, it should be noted that most vendors of serious mathematical libraries, including the hardware vendors, are now committing themselves to implementations that are fully accurate throughout the domain, since practical software techniques for achieving that accuracy are becoming more widely known. The accuracy requirements in Ada 95 are not as stringent as those which vendors are now striving to achieve.

Certain results (for example, the exponential of zero) are prescribed to be exact, even in the relaxed mode, because of the frequent occurrence of the corresponding degenerate cases in calculations and because they are inexpensively provided. Also, although the accuracy is implementation-defined in relaxed mode, nothing gives an implementation license to raise a spurious exception when an intermediate result overflows but the final result does not. Thus, implementations of the forward hyperbolic functions need to be somewhat more sophisticated than is suggested by the usual textbook formulae that compute them in terms of exponentials.

An implementation that accommodates signed zeros, such as one on IEEE hardware (where Float_Type'Signed_Zeros is true), is required to exploit them in several important contexts, in particular the signs of the zero results from the "odd" functions Sin, Tan, and their inverses and hyperbolic analogs, at the origin, and the sign of the half-cycle result from Arctan and Arccot; this follows a recommendation [Kahan 87] that provides important benefits for complex elementary functions built upon the real elementary functions, and for applications in conformal mapping. Exploitation of signed zeros at the many other places where the elementary functions can return zero results is left implementation-defined, since no obvious guidelines exist for these cases.

A.3.2 Random Number Generation

The capability of generating random numbers is required for many applications. It is especially common in simulations, even when other aspects of floating point computation are not heavily stressed. Indeed, some applications of random numbers have no need at all for floating point computation. For these reasons, Ada 95 provides in the predefined language environment a package, Numerics.Float_Random, that defines types and operations for generating random floating point numbers uniformly distributed over the range 0.0 .. 1.0 and a generic package, Numerics.Discrete_Random, that defines types and operations for generating uniformly distributed random values of a discrete subtype specified by the user.

As a simple example, various values of a simulated uniform risk could be generated by writing

```
use Ada.Numerics.Float_Random;
Risk: Float range 0.0 .. 1.0;
G: Generator;
...
loop
   Risk := Random(G);    -- a new value for risk
   ...
end loop;
...
```

It has been the custom in other languages (for example, Fortran 90) to provide only a generator of uniformly distributed random floating point numbers and to standardize the range to 0.0 .. 1.0. Usually it is also stated that the value 1.0 is never generated, although values as close to 1.0 as the hardware permits may be generated. Sometimes the value 0.0 is excluded from the range instead, or in addition. The user who requires random floating point numbers uniformly distributed in some other range or having some other distribution, or who requires uniformly distributed random integers, is required to figure out and implement a conversion of what the language provides to the type and range desired. Although some conversion techniques are robust with respect to whether 0.0 or 1.0 can occur, others might fail to stay within the desired range, or might even raise an exception, should these extreme values be generated; with a user-designed conversion, there is also a risk of introducing bias into the distribution.

The random number facility designed for Ada 95 initially followed the same custom. However, concerns about the potential difficulties of user-designed post-generation conversion, coupled with the assertion that the majority of applications for random numbers actually need random integers, led to the inclusion of a capability for generating uniformly distributed random integers directly. The provision of that capability also allows for potentially more efficient implementations of integer generators, because it gives designs that can stay in the integer domain the freedom to do so.

Thus a random integer in the range 1 to 49 inclusive can be generated by

```
subtype Lotto is Integer range 1 .. 49;
package Lottery is new Ada.Numerics.Discrete_Random(Lotto);
use Lottery;
G: Generator;
Number: Lotto;
...
loop
   Number := Random(G);    -- next number for lottery ticket
   ...
end loop;
...
```

The use of generics to parameterize the integer range desired seemed obvious and appropriate, because most applications for random integers need a sequence of values in some fixed, problem-dependent subtype. As an alternative or a potential addition, we considered specifying the range dynamically on each call for a random number; this would have been convenient for those applications that require a random integer from a different range on each call. Reasoning that such applications are rare, we left their special needs to be addressed by using the floating point generator, coupled with post-generation conversion to the dynamically varying integer range. Help for the occasional user who faces the need to perform such a conversion is provided by a note in the reference manual, which describes a robust conversion technique [RM95 A.5.2(50..52)].

Note that the parameter of `Discrete_Random` can be of any discrete subtype and so one can easily obtain random Boolean values, random characters, random days of the week and so on.

Once the potential conversion problems had been solved by the combination of providing a generic discrete generator and documenting a robust conversion technique for the small number of applications that cannot use the generic generator, some of the pressure on the floating point generator was relieved. In particular, it was no longer necessary to specify that it must avoid generating 0.0 or 1.0. The floating point generator is allowed to yield any value in its range, which can be described as the range 0.0 .. 1.0 without further qualification. Of course, some implementations may be incapable of generating 0.0 or 1.0, but the user does not need to know that and would be better off not knowing it (portability could be compromised by exploiting knowledge that a particular implementation of the random number generator cannot deliver one or both bounds of the range). A note in the reference manual [RM95 A.5.2(52..54)] discusses ways of transforming the result of the floating point generator, using the `Log` function, into exponentially distributed random floating point numbers, illustrating a technique that avoids the `Argument_-Error` exception that `Log` would raise when the value of its parameter is zero.

Generators

With the obvious exception of the result subtype, the two predefined packages declare the same types and operations, thereby simplifying their description and use. In the remainder of this section, we therefore discuss the contents of the packages without (in most cases) naming one or the other.

Applications vary widely in their requirements for random number generation. Global floating point and discrete random number generators would suffice for most applications, but more demanding applications require multiple generators (either one in each of several tasks or several in one task), with each generator giving rise to a different sequence of random numbers. For this reason, we provide in both packages a type called `Generator`, each of whose objects is associated with a distinct sequence of random numbers.

Operations on generators, such as obtaining the "next" random number from the associated sequence, are provided by subprograms that take an object of type `Generator` as a parameter. Applications requiring multiple generators can declare the required number of objects of type `Generator` in the tasks where they are needed. The mechanism is simple enough, however, not to be burdensome for applications requiring only a single global generator, which can be declared in the main program or in a library package.

(We entertained the idea of also having an implicit generator, which would be used when the `Generator` parameter is omitted from an operation on generators. This idea was abandoned, however, when agreement could not be reached on the question of whether the implicit generator should be local to each task or global to the tasks in a partition, and, in the latter case, whether serialization should be automatically provided for concurrent operations on the default generator performed in different tasks. To do so would be likely to impose an unnecessary overhead on applications that do no tasking and require only a single generator. The mechanisms provided in the random number packages and elsewhere in the language, particularly protected types and the generic package `Ada.Task_Attributes`, are sufficient to allow the developer of an advanced application, or the designer of a secondary library, to provide these capabilities, if desired.)

State Information

A generator obviously has state information associated with it, which reflects the current position in the associated sequence of random numbers and provides the basis for the computation of the next random number in the sequence. To allow the implementation wide latitude in choosing appropriate algorithms for generating random numbers, and to enforce the abstraction of a generator, the `Generator` type is a private type; furthermore, to enforce the distinctness of different generators, the type is limited. The full type is implementation defined.

For convenience of use, we chose to make `Random` a function. Since its parameter must therefore be of mode in, the `Generator` type in practice has to be realized either as an access type or (if its storage is to be reclaimed through finalization on exit from the generator's scope) as a controlled type containing an access type.

Applications that use random numbers vary also in their requirements for repeatability as opposed to uniqueness of the sequence of random numbers. Repeatability is desired during development and testing but often not desired in operational mode when a unique sequence of random numbers is required in each run. To meet both of these needs, we have specified that each generator always starts in the same, fixed (but implementation-defined) state, providing repeatable sequences by default, and we have provided several operations on generators that can be used to alter the state of a generator.

Calling the `Reset` procedure on a generator without specifying any other parameter sets the state to a time-dependent value in an implementation-dependent way.

The `Reset` procedure can also be used to ensure that task-local generators yield different, but repeatable, sequences. Note that by default, the fixed initial state of generators will result in all such generators yielding the same sequence. This is probably not what is desired. We considered specifying that each generator should have a unique initial state, but there is no realistic way to provide for the desired repeatability across different runs, given that the nondeterministic nature of task interactions could result in the "same" tasks (in some logical sense) being created in a different order in different runs.

Assuming that each task has a generator, different-but-repeatable sequences in different tasks are achieved by invoking the `Reset` procedure with an integer `Initiator` parameter on each generator prior to generating random numbers. The programmer typically must provide integer values uniquely associated with each task's logical function, independent of the order in which the tasks are created. The specified semantics of `Reset` are such that each distinct integer initiator value will initiate a sequence that will not overlap any other sequence in a practical sense, if the period of a generator is long enough to permit that. At the very least, consecutive integers should result in very different states, so that the resulting sequences will not simply be offset in time by one element or a small number of elements.

Saving the State

Most applications will have no need for capabilities beyond those already described. A small number of applications may have the need to save the current state of a generator and restore it at a later time, perhaps in a different run. This can be done by calling the `Save` procedure and another overloading of the procedure `Reset`. The state is saved in a variable of the private type `State`.

As was said earlier, the realization of the internal state of a generator is implementation defined, so as to foster the widest possible innovation in the design of generators and generation algorithms. The state is thus private and might be represented by a single integer or floating point value, or it might be represented by an array of integer or floating point values together with a few auxiliary values, such as indices into the array.

Internal generator states can be exported to a variable of the type `State`, saved in a file, and restored in a later run, all without knowing the representation of the type.

We also provide an `Image` function, which reversibly converts a value of type `State` to one of type `String` in an implementation-defined way, perhaps as a concatenation of one or more integer images separated by appropriate delimiters. The maximum length of the string obtained from the `Image` function is given by the named number `Max_Image_Width`; images of states can be manipulated conveniently in strings of this maximum length obtained by the use of `Ada.Strings.Bounded`. Using `Save` and `Image`, one can examine (a representation of) the current internal state for debugging purposes; one might use these subprograms in an interactive debugger, with no advanced planning, to make a pencilled note of the current state with the intention of typing it back in later. This does not require knowledge of the mapping between states and strings.

The inverse operation, Value, converts the string representation of an internal state back into a value of type State, which can then be imported into a generator by calling the Reset procedure. This pair of subprograms supports, without knowledge of the mapping between states and strings, the restoration of a state saved in the form of a string. Of couse if one does know the implementation's mapping of strings to states, then one can use Value and Reset to create arbitrary internal states for experimentation purposes. If passed a string that cannot be interpreted as the image of a state, Value raises Constraint_Error. This is the only time that the possibly expensive operation of state validation is required; it is not required every time Random is called, nor even when resetting a generator from a state.

We considered an alternative design, perhaps closer to the norm for random number generators, in which Random is a procedure that acts directly on the state, the latter being held in storage provided by the user. There would be no need for the Save and Reset (from-saved-state) procedures in this design, since the generator and state types would effectively be one and the same. The only real problem with this design is that it necessitates making Random a procedure, which would interfere with the programmer's ability to compose clear and meaningful expressions.

Of course, most simple applications will have no need to concern themselves with the State type: no need to declare variables of type State, and no need to call Save or Reset with a state parameter.

Statistical Considerations

The result subtype of the Random function in Float_Random is a subtype of Float with a range of 0.0 .. 1.0. The subtype is called Uniformly_Distributed to emphasize that a large set of random numbers obtained from this function will exhibit an (approximately) uniform distribution. It is the only distribution provided because it is the most frequently required distribution and because other distributions can be built on top of a uniform distribution using well-known techniques. In the case of Discrete_Random, it does not really make sense to consider other than uniform distributions.

No provision is made for obtaining floating point random numbers with a precision other than that of Float. One reason is that applications typically do not have a need either for extremely precise random floating point numbers (those with a very fine granularity) or for random floating point numbers with several different precisions. Assuming that they are to be used as real numbers, and not converted to integers, the precision of a set of random floating point numbers generally does not matter unless an immense quantity of them are to be consumed. High precision random floating point numbers would be needed if they were to be converted to integers in some very wide range, but the provision of Discrete_Random makes that unnecessary. A second reason for providing random floating point numbers only with the precision of Float, and especially for not providing them with a precision of the user's choice, is that algorithms for random number generation are often tied to the use of particular hardware representations, which essentially dictates the precision obtained.

Nothing is said about the number of distinct values between 0.0 and 1.0 that must be (capable of being) delivered by the Random function in Float_Random. Indeed, in the spirit of not requiring guaranteed numerical performance unless the Numerics Annex is implemented, the specification of Float_Random says nothing about the quality of the result obtained from Random, except that a large number of such results must appear to be approximately uniformly distributed. On the other hand, the Numerics Annex specifies the minimum period of the generation algorithm, a wide range of statistical tests that must be satisfied by that algorithm, and the resolution of the time-dependent Reset function. In implementations in which Float corresponds to the hardware's double-precision type, the floating point random number algorithm can be based on the use of single-precision hardware, and can coerce the single-precision results to double precision at the final step, provided that the statistical tests are satisfied, which is perfectly feasible.

Details of the statistical tests, which are adapted from [Knuth 81] and other sources, are provided in an annotation in the [AARM]. The tests applicable to the floating point random number generator facility all exploit the floating point nature of the random numbers directly; they do not convert the numbers to integers. Different tests are applicable to the discrete random number generator.

In the rare case that random floating point numbers of higher precision (finer granularity) than that of Float are needed, the user should obtain them by suitably combining two or more successive results from Random. For example, two successive values might be used to provide the high-order and the low-order parts of a higher-precision result.

Guaranteeing that all the values in a wide integer range will eventually be generated is, in general, rather difficult and so is not required for the discrete generator. Nevertheless, some guarantee of this nature is desirable for more modest ranges. We thus require that if the range of the subtype has 2^{15} or fewer values then each value of the range will be delivered in a finite number of calls. This coverage requirement is in the specification of Discrete_Random in the Predefined Language Environment Annex; because it so directly affects the usability of the discrete random number generator facility, it was not thought appropriate to relegate the coverage requirement to the (optional) Numerics Annex. It is practical to verify by testing that the coverage requirement is satisfied for ranges up to this size, but it is not practical to verify the same for significantly wider ranges; for that matter, only a very long-running application could detect that a wide integer range is not being completely covered by the random numbers that are generated. Satisfying the coverage requirement is easily achieved by an underlying floating point algorithm, even one implemented in single precision, that converts its intermediate floating point result to the integer result subtype by appropriate use of scaling and type conversion.

The modest requirement discussed above does not completely eliminate all the difficulty in implementing Discrete_Random. Even the straightforward scaling and conversion technique faces mundane problems when the size of the integer range exceeds Integer'Last. Note that the size of the range of the predefined subtype Integer exceeds Integer'Last by about a factor of two, so that an instantiation of Discrete_Random for that predefined subtype will have to confront certain mundane problems, even if it does not purport to cover that range completely. These implementation burdens could have been eliminated by imposing restrictions on the (size of the ranges of the) subtypes with which Discrete_Random could be instantiated, but such restrictions are inimical to the spirit of Ada.

Of course, implementations of Discrete_Random need not be based on an underlying floating point algorithm, and indeed, as has already been said, part of the justification for providing this package separately from Float_Random has to do with the efficiency gains that can be realized when the former is implemented in terms of an underlying integer algorithm, with no use of floating point at all. Nevertheless, it may be convenient and sufficiently efficient for the discrete generator facility to be implemented in terms of a floating point algorithm. There are implementations of the venerable multiplicative linear congruential generator with multiplier 7^5 and modulus 2^{31}-1 of [Lewis 69] and both the add-with-carry and subtract-with-borrow Fibonacci generators of [Marsaglia 91] that remain entirely within the floating point domain, and which therefore pay no premium for conversion from integer to floating point. These algorithms have been verified to pass the statistical requirements of the Numerics Annex. (Other algorithms that might be expected to pass, but that have not been explicitly tested, include the combination generators of [Wichmann 82] and [L'Ecuyer 88] and the $x^2 \bmod N$ generators of [Blum 86]; each of the algorithms mentioned here has much to recommend it.)

A.3.3 Attributes of Real Types

Most of the attributes of floating and fixed point types are defined in the Predefined Language Environment Annex. These attributes are discussed elsewhere in this Rationale (see 6.2).

A.4 Input-Output

Enhancements to input-output include a facility for heterogeneous streams, additional flexibility for `Text_IO`, and further file manipulation capabilities.

A.4.1 Stream Input and Output

The packages `Sequential_IO` and `Direct_IO` have not proved to be sufficiently flexible for some applications because they only process homogeneous files. Even so this is fairly liberal in the case of `Sequential_IO` which now has the form

```
generic
    type Element_Type(<>) is private;
package Ada.Sequential_IO is ...
```

since the actual parameter can be any indefinite type and hence can be a class-wide type. This does not apply to `Direct_IO` which can only take a definite type as a parameter because of the need to index individual elements.

In order to provide greater flexibility, totally heterogeneous streams can be processed using the new package `Streams` [RM95 13.13] and several child packages [RM95 A.12].

The general idea is that there is a stream associated with any file declared using the package `Ada.Streams.Stream_IO`. Such a file may be processed sequentially using the stream mechanism and also in a positional manner similar to `Direct_IO`. We will consider the stream process first and return to positional use later.

The package `Streams.Stream_IO` enables a file to be created, opened and closed in the usual manner. Moreover, there is also a function `Stream` which takes a stream file and returns (an access to) the stream associated with the file. In outline the first part of the package is

```
package Ada.Streams.Stream_IO is
    type Stream_Access is access all Root_Stream_Type'Class;
    type File_Type is limited private;
    -- Create, Open, ...
    function Stream(File: in File_Type) return Stream_Access;
    ...
end Ada.Streams.Stream_IO;
```

Observe that all streams are derived from the abstract type `Streams.Root_Stream_Type` and access to a stream is typically through an access parameter designating an object of the type `Streams.Root_Stream_Type'Class`. We will return to the package `Streams` and the abstract type `Root_Stream_Type` in a moment.

Sequential processing of streams is performed using attributes `T'Read`, `T'Write`, `T'Input` and `T'Output`. These attributes are predefined for all nonlimited types. The user can replace them by providing an attribute definition clause and can also define such attributes explicitly for limited types. This gives the user fine control over the processing when necessary. The attributes `T'Read` and `T'Write` will be considered first; `T'Input` and `T'Output` (which are especially relevant to indefinite subtypes) will be considered later.

The attributes `Read` and `Write` take parameters denoting the stream and the element of type `T` thus

```
procedure T'Write(Stream : access Streams.Root_Stream_Type'Class;
                  Item    : in T);

procedure T'Read(Stream : access Streams.Root_Stream_Type'Class;
                 Item    : out T);
```

As a simple example, suppose we wish to write a mixture of integers, month names and dates where type Date might be

```
type Date is
   record
      Day   : Integer;
      Month : Month_Name;
      Year  : Integer;
   end record;
```

We first create a file using the normal techniques and then obtain an access to the associated stream. We can then invoke the Write attribute procedure on the values to be written to the stream. We have

```
use Streams.Stream_IO;
Mixed_File : File_Type;
S          : Stream_Access;
...
Create(Mixed_File);
S := Stream(Mixed_File);
...
Date'Write(S, Some_Date);
Integer'Write(S, Some_Integer);
Month_Name'Write(S, This_Month);
...
```

Note that Streams.Stream_IO is not a generic package and so does not have to be instantiated; all such heterogeneous files are of the same type. Note also that they are binary files. A file written in this way can be read back in a similar manner, but of course if we attempt to read things with the inappropriate subprogram then we will get a funny value or Data_Error.

In the case of a simple record such as Date the predefined Write attribute simply calls the attributes for the components in order. So conceptually we have

```
procedure Date'Write(Stream : access Streams.Root_Stream_Type'Class;
                     Item    : in Date) is
begin
   Integer'Write(Stream, Item.Day);
   Month_Name'Write(Stream, Item.Month);
   Integer'Write(Stream, Item.Year);
end;
```

We can supply our own version of Write. Suppose for some reason that we wished to output the month name in a date as the corresponding integer; we could write

```
procedure Date_Write(Stream : access Streams.Root_Stream_Type'Class;
                     Item    : in Date) is
begin
   Integer'Write(Stream, Item.Day);
   Integer'Write(Stream, Month_Name'Pos(Item.Month) + 1);
   Integer'Write(Stream, Item.Year);
end Date_Write;
```

```
for Date'Write use Date_Write;
```

and then the statement

```
Date'Write(S, Some_Date);
```

will use the new format for the output of dates. Similar facilities apply to input and indeed if we wish to read the dates back in we would need to declare the complementary version of Date'Read to read the month as an integer and convert to the appropriate value of Month_Name.

Note that we have only changed the output of months in dates, if we wish to change the format of all months then rather than redefining Date'Write we could simply redefine Month_Name'Write and this would naturally have the indirect effect of also changing the output of dates.

Note carefully that the predefined attributes T'Read and T'Write can only be overridden by an attribute definition clause in the same package specification or declarative part where T is declared (just like any representation item). As a consequence these predefined attributes cannot be changed for the predefined types. But they can be changed for types derived from them.

The situation is slightly more complex in the case of arrays, and also records with discriminants, since we have to take account of the "dope" information represented by the bounds and discriminants. (In the case of a discriminant with defaults, the discriminant is treated as an ordinary component.) This is done using the additional attributes Input and Output. The general idea is that Input and Output process dope information (if any) and then call Read and Write to process the rest of the value. Their profiles are

```
procedure T'Output(Stream : access Streams.Root_Stream_Type'Class;
                   Item   : in T);

function T'Input(Stream: access Streams.Root_Stream_Type'Class)
     return T;
```

Note that Input is a function since T may be indefinite and we may not know the constraints for a particular call.

Thus in the case of an array the procedure Output outputs the bounds of the value and then calls Write to output the value itself.

In the case of a record type with discriminants, if it has defaults (is definite) then Output simply calls Write which treats the discriminants as just other components. If there are no defaults then Output first outputs the discriminants and then calls Write to process the remainder of the record. As an example consider the case of a definite subtype of a type whose first subtype is indefinite such as

```
subtype String_6 is String(1 .. 6);
S: String_6 := "String";
...
String_6'Output(S);      -- outputs bounds
String_6'Write(S);       -- does not output bounds
```

Note that the attributes Output and Write belong to the types and so it is immaterial whether we write String_6'Write or String'Write.

The above description of T'Input and T'Output applies to the default attributes. They could be redefined to do anything and not necessarily call T'Read and T'Write. Note moreover that Input and Output also exist for definite subtypes; their defaults just call Read and Write.

There are also attributes T'Class'Output and T'Class'Input for dealing with class-wide types. For output, the external representation of the tag (see [RM95 3.9]) is output and then the procedure Output for the specific type is called (by dispatching) in order to output the specific value (which in turn will call Write). Similarly on input, the tag is first read and then, according to its value, the corresponding function Input is called by dispatching. For completeness, T'Class'Read (T'Class'Write) is defined to dispatch to the subprogram denoted by the Read (respectively, Write) attribute of the specific type identified by the tag.

The general principle is, of course, that whatever is written can then be read back in again by the appropriate reverse operation.

We now return to a consideration of the underlying structure. All streams are derived from the abstract type Streams.Root_Stream_Type which has two abstract operations, Read and Write thus

```
procedure Read(Stream : in out Root_Stream_Type;
               Item   : out Stream_Element_Array;
               Last   : out Stream_Element_Offset) is abstract;

procedure Write(Stream : in out Root_Stream_Type;
                Item   : in Stream_Element_Array) is abstract;
```

These work in terms of stream elements rather than individual typed values. Note the difference between stream elements and storage elements (the latter being used for the control of storage pools which was discussed in 13.4). Storage elements concern internal storage whereas stream elements concern external information and are thus appropriate across a distributed system.

The predefined Read and Write attributes use the operations Read and Write of the associated stream, and the user could define new values for the attributes in the same way. Note, however, that the parameter Stream of the root type is of the type Root_Stream_Type whereas that of the attribute is an access type denoting the corresponding class. So any such user-defined attribute will have to do an appropriate dereference thus

```
procedure My_Write(Stream : access Streams.Root_Stream_Type'Class;
                   Item   : T) is
begin
   ... -- convert value into stream elements
   Streams.Write(Stream.all, ...);   -- dispatches
end My_Write;
```

We conclude by remarking that Stream_IO can also be used for indexed access. This is possible because the file is structured as a sequence of stream elements. Indexing then works in terms of stream elements much as Direct_IO works in terms of the typed elements. Thus the index can be read and reset. The procedures Read and Write process from the current value of the index and there is also an alternative Read that starts at a specified value of the index. The procedures Read and Write (which take a file as parameter) correspond precisely to the dispatching operations of the associated stream.

A.4.2 Text_IO

The main changes to Ada.Text_IO are the addition of internal generic packages Modular_IO (similar to Integer_IO) and Decimal_IO (similar to Fixed_IO).

There is also a completely distinct package Ada.Wide_Text_IO which provides identical facilities to Ada.Text_IO except that it works in terms of the types Wide_Character and Wide_String rather than Character and String. Text_IO and Wide_Text_IO declare distinct file types.

Both Text_IO and Wide_Text_IO have a child package Editing defined in the Information Systems Annex. This provides specialized facilities for the output of decimal values controlled by picture formats; for details see F.1. Similarly both packages have a child Complex_IO defined in the Numerics Annex; see G.1.3.

Small but important changes to Text_IO are the addition of subprograms Look_Ahead, Get_Immediate and Flush. The procedure Look_Ahead enables the next character to be determined without removing it and thereby enables the user to write procedures with similar behavior to predefined Get on numeric and enumeration types. The procedure Get_Immediate removes a single character from the file and bypasses any buffering that might otherwise be used; it is designed for interactive use. A call of Flush causes the remainder of any partly processed output buffer to be output.

A minor point is that the procedures Get for real types accept a literal in more liberal formats than in Ada 83. Leading and trailing zeros before or after the point are no longer required and indeed the point itself can be omitted. Thus the following are all acceptable forms for input for real types:

```
0.567
123.0
.567
123.
123
```

whereas in Ada 83 only the first two were acceptable. This is in some respects an incompatibility since a form such as .567 would cause Data_Error to be raised in Ada 83. However, the main advantage is interoperability with other languages; data produced by Fortran programs can then be processed directly. Furthermore, the allowed formats are in accordance with ISO 6093:1985 which defines language independent formats for the textual representation of floating point numbers.

There are also nongeneric equivalents to Integer_IO and Float_IO for each of the predefined types Integer, Long_Integer, Float, Long_Float and so on. These have names such as Ada.Integer_Text_IO, Ada.Long_Integer_Text_IO, and Ada.Float_Text_IO. Observe that they are not child packages of Ada.Text_IO but direct children of Ada, thus allowing the names to be kept reasonably short.

A major reason for introducing these nongeneric equivalents was to facilitate teaching Ada to new users. Experience with teaching Ada 83 has shown that fundamental input-output was unnecessarily complicated by the reliance on generics, which gave the language an air of difficulty. So rather than writing

```
with Ada.Text_IO;
procedure Example is
   package Int_IO is new Ada.Text_IO.Integer_IO(Integer);
   use Int_IO;
   N: Integer;
begin
   ...
   Put(N);
   ...
end Example;
```

one can now perform simple output without needing to instantiate a generic

```
with Ada.Integer_Text_IO; use Ada.Integer_Text_IO;
procedure Example is
   N: Integer;
begin
   ...
   Put(N);
   ...
end Example;
```

Another advantage of the nongeneric equivalents is that the user does not have to worry about an appropriate name for the instantiated version (and indeed fret over whether it might also be called Integer_IO without confusion with the generic version, or some other name such as we chose above). Having standard names also promotes portability since many vendors had provided such nongeneric equivalents but with different names.

Note carefully that these packages are said to be nongeneric equivalents rather than preinstantiated versions. This is so that implementations can use special efficient techniques not possible in the generic versions. A minor consequence is that the nongeneric equivalents cannot be used as actual package parameters corresponding to the generic package. Thus we cannot use Ada.Integer_Text_IO as an actual parameter to

```
generic
    with package P is new Ada.Text_IO.Integer_IO;
package Q is ...
```

Similar nongeneric equivalents apply to the generic packages for elementary functions, complex types and complex elementary functions, see A.3.1 and G.1.

Finally, it is possible to treat a Text_IO file as a stream and hence to use the stream facilities of the previous section with text files. This is done by calling the function Stream in the child package Text_IO.Text_Streams. This function takes a Text_IO file as parameter and returns an access to the corresponding stream. It is then possible to intermix binary and text input-output and to use the current file mechanism with streams.

A.4.3 File Manipulation

The Ada 83 package Sequential_IO did not make provision for appending data to the end of an existing file. As a consequence implementations provided a variety of solutions using pragmas and the form parameter and so on. In Ada 95 we have overcome this lack of portability by adding a further literal Append_File to the type File_Mode for Sequential_IO and Text_IO. It also exists for Stream_IO but not for Direct_IO.

The concept of a current error file for Text_IO is introduced, plus subprograms Standard_-Error, Current_Error and Set_Error by analogy with the similar subprograms for current input and current output. The function Standard_Error returns the standard error file for the system. On some systems standard error and standard output might be the same.

Error files are a convenience for the user; the ability to switch error files in a similar manner to the default output file enables the user to keep the real output distinct from error messages in a portable manner.

A problem with the Ada 83 subprograms for manipulating the current files is that it is not possible to store the current value for later use because the file type is limited private. As mentioned in 7.3, it is possible to temporarily "hang on" to the current value by the use of renaming thus

```
Old_File: File_Type renames Current_Output;
... -- set and use a different file
Set_Output(Old_File);
```

and thus permits some other file to be used and then the preexisting environment to be restored afterwards. This works because the result of a function call is treated like an object and can then be renamed. However, this technique does not permit a file value to be stored in an arbitrary way.

In order to overcome this difficulty, further overloadings of the various functions are introduced which manipulate an access value which can then be stored. Thus

```
type File_Access is access constant File_Type;
function Current_Input  return File_Access;
function Current_Output return File_Access;
function Current_Error  return File_Access;
```

and similarly for Standard_Input and so on. Additional procedures for setting the values are not required. We can then write

```
procedure P(...) is
   New_File     : File_Type;
   Old_File_Ref : constant File_Access := Current_Output;
begin
   Open(New_File, ...);
   Set_Output(New_File);
   -- use the new file
   Set_Output(Old_File_Ref.all);
   Close(New_File);
end P;
```

More sophisticated file manipulation is also possible. We could for example have an array or linked list of input files and then concatenate them for output. As another example, a utility program for pre-processing text files could handle nested "include"s by maintaining a stack of File_Access values.

Making the access type an access to constant prevents passing the reference to subprograms with **in out** parameters and thus prevents problems such as might arise from calling Close on Current_Input.

A.5 Command Line

The package Ada.Command_Line provides an Ada program with a simple means of accessing any arguments of the command which invoked it. The package also enables the program to set a return status. Clearly the interpretation and implementation of these facilities depends very much on the underlying operating system.

The function Command_Name returns (as a string) the command that invoked the Ada program and the function Argument_Count returns the number of arguments associated with the command. The function Argument takes an integer and returns the corresponding individual command argument also as a string.

The exit status can be set by a call of Set_Exit_Status which takes an integer parameter.

An alternative scheme based on using the parameters and results of the Ada main subprogram as the command arguments and exit status was rejected for a number of reasons. The main reason was that the start and end of the main subprogram are not the start and end of the execution of the Ada program as a whole; elaboration of library packages occurs before and might want access to command arguments and similarly, library tasks can outlive the main subprogram and might want to set the exit status.

A.6 Requirements Summary

The study topic

S10.4-A(1) — Varying-length String Package

is met by the bounded and unbounded-length string packages, and the study topic

S10.4-A(2) — String Manipulation Functions

is met in part by the string handling packages.
The requirement

R11.1-A(1) — Standard Mathematics Packages

is met by the generic elementary functions and random number packages.
The somewhat general requirement

R4.6-B(1) — Additional Input/Output Functions

calls for additional capability. In particular it suggests that there should be a standard way to append data to an existing file and the ability to have heterogeneous files. These specific requirements (and others) have been met as we have seen. Moreover the requirement

R4.6-A(1) — Interactive TEXT_IO

is specifically addressed by the introduction of the subprograms Get_Immediate, Look_Ahead and Flush; see A.4.2.

B Interface to Other Languages

It is very important for Ada 95 programs to be able to interface effectively with systems written in other languages. For example, the success of Ada 95 depends in part on its ability to cleanly and portably support interfaces to such systems as X Windows, POSIX, and commercial windows-based personal computer environments. (The portability in question is the ability to take a given Ada program or binding that interfaces with an external system, and move it to an environment with the same external system but a different Ada implementation.) To achieve this goal we have supplied three pragmas for interfacing with non-Ada software, and child packages Interfaces.C, Interfaces.COBOL, and Interfaces.Fortran which declare types, subprograms and other entities useful for interfacing with the three languages. The root package Interfaces contains declarations for hardware-specific numeric types, described in 3.3.

B.1 Interfacing Pragmas

Experience with pragma Interface in Ada 83 has uncovered a number of issues that may interfere with developing portable Ada code that is to be linked with foreign language modules. We have therefore removed pragma Interface (though the implementation may choose still to support it for upward compatibility) and have added the three pragmas Import (effectively replacing Interface), Export and Convention which provide the following capabilities:

- Calling Ada subprograms from other languages. Ada 83 only supported calls in one direction, from Ada to external code modules.

- Communicating with external systems via access to subprogram types.

- Specifying external names (and link names) where appropriate. Most Ada 83 implementations supported such an ability and it is beneficial to users that it be standardized [Fowler 89].

- Communicating with external systems via objects and other entities. Ada 83 only supported interfacing via subprogram calls.

The following example illustrates how Ada 95 procedures can call and be called from a program written in the C language.

```
type XT_Callback is access
    procedure (Widget_Id : in out XT_Intrinsics.Widget;
               Closure   : in X_Lib.X_Address;
               Call_Data : in X_Lib.X_Address);

pragma Convention(C, XT_Callback);

procedure XT_Add_Callback
        (The_Widget    : in out XT_Intrinsics.Widget;
         Callback_Name : in String;
         Callback      : in XT_Callback;
         Client_Data   : in XT_Intrinsics.XT_Pointer);
```

```
pragma Import(C, XT_Add_Callback, External_Name => "XtAddCallBack");

procedure My_Callback(Widget_Id : in out XT_Intrinsics.Widget;
                      Closure    : in X_Lib.X_Address;
                      Call_Data  : in X_Lib.X_Address) is separate;

pragma Convention(C, My_Callback);

My_Widget : XT_Intrinsics.Widget;
...
XT_Add_Callback(My_Widget,
                "Mousedown" & ASCII.Nul,
                My_Callback'Access,
                XT_Intrinsics.Null_Data);
```

The pragma Convention applies to the type XT_Callback, and indicates that values of this type designate subprograms callable from programs written in C. The machine code generated for calls through the access values of the type XT_Callback will follow the conventions of the C compiler.

The pragma Import indicates that the procedure XT_Add_Callback is written with the calling conventions of a C compiler. The third parameter of the pragma specifies the external name (in this case the C name) of the subprogram.

The pragma Convention also applies to My_Callback. This informs the compiler that the procedure is written in Ada but is intended to be called from a C program, which may affect how it will reference its parameters.

My_Callback'Access will yield a value compatible with XT_Callback, because the same calling convention is specified for both. Note that it is unnecessary to apply the pragma Export to My_Callback since, although called from the C program, it is called indirectly through the access to subprogram value and the Ada identifier itself is not required externally.

The pragmas Import and Export may omit the external name if it is the same as the Ada identifier. A fourth parameter may be used to specify the link name if necessary.

The pragmas Import and Export may also be applied to objects. In particular a deferred constant can be completed by a pragma Import; this specifies that the object is defined externally to the Ada program. Similarly a pragma Export can be used to indicate that an object is used externally.

A programmer would typically use pragma Export in situations where the main subprogram is written in the external language. This raises some semantic issues, because correct execution of the exported Ada subprogram might depend on having certain Ada library units elaborated before the subprogram is invoked. For example, the subprogram might reference library package data objects that are initialized by the package body; or the subprogram might execute a construct (such as an allocator) that requires the Ada run-time system to have been elaborated. To handle such situations, Ada 95 advises the implementation [RM95 B.1(39)] to supply subprograms with link names "adainit" and "adafinal". The adainit subprogram contains elaboration code for the Ada library units, and adafinal contains any needed finalization code (such as finalization of the environment task). Thus a main subprogram written in the external language should call adainit before the first call to an Ada subprogram, and adafinal after the last.

B.2 C Interface Package

The C interface package, Interfaces.C, supports importing C functions into Ada, and exporting Ada subprograms to C. Since many bindings and other external systems are written in C, one of the more important objectives of Ada 95 is to ease the job of having Ada code work with such software.

Part of the issue in arranging an interface to a foreign language, of particular importance with C, is to allow an Ada subprogram to be called from code written in the foreign language. This is handled in Ada 95 through a combination of pragma Convention and access to subprogram types, as illustrated above.

Further child packages Interfaces.C.Strings and Interfaces.C.Pointers provide specialized functionality for dealing with C strings and pointers.

B.2.1 Scalar Types

C's predefined integer, floating point, and character types are modelled directly in Interfaces.C. The Ada implementation is responsible for defining the Ada types such that they have the same representation as the corresponding C types in the supported C implementation.

Since C parameters are passed copy-in, interfacing to a C function taking a scalar parameter is straightforward. The program declares an Ada subprogram with an in parameter of the corresponding type.

A C function may have a t* parameter, where t is a scalar type, and where the caller is supposed to pass a reference to a scalar. If such a function is imported, then the corresponding Ada subprogram would declare either an **access** T parameter, or an **in out** T parameter.

B.2.2 Strings

C's string representation and manipulation come in several varieties, and we have tried to define the interface package so as to support the most typical applications. The Interfaces.C package provides an implementation-defined character type, char, designed to model the C run-time character type. This may or may not be the same as Ada's type Character; thus the package provides mappings between the types char and Character. Unlike COBOL, the mappings between the C and Ada character types do not need to be dynamically modifiable; hence they are captured by functions. In the common case where the character set is the same in C and Ada, the implementation should define the conversion functions through unchecked conversions expanded inline, with thus no run-time overhead.

One important application of the C interface package is for the programmer to compose a C string and pass it to a C function. We provide several ways to accomplish this goal. One approach is for the programmer to declare an object that will hold the C array, and then pass this array to the C function. This is realized via the type char_array:

type char_array **is array** (size_t **range** <>) **of** char;

The programmer can declare an Ada String and convert it to a char_array (or simply declare a char_array directly), and pass the char_array as actual parameter to the C function that is expecting a char *. The implication of pragma Import on the subprogram is that the char_array will be passed by reference, with no "descriptor" for the bounds; the compiler needs to implement this in such a way that what is passed is a pointer to the first element.

The package Interfaces.C , which provides the above conversions, is Pure; this extends its applicability in distributed applications that need to interface with C code.

An alternative approach for passing strings to C functions is for the programmer to obtain a C char pointer from an Ada String (or from a char_array) by invoking an allocation function. The child package Interfaces.C.Strings provides a private type chars_ptr that corresponds to C's char *, and two allocation functions. To avoid storage leakage, we also provide a Free procedure that releases the storage that was claimed by one of these allocate functions. If one of these allocate functions is invoked from an Ada program, then it is the responsibility of the Ada program (rather than the called C function) to reclaim that storage.

It is typical for a C function that deals with strings to adopt the convention that the string is delimited by a nul character. The C interface package supports this convention. A constant nul of type char is declared, and the function Value(chars_ptr) in Interfaces.C.Strings returns a char_array up to and including the first nul in the array that the chars_ptr points to.

Some C functions that deal with strings do not assume nul termination; instead, the programmer passes an explicit length along with the pointer to the first element. This style is also supported by Interfaces.C, since objects of type char_array need not be terminated by nul.

B.2.3 Pointers and Arrays

The generic package Interfaces.C.Pointers allows the Ada programmer to perform C-style operations on pointers. It includes an access type Pointer, Value functions that dereference a Pointer and deliver the designated array, several pointer arithmetic operations, and "copy" procedures that copy the contents of a source pointer into the array designated by a destination pointer. As in C, it treats an object Ptr of type Pointer as a pointer to the first element of an array, so that for example, adding 1 to Ptr yields a pointer to the second element of the array.

This generic package allows two styles of usage: one in which the array is terminated by a special terminator element; and another in which the programmer needs to keep track of the length.

This package may be used to interface with a C function that takes a "*" parameter. The Pointer type emerging from an instantiation corresponds to the "*" parameter to the C function.

B.2.4 Structs

If the C function expects a "struct *", the Ada programmer should declare a corresponding simple record type and apply pragma Convention to this type. The Ada compiler will pass a reference to the record as the argument to the C function. Of course, it is not realistic to expect that any Ada record could be passed as a C struct; [RM95, B.1] allows restrictions so that only a "C-eligible" record type T need be supported for pragma Convention(C, T). For example, records with discriminants or dynamically-sized components need not be supported. Nevertheless, the set of types for which pragma Convention needs to be supported is sufficiently broad to cover the kinds of interfaces that arise in practice.

In the (rare) situation where the C function takes a struct by value (for example a struct with a small number of small components), the programmer can declare a C function that takes a struct * and which then passes the value of its argument to the actual C function that is needed.

B.2.5 Example

The following example shows a typical use of the C interface facilities.

```
-- Calling the C Library Function strcpy

with Interfaces.C;
procedure Test is
   package C renames Interfaces.C;
   use type C.char_array;
   -- Call <string.h>strcpy:
   -- C definition of strcpy:
   --   char *strcpy(char *s1, const char *s2);
   --      This function copies the string pointed to by s2
   --      (including the terminating null character) into the
```

```
--      array pointed to by s1.  If copying takes place
--      between objects that overlap, the behavior is undefined.
--      The strcpy function returns the value of s1.
-- Note: since the C function's return value is of no interest,
-- the Ada interface is a procedure

procedure Strcpy(Target : out C.char_array;
                 Source : in  C.char_array);
pragma Import(C, Strcpy, "strcpy");
Chars1:  C.char_array(1 .. 20);
Chars2:  C.char_array(1 .. 20);
begin
   Chars2(1 .. 6) := "qwert" & C.Nul;
   Strcpy(Chars1, Chars2);
   -- Now Chars1(1 .. 6) = "qwert" & C.Nul
end Test;
```

B.3 COBOL Interface Package

The package Interfaces.COBOL allows an Ada program to pass data as parameters to COBOL programs, allows an Ada program to make use of "external" data created by COBOL programs and stored in files or databases, and allows an Ada program to convert an Ada decimal type value to or from a COBOL representation.

In order to support the calling of and passing parameters to an existing COBOL program, the interface package supplies types that can be used in an Ada program as parameters to subprograms whose bodies will be in COBOL. These types map to COBOL's alphanumeric and numeric data categories.

Several types are provided for support of alphanumeric data. Since COBOL's run-time character set is not necessarily the same as Ada's, Interfaces.COBOL declares an implementation-defined character type COBOL_Character and mappings between Character and COBOL_Character. These mappings are visible variables (rather than, say, functions or constant arrays), since in the situation where COBOL_Character is EBCDIC, the flexibility of dynamically modifying the mappings is needed. Corresponding to COBOL's alphanumeric data is the array type Alphanumeric.

Numeric data may have either a "display" or "computational" representation in COBOL. On the Ada side, the data is of a decimal fixed point type. Passing an Ada decimal data item to a COBOL program requires conversion from the Ada decimal type to some type that reflects the representation expected on the COBOL side.

•   Computational Representation

    Floating point representation is modelled by Ada floating point types, Floating and Long_Floating. Conversion between these types and Ada decimal types is obtained directly, since the type name serves as a conversion function.

    Binary representation is modelled by an Ada integer type, Binary, and possibly other types such as Long_Binary. Conversion between, say, Binary and a decimal type is through functions from an instantiation of the generic package Decimal_Conversions. An integer conversion using say Binary as the target and an object of a decimal type as the source does not work, since there would be no way to take into account the scale implicitly associated with the decimal type.

Packed decimal representation is modelled by the Ada array type `Packed_Decimal`. Conversion between packed decimal and a decimal type is through functions from an instantiation of the generic package `Decimal_Conversions`.

• Display Representation

Display representation for numeric data is modelled by the array type `Numeric`. Conversion between display representation and a decimal type is through functions from an instantiation of the generic package `Decimal_Conversions`. A parameter to the conversion function indicates the desired interpretation of the data (e.g., signed leading separate, etc.)

The pragma `Convention(COBOL, T)` may be applied to a record type `T` to direct the compiler to choose a COBOL-compatible representation for objects of the type.

The package `Interfaces.COBOL` allows the Ada programmer to deal with data from files or databases created by a COBOL program. For data that is alphanumeric, or in display or packed decimal format, the approach is the same as for passing parameters: instantiate `Decimal_Conversions` to obtain the needed conversion functions. For binary data, the external representation is treated as a `Byte` array, and an instantiation of `Decimal_Conversions` produces a package that declares the needed conversion functions. A parameter to the conversion function indicates the desired interpretation of the data (e.g., high- versus low-order byte first).

We had considered defining the binary conversion functions in terms of a `Storage_Array` rather than a `Byte_Array` for the "raw data". However, `Storage_Array` reflects the properties of the machine that is running the Ada program, whereas the external file may have been produced in a different environment. Thus it is simpler to use a model in terms of COBOL-character-sized units.

The following examples show typical uses of the COBOL interface.

```
with Interfaces.COBOL;
procedure Test_Call is
    -- Calling a foreign COBOL program
    -- Assume that a COBOL program PROG has the following declaration
    --    in its LINKAGE section:
    --    01 Parameter-Area
    --        05 NAME   PIC X(20).
    --        05 SSN    PIC X(9)
    --        05 SALARY PIC 99999V99 USAGE COMP.
    -- The effect of PROG is to update SALARY based on some algorithm

    package COBOL renames Interfaces.COBOL;
    type Salary_Type is delta 0.01 digits 7;

    type COBOL_Record is
        record
            Name   : COBOL.Numeric(1 .. 20);
            SSN    : COBOL.Numeric(1 .. 9);
            Salary : COBOL.Binary;   -- Assume Binary = 32 bits
        end record;
    pragma Convention(COBOL, COBOL_Record);

    procedure Prog(Item : in out COBOL_Record);
    pragma Import(COBOL, Prog, "PROG");

    package Salary_Conversions is
        new COBOL.Decimal_Conversions(Salary_Type);

    Some_Salary : Salary_Type := 12_345.67;
```

```
   Some_Record : COBOL_Record :=
      (Name    => "Johnson, John        ",
       SSN     => "111223333",
       Salary  => Salary_Conversions.To_Binary(Some_Salary));

begin
   Prog(Some_Record);
   ...
end Test_Call;


with Interfaces.COBOL;
with COBOL_Sequential_IO; -- Assumed to be supplied by implementation
procedure Test_External_Formats is
   -- Using data created by a COBOL program
   -- Assume that a COBOL program has created a sequential file with
   --   the following record structure, and that we need to
   --   process the records in an Ada program
   --   01 EMPLOYEE-RECORD
   --        05 NAME    PIC X(20).
   --        05 SSN     PIC X(9)
   --        05 SALARY  PIC 99999V99 USAGE COMP.
   --        05 ADJUST  PIC S999V999 SIGN LEADING SEPARATE
   -- The COMP data is binary (32 bits), high-order byte first
package COBOL renames Interfaces.COBOL;

type Salary_Type is delta 0.01 digits 7 range 0.0 .. 99_999.99;
type Adjustments_Type is delta 0.001 digits 6;

type COBOL_Employee_Record_Type is  -- External representation
   record
      Name   : COBOL.Alphanumeric(1 .. 20);
      SSN    : COBOL.Alphanumeric(1 .. 9);
      Salary : COBOL.Byte_Array(1 .. 4);
      Adjust : COBOL.Numeric(1 .. 7);  -- Sign and 6 digits
   end record;
pragma Convention(COBOL, COBOL_Employee_Record_Type);

package COBOL_Employee_IO is
   new COBOL_Sequential_IO(COBOL_Employee_Record_Type);
use COBOL_Employee_IO;

COBOL_File : File_Type;

type Ada_Employee_Record_Type is  -- Internal representation
   record
      Name   : String(1 .. 20);
      SSN    : String(1 .. 9);
      Salary : Salary_Type;
      Adjust : Adjustments_Type;
   end record;

COBOL_Record : COBOL_Employee_Record_Type;

Ada_Record   : Ada_Employee_Record_Type;

package Salary_Conversions is
   new COBOL.Decimal_Conversions(Salary_Type);
use Salary_Conversions;
```

```
        package Adjustments_Conversions is
           new COBOL.Decimal_Conversions(Adjustments_Type);
        use Adjustments_Conversions;
begin
        Open(COBOL_File, Name => "Some_File");
        loop
           Read(COBOL_File, COBOL_Record);
           Ada_Record.Name := To_Ada(COBOL_Record.Name);
           Ada_Record.SSN  := To_Ada(COBOL_Record.SSN);
           begin
              Ada_Record.Salary :=
                 To_Decimal(COBOL_Record.Salary, High_Order_First);
           exception
              when Conversion_Error =>
                 ... -- Report "Invalid Salary Data"
           end;
           begin
              Ada_Record.Adjust :=
                 To_Decimal(COBOL_Record.Adjust, Leading_Separate);
           exception
              when Conversion_Error =>
                 ... -- Report "Invalid Adjustment Data"
           end;
           ... -- Process Ada_Record
        end loop;
exception
        when End_Error => ...
end Test_External_Formats;
```

B.4 Fortran Interface Package

Much mathematical software exists and continues to be written in Fortran and so there is a strong need for Ada programs to be able to interface to Fortran routines. Ada programs should be able to call Fortran subprograms, or Fortran library routines, passing parameters mapped the way Fortran would map them. Similarly, with increasing frequency, there will also be reasons for Fortran programs to call Ada subprograms as if they were written in Fortran (that is, with parameters passed in the normal way for Fortran). The Numerics Annex recommends that the facilities for interfacing to Fortran described in the annex on Interface to Other Languages be implemented if Fortran is widely supported in the target environment. Some high-performance mathematical software is also written in C, so a similar recommendation is made with regard to the facilities for interfacing to C. We discuss only the Fortran interfacing facilities here.

Interfacing to Fortran is provided by the child package Interfaces.Fortran and the convention identifier Fortran in the interfacing pragmas.

The package Interfaces.Fortran defines types having the same names as the Fortran intrinsic types (except where they would conflict with the names of Ada types predefined in Standard, in which case they are given different names) and whose representations match the default representations of those types in the target Fortran implementation. Multiple Fortran interface packages may be provided if several different implementations of Fortran are to be accommodated in the target environment; each would have an identifier denoting the corresponding implementation of Fortran. The same identifier would be used to denote that implementation in the interfacing pragmas.

Additional types may be added to a Fortran interface package as appropriate. For example, the package for an implementation of Fortran 77 might add declarations for Integer_Star_2, Integer_Star_4, Logical_Star_1, Logical_Star_4, and so on, while one for an implementation of Fortran 90 might add declarations for `Integer_Kind_0`, `Integer_Kind_1`, `Real_Kind_0`, `Real_Kind_1`, and so forth.

Use of the types defined in a Fortran interface package suffices when the application only requires scalar objects to be passed between Ada and Fortran subprograms. The `Convention` pragma can be used to indicate that a multidimensional array is to be mapped in Fortran's column-major order, or that a record object declared in a library subprogram or package is to be mapped the way Fortran would map a common block (the `Import` or `Export` pragma would also be specified for the object), or that a record type is to be mapped the way Fortran 90 would map a corresponding type (called a "derived type" in Fortran 90). Compatibility with Fortran 90's pointer types is provided by applying the `Convention` pragma to appropriate access types.

B.5 Requirements Summary

The requirement

> *R4.1-B(2) — Pragma Interface*

is met by the introduction of the pragmas `Convention`, `Import` and `Export` for the better control of interfaces to programs in other languages.

The study topic

> *S10.1-A(2) — Specification of Decimal Representation*

is met in part by the generic package `Interfaces.COBOL.Decimal_Conversions`.

The study topic

> *S10.2-A(1) — Alternate Character Set Support*

is satisfied in part by the facilities provided in `Interfaces.COBOL.Decimal_Conversions`.

The study topic

> *S10.3-A(1) — Interfacing with Data Base Systems*

is satisfied in part by the types and conversions in the package `Interfaces.COBOL`.

The study topic

> *S11.2-A(1) — Array Representation*

is met by the pragma `Convention` with a Fortran convention identifier, and more generally by the package `Interfaces.Fortran`.

C Systems Programming

The Systems Programming Annex specifies additional capabilities for low-level programming. These capabilities are also required in many real-time, embedded, distributed, and information systems.

The purpose of the Annex is to provide facilities for applications that are required to interface and interact with the outside world (i.e. outside the domain of an Ada program). Examples may be other languages, an operating system, the underlying hardware, devices and I/O channels. Since these kinds of interfaces lie outside the Ada semantic model, it is necessary to resort to low-level, environment specific programming paradigms. Such sections of the application are often implementation dependent and portability concerns are less critical. However, rigid isolation of these components helps in improving the portability of the rest of the application.

The application domains of such systems include: real-time embedded computers, I/O drivers, operating systems and run-time systems, multilingual/multicomponent systems, performance-sensitive hardware dependent applications, resource managers, user-defined schedulers, and so on. Accordingly, this annex covers the following facilities needed by such applications:

- Access to the underlying hardware (machine instructions, hardware devices, etc.);

- Access to the underlying operating or runtime system;

- Low-level, direct interrupt handling;

- Unchecked access to parts of the run-time model of the implementation;

- Specifying the representation and allocation of program data structures;

- Access to shared variables in a multitasking program;

- Access to the identity of tasks and the allocation of data on a per-task basis.

Note that implementation of this annex is a prerequisite for the implementation of the Real-Time Systems annex.

C.1 Access to Machine Operations

In systems programming and embedded applications, we need to write software that interfaces directly to hardware devices. This might be impossible if the Ada language implementation did not permit access to the full instruction set of the underlying machine. A need to access specific machine instructions arises sometimes from other considerations as well. Examples include instructions that perform compound operations atomically on shared memory, such as test-and-set and compare-and-swap, and instructions that provide high-level operations, such as translate-and-test and vector arithmetic.

It can be argued that Ada 83 already provides adequate access to machine operations, via the package Machine_Code. However, in practice, the support for this feature was optional, and some implementations support it only in a form that is inadequate for the needs of systems programming and real-time applications.

The mechanisms specified in this Annex for access to machine code are already allowed in Ada 83. The main difference is that now it is intended that the entire instruction set of a given machine should be accessible to an Ada program either via the Machine_Code package or via intrinsic subprograms (or indeed both). In addition, implementation-defined attributes ought to allow machine code to refer to the addresses or offsets of entities declared within the Ada program.

This Annex leaves most of the interface to machine code implementation defined. It is not appropriate for a language standard to specify exactly how access to machine operations must be provided, since machine instructions are inherently dependent on the machine.

We considered providing access to machine instructions only through interface to assembly language. This would not entirely satisfy the requirements, however, since it does not permit insertion of machine instructions in-line. Because the compiler cannot always perform register allocation across external subprogram calls, such calls generally require the saving and restoring of all registers. Thus, the overhead of assembly language subprogram calls is too high where the effect of a single instruction (e.g. test-and-set or direct I/O) is desired. For this, an in-line form of access is required. This requirement is satisfied by machine-code inserts or intrinsic subprograms.

To be useful, a mechanism for access to machine code must permit the flow of data and control between machine operations and the rest of the Ada program. There is not much value in being able to generate a machine code instruction if there is no way to apply it to operands in the Ada program. For example, an implementation that only permits the insertion of machine code as numeric literal data would not satisfy this requirement, since there would be no way for machine code operations to read or write the values of variables of the Ada program, or to invoke Ada procedures. However, this can be entirely satisfied by a primitive form of machine-code insertion, which allows an instruction sequence to be specified as a sequence of data values, so long as symbolic references to Ada entities are allowed in such a data sequence.

For convenience, it is desirable that certain instructions that are used frequently in systems programming, such as test-and-set and primitive I/O operations, be accessible as intrinsic subprograms, see [RM95 6.3.1]. However, it is not clear that it is practical for an implementation to provide access to all machine instructions in this form. Thus, it might be desirable to provide machine code inserts for generality, and intrinsic operations for convenient access to the more frequently needed operations.

The Pragma Export

The implementation advice concerning the pragma Export [RM95 B.1] addresses unintended interactions between compiler/linker optimizations and machine code inserts in Ada 83. A machine code insert might store an address, and later use it as a pointer or subprogram entry point — as with an interrupt handler. In general, the compiler cannot detect how the variable or subprogram address is used. When machine code is used in this way, it is the programmer's responsibility to inform the compiler about these usages, and it is the language's responsibility to specify a way for the programmer to convey this information. Without this information, the compiler or linker might perform optimizations so that the data object or subprogram code are deleted, or loads and stores referencing the object are suppressed.

In Ada 95, machine code subprograms are like external subprograms written in another language, in that they may be opaque to optimization. That is, in general, the compiler cannot determine which data objects a machine code subprogram might read or update, or to where it might transfer control. The Export pragma tells the compiler not to perform optimizations on an exported object. By requiring the user to specify as exported anything that might be modified by an external call, the compiler is provided with information that allows better optimization in the general case.

Export can also be used to ensure that the specified entity is allocated at an addressable location. For example, this might mean that a constant must actually be stored in memory, rather than only inserted in-line where used.

Interface to Assembly Language

An Ada implementation conforming to this Annex should also support interface to the traditional "systems programming language" for that target machine. This might be necessary to interface with existing code provided by the hardware vendor, such as an operating system, device drivers, or built-in-test software. We considered the possibility of requiring support for an assembler, but this has obvious problems. It is hard to state this requirement in a way that would not create enforcement problems. For example, what if there are several assemblers available for a given target, and new assemblers are developed from time to time? Which ones must an implementor support? Likewise, how hard does an implementor need to look before concluding there are no assemblers for a given target? However, we believe that stating the requirement simply as "should support interface to assembler" together with market forces will provide the appropriate direction for implementors in this area, even though compliance can not be fully defined.

Documentation Requirements

The intent of the documentation requirements is to ensure that the implementation provides enough information for the user to write machine code subprograms that interact with the rest of the Ada program. To do so effectively, the machine code subprograms ought to be able to read constants and read and update variables (including protected objects), to call subprograms, and to transfer control to labels.

Validation

The specifications for machine code are not likely to be enforceable by standard validation tests, but it should be possible to check for the existence of the required documentation and interfaces by examination of vendor supplied documentation, and to carry out spot checks with particular machine instructions.

C.2 Required Representation Support

The recommended levels of support defined in [RM95 13] are made into firm requirements if this annex is implemented because systems programming applications need to control data representations, and need to be able to count on a certain minimum level of support.

C.3 Interrupt Support

The ability to write handlers for interrupts is essential in systems programming and in real-time embedded applications.

The model of interrupts and interrupt handling specified in Ada 95 is intended to capture the common elements of most hardware interrupt schemes, as well as the software interrupt models used by some application interfaces to operating systems, notably POSIX [1003.1 90]. The specification allows an implementation to handle an interrupt efficiently by arranging for the interrupt handler to be invoked directly by the hardware. This has been a major consideration in the design of the interrupt handling mechanisms.

The reason for distinguishing *treatments* from handlers is that executing a handler is only one of the possible treatments. In particular, executing a handler constitutes delivery of the interrupt. The default treatment for an interrupt might be to keep the interrupt pending, or to discard it without delivery. These treatments cannot be modelled as a default handler.

The notion of *blocking* an interrupt is an abstraction for various mechanisms that may be used to prevent delivery of an interrupt. These include operations that "mask" off a set of interrupts, raise the hardware priority of the processor, or "disable" the processor interrupt mechanism.

On many hardware architectures it is not practical to allow a direct-execution interrupt handler to become blocked. Trying to support blocking of interrupt handlers results in extra overhead, and can also lead to deadlock or stack overflow. Therefore, interrupt handlers are not allowed to block. To enable programmers to avoid unintentional blocking in handlers, the language specifies which operations are potentially blocking, see [RM95 9.5.1].

We introduced the concept of *reserved* interrupts to reflect the need of the Ada run-time system to install handlers for certain interrupts, including interrupts used to implement time delays or various constraint checks. The possibility of simply making these interrupts invisible to the application was considered. This is not possible without restricting the implementation of the Interrupt_ID type. For example, if this type is an integer type and certain values within this range are reserved (as is the case with POSIX signals, for example), there is no way to prevent the application from *attempting* to attach a handler to one of the reserved interrupts; however, any such attempt will raise Program_Error. Besides, other (implementation-defined) uses for an interrupt-id type are anticipated for which the full range of values might be needed; if the standard interrupt-id type did not include all values, the implementation would have to declare an almost identical type for such purposes.

We also need to reserve certain interrupts for task interrupt entries. There are many ways in which implementations can support interrupt entries. The higher-level mechanisms involve some degree of interaction with the Ada run-time system. It could be disastrous if the run-time system is relying on one of these high-level delivery mechanisms to be in place, and the user installs a low-level handler. For this reason, the concept of reserved interrupt is used here also, to prevent attachment of another handler to an interrupt while an interrupt entry is still attached to it.

On some processor architectures, the priority of an interrupt is determined by the device sending the interrupt, independent of the identity of the interrupt. For this reason, we need to allow an interrupt to be generated at different priorities at different times. This can be modelled by hypothesizing several hardware tasks, at different priorities, which may all call the interrupt handler.

A consequence of direct hardware invocation of interrupt handlers is that one cannot speak meaningfully of the "currently executing task" within an interrupt handler (see [RM95 C.7.1]). The alternative, of requiring the implementation to create the illusion of an Ada task as context for the execution of the handler would add execution time overhead to interrupt handling. Since interrupts may occur very frequently, and require fast response, any such unnecessary overhead is intolerable.

For these and other reasons, care has been taken not to specify that interrupt handlers behave exactly as if they are called by a hardware "task". The language must not preclude the writing of efficient interrupt handlers, just because the hardware does not provide a reasonable way to preserve the illusion of the handler being called by a task.

The Annex leaves as implementation-defined the semantics of interrupts when more than one interrupt subsystem exists on a multi-processor target. This kind of configuration may dictate that different interrupts are delivered only to particular processors, and will require that additional rules be placed on the way handlers are attached. In essence, such a system cannot be treated completely as a homogeneous multi-processor. The means for identifying interrupt sources, and the specification of the circumstances when interrupts are blocked are therefore left open by the Annex. It is expected that these additional rules will be defined as a logical extension of the existing ones.

From within the program the form of an interrupt handler is a protected procedure. Typically we write

```
protected Alarm is
   procedure Response;
   pragma Attach_Handler(Response, Alarm_Int);
end Alarm;

protected body Alarm is
   procedure Response is
   begin
      ...  -- the interrupt handling code
   end Response;
end Alarm;
```

where Alarm_Int identifies the physical interrupt as discussed in C.3.2.

Protected procedures have appropriate semantics for fast interrupt handlers; they are directly invoked by the hardware and share data with tasks and other interrupt handlers. Thus, once the interrupt handler begins to execute it cannot block; on the other hand while any shared data is being accessed by other threads of control, an interrupt must be blocked.

For upward compatibility, the Ada 83 interrupt entry mechanism is retained although classified as obsolescent. It has been extended slightly, as a result of the integration with the protected procedure interrupt-handling model. In addition, this Annex does not preclude implementations from defining other forms of interrupt handlers such as protected procedures with parameters. The recommendation is that such extensions will follow the model defined by this Annex.

Exceptions and Interrupt Handlers

Propagating an exception from an interrupt handler is specified to have no effect. (If interrupt handlers were truly viewed as being "called" by imaginary tasks, the propagation of an exception back to the "caller" of an interrupt handler certainly should not affect any user-defined task.)

The real question seems to be whether the implementation is required to hide the effect of an interrupt from the user, or whether it can be allowed to cause a system crash. If the implementation uses the underlying interrupt mechanism directly, i.e. by putting the address of a handler procedure into an interrupt vector location, the execution context of the handler will be just the stack frame that is generated by the hardware interrupt mechanism. If an exception is raised and not handled within the interrupt handler, the exception propagation mechanism will try to unroll the stack, beyond the handler. There needs to be some indication on the stack that it should stop at the interrupt frame, and not try to propagate beyond. Lacking this, either the exception might just be propagated back to the interrupted task (if the hardware interrupt frame structure looks enough like a normal call), or the difference in frame structures will cause a failure. The failure might be detected in the run-time system, might cause the run-time system to crash, or might result in transfer of control to an incorrect handler, thereby causing the application to run amok. The desired behavior is for the exception mechanism to recognize the handler frame as a special case, and to simply do an interrupt return. Unless the hardware happens to provide enough information in the handler frame to allow recognition, it seems an extra layer of software will be needed, i.e. a software wrapper for the user interrupt handler. (This wrapper might be provided by the compiler, or by the run-time system.)

Thus, the requirement that propagating an exception from a handler be "safe" is likely to impose some extra run-time overhead on interrupt handlers but is justified by the additional safety it provides. It is not expected that exceptions will be raised intentionally in interrupt handlers, but when an unexpected error (a bug) causes an exception to be raised, it is much better to contain the effect of this error than to allow the propagation to affect arbitrary code (including the RTS itself).

Implementation Requirements

It is not safe to write interrupt handlers without some means of reserving sufficient stack space for them to execute. Implementations will differ in whether such handlers borrow stack space from the task they interrupt, or whether they execute on a separate stack. In either case, with dynamic attachment of interrupt handlers, the application needs to inform the implementation of its maximum interrupt stack depth requirement. This could be done via a pragma or a link-time command.

Documentation Requirements

Where hardware permits an interrupt to be handled but not to be blocked (while in the handler), it might not be possible for an implementation to support the protected object locking semantics for such an interrupt. The documentation must describe any variations from the model.

For example, in many implementations, it may not be possible for an interrupted task to resume execution until the interrupt handler returns. The intention here is to allow the implementation to choose whether to run the handler on a separate stack or not. The basic issue is whether the hardware (or underlying operating system) interrupt mechanism switches stacks, or whether the handler begins execution on the stack of the interrupted task. Adding software to the handler to do stack switching (in both directions) can add significantly to the run-time overhead, and this may be unacceptable for high frequency interrupts.

Situations in which this would make a difference are rather unusual. Since the handler can interrupt, the task that it interrupts must have a lower active priority at that time. Therefore, the only situations where the interrupted task would need to resume execution before the handler returns are:

- If there is more than one processor, and the interrupted task could migrate to another available processor;

- If the handler or some higher priority task causes the priority of the interrupted task to be raised (via a call to Set_Priority); or

- If priorities are not supported.

The semantic model, when the interrupt handler uses the stack of the interrupted task, is that the handler has taken a non-preemptable processing resource (the upper part of the stack) which the interrupted task needs in order to resume execution. Note that this stack space was not in use by the interrupted task at the time it was preempted, since the stack did not yet extend that far, but it is needed by the interrupted task before it can resume execution.

C.3.1 Protected Procedure Handlers

A handler can be statically attached to an interrupt by the use of the pragma Attach_Handler as in the example above. Alternatively the connection can be made dynamic by using the pragma Interrupt_Handler together with the procedure Attach_Handler. The example might then become

```
protected Alarm is
   procedure Response;
   pragma Interrupt_Handler(Response);
end Alarm;

protected body Alarm is
```

```
    procedure Response is
    begin
    ...  -- the interrupt handling code
    end Response;
end Alarm;
...
Attach_Handler(Alarm.Response, Alarm_Int);
```

Note therefore that the name Attach_Handler is used for both the pragma and for the procedure.

The procedure form is needed to satisfy the requirement for dynamic attachment. The pragma form is provided to permit attachment earlier, during initialization of objects, or possibly at program load time. Another advantage of the pragma form is that it permits association of a handler attachment with a lexical scope, ensuring that it is detached on scope exit. Note that while the protected type is required to be a library level declaration, the protected object itself may be declared in a deeper level.

Under certain conditions, implementations can preelaborate protected objects, see [RM95 10.2.1] and [RM95 C.4]. For such implementations, the Attach_Handler pragma provides a way to establish interrupt handlers truly statically, at program load time.

The Attach_Handler and Interrupt_Handler pragmas specify a protected procedure as one that is or may be used as an interrupt handler and (in the latter case) be attached dynamically. This has three purposes:

*   It informs the compiler that it might need to generate code for a protected procedure that can be invoked directly by the hardware interrupt mechanism, and to generate appropriate calls to procedures contained in such an object if they are called from software.

*   It allows the implementation to allocate enough space for the corresponding protected object to store the interrupt-id to which the handler is attached. (This might be needed on some implementations in order to mask that interrupt when operations on the protected object are called from software.)

*   It serves as important documentation about the protected object.

In general, the hardware mechanism might require different code generation than for procedures called from software. For example, a different return instruction might be used. Also, the hardware mechanism may implicitly block and unblock interrupts, whereas a software call may require this to be done explicitly. For a procedure that can be called from hardware or software, the compiler generally must choose between:

*   Compiling the procedure in the form for hardware invocation and adding some sort of glue-code when it is called via software;

*   Compiling the procedure in the form for software invocation, and call it indirectly, from an extra layer of interrupt handler, when a hardware interrupt occurs.

Because code generation is involved, the pragma is associated with the protected type declaration, rather than with a particular protected object.

The restrictions on protected procedures should be sufficient to eliminate the need for an implementation to place any further restrictions on the form or content of an interrupt handler. Ordinarily, there should be no need for implementation-defined restrictions on protected procedure interrupt handlers, such as those imposed by Ada 83 on tasks with fast interrupt handler entries. However, such restrictions are permitted, in case they turn out to be needed by implementations.

This Annex requires only that an implementation support parameterless procedures as handlers. In fact, some hardware interrupts do provide information about the cause of the interrupt and the state of the processor at the time of the interrupt. Such information is also provided by operating systems that support software interrupts. The specifics of such interrupt parameters are necessarily dependent on the execution environment, and so are not suitable for standardization. Where appropriate, implementation-defined child packages of Ada.Interrupts should provide services for such interrupt handlers, analogous to those defined for parameterless protected procedures in the package Ada.Interrupts itself.

Note that only procedures of library-level protected objects are allowed as dynamic handlers. This is because the execution context of such procedures persists for the full lifetime of the partition. If local procedures were allowed to be handlers, some extra prologue code would need to be added to the procedure, to set up the correct execution environment. To avoid problems with dangling references, the attachment would need to be broken on scope exit. This does not seem practical for the handlers that might be attached and detached via a procedure interface. On the other hand, it could be practical for handlers that are attached via a pragma. Some implementations may choose to allow local procedures to be used as handlers with the Attach_Handler pragma.

For some environments, it may be appropriate to also allow ordinary subprograms to serve as interrupt handlers; an implementation may support this, but the mechanism is not specified. Protected procedures are the preferred mechanism because of the better semantic fit in the general case. However, there are some situations where the fit might not be so good. In particular, if the handler does not access shared data in a manner that requires the interrupt to be blocked, or if the hardware does not support blocking of the interrupt, the protected object model may not be appropriate. Also, if the handler procedure needs to be written in another language, it may not be practical to use a protected procedure.

Issues Related to Ceiling Priorities

With priority-ceiling locking, it is important to specify the active priority of the task that "calls" the handler, since it determines the ability of the interrupt to preempt whatever is executing at the time. It is also relevant to the user, since the user must specify the ceiling priority of the handler object to be at least this high, or else the program will be erroneous (might crash).

Normally, a task has its active priority raised when it calls a protected operation with a higher ceiling than the task's own active priority. The intent is that execution of protected procedures as interrupt handlers be consistent with this model. The ability of the interrupt handler "call" from the hardware to preempt an executing task is determined by the hardware interrupt priority. In this respect, the effect is similar to a call from a task whose active priority is at the level of the hardware interrupt priority. Once the handler begins to execute, its active priority is set to the ceiling priority of the protected object. For example, if a protected procedure of an object whose ceiling priority is 5 is attached as a handler to an interrupt of priority 3, and the interrupt occurs when a task of priority 4 runs, the interrupt will remain pending until there is no task executing with active priority higher than or equal to 3. At that point, the interrupt will be serviced. Once the handler starts executing, it will raise its active priority to 5.

It is impractical to specify that the hardware must perform a run-time check before calling an interrupt handler, in order to verify that the ceiling priority of the protected object is not lower than that of the hardware interrupt. This means that checks must either be done at compile-time, at the time the handler is attached, or by the handler itself.

The potential for compile-time checking is limited, since dynamic attachment of handlers is allowed and the priority can itself be dynamic; all that can be done is to verify that the handler ceiling is specified via the Interrupt_Priority pragma thus

```
protected Alarm is
    pragma Interrupt_Priority(N);
    procedure Response;
    pragma Interrupt_Handler(Response);
end Alarm;
```

Doing the check when the handler is attached is also limited on some systems. For example, with some architectures, different occurrences of the same interrupt may be delivered at different hardware priorities. In this case, the maximum priority at which an interrupt might be delivered is determined by the peripheral hardware rather than the processor architecture. An implementation that chooses to provide attach-time ceiling checks for such an architecture could either assume the worst (i.e. that all interrupts can be delivered at the maximum priority) or make the maximum priority at which each interrupt can be delivered a configuration parameter.

A last-resort method of checking for ceiling violations is for the handler to start by comparing its own ceiling against the active priority of the task it interrupted. Presumably, if a ceiling violation were detected, the interrupt could be ignored or the entire program could be aborted. Providing the run-time check means inserting a layer of "wrapper" code around the user-provided handler, to perform the check. Executing this code will add to the execution time of the handler, for every execution. This could be significant if the interrupt occurs with high frequency.

Because of the difficulty of guaranteeing against ceiling violations by handlers on all architectures, and the potential loss of efficiency, an implementation is not required to detect situations where the hardware interrupt mechanism violates a protected object ceiling. Incorrect ceiling specification for an interrupt handler is "erroneous" programming, rather than a bounded error, since it might be impractical to prevent this from crashing the Ada RTS without actually performing the ceiling check. For example, the handler might interrupt a protected action while an entry queue is being modified. The epilogue code of the handler could then try to use the entry queue. It is hard to predict how bad this could be, or whether this is the worst thing that could happen. At best, the effect might be limited to loss of entry calls and corresponding indefinite blocking of the calling tasks.

Since the priorities of the interrupt sources are usually known a priori and are an important design parameter, it seems that they are not likely to vary a lot and create problems after the initial debugging of the system. Simple coding conventions can also help in preventing such cases.

Non-Suspending Locks

With interrupt handlers, it is important to implement protected object locking without suspension. Two basic techniques can be applied. One of these provides mutual exclusion between tasks executing on a single processor. The other provides mutual exclusion between tasks executing on different processors, with shared memory. The minimal requirement for locking in shared memory is to use some form of spin-wait on a word representing the protected object lock. Other, more elaborate schemes are allowed (such as priority-based algorithms, or algorithms that minimize bus contention).

Within a single processor, a non-suspending implementation of protected object locking can be provided by limiting preemption. The basic prerequisite is that *while a protected object is locked, other tasks that might lock that protected object are not allowed to preempt.* This imposes a constraint on the dispatching policy, which can be modelled abstractly in terms of *locking sets*. The locking set of a protected object is the set of tasks and protected operations that might execute protected operations on that object, directly or indirectly. More precisely, the locking set of a protected object R includes:

•   Tasks that call protected operations of R directly.

•   Protected procedures and entries whose bodies call a protected operation of R.

•   The locking set of Q, if Q is a protected object with a procedure or entry whose body contains a call to an operation (including a requeue) in the locking set of R.

While a protected object is held locked by a task or interrupt handler, the implementation must prevent the other tasks and interrupt handlers in the locking set from executing on the same processor. This can be enforced conservatively, by preventing a larger set of tasks and interrupt handlers from executing. At one extreme, it may be enforced by blocking all interrupts, and disabling the dispatching of any other task. The priority-ceiling locking scheme described in [RM95 D.3] approximates the locking set a little less conservatively, by locking out all tasks and interrupt handlers with lower or equal priority to the one that is holding the protected object lock.

The above technique (for a single processor) can be combined with the spin-wait approach on a multiprocessor. The spinning task raises its priority to the ceiling or mask interrupts before it tries to grab the lock, so that it will not be preempted after grabbing the lock (while still being in the "wrong" priority).

Metrics

The interrupt handler overhead metric is provided so that a programmer can determine whether a given implementation can be used for a particular application. There is clearly imprecision in the definition of such a metric. The measurements involved require the use of a hardware test instrument, such as a logic analyzer; the inclusion of instructions to trigger such a device might alter the execution times slightly. The validity of the test depends on the choice of reference code sequence and handler procedure. It also relies on the fact that a compiler will not attempt in-line optimization of normal procedure calls to a protected procedure that is attached as an interrupt handler. However, there is no requirement for the measurement to be absolutely precise. The user can always obtain more precise information by carrying out specific testing. The purpose of the metric here is to allow the user to determine whether the implementation is close enough to the requirements of the application to be worth considering. For this purpose, the accuracy of a metric could be off by a factor of two and still be useful.

C.3.2 The Package Interrupts

The operations defined in the package Ada.Interrupts are intended to be a minimum set needed to associate handlers with interrupts. The type Interrupt_ID is implementation defined to allow the most natural choice of the type for the underlying computer architecture. It is not required to be private, so that if the architecture permits it to be an integer, a non-portable application may take advantage of this information to construct arrays and loops indexed by Interrupt_ID. It is, however, required to be a discrete type so that values of the type Interrupt_ID can be used as discriminants of task and protected types. This capability is considered necessary to allow a single protected or task type to be used as handler for several interrupts thus

```
Device_Priority: constant array (1 .. 5) of Interrupt_Priority :=
                                                      ( ... );
protected type Device_Interface(Int_ID: Interrupt_ID) is
   procedure Handler;
   pragma Attach_Handler(Handler, Int_ID);
   ...
   pragma Interrupt_Priority(Device_Priority(Int_ID));
end Device_Interface;
...
Device_1_Driver: Device_Interface(1);
...
Device_5_Driver: Device_Interface(5);
...
```

Some interrupts may originate from more than one device, so an interrupt handler may need to perform additional tests to decide which device the interrupt came from. For example, there might be several timers that all generate the same interrupt (and one of these timers might be used by the Ada run-time system to implement delays).   In such a case, the implementation may define multiple logical interrupt-id's for each such physical interrupt.

The atomic operation `Exchange_Handler` is provided to attach a handler to an interrupt and return the previous handler of that interrupt. In principle, this functionality might also be obtained by the user through a protected procedure that locks out interrupts and then calls `Current_Handler` and `Attach_Handler`. However, support for priority-ceiling locking of protected objects is not required. Moreover, an exchange-handler operation is already provided in atomic form by some operating systems (e.g. POSIX). In these cases, attempting to achieve the same effect via the use of a protected procedure would be inefficient, if feasible at all.

The value returned by `Current_Handler` and `Exchange_Handler` in the case that the default interrupt treatment is in force is left implementation-defined. It is guaranteed however that using this value for `Attach_Handler` and `Exchange_Handler` will restore the default treatment. The possibility of simply requiring the value to be null in this case was considered but was believed to be an over-specification and to introduce an additional overhead for checking this special value on each operation.

Operations for blocking and unblocking interrupts are intentionally not provided. One reason is that the priority model provides a way to lock out interrupts, using either the ceiling-priority of a protected object or the `Set_Priority` operation (see [RM95 D.5]). Providing any other mechanism here would raise problems of interactions and conflicts with the priority model. Another reason is that the capabilities for blocking interrupts differ enough from one machine to another that any more specific control over interrupts would not be applicable to all machines.

In Ada 83, interrupt entries are attached to interrupts using values of the type `System.Address`. In Ada 95, protected procedures are attached as handlers using values of `Interrupt_ID`. Changing the rules for interrupt entries was not considered feasible as it would introduce upward-incompatibilities, and would require support of the `Interrupts` package by all implementations. To resolve the problem of two different ways to map interrupts to Ada types, the `Reference` function is provided. This function is intended to provide a portable way to convert a value of the type `Interrupt_ID` to a value of type `System.Address` that can be used in a representation clause to attach an interrupt entry to an interrupt source.

The Interrupts.Names Package

The names of interrupts are segregated into the child package `Interrupts.Names`, because these names will be implementation-defined. In this way, a use clause for package `Interrupts` will not hide any user-defined names.

C.3.3 Task Entries as Handlers

Attaching task entries to interrupts is specified as an obsolescent feature (see [RM95 J.7.1]). This is because support of this feature in Ada 83 was never required and important semantic details were not given. Requiring every implementation to support attaching both protected procedures and task entries to interrupts was considered to be an unnecessarily heavy burden. Also, with entries the implementation must choose between supporting the full semantics of rendezvous for interrupts (with more implementation overhead than protected procedures) versus imposing restrictions on the form of handler tasks (which will be implementation-dependent and subtle). The possibility of imposing standard restrictions, such as those on protected types, was considered. It was rejected on the grounds that it would not be upward compatible with existing implementations of interrupt entries (which are diverse in this respect). Therefore, if only one form of handler is to be supported, it should be protected procedures.

As compared to Ada 83, the specifications for interrupt entries are changed slightly. First, the implementation is explicitly permitted to impose restrictions on the form of the interrupt handler task, and on calls to the interrupt entry from software tasks. This affirms the existing practice of language implementations which support high-performance direct-execution interrupt entries. Second, the dynamic attachment of different handlers to the same interrupt, sequentially, is explicitly allowed. That is, when an interrupt handler task terminates and is finalized, the attachment of the interrupt entry to the interrupt is broken. The interrupt again becomes eligible for attachment. This is consistent with the dynamic attachment model for protected procedures as interrupt handlers, and is also consistent with a liberal reading of the Ada 83 standard. Finally, in anticipation of Ada 95 applications that use protected procedures as handlers together with existing Ada 83 code that uses interrupt entries, interrupts that are attached to entries, are specified as reserved, and so effectively removed from the set of interrupts available for attachment to protected procedures. This separation can therefore eliminate accidental conflicts in the use of values of the Interrupt_ID type.

C.4 Preelaboration Requirements

The primary systems programming and real-time systems requirement addressed by preelaboration is the fast starting (and possibly restarting) of programs. Preelaboration also provides a way to possibly reduce the run-time memory requirement of programs, by removing some of the elaboration code. This section is in the Systems Programming Annex (rather than the Real-Time Annex) because the functionality is not limited to real-time applications. It is also required to support distribution.

Rejected Approaches

There is a spectrum of techniques that can be used to reduce or eliminate elaboration code. One possible technique is to run the entire program up to a certain point, then take a snap-shot of the memory image, which is copied out and transformed into a file that can be reloaded. Program start-up would then consist of loading this check-point file and resuming execution. This "core-dump" approach is suitable for some applications and it does not require special support from the language. However, it is not really what has been known as preelaboration, nor does it address all the associated requirements.

The core-dump approach to accelerating program start-up suffers from several defects. It is error-prone and awkward to use or maintain. It requires the entire active writable memory of the application to be dumped. This can take a large amount of storage, and a proportionately long load time. It is also troublesome to apply this technique to constant tables that are to be mapped to read-only memory; if the compiler generates elaboration code to initialize such tables, writable memory must be provided in the development target during the elaboration, and replaced by read-only memory after the core-dump has been produced; the core-dump must then be edited to separate out the portions that need to be programmed into read-only memory from those that are loaded in the normal way. This technique presumes the existence of an external reload device, which might not be available on smaller real-time embedded systems. Finally, effective use of this method requires very precise control over elaboration order to ensure that the desired packages, and only those packages, are elaborated prior to the core-dump. Since this order often includes implementation packages, it is not clear that the user can fully control this order.

The Chosen Approach

Preelaboration is controlled by the two pragmas Pure and Preelaborate as mentioned in 10.3. Many predefined packages are Pure such as

```
package Ada.Characters is
   pragma Pure(Characters);
end Ada.Characters;
```

The introduction of pure packages together with shared passive and remote call interface packages (see [RM95 E.2]) for distribution, created the need to talk about packages whose elaboration happens "before any other elaboration". To accommodate this, the concept of a *preelaborable* construct is introduced in [RM95 10.2.1]. (Preelaborability is naturally the property of an entity which allows it to be preelaborated.) Pure packages are always preelaborated, as well as packages to which the pragma `Preelaborate` specifically applies such as

```
package Ada.Characters.Handling is
   pragma Preelaborate(Handling);
   ...
```

The difference between pure packages and any other preelaborated package is that the latter may have "state". In the core, being preelaborated does not necessarily mean "no code is generated for preelaboration", it only means that these library units are preelaborated before any other unit.

The Systems Programming Annex defines additional implementation and documentation requirements to ensure that the elaboration of preelaborated packages does not execute any code at all.

Issues Related to Preelaboration

Given this approach, some trade-offs had to be made between the generality of constructs to which this requirement applies, the degree of reduction in run-time elaboration code, the complexity of the compiler, and the degree to which the concerns of the run-time system can be separated from those of the compiler.

Bodies of subprograms that are declared in preelaborated packages are guaranteed to be elaborated before they can be called. Therefore, implementations are required to suppress the elaboration checks for such subprograms. This eliminates a source of a distributed overhead that has been an issue in Ada 83.

Tasks, as well as allocators for other than access-to-constant types, are not included among the things specified as preelaborable, because the initialization of run-time system data structures for tasks and the dynamic allocation of storage for general access types would ordinarily require code to be executed at run time. While it might be technically possible to preelaborate tasks and general allocators under sufficiently restrictive conditions, this is considered too difficult to be required of every implementation and would make the compiler very dependent on details of the run-time system. The latter is generally considered to be undesirable by real-time systems developers, who often express the need to customize the Ada run-time environment. It is also considered undesirable by compiler vendors, since it aggravates their configuration management and maintenance problem. (Partial preelaboration of tasks might be more practical for the simple tasking model, described in [RM95 D.7].)

Entryless protected objects are preelaborable and are essential for shared passive packages. They are therefore allowed in preelaborated packages. The initialization of run time data structures might require run-time system calls in some implementations. In particular, where protected object locking is implemented using primitives of an operating system, it might be necessary to perform a system call to create and initialize a lock for the protected object. On such systems, the system call for lock initialization could be postponed until the first operation that is performed on the protected object, but this means some overhead on every protected object operation (perhaps a load, compare, and conditional jump, or an indirect call from a dispatching table). It seems that this kind of distributed overhead on operations that are intended to be very efficient is too high a price to pay for requiring preelaboration of protected objects. These implementations can conform to the requirements in this Annex by doing all initializations "behind-the-scene" before the program actually starts. On most other systems, it is expected that protected objects will be allocated and initialized statically and thus be elaborated when the program starts. Thus, the difference between these two cases is not semantic, and can be left to metrics and documentation requirements.

C.5 Shared Variable Control

Objects in shared memory may be used to communicate data between Ada tasks, between an Ada program and concurrent non-Ada software processes, or between an Ada program and hardware devices.

Ada 83 provided a limited facility for supporting variables shared between otherwise unsynchronized tasks. The pragma Shared indicated that a particular elementary object is being concurrently manipulated by two or more tasks, and that all loads and stores should be indivisible. The pragma Shared was quite weak. The semantics were only defined in terms of tasks, and not very clearly. This made it inadequate for communication with non-Ada software or hardware devices. Moreover, it could be applied only to a limited set of objects. For example, it could not be applied to a component of an array. One of the most common requirements for shared data access is for buffers, which are typically implemented as arrays. For these reasons, the pragma Shared was removed from the language and replaced by the pragmas Atomic and Volatile.

This Annex thus generalizes the capability to allow data sharing between non-Ada programs and hardware devices, and the sharing of composite objects. In fact, two levels of sharability are introduced:

atomic This indicates that all loads and stores of the object should be indivisible, and that no local copies of the object may be retained. It need only be supported for types where the underlying hardware memory access allows indivisible load and store operations. This imposes requirements on both the size and the alignment of the object.

volatile This indicates that the object can be updated asynchronously. However, there is no need for indivisible load and store.

So we can write

```
type Data is new Long_Float;
pragma Atomic(Data);        -- applying to a type
...
I: Integer;
pragma Volatile(I);         -- applying to a single object
```

Atomic types and objects are implicitly volatile as well. This is because it would make little sense to have an operation applied to an atomic object while allowing the object itself not to be flushed to memory immediately afterwards.

Since the atomicity of an object might affect its layout, it is illegal to explicitly specify other aspects of the object layout in a conflicting manner.

These pragmas may be applied to a constant, but only if the constant is imported. In Ada, the constant designation does not necessarily mean that the object's value cannot change, but rather that it is read-only. Therefore, it seems useful to allow an object to be read-only, while its value changes from the "outside". The rules about volatile objects ensure that the Ada code will read a fresh value each time.

The run-time semantics of atomic/volatile objects are defined in terms of external effects since this is the only way one can talk formally about objects being flushed to or refreshed from memory (as is required to support such objects).

When using such pragmas, one would not want to have the effect of the pragma more general than is minimally needed (this avoids the unnecessary overhead of atomic or load/store operations). That is why separate forms of the pragmas exist for arrays. Writing

```
Buffer: array (1 .. Max) of Integer;
pragma Atomic_Components(Buffer);
```

indicates that the atomicity applies individually to each component of the array but not to the array Buffer as a whole.

These pragmas must provide all the necessary information for the compiler to generate the appropriate code each time atomic or volatile objects are accessed. This is why the indication is usually on the type declaration rather than on the object declaration itself. For a stand-alone object there is no problem for the designation to be per-object, but for an array object whose components are atomic or volatile complications would arise. Specifying array components as atomic or volatile is likely to have implications on the layout of the array objects (e.g. components have to be on word boundaries). In addition, if the type of a formal parameter does not have volatile components and the actual parameter does, one would have to pass the parameter by copy, which is generally undesirable. Anonymous array types (as in the example above) do not present this problem since they cannot be passed as parameters directly; explicit conversion is always required, and it is not unreasonable to presume that a copy is involved in an explicit conversion.

The rules for parameter passing distinguish among several cases according to the type; some must be passed by copy, some must be passed by reference and in some cases either is permitted. The last possibility presents a problem for atomic and volatile parameters. To solve this, the rules in this section make them by reference if the parameter (or a component) is atomic or volatile. Moreover, if the actual is atomic or volatile and the formal is not then the parameter is always passed by copy; this may require a local copy of the actual to be made at the site of the call.

The following example shows the use of these pragmas on the components of a record for doing memory-mapped I/O

```
type IO_Rec_Type is
   record
      Start_Address: System.Address;
      pragma Volatile(Start_Address);
      Length: Integer;
      pragma Volatile(Length);
      Operation: Operation_Type;
      pragma Atomic(Operation);
      Reset: Boolean;
      pragma Atomic(Reset);
   end record;

-- A store into the Operation field triggers an I/O operation.
-- Reading the Reset field terminates the current operation.

IO_Rec: IO_Rec_Type;

for IO_Rec'Address use ... ;
```

By using the pragmas to indicate the sharability of data, the semantics of reading and writing components can be controlled. By declaring Operation and Reset to be atomic, the user ensures that reads and writes of these fields are not removed by optimization, and are performed indivisibly. By declaring Start_Address and Length to be volatile, the user forces any store to happen immediately, without the use of local copies.

Other Alternatives

Another concept considered was a subtype modifier which would appear in a subtype indication, an object declaration, or parameter specification. However, for simplicity, pragmas were chosen instead.

Other possibilities included an "independent" indication. This would mark the object as being used to communicate between synchronized tasks. Furthermore, the object should be allocated in storage so that loads and stores to it may be performed independently of neighboring objects. Since in Ada 83, all objects were implicitly assumed as independent, such a change would have created upward-compatibility problems. For this reason, and for the sake of simplicity, this feature was rejected.

C.6 Task Identification and Attributes

In order to permit the user to define task scheduling algorithms and to write server tasks that accept requests in an order different from entry service order, it is necessary to introduce a type which identifies a general task (not just of a particular task type) plus some basic operations. This Task_ID type is used also by other language-defined packages to operate on task objects such as Dynamic_Priorities and Asynchronous_Task_Control. In addition, a common need is to be able to associate user-defined properties with all tasks on a per-task basis; this is done through task attributes.

C.6.1 The Package Task_Identification

The Task_ID type allows the user to refer to task objects using a copyable type. This is often necessary when one wants to build tables of tasks with associated information. Using access-to-task types is not always suitable since there is no way to define an access-to-any-task type. Task types differ mostly in the entry declarations. The common use of task-id's does not require this entry information, since no rendezvous is performed using objects of Task_ID. Instead, the more generic information about the object as being a task is all that is needed. Several constructs are provided to create objects of the Task_ID type. These are the Current_Task function to query the task-id of the currently executing task; the Caller attribute for the task-id of entry callers; and the Identity attribute for the task-id of any task object. It is believed that together these mechanisms provide the necessary functionality for obtaining task-id values in various circumstances. In addition, the package provides various rudimentary operations on the Task_ID type.

Thus using the example from 9.6, the user might write

```
Joes_ID: Task_ID := Joe'Identity;
...
Set_Priority(Urgent, Joes_ID);   -- see D.5
...
Abort_Task(Joes_ID);             -- same as abort Joe;
```

Another use might be for remembering a caller in one rendezvous and then recognizing the caller again in a later rendezvous, thus

```
task body Some_Service is
   Last_Caller: Task_ID;
begin
   ...
   accept Hello do
      Last_Caller := Hello'Caller;
```

```
      . . .
   end Hello;
   . . .
   accept Goodbye do
      if Last_Caller /= Goodbye'Caller then
         raise Go_Away;   -- propagate exception to caller
      end if;
      . . .
   exception
      when Go_Away => null;
   end Goodbye;
   . . .
end Some_Service;
```

Since objects of Task_ID no longer have the corresponding type and scope information, the possibility for dangling references exist (since Task_ID objects are nonlimited, the value of such an object might contain a task-id of a task that no longer exists). This is particularly so since a server is likely to be at a library level, while the managed tasks might be at a deeper level with a shorter life-time. Operating on such values (here and in other language-defined packages) is defined to be erroneous. Originally, the possibility of requiring scope checking on these values was considered. Such a requirement would impose certain execution overhead on operations and space overhead on the objects of such a type. Since this capability is mainly designed for low-level programming, such an overhead was considered unacceptable. (Note, however, that nothing prevents an implementation from implementing a Task_ID as a record object containing a generation number and thereby providing a higher degree of integrity.)

The Task_ID type is defined as private to promote portability and to allow for flexibility of implementation (such as with a high degree of integrity). The possibility of having a visible (implementation-defined) type was considered. The main reason for this was to allow values of the type to be used as indices in user-defined arrays or as discriminants. To make this usable, the type would have to be discrete. However a discrete type would not allow for schemes that use generation numbers (some sort of a record structure would then be required as mentioned above). A visible type would also reduce portability. So, in the end, a private type approach was chosen. As always, implementations can provide a child package to add hashing functions on Task_ID values, if indexing seems to be an important capability.

Other Alternatives

In an earlier version of Ada 9X, the Task_ID type was defined as the root type of the task class. Since that class was limited, a language-defined access type was also defined to accommodate the need for a copyable type. This definition relied on the existence of untagged class types which were later removed from the language. The approach provided a nice encapsulation of the natural properties of such a type. The general rules of derivations and scope checking could then be fitted directly into the needs of the Task_ID type. Since the underlying model no longer exists, the simpler and more direct approach of a private type with specialized semantics and operation, was adopted.

Another possibility that was considered was to define a special, language-defined, access-to-task type which, unlike other access types, would be required to hold enough information to ensure safe access to dereferenced task objects. This type could then be used as the task-id. Values of such a type would necessarily be larger. This was rejected on the grounds that supporting this special access type in the compiler would be more burdensome to implementations.

Obtaining the Task Identity

The Current_Task function is needed in order to obtain the identity of the currently executing task when the name of this task is not known from the context alone; for example when the identity of the environment task is needed or in general service routines that are used by many different tasks.

There are two situations in which it is not meaningful to speak of the "currently executing task". One is within an interrupt handler, which may be invoked directly by the hardware. The other is within an entry body, which may be executed by one task on behalf of a call from another task (the Caller attribute may be used in the latter case, instead). For efficiency, the implementation is not required to preserve the illusion of there being an interrupt handler task, or of each execution of an entry body being done by the task that makes the call. Instead, calling Current_Task in these situations is defined to be a bounded error.

The values that may be returned if the error is not detected are based on the assumption that the implementation ordinarily keeps track of the currently executing task, but might not take the time to update this information when an interrupt handler is invoked or a task executes an entry body on behalf of a call from another task. In this model, the value returned by Current_Task would identify the last value of "current task" recorded by the implementation. In the case of an interrupt handler, this might be the task that the interrupt handler preempted, or an implementation task that executes when the processor would otherwise be idle.

If Current_Task could return a value that identifies an implementation task, it might be unsafe to allow a user to abort it or change its priority. However, the likelihood of this occurring is too small to justify checking, especially in an implementation that is sufficiently concerned with efficiency not to have caught the error in the first place. The documentation requirements provide a way for the user to find out whether this possibility exists.

Conversion from an object of any task type to a Task_ID is provided by the Identity attribute. This conversion is always safe. Support for conversion in the opposite direction is intentionally omitted. Such a conversion is rarely useful since Task_ID is normally used when the specific type of the task object is not known, and would be extremely error-prone; (a value of one task type could then be used as another type with all the dangerous consequences of different entries and masters).

Caller and Identity are defined as attributes and not as functions. For Caller, an attribute allows for an easier compile-time detection of an incorrect placement of the construct. For Identity, a function would require a formal parameter of a universal task type which does not exist.

The Caller attribute is allowed to apply to enclosing accept bodies (not necessarily the innermost one) since it seems quite useful without introducing additional run-time overhead.

Documentation Requirements

In some implementations, the result of calling Current_Task from an interrupt handler might be meaningful. Non-portable applications may be able to make use of this information.

C.6.2 The Package Task_Attributes

The ability to have data for which there is a copy for each task in the system is useful for providing various general services. This was provided for example in RTL/2 [Barnes 76] as SVC data.

For Ada 95, several alternatives were considered for the association of user-defined information with each task in a program.

The approach which was finally selected is to have a language-defined generic package whose formal type is the type of an attribute object. This mechanism allows for multiple attributes to be associated with a task using the associated Task_ID. These attributes may be dynamically defined, but they cannot be "destroyed". A new attribute is created through instantiation of the generic package.

Thus if we wished to associate some integer token with every task in a program we could write

```
package Token is
   new Ada.Task_Attributes(Attribute => Integer, Initial_Value => 0);
```

and then give the task Joe its particular token by

```
Token.Set_Value(99, Joes_ID);
```

Note that the various operations refer to the current task by default, so that

```
Token.Set_Value(101);
```

sets the token of the task currently executing the statement.

After being defined, an object of that attribute exists for each current and newly created task and will be initialized with a user-provided value. Internally the hidden object will typically be derived from the type Finalization.Controlled so that finalization of the attribute objects can be performed. When a task terminates, all of its attribute objects are finalized. Note that the attribute objects themselves are allocated in the RTS space, and are not directly accessible by the user program. This avoids problems with dangling references. Since the object is not in user space, it cannot live longer than the task that has it as an attribute. Similarly, this object cannot be deallocated or finalized while the run-time system data structures still point to it.

Obviously, other unrelated user objects might still contain references to attribute objects after they have gone (as part of task termination). This can only happen when one dereferences the access value returned by the Reference function since the other operations return (or store) a copy of the attribute. Such dereference (after the corresponding task has terminated) is therefore defined as erroneous. Note that one does not have to wait until a master is left for this situation to arise; referencing an attribute of a terminated task is equally problematic. In general, the Reference function is intended to be used "locally" by the task owning the attribute. When the actual attribute object is large, it is sometimes useful to avoid the frequent copying of its value; instead a pointer to the object is obtained and the data is read or written in the user code. When the Reference function is used for tasks other then the calling task, the safe practice should be to ensure, by other means, that the corresponding task is not yet terminated.

The generic package Task_Attributes can be instantiated locally in a scope deeper than the library level. The effect of such an instantiation is to define a new attribute (for all tasks) for the lifetime of that scope. When the scope is left, the corresponding attribute no longer exists and cannot be referenced anymore. An implementation may therefore deallocate all such attribute objects when that scope is left.

For the implementation of this feature, several options exist. The simplest approach is of a single pointer in the task control block (TCB) to a table containing pointers to the actual attributes, which in turn are allocated from a heap. This table can be preallocated with some initial size. When new attributes are added and the table space is exhausted, a larger one can be allocated with the contents of the old one being copied to the new one. The index of this table can serve as the attribute-id. Each instantiated attribute will have its own data structure (one per partition, not per task), which will contain some type information (for finalization) and the initial value. The attribute-id in the TCB can then point to this attribute type information. Instead of having this level of indirection, the pointer in the TCB can point to a linked list of attributes which then can be dynamically extended or shrunk. Several optimizations on this general scheme are possible. One can preallocate the initial table in the TCB itself, or store in it a fixed number of single-word attributes (presumably, a common case). Since implementations are allowed to place restrictions on the maximum number of attributes and their sizes, static allocation of attribute space is possible, when the application demands more deterministic behavior at run time. Finally, attributes that have not been set yet, or have been reinitialized, do not have to occupy space at all. A flag indicating this state is sufficient for the Value routine to retrieve the initial value from the attribute type area instead of requiring per-task replication of the same value.

Other Approaches

A number of other approaches were considered. One was the idea of a per-task data area. Library-level packages could have been characterized by a pragma as Per_Task, meaning that a fresh copy of the data area of such a package would be available for each newly created task.

Several problems existed with this approach. These problems related to both the implementation and the usability aspects. A task could only access its own data, not the data of any other task. There were also serious problems concerning which packages actually constituted the per-task area.

Another approach considered was a singe attribute per task. Operations to set and retrieve the attribute value of any task were included in addition to finalization rules for when the task terminates. This approach was quite attractive. It was simple to understand and could be implemented with minimal overhead. Larger data structures could be defined by the user and anchored at the single pointer attribute. Operations on these attributes were defined as atomic to avoid race conditions. But the biggest disadvantage of this approach, which eventually led to its rejection, was that such a mechanism does not compose very well and is thus difficult to use in the general case.

C.7 Requirements Summary

The requirements

> *R6.3-A(1) — Interrupt Servicing*

> *R6.3-A(2) — Interrupt Binding*

are met by the pragmas Interrupt_Handler and Attach_Handler plus the package Ada.Interrupts.

The requirement

> *R7.1-A(1) — Control of Shared Memory*

is met by the pragmas Atomic and Volatile discussed in C.5.

D Real-Time Systems

The purpose of this Annex is to supplement the core language with features specific to real-time systems. Since Ada is a general-purpose language with a large and diverse audience, not all the capabilities that are required to build applications can be sensibly put in the core language without prohibitively increasing its size and hurting other application domains.

As is the case with Ada 95 in general, this Annex tries to provide a single solution to each recognized problem, even though we acknowledge that several alternatives exist in the marketplace. The mechanisms that we have provided can serve as building blocks when more sophisticated solutions are needed. The models that we specify allow for extensions, and accommodate a certain degree of variability. The primary goal was to allow the user to rely on a portable, yet usable, set of capabilities. These capabilities will always be present in an implementation that supports this Annex. Therefore, the default behavior is well-specified, and the user must explicitly request implementation-provided additions. In addition, optionality within this Annex was kept to a minimum.

This annex addresses the following topics

- Priorities of tasks in general and especially the ability to change priorities (they were fixed in Ada 83) either explicitly or as a result of interaction with other tasks and protected objects;

- Scheduling issues including the entry queue discipline;

- Specific measurements on the effect of the abort statement including the formalization of the concept of an abort-deferred region;

- Restrictions on the use of certain aspects of the tasking model that should permit the use of specialized runtime systems;

- Resolution of a number of timing issues in Ada 83, including the introduction of a distinct monotonic clock;

- The addition of explicit synchronous and asynchronous task control protocols.

Note that several features in this Annex are invoked by using configuration pragmas (see [RM95 10.1.5]). This means that the corresponding semantics are defined on a per-partition basis; thus priority scheduling, the queuing policy and time are only specified in the scope of the one active partition containing the unit where the pragma applies. Ada 95 does not address issues concerning multipartition execution beyond the minimum that is in the Distributed Systems Annex. Interactions among partitions are left to implementations or to the providers of partition communication software.

D.1 Task Priorities

In real-time applications, it is necessary to schedule the use of processing resources to meet timing constraints. One approach is to use priority scheduling; this has a well developed theory, and is adequate for a wide range of real-time applications; see [Sha 90a] and [Klein 93].

Ada 83 specified preemptive task scheduling based on static priorities, but left certain aspects implementation dependent. This scheduling model, however, has raised issues in practice. On the one hand, it is viewed as not sufficiently specified for portable real-time system designs. On the other hand, it is viewed as too restrictive to permit the implementation of important real-time programming paradigms.

It is important that a language not limit the application to a particular scheduling model. There are many appropriate scheduling techniques, and more are continually being developed. No one scheduling model is accepted as adequate for all real-time applications.

It is also important to permit Ada to take advantage of the concurrent programming support of commercial real-time operating systems or executives. This is especially so with the growing acceptance of the "open systems" approach to software architecture, and the development of standards for application program interfaces to operating system services, such as POSIX [1003.1 90]. Ada should not impose any requirements on the language implementation that conflict with the scheduling model of an underlying operating system.

For these reasons, the Ada 83 priority scheduling model has been removed from the core of the language. However, this leaves a gap. Some users have found the Ada 83 scheduling model useful and it is clearly essential to continue to support those users. This argues for the inclusion of a priority scheduling model in this Annex, and for it to be compatible with Ada 83.

A second reason for specifying a standard scheduling model in this Annex is economy. Even though a single scheduling model cannot satisfy the requirements of all Ada users, it seems that a large number can be satisfied with priority scheduling, provided that the obvious adjustments to Ada 83 are made. This model thus provides a useful base for vendors and users alike.

The priority model specified in this Annex thus subsumes the Ada 83 model and provides several important improvements: support for dynamic priorities; solutions to the problem of priority inversion; and a unified model of the interactions of task priorities with protected objects and interrupts.

The specification of the priority model is spread over several clauses in [RM95 D.1-5]. Besides readability, the main reason for this organization is to permit the designation of options within the Annex. In particular, while the overall task dispatching model is essential, the standard policies for Task Dispatching, Priority Ceiling Locking, and Entry Queuing may optionally be replaced by other implementation defined alternatives.

D.1.1 Priority Subtypes

The range of possible task priorities is extended so that it can overlap with interrupt priorities as on some hardware architectures. We now have

```
subtype Any_Priority is Integer range implementation-defined;
subtype Priority is Any_Priority
                range Any_Priority'First .. implementation-defined;
subtype Interrupt_Priority is Any_Priority
                range Priority'Last+1 .. Any_Priority'Last;
```

The subtype Any_Priority is introduced (rather than simply allowing Priority to include interrupt priorities) because existing Ada 83 programs may assume that Priority'Last is below interrupt priority. Moreover, since giving a task a priority that blocks interrupts is sufficiently dangerous that it should be very visible in the source code, the subtype Interrupt_Priority is introduced. The ranges of Priority and Interrupt_Priority do not overlap.

A minimum number of levels of priority is specified, in the interest of promoting portability of applications and to ensure that an implementation of this Annex actually supports priority scheduling in a useful form. Research in Rate Monotonic scheduling [Lehoczky 86] has shown that approximately 32 levels of priority is the minimum needed to ensure adequate schedulability in systems with 32 or more tasks. Moreover, it is desirable that where hardware provides support for priority scheduling, it should be possible to use such support. Certain hardware architectures are reported to support only 32 levels of priority, including interrupt priority levels. Therefore the combined number of priority levels is not required to be higher than 32. In order to permit the use of efficient bit-vector operations on 32-bit machines, where one bit may need to be reserved, the actual requirement is reduced to 31 of which one must be an interrupt priority.

As in Ada 83, priority subtypes need not be static, so an implementation that is layered over an operating system can query the underlying operating system at elaboration-time to find out how many priority levels are supported.

D.1.2 Base and Active Priorities

The distinction between base and active priority is introduced in order to explain the effect of priority inheritance. The base priority of a task is the priority the task would have in the absence of priority inheritance of any sort.   Priority inheritance is already present in Ada 83, during rendezvous. It is extended here, to bound priority inversion (see D.3.1 for the definition of priority inversion) during protected operations.

In the default scheduling policy, priority inheritance is limited to a few simple forms, in order to permit more efficient implementations. These forms do not cause the active priority of a task to change asynchronously. Inheritance happens only as a direct result of the execution of the affected task, when the task is being resumed, or before the task has ever executed. If inheritance is via protected operations, the priority is raised at the start of the operation and lowered at the end. If inheritance is via rendezvous, the priority is raised at the beginning of rendezvous (either by the accepting task itself, or by the caller before the acceptor is resumed) and then lowered at the end of the rendezvous (by the acceptor). The case of activation is slightly different, since if the active priority of the task is raised, it is raised by the *creator*. However, this change is synchronous for the affected task, since the task has not yet started to execute; the lowering of the priority is done at the end of activation by the action of the activated task.

Priority inheritance via queued entry calls, via abortion, and via a task master waiting for dependents to terminate is intentionally not specified, mainly because the effects are asynchronous with respect to the affected task, which would make implementation significantly more difficult. An additional reason for not specifying inheritance through task masters waiting for dependents is that it would be a one-to-many relation, which would also introduce extra implementation difficulty. Other reasons for not doing inheritance via abortion are stated in D.6.

D.1.3 Base Priority Specification

The initial specification of the base priority of a task is by means of the pragma `Priority`. This is compatible with Ada 83.

The pragma `Interrupt_Priority` is provided for specifying a base priority that may be at an interrupt level. The pragma is different in order to make it very visible in the source code wherever a base priority is being assigned that might have the side-effect of blocking interrupts. The `Interrupt_Priority` pragma is also allowed to specify priorities below interrupt level, so that it is possible to write reusable code modules containing priority specifications, where the actual priority is a parameter.

The rule that the priority expression is evaluated for each task object, at the time of task initialization satisfies the requirement for having task objects of the same type but with different priorities. The expression specifying the priority is evaluated separately for each task. This means that it is possible, for example, to define an array of tasks of different priorities, by specifying the priority as a discriminant of the task, or by a call to a function that steps through the desired sequence of priority values thus

```
task type T is
   pragma Priority(Next_One);    -- call function Next_One
   ...
```

and similarly for protected objects.

A default base priority is specified, so that the behavior of applications is more predictable across implementations that conform to this Annex. This does not prevent implementations from supporting priority inheritance or other implementation-defined scheduling policies, which relied for legality under Ada 83 on the task priority being unspecified. This is because an implementation need not support this Annex at all but if it does then it may still conform and provide user-selectable task scheduling policies that define additional forms of priority inheritance. Such inheritance may raise the active priority of a task above its base priority, according to any policy the implementation chooses.

The main reason for choosing the default priority of a task to be the base priority of the task that activates it (the base priority of its creator) is that the creator must wait for the new task to complete activation. For the same reason, AI-00288 specifies that during this time the task being activated should inherit the priority of the creator.

The default base priority of the environment task (System.Default_Priority) is chosen to be the midpoint of the priority range so that an application has equal freedom to specify tasks with priorities higher and lower than that of the default. It does not seem to always be the case that "normal" tasks (i.e. those that do not have a particular priority requirement), necessarily have the lowest priority in all circumstances.

D.2 Priority Scheduling

The purpose of this section is to define the operational semantics of task priority, and to define a specific default scheduling policy. The definitions introduced here are also used for priority ceiling locking [RM95 D.3] and entry queuing policies [RM95 D.4].

D.2.1 The Task Dispatching Model

Ada 95 provides a framework for a family of possible task dispatching policies, including the default policy which is specified in [RM95 D.2.2] as well as other policies which may be defined by an implementation.

The phrase *task dispatching* is used here to denote the action of choosing a task to execute on a processor at a particular instant, given that one already knows the set of tasks that are eligible for execution on that processor at that instant, and their priorities. This is distinguished from the more general concept of *task scheduling*, which includes determination of the other factors, i.e. which tasks are eligible to execute (in the logical sense), which tasks are allowed to be executed on each processor, and what is the active priority of each task.

The term "processing resource", which was introduced in Ada 83, is developed further. Informally, a processing resource is anything that may be needed for the execution of a task, and whose lack can prevent a task from execution even though the task is eligible for execution according to the rules of the language.

Besides processors, the only specific processing resources that are specified by the Annex are the logical "locks" of protected objects — i.e. the rights to read or update specific protected objects. An important feature of the protected type model (explained more fully in D.3) is that protected objects can be implemented in a way that never requires an executing task to block itself in order to execute a protected subprogram call. As explained in D.3, it is a consequence of the priority-ceiling rules that, if there is only one processor, the highest priority task that is eligible for execution will never attempt to lock a protected object that is held by another task. Thus, based on single-processor systems alone, there would be no need to treat protected objects as processing resources. However, on a multiprocessor system, regardless of how protected types are implemented, a task may be forced to wait for access to a protected object. Thus, access to a protected object must be viewed as a processing resource. Even on a single-processor system, if the implementation chooses not to use priority-ceiling locking, a task may need to wait for access to a protected object. This might be the case, for example, if tasks are implemented using the services of an underlying operating system which does not support economical priority changes. (Note that this potential waiting is not formally considered to be "blocking" by the rules of the language.)

In some systems there may be other processing resources. A likely example is access to a page of virtual memory. This might require a task to wait for a page of real memory to be allocated, and the desired page of virtual memory to be read into it. I/O operations may require access to an I/O device that is in use by another task (or operating system process).

The use of conceptual ready queues in the specification of the task dispatching model is derived from POSIX 1003.4 (Realtime Extension) [1003.4 93] and 1003.4a (Threads Extension) [1003.4a 93] standards.

A separate queue for each processor is specified in the model, in order to allow models of multiprocessor scheduling in which certain tasks may be restricted to execute only on certain processors. If the implementation allows all tasks to run on any processor, then the conceptual ready queues of all processors will be identical. Since this is only a conceptual model, the implementation is free to implement the queues as a single physical queue in shared memory. The model thus accommodates a full range of task-to-processor assignment policies, including the extremes of a single task dispatching queue and a separate queue per processor.

To allow for multiprocessor implementations, it is implementation defined whether a task may hold the processor while waiting for access to a protected object. This allows the implementation to directly use a "spin-lock" mechanism, or to use a (higher-level) suspending lock mechanism such as might be provided by an underlying multiprocessor operating system.

Though it is not specified here, it is desirable for delay queues to be ordered by priority within sets of tasks with the same wake-up time. This can reduce priority inversion when several tasks wake up at once. Ideally, run-time system processing for wake-ups of lower priority tasks should also be postponed, while a high-priority task is executing. This behavior is allowed by the model, but it is not required, since the implementation cost may be high.

Though we hope that the default scheduling policy defined in [RM95 D.2.2] will be adequate for most real-time applications, it is inevitable that there will be a demand for implementation-defined variations. We will consider how several such policies can be accommodated within the framework.

Consider the Earliest-Deadline-First (EDF) scheduling technique. The EDF scheduling algorithm is known to be optimal for systems of independent tasks on a single processor. The EDF priority of a task is the number of ready tasks with later (absolute) deadlines. In general, this value may need to be adjusted for every change in the set of tasks that are eligible for execution. Since there is no mechanism by which a user-defined scheduler can be notified to make such changes, the Dynamic_Priorities package (see D.5) is insufficient for a user to implement EDF scheduling. However, an implementation is free to provide EDF scheduling via an implementation-defined mechanism. The implementation could dynamically adjust base priorities to reflect EDF task ordering, in which case the semantics could be defined in terms of the run-time system calling Set_Priority to affect the changes. Alternatively, an implementation could model EDF scheduling by means of "priority inheritance", where tasks inherit priority dynamically from some implementation-defined abstraction. For this to work well, the base priorities of all tasks would need to be set to Any_Priority'First, since the active priority would need to be lowered dynamically, as well as raised.

Another anticipated application requirement is for time slicing. Implementation-defined time-slicing schemes may conform to this specification by modifying the active or base priority of a task, in a fashion similar to that outlined for EDF scheduling.

D.2.2 The Standard Task Dispatching Policy

The standard dispatching policy can be explicitly requested by writing

pragma Task_Dispatching_Policy(FIFO_Within_Priorities);

for the partition. An implementation may provide alternatives but none are required. If no such pragma appears then the policy is implementation defined.

As mentioned above, the purpose of specifying a standard task dispatching policy is to achieve more predictable task scheduling and more portability of applications that use priority scheduling, as compared to the Ada 83 task scheduling model. This leads to a dilemma. On one hand, the ideal is to completely specify which task will be chosen to execute. On the other hand, such specification will prevent (efficient) implementation on certain machines. In particular, there are inherent differences between multiprocessor and single-processor machines, and there may be constraints on task dispatching policies imposed by underlying operating systems. It seems there is no one task dispatching policy that will be acceptable to all users and implementable for all execution environments. Nevertheless, if there is a dispatching policy that will satisfy the needs of a large segment of real-time applications and is implementable on most execution platforms, there are benefits to making it always available.

While implementations are allowed to provide additional dispatching policies, there is no requirement that more than one such policy will be supported in the same active partition. This is based on the assumption that usually it does not make a lot of sense to talk about two independent dispatching policies in the same partition. Interactions must be defined and by doing so the two policies become essentially one. However, the support of two such unrelated policies is not precluded whenever it makes sense for the application and/or the underlying system. In addition, the dispatching policy is unspecified (as opposed to implementation-defined) if the user does not specify the pragma Task_Dispatching_Policy. This is because presumably, if the pragma is not provided, the user is not concerned about the dispatching specifics, and in addition, in many cases the actual policy (in the absence of the pragma) can simply be the policy of the underlying OS. This might not be specified, not documented precisely enough, or may even vary from one execution of the program to the next (as would be the case if the policy is controlled from outside the program).

The standard task dispatching policy specified in this Annex can be implemented on both single-processor and multiprocessor machines. It can be implemented by an Ada RTS that runs on a bare machine, and it is also likely to be implementable over some operating systems. In particular, the standard dispatching policy is intended to be compatible with the SCHED_FIFO policy of the Realtime Extension of the POSIX operating system interface standard.

A special feature of the delay statement, whether it appears as a simple statement or in a select statement, is that it always causes the executing task to go to the tail of its ready queue of its active priority. This is true even for delay statements with a zero or negative duration. It means that if there is another task of equal priority competing for the same processor, the task executing the delay will yield to this task. Imposing this rule makes the delay behavior uniform. It is also desired for predictable execution behavior, especially in situations where the delay duration or time is a value computed at run time, and which may have positive, zero, or negative values. As mentioned in UI-0044, causing a task to yield its processor to equal-priority tasks is a side-effect of delay statements in many existing Ada 83 implementations. Some current Ada users rely on this feature to achieve a form of voluntary round-robin scheduling of equal-priority tasks, under application control. Supporting this feature is expected to increase the execution time overhead of zero and negative delays, but the overhead does not seem to be greater than that which would be experienced if the shortest possible nontrivial delay (i.e. one that requires the task to be blocked) were executed.

D.3 Priority Ceiling Locking

Priority-ceiling locking of protected objects serves the following purposes, in order of decreasing importance

- Priority inversion can be bounded.

- A very efficient implementation of locking is permitted.

- Protected subprograms can be called safely from within direct-execution hardware interrupt handlers.

- On a single processor, deadlock is prevented.

Priority ceiling locking is specified by writing

```
pragma Locking_Policy(Ceiling_Locking);
```

in a unit of the partition. Other policies are permitted but not required. As with task dispatching, if no pragma appears for the locking policy, then the policy is implementation defined.

Note that if FIFO_Within_Priorities is requested as the task dispatching policy then Ceiling_Locking must also be specified.

D.3.1 Bounding Priority Inversion

By specifying that the task executing a protected operation inherits the priority of the protected object, we permit the duration of priority inversion (due to enforcement of mutual exclusion between operations on a protected object) to be bounded. A priority inversion is a deviation from the ideal model of preemptive priority scheduling; that is, a situation where a higher (base) priority task is waiting for a processing resource that is being used by a lower (base) priority task. Priority inversion is undesirable in a priority-based scheduling system, since it represents a failure to honor the intent of the user, as expressed by the task priorities.

Bounding priority inversion is important in schedulability analysis. In particular, if priority inversion can be bounded, Rate Monotonic Analysis can be used to predict whether a set of Ada tasks will be able to meet their deadlines [Sha 90a]. The technique has been successfully applied to several hard real-time systems written in Ada.

The ceiling locking scheme specified in this Annex is similar to the "priority ceiling emulation" in [Sha 90b], and to the "stack resource protocol" described in [Baker 91]. On a single processor, these schemes have the property that, once a task starts to run, it cannot suffer priority inversion until it blocks itself. Thus, the only points at which a task can suffer priority inversion are where the task has been unblocked (e.g. delay or rendezvous) and is waiting to resume execution. At these points, it may need to wait for one task with lower base priority (but a higher inherited priority) to complete the execution of a protected operation.

Among the locking policies that bound priority inversion, the policy specified here is the simplest to implement, and has been shown to be more or less indistinguishable from other policies in effectiveness. Support for this policy is also included in the mutex locking model of the proposed POSIX Threads Extension standard [1003.4a 93].

With priority inheritance through protected object ceilings, the duration of priority inversion encountered by a task T that has been unblocked will not be longer than the longest execution time of any one protected operation, over all the protected objects with ceilings higher than or equal to the base priority of T. In estimating this bound, the worst case execution time of each operation must be used, including the entry-servicing code. For a protected object with entries, this time bound must include the case where the maximum number of queued entry calls are served. (This number is bounded by the number of tasks that share access to the protected object.)

Checking of priority ceiling violations by the implementation can be helpful to the programmer, even if the implementation is not relying on the accuracy of this information for locking, since it amounts to verifying important assumptions that are made in schedulability analysis.

D.3.2 Efficient Implementation Techniques

Note that the Annex does not require that protected objects be implemented in any specific way. However, it is intended that the model be implementable via an efficient non-suspending mutual exclusion mechanism, based on priorities. Such mechanisms are well understood for static priority systems where the only priority inheritance is through locks, but the inclusion of dynamic base priorities and other forms of priority inheritance complicates the picture.

We will argue the adequacy of the specifications in this Annex to permit an efficient non-suspending mutual exclusion mechanism based on priorities, under certain assumptions. In this discussion it is assumed that priority inheritance occurs only via the mechanisms specified in this Annex, and the only processing resources that can be required by a task are a processor and protected object locks. Here, a lock is an abstraction for having mutually exclusive access to a protected object. The operations on locks are *seize* a lock, and *release* a lock. Locks are not transferable; once seized, a lock is not allowed to be seized by another task until it is released by the last task that seized it. It is assumed that protected objects can be implemented using locks. It is also assumed here that when the base priority of a task is lowered, it yields its processor to any task with active priority equal to the new base priority, in particular to one that is holding a protected object lock with that priority as its ceiling, if such a task exists. The cases of a single processor and a multiprocessor will be considered separately.

Suppose there is only one processor. Assume that the implementation of the seize operation is not able to block the task. We will argue that mutual exclusion is still enforced, by the scheduling policy. In particular, suppose a task, T1, is holding a lock on a protected object, R1. Suppose T2 is another task, and T2 attempts to seize R1 while T1 is holding it. We will show that this leads to a contradiction.

Let $C(R)$ denote the ceiling of a protected object R, $Bp(T)$ denote the base priority of a task T, and $Ap(T)$ denote the active priority of a task T. If $Ap(T2) > C(R1)$, T2 would not be allowed to attempt to lock R1. (This rule is enforced by a run-time check.) Therefore, $Ap(T2) \leq C(R1)$.

T1 must run in order to seize R1, but it cannot be running when T2 attempts to seize R1. So long as T1 is holding R1, it cannot be blocked. (This rule can be enforced statically, or by a run-time check.) Thus T1 must be preempted after it seizes R1 but before T2 attempts to seize R1. When T1 is preempted, it goes to the head of the ready queue for its active priority, where it stays until it runs again. Note that the active priority of T1 cannot be changed until it runs again, according to the reasoning in D.1.2: changes to base priority are deferred while T1 is holding the lock of R1, and T1 cannot inherit higher priority since it is not blocked (and not running) and must already have started activation.

For T2 to attempt to seize R1 while T1 is on the ready queue, T2 must have higher active priority than T1, or have been inserted at the head of T1's queue after T1 was preempted. The latter case can be eliminated: for T2 to be inserted at the head of T1's ready queue, T2 must be preempted after T1; to be preempted after T1, T2 must be running after T1 is preempted; to be running after T1 is preempted, T2 must be at the head of the highest priority non-empty queue; this queue must have higher priority than $Ap(T1)$, since T1 is at the head of its own queue. Thus, in either case, T2 must be executing with higher active priority than $Ap(T1)$, some time after T1 is preempted and while T1 is still on the same priority queue. That is $Ap(T1) < Ap(T2)$.

Since T1 is holding R1, it follows that $C(R1) \leq Ap(T1) < Ap(T2)$ at the first point where T2 runs after T1 is preempted, and while T1 is still on the same ready queue. Before T2 attempts to seize R1, the active priority of T2 must drop to a value no greater than $C(R1)$. (This is enforced by a run-time check.) The active priority of T2 cannot drop below $Ap(T1)$, or T1 would preempt. This leaves the possibility that the active priority of T2 drops to exactly $Ap(T1)$. But in this case, the implementation must cause T2 to yield to T1, as part of the operation that changes the base priority of T2 (see [RM95 D.5]). Thus, T2 cannot execute and so cannot attempt to lock R1.

In conclusion, for a single processor, the scheduling policy guarantees that there is no way a task can execute to attempt to seize a lock that is held by another task, and thus, no explicit locking mechanism is required.

On a multiprocessor, it is clear that priorities alone will not be sufficient to enforce mutual exclusion. Some form of interprocessor locking is required. Suppose this is accomplished by means of a busy-wait loop, using an atomic read-modify-write operation such as test-and-set. That is, a processor attempting to seize a protected object lock "spins" until it is able to set some variable in shared memory, which indicates that the protected object is locked. Thus, there is no danger of loss of mutual exclusion. The new problem is deadlock.

A necessary (but not sufficient) condition for deadlock is a cycle of "wait-for" relationships between pairs of tasks. In this case, there are two kinds of wait-for relationships. The obvious kind is where task T is spinning for a lock R held by task T'. The less obvious kind is where T is waiting for a processor that is being held by the spinning task T'.

The priority locking scheme does not prevent a direct deadlock situation of the obvious kind, in which task T1 is spinning waiting for a lock held by task T2, and task T2 is spinning (on another processor) waiting for a lock held by task T1. Fortunately, the user can prevent this kind of a deadlock, by not using nested protected operation calls, or by imposing a fixed ordering on nested protected operation calls.

A more serious problem, if it could occur, would be a deadlock involving a task waiting for a processor that is busy spinning for a lock. For example, suppose task T1 seizes R1, T1 is preempted by T2, and then T2 starts spinning in an attempt to seize R1. This would result in a deadlock if T2 is spinning on the only processor where T1 can execute at this time. This kind of deadlock would be serious, since it would be hidden inside the implementation, where the user could not prevent it.

Fortunately, this kind of deadlock is prevented by the priority ceiling locking scheme. For tasks executing on the same processor, this is obvious. Since T1 inherits the ceiling priority of R1, an exception will be raised if T2 tries to lock R1 while its active priority is high enough to preempt T1. The priority ceiling scheme also prevents such deadlocks in situations involving tasks executing on different processors. For example, suppose task T1 (executing on processor M1) locks R1 and task T2 (executing on M2) locks R2. Suppose task T3 preempts T1 and attempts to lock R2, while T4 preempts T2 and tries to lock R1. For this to happen, either T3 or T4 must fail the priority ceiling check. We will show this for the general case. Suppose there is a cycle of wait-for relationships. If T is waiting for T', we have either:

1   T is spinning for a lock L held by T', so $Ap(T) = C(L) \leq Ap(T')$. (Note that we may have $C(L) < Ap(T')$ if T' performs a nested protected operation with higher ceiling, while it is still holding the lock L.)

2   T is waiting for a processor held by T', which is spinning for some lock L', so $Ap(T) < Ap(T') = C(L')$.

In order for the cycle to happen, both relationships have to hold for at least one pair of tasks, but then we have a contradiction.

D.3.3 Deadlock Prevention

It is a consequence of the priority ceiling locking scheme that an application cannot create a deadlock using protected subprograms on a single processor. This follows directly from the fact that a task executing a protected object operation cannot be preempted by any other task that requires access to that protected object.

Note that this is distinct from the problem of deadlock discussed above, which is within a particular multiprocessor implementation of ceiling locking. In the case of a multiprocessor, the priority ceiling locking does not prevent an application from constructing a deadlock with protected subprograms, but it still can be used to prevent deadlocks that might be caused by the implementation.

D.3.4 Implementing Over an OS

Priority ceiling locking may be very costly (possibly even impossible) where Ada tasks are implemented using the services of certain operating systems or executives. In particular, locking a protected object requires setting the active priority of a task to the protected object ceiling, or making the task entirely non-preemptable in some way, or using specialized operating system primitives. If there is no way to do this at all over a particular OS or executive, [RM95 1.1.3(6)] may be used to relieve the implementation from supporting priority ceiling locking. A more difficult case would be where there is a way to change a task's priority, but this operation is very costly. This might be true, for example, where Ada is implemented over a version of POSIX threads which does not support the priority ceiling emulation option for mutexes.

We considered whether an implementation of this Annex should be allowed to support priority ceiling locking but to only use it on those protected objects for which it is requested explicitly. The rationale is that the cost of priority changes may be too high to tolerate in general, but the user may determine that it is worthwhile in some specific cases. The extra implementation overhead of supporting two kinds of locks would be offset by the gain in efficiency for those cases (perhaps the majority) where ceiling locking is not used. Presumably, an implementation could still use priority ceiling locking with a default priority ceiling when no ceiling is specified, but could also use some other locking protocol in this case.

If this proposal had been accepted, then there would have been a problem with the check for ceiling violations. To reap the maximum benefit in efficiency from not raising the active priority of a task when it locks a protected object, no check for ceiling violations should be required either. This would result in portability problems going from implementations that use a mixture of priority-ceiling and non-priority-ceiling locking (A) to implementations that use priority-ceiling locking for all protected objects (B). For example, suppose PR1 has no specified ceiling, PR2 has a ceiling specified that is somewhere below Priority'Last, and all callers of PR1 and PR2 happen to have active priorities below Priority'Last. Suppose some operation of PR1 calls some operation of PR2. With implementation (A), this call to PR2 would always be safe, since the active priority of a task is not raised by calling PR1. With implementation (B), the call to PR2 from inside PR1 would be made at the default ceiling priority of PR1, which is Priority'Last. This would violate the ceiling of PR2, causing Program_Error to be raised.

While this approach could have worked, it did not seem that there was enough user benefit to justify the loss of portability. If the implementation did not support priority-ceiling locking, because the cost of priority changes is prohibitive, but the application designer judged that avoiding priority inversion justifies the overhead of the priority changes, the application might have to adjust the active priority explicitly, by setting the base priority. This would mean calling Set_Priority before and after calls to the protected operations where priority inversion is of concern. Naturally, techniques like this are prone to race conditions, especially in the presence of interrupts. Also, it is not clear that the overhead of Set_Priority would be any smaller than the direct OS support for priority ceilings.

This Annex provides a prioritized model of mutual-exclusion which is integrated with interrupt disabling when shared data is used between the interrupt handler and normal tasks. There may be situations where this model will be too elaborate and costly. Examples of this may be certain operating systems, or implementations over bare machines which traditionally have disabled preemption and/or interruption for this purpose. This implementation model is allowed by the Annex and is consistent with the other priority rules. In particular, the tasks' priorities still maintain the *granularity* and the range of the type. However, for protected object ceilings, implementations are allowed to round all priority values in the `Priority` range to `Priority'Last`, and those in the `Interrupt_Priority` range to `Interrupt_-Priority'Last`. The net effect of such rounding is that on each call of a protected object with ceiling in the lower range, preemption (or dispatching) is disabled. When a protected object in the interrupt range is involved, all interrupts are disabled. This reduces the number of protected object ceilings to only two values which makes the approach quite similar to the disable preemption/interruption employed by existing kernels. The rest of the priority rules are not affected by this approach.

D.3.5 Implementation and Documentation Requirements

The implementation will require protection of certain processing resources, not visible to the application, from concurrent access. For example, a storage allocation operation generally requires exclusive access to the data structure that is used to keep track of blocks of free storage. Likewise, run-time system operations involved in rendezvous generally require exclusive access to an entry queue. It would be natural to implement such critical sections in the run-time system using protected objects. If this is done, it is important that an application task with high active priority does not unwittingly violate the priority ceiling of one of these run-time system structures.

In order to reduce the likelihood of such problems, the implementation requirement is for the ceilings of such resources to be at least `Priority'Last`. This is intended to make such unwitting ceiling violations impossible unless the application uses interrupt priorities. An application that does use interrupt priorities is responsible for ensuring that tasks avoid operations with low ceilings while they are operating at interrupt priority. The rules against performing potentially blocking operations in protected bodies are expected to help in this respect, by ruling out most of the operations (other than storage allocation) that are likely to require locking run-time system data structures. In addition, the implementation is allowed to limit the RTS operations that are allowed from an interrupt handler.

An application that uses interrupt priority levels will need to know of any implementation uses of resources with lower ceilings, in order to avoid ceiling violations. The implementation is required to provide this information.

D.4 Entry Queuing Policies

The Ada 83 rule that entry calls be served in FIFO order may result in priority inversion, which can cause a loss of schedulable processor utilization. The same issue has been raised regarding the choice between open alternatives of a selective accept statement, which is unspecified by Ada 83. However, for upward compatibility reasons any existing Ada applications that rely on FIFO entry queuing order should continue to work with Ada 95. For this reason, the default entry queuing policy, specified in [RM95 9.5.3] and [RM95 9.7.1] is still FIFO. (This contrasts with the other two policies where, if no pragma is supplied, the policies are implementation defined.)

In addition, the user can override the default FIFO policy with the pragma `Queueing_Policy` thus

```
pragma Queuing_Policy(Priority_Queuing);
```

which stipulates the alternative policy which all implementations supporting this Annex must provide.

An approach that we rejected was for a user to be able to specify different entry service policies for each entry or task. Based on analysis of existing Ada run-time system technology, it appeared that requiring the Ada implementation to support per-entry or per-task selection would impose significant distributed execution-time overhead and would significantly complicate the Ada run-time system. Moreover, the need for mixed policies for entry service has not been demonstrated.

The solution adopted here is that a user can rely on applications that select priority queuing on a partition-wide basis being portable to any implementation that complies with this Annex. It is left to the implementor to decide whether to support finer-grained (i.e. per-task or per-entry) selection of queuing policy, based on customer demand.

It is possible that the choice of entry queuing policy may cause different code to be generated. Thus, the entry queuing policy must be specified no later than the point where each affected entry is declared.

Since certain compilation units (including packages that are intended to be reusable) may depend for correctness on a particular policy, it is important for the compiler or linker to be able to detect inconsistencies in such dependences. This can be guaranteed so long as the choice of policy is fixed at the time the entry is declared, and achieved through the general mechanism of compatible configuration pragmas (see [RM95 10.1.5]).

D.4.1 FIFO Queuing

FIFO queuing is provided for upward compatibility with Ada 83. If the correctness of a particular unit relies on FIFO entry queuing, it may specify this policy explicitly by

```
pragma Queueing_Policy(FIFO_Queuing);
```

This is important when other units that are included in the same partition specify Priority_- Queuing. If FIFO_Queuing was just the default, all units in the partition would have inherited, in this case, the Priority_Queuing policy, as opposed to being illegal (due to conflicts) which is the desired behavior. Implementations may support both policies in the same partition, but then the interactions between the policies are implementation-defined.

Nothing is specified about the rules for choosing between open alternatives of a selective accept statement, since there is no consensus among existing Ada compilers or Ada users as to how this choice should be resolved in a FIFO queuing environment. Leaving the rule unspecified provides upward compatibility.

D.4.2 Priority Queuing

Substantial consensus seems to have evolved that priority scheduling requires priority-ordered entry service. Priority-ordered entry service eliminates a source of unnecessary priority inversion and more consistently expedites the execution of higher priority tasks. Therefore, the Priority_Queuing policy is specified as a user-selectable option that must be supported by all real-time implementations.

Priority inheritance through queued entry calls was intentionally omitted from the Priority_Queuing policy. Several models for priority inheritance through queued calls have been proposed in the literature. However, there is no hard analytical data to support choosing one of these priority inheritance models over another. The basic need for providing access to shared data without unbounded priority inversion is already supported by the inheritance feature of priority-based protected objects. The implementation overhead of more complex forms of priority inheritance is sufficiently high that requiring it is not sensible, if only one standard entry queuing and priority inheritance policy is specified.

The decision to require priority-order selection among open alternatives of selective accept statements, and among open entries of a protected object is based on the desire to avoid unnecessary priority inversion. It is understood that there will be some additional implementation overhead, but this overhead is believed to be justified by the potential gain in schedulability.

Priority ties can occur. If there are several open accept alternatives of a selective accept statement, or several open entries of a protected object, there may be several highest priority calls. For predictable behavior, a tie-breaking rule is needed. Textual order of the select alternatives or entry declarations is specified, on the grounds that this provides the greatest degree of predictability and direct control to the programmer. In addition, it is believed to be easy to implement.

The choice of tie-breaker rules does limit implementation choices. Even though the semantic model for entries is based on there being a separate queue for each entry, the implementation may choose not to provide separate physical queues. For example, when a task reaches a selective accept statement or is exiting a protected object the implementation might do one of the following:

- Do a full scan of all tasks in the system, in priority order, to see whether any of them is trying to call one of the currently open entries. (This might already be very inefficient, due to the rules about the effects of priority changes on queued calls.)

- Search a single priority-ordered queue, which is associated with the accepting task or the protected object, to find the first caller that is calling one of the currently open entries.

With data structures that combine calls to different entries, it would be harder to select the call that corresponds to the lexically-first accept alternative or entry body declaration. The most natural tie-breaker between equal priority calls would be some form of FIFO. On the other hand, if the implementation does maintain a separate queue for each entry, then it may be easier to break ties based on textual order. The present rule takes the point of view that pinning down the choice of tie-breaker rule is important enough to the application that the implementation choice can be so limited.

Reordering of Entry Queues

The decision to specify what effect task priority changes have on queued entry calls is based on the goal of implementation uniformity. The rules distinguish between "synchronous" entry calls and those associated with asynchronous select statements.

Entry calls associated with asynchronous select statements are not reordered when the priority of the task that queued the entry call changes. This decision is largely based on consideration of implementation efficiency and the fact that the task is not waiting for these entry calls. Otherwise, every time the priority of a task changed, its asynchronous calls would be deleted and reinserted in their various entry queues. This would conceivably happen even for temporary changes in active priority associated with starting and completing a protected action in the abortable part.

The priority of an entry call must be determined before the task has locked the protected object, because it is a consequence of the priority ceiling locking mechanism that, at the time the protected object lock is seized, the active priority of the task making the entry call will always be equal to the ceiling of the protected object. If the priority of the call were taken at this time, it would be the same for all callers to the entry, which would defeat the purpose of priority queuing. The desired semantics can be implemented by recording the calling priority as an implicit parameter associated with the queued call, before the protected object is locked.

In an earlier version, asynchronous entry calls were reordered as well, but only upon base priority changes. However, this introduced certain problems. In particular, the task that caused the priority to change would probably have to do the reordering itself, which would imply getting the locks on the various protected objects with asynchronous calls. This would not be possible if the ceiling of the protected object were below the active priority of the task causing the priority change. By contrast, a task waiting on a synchronous entry call can do its own queue reordering, presuming its new priority is not above the ceiling. If it is, it is considered a bounded error, and Program_Error might be raised in the waiting task. This is consistent with the behavior which would have occurred if the priority had been raised above the ceiling just before the task originated the entry call, so it was deemed appropriate.

We also considered the idea of requiring that the priority of a task not change while it is on an entry queue. This would eliminate the question of queue reordering, but it has several complicated consequences. Most serious of these seems to be that a task could not lock a protected object while it is on an entry queue and executing the abortable part of an asynchronous select statement. Other limitations would also need to be imposed, including extension of the deferral of base priority changes to cover the case where a task is on an entry queue. This would in turn increase the overhead of entry calls.

More serious is that this limitation would interfere with the use of an entry queue to control user-defined scheduling. It seems plausible to create the equivalent of a ready queue using a protected entry queue, and then use dynamic priority changes coupled with other operations on the protected object to implement a scheduling policy. If dynamic priority changes were not permitted, a hypothetical scheduler would have significantly less flexibility in controlling the order of service of the various tasks on the entry queue.

In contrast to asynchronous calls, a synchronous entry call is reordered upon a priority change in the waiting task. This was deemed important for consistency of the priority model, for example when dynamic priority changes are used to implement mode changes or a user-defined scheduling policy. Moreover, since dynamic priority changes are not expected to be frequent and there are other factors that are already likely to make the Set_Priority operation complicated, the extra complexity of checking whether the task is waiting on a (synchronous) entry call does not seem too high.

We considered whether, when a task's priority changes, the new position of its queued call should be based on the new base priority or the new active priority. Since a waiting task could not be inheriting priority from a protected object, the active priority will be the same as the base unless the task is in a rendezvous or activating. (This assumes there are no extra implementation-defined sources of priority inheritance.) In these latter cases, it seems the call should continue to inherit the priority from the activator or entry caller. Therefore, the new priority of the call is specified as the new active priority of the caller after the new base priority is set.

Another semantic detail is whether adjustment of priority causes loss of FIFO position within a priority queue, in the case that the new active priority is the same as the old active priority. For conceptual consistency, Set_Priority is specified as having the same round-robin effect on queued entry calls as it does on the task's position in the ready queue(s).

D.4.3 Other Queuing Policies

The possibility of specifying other standard entry queuing policies, including some with priority inheritance, was also considered. The decision not to specify such alternative policies in the Annex was based on a general design goal of avoiding multiple solutions for a single problem. This would be contrary to the intent of the Annex to encourage uniformity among implementations and portability among applications. Moreover, supporting each alternative policy would involve significant implementation cost. Therefore, requiring every implementation of the Real-Time Systems Annex to support several alternative policies would not be sensible. The intent is that there be one policy that all Annex implementations are required to support; this is the Priority_Queuing. For applications that require upward compatibility with Ada 83, FIFO_Queuing is also specifiable. The basic model defined in this Annex allows experimentation with new policies, and the introduction of new solutions based on market demands. Therefore, implementations are permitted to define alternatives, but portable applications should rely only on the Priority_Queuing and FIFO_Queuing policies.

D.5 Dynamic Priorities

The ability to vary the priorities of tasks at run-time has been so widely demanded that most Ada implementations provide some form of dynamic priority facility. The package Ada.Dynamic_- Priorities provides such a capability in a portable manner. The interactions of priority changes with other aspects of Ada task semantics are also defined. The following subprograms are provided

```
procedure Set_Priority(Priority: Any_Priority;
                       T: Task_ID := Current_Task);

function Get_Priority(T: Task_ID := Current_Task)
                     return Any_Priority;
```

where the priority is the base priority rather than the active priority.

Versions of Get_Priority and Set_Priority with no explicit task parameter (and so applying implicitly to the calling task) are unnecessary since this capability is provided by the Current_Task as a default parameter. Calling such operations might be slightly faster, but they would clutter the interface, and since these operations are not trivial anyway, the benefit did not seem to be worthwhile. (Compilers recognizing this special case can still optimize it by calling a separate entry point in the RTS.)

Calling Get_Priority for a terminated task raises Tasking_Error. This allows the implementation to reclaim the storage devoted to the task control block upon task termination. Querying the priority of a completed or abnormal task is allowed and has a well-defined meaning since such tasks may still be executing and may still use the CPU, so providing user access to their priorities makes sense.

A function for querying the active priority of a task was intentionally omitted. This is partly because the active priority can be volatile, making the result unreliable. In particular, querying the active priority inside a protected body will not return useful information, since the task will always be executing at the priority ceiling of the protected object. Another reason is that it is likely to be difficult to implement such a function on some systems. Moreover, requiring this value to be available would rule out at least one efficient technique for priority inheritance, in which inheritance relationships are represented only by links from donor to inheritor, and the implementation does not need to explicitly compute the active priority of a task or to store it.

When the base priority of a running task is set, the task is required to go to the tail of the ready queue for its active priority. There are several reasons for this. First, this is what is specified in the SCHED_FIFO policy of [1003.4 93], after which the default task dispatching policy is modelled. Second, this is needed to prevent priority changes from violating the ceiling rules if priority inheritance is used to enforce mutual exclusion. For example, suppose task T1 is executing a protected operation of PR1, and task T2 preempts. Suppose T2 then lowers its own base priority to the ceiling of PR1. T2 is required to go to the tail of the ready queue at this point. This ensures that there is no danger of T2 trying to perform a protected operation on PR1. (Allowing T1 to preempt under these circumstances might also be desirable from the point of view of expediting the release of PR1.)

Deferral of the Effect of Priority Changes

The effect of Set_Priority on a task is deferred while the task is executing a protected operation, for several reasons. One reason is to prevent Set_Priority from forcing a task that is executing in a protected object to give up the processor to a task of the same active priority.

Another reason is to permit more efficient implementation of priority inheritance and priority changes. In particular, when entering a protected operation body, or starting a rendezvous, it is permissible to push the old active priority on a stack, from which it is popped when the protected operation is left, or the rendezvous ends. Note that there need be no additional execution time overhead for implementing this deferral, over that already imposed by deferring abortion, in the case that no priority change is attempted during the time the protected operation is executed.

For simplicity of implementation, priority changes are allowed to be deferred until the next abort completion point. This will be primarily useful in the context of target environments that have limited support for preemptive interthread or interprocessor signalling.

Taken from a user's point of view, deferring a change to the base priority of a task during protected operations should make no difference if the change is in the downward direction, since this would not affect the active priority of the task anyway. If the change is in the upward direction, the difference could be noticeable, but no requirement for immediate upward change of base priority during protected operations has been demonstrated. There may be a requirement for a temporary change to the active priority, but this is possible by calling an operation of a protected object with high enough ceiling.

Deferring the effect of changing the base priority also eliminates some semantic questions. One of these is whether the base priority of a task should be allowed to be raised higher than the ceiling priority of a protected object in which the task is currently executing. Allowing this would constitute a retroactive violation of the rule that a task cannot call a protected operation of a protected object while its active priority is higher than the protected object ceiling (the active priority is of course never less than the base priority).

Dynamic Priorities and Ceilings

When ceiling priorities and dynamic changes to priorities are supported in the same environment, some interactions with other language features are unavoidable. The source of these problems is mainly the inherent conflict between the need to arbitrarily and asynchronously change the task base priorities, and the ceiling model where a more disciplined usage of priorities is required. The problems get more serious if the effect of such misuse affects not just the program behavior, but also the correctness of the implementation. At least two interesting cases exist:

1   As part of the Set_Priority operation, a protected entry queue may have to be reordered. This happens when the affected task is waiting on a protected entry call (see [RM95 D.4]). If the task calling Set_Priority has an active priority higher than the ceiling of the relevant protected object, it will not be able to accomplish this reordering due to a ceiling violation. To circumvent this problem, it can awaken the waiting task which can then itself reorder the queue and continue waiting.

2   A call queued on a protected entry queue may sometimes need to be cancelled. This happens when the task is aborted, its currently executing abortable_part is aborted (and it has some nested calls), or when the abortable_part completes normally and the triggering call needs to be removed from its queue. If the task's base priority was raised after the call was initially queued and remains too high when the call needs to be removed, it might fail to remove the call due to ceiling violations (since such removal involves locking the protected object). This situation is considered a bounded error, and can result in the task's priority being temporarily lowered to accomplish the cancellation of its call.

We considered other alternatives as solutions to the above problems. For the first case, we looked into the possibility of temporarily lowering the priority of the task calling Set_Priority. This has the obvious problems of potentially introducing priority inversions, complicating implementations, and presenting a non-intuitive model to the user. We also looked at allowing the reordering to be deferred. This is also undesirable: the deferral may be too long and there may be several priority changes during this time. Resuming the affected task in order to accomplish the reordering was chosen as the suggested implementation model, since a similar mechanism is already required to support abort of a low-priority task by a high-priority task. We also looked at the possibility of limiting the effect of the Set_Priority call such that it will raise the priority only to the minimum of the ceilings of protected objects either held by or being queued on by the task. Again, it was not clear that these semantics are desired, and it would certainly add a substantial cost to the implementation.

The second situation introduces a problem that if not addressed might make the implementation of finalization (as part of abortion) impossible. Here, a call is already queued and it must be removed; just raising an exception is not acceptable since this will not solve the problem. We considered various solutions, but ultimately declared the situation a bounded error, and allowed the task when it needs to cancel its call to have its priority temporarily lowered. The temporary priority inversion was not felt to be serious since this is considered an error situation anyway.

Example of Changing Priorities of a Set of Tasks

```
type Task_Number is range 1 .. 4;
type Mode_Type is range 0 .. 2;
Task_Priority: array (Task_Number, Mode_Type) of Priority := ... ;

protected Mode_Control is
   procedure Set(Mode: Mode_Type);
   pragma Priority(System.Priority'Last);
end Mode_Control;

protected High_Priority_Mode_Control is
   procedure Set(Mode: Mode_Type);
   pragma Interrupt_Priority;
end High_Priority_Mode_Control;

use Dynamic_Priorities;
protected body Mode_Control is
   procedure Set(Mode: Mode_Type) is
   begin
      High_Priority_Mode_Control.Set(Mode);
      Set_Priority(Task_Priority(1, Mode),T1);
      Set_Priority(Task_Priority(2, Mode),T2);
   end Set;
end Mode_Control;

protected body High_Priority_Mode_Control is
   procedure Set(Mode: Mode_Type) is
   begin
      Set_Priority(Task_Priority(3, Mode),T3);
      Set_Priority(Task_Priority(4, Mode),T4);
   end Set;
end High_Priority_Mode_Control;
```

The table Task_Priority specifies the priorities that the tasks T1 through T4 should have, for every mode. Here, in order to avoid blocking every task for a long time, the priority changes are done in stages, at two different active priorities, via two protected objects. The task doing the priority change starts with a call to the lower-priority protected object. This calls the next higher level. The priority adjustments of lower priority tasks can be preempted by the execution of the higher priority tasks.

Metrics

The purpose of the metric for Set_Priority is to specify the cost of this operation, compared to other operations, for a case where it should be about as low as can be expected. This metric may be critical for some applications, which need to perform priority changes under time constraints, but the inherent complexity of Set_Priority is likely to make it time-consuming.

Of course, complicating factors such as entry queue reordering may make the execution time of Set_Priority worse than would be indicated by this metric. The possibility of including more metrics, such as for a situation involving entry-queue reordering, was considered. This idea was rejected on the grounds that it would only be of interest for applications that change the priority of tasks with queued entry calls. Special cases could not be covered uniformly to this level of detail without greatly increasing the number of metrics. Finally, this metric would cover a large part of the RTS code itself, and not just the priority change operation proper, thus it will be influenced by many factors diminishing the value of the specific metric to the user.

D.6 Preemptive Abort

A requirement has been expressed for "immediate" task abortion. There appear to be several motivations for wanting immediate abortion:

1   To stop the task from doing what it is currently doing before it can "contaminate" the application further, possibly with dangerous consequences. A task can contaminate the application by changing the system state or wasting processing resources.

2   To be certain that the task has stopped executing, so that the aborter can proceed without fear of interference from the aborted task (e.g. I/O, rendezvous, writing on shared variables).

3   To be certain that the aborted task does not continue executing indefinitely, as it might if it were (due to error) in an infinite loop without any abort completion points (see [RM95 9.8]).

There are several possible meanings of "immediate" in this context:

•   Before the abort statement completes. This is easy to define and implement, but it may take a long or indeterminate time to complete, and so might require blocking the task that executes the abort. It satisfies requirement (2) only.

•   Before the affected task(s) are allowed to execute further. This is easy on a single processor, but may be too costly or impossible on a multiprocessor. It satisfies all three requirements.

•   As soon as the implementation can do it, and certainly within a bounded time. On a single processor, this would have the same meaning as above, but would allow some delay on a multiprocessor. It satisfies requirements (2) and (3). Whether it satisfies (1) depends on the implementation.

The third meaning of "immediate" seems like the best compromise. This is the basis for the specifications in this section. With respect to what actually has to happen as part of the immediate activity, [RM95 9.8] defines what is included in the completion of an aborted construct. Specifically, [RM95 9.8] requires part of the effect of the abort statement to occur before that statement returns (e.g. marking the affected tasks and their dependents as abnormal). The requirements in the Annex go further and address the completion and finalization of the aborted constructs.

The key requirement here is that the abortion be preemptive, in the sense that abortion should preempt the execution of the aborted task, and if abortion requires the attention of another processor, the abortion request should preempt any activity of the other processor that is not higher in priority than the aborted tasks.

Note that the requirement for bounding the delay in achieving the effect of abortion can be satisfied on a multiprocessor, even if it is not possible for one processor to interrupt another. One technique is to use a periodic timer-generated interrupt on each processor, which causes the processor to check whether the currently executing task has become abnormal.

An alternative was considered to allow the task calling the abort statement to be blocked until all the aborted tasks have completed their finalization, and for those tasks to inherit the blocked task's priority while it is blocked. This would be a change from Ada 83, where it is only necessary to wait for the aborted tasks to become "abnormal", and Ada 83 did not have user-defined finalization. Certainly, one of the reasons for aborting a task may be to release resources that it is holding. The actual release of such resources may be done during task finalization. However, waiting for finalization is not always possible, since a task may abort itself (perhaps indirectly, by aborting some other task on which it indirectly depends). In this case, it is not possible for the task calling for the abortion to wait for all the aborted tasks (including itself) to complete their finalization. Another problem is where the abort statement is inside an accept statement, and the task being aborted is the caller in the rendezvous. In this case, forcing the aborter to wait for the aborted task to complete finalization would result in a deadlock. The problem with self-abortion could be resolved by releasing the aborter to perform finalization, but the problem with rendezvous does not seem to be so easily resolved.

The ability to wait for a collection of tasks to complete finalization is partially satisfied by two other mechanisms. One of these is the rule that requires blocking of a completed task master until its dependent tasks are terminated. If the tasks being aborted are not dependent, another partial solution is to use the delay statement and the Terminated attribute to poll the aborted tasks until they have all terminated. However, none of these mechanisms fully accomplishes the objective.

Not allowing abortion to cause blocking has several benefits. In real-time applications, there are situations where the task executing the abort statement does not wish to wait for the aborted task to complete; in this case it could also be said that requiring the task to block is not "immediate" abortion. If the task executing the abort statement were to be blocked, unbounded priority inversion would be possible unless the tasks being aborted inherit the priority of the blocked task. This form of inheritance is undesirable for reasons explained in the next paragraph. A final benefit is that in this way, the treatment of abortion of a task via the abort statement is more similar to the abortion of a sequence of statements via a change to a barrier caused by a protected operation, since executing the body of a protected operation can never involve blocking of the calling task.

Irrespective of the decision not to block the task executing the abort statement, there are other reasons for not requiring that aborted tasks executing finalization code inherit the priority of the task executing the abort. First, this would introduce a new form of one-to-many inheritance, with the associated additional implementation complexity. Second, if the aborted task is a low-priority task, and the aborter has high priority, it might not be appropriate to suspend the aborter while the aborted task finalizes. Third, if the active priority of the aborted task could be raised by abortion, it would be necessary to take into account all abort statements, as well as task dependency hierarchies, in determining protected object ceiling priorities; otherwise, the active priority of a task might violate the ceiling of a protected object during finalization code.

Note finally, that if the user does want to make the finalization of the aborted task happen faster, the only solution is to raise the aborted task's base priority either before or after issuing the abort. Doing it afterwards enables the priority to be set higher than that of the aborting task; if the aborted task is already terminated no harm is done

```
Abort_Task(Joes_ID);                     -- take that
Set_Priority(Priority'Last, Joes_ID);    -- die quickly you dog
```

While this approach is not that elegant, it is expected to satisfy such a need.

Documentation Requirements

It is clear that interprocessor communication delays may cause abortion to take longer on some multiprocessor systems. The predictability of such delays is bound to depend on the implementation, and the duration may depend on what other activities are going on in the system at the time. It is important that the designer of an application that uses abortion be able to determine whether this is going to be a problem for a particular application.

Metrics

The execution time of an abort statement is intended only to be a sample of the execution time, in a non-pathological case. Of course the actual execution time will vary, depending on factors such as the number of tasks being aborted, their current states, and their dependence relationships. Providing an upper bound would therefore require specification of more conditions.

The intent of the upper bound on the additional delay for a multiprocessor is primarily to require the implementor to verify that such an upper bound exists. The specific value is less important than the existence of such a value. There must be some upper bound on the delay if abortion is to be useful in a real-time system. An upper bound may not be able to be measured directly, but it should be possible to (over-) estimate a bound by adding the upper bound of the communication delay to the upper bound of the local processing time.

The intent of the metrics for asynchronous transfer of control is to tell whether this capability is implemented efficiently enough to be useful in time-critical applications. Potentially, there is a great gap in performance between an implementation of asynchronous transfer of control that is based on creating a separate thread of control for the abortable part, versus an implementation that uses the context of the same task. The intent is that such a gap can be discovered by the metrics.

D.7 Tasking Restrictions

This section establishes that the Ada standard permits the development of highly optimized implementations for restricted tasking models. It also defines a specific set of restrictions, that both serves as an example of what an implementation can do, and may encourage convergent development and usage.

Builders of hard real-time systems have observed that the full Ada tasking model is more general than they require, and imposes more overhead than they can afford. The existence of very lightweight executives for other tasking models suggests that significant performance improvements are possible for Ada tasking implementations, if some usage restrictions are observed.

Any Ada implementor can define a restricted tasking model and provide a run-time system that is optimized for this model. (In fact many implementations do so currently, but in a non-portable way.) However, Ada 83 has been misinterpreted to give the (incorrect) impression that this is a form of "subsetting", and therefore is not allowed by the language standard. It is not subsetting, as long as the implementor also provides support for the full tasking model, perhaps with different compilation and linking options. Thus, it appears desirable for the Real-Time Annex to endorse this form of optimization.

A restricted tasking model should permit simple and useful multitasking applications to be expressed, but simplify the implementation problem enough so that the size and execution time overhead of the run-time system need be no greater than with traditional real-time executives.

Therefore, the intent behind the model defined here is to satisfy the needs of many of the real-time embedded applications that have rejected the full Ada tasking model for being too heavyweight. These applications include some that consist of a fixed set of cyclic tasks, with periodic and aperiodic timing constraints. This has traditionally been a stronghold of the cyclic executive and rate-monotonic scheduling models. The intended scope of restricted tasking applications also includes some more complex applications, which are event-driven. These applications have traditionally used real-time executives that can dynamically create and schedule extremely lightweight tasks. This kind of system is organized into groups of simple tasks. A task group is created in response to an event, executes for a while, and goes away. There may be precedence relations and delays among tasks within a group, but an individual task never blocks to wait for another task. Each task within a group is very simple: it may be preempted, but otherwise it runs to completion without blocking. The events that can trigger the invocation of task groups include interrupts and actions performed by other tasks. This is a well established model of software architecture, and has been used for more than a decade in guidance and control systems, including radar and sonar tracking systems, process control, railroad signalling and so on. This is also the task model of classical scheduling theories (see [Coffman 73]).

D.7.1 The Chosen Approach To Restrictions

This Annex specifies a set of restrictions which should be such that the potential performance improvement justifies producing one or more special versions of the RTS according to the combinations of restrictions asserted in a particular program.

The Restrictions pragma (see [RM95 13.12]), which is a configuration pragma, takes two forms. One such as

```
pragma Restrictions(No_Task_Hierarchy);
```

indicates a simple yes/no restriction, whereas

```
pragma Restrictions(Max_Select_Alternatives => 5);
```

indicates some numerical restriction on the feature concerned.

Compliance

Compliance with this pragma means that all the parameters must be recognized by the implementation, and the associated limitations must be enforced. It is clearly important for the implementation to reject violations of the restrictions. Without such checking, much of the value of the pragma is lost. Checking itself can be of value as well. Where the implementation is for a development host, if the host is used in preliminary testing of an application that is eventually intended for an embedded target, enforcement of the pragma by the development host will help to identify code that will cause problems arising when the time comes to move the application to the final target.

Some of these limitations are to be checked at compile-time (such as for task hierarchies and the presence of finalization). For those that can only be checked at run-time, implementations are allowed to omit the checking code. Programs that violate the corresponding restrictions are considered erroneous. If a run-time check fails, Storage_Error should be raised. This exception is chosen because failure of these checks often indicates shortage of the storage allocated for a task — either the run-time stack storage or storage allocated within the task control block.

The permission to omit the run-time checks is given due to the recognition that a check for a given violation may be as complex and costly as the support for the restricted construct. One does not want the checks to be difficult to implement or for the checks to add any overhead to a model that is intended to allow a simple implementation. The resource utilization checks need to be done at run time, and may incur some run-time overhead, but they may be very important during the testing of a system. The decision on whether to omit the checks is therefore left to the implementation based on the particular situation.

The Specific Restrictions

The basic criteria for deciding upon the restrictions were:

- The restriction allows a faster or smaller run-time system.

- The advantage is distributed. If it is a speed improvement, it applies to operations other than those ruled out by the restriction. If it is a size reduction, it is not simply due to deletion of unused run-time system components, such as might be done automatically by a linker.

- Taking advantage of the restriction does not require a major change in compilation strategy for programs that follow the restriction from those that do not.

- A sample of real-time embedded systems developers felt that the restricted feature is not essential for a significant portion of their applications.

In addition, some restrictions have been included because a significant number of users and vendors felt that they were appropriate.
Some of the specific restrictions and the benefits they bring are as follows

- Max_Tasks (maximum number of task creations over the lifetime of the partition) plus Max_Task_Entries (maximum number of entries per task). These enable fixed RTS and task storage size. The amount of storage required by the run-time system for its own data structures and task workspace should be determinable statically, no later than load time.

- Max_Task_Entries plus Max_Asynchronous_Select_Nesting (maximum nesting of asynchronous selects). These enable a fixed Task Control Block (TCB) size. If each task can be represented in the RTS by a fixed-size task control block, the complexity of the RTS is reduced. A list of free TCBs may be allocated at load time, speeding up task creation.

- No_Task_Hierarchy; all tasks are library tasks. This means no overhead due to code executed to keep track of potential task masters, or to check for unterminated dependent tasks. Likewise, there should be no storage overhead for data structures to keep track of task master nesting. Abortion and task termination should not be complicated by the need to support hierarchies.

- No_Task_Hierarchy plus No_Nested_Finalization (all controlled objects at library level). These permit the storage for non-library-level collections to be allocated on the stack, and the stack space can be recovered without finalization when the stack frame is popped.

- No_Dynamic_Priorities. There are several known scheduling algorithms that do not use the capability to dynamically change the task's base priority. If it is known that the base priority of a task is static, then it is possible to have much simpler and more efficient queue management and dispatching algorithms in the run-time system.

- `No_Asynchronous_Control`. Even though the semantics of this package are defined in terms of priorities, it is not clear that an implementation approach based on this semantic model is feasible on all possible targets. In general, the ability to asynchronously suspend the execution of another task is considered dangerous from the user's point of view, and may have distributed ramifications on the rest of the run-time system. Since in some applications, this feature will not be used (and may even be disallowed) it makes sense to allow for the corresponding restriction.

- `Max_Protected_Entries`. There are several very efficient algorithms for servicing protected entry queues when the maximum number of entries is statically known and relatively small. The main issue here is the requirement for evaluating barriers whenever the state of the protected objects changes. The language rules in [RM95 9.5.2, 9.5.3] make it possible to evaluate the barrier less often than it would otherwise be needed (provided that the compiler can determine that no "interesting" change has occurred since the last check). It was suggested that the implementation can use a bit-vector (usually of one word length) to represent the true/false state of the barriers, and then check this bit-vector (using only a small number of machine instructions) in appropriate places instead of reevaluating all the barrier expressions. For this approach to work, the number of possible entries should be known a priori. Since the implementation of such a technique often involves the compiler, it might be necessary for this information to be known before any unit is compiled.

- `No_Abort_Statements` plus `No_Asynchronous_Control`. These enable a number of further simplifications to the model.

- `Max_Task_Entries = 0`. Forbidding task entries could reduce the size of the run-time system code. It could also reduce the amount of rendezvous-related information that must be stored in task control blocks. Processing this information during task creation and termination is a source of distributed overhead. The implementation of abortion might also benefit by not having to take into account the special case of tasks engaged in a rendezvous as callers, though the rules requiring deferral during protected operations and finalization operations cast this into doubt. Protected objects provide a lighter-weight mechanism that is more suitable than rendezvous for data and control synchronization in small real-time embedded systems.

- `No_Terminate_Alternatives`. The terminate alternative may add distributed overhead but is less valuable in Ada 95 since a protected object will typically be used rather than a server task.

- `No_Implicit_Heap_Allocation`. We considered adding a restriction forbidding the compiler from using the heap implicitly (i.e. not as a direct result of using an allocator). Such a restriction can improve the deterministic behavior of the memory in the system, by making all memory usage visible and user-invoked. However, this was difficult to mandate as a requirement on the compiler and so we have adopted a slightly different approach. The compiler is allowed to reject (and document) such user constructs that require implicit heap allocation. This way, it can ensure that no such heap requests will be present at run-time, and so the heap usage will be avoided.

Certain other restrictions were considered, but were not included.

Specifying a mechanism for configuring the run-time system size limits was also considered. It was left implementation-defined, because the practical mechanism is outside the scope of the language. For example, one method is for the implementor to provide source code of a few run-time system packages, which contain configuration constants. The user could edit these, recompile them, and link them in with the rest of the run-time system and the user's application. Another method is to provide a configuration tool that edits the run-time system object code, inserting constants for the required limits at the required points. This same function might be performed by a linker or a loader.

Max_Storage_At_Blocking

This restriction deserves special mention. If a task is not permitted to be blocked while it is holding more than a fixed amount of stack storage, a much larger number of tasks can be supported, since only one dynamic stack storage area is required for each priority level (essentially, only the TCB of a blocked task needs to be saved). Traditional real time systems are designed to make this possible. Practical ramifications of this requirement include:

- Tasks should not have large local data objects or access collections.

- Tasks should not have entries whose parameters require a large amount of storage.

- Operations that may cause a task to be blocked should not be performed within deeply nested procedure calls or within a block statement that has large local data requirements.

One implementation model is to have a fixed pool of stack spaces that are shared by all tasks, or all the tasks at a priority level. On each processor, not more than one stack space will be needed for each priority level. The stack space for a given level must be configured (by the user) to be large enough to meet the largest stack requirement of any task that executes at that priority level. A task releases its stack area when it blocks, and is allocated a stack area when it wakes up again. Depending on how ready queues are structured, allocation of a stack area might be done at the point where the task wakes up, or as a special case in the dispatcher when it gets ready to do a context switch to a stack-less task. A slight variation of this approach would be to always allocate a small and fixed-size part of the stack to the task, and to allocate the larger part only when the task is ready. In any case, the implementation can go to a linked list of stack spaces, remove one, and link it to the fixed-size part of the stack. This could be kept simple, maybe to the point of just setting the saved stack pointer value and a link to the fixed part of the stack. For example, on a machine with register windows, the implementation could keep one register window stored in the TCB. When allocating a stack area, it would write the new stack pointer (base) into this saved register window. Then, when the task is resumed, the implementation would load registers from the TCB and the task would be running with the new stack.

The intention is that all requirements for non-volatile storage associated with a task be met by the task control block (or by a fixed-size extension of it). For example, this includes storage for the implementation of select statements, entry parameters, local variables, and local access collections. This means that any large non-volatile data used by a task must be declared in library-level packages or passed to the task by means of access values. The size of the task control block and the fixed part of each task's run-time stack is intended to be determinable no later than link time, so that a fixed-size pool of identical task control blocks can be pre-allocated at system initialization time.

D.8 Monotonic Time

The package Ada.Real_Time is similar to the package Calendar. It has a type Time, a function Clock, relational operations on time, and arithmetic operations for combining times and durations. In order to explain why such a "duplicate" of Calendar is needed, we first review why some real-time applications need facilities beyond those in package Calendar.

The inclusion of a standard calendar package and clock function in Ada seems useful. Certainly, the existence of a standard interface to time-keeping services that hides unimportant details of specific execution environments can be an aid to writing portable applications. However, a sample of existing practice in real-time Ada applications reveals that they frequently choose not to use the package Calendar. Perhaps the main reason is simply that Calendar is typically "political" time and so is not guaranteed to be monotonic since it may be adjusted by the effects of time zones and daylight saving changes.

Another issue is the diversity of time-keeping requirements among real-time applications. It does not seem feasible to meet all these with a single solution. Both the requirements and the hardware (or operating system) support available differ widely from one real-time application to another. At one extreme, a simple real-time controller might be able to use a single 16-bit counter-timer circuit, with very fine granularity but a rather narrow range. At the other extreme, a complex electronic navigation system may require an atomic clock that is precisely synchronized with a global time reference, and may have precision and range requirements that demand 64-bit time representation.

Given this diversity, it is natural to wonder whether Ada 95 should attempt to provide any standard time services at all other than the package Calendar which has to be retained for compatibility. To the extent that there are common requirements for such services within certain application domains, they should perhaps be the subject of a language-independent standard; but no such standard exists.

The exisiting delay statement and the delay alternative require the language to provide a clock for two reasons:

• *Coordination of Clock and delay.* If the application uses delay statements to control timing, the application's view of the time should be consistent with that of the implementation.

• *Timer resource sharing.* The implementation needs access to a timer for the implementation of the delay statements. If there is only one such timer (as is the case on some execution platforms), the implementation and application must share it.

Real-time applications clearly need the capability to block task execution until a specified time, and to impose a time limit on how long a task can stay blocked waiting for other operations.

We considered an approach of providing general mechanisms for an application to wait for an event, and to abort blocking operations in response to events. This would have allowed the application to provide its own timer services. The delay statement could then just be a special case of waiting for a time-out event signalled by the user-defined timer, rather than the implementation's default timer. This solution was dropped since the added complexity seemed out of proportion to the benefits.

The inclusion of the Real_Time package in this Annex is based on the realization that there was no choice but to provide a real-time clock which applications could use. Specifically, an application that requires time-outs on select statements must use the standard delay statement implementation. If the application needs to know what time it is, based on a time reference that is consistent with the delay, it must use a clock provided by the implementation.

The following general requirements can be identified for a clock that is used in conjunction with the delay statement, to schedule task execution and specify time-outs:

- Monotonically non-decreasing time value, incremented at a steady rate, with bounded discontinuities.

- Fine granularity.

- The ability to be used as the time reference in all forms of delay statement.

- Efficient implementability using clock facilities that are typical of most existing hardware, and real-time operating systems.

- Exact arithmetic on time and duration values, and precise conversion of rational-number durations to time intervals.

- A defined relationship to other time-related features of the language, including the Calendar package, System.Tick, and the Standard.Duration type.

The package Ada.Real_Time is intended to provide facilities that satisfy these requirements.
  Some real-time applications have other requirements, such as

- Unique time-stamps. With fast processors and multiprocessor architectures, it is possible that for some implementations the clock may be read several times in one tick. Enforcing uniqueness in such an environment would amount to slowing down the clock reading operation.

- Synchronization with external time references. In some situations (such as where the external time reference is non-monotonic, or synchronization cannot be performed frequently enough to avoid large adjustments), synchronization may be incompatible with the requirements for monotonicity and bounded discontinuity of the clock.

These were considered but appeared to conflict with satisfying one or more of the other requirements and so were dropped.

D.8.1 An Ideal Clock

International Atomic Time (TAI), regulated by the Bureau International de l'Heure (BIH) and supported by the various national time references, is currently accepted as the most precise physical time reference. It is monotonic and does not have leap-seconds or seasonal changes. All the other time standards can be defined as a function of TAI. That is, any other standard of political or physical time can be defined as a function $C = TAI + D(TAI)$, where $D(TAI)$ is a piecewise constant function, depending on the current value of TAI. In an ideal world, and an ideal implementation of the language for real-time applications, there would be a clock function that returns the current TAI clock value. Language-defined functions could be provided to convert this time to an arbitrary time zone.
  In practice, most Ada execution environments will not have access to an atomic clock. Even if such a clock is available, there may be a need to use other (less accurate) clocks, including the local time as perceived by a human operator or an operating system, or counter-timer circuits that are capable of generating interrupts.

D.8.2 Time Sources

A language implementation is limited by the actual time-keeping resources provided by the hardware, which are possibly filtered through an operating system interface.

In practice, several different kinds of time references are likely to be available to an Ada implementor. These have significantly different characteristics:

- Counter-timer circuit

- Calendar clock circuit

- Externally synchronized clock

A counter-timer circuit is a programmable hardware device which can be viewed as a register counting clock ticks. Such a timer is typically driven by a crystal oscillator, and can be read and reset to a specified value. A typical tick duration might be one microsecond.

A counter-timer can typically be used to generate an interrupt when a specified number of ticks have elapsed. It might then restart automatically at a specified value (a periodic timer) or wait to be reset (a one-shot timer).

Counter-timer circuits are comparatively inexpensive, and are easily added to a microprocessor-based design. Thus, in a specific hardware configuration of an embedded application, there may be several counter-timer circuits. However, these are not likely to be known and available to the implementation. The standard configuration of most processors typically has only a small number of counter-timer circuits (possibly one) that can be relied upon to always be available for use by the application and the language implementation. In small embedded real-time applications, these counter-timer circuits may be the only time reference available. The strengths of counter-timer circuits include:

- Small clock-tick, typically one microsecond or smaller;

- Monotonicity, subject to periodic wrap-around to zero;

- Very regular ticks;

- Ability to generate interrupts;

- Very regular periodic interrupts, in periodic mode.

Some limitations of counter-timer circuits include: jitter up to one clock-tick, variation in interval from one timer to another and with temperature, and a limited range before wrap-around.

A calendar-clock circuit is a programmable hardware device that is very similar to a counter-timer-circuit. The main differences are:

- The visible update rate (granularity) of the clock may be coarser (e.g. once per second). However, the underlying oscillator rate, and hence the accuracy, is likely to be just as high as the counter-timer.

- The range of times representable by the clock is large, perhaps 100 years.

- The clock may be programmable to automatically take into account leap years and seasonal political time changes, such as daylight savings time.

- Time values, instead of being a simple count of ticks, may be represented in terms of second, minute, hour, day, month, and year.

Various forms of externally synchronized time references may be available in a specific application. In a system requiring very precise global positioning there might be a local atomic clock, periodically synchronized with the TAI via a communications link. In a network, there might be a broadcast periodic "heartbeat", or a message-based averaging algorithm for keeping the local clocks of various network nodes synchronized within some tolerance.   Generally, the frequency of external synchronization is limited, and if it relies on communications with external systems there may be times when the local system is cut off from its source of external synchronization. Typically, local clock or timer circuits are used to keep time between external synchronization points, so that a finer granularity of time is available locally.

In general, synchronization conflicts with regularity and fine granularity. That is, if the granularity of the clock is fine enough, synchronization will cause discernible irregularities in the rate of progress of the clock. Clock synchronization may require the local clock to jump forward or backward. Of these two, backward jumps are especially troublesome, since they can induce apparent ordering inversion if the clock happens to be used to determine the times of events immediately before and after a jump. However, an error in the measurement of an interval due to a forward jump can also be serious.

A good synchronization method can reduce the impact of clock adjustments by several techniques. Backward jumps may be avoided by arranging to skip some ticks of the local time reference until the desired adjustment is reached. Discontinuities due to forward jumps and skipped ticks may be smoothed by splitting a large adjustment into several smaller adjustments, separated by intervals.   Better, the size of adjustments may be kept small by frequent synchronization. Still, these techniques are limited. In less than ideal circumstances, one must anticipate that a synchronized clock may be available but not be able to deliver as fine a granularity, or as regular a rate of progress, as unsynchronized time references that may be available locally.

Where Ada is implemented over an operating system, and so does not have direct access to time-keeping hardware circuits, it may be necessary to rely on the time-keeping services of the operating system. The operating system ultimately must rely on hardware devices similar to those described above, and it may or may not attempt to synchronize with other clocks; therefore, operating system time sources are subject to the same diversity of characteristics discussed above. In addition, they are subject to other limitations, including:

- Inability to access the full accuracy of the hardware, due to timer-programming decisions made by the OS implementor.

- Loss of accuracy as viewed by the user, due to system-call overhead.

- Delay between expiration of a wake-up time and notification being delivered to a waiting process, due to system overhead.

- Discontinuities, due to setting of the clock by a human operator or an unrelated application program.

- Disparate views, due to "environment variables" specifying different time zones for different processes within a system.

While these factors may affect the suitability of a particular operating system for a real-time application, they must be accepted as inherent limitations from the point of view of the Ada language. One is forced to assume that the time services provided by the OS have sufficient accuracy and low enough overhead to meet the needs of Ada applications on that system.

For the purposes of this discussion, whatever time sources are provided by an operating system are presumed to have characteristics similar to one of the three basic types of clocks mentioned above.

A Single-Clock Model

In a real-time application, there may be requirements that cannot be satisfied by any single time source that is available. As explained above, the actual time-keeping resources available in a specific environment may have significant limitations, and the choice of time references may require that one thing be sacrificed for another. For example, fine granularity may mean sacrificing range or synchronization, greater range may mean sacrificing granularity, and synchronization may mean sacrificing the regularity or fine granularity, all at the cost of higher overhead. It follows that if all of these properties are important for a given application, a combination of different time references must be used.

In some cases, it may be possible to provide a virtual interface that creates the illusion of a single time reference, using multiple time references in the implementation. For example, this is the case when a local timer is used to interpolate between points of synchronization with a remote clock. However, preserving this illusion is not always possible, or practical. In the extreme, there may be a fundamental conflict, as between steady tick rate and synchronization with an external reference. An implementation of a single-clock interface may be useless if it ends up exhibiting the same time anomalies such as sudden jumps, insufficient granularity, or insufficient accuracy. In this case, the promise of portability becomes a dangerous illusion.

The Ada 83 `Calendar` package attempts to provide a single-clock interface. In order to ensure that it can be implemented in most execution environments, very little is specified about `Calendar.Clock` and, as mentioned, the predominant practice among existing implementations is to treat `Calendar.Clock` as political time. The values are likely not to be monotonic, and the resolution may be rather coarse. In effect, `Calendar.Clock` cannot be relied upon for measurement of "physical time" in real-time applications.

A Two-Clock Model

For the Real-Time Annex, we considered adding requirements to `Calendar.Clock` so that it would satisfy real-time requirements. For example, it could be required to be monotonic and have at least one millisecond precision. This idea was rejected. One reason is that the requirement for monotonicity might conflict with existing practice and other (non-real-time) requirements for a standard clock that returns local political time. A second reason is that requiring fine precision for `Calendar.Clock` might prevent an implementation from using hardware calendar-clock circuits. Thus `Calendar.Clock` is essentially as in Ada 83.

In contrast, `Real_Time.Clock` is used for computations of physical parameters based on time, and scheduling of task execution to satisfy real-time constraints. The implementation must ensure that the value of the clock progresses monotonically, and that irregularities are strictly bounded. After the system starts, the clock is not allowed to be reset by an operator, the underlying operating system, or the run-time environment.

Of course, there is no requirement for an implementation to have multiple clocks internally. The implementation may simply provide two package interfaces to a single underlying (monotonic) clock. The capability of supporting clock adjustments and seasonal time changes for `Calendar.Clock` is not mandated by the language, so the values of the two clocks could be the same. Moreover, where the application requires `Calendar.Clock` to do things that are incompatible with the specification of `Real_Time.Clock`, such as seasonal time changes and clock adjustments, the effect may be accomplished by computing a transformation of the value of `Real_Time.Clock`. It is in fact recommended that both `Calendar.Clock` and `Real_Time.-Clock` be transformations of the same underlying timebase.

The suggestion was made that a way might be provided for the application to modify the rate of the clock, so that the application could do clock synchronization, and do it in a way that would not compromise monotonicity. However, such a requirement would be applicable to only a small subset of applications, and the cost of providing the capability would be unwelcome for applications not needing it. In fact, for most existing general purpose processors, such a facility is not provided in the hardware, and providing it in software would introduce significant overhead in the clock driver. Alternatively, this capability, as well as the capability to do other low-level clock functions, is better provided by expecting the implementation to export the interface to its low-level clock driver in these systems, allowing it to be replaced by applications with special clock requirements.

D.8.3 Clock Accuracy Requirements

The average clock tick given by the constant Real_Time.Tick is specified as not being larger than one millisecond. This number is conservative in the direction of not imposing extreme requirements on implementors, and seems adequate for the task scheduling needs of many real-time applications. Finer clock resolution is recommended.

D.8.4 Relationship to Delays

The requirement that Real_Time.Clock be consistent with the effect of delay statements may be problematic for some implementations, but the conceptual consistency is seen as outweighing the implementation difficulty. One problem is that the range of times measurable directly by the available counter-timer circuit may be very narrow. In this case, the clock may need to be implemented in two parts. The low-order part may be decremented by every tick of the hardware timer, and the high-order part may be incremented by an interrupt handler that is driven by underflow of the timer. Another possible problem is that a separate timer circuit may be used for delays. It is desirable to utilize one timer to implement the real-time clock, using the simple treatment of timer underflow explained above, and to program another timer to generate an interrupt at the next point a delay is due to expire. However, in this case, since the delay timer is used only to express offsets from the clock, any difference between the two timers may not be noticeable.

D.8.5 Representation of Duration, Time_Span, and Real_Time.Time

The Time_Span type is introduced to allow more precise representation of durations. A new type is introduced because the need for upward compatibility rules out changes to the range requirement for Standard.Duration.

Requirements and Representation

Lack of sufficient precision is one of the issues with the Calendar package and delay statements in Ada 83. The Duration type is required to be able to represent a full day, in the positive or negative direction. The hardware arithmetic on many machines today is limited to 32 bits. If Duration values are represented with 32 bits, then Duration'Small cannot be smaller than $2.0**(-14)$ seconds. This is coarser than the resolution of timer circuits. If the resolution of the timer is not exactly equal to an integer multiple (or divisor) of Duration'Small, additional precision can be lost in conversion. For example, suppose the clock is implemented using a timer with microsecond resolution, and the difference of two clock values is 100 microseconds. If Duration'Small is $2.0**(-14)$, the nearest Duration value to 100 microseconds is $2*$Duration'Small, or about 122 microseconds. Conversion to Duration in this example has introduced an error of 22 percent!

The required minimum range and precision of Time_Span represent a compromise, given the assumption that the value should be representable in 32 bits. Originally, we required that Time_Span_Unit be equivalent to at most one microsecond and the range, equivalent to at least

-2.0 .. 2.0 seconds. These requirements would still allow for a nanosecond representation in 32 bits (for example, the real-time extensions to POSIX specify nanosecond precision for timers). On the other hand, it would allow a range of up to an hour (with one microsecond precision). However, reviewers have commented that a portable range of -2.0 .. 2.0 is too small to be useful. We have changed the requirements so that a minimum resolution of twenty microseconds, and a minimum range of ± one hour are mandated. This compromise still allows for "spare" bits in each direction, so that implementations, using 32 bits, can still have some flexibility in responding to stricter application needs without violating the range or precision requirements. Of course, this freedom sacrifices portability for users who require a greater range or finer precision than these minimum specifications. It is expected that in many implementations, the representation of Time_Span will use 64 bits (just as for the type Time). Since this type is private, such an implementation approach will not require 64-bit arithmetic in general.

Since these requirements are based on a 32-bit machine architecture, for machines with a smaller word size, we have provided an escape clause in the form of an implementation permission. For example, some machines have only 24-bit words with no easy way to manipulate double-words. If we want to maintain the model of one word for Time_Span and two for Time, we must relax the range/accuracy requirements. On the other hand, a 16-bit machine such as the 1750A, which has built-in double-word operations, can easily use one double-word for Time_Span and two double-words for Time, and thus meet the requirements.

The possibility was also considered of having Time_Span as a visible integer type, which could be a count of ticks. This is appealing, since clocks count time in ticks, and arithmetic on real numbers tends to introduce unnecessary loss of accuracy. Under the Ada 83 rules, the multiplication and division operations on fixed point types require much greater precision than for integer types of the same size. Moreover, real-time systems often involve computations in which time is viewed as cyclic. Such computations are naturally expressed in terms of the integer division and rem operations, rather than fixed point operations. This idea was discarded because there was a potential for confusion arising from different units for logically similar types. For example, the assignment statements in

```
T: Time_Span;
...
T := T + 3        -- add 3 ticks to T
...
T := T + 3.0;     -- add three seconds duration to T
```

would have a vastly different meaning and yet both be allowed because both relevant overloadings of the "+" operator would exist.

The concept of a Time_Unit is introduced to ensure that the choice of representations for Time and Time_Span do not cause loss of information in time arithmetic. That is, the value obtained by subtracting two Time values should be exactly representable as a Time_Span, and adding a Time_Span value to a Time value should yield an exact Time value. This is the origin of the requirement that Time_Span_Unit be equal to Time_Unit.

Fixed point Issues

An alternative considered was to replace both Time and Time_Span by a single (64-bit) fixed point type. This would have simplified the interface and allowed a full range of user needs to be met. However, we concluded that supporting fixed point arithmetic on 64 bits would have been an unreasonable requirement to impose on all real-time implementations. Moreover, users who do not require extreme range or precision would have suffered from the overhead of arithmetic operations on objects of such a type. Finally, the requirements for accuracy and determinism on these types would have disturbed the general model of fixed point types in the core too much. Some of the needed changes would have been in direct conflict to the changes needed to support decimal types. Also, they would have been upward incompatible and too much of an implementation burden. Below, we provide more details about this alternative and related issues.

D.8.6 Arithmetic and Relational Operators

In Ada 83 [RM83 9.6(5)], nothing is specified about the semantics of arithmetic and relational operators on times and durations except that the operations "have the conventional meaning". One of the objectives of this Annex is to give a more precise specification. Several approaches were considered. One of these is to specify a representation for Time, and then define the effects of the operations in terms of the representation. Possibilities considered included: a two-part record, analogous to the POSIX "timespec" type (a two-part record, consisting of a signed integer count of seconds and an unsigned integer count of nanoseconds); a very long integer type; and a very long fixed point type. This approach was rejected on the grounds that it would not allow the natural implementation for a wide enough variety of machines and operating systems. On the assumption that Time must be a private type, the possibility of providing an axiomatic specification of time arithmetic was considered. This approach was rejected on the grounds that it is inconsistent with the style of the rest of the Ada language definition. The present approach draws on analogy to the definition of arithmetic on integer types. In addition, for the conversion functions, rounding is specified (away from zero) to ensure deterministic results.

Another possibility considered was of specifying that the time values are unsigned integers. As such, there is no overflow or underflow, and arithmetic is modular. One unfortunate aspect of using modular arithmetic for time is that the relational operations must be used with great care. For example, on a 12-hour clock it is not possible to say whether eleven o'clock is earlier or later than one o'clock, without further information. Because of this potential for confusion, the idea of arithmetic on time values being modular was dropped. This means that the Time type cannot be practically represented in 32 bits.

If Time is going to take 64 bits, there is no problem representing a large range. A 32-bit signed count of seconds can represent a range of about 136 years. The requirement for a range of 50 years has been chosen because it is well within this range, and appears more than adequate to handle the continuous running time of most real-time systems.

The operations Nanoseconds, Microseconds, and Milliseconds construct values of the type Time_Span. We considered having constants for one nanosecond, one microsecond, etc. However, the possibility that such real time values might not be representable accurately as Time_Span values, when using the constants to convert multiples of these values, leads to the danger of introducing cumulative errors. For example, if one wants to have a value of Time_Span equal to five milliseconds, calling Milliseconds(5) will return a more accurate result than doing 5*One_Millisecond, where One_Millisecond is a constant of Time_Span representing one millisecond. Using Milliseconds, one can convert up to almost 25 days worth of milliseconds (assuming a 32-bit implementation of Integer). This range seems large enough for this purpose, so a function that takes seconds as a parameter is not provided.

D.8.7 Other Issues

In order to allow direct mapping of Real_Time.Time onto the most natural time reference that is available for a particular implementation, it is not required that there be any fixed correspondence between time values and specific real-time intervals. For example, Real_Time.Time could be a simple count of ticks since the clock was started. Given a fixed size representation of time values, this gives the widest possible range of values in the direction of interest, which is forward from the time of system start-up. It is also easy to implement, since there is no requirement for synchronization to obtain the initial clock value.

In a model with this degree of implementation freedom, it is difficult to specify meaningful counterparts of Calendar.Split and Calendar.Time_Of. In this context, Split and

Time_Of are likely to be used as a communication means to the outside world (since both Time and Time_Span are private). Examples include constructing a (local) time value from information read from a network, and logging event times in a readable format. Two possible approaches were considered.

One approach was to provide functions for conversion between Real_Time.Time and Calendar.Time. The Split and Time_Of operations on Calendar.Time could then be used. The other approach was to define Time_Of and Split as operations that would convert a Time value into a seconds value and Duration part, or construct a Time value from these values. The seconds value would then be interpreted as an extended duration since clock start-up. Both of these approaches could be implemented, within some degree of tolerance for error, if the implementation reads both Real_Time.Clock and Calendar.Clock at the time of system start-up to establish a common reference point.

The second approach, with a slight variation, was chosen for two reasons. First, it does not seem appropriate to require applications to include the package Calendar, just for this I/O purpose, if it is not needed otherwise (as is often the case). Second, as was discussed above, the package Calendar allows for certain implementation-defined behavior; it is not clear that the operations of this package will always be capable of serving as a transparent filter, one that provides the appropriate range and accuracy needed by the Real_Time.Time type representation.

Accordingly, an integer type, Seconds_Count, is introduced. It represents the elapsed time from the epoch (the origin point) in seconds. (Since the epoch of the time is not specified by this Annex, the meaning of the Seconds parameter has to be interpreted based on implementation and application conventions.) A seconds representation was chosen based on range considerations. Even a 32 bit representation is enough to hold 50 years. Seconds_Count is a signed integer since the Annex does not specify that Time_First equals the epoch. In fact, it is legal to have the epoch defined somewhere in the future, and have Time values as negative offsets from that point. Hence, Seconds_Count should be able to hold both positive and negative values.

For the fraction part, we had originally chosen the type Duration (as opposed to Time_Span). This was done in light of the fact that the primary purpose of the Split and Time_Of operation is communication with the outside world. A visible and printable type is much more convenient in this case. However, some reviewers commented that by doing so we introduce the possibility of an error "at the source", and that Time_Span should be used instead of Duration as the parameter for these operations. Since there exist other conversion routines that return a Duration value, and since the suggestion seemed to provide more flexibility, it was accepted.

Metrics

The intent of the upper bounds on clock ticks and clock jumps is to quantify the maximum fine-grain clock variation that can be expected.

The upper bound on clock drift rate is intended to provide an estimate of the long-term accuracy of the clock.

The upper bound on the execution time of a call to the Clock function is intended to expose implementations where reading the clock is extremely time-consuming. This might be the case, for example, where the clock function involves an operating system call, which involves context switches in and out from the operating system kernel.

The reason for the metric on time arithmetic is to expose extremely inefficient time representations. For example, this is likely to expose the difference between an implementation based on a record containing years, months, days, etc. and an implementation based on a 64-bit count of clock ticks.

Not all of these metrics are intended to be testable by pure Ada benchmark programs, such as the PIWG performance tests. That measurement technique is inherently limited, especially by the accuracy and precision of the software clock. Instead, it is intended that an external timing instrument, such as a logic analyzer, plus some knowledge of the implementation, may be needed to obtain the values of some metrics. In particular, this applies to measurements of the accuracy of the clock itself. Benchmark programs that rely on the internal clock for a time reference are inherently incapable of measuring the behavior of the clock itself. Moreover, for fine measurements such programs must settle for average execution times, since they must perform many iterations before they can accumulate enough execution time that is measurable on the internal clock. Thus, benchmarks are intrinsically incapable of deriving worst-case bounds for short execution times.

D.9 Delay Accuracy

Real-time applications require that a task of sufficiently high priority be able to delay itself for a period of time with the assurance that it will resume execution immediately when the delay expires — i.e. that the duration of the interval between the start of the delay and the time the task resumes execution must be equal to the requested duration, within a predictable tolerance.

[RM95 9.6] only requires that execution of the task that executes the delay be blocked for at least the duration specified. It is not in general possible to require an upper bound on the duration of the execution of any statement, due to possible interleaved operations of other tasks on the same processor. However, it is both possible and necessary to have an upper bound on the duration of the interval between the start of a delay and the time the expiration of the delay is detected. It is also possible to guarantee that if the task whose delay has expired has higher priority than all the other tasks it will resume execution as soon as the expiration of the delay is detected.

This section of the Annex tightens the core requirements on the implementation of delays, and requires documentation of implementation characteristics. These tighter semantics also apply to uses of delay statements within select statements. These tighter semantics will permit better prediction of application timing behavior.

Coordination with Real_Time.Clock

An important reason for a language to provide a standard clock is to present a view of time that is coordinated with the implementation of the delay statement. Without such coordination, the utility of both delays and the clock is significantly diminished.

The measurement of delays relative to a time reference that may be reset or adjusted (i.e. the time-of-day/calendar clock) is unacceptable, due to possible anomalies. In general, it may be necessary to adjust the calendar clock, for such things as leap-seconds or time zones. Maintaining a relationship between the actual delay duration and the time, relative to such a non-continuous clock, would make delays useless for most hard real-time applications, and would impose extra complexity on the delay implementation.

The specific requirements in this section for coordination with Real_Time.Clock are minimal, since a delay statement is only required to delay a task for "at least" a specified time. However, taken together, the metrics on delay accuracy and clock accuracy permit a user to determine more precisely how well coordinated delays are with Real_Time.Clock.

We also considered specifying a relationship between the clock resolution and the delay resolution. It is not reasonable to require that the delay resolution be at least as fine as that of the clock itself. The internal resolution can have very fine granularity if it is implemented via a hardware timer, much finer than the overhead of setting up a delay or reading the clock. If a periodic timer-generated interrupt is used to check for delay expirations, the interval between interrupts must be kept long enough to get useful work done; this limits delay granularity. If delay expirations are implemented via a programmed-interval timer, delay accuracy is limited by the overhead of receiving an interrupt and reprogramming the timer. It is possible to achieve finer granularity (without blocking) via execution of a timed sequence of "idle" instructions. This may provide delay resolution below the level of granularity achievable by a timer, provided the task is able to execute without preemption. Otherwise, if the task is preempted, it may delay longer than desired. To remain accurate in the face of preemption, the task could loop, reading the clock and comparing the clock value against the desired wake-up time; in this case, the precision is limited by the time it takes to execute an iteration of this loop. Of course, such busy-waiting techniques would not be sensible where delays are used within select statements, if the task is waiting for a rendezvous with a task that must execute on the same processor. It is not reasonable to require that the clock resolution be at least as fine as the delay resolution, either, since this could rule out the high-resolution delay implementation techniques described above.

Uniform Behavior Near Zero

A problem with timed entry calls was pointed out by the Third International Workshop on Real-Time Ada Issues [Baker 89]. Suppose the requested delay duration is a variable, and consider the effect of the timed entry call as the requested duration approaches zero from above. For large positive requests, an attempt will be made to perform a rendezvous. For small enough positive requests, an implementation is permitted to not make any attempt to rendezvous, on the presumption that simply determining whether a rendezvous is possible will take longer than the requested delay. The effect is that for small positive requests there will certainly be no rendezvous, and the total execution time of the timed entry call will be short. Then, as the requested delay approaches zero, the semantics change abruptly, back to what they would be for large positive requests (this is because of the conditional entry call semantics as specified in [RM95 9.7.2, 9.7.3]). The implementation must check whether a rendezvous is possible. This may take a long time. There is again a possibility of rendezvous, and the execution time of the timed call will be longer than it is for requests with small positive delays. An implementation that conforms to this Annex should avoid this anomalous behavior for small positive values, by always attempting to make a rendezvous (even if the requested duration is very short).

Similar issues come up with timed entry calls using the absolute form of the delay statement, and for delay alternatives in selective accept and asynchronous select statements. However, for asynchronous select statements, the required behavior is modelled after the case where an entry call replaces the delay statement. In this situation, if the entry call can proceed immediately, the abortable part never starts. Similarly, when the delay amount is zero, the alternative is chosen, and the abortable part does not start.

An Alternative Proposal

The Third International Workshop on Real-Time Ada Issues proposed a more detailed accuracy model for delays [Baker 89]. One possibility that we considered was to incorporate this approach into the implementation requirements. This proposal has not been adopted, because it is expressed in terms of events in the implementation that are not directly visible to the user, and it was believed to be too complex.

Documentation Requirements

The implementation is required to document the thresholds that it uses to determine whether a delay statement will result in the blocking of the task.

Metrics

The specifications given here are intended to allow enough flexibility that they can be applied to a variety of different implementation techniques.

The upper bound on the execution time of a relative delay statement with zero duration, and the execution time of an absolute delay whose wake-up time has already arrived, are intended to give the user an approximate idea of the minimum execution time overhead of the statement, excluding blocking.

The upper bounds on the lateness of delay statements are intended to give the user an idea of the accuracy with which delays are implemented. As with other upper bounds, its mere existence is actually more important than the precise value of the bound.

It is understood that these metrics will not expose the full implementation behavior. For example, if busy-wait delays are used for short durations, the granularity there may be much finer than further up the scale. The present metric ignores this issue. Likewise, if the hardware timer has limited range, a timer-task might be used for delays outside this range. Thus, there might be another shift in granularity farther out. The metrics chosen here do not require the implementor to expose such details. However, the implementor is free to provide more detailed information, by expressing the bound as a function of the requested delay.

D.10 Synchronous Task Control

During the 9X revision, the term *suspension* was replaced with *blocking* since it was considered to better describe the actual state (i.e. waiting for something to happen — being blocked as opposed to just being suspended). We recognize that traditionally suspend and resume were the common terms used when discussing these primitives. In this and the following section, we use the term *blocked* when referring to the "official" Ada state, and the term *suspended* when referring to the generic capability.

An important goal for Ada 95 was to allow protected objects for a simple suspend/resume mechanism that in turn could be used to build higher-level synchronization primitives. Here, by suspend, we mean the ability to block only the calling task itself, not another (for the latter, see the next section). Even for such a simple mechanism, some guarantees have to be made. This is commonly known as the *two-stage suspend* problem. (Strictly speaking, this name refers more to the solution, rather to the problem itself.) The problem that needs to be solved can be briefly described as follows. A task may want to block itself, after it has checked some data structure, and found that a particular system state is not present yet. The data structure is used by other tasks as well. One of these tasks will eventually set the data structure to the appropriate state and will resume the blocked task. Therefore, this data structure must be protected from concurrent access, i.e. a lock is needed. This in turn leads to the requirement that a task will be able to atomically release the lock and block itself. If it first releases the lock, the state might change just before it is about to be blocked (for example, the desired state may now be present, but there will be no way to detect it). On the other hand, if the task is blocked while still holding the lock, another task will not be able to access the shared data structure, and to record the new state — a deadlock.

If the state that is being waited upon can be easily expressed using a protected entry barrier expression, then such functionality already exists in the language. However, this is not always the case. When user-defined schedulers or servers are being implemented, it is often much more natural to separate the blocked state (and the corresponding operations) from the actual reason the task is waiting (it might be waiting for multiple events).

There are several approaches to solve this problem. They all depend on the kinds of primitives the underlying system provides.

1   Allow the calling task to suspend while it still holds the lock. When the task is suspended, it loses the lock, and has to reacquire it when it wakes up.

2   Register a *pending suspension* request while still holding the lock. After the task releases the lock (presumably soon after registering the request), it will be suspended.

3   Atomically clear a bit in the user space marking the suspension intention, and then suspend waiting for the bit to be set. A task wishing to resume the suspended task does so by atomically setting the bit. If the protocol of manipulating this bit is well-coordinated, such a technique can work safely and efficiently.

It is beyond the scope of this discussion to analyze the trade-offs of the approaches described above. For Ada 95, we have chosen the third approach mainly for its simplicity and the fact that it does not require any changes to the semantics of protected types and does not have complex interactions with other existing semantics. Here, the two-stage suspend means that first the task announces its intention to suspend itself, and then it actually does so. Between these two operations, the task is logically suspended as viewed by other tasks in the system, and so they may reliably resume it even before the actual suspension is done. For example, it would be wrong for the suspending task to clear the bit again without first checking its state to ensure that no other task has resumed it in the meantime. Failing to do so will effectively result in losing the resume operation.

Originally, we proposed to express the needed functionality as visible operations of a language-defined protected type. The abstraction presented by a simple protected type with Set_True and Set_False operations and a Suspend_Until_True entry, in addition to one boolean flag, seemed appropriate. Having this type known to the implementation would ensure that optimization was straightforward.

We rejected this idea for two reasons: a procedural interface enables the implementation to choose the most efficient technique by isolating this feature from the general support of the protected types. Second, by not having a visible protected entry for the Suspend_Until_True operation, the user is not able to use it in a select statement. While this may be considered as a loss of functionality, it has not been demonstrated that such functionality (timed, conditional, and asynchronous waits) is needed with such a low-level primitive. Not having to support the various kinds of select statements allows a much simpler, and hence, more efficient implementation.

The chosen solution is thus to make the suspension object of a private type with the operations described above (that is, Set_True, Set_False, and Suspend_Until_True). In addition, we provide a function Current_State to query the state of the object. This function should be used with care since the state may change asynchronously, and in particular, immediately after the function returns. We considered providing additional operations, to atomically change the state of the object and to return its previous state. We did not provide these operations since they really do not belong to this abstraction and we could not find a practical use for them; they were unreliable and they required an extra locking mechanism inside the implementation. This locking would be required when Set_False and Set_True (both with a return parameter) were called at the same time.

A suspension object can be viewed as a private binary semaphore in that it can be assumed to belong to one task only. This assumption is not enforced by the language, but a check is provided that only one task may wait on such an object at any point in time, Program_Error being raised if it fails. This rule makes it unnecessary to maintain a queue — a major saving in run-time cost.

A suspension object (or a pointer to it) can be passed to other components, thus indirectly maintaining the identity of the task that needs to be resumed when a certain state becomes true.

A typical example of the use of suspension objects is as follows

```
-- Assume that the protected object state
-- contains just a simple (protected) indication of the state;
-- the rest is elsewhere.

use Ada.Synchronous_Task_Control;
type Token is access all Suspension_Object;
protected State is
   procedure Check(T : in Token; Result : out Boolean);
   procedure Set(D : in Some_Data_Structure);
private
```

```ada
   Data : Some_State_Structure;
   Waiting_Task : Token;
end State;

protected body State is
   procedure Check(T : in Token; Result : out Boolean) is
   begin
      if Data = Desired_State then
         Result := True;
      else
         -- Mark intention to suspend
         Set_False(T.all);
         Waiting_Task := T;
         Result := False;
      end if;
   end Check;

   procedure Set(D : in Some_Data_Structure) is
   begin
      Data := D;
      if Data = Desired_State then
         if Waiting_Task /= null then
            -- Resume waiting task
            Set_True(Waiting_Task.all);
         end if;
      end if;
   end Set;
end State;

-- Task wishing to suspend
task body T1 is
   SO : aliased Suspension_Object;
   In_Desired_State : Boolean;
begin
   State.Check(SO'Unchecked_Access, In_Desired_State);
   if In_Desired_State then
      process-data
   else
      Suspend_Until_True(SO);        -- suspend
   end if;
   ...
end T1;

-- Another task detects that the waiting task needs
-- to be resumed
task body T2 is
   Data : Some_Data_Structure;
begin
   State.Set(Data);
end T2;
```

When Check is called by T1, the state is checked. If it is possible to continue, T1 does so and processes the data. Otherwise, T1 suspends itself until the object becomes true. When T2 updates a new state, it checks to see if the updated state is a desired one. If it is, and a task is waiting, it is resumed (Set_True). The new state is saved, so when T1 checks again, it will not have to be suspended. The important thing to remember is that it makes no difference whether the Set_True is called before or after the Suspend_Until_True. Since the semantics of suspension objects are defined to be persistent in the sense that there is a bit to keep the state, the suspending task will always notice the resume request.

D.11 Asynchronous Task Control

An important facility for some real-time aplications is a very low-level, simple, and efficient capability to suspend the execution of another task (and resume it later).

The core part of Ada 95 intentionally omitted this capability because of the well-known problems with integrating such a feature into a multi-tasking environment. The asynchronous transfer of control is the feature that comes closest to this requirement, but it is not the full answer; it requires cooperation of the "to-be-suspended" task, and does not allow the continuation of the affected task from exactly the same point where it was interrupted. There are very good reasons for these limitations in the general case. Suspending a task asynchronously at an arbitrary point is likely to leave the system state in an inconsistent state. This state would then become visible to the remaining tasks in the system. In addition, the interaction of such suspension with the other blocking primitives of the language is quite problematic (particularly, when priority scheduling is in effect).

In practice, two choices exist. One is to define the complete semantic model of such a feature and how it interacts with the rest of the language. Such a model would then require additions to the core and was believed to be very complex to understand and implement, especially for those users that do not need this capability. The other option is to leave all these interactions as implementation-defined. This is obviously undesirable since many of the benefits of standardizing such a capability would be lost. In addition, using such features is likely to move the program into the "erroneous zone", since the semantic model of tasking would not apply. Finally, and probably due to the above, experience with such primitives has proven in the past to be quite error-prone.

However, for a certain class of applications, such a capability is considered essential. These applications can be characterized as small, time-critical, and often safety-critical. They usually do not use the full power of the language, especially its tasking model. For certification reasons, as much as possible of the code needs to be visible in the actual program as opposed to be "hidden" inside the run-time system support supplied by the vendor. So even though this capability by itself may be considered unsafe, using it on top of a very simple run-time system, and applying strict guidelines, can make a system easier to certify. A final argument in favor of adding such a capability is that within certain application domains, this paradigm is well-understood, has been heavily used in the past, and is known to be implementable efficiently. Note that the issue of feature interaction with the rest of the tasking primitives is less of a concern here, since most of these primitives are not likely to be used by such an application.

Existing capabilities in the language and annexes allow a task to block itself until a specified state becomes true. This is not the same as a capability to asynchronously suspend another task. Because of this difference, the problems mentioned above, and issues concerning the best way to define such a feature in Ada, the straightforward approach of just defining a Suspend_Other primitive was rejected. Such an approach would necessitate introducing another task state ("suspended"), in addition to the existing states, and defining all the necessary interactions.

Instead, the approach taken by this Annex is based on the observation that a "suspend-other" capability is quite similar to the capability to lower a task's priority to a value that is so low as to effectively prevent the task from being dispatched. (In fact, using dynamic priorities is a known workaround to this problem, but it does not scale well to multiprocessors.)

The package Asynchronous_Task_Control introduces a conceptual *idle task* for each processor in the system, in addition to a priority level which is so low as to be below any other task in the system including the idle task. This level is also conceptual; it need not actually exist as a separate level in the ready queue. The Hold procedure is defined in terms of sources of priority inheritance. The general model of priority inheritance as defined in [RM95 D.3] states that the task's own base priority is always a source of priority inheritance. However, when the task is being held, its own base priority is no longer such a source, and instead the value of the special priority level becomes such a source. For reasons similar to those discussed in D.10, we do not want to stop the task's execution while it is inside a protected action. With this approach, a held task will still inherit the ceiling priority of the protected object in which it is executing, and will therefore continue to run until it leaves the protected action. When the task does not inherit any other priority, its active priority becomes lower than the conceptual task; therefore it does not run. The Continue operation simply changes the inheritance sources back to the default.

The benefit of this approach is that nothing else has to be said with respect to interactions with other tasking constructs. All the rules are ramifications of the above definitions and the general priority rules. (For a more detailed analysis of the various cases, see the notes in [RM95 D.11].) In this way, no additional mechanism is needed in the run-time system, and the feature can be implemented efficiently while still presenting a consistent and safe interface to the user. For implementation flexibility, nothing in this section really requires the use of dynamic priorities inside the implementation; priorities are used just to describe the semantic model. A straightforward implementation approach that uses traditional states is therefore possible.

D.12 Other Optimization and Determinism Rules

This section of the Annex describes various requirements for improving the response and determinism in a real-time system.

The maximum duration that interrupts are blocked by the implementation (in supporting the language features) must be bounded and documented. Clearly, this value is very important to the application for schedulability analysis. In addition, a real-time application often needs to interact with an external device at a certain frequency. If the implementation-induced interrupt blocking time is too long, such a device interface is not feasible.

Another requirement addresses the problem of the storage associated with terminated tasks. In a real-time system, tasks are often allocated using a library-level access type, and their storage is sometimes released only upon exit from the access type's scope. In this case, this will mean not until the partition as a whole terminates, which is clearly too late. Ada 83 did not require Unchecked_Deallocation of tasks to actually release the task's storage, and this is the motivation for the new requirement.

When a protected object does not have entries, it acts similarly to a simple lock (mutex) abstraction with no need for any overhead associated with checking barriers and servicing queues. It is expected that such protected objects will be used heavily by concurrent applications to achieve simple mutual exclusion. It is therefore important that implementations will recognize such cases, and avoid any unnecessary run-time costs. In general, performance can be neither legislated nor validated; the purpose of the requirement is to direct the attention of implementors to this important case. The corresponding metrics are provided for the purpose of exposing the degree to which such an optimization is carried out in a given implementation.

D.13 Requirements Summary

The requirements

>   *R5.1-A(1) — Elapsed Time Measurement*

>   *R5.1-B(1) — Precise Periodic Execution*

are met by the introduction of Real_Time.Time and the precise requirements on the delay statement.

The requirement

>   *R5.2-A(1) — Alternative Scheduling Algorithms*

is generally addressed by the various pragmas such as `Task_Dispatching_Policy`, `Locking_Policy` and `Queueing_Policy` plus the facilities for priority control. The packages for synchronous and asynchronous task control provide facilities for special techniques.

E Distributed Systems

The Ada 95 model for programming distributed systems specifies a partition as the unit of distribution. A partition comprises an aggregation of library units that executes in a distributed target execution environment. Typically, each partition corresponds to a single execution site, and all its constituent units occupy the same logical address space. The principal interface between partitions is one or more package specifications. The semantic model specifies rules for partition composition, elaboration, execution, and interpartition communication. Support for the configuration of partitions to the target execution environment and its associated communication connectivity is not explicitly specified in the model.

The rationale for this model derives from the Ada 9X Requirements for Distributed Processing (see R8.1-A(1) and R8.2-A(1)); namely, that the language shall facilitate the distribution and dynamic reconfiguration of Ada applications across a homogeneous distributed architecture. These requirements are satisfied by a blend of implementor- and user-provided (or third-party) capabilities.

In addition, the following properties are considered essential to specifying a model for distributed program execution:

*   The differences between developing a distributed versus a nondistributed system should be minimal. In particular, the same paradigms, rules for type safety, and interface consistency for a nondistributed system should apply to a distributed system. Furthermore, it must be possible to partition an Ada library for varying distributed configurations without recompilation.

*   The implementation should be straightforward. In particular, the run-time system of each partition should be autonomous. In this way, robust type-safe distributed systems can be implemented using off-the-shelf Ada compilers that support the model, rather than depending upon custom adaptations of a compiler to a specific distributed environment.

*   The partitioning should be separated from the details of the communications network architecture supporting the distributed system. Similarly, inter-partition communication should avoid specifying protocols more appropriately provided by an application or by standard layers of the network communications software.

*   The model should facilitate programming fault-tolerant applications to the extent that an active partition failure should not cause the distributed program to fail. In particular, it should be possible to replace the services provided by a failed partition with those of a replacement partition.

*   The model should be compatible with other standards that support open distributed applications.

The requirements and properties are satisfied in the Annex by specifying a simple, consistent, and systematic approach towards composing distributed systems based upon the partition concept. Partitions are specified before runtime, usually during or after the linking step. Programming the cooperation among partitions is achieved by library units defined to allow access to data and subprograms in different partitions. These library units are identified at compile-time by categorization pragmas. In this way, strong typing and unit consistency is maintained across a distributed system. Finally, separation of implementor and user responsibility is allowed by specifying a common interface to a partition communication subsystem (PCS) that performs message passing among partitions. The PCS is internally responsible for all routing decisions, low-level message protocols, etc. By separating the responsibilities, an implementation need not be aware of the specific network connectivity supporting the distributed system, while the communication subsystem need not be aware of the types of data being exchanged.

E.1 The Partition Model

An Ada 83 program corresponds to an Ada 95 active partition (see below); an Ada 95 program is defined in [RM95 10.2] as a set of one or more partitions. The description in the Core is kept purposefully non-specific to allow many different approaches to partitioning a distributed program, either statically or dynamically.   In the Annex, certain minimal capabilities are specified to enhance portability of distributed systems across implementations that conform to these specifications.

This Annex develops the partitioning concept for distributed systems in terms of *active* and *passive* partitions. The library units comprising an active partition reside and execute upon the same processing node. In contrast, library units comprising a passive partition reside at a storage node that is accessible to the processing nodes of different active partitions that reference them. Library units comprising a passive partition are restricted to ensure that no remote access (such as for data) is possible and that no thread of control is needed (since no processing capabilities are available and no tasking runtime system exists in such a partition). Thus, a passive partition provides a straightforward abstraction for representing an address space that is shared among different processing nodes (execution sites).

It is implementation-defined (and must therefore be documented) whether or not more than one partition may be associated with one processing or storage node. The characteristics of these nodes are target dependent and are outside the scope of the Annex.

Similar to an Ada 83 program, each active partition is associated with an environment task that elaborates the library units comprising the partition. This environment task calls the main subprogram, if present, for execution and then awaits the termination of all tasks that depend upon the library units of the partition. Therefore, there is no substantive difference between an active partition and an Ada 83 program.

A partition is identified as either active or passive by the post-compilation (link-time) aggregation of library units. Post-compilation tools provide the necessary functionality for composing partitions, linking the library units of a partition, and for resolving the identities of other partitions. A passive partition may include only shared passive and pure library units.

By naming a shared passive library unit (which resides in a passive partition) in a context clause, the referencing unit gains access to data and code that may be shared with other partitions. Different active partitions (executing on separate nodes) may thus share protected data or call subprograms declared in such shared passive library units. An active partition can obtain mutually exclusive access to data in a shared partition package if the data is encapsulated in a protected object or is specified as atomic.

An active partition may call subprograms in other active partitions. Calls to subprograms in a different active partition are allowed only if the called subprogram is declared in a library unit with a `Remote_Call_Interface` pragma. Each active partition calling the subprogram must name the corresponding remote call interface (RCI) library unit in its context clause. So we might have

```
package A is                        -- in one active partition
   pragma Remote_Call_Interface(A);
   procedure P( ... );
   ...
end A;

--------------
```

```
with A;
package B is                              -- in another active partition
   ...
      A.P( ... );                         -- a remote call
   ...
end B;
```

When an active partition calls such a subprogram, the call is termed a remote procedure call (RPC). Stubs are inserted in the calling code and in the called code to perform the remote communication; these are termed the calling stub and receiving stub respectively. In addition, an asynchronous procedure call capability is provided to allow the caller and the remote subprogram to execute independently once the call has been sent to the remote partition.

The categorization of library units establishes potential interfaces through which the partitions of a distributed system may cooperate. In a distributed system where no remote subprogram calls or shared library units are required, e.g., all inter-partition data is exchanged through other communication facilities, library unit categorization is unnecessary. In such a case the multipartition program is similar to the multiprogramming approach allowed by Ada 83 (using a set of quite distinct programs).

The library unit categorization and link-time identification of partitions provides a flexible and straightforward approach for partitioning the library units of an Ada program library. Library units may be aggregated to form partitions exploiting the target execution environment for the distributed system, with the single stipulation that any given shared passive or RCI library unit may be assigned to only one partition. Different distributed configurations of the same target execution environment may then be supported by a single version of an Ada library. (A change to the configuration does not require recompilation of library units.) Library units are elaborated and executed within the context of the environment task associated with the active partition, and until they communicate with another partition, their execution proceeds independently (since all the library units in a passive partition must be preelaborated, the environment task in such a partition is purely conceptual).

The runtime system of each active partition is independent of all other runtime systems in a multi-partition program. This is achieved by first disallowing tasks and protected types with entries in the visible parts of the interface library units, and second, by declaring the library units Calendar and Real_Time, as well as the subtype Priority, as local to each active partition. In consequence, tasks (and hence entry queues) are not visible across partitions. This allows each active partition to manage its own tasking subsystem independently, avoiding such complexities as remote rendezvous, distributed time management, and distributed activation and termination management. (Protected objects without entries are allowed in passive partitions, since access to their data requires only a simple mutual-exclusion, a capability assumed to be present for a passive partition.)

Mechanisms to specify the allocation of partitions to the target execution environment are not included in the Annex; similarly, the dynamic creation and replication of partitions is not explicitly specified. These capabilities are deemed beyond the scope of the requirements. However, because partition replication is essential towards programming fault-tolerant applications, remote calls may be directed to different partitions using one of the two forms of dynamic binding, by dereferencing an access-to-subprogram object or access-to-class-wide tagged object. Thus, implementations that support the replication of partitions can allow a failed partition to be replaced transparently to other partitions.

In summary, this approach allows for flexible, link-time partitioning, with type-safety ensured at compile-time. The model separates categorization and partitioning from configuration and communication thus promoting compiler/linker independence from the target execution environment. The objective is to maintain the properties of a single Ada program for distributed execution with minimal additional semantic and implementation complexity. Fundamental to this objective is the ability to dynamically call remote subprograms.

E.2 Categorization of Library Units

Several library unit categorization pragmas exist. They are

```
pragma Shared_Passive( ... );
pragma Remote_Types( ... );
pragma Remote_Call_Interface( ... );
```

where in each case the optional parameter simply names the library unit. These pragmas identify library units used to access the types, data, and subprograms of other partitions. In other words, the library units that are associated with categorization pragmas provide the visible interface to the partitions to which they are assigned.   These pragmas place specific restrictions upon the declarations that may appear in the visible part of the associated library units and the other library units that they may name in their context clauses. In addition, such library units are preelaborated.

The pragma Pure, which is defined in the core since it also relates to preelaboration, is also important for distribution and has the most severe restrictions.

The various categories form a hierarchy, in the order given above with Pure at the top. Each can only "with" units in its own or higher categories (although the bodies of the last two are not restricted).   Thus a package marked as Shared_Passive can only with packages marked as Shared_Passive or Pure.

Restricting the kinds of declarations that may be present in such library units simplifies the semantic model and reduces the need for additional checking when the library unit is named in the context clause of another library unit.   For example, by disallowing task declarations (and protected types with entries), we avoid the interaction among the run-time systems of different partitions that is required to support entry calls across partitions.

Pure library units [RM95 10.2.1] may be named in the context clauses of other interface library units. For example, a pure library unit may contain type declarations that are used in the formal parameter specifications of subprograms in RCI library units.   To achieve remote dispatching, a library unit specified with pragma Pure must declare the corresponding dispatching operations. Such a library unit is replicated in all referencing partitions. The properties of a pure library unit allow it to be replicated consistently in any partition that references it, since it has no variable state that may alter its behavior.

When no categorization pragma is associated with a library unit, such a unit is considered normal; it may be included in multiple active partitions with no restrictions on its visible part. Unlike a pure library unit, replication of such a unit in different partitions does not necessarily maintain a consistent state. The state of the unit in each partition is independent.

E.2.1 Shared Passive Library Units

The rules for a shared passive library unit ensure that calling any of its subprograms from another partition cannot result in an implicit remote call, either directly or indirectly.   Moreover, the restrictions eliminate the need for a run-time system (e.g., to support scheduling or real-time clocks) to be associated with a passive partition. Thus a passive partition corresponds to a logical address space that is common to all partitions that reference its constituent library units.

As mentioned earlier, a shared passive unit must be preelaborable and can only depend on pure and other shared passive units. There are also restrictions on access type declarations which ensure that it is not possible to create an access value referring back to an active partition.

E.2.2 Remote Types Library Units

Originally, this Annex provided only the Shared_Passive and Remote_Call_Interface pragmas (in addition to the core pragma Pure). However, this omitted an important functionality.

Often one needs to be able to pass access values among partitions. Usually, such access values have no meaning outside their original partition (since their designated object is still in that partition). Hence we generally disallow access types for remote subprograms' formal parameters. However, there are cases in which the access type has a user-defined meaning (such as a handle to a system-wide resource) that can be "understood" in other partitions as well. Since the implementation is not aware of such a meaning, the user must supply specific Read and Write attributes to allow the meaningful transfer of the information embodied in such access values. In addition, such a library unit often needs to be able to maintain specific (per-partition) state, to support such conversions. This is the main reason for introducing the Remote_Types categorization pragma. The restrictions enforced by this pragma are quite similar to those enforced by pragma Pure; a separate copy of a remote types package is placed in every partition that references it. Since a remote types library unit may be withed by a remote call interface, the types declared in the former may be used as formals of remote subprograms.

E.2.3 Remote Call Interface Library Units

For RCI library units the restrictions ensure that no remote accesses need be supported, other than remote procedure calls. These calls may be

- direct, through static binding,

- indirect, through a remote access to subprogram type,

- dispatching, through a remote access to class wide type.

Furthermore, the types of all formal parameters may be converted to and from a message stream type using the Write and Read attributes respectively [RM95 13.13.2]. This message stream type is the primary interface to the partition communication subsystem.

Child library units of an RCI library unit must be assigned to the same partition as the RCI library unit. As a consequence, visible child library units of an RCI library unit have the same restrictions as RCI library units. That is, the private part and the body of a child library unit have visibility to the private part of the parent. Thus a child library unit, unless included in the same partition as its parent, may make an unsupported remote access to its parent's private part. By constraining a child to the same partition, its visible part must be as restricted as the root RCI library unit.

The support for remote call interface library units is optional in the Annex, since RPC is not always the appropriate communication paradigm for a particular application. The other capabilities introduced by this Annex might still be useful in such a case.

Pragma All_Calls_Remote

For some applications, it is necessary that the partition communication subsystem get control on each remote procedure call. There are several motivations for such a requirement, including support for debugging (for example, isolating problems to either the PCS or to the generated code) and the need in some circumstances to have the PCS perform application-specific processing (e.g. supporting broadcasts) on each remote call. For such techniques to be feasible, users need to be assured that remote calls are never "optimized away". This can be assured by inserting

```
pragma All_Calls_Remote;
```

in the unit concerned.

Note that opportunities for such optimizations arise often, for example when the calling library unit and the called RCI library unit are assigned to the same active partition. In such cases, the linker can transform the remote call to a local call, thereby bypassing the stubs and the PCS. (In fact, such an optimization is extremely important in general, to allow the design of library units independent of their eventual location.) Similar optimization is possible (although probably not as straightforward) when multiple active partitions are configured on the same processing node.

When a call on a subprogram declared in the visible part of an RCI library unit (usually a remote call) is generated from either the body of that library unit or from one of its children, it is always guaranteed to be local (regardless of the specific configuration). This is because the Annex rules ensure that all corresponding units end up in the same partition. For this reason, the All_Calls_Remote pragma does not apply to such calls, and they remain local. Doing otherwise would constitute a change of the program semantics (forcing a local call to be remote), would introduce implementation difficulties in treating otherwise normal procedure calls as special, and would introduce semantic difficulties in ensuring that such a local-turned-remote call did not violate the privacy rules that guarantee that remote references are not possible.

E.3 Consistency of a Distributed System

Consistency is based on the concept of a version of a compilation unit. The exact meaning of version is necessarily implementation-defined, and might correspond to a compilation time stamp, or a closure over the source text revision stamps of all of the semantic dependences of the unit.

E.4 Remote Subprogram Calls

RCI library units allow communication among partitions of a distributed system based upon extending the well-known remote procedure call (RPC) paradigm. This is consistent with the ISO RPC Committee Draft that presents a proposed RPC Interaction Model (see subsequent section) and Communication Model for cooperating applications in a distributed system. Calls to remote partitions may be bound either statically or dynamically.

The task executing a synchronous remote call suspends until the call is completed. Remote calls are executed with at-most-once semantics (i.e., the called subprogram is executed at most once; if a successful response is returned, the called subprogram is executed exactly once). If an exception is raised in executing the body of a remote subprogram, the exception is propagated to the calling partition.

Unless the pragma Asynchronous (see below) is associated with a procedure (for a direct call) or an access type (for an indirect call), the semantics of a call to a remote subprogram are nearly identical to the semantics of the same subprogram called locally. This allows users to develop a distributed program where a subprogram call and the called subprogram may be in the same or different partitions. The location of the subprogram body, determined when the program is partitioned, only affects performance.

The exception System.RPC.Communication_Error may be raised by the PCS (the package System.RPC is the interface to the PCS). This exception allows the caller to provide a handler in response to the failure of a remote call as opposed to the result of executing the body of the remote subprogram; for example, if the partition containing the remote subprogram has become inaccessible or has terminated. This exception may be raised for both synchronous and asynchronous remote calls. For asynchronous calls, the exception is raised no later than when control would be returned normally to the caller; any failure after that point is invisible to the caller.

E.4.1 Pragma Asynchronous

An asynchronous form of interaction among partitions is provided by associating the pragma `Asynchronous` with a procedure accessible through an RCI library unit. Thus using the previous example we might write

```
package A is
   pragma Remote_Call_Interface(A);
   procedure P( ... );
   pragma Asynchronous(P);
   ...
end A;
```

When this pragma is present, a procedure call may return without awaiting the completion of the remote subprogram (the task in the calling partition is not suspended waiting the completion of the procedure). This extends the utility of the remote procedure call paradigm to exploit the underlying asynchronism that may be available through the PCS. As a consequence, synchronous and asynchronous interactions among partitions are maintained at a consistent level of abstraction; an agent task is not required to await the completion of a remote call when asynchronism is desired. Asynchronous procedure calls are necessarily restricted to procedures with all parameters of mode in (and of course a function cannot be asynchronous).

Unhandled exceptions raised while executing an asynchronous remote procedure are not propagated to the calling partition but simply lost. When the call and called procedure are in the same partition, the normal synchronous call semantics apply.

The use of asynchronous procedure calls, when combined with the capability to dynamically bind calls using remote access values, allows the programming of efficient communication paradigms. For example, an asynchronous procedure call may pass a remote access value designating a procedure (in the sending partition) to be called upon completion. In this way, the results of the asynchronous call may be returned in some application-specific way.

E.5 Post-Compilation Partitioning

Aggregating library units into partitions of a distributed system is done after the units have been compiled. This post-compilation approach entails rules for constructing active and passive partitions. These rules ensure that a distributed system is semantically consistent with a nondistributed system comprising the same library units. Moreover, the required implementation is within the capability of current post-compilation tools. Therefore, in order to allow the use of existing tools and to avoid constraining future tools, the Annex omits specifying a particular method for constructing partitions.

Each RCI library unit may only be assigned to a single active partition. Similarly, each shared passive library unit may only be assigned to a single passive partition. Following the assignment of a library unit to a partition, a value for the attribute `Partition_ID` is available that identifies the partition after it is elaborated. (This attribute corresponds to values of the type `Partition_ID` declared in `System.RPC`; see E.7. This library unit provides the interface to the PCS; however, it is not required that this unit be visible to the partition using the attribute and hence the attribute returns *universal_integer*.)

In order to construct a partition, all RCI and shared passive library units must be explicitly assigned to a partition. Consequently, when a partition is elaborated, the `Partition_ID` attribute for each RCI or shared passive library unit referenced by this partition has a known value. The construction is completed by including in a partition all the other units that are needed for execution.

An exception is that a shared passive library unit is included in one partition only. Similarly, the body of an RCI library unit is in one partition only; however the specification of an RCI library unit is included in each referencing partition (with the code for the body replaced by the calling stubs).

A library unit that is neither an RCI nor shared passive library unit may be included in more than one partition. Unlike a nondistributed system, a normal library unit does not have a consistent state across all partitions. For example, the package Calendar does not synchronize the value returned by the Clock function among all partitions that include the package.

A type declaration within the visible part of a library unit elaborated in multiple partitions yields matching types. For pure, RCI, and shared passive library units, this follows either from the rule requiring library unit preelaboration (RCI and shared passive) or the restrictions on their declarations. For normal library units, since non-tagged types are not visible across partitions, this matching is of little significance. However, a special check is performed when passing a parameter of a class-wide type to make sure that the tag identifies a specific type declared in a pure or shared passive library unit, or the visible part of a remote types or RCI library unit. Type extensions declared elsewhere (in the body of a remote types or RCI library unit, or anywhere in a normal library unit) might have a different structure in different partitions, because of dependence on partition-specific information. This check prevents passing parameters of such a type extension, to avoid erroneous execution due to a mismatch in representation between the sending and the receiving partition. An attempt to pass such a parameter to a remote subprogram will raise Program_Error at run-time. For example, consider the following declarations:

```
package Pure_Pkg is
   pragma Pure;
   type Root_Type is tagged ...
   ...
end Pure_Pkg;

with Pure_Pkg;
package RCI_Pkg is
   pragma Remote_Call_Interface;
   -- Class-wide operation
   procedure Cw_OP(Cw : in Pure_Pkg.Root_Type'Class);
end RCI_Pkg;

with Pure_Pkg;
package Normal_Pkg is
   ...
   type Specific_Type is new Pure_Pkg.Root_Type with
      record
         Vector : Vector_Type(1 .. Dynamic_Value);
      end record;
end Normal_Pkg;

with RCI_Pkg;
package body Normal_Pkg is
   Value : Specific_Type;
begin
   -- The following call will result in Program_Error
   -- when the subprogram body is executed remotely.
   RCI_Pkg.Cw_OP(Cw => Value);
end Normal_Pkg;
```

In the above example, if Normal_Pkg is included in a partition that is not assigned RCI_Pkg, then a call to Cw_OP will result in a remote call. When this call is executed in the remote partition, Program_Error is raised.

The following library units are a simple example of a distributed system that illustrate the post-compilation partitioning approach. In this particular example, the system uses mailboxes to exchange data among its partitions. Each partition determines the mailbox of its cooperating partitions by calling a subprogram specified in an RCI library unit.

The mailboxes for each partition are represented as protected types. Objects of the protected types are allocated in a shared passive library unit. RCI library units (instantiations of Gen_Mbx_Pkg) are included in active partitions, and they with the shared passive package Ptr_Mbx_Pkg. When an allocator for Ptr_Safe_Mbox is executed (on behalf of a library unit in another partition), the protected object is allocated in the passive partition, making it accessible to other partitions. Consequently, no remote access is required to use mailbox data. However, to access a mailbox of another partition, a remote subprogram call is required initially.

```ada
package Mbx_Pkg is
   pragma Pure;
   type Msg_Type is ...
   type Msg_Array is array (Positive range <>) of Msg_Type;
   type Key_Type is new Integer;

   protected type Safe_Mbx(Lock : Key_Type;
                           Size : Positive) is
      procedure Post(Note : in Msg_Type);
      -- Post a note in the mailbox
      procedure Read(Lock : in Key_Type;
                     Note : out Msg_Type);
      -- Read a note from the mailbox if caller has key
   private
      Key : Key_Type := Lock;
      Mbx : Msg_Array(1 .. Size);
   end Safe_Mbx;
end Mbx_Pkg;

with Mbx_Pkg;
package Ptr_Mbx_Pkg is
   pragma Shared_Passive;
   type Ptr_Safe_Mbx is access Mbx_Pkg.Safe_Mbx;
   -- All mailboxes are allocated in a passive partition and
   -- therefore remote access is not required.
end Ptr_Mbx_Pkg;

with Mbx_Pkg;
with Ptr_Mbx_Pkg;
generic
   Mbx_Size : Positive;
   Ptn_Lock : Mbx_Pkg.Key_Type;
package Gen_Mbx_Pkg is
   -- This package creates a mailbox and makes the
   -- access value designating it available through
   -- a remote subprogram call.
   pragma Remote_Call_Interface;
   function Use_Mbx return Ptr_Mbx_Pkg.Ptr_Safe_Mbx;
end Gen_Mbx_Pkg;

with Mbx_Pkg;
package body Gen_Mbx_Pkg is
   New_Mbx : Ptr_Mbx_Pkg.Ptr_Safe_Mbx :=
                    new Mbx_Pkg.Safe_Mbx(Ptn_Lock, Mbx_Size);
   -- A mailbox is created in the passive partition.
   -- The key to read from the mailbox is the elaborating
   -- partition's identity.
   function Use_Mbx return Ptr_Mbx_Pkg.Ptr_Safe_Mbx is
```

```
        -- The access value designating the created mailbox is
        -- made available to the calling unit.
        begin
           return New_Mbx;
        end Use_Mbx;
    end Gen_Mbx_Pkg;

    with Ptr_Mbx_Pkg, Gen_Mbx_Pkg;
    package RCI_1 is
        -- This package is the interface to a set of library units that
        -- is conveniently identified by the library unit Closure_1.
        pragma Remote_Call_Interface;
        package Use_Mbx_Pkg is new Gen_Mbx_Pkg(1_000, RCI_1'Partition_ID);
        function Use_Mbx return Ptr_Mbx_Pkg.Ptr_Safe_Mbx
           renames Use_Mbx_Pkg.Use_Mbx;
        -- All partitions include this remote subprogram in
        -- their interface.
        ...
    end RCI_1;

    with Ptr_Mbx_Pkg, Gen_Mbx_Pkg;
    package RCI_2 is
        -- This package is the interface to a set of library units that
        -- is conveniently identified by the library unit Closure_2.
        pragma Remote_Call_Interface;
        ...
    end RCI_2;

    with Ptr_Mbx_Pkg, Gen_Mbx_Pkg;
    package RCI_3 is
        -- This package is the interface to a set of library units that
        -- is conveniently identified by the library unit Closure_3.
        pragma Remote_Call_Interface;
        ...
    end RCI_3;

    with Closure_1;
        -- Names library units that execute locally.
    with RCI_2, RCI_3;
      -- Names RCI packages for interfacing to other
      -- partitions executing at different sites.
    package body RCI_1 is
        My_Mbx : Ptr_Mbx_Pkg.Ptr_Safe_Mbx := Use_Mbx_Pkg.Use_Mbx;
        Mbx_2,
        Mbx_3 : Ptr_Mbx_Pkg.Ptr_Safe_Mbx;
        ...
        -- Obtain access values to other partition mailboxes.
        -- For example
        Mbx_2 := RCI_2.Use_Mbx;
        Mbx_3 := RCI_3.Use_Mbx;
        ...
        My_Mbx.Read(RCI_1'Partition_ID, Next_Note);
        Mbx_2.Post(Next_Note);
        Mbx_3.Post(Next_Note);
        -- Read note in local mailbox and pass to other mailboxes.
        ...
    end RCI_1;
```

```
with Closure_2;
   -- Names library units that execute locally.
with RCI_1, RCI_3;
   -- Names RCI packages for interfacing to other
   -- partitions executing at different sites.
package body RCI_2 is
   ...
   -- Obtain access values to other partition mailboxes.
   -- For example
   Mbx_1 := RCI_1.Use_Mbx;
   Mbx_3 := RCI_3.Use_Mbx;
   ...
end RCI_2;

with Closure_3;
   -- Names library units that execute locally.
with RCI_1, RCI_2;
   -- Names RCI packages for interfacing to other
   -- partitions executing at different sites.
package body RCI_3 is
   ...
   -- Obtain access values to other partition mailboxes.
   -- For example
   Mbx_1 := RCI_1.Use_Mbx;
   Mbx_2 := RCI_2.Use_Mbx;
   ...
end RCI_3;
```

The following post-compilation partitioning support is implementation defined; the syntax is for illustration only. Several possible combinations for partitioning are presented. In each combination, the first partition specified is a passive partition where the mailboxes are allocated. This partition is accessible to other partitions by simply calling the protected operations of the mailbox.

The minimally distributed partitioning comprises two partitions; one passive partition and one active partition. All RCI library units in the application are assigned to a single active partition. There would be no remote calls executed as a result of this partitioning.

```
Partition(Ptn => 0, Assign => (Ptr_Mbx_Pkg))            -- passive
Partition(Ptn => 1, Assign => (RCI_1, RCI_2, RCI_3))    -- active
```

A more distributed version comprises three partitions. The RCI library units in the application are assigned to two active partitions.

```
Partition(Ptn => 0, Assign => (Ptr_Mbx_Pkg))    -- passive
Partition(Ptn => 1, Assign => (RCI_1))          -- active
Partition(Ptn => 2, Assign => (RCI_2, RCI_3))   -- active
```

A fully distributed version comprises four partitions. The RCI library units in the application are assigned to three active partitions.

```
Partition(Ptn => 0, Assign => (Ptr_Mbx_Pkg))    -- passive
Partition(Ptn => 1, Assign => (RCI_1))          -- active
Partition(Ptn => 2, Assign => (RCI_2))          -- active
Partition(Ptn => 3, Assign => (RCI_3))          -- active
```

Note that there is no need to mention the pure unit Mbx_Pkg because it can be replicated as necessary. Moreover, generic units do not have to be mentioned since it is only their instances that really exist.

E.5.1 Dynamically Bound Remote Subprogram Calls

In Ada 95, the core language supports dynamically bound subprogram calls. For example, a program may dereference an access-to-subprogram object and call the designated subprogram, or it may dispatch by dereferencing an access-to-class-wide type controlling operand. These two forms of dynamic binding are also allowed in distributed systems to support the programming of fault-tolerant applications and changes in communication topology. For example, through dynamically bound calls, a distributed program may reference subprograms in replicated partitions to safeguard against the failure of active partitions. In the event of a failure in a called active partition, the caller can simply redirect the call to a subprogram backup partition.

An advantage of these two forms of dynamic binding is that they relax the requirement for library units in the the calling partition to semantically depend on the library units containing the actual remote subprograms. Partitions need only name an RCI or Remote-Types library unit that includes the declaration of an appropriate general access type; objects of such types may contain remote access values.

A remote access value designating a subprogram allows naming a subprogram indirectly. The remote access value is restricted to designating subprograms declared in RCI library units. This ensures that the appropriate stubs for the designated subprograms exist in a receiving (server) partition. In order to pass remote access values designating subprograms among partitions, subprograms declared in RCI library units may specify formal parameters of access-to-subprogram types.

The remote access-to-class-wide type provides an alternative dynamic binding capability that facilitates encapsulating both data and operations. The remotely callable subprograms are specified as the primitive operations of a tagged limited type declared in a pure library unit. In an RCI or Remote-Types library unit, a general access type designating the class-wide type is declared; this declaration allows the corresponding primitive operations to be remote dispatching operations when overridden. Similar to the binding using access-to-subprogram types, library units in the calling partition need only include the RCI or Remote-Types library unit (that declares the access-to-class-wide type) in their context clause in order to dispatch to subprograms in library units included in other active partitions.

By restricting dereferencing of such remote access values to occur as part of a dispatching operation, there is no need to deal with remote addresses elsewhere. The existing model for dispatching operations corresponds quite closely to the dispatching model proposed for the linker-provided RPC-receiver procedure suggested in [RM95 E.4].

These dynamic binding capabilities are enhanced further when combined with a name server partition. Typically, the name server partition provides a central repository of remote access values. When a remote access value is made available to a client partition, the value can be dereferenced to execute a remote subprogram call. This avoids a link-time dependence on the requested service and achieves the dynamic binding typical of a client/server paradigm.

The following library units illustrate the use of access-to-class-wide types to implement a simple distributed system. The system comprises multiple client partitions, which are instantiations of Client_Ptn, a mailbox server partition named Mbx_Server_Ptn, and two partitions to access local and wide-area network mailboxes named Lan_Mbx_Ptn and Wan_Mbx_Ptn respectively. A client partition may communicate with other partitions in the distributed system through a mailbox that it is assigned by the mailbox server. It may post a message to its mailbox for delivery to another partition (based on the address in the message), or wait for a message to be delivered to its mailbox. A client may be connected either to the LAN or the WAN, but this is transparent to the application.

```ada
package Mbx_Pkg is
   pragma Pure;
   type Mail_Type is ...
   type Mbx_Type is abstract tagged limited private;
   procedure  Post(Mail : in Mail_Type;
                   Mbx  : access Mbx_Type) is abstract;
   procedure  Wait(Mail : out Mail_Type;
                   Mbx  : access Mbx_Type) is abstract;
private
   type Mbx_Type is abstract tagged limited null record;
end Mbx_Pkg;

with Mbx_Pkg; use Mbx_Pkg;
package Mbx_Server_Ptn is
   pragma Remote_Call_Interface;
   type Ptr_Mbx_Type is access all Mbx_Type'Class;
   function Rmt_Mbx return Ptr_Mbx_Type;
end Mbx_Server_Ptn;

with Mbx_Server_Ptn;
package Lan_Mbx_Ptn is
   pragma Remote_Call_Interface;
   function New_Mbx return Mbx_Server_Ptn.Ptr_Mbx_Type;
end Lan_Mbx_Ptn;

with Mbx_Server_Ptn;
package Wan_Mbx_Ptn is
   pragma Remote_Call_Interface;
   function New_Mbx return Mbx_Server_Ptn.Ptr_Mbx_Type;
end Wan_Mbx_Ptn;

with Mbx_Pkg;
package body Lan_Mbx_Ptn is
   type Lan_Mbx_Type is new Mbx_Pkg.Mbx_Type with ...;

   procedure Post(Mail : in Mail_Type;
                  Mbx  : access Lan_Mbx_Type);
   procedure Wait(Mail : out Mail_Type;
                  Mbx  : access Lan_Mbx_Type);
   ...

   function New_Mbx return Ptr_Mbx_Type is
   begin
      return new Lan_Mbx_Type;
   end New_Mbx;
end Lan_Mbx_Ptn;

with Mbx_Pkg;
package body Wan_Mbx_Ptn is ...

with Lan_Mbx_Ptn, Wan_Mbx_Ptn;
package body Mbx_Server_Ptn is
   function Rmt_Mbx return Ptr_Mbx_Type is
   begin
      if ... then
         return Lan_Mbx_Ptn.New_Mbx;
      elsif ... then
         return Wan_Mbx_Ptn.New_Mbx;
      else
```

```
            return null;
         end if;
      end Rmt_Mbx;
end Mbx_Server_Ptn;

   -- The client partitions do not need to with the specific
   -- LAN/WAN mailbox interface packages.
with Mbx_Pkg, Mbx_Server_Ptn, ...
use Mbx_Pkg, Mbx_Server_Ptn, ...
procedure Use_Mbx is
   Some_Mail : Mail_Type;
   This_Mbx  : Ptr_Mbx_Type := Rmt_Mbx;
   -- Get a mailbox pointer for this partition
begin
   ...
   Post(Some_Mail, This_Mbx);
   -- Dereferencing controlling operand This_Mbx
   -- causes remote call as part of Post's dispatching
   ...
   Wait(Some_Mail, This_Mbx);
   ...
end Use_Mbx;

generic
   ...
package Client_Ptn is
   pragma Remote_Call_Interface;
end Client_Ptn;

with Use_Mbx;
package body Client_Ptn is
begin
   ...
end Client_Ptn;

package Client_Ptn_1 is new Client_Ptn ...
...
package Client_Ptn_N is new Client_Ptn ...

   -- Post-compilation partitioning
Partition(Ptn => 0, Assign => (Mbx_Server_Ptn))
Partition(Ptn => 1, Assign => (Lan_Mbx_Ptn))
Partition(Ptn => 2, Assign => (Wan_Mbx_Ptn))
Partition(Ptn => 3, Assign => (Client_Ptn_1))
...
Partition(Ptn => N+2, Assign => (Client_Ptn_N))
```

In this next example, there is one controlling partition, and some number of worker partitions, in a pipeline configuration. The controller sends a job out to a worker partition, and the worker chooses either to perform the job, or if too busy, to pass it on to another worker partition. The results are returned back through the same chain of workers through which the original job was passed. Here is a diagram for the flow of messages:

```
               Job        Job        Job        Job
   Controller ---->   W1 --->    W2 --->    W3 --->    W4 ...
              <---       <---       <---       <---
              Result     Result     Result     Result
```

The elaboration of each worker entails registering that worker with the controller and determining which other worker (if any) the job will be handed to when it is too busy to handle the job itself. When it receives a job from some other worker, it also receives a "return" address to which it should return results. The workers are defined as instances of a generic RCI library unit.

The first solution uses (remote) access-to-subprogram types to provide the dynamic binding between partitions. Two access-to-subprogram types are declared in the RCI library unit (Controller) that designate the procedures to perform the work and return the results. In addition, this library unit declares two procedures; one to register and dispense workers for the pipeline and one to receive the final results. An instantiation of a generic RCI library unit (Worker) declares the actual subprograms for each worker. The locations of these procedures are made available as remote access values; elaboration of Worker registers the Receive_Work procedure with the Controller.

```ada
package Controller is
   pragma Remote_Call_Interface;
   type Job_Type is ...;
   -- Representation of job to be done
   type Result_Type is ...;
   -- Representation of results
   type Return_Address is access procedure (Rslt : Result_Type);
   -- Return address for sending back results
   type Worker_Ptr is access
                  procedure(Job : Job_Type; Ret : Return_Address);
   -- Pointer to next worker in chain
   procedure Register_Worker(Ptr  : Worker_Ptr;
                             Next : out Worker_Ptr);
   -- This procedure is called during elaboration
   -- to register a worker.  Upon return, Next contains
   -- a pointer to the next worker in the chain.
   procedure Give_Results(Rslt : Result_Type);
   -- This is the controller procedure which ultimately
   -- receives the result from a worker.
end Controller;

with Controller; use Controller;
generic
   -- Instantiated once for each worker
package Worker is
   pragma Remote_Call_Interface;
   procedure Do_Job(Job : Job_Type;
                    Ret : Return_Address);
   -- This procedure receives work from the controller or
   -- some other worker in the chain
   procedure Pass_Back_Results(Rslt : Result_Type);
   -- This procedure passes results back to the worker in the
   -- chain from which the most recent job was received.
end Worker;

package body Worker is
   Next_Worker : Worker_Ptr;
   -- Pointer to next worker in chain, if any
   Previous_Worker : Return_Address;
   -- Pointer to worker/controller who sent a job most recently

   procedure Do_Job(Job : Job_Type;
                    Ret : Return_Address) is
   -- This procedure receives work from the controller or
   -- some other worker in the chain
```

```
begin
    Previous_Worker := Ret;
    -- Record return address for returning results
    if This_Worker_Too_Busy
        and then Next_Worker /= null then
        -- Forward job to next worker, if any, if
        -- this worker is too busy
        Next_Worker(Job, Pass_Back_Results'Access);
        -- Include this worker's pass-back-results procedure
        -- as the return address
    else
        declare
            Rslt : Result_Type;   -- The results to be produced
        begin
            Do The Work(Job, Rslt);
            Previous_Worker(Rslt);
        end;
    end if;
end Do_Job;

procedure Pass_Back_Results(Rslt : Result_Type) is
    -- This procedure passes results back to the worker in the
    -- chain from which the most recent job was received.
begin
    -- Just pass the results on...
    Previous_Worker(Rslt);
end Pass_Back_Results;
begin
    -- Register this worker with the controller
    -- and obtain pointer to next worker in chain, if any
    Controller.Register_Worker(Do_Job'Access, Next_Worker);
end Worker;

    -- Create multiple worker packages
package W1_RCI is new Worker;
...
package W9_RCI is new Worker;

    -- Post-Compilation Partitioning
    -- Create multiple worker partitions
Partition(Ptn => 1, Assign => (W1_RCI))
...
Partition(Ptn => 9, Assign => (W9_RCI))
    -- create controller partition
Partition(Ptn => 0, Assign => (Controller))
```

The second solution uses (remote) access-to-class-wide types to provide the dynamic binding between partitions. A root tagged type is declared in a pure package Common. Two derivatives are created, one to represent the controller (Controller_Type), and one to represent a worker (Real_Worker). One object of Controller_Type is created, which will be designated by the return address sent to the first worker with a job. An object for each worker of the Real_Worker type is created, via a generic instantiation of the One_Worker generic. All of the data associated with a single worker is encapsulated in the Real_Worker type. The dispatching operations Do_Job and Pass_Back_Results use the pointer to the Real_Worker (the formal parameter W) to gain access to this worker-specific data.

The access type `Worker_Ptr` is used to designate a worker or a controller, and can be passed between partitions because it is a remote access type. Normal access types cannot be passed between partitions, since they generally contain partition-relative addresses.

```ada
package Common is
   -- This pure package defines the root tagged type
   -- used to represent a worker (and a controller)
   pragma Pure;
   type Job_Type is ...;
   -- Representation of Job to be done
   type Result_Type is ...;
   -- Representation of results
   type Worker_Type is abstract tagged limited private;
   -- Representation of a worker, or the controller
   procedure Do_Job(W : access Worker_Type;
                    Job : Job_Type;
                    Ret : access Worker_Type'Class) is abstract;
   -- Dispatching operation to do a job
   -- Ret may point to the controller
   procedure Pass_Back_Results(W : access Worker_Type;
                               Rslt : Result_Type) is abstract;
   -- Dispatching operation to pass back results
private
   ...
end Common;

with Common; use Common;
package Controller is
   pragma Remote_Call_Interface;
   type Worker_Ptr is access all Common.Worker_Type'Class;
   -- Remote access to a worker
   procedure Register_Worker(Ptr  : Worker_Ptr;
                             Next : out Worker_Ptr);
   -- This procedure is called during elaboration
   -- to register a worker.  Upon return, Next contains
   -- a pointer to the next worker in the chain.
end Controller;

package body Controller is
   First_Worker : Worker_Ptr := null;
   -- Current first worker in chain
   type Controller_Type is new Common.Worker_Type;
   -- A controller is a special kind of worker,
   -- it can receive results, but is never given a job
   The_Controller : Controller_Type;
   -- The tagged object representing the controller
   Controller_Is_Not_A_Worker : exception;
   procedure Do_Job(W : access Controller_Type;
                    Job : Job_Type;
                    Ret : access Worker_Type'Class) is
   -- Dispatching operation to do a job
   begin
      raise Controller_Is_Not_A_Worker;
      -- Controller never works (lazy pig)
   end Do_Job;

   procedure Pass_Back_Results(W : access Controller_Type;
                               Rslt : Result_Type) is
   -- Dispatching operation to receive final results
```

```
    begin
        Do Something With Result(Rslt);
    end Pass_Back_Results;

    procedure Register_Worker(Ptr : Worker_Ptr;
                              Next : out Worker_Ptr) is
        -- This procedure is called during elaboration
        -- to register a worker.  It receives back
        -- a pointer to the next worker in the chain.
    begin
        -- Link this worker into front of chain gang
        Next := First_Worker;
        First_Worker := Ptr;
    end Register_Worker;
begin
    -- Once all workers have registered, Controller initiates
    -- the pipeline by dispatching on Do_Job with First_Worker
    -- as the controlling operand; Controller then awaits the
    -- results to be returned (this mechanism is not specified).
end Controller;

with Common; use Common;
with Controller; use Controller;
package Worker_Pkg is
    -- This package defines the Real_Worker type
    -- whose dispatching operations do all the
    -- "real" work of the system.
    -- Note: This package has no global data;
    -- All data is encapsulated in the Real_Worker type.
    type Real_Worker is new Common.Worker_Type with
        record
            Next : Worker_Ptr;
            -- Pointer to next worker in chain, if any
            Previous : Worker_Ptr;
            -- Pointer to worker/controller who sent
            -- us a job most recently
            ... -- other data associated with a worker
        end record;

    procedure Do_Job(W : access Real_Worker;
                     Job : Job_Type;
                     Ret : access Worker_Type'Class);
    -- Dispatching operation to do a job
    procedure Pass_Back_Results(W : access Real_Worker;
                                Rslt : Result_Type);
    -- Dispatching operation to pass back results
end Worker_Pkg;

package body Worker_Pkg is
    procedure Do_Job(W : access Real_Worker;
                     Job : Job_Type;
                     Ret : access Worker_Type'Class) is
    -- Dispatching operation to do a job.
    -- This procedure receives work from the controller or
    -- some other worker in the chain.
    begin
        W.Previous := Worker_Ptr(Ret);
        -- Record return address for returning results
```

```
         if W.This_Worker_Too_Busy
             and then W.Next /= null then
          -- Forward job to next worker, if any, if
          -- this worker is too busy
          Common.Do_Job(W.Next, Job, W);
          -- now dispatch to appropriate Do_Job,
          -- include a pointer to this worker
          -- as the return address.
       else
          declare
             Rslt : Result_Type;   -- The results to be produced
          begin
             Do The Work(Job, Rslt);
             Common.Pass_Back_Results(W.Previous, Rslt);
             -- dispatch to pass back results
             -- to another worker or to the controller
          end;
       end if;
    end Do_Job;

    procedure Pass_Back_Results(W : access Real_Worker;
                                Rslt : Result_Type) is
       -- Dispatching operation to pass back results
       -- This procedure passes results back to the worker in the
       -- chain from which the most recent job was received.
    begin
       -- Pass the results to previous worker
       Common.Pass_Back_Results(W.Previous, Rslt);
    end Pass_Back_Results;
 end Worker_Pkg;

generic
    -- Instantiated once for each worker
package One_Worker is
    pragma Remote_Call_Interface;
end One_Worker;

with Worker_Pkg;
with Controller;
package body One_Worker is
    The_Worker : Worker_Pkg.Real_Worker; -- The actual worker
begin
    -- Register this worker "object"
    Controller.Register_Worker(The_Worker'Access, The_Worker.Next);
end One_Worker;

-- Create multiple worker packages
package W1_RCI is new One_Worker;
...
package W9_RCI is new One_Worker;

-- Post-Compilation Partitioning
-- Create multiple worker partitions
Partition(Ptn => 1, Assign => (W1_RCI))
...
Partition(Ptn => 9, Assign => (W9_RCI))
-- create controller partition
Partition(Ptn => 0, Assign => (Controller))
```

E.6 Configuring a Distributed System

In the previous examples, post-partitioning has been illustrated in terms of the library units that comprise a partition. The configuration of partitions to nodes has been omitted since this is beyond the scope of the Annex. For example, whether partitions may share the same node is implementation defined. The capability for a passive partition to share a node with multiple active partitions would allow a distributed system to be configured into a standard, multiprogramming system, but this may not be practical for all environments.

The mapping of partitions to the target environment must be consistent with the call and data references to RCI and shared passive library units, respectively. This requires only that the target environment support the necessary communication connectivity among the nodes; it does not guarantee that active partitions are elaborated in a particular order required by the calls and references. To allow partitions to elaborate independently, a remote subprogram call is held until the receiving partition has completed its elaboration. If cyclic elaboration dependencies result in a deadlock as a result of remote subprogram calls, the exception Program_Error may be raised in one or all partitions upon detection of the deadlock.

The predefined exception Communication_Error (declared in package System.RPC) is provided to allow calling partitions to implement a means for continuing execution whenever a receiving partition becomes inaccessible. For example, when the receiving partition fails to elaborate, this exception is raised in all partitions that have outstanding remote calls to this partition.

To maintain interface consistency within a distributed system, the same version of an RCI or a shared passive library unit specification must be used in all elaborations of partitions that reference the same library unit. The consistency check cannot happen before the configuration step. (The detection of unit inconsistency, achievable when linking a single Ada program, cannot be guaranteed at that time for the case of a distributed system.) It is implementation defined how this check is accomplished; Program_Error may be raised but in any event the partions concerned become inaccessible to one another (and thus later probably resulting in Communication_Error); see [RM95 E.3].

In addition to the partition termination rules, an implementation could provide the capability for one partition to explicitly terminate (abort) another partition; the value of the attribute Partition_ID may be used to identify the partition to be aborted. If a partition is aborted while executing a subprogram called by another partition, Communication_Error will be raised in the calling partition since the receiving partition is no longer accessible.

E.7 Partition Communication Subsystem

The partition communication subsystem (PCS) is notionally compatible with the proposed Communications Model specified by the in-progress recommendations of the ISO RPC Committee Draft. The Annex requires that, as a minimum capability, the PCS must implement the standard package RPC to service remote subprogram calls. Standardizing the interface between the generated stubs for remote subprogram calls and the message-passing layer of the target communications software (the RPC package) facilitates a balanced approach for separating the implementation responsibilities of supporting distributed systems across different target environments.

The remote procedure call (RPC) paradigm was selected as the specified communication facility rather than message passing or remote entry call because of the following advantages of RPC:

- The RPC paradigm is widely implemented for interprocess communication between processes in different computers across a network. Several standards have been initiated by organizations such as ISO and OSF. Furthermore, emerging distributed operating system kernels promote support for RPC. Such considerations require that a language for programming distributed systems provide RPC as a linguistic abstraction. Finally, the need for RPC support is identified in U.S. Government initiatives towards developing open systems.

• A tenet of the revision is to maintain the type safety properties of the existing standard. Type-safe interfaces among partitions are a consequence of using the RPC paradigm. RPC is a compatible extension of the standard which, unless included in the Annex, would be difficult to support (by user-defined facilities) since detailed information on the compiler implementation is required.

• The RPC paradigm allows programs to be written with minimal regard for whether the program is targeted for distributed or nondistributed execution. Except in the instance of asynchronous procedure calls, the execution site implies no change in semantics from that of a local subprogram call. This is necessary for partitioning library units into various distributed configurations in a seamless or transparent manner. Furthermore, the use of RPC maintains concurrency/parallelism as orthogonal to distribution. This orthogonality reduces the complexity of the run-time system and allows remote references to be controlled through straightforward restrictions.

• The asynchronous form of RPC relaxes the normal synchronous semantics of RPC. This facilitates programming efficient application-specific communication paradigms where at-most-once semantics are not required.

Ada 95 includes important enhancements that allow dynamic subprogram calls using access-to-subprogram types and tagged types. To restrict these enhancements to nondistributed programs is likely to promote criticism similar to the absence of dynamic calls in Ada 83. In addition, the capability to support remote dispatching is an important discriminator between Ada 95 and other competing languages.

Package System.RPC

This package specifies the standard interface necessary to implement stubs at both the calling and receiving partitions for a remote subprogram call. The interface specifies both the actual operations and the semantic conditions under which they are to be used by the stubs. It is also adaptable to different target environments. Additional non-standard interfaces may be specified by the PCS. For example, a simple message passing capability may be specified for exchanging objects of some message type using child library units.

(Note that the normal user does have to use this package but only the implementer of the communication system.)

The package specifies the primitive operations for Root_Stream_Type to marshall and unmarshall message data by using the attributes Read and Write within the stubs. This allows an implementation to define the format of messages to be compatible with whatever message-passing capability between partitions is available from the target communication software.

The routing of parameters to a remote subprogram is supported by the Partition_ID type that identifies the partition, plus implementation-specific identifiers passed in the stream itself to identify the particular RCI library unit and remote subprogram. A value of type Partition_ID identifies the partition to which a library unit is assigned by the post-compilation partitioning.

The procedures RPC and APC support the generation of stubs for the synchronous and asynchronous forms of remote subprogram call. Each procedure specifies the partition that is the target of the call and the appropriate message data to be delivered. For the synchronous form, the result data to be received upon the completion the call is specified. As a consequence, the task originating the remote subprogram call is suspended to await the receipt of this data. In contrast, the asynchronous form does not suspend the originating task to await the receipt of the result data.

To facilitate the routing of remote calls in the receiving partition, the procedure Establish_RPC_Receiver is specified to establish the interface for receiving a message and for dispatching to the appropriate subprogram. The interface is standardized through the parameters specified for an access-to-subprogram type that designates an implementation-provided RPC-receiver procedure. In this way, post-compilation support can link the necessary units and data to the RPC-receiver procedure. Once the RPC-receiver procedure has been elaborated, it may be called by the PCS.

A single exception Communication_Error is specified to report error conditions detected by the PCS. Detailed information on the precise condition may be provided through the exception occurrence. These conditions are necessarily implementation-defined, and therefore, inappropriate for inclusion in the specification as distinct exception names.

E.7.1 The Interaction Between the Stubs and the PCS

The execution environment of the PCS is defined as an Ada environment. This is done in order to provide Ada semantics to serving partitions. In the calling and receiving partitions, the canonical implementation relies upon the Ada concurrency model to service stubs. For example, in the calling partition, cancellation of a synchronous remote call, when the calling task has been aborted, requires that the PCS interrupt the Do_RPC operation to execute the cancellation. In the receiving partition, the stub for a remote subprogram is assumed to be called by the RPC-receiver procedure executing in a task created by the PCS.

E.8 Requirements Summary

The facilities of the Distributed Systems annex relate to the requirements in 8.1 (Distribution of Ada Applications) and 8.2 (Dynamic Reconfiguration of Distributed Systems).

More specifically, the requirement

>   *R8.1-A(1) — Facilitating Software Distribution*

is met by the concept of partitions and the categorization of library units and the requirement

>   *R8.2-A(1) — Dynamic Reconfiguration*

is addressed by the use of remote access to subprogram and access to class wide types for dynamic calls across partitions.

F Information Systems

One of the major goals of Ada 95 is to provide the necessary language facilities for the development of large-scale information systems that previously have been produced in COBOL and 4GLs. To a large extent, core language enhancements such as child units and object-oriented programming, and the new support for distribution, serve to meet this goal. However, there are also specific requirements at the computational level and for report-oriented output that must be addressed in order to ensure applicability to financial and related Information Systems applications. The major needs are

- Exact, decimal arithmetic for quantities up to at least 18 digits of precision;

- The ability to produce human-readable formats for such values, with control over the form and placement of currency symbol, sign, digits separator, and radix mark;

- The ability to interface with data produced by, or programs written in, other languages (in particular C and COBOL).

This chapter describes the facilities and gives the reasons for the major decisions taken in Ada 95 to satisfy these requirements.

F.1 Decimal Computation

A numeric model highly appropriate for information systems, especially for financial applications, is that supplied by the COBOL language. In COBOL the programmer defines numeric items via a "picture" in terms of a specified number of decimal digits and the placement of the decimal point. The arithmetic verbs provide exact arithmetic, with control over truncation versus rounding on a per-computation basis. For example:

```
05 FRACTION          PIC S9V99      VALUE .25.
05 ALPHA             PIC S9999V9    VALUE 103.
05 BETA              PIC S9999V9.
```

FRACTION has values in the range -9.99 through 9.99, and each of ALPHA and BETA is in the range -9999.9 through 9999.9.

```
    MULTIPLY ALPHA BY FRACTION GIVING BETA ROUNDED.
  * Now BETA = 25.8, the rounded value of 25.75
    ADD ALPHA TO BETA.
  * Now BETA = 128.8
    DIVIDE BETA BY 10.
  * Now BETA = 12.8, since truncation is the default
```

It is also possible to express the above calculation more succinctly in COBOL:

```
COMPUTE BETA = (ALPHA * FRACTION + ALPHA) / 10.
```

However, the effect of rounding versus truncation is now implementation dependent, so the result may be either 12.8 or 12.9.

F.1.1 Decimal Arithmetic through Discriminated Type

In addressing the exact computational requirements, we examined several alternatives. One was to rely on a private discriminated type, with discriminants reflecting scale and precision. (The terminology here is the same as in SQL [ISO 92]: precision is the total number of decimal digits; scale is the number of digits after the decimal point.) For example

```
package Computation is
    subtype Scale_Range is
      Integer range implementation-defined .. implementation-defined;
    subtype Precision_Range is
      Positive range 1 .. implementation-defined;
    type Decimal(Precision : Precision_Range;
                  Scale     : Scale_Range) is private;
    ... -- Subprograms for arithmetic
end Computation;
```

Such an approach would have the benefit of separability from the core features, but its numerous drawbacks led to its rejection:

- Literals are unavailable for private types, hence the programmer would need to perform explicit conversions either from String or from a specific real type. Such a style would be both inefficient and aesthetically displeasing. In an early version of the Ada 9X mapping there was a capability to obtain numeric literals for private types, but this was removed as a simplification.

- Non-trivial optimizations are needed to avoid time and space overhead. In COBOL precision and scale are known at compile time, so the compiler can generate efficient code. The discriminated type approach lets the programmer defer specifying the precision and scale until run time, but the generality comes at a price.

- A problem often cited with the COBOL model is the lack of typing. For example, if by mistake a COBOL programmer adds a unitless fraction to a salary, this error will not be detected by the compiler. To obtain compile-time protection from such an error in Ada, the programmer would need to derive from type Decimal, for example to declare the types Fraction and Salary. However, derivation provides more operations than make sense and hence other kinds of errors could still arise (for example, multiplying a Salary by a Salary to obtain a Salary). At the same time it yields less than what is needed; for example, it would be useful to be able to divide two Salary values and obtain a Fraction, but this would not be provided automatically. Although both of these problems could be solved by the programmer providing some additional explicit declarations, programmers might be tempted to forego the type derivations (and the resulting safety) and to simply declare all their data of type Decimal.

- Specifying just precision and scale allows more values than might be sensible. For example, if we want a fraction value to be in the range 0.00 .. 1.00, we need to specify Decimal(Precision=>3, Scale=>2), but this allows all values in the range -9.99 .. 9.99.

Another major problem with the discriminated type approach is the error-prone effects of having arithmetic operators take parameters of type Decimal and deliver a result of type Decimal.

Division in particular is troublesome; languages that attempt to address the issue lead inevitably to anomalies. For example, the well-known curiosity in PL/I is that the operation 10+1/3 overflows, since the language rules attempt to maximize the precision of the quotient. Moreover, the rules for precision and scale of an arithmetic result would clash with the need for discriminant identity on assignment. For example, consider the simple fragment:

```
declare
    Salary : Decimal(Precision => 9, Scale => 2);
            -- Values in -99_999_99.99 .. 99_999_999.99
    Fraction : Decimal(Precision => 2, Scale => 2);
            -- Values in -0.99 .. 0.99
begin
    ...
    Salary := Salary * Fraction;
    ...
end;
```

The intuitive rule for "*" would be to define the precision of the result as the sum of the precisions of the operands, and similarly for the scale. Thus Salary*Fraction would have precision 11 and scale 4, sufficient to hold any product. But then the rules for discriminant matching would cause Constraint_Error to be raised by the assignment to Salary.

A possible solution would be to introduce special rules for discriminant matching in such cases, but this adds complexity. An alternative would be to omit the operator forms for the arithmetic subprograms and instead to provide a procedural interface with an out parameter, thereby making the result precision and scale known at the point of call. For example:

```
procedure Multiply
    (Left, Right : in Decimal;
     Result      : out Decimal;
     Rounding    : in Boolean := False);
```

Although such an approach has been successfully applied in the Ada 83 Decimal Arithmetic and Representation components [Brosgol 92], the other drawbacks led us to seek alternative solutions for Ada 95.

F.1.2 Decimal Arithmetic and Ada 83 Numeric Types

The Ada 83 numeric types give us a choice among integer, floating point, and fixed point. In some sense integer arithmetic provides the most appropriate computational model, since it matches the requirements for exact results. For example, one might consider using an integer type Pennies to represent monetary values. However, this would be impractical for several reasons: the absence of real literals is a hardship, keeping track of implicit scaling is awkward, and many compilers do not support the 64-bit integer arithmetic that would be needed for 18 digits of accuracy.

Floating point is unacceptable because of the inherent inexactness of representing decimal quantities. Consider the following program fragment, where X is a floating point variable:

```
X := 0.0;
for I in 1 .. 10 loop
    X := X + 0.10;
end loop;
```

After execution of the loop using typical floating point hardware, X will not equal 1.00. Moreover, 64-bit floating point does not have enough mantissa bits to represent 18 decimal digits.

At first glance, fixed point seems no better. The apparent motivations behind the fixed point facility in Ada were to deal with scaled data coming in from sensors in real-time applications, and to provide a substitute for floating point in target environments lacking floating point hardware. Indeed, the inherent bias toward powers of 2 for the attribute Small in the Ada 83 fixed point model seems at odds with the needs of decimal computation.

However, fixed point provides a closer fit than might be expected [Dewar 90b]. The Ada 83 unification of floating point and fixed point under the category of "approximate" computation is more artificial than real, since the model-number inaccuracy that is appropriate in the floating point case because of differences in target hardware is not applicable at all to fixed point. The fixed point arithmetic operations "+", "-", "*", "/" are exact, and through a Small representation clause the programmer can specify decimal scaling. Thus consider a COBOL declaration

```
05   SALARY PICTURE S9(6)V9(2) USAGE COMPUTATIONAL.
```

which defines SALARY as a signed binary data item comprising 8 decimal digits, of which 2 are after the assumed decimal point. This can be simulated in Ada:

```
type Dollars is delta 0.01 range -999_999.99 .. 999_999.99;
for Dollars'Small use 0.01;

Salary : Dollars;
```

The programmer-specified Small not only provides the required decimal scaling, it also prevents the implementation from supplying extra fractional digits. This is important in financial applications: if the programmer requests 2 fractional digits, it would be incorrect for a compiler to provide 3.

The fixed point approach immediately avoids several of the problems with discriminated types: we get numeric literals, compile-time known scales and precisions, strong typing, and the ability to specify logical ranges. Moreover, the rules for the arithmetic operators are fitting. The "+" and "-" operators require identical operand types and deliver a result of the same type, which is an intuitively correct restriction. Adding or subtracting quantities with different scales is not a frequent situation; when it arises, it is reasonable to require an explicit conversion to indicate the rescaling. Automatic availability of mixed-type "*" and "/" also makes sense.

There are, however, several problems with adopting the Ada 83 fixed point model unchanged for decimal arithmetic.

- The Ada fixed point model leads to occasional surprises, even in the presence of a Small representation clause. For example, one or both endpoints supplied in the definition of a fixed point type may be absent from the implemented range for the type.

- The Ada 83 fixed point rules require conversions of real literals (and named numbers of type *universal_real*) that appear as factors in multiplication or division. Without the programmer providing an explicit declaration of an applicable "*" operator, it would be illegal to write:

```
Worker_Salary := 1.05 * Worker_Salary;
```

Instead, something like the following circumlocution is required:

```
Worker_Salary := Dollars(Some_Type(1.05) * Worker_Salary);
```

The need for the programmer to supply either these explicit conversions or an explicit overloading of "*", is somewhat embarrassing. In COBOL the equivalent functionality can be obtained directly:

```
MULTIPLY WORKER-SALARY BY 1.05.
```

• The previous example illustrates another serious problem: Ada fixed point does not give a well-defined result for the conversion of values. That is, the language does not guarantee whether the result of a fixed point conversion is to be rounded or truncated. In fact, different evaluations of the same expression in the same program could yield different results, an unwelcome nondeterminism.

• Facilities such as edited output, and a division operation delivering both a quotient and remainder, are not defined for fixed point types.

F.1.3 Decimal Arithmetic through Decimal Types

Since fixed point comes reasonably close to satisfying the requirements for decimal arithmetic, our decision was to use that facility as the basis for a solution. Ada 95 thus introduces a new class of fixed point types, the *decimal* types, distinguished syntactically by the presence of a positive integer **digits** value following the **delta** in a fixed point definition. The **delta** .. **digits** .. syntax, suggested by David Emery [Emery 91], has the advantage of identifying the type immediately as a special kind of fixed point type (the **delta**) without requiring new reserved words.

The **delta** value must be a power of 10. For example:

```
type Francs is delta 0.01 digits 9;
```

This declaration is similar in effect to the Ada 83 fragment:

```
type Francs is delta 0.01 range -(10.0**9 - 1.0) .. 10.0**9 - 1.0;
for Francs'Small use 0.01;
```

The **digits** value in a decimal fixed point type definition thus implies a range constraint. For a decimal type with delta D and digits N (both of which must be static), the implied range is $-(10.0^{**}N - 1.0)^{*}D$ .. $(10.0^{**}N - 1.0)^{*}D$. Moreover, a range constraint may be further supplied at the definition of a decimal type or subtype, and at the declaration of objects. For example:

```
type    Salary is delta 0.01 digits 8 range 0.00 .. 100_000.00;
subtype Price  is Francs              range 0.00 .. 1000.00;
Worker_Salary : Salary range 0.00 .. 50_000.00;
```

The ordinary fixed point operations, such as the arithmetic operators and fixed point attributes, are available for decimal types. There are, however, several important differences:

• For a decimal subtype S, the conversion S(*expr*) where *expr* is of some numeric type is defined to truncate (towards 0) rather than having an unspecified effect.

• To obtain a rounded result for an expression *expr* having a real type, the function attribute S'Round(*expr*) can be used. This attribute is not available for ordinary fixed point types.

• Other attributes apply only to decimal subtypes: for example, S'Digits and S'Scale. The former reflects the value of digits supplied for the declaration of S. The latter is the number of digits after the decimal point in values of S and is related to S'Delta by the equation

```
10.0**(-S'Scale) = S'Delta
```

A stylistic issue noted above, namely the inability in Ada 83 to write simple statements such as:

```
Worker_Salary := 1.05 * Worker_Salary;
```

has been solved in Ada 95 for fixed point types in general. The revised rules permit a *universal_fixed* value to be implicitly converted to a specific target type if the context uniquely establishes the target type. Thus there is no need to convert to Salary the product on the right side of the assignment. Another new rule allows a *universal_real* value to be used as an operand to a fixed point "*" and "/"; thus there is no need to convert the literal 1.05 to a specific type. Although these enhancements are motivated by considerations with decimal types, it makes no sense either from an implementation or user viewpoint to apply the new rules only to decimal types, and thus they have been generalized for ordinary fixed point types as well.

Given that decimal types come equipped with their own operations, it is natural to introduce a category of generic formal type that can only be matched by decimal subtypes. The syntax for such a generic formal type is what one would expect:

type T **is delta** <> **digits** <>;

The actual subtype supplied for a formal decimal type must be a decimal subtype. This makes sense, since an ordinary fixed point subtype does not have all the necessary operations. On the other hand, there is a design issue whether to permit an actual decimal subtype to match a formal fixed point type (one given by **delta** <>). Such permission would seem to be useful, since it would allow existing Ada 83 fixed point generics to be matched by Ada 95 decimal subtypes. However, it would introduce some implementation difficulties, especially for those compilers that attempt to share the code of the template across multiple instances. The fact that some operations (in particular numeric conversion) behave differently for decimal and ordinary fixed point would also cause complications if decimal subtypes were permitted to match formal fixed point types. Thus the decimal fixed point types are defined to form a class disjoint from ordinary fixed point types with respect to generic matching.

Formal decimal types are exploited to provide edited output (see below) as well as division delivering both a quotient and a remainder.

One of the requirements for information systems applications is the ability to perform edited output of decimal quantities. We considered introducing decimal subtype attributes for this effect; for example S'Image(X, Picture) would return a String based on the value of X and the formatting conventions of Picture. However, this approach would have introduced implementation complexity out of proportion to the notational benefit for users. The type of Picture is defined in an external package, making such an attribute rather atypical, and support would affect the compiler and not simply require a supplemental package. Instead, picture-based output is obtained via generics, as described below.

F.1.4 Internal Representation for Decimal Objects

Ada and COBOL have a somewhat different philosophy about internal data representation. Through the USAGE clause the COBOL programmer furnishes information about how numeric items will be represented, either explicitly (such as BINARY, DISPLAY, PACKED-DECIMAL) or by default (DISPLAY). COBOL's default representation opts for data portability versus computational efficiency.

Ada's approach to data representation, for types in general and not just decimal, is to let the compiler decide based on efficiency, and to let the programmer override this choice explicitly when necessary. For decimal types this is achieved through the Machine_Radix attribute and the corresponding attribute definition clause.

An object of a decimal type, as with fixed point in general, may be viewed as the product of an integer mantissa (represented explicitly at run time) and the type's delta (managed at compile time). The type's Machine_Radix determines the representation of the mantissa: a value of 2 implies binary, while a value of 10 implies decimal. The compiler will choose an implementation-defined machine radix by default, which the programmer can override with an explicit attribute definition clause. Consider the following example, where the implementation's default for all decimal types is binary machine radix:

```
type Money_2  is delta 0.01 digits 18;
type Money_10 is delta 0.01 digits 18;
for Money_10'Machine_Radix use 10;
```

An object of type Money_2 is represented in binary; on typical machines it will occupy 64 bits (including a sign).

An object of type Money_10 is represented in decimal; it will take 18 digits (and a sign). The exact representation is unspecified, and in fact different machines have different formats for packed decimal concerning how the sign is encoded. If a decimal type's machine radix is 10, then the compiler may also generate packed-decimal instructions for arithmetic computation. Whether it chooses to do so, rather than converting to/from binary and using binary arithmetic, depends on which is more efficient.

The only difference in behavior between decimal and binary machine radix, aside from performance, is that some intermediate results might overflow in one case but not the other. For example, if Money_10 values are represented in 19 digits (an odd number is typical for packed decimal, since the sign can be stored in the same byte as a digit), and Money_2 values occupy 64 bits, then a computation such as (100.0 * Money)/100.0 will overflow if Money has type Money_10, but not if Money has type Money_2, where Money is $10.0**18 - 1.0$.

Implementations using packed decimal are encouraged to exploit subtype digits constraints for space economization. For example:

```
Pay : Money_10 digits 9;
```

The compiler can and should represent Pay in 9 digits rather than 18 as would be needed in general for Money_10.

Ada does not provide the equivalent of DISPLAY usage for decimal data, since computation on character strings would be inefficient. If the programmer wishes to store decimal data in an external file in a portable fashion, the recommended approach is to convert via the To_Display function in Interfaces.COBOL.Decimal_Conversions; see B.3.

F.1.5 Compliance

The decimal type facility is part of the core language; thus the syntax for decimal types and for formal generic decimal types must be supported by all implementations. However, since a compiler needs to implement ordinary fixed point only for values of Small that are powers of 2, it may reject the declaration of a decimal type and also the declaration of a generic unit with a formal decimal type parameter. To be compliant with the Information Systems Annex a compiler must implement decimal types and must also allow digits values up to at least 18.

We had considered requiring support for decimal types (but without the 18 digit capacity) for all implementations. However, this was judged a heavy implementation burden for a facility whose usage is fairly specialized.

F.2 Edited Output

A facility essential for financial and other Information Systems applications and long established in COBOL is the ability for the programmer to dictate the appearance of numeric data as character strings, for example for reports or for display to human readers. Known as edited output, such a facility allows control over the placement and form of various elements:

- The sign;

- The radix mark, which separates the integer part of the number from the fraction;

- The digits separator, which separates groups of digits to improve readability;

- The currency symbol;

- The treatment of leading zeros, for example whether they should appear explicitly as '0' characters, as blank space, or as a string of occurrences of a "check protection" character.

COBOL's approach is to associate a "picture string" with the target data item for the edited output string. When a numeric value is moved to that target item, the associated picture determines the form of the output string. For example:

```
05 OUTPUT-FIELD PIC S$,ZZ9.99.
05 DATA-1       PIC S9999V99    VALUE -1234.56.
...
MOVE DATA-1 TO OUTPUT-FIELD.
```

The contents of OUTPUT-FIELD after the move are "-$bb1,234.56" where 'b' denotes the blank character.

F.2.1 General Approach

Textual I/O for decimal types is obtained in the same fashion as for other numeric types, by generic instantiation. The generic package Decimal_IO in Text_IO supplies Get and Put procedures for a decimal type with analogous effects to Get and Put in Text_IO.Fixed_IO for an ordinary fixed point type. Supplementing these facilities is a child package Text_IO.Editing in the Information Systems Annex, which provides several facilities:

- A private type Picture and associated operations. A Picture object encodes the formatting information supplied in a "picture string" concerning the placement of so-called "editing characters" in an output string;

- Constants for the default localization elements. These elements comprise the currency string, and the characters for fill of leading zeros, for digits separation, and for the radix mark;

- A generic package Decimal_Output allowing COBOL-style edited output for decimal types.

The Decimal_Output package supplies an Image function and several Put procedures, each taking an Item parameter (of the decimal type), a Pic parameter (of type Picture), and parameters for the localization effects. The default values for the localization parameters can be supplied as generic parameters; if not, then the default values declared in the enclosing package Text_IO.Editing are used.

An alternative that we considered for the picture parameter was to have it directly as a String, but this would make optimizations difficult. Hence package Editing supplies a private type Picture, conversion functions between String and Picture, and a function Valid that checks a string for well-formedness. Since picture strings are dynamically computable, the approach provides substantial flexibility. For example, an interactive program such as a spreadsheet could obtain the picture string at run time from the user. On the other hand, if the programmer only needs static picture strings, the compiler can exploit this and produce optimized inline expansions of calls of the edited output subprograms.

An example of a typical usage style is as follows:

```
with Text_IO.Editing;
procedure Example is
    use Text_IO.Editing;
    type Salary is delta 0.01 digits 9;
    package Salary_Output is new Decimal_Output(Salary);
    S     : Salary;
    S_Pic : constant Picture := To_Picture("$*_***_**9.99");
begin
    S := 12345.67;
    Salary_Output.Put(S, S_Pic);   -- Produces "$***12,345.67"
end Example;
```

We recognize that someone coming to Ada from COBOL may find the style somewhat unusual. In COBOL, performing edited output involves simply defining a picture and doing a MOVE, whereas in Ada 95 it is necessary to instantiate a generic, convert a string to a private type, and invoke a subprogram. However, this is principally a training and transition issue, which experience has shown to be solvable via an appropriate pedagogical style. Moreover, generics and private types are features of Ada that all programmers will need to understand and employ. Since these features apply naturally to the problem of edited output, there is little point in trying to disguise this.

F.2.2 Relationship to COBOL Edited Output

There are several reasons for basing the Ada 95 edited output facility directly on COBOL. First, the programmer population toward whom Ada 95's information systems support is targeted comprises largely COBOL users. Second, although enhanced edited output mechanisms have appeared in modern spreadsheet utilities, their proprietary nature makes commercial products an unappealing candidate as a source of specific features.

Still there was the issue of whether to adopt COBOL's "picture" approach as closely as possible, or to use it more loosely as the basis for a more comprehensive but possibly incompatible facility. We have taken the former approach for several reasons:

• To redesign the edited output facility from starting principles would have required a detailed review of the entire history behind the current COBOL standard's approach, an effort that would have been outside the scope of the Ada 9X project.

• Basing the Ada 95 edited output rules directly on COBOL obviously reduces the learning curve for COBOL programmers.

As a result the rules for picture string formation and interpretation for edited output are identical to those in ISO standard COBOL, except for the following:

• In Ada the picture characters for currency symbol, digits separator, and radix mark are not overridable. '$' and '#' are the currency symbols, '_' is the digits separator and '.' is the radix mark. No other characters can be used for these purposes *in the picture string*.

• On the other hand, Ada provides more flexibility than COBOL in the run-time localization of currency symbol, digits separator, radix mark, and "fill character" (also known as the "check protection character"). The programmer can arrange localization by passing explicit parameters to the edited output subprograms, or by instantiating the generic Decimal_Output package with values to be used as defaults for the localization elements.

• The currency symbol can be localized to a multi-character string; each of the other localization elements can be localized to any single character. The first (or only) occurrence of '$' in a picture string represents as many positions in the edited output result as there are characters in the current currency string. Subsequent occurrences of the symbol represent just one position in the edited output string.

• Ada allows a multi-character currency substring of the picture string to stand for a substring with the same length in the edited output string, if '#' is the currency symbol. This "length invariant" property can be useful in programs that need to deal with different currencies.

• Ada also allows the use of parentheses for negative quantities in the edited output string. The angle bracket characters '<' and '>' in the picture string denote positions where '(' and ')' can appear in the edited output. (The parentheses characters themselves have other meaning in picture strings, surrounding a count indicating repetition of the preceding picture character as in COBOL. The angle brackets were chosen since they look enough like parentheses to remind the user of their effect.)

• Ada allows the currency symbol to the right of the number as well as to the left.

There are several reasons why we have not adopted the COBOL-style permission to provide a single-character replacement in the picture string for the '$' as currency symbol, or to interchange the roles of '.' and ',' in picture strings:

• It would have introduced considerable complexity into Ada, as well as confusion between run-time and compile-time character interpretation, since picture strings are dynamically computable in Ada, in contrast with COBOL.

• Ada's rules for real literals provide a standard and natural interpretation of '_' as digits separator and '.' for radix mark; it is not essential to allow these to be localized in picture strings, since Ada does not allow them to be localized in real literals.

• The COBOL restriction for the currency symbol in a picture string to be replaced by a single character currency symbol is a compromise solution. In any event a mechanism is needed to localize the edited output to be a multi-character currency string. Allowing a single-character localization for the picture character, and a multiple-character localization for the currency string, would be an unwelcome complication.

The enhancement of the picture string form to allow parentheses for negative quantities is not in the current COBOL standard, but it is a real need in many financial applications. Thus the additional rules were judged to be worth the cost.

The approach to currency symbol localization is consistent with the directions that the ISO COBOL standardization group (WG4) is taking [Sales 92]. Thus we are attempting to preserve compatibility not just with the existing COBOL standard but also with the version currently under development.

In COBOL, the BLANK WHEN 0 clause for a numeric edited item interacts with edited output. For example, if OUTPUT-ITEM is defined as follows:

```
05    OUTPUT-ITEM  PIC -9999.99 BLANK WHEN 0.
...
MOVE 0 to OUTPUT-ITEM.
```

then OUTPUT-ITEM will contain a string of 8 blanks. In the absence of the BLANK WHEN 0 clause, OUTPUT-ITEM would contain "b0000.00". The effect of the BLANK WHEN 0 clause is considered in Ada to be part of the Picture value; thus the function To_Picture takes not just a picture string but also a Boolean value reflecting whether a 0 value is to be treated as all blanks.

The edited output rules in the Ada standard are given by a combination of BNF (for "well-formed picture strings") and expansion rules that define the edited output of a non-terminal in terms of the edited output for the right sides of the rules. We had considered defining the rules instead by a direct reference to the COBOL standard, but that would have had two undesirable consequences. First, it would have required the reader to be familiar with a rather complicated section of a document (the COBOL standard) that would not necessarily be easily accessible. Second, the reference would become obsolete when the COBOL standard is revised.

F.2.3 Example

The following example illustrates edited output with localization:

```
with Text_IO.Editing;
procedure Example is
   use Text_IO.Editing;
   type Money is delta 0.01 digits 8;
   package Money_Output is new Decimal_Output(Money);

   package Money_Output_FF is
      new Decimal_Output(
         Money,
         Default_Currency   => "FF",
         Default_Fill       => '*',
         Default_Separator  => '.',
         Default_Radix_Mark => ',');

   Amount     : Money range 0.0 .. Money'Last;
   Amount_Pic : constant Picture := To_Picture("$$$$_$$9.99");

begin
   Amount := 1234.56;

   Money_Output.Put(Item => Amount,
                    Pic  => Amount_Pic );
   -- Outputs the string "bb$1,234.56"
   -- where 'b' designates the space character

   Money_Output_FF.Put(Item => Amount,
                        Pic  => Amount_Pic );
   -- Outputs the string "bbFF1.234,56"

   Money_Output.Put(Item       => Amount,
                    Pic        => Amount_Pic,
                    Currency   => "CHF",
                    Fill       => '*',
                    Separator  => ',',
                    Radix_Mark => '.' );
   -- Outputs the string "bbCHF1,234.56"
```

```
Money_Output.Put(Item        => Amount,
                 Pic         => To_Picture("####_##9.99")
                 Currency    => "CHF",
                 Fill        => '*',
                 Separator   => ',',
                 Radix_Mark  => '.' );
-- Outputs the string "CHF1,234.56"

end Example;
```

F.3 Requirements Summary

The facilities of the Information Systems Annex relate to the requirements in 10.1 (Handling Currency Quantities for Information Systems), 10.2 (Compatibility with Other Character Sets), 10.3 (Interfacing with Data Base Systems), and 10.4 (Common Functions).
   The requirement

   R10.1-A(1) — Decimal-Based Types

is satisfied by the Ada 95 decimal fixed point type facility.
   The study topic

   S10.1-A(2) — Specification of Decimal Representation

is met in part by the Machine_Radix attribute definition clause.
   The study topic

   S10.2-A(1) — Alternate Character Set Support

is satisfied in part by the permission of an implementation to localize the declaration of type Character.
   The study topic

   S10.3-A(1) — Interfacing with Data Base Systems

is satisfied in part by the provision of decimal types and also the package Interfaces.COBOL (see B.3).
   The study topic

   S10.4-A(2) — String Manipulation Functions

is met in part by the edited output facilities.

G Numerics

The Numerics Annex addresses the particular needs of the numerically intensive computing community. Like the other specialized needs annexes, support of this annex is optional. The annex covers the following topics

- Various generic packages are provided for the manipulation of complex numbers including the computation of elementary functions and input-output.

- The annex specifies two modes of operation, a strict mode in which certain accuracy requirements must be met and the relaxed mode in which they need not be met. The accuracy requirements for the strict mode cover both arithmetic and the noncomplex elementary functions and random number generation of the core language.

- The models of floating point and fixed point arithmetic applicable to the strict mode are described; these differ from those of Ada 83.

- Various model attributes are defined which are applicable to the strict mode for floating point types; again these differ from Ada 83.

Note that since the elementary functions and random number generation are in the core language, they and their accuracy requirements are discussed elsewhere (see A.3). The majority of attributes (including the so-called "primitive function" attributes) are also defined in the core language.

Implementations conforming to the numerics annex should also support the package `Interfaces.Fortran`, which is discussed in B.4.

G.1 Complex Arithmetic

Several application areas depend on the use of complex arithmetic. Complex fast Fourier transforms are used, for example, in conjunction with radar and similar sensors; conformal mapping uses complex arithmetic in fluid-flow problems such as the analysis of velocity fields around airfoils; and electrical circuit analysis is classically modelled in terms of complex exponentials.

The Ada 95 facilities for complex arithmetic consist of the generic packages

```
Numerics.Generic_Complex_Types
Numerics.Generic_Complex_Elementary_Functions
Text_IO.Complex_IO
```

which are children of `Ada`.

G.1.1 Complex Types and Arithmetic Operations

When first designed, `Numerics.Generic_Complex_Types` was patterned after the version of the generic package, `Generic_Complex_Types`, that was then being developed in the SIGAda Numerics Working Group for proposal as an ISO standard for Ada 83. At that time, roughly mid-

1992, the latter defined a complex type as well as types for vectors and matrices of complex components, together with a large set of scalar, vector, and matrix operations on those types. A decision was made to abbreviate the Ada 95 package by omitting the vector and matrix types and operations. One reason was that such types and operations were largely self-evident, so that little real help would be provided by defining them in the language. Another reason was that a future version of Ada might add enhancements for array manipulation and so it would be inappropriate to lock in such operations prematurely.

The initial design for `Numerics.Generic_Complex_Types` also inherited a rather pedestrian approach to defining the complex type from the same proposed standard. The Ada 9X Distinguished Reviewers recommended a different approach that enabled the writing of expressions whose appearance closely matches that of the standard mathematical notation for complex arithmetic. The idea was to define not just a complex type, but also a pure imaginary type `Imaginary` and a constant `i` of that type; operations could then easily be defined to allow one to write expressions such as

```
3.0 + 5.0*i    -- of type Complex
```

which has the feel of a complex literal.

Another advantage of this approach is that by providing mixed mode operations between complex and imaginary as well as between complex and real, it is possible to avoid unnecessary arithmetic operations on degenerate components. Moreover, avoiding such unnecessary operations is crucial in environments featuring IEEE arithmetic [IEC 89], where signed infinities can arise and can be used in meaningful ways.

(Ada 95 does not support infinite values, but in an implementation in which the `Machine_Overflows` attribute is `False`, an overflow or a division by zero yields an implementation-defined result, which could well be an infinite value. Thus a future Ada binding to IEEE arithmetic could capitalize on exactly that opportunity by providing semantics of arithmetic with infinities as in [IEC 89].)

To see how avoiding unnecessary operations provides more than just a gain in efficiency, consider the multiplication of a complex value $x + iy$ by a pure imaginary value iv. The result of the multiplication should, of course, be $-vy + ivx$. Without a pure imaginary type, we have to represent the pure imaginary value as the complex value $0.0 + iv$ and perform a full complex multiplication, yielding $(0.0x-vy) + i(vx+0.0y)$. This, of course, reduces to the same value as before, unless x or y is an infinity.

However, if x is infinity, y is finite, and v is nonzero (say, positive), the result should be $-vy + i\cdot\infty$, but instead we get $NaN + i\cdot\infty$, since multiplication of zero and infinity yields a NaN ("Not-a-Number") in IEEE arithmetic, and NaNs propagate through addition. See [Kahan 91].

A similar situation can be demonstrated for the multiplication of a complex value and a pure real value, but in that case we expect to have such a mixed-mode operation, and if we use it the generation of the NaN is avoided.

Another subtle problem occurs when the imaginary value iv is added to the complex value $x + iy$. The result, of course, should be $x + i(y+v)$. Without an imaginary type, we have to represent the imaginary value as the complex value $0.0 + iv$ and perform a full complex addition, yielding $(x+0.0) + i(y+v)$. The problem here [Kahan 91] is that if x is a negative zero, the real component of the result of the full complex addition will have the wrong sign; it will be a positive zero instead of the expected negative zero. This phenomenon, also a consequence of the rules of IEEE arithmetic, can and does occur in existing Ada 83 implementations, since it does not require an extension permitting infinities.

In both cases, the pure imaginary type gives the programmer the same opportunity to avoid problems in mixed complex/imaginary arithmetic as in mixed complex/real arithmetic.

With the inclusion of a pure imaginary type and mixed complex/imaginary operations, the generic complex types package in Ada 95 could have diverged from the proposed standard under development in the SIGAda NumWG. This was averted, however, when the working group changed its proposed standard to agree with the Ada 95 version. It also removed the vector and matrix types and operations from its generic complex types package and put them in a separate package. And so, `Numerics.Generic_Complex_Types` is just a slight variation of the generic package proposed for standardization for Ada 83. (The differences have to do with the use of `Real'Base`, rather than just `Real`, as the subtype mark for the components of the complex type and for the parameter and result subtypes of some of the operations, `Real` being the name of the generic formal parameter. This capability is lacking in Ada 83.)

The type `Complex` defined by `Numerics.Generic_Complex_Types` is a visible record type thus

```
type Complex is
   record
       Re, Im: Real'Base;
   end record;
```

corresponding to the cartesian representation of a complex value. We have made the type visible to allow one to write complex "literals" using aggregate notation as in some other languages (and to ensure efficiency). The cartesian representation was chosen over a polar representation to avoid canonicalization problems and because it is normal practice. An explicit choice of representation is required in any case to give meaning to the accuracy requirements. Operations are provided, however, to compute the modulus (length) and argument (angle) of a complex value and to construct a complex value from a given modulus and argument, so that it is easy to convert between the built-in cartesian representation and a polar representation, if needed.

It is perhaps unusual that the components of the complex type are of the unconstrained subtype of the generic formal parameter, `Real'Base`, rather than just `Real`, but this is intended to increase the chances of being able to deliver the result computed by a complex arithmetic operation even when their operands belong to some restricted domain. This provides behavior analogous to that of the elementary functions (see A.3.1), which also yield results in the unconstrained subtype of the relevant generic formal parameter. It is also similar to the behavior of the predefined arithmetic operations, which yield results of an unconstrained subtype, even when their operands are of a constrained subtype. A consequence is that we cannot create complex types with constrained components, but that does not seem so severe in view of the fact that applications of complex arithmetic typically have a naturally circular domain, rather than a rectangular domain.

The type `Imaginary`, on the other hand, is private, its full type being derived from `Real'Base` thus

```
type Imaginary is new Real'Base;
```

Making it private prevents the implicit conversion of a real literal to the type `Imaginary`, which would be available if `Imaginary` were visibly derived from `Real'Base`. This avoids various ambiguous expressions and enables overload resolution to work properly. It has the additional advantage of suppressing the implicit declaration of multiplying operators for the `Imaginary` type, which would incorrectly yield a result of the type `Imaginary`, when it should be `Real'Base`. Operations with the correct result type such as

```
function "*" (Left, Right: Imaginary) return Real'Base;
```

are, of course, explicitly declared. The same benefits could have been achieved by defining `Imaginary` as a visible record type with a single component, but the method chosen prevents the writing of expressions containing pure imaginary values as aggregates, whose meaning would not be intuitively obvious.

The imaginary constant i (and its equivalent, j, provided for the engineering community), has the value 1.0, and so unoptimized expressions like 5.0*i will have the proper numerical value. However, it is expected that compilers will optimize this and effectively convert the real literal 5.0 to the imaginary type. Similarly, an expression such as 3.0 + 5.0*i can be optimized to perform no arithmetic at all since it is functionally equivalent to the aggregate (3.0, 5.0) of the type Complex.

Note that there are also constructor and selector functions such as Compose_From_-Cartesian. The following expressions are thus equivalent

```
X + i*Y                          -- using operators

(X, Y)                           -- using an aggregate

Compose_From_Cartesian(X, Y)     -- using the constructor
```

The constructor function has the merit that it can be used as a generic actual parameter, if it should be necessary.

Nongeneric equivalents of Numerics.Generic_Complex_Types are provided corresponding to instantiations with the predefined types Float, Long_Float and so on with names such as

```
Numerics.Complex_Types           -- for Float
Numerics.Long_Complex_Types      -- for Long_Float
```

This means that applications can effectively treat single-precision complex, double-precision complex, etc., as predefined types with the same convenience that is provided for the predefined floating point types (or, more importantly, so that independent libraries assuming the existence and availability of such types without the use of generics can be constructed and freely used in applications). The nongeneric forms also have the advantage that Fortran programmers migrating to Ada do not have to learn generics in order to use complex arithemtic.

Accuracy requirements are generally specified for the complex arithmetic operations only in the strict mode. Nevertheless, certain special cases are prescribed to give the exact result even in the relaxed mode, ensuring high quality at negligible implementation cost. Examples are where one operand is pure real or pure imaginary. (These prescribed results are likely to be achieved even without special attention by the implementation.) Accuracy requirements are not given for exponentiation of a complex operand by an integer, owing to the variety of implementations that are allowed (ranging from repeated complex multiplication to well-known operations on the polar representation).

Note finally that spurious overflows (those occurring during the computation of an intermediate result, when the final result, or its components, would not overflow) are not allowed. Thus, implementations of complex multiplication and division need to be somewhat more sophisticated than the textbook formulae for those operations.

G.1.2 Complex Elementary Functions

The package Numerics.Generic_Complex_Elementary_Functions differs from the corresponding proposed standard for Ada 83 by taking advantage of the formal package parameter facility of Ada 95. Thus it imports the one parameter which is an instance of Numerics.Generic_Complex_Types instead of the complex type and a long list of operations exported by such an instance.

In the Ada 83 version, the complex type has to be imported as a private type, and implementations of the complex elementary functions there have no choice but to use the imported selector functions, Re and Im, to extract the real and imaginary components of a complex value, and the imported constructor function, Compose_From_Cartesian, to assemble such components into a complex value. Implementations of the Ada 95 version see that type as the record type that it is, allowing more efficient composition and decomposition of complex values; they also have available the complete set of operations, not just the partial (albeit long enough) list of operations imported in the Ada 83 version.

Nonngeneric equivalents of `Numerics.Generic_Complex_Elementary_Functions` are also provided for each of the predefined floating point types.

The overloading of the `Exp` function for a pure imaginary parameter is provided to give the user an alternative way to construct the complex value having a given modulus and argument. Thus, we can write either

```
Compose_From_Polar(R, Theta)
```

or

```
R * Exp(i * Theta)
```

where the latter corresponds more naturally to the mathematical $Re^{i\theta}$.

The treatment of accuracy requirements and prescribed results for the complex elementary functions is analogous to that discussed above for the complex arithmetic operations. However, since the avoidance of spurious overflows is difficult and expensive to achieve in several of the functions, it is explicitly permitted, allowing those functions to be implemented in the obvious way. No accuracy requirement is imposed on complex exponentiation (the operator `"**"`) by a pure real, pure imaginary, or complex exponent, because the obvious implementation in terms of complex exponentials and logarithms yields poor accuracy in some parts of the domain, and better algorithms are not available.

G.1.3 Complex I/O

Complex I/O is performed using the procedures in the generic child package, `Text_IO.-Complex_IO`. As with `Numerics.Generic_Complex_Elementary_Functions`, the user instantiates this generic package with an instance of `Numerics.Generic_Complex_Types`. (Note that nongeneric equivalents do not exist.)

A fundamental design decision underlying `Text_IO.Complex_IO` is that complex values are represented on the external medium in parenthesized aggregate notation, as in Fortran list-directed I/O. This is the format produced on output, and it is the format expected on input, except that the comma, the parentheses, or both may be omitted when the real and imaginary components are separated by appropriate white space. (This allows the reading of existing Fortran files containing complex data written by a variety of techniques.)

An implementation of `Text_IO.Complex_IO` can easily be built around an instance of `Text_IO.Float_IO` for `Real'Base`; the optional parentheses on input requires the use of the procedure `Text_IO.Look_Ahead`; see A.4.2.

`Text_IO.Complex_IO` defines similar `Get` and `Put` procedures to `Text_IO.Float_IO` with analogous semantics. The only somewhat arbitrary decision that we made concerns the mechanism for filling the target string in the case of output to a string. The question is where to put any extra blanks that are needed to fill the string. A rule like the one for `Text_IO.Float_-IO.Put` to a string might read:

> *Outputs the value of the parameter* Item *to the given string, following the same rule as for output to a file, using a value for* Fore *such that the sequence of characters output exactly fills, or comes closest to filling, the string; in the latter case, the string is filled by inserting one extra blank immediately after the comma.*

Such a rule essentially allocates the available space equally to the real and imaginary components. But that is not desirable when the value of the `Exp` parameter is zero and the two components of the `Item` parameter have disparate magnitudes, so that the integer part of one requires more characters than the integer part of the other. To accommodate this case, we have chosen a rule, simple to implement, that left justifies the left parenthesis, real component, and comma and right justifies the imaginary component and right parenthesis. All the extra spaces are placed between the comma and the imaginary component; they are available to accommodate either component, should it be unusually long. If strings produced by this rule are eventually displayed in the output, the real and imaginary components will not line up in columns as well as with the previously cited rule, but it can be argued that output to a string is intended for further computation, rather than for display.

Early implementation experience indicated that it might also have been profitable to consider yet another rule for output to a string, namely, that all the components be right justified, with all the padding placed at the beginning of the string. This rule would be extremely easy to implement if `Text_IO.Float_IO.Put` to a string (which right justifies its output in the target string), had an additional out parameter which gave the index of the first non-blank character that it put into the output string.

G.2 Floating Point Machine Numbers

Many of the attributes of floating point types are defined with reference to a particular mathematical representation of rational numbers called the *canonical form*, which is defined, together with those attributes, in the Predefined Language Environment. The definitions clarify certain aspects of the floating point machine numbers. Several new representation-oriented attributes of floating point machine numbers are also defined, together with a group of functional attributes called the "primitive function" attributes.

G.2.1 Clarification of Existing Attributes

The machine numbers of a floating point type are somewhat informally defined as the values of the type that are capable of being represented to full accuracy in all unconstrained variables of the type. The intent is to exclude from the set of machine numbers any extra-precise numbers that might be held in extended registers in which they are generated as a consequence of performing arithmetic operations. In other words, it is the stored values that matter and not values generated as intermediate results.

The representation-oriented attributes `S'Machine_Mantissa`, `S'Machine_Emin`, and `S'Machine_Emax` of a floating point subtype S are defined in terms of bounds on the components of the canonical form. The attribute `S'Machine_Radix` is the radix of the hardware representation of the type and is used as the radix of the mantissa in the canonical form.

These definitions clarify that `S'Machine_Emin` is the minimum canonical-form exponent such that *all* numbers expressible in the canonical form, with that exponent, are indeed machine numbers. In other words, `S'Machine_Emin` is determined by the normalized floating point numbers only; the presence of IEEE denormalized numbers in the implementation does not affect (reduce) the value of `S'Machine_Emin`. A consequence of this definition of `S'Machine_Emin` is that the primitive function attribute `S'Exponent(X)` can yield a result whose value is less than that of `S'Machine_Emin` if X is denormalized.

The definitions also clarify that `S'Machine_Emax` is the canonical-form exponent of the machine number of largest magnitude whose negation is also a machine number; it is not the canonical-form exponent of the most negative number on radix-complement machines.

Alternative definitions for `S'Machine_Emin` and `S'Machine_Emax` were considered, namely, that they yield the minimum and maximum canonical-form exponents for which some combination of sign, exponent, and mantissa yields a machine number. This would have allowed denormalized numbers to be accommodated without relaxing the normalization requirement (see the next section) in the definition of the canonical form, and the result of `S'Exponent(X)` would have necessarily remained within the range `S'Machine_Emin` .. `S'Machine_Emax`, which is appealing. Nevertheless, it was judged to be too much of a departure from current practice and therefore too likely to cause compatibility problems.

G.2.2 Attributes Concerned With Denormalized Numbers and Signed Zeros

Many implementations of Ada do provide IEEE denormalized numbers and "gradual underflow", as defined in [IEC 89], even though the full capabilities of IEEE arithmetic are not provided and must await an Ada binding to IEEE arithmetic. (Denormalized numbers come for free with IEEE hardware chips and have always been consistent with the Ada model of floating point arithmetic; it would require extra code generation to suppress them.) Since denormalized numbers are capable of being stored in variables of an unconstrained floating point type, they are machine numbers. What characterizes the denormalized numbers is that they can be represented in the canonical form with an exponent of S'Machine_Emin, provided that the normalization requirement on the mantissa is relaxed. If every nonzero number expressible in this weakened canonical form is a machine number of the subtype S, then the new representation-oriented attribute, S'Denorm, is defined to have the value True.

Many implementations also provide IEEE signed zeros, which similarly come for free. The new representation-oriented attribute, S'Signed_Zeros, is True if signed zeros are provided by the implementation and used by the predefined floating point operations as specified in [IEC 89]. The idea behind a signed zero is that a zero resulting from a computation that underflows can retain the sign of the underflowing quantity, as if the zero represented an infinitesimal quantity instead; the sign of a zero quantity, interpreted as if it were infinitesimal, can then affect the outcome of certain arithmetic operations.

Moreover, various higher-level operations, such as the elementary functions, are defined to yield zeros with specified signs for particular parameter values when the Signed_Zeros attribute of the target type is True. And indeed, some such operations, for example, Arctan and Arccot produce different (nonzero) results in certain cases, depending on the sign of a zero parameter, when Signed_Zeros is True.

In some cases, no conventions exist yet for the sign of a zero result. We do not specify the sign in such cases, but instead require the implementation to document the sign it produces. Also, we have not carried over into the facilities for complex arithmetic and the complex elementary functions the specifications for the signs of zero results (or their components) developed by the SIGAda NumWG, largely because of their excessive complexity. Instead we merely suggest that implementations should attempt to provide sensible and consistent behavior in this regard (for example, by preserving the sign of a zero parameter component in a result component that behaves like an odd function).

G.2.3 The Primitive Function Attributes

A group of attributes of floating point types called the "primitive function" attributes is provided, in support of Requirement R11.1-A(1), to facilitate certain operations needed by the numerical specialists who develop mathematical software libraries such as the elementary functions.

These attributes are modelled on the various functions in the standard package Generic_Primitive_Functions for Ada 83 [ISO 94b], but made available in the language as attributes of a floating point subtype rather than as functions in a generic package. These attributes support

- error-free scaling by a power of the hardware radix,

- decomposition of a floating point quantity into its components (mantissa and exponent), and construction of a floating point quantity from such components,

- calculation of exact remainders, and various directed rounding operations.

All of these attributes yield the mathematically specified results, which are either machine numbers or have the accuracy of the parameters. For a general rationale for the design of the primitive functions, see [Dritz 91b]. (Some of the attributes have different names from the corresponding functions in [ISO 94b], since some of the names in the latter had already been used for other new, but unrelated, attributes.)

The casting of the primitive functions as attributes, rather than as functions in a generic package, befits their primitive nature and allows them to be used as components of static expressions, when their parameters are static.

The Exponent and Fraction attributes decompose a floating point number into its exponent and (signed) fraction parts. (These attributes, along with Scaling and Leading_Part, are useful in the argument reduction step of certain kinds of function approximation algorithms in high-quality mathematical software; Scaling and Compose are similarly useful in the final result assembly steps of such algorithms.)

T'Exponent(X) is defined in such a way that it gives an indication of the gross magnitude of X, even when X is denormalized. In particular, if X is repetitively scaled down by a power of the hardware radix, T'Exponent(X) will decrease by one and will continue to do so (on machines with denormalized numbers) even after X becomes denormalized. T'Fraction(X) will *not* change as X is scaled in this way, even when X becomes denormalized. To achieve this behavior, an implementation of Exponent must do more than just pick up the hardware exponent field and unbias it, and an implementation of Fraction must do more than just pick up the hardware fraction field; both attributes must be sensitive to denormalized numbers.

(Indeed, the presence or absence of the leading fraction digit is dependent on whether a number is denormalized or not, on IEEE hardware. Probably the most efficient solution to the problem is for the implementation of Exponent to scale the operand up by an appropriate fixed amount *k* sufficient to normalize it when the operand is in the denormalized range, as evidenced by its having the minimum exponent or by other means; extract and unbias the exponent field; and then subtract *k* to obtain the result. The implementation of Fraction can simply extract the fraction field after a similar scaling up when the operand is in the denormalized range, and then attach the appropriate fixed exponent; what the scaling accomplishes is the left shifting of the fraction field and the removal of its leading digit.)

The Copy_Sign attribute transfers the sign of one value to another. It is provided for those applications that require a sign to be propagated, even (on machines with signed zeros) when it originates on a zero; such a need cannot be met by the predefined comparison operators and various sign-changing operations (like **abs** and negation), because comparison ignores the sign of zero and therefore cannot be used to determine the sign of a zero. By the same token, the implementation of Copy_Sign must likewise use some other technique, such as direct transfer of the sign bit or some other examination of the Sign operand to determine its sign. An application can use the Copy_Sign attribute to determine the sign of a zero value, when required, by transferring that sign to a nonzero value and then comparing the latter to zero.

The Remainder attribute computes the remainder upon dividing its first floating point parameter by its second. It considers both parameters to be exact, and it delivers the exact remainder, even when the first parameter is many orders of magnitude larger than the second; for this reason, its implementation can be tricky. This attribute is useful in implementing the argument reduction step of algorithms for computing periodic functions (when the period is given exactly).

The function T'Remainder(X, Y) is defined so that the magnitude of the result is less than or equal to half the magnitude of Y; it may be negative, even when both parameters are positive. Note that the Remainder attribute cannot be considered to be a natural extension of the predefined **rem** operator for floating point operands (and, indeed, that is one reason why the functionality was not made available by overloading **rem**). To see this, observe that

```
Float'Remainder(14.0, 5.0)    -- yields -1.0
```

whereas

```
14 rem 5                      -- yields 4
```

and so are quite different. The rationale for defining Remainder this way is twofold: it exhibits the behavior preferred by numerical analysts (i.e., it yields a reduced argument of generally smaller magnitude), and it agrees with the IEEE rem operator. Indeed, the latter is implemented in hardware on some machines; when available, it should certainly be used instead of the painful alternative documented in [Dritz 91b].

The functionality of the Successor and Predecessor functions of [ISO 94b] is provided by extending the existing attributes Succ and Pred to floating point types. Note that T'Succ(0.0) returns the smallest positive number, which is a denormalized number if T'Denorm is True and a normalized number if T'Denorm is False; this is equivalent to the "fmin" derived constant of LIA-1 (Language Independent Arithmetic) [ISO 93]. (Most of the other constants and operations of LIA-1 are provided either as primitive functions or other attributes in Ada 95; those that are absent can be reliably defined in terms of existing attributes.)

G.3 Assignments to Variables of Unconstrained Numeric Types

Ada 83 did not make a distinction between unconstrained and constrained numeric subtypes. Any subtype T was considered constrained by the values given by T'First and T'Last; if no range constraint was declared for T, then T'First = T'Base'First and T'Last = T'Base'Last.

It was technically not possible for a variable of an unconstrained subtype to be assigned a value outside the range T'Base'First .. T'Base'Last. This prevented the optimization of leaving a value in an extended register beyond an assignment, fulfilling subsequent references to the target variable from the register. To guarantee that the new value of the target variable after an assignment is not outside the range T'Base'First .. T'Base'Last, it is necessary in Ada 83 either to store the register into the variable's assigned storage location (if such a store operation could signal violation of the range check by generating an overflow condition) or to compare the value in the register to the values of T'Base'First and T'Base'Last; if the range check succeeds, the value in the register can be used subsequently.

Ada 95 does not perform a range check on the value assigned to a variable of an unconstrained numeric subtype; consequently, such a target variable can acquire a value outside its base range (T'Base'First .. T'Base'Last). This allows the value to be retained in the register in which it was generated and never stored (if all subsequent references to the target variable can be fulfilled from the register) nor checked by comparison for inclusion in the base range.

A consequence of this change, which generally allows more efficient object code to be generated, is that an Ada 83 program that raised Constraint_Error for a range violation on assignment to a variable of an unconstrained numeric subtype may raise the exception later (at a different place) or not at all. The first possibility arises because it may be necessary to store the extended register in the storage format for any of several reasons at a place far removed from the original assignment. The opportunity to raise the exception at such remote places is provided by a new rule that allows Constraint_Error to be raised at the place where a variable is referenced (fetched), if its value is outside its base range.

G.4 Accuracy and Other Performance Issues

The Numerics Annex specifies the accuracy to be delivered by the elementary functions, the complex arithmetic operations, and the complex elementary functions, and the performance to be expected from the random number generator. It also specifies the accuracy expected of the predefined floating point and fixed point arithmetic operators. If the Numerics Annex is not implemented, the predefined arithmetic operations and the various numerical packages do not have to yield any particular language-defined accuracy or performance, except where specified outside the Numerics Annex.

Even though the accuracy and performance requirements of the Numerics Annex are realistic, strict conformance may, in certain implementations, come only at a price. One or more native floating point instructions may produce slightly anomalous behavior that cannot conform to the model without some kind of sacrifice; for example, the purported maximum precision may have to be reduced, or some operations may have to be simulated in software. Similarly, achieving the specified accuracy in the elementary functions (say) may mean abandoning less accurate but much faster versions available on a hardware chip. Thus, to allow the user to trade accuracy for other considerations, the Numerics Annex specifies a pair of modes, strict mode and relaxed mode, that may be selected by the user. The accuracy and other performance requirements apply only when the strict mode is selected; the relaxed mode exempts implementations from these requirements, exactly as if the Numerics Annex had not been implemented.

A program that is intended for wide distribution, and whose numerical performance is to be guaranteed and portable across implementations, must be compiled and linked in the strict mode. Its portability will clearly extend, in that case, only to implementations that support the Numerics Annex.

The language does not specify how the modes should be implemented. It is clear, however, that the choice of mode can affect code generation, the values of the model-oriented attributes, and the version of the numerical libraries that is used. In implementations that meet the requirements without any undue sacrifices, or that have nothing substantial to gain from their relaxation, the two modes may, in fact, be identical.

G.4.1 Floating Point Arithmetic and Attributes

The strict-mode accuracy requirements for predefined floating point arithmetic operations are based on the same kind of model that was used in Ada 83, but with several changes. The Ada 83 model of floating point arithmetic was a two-level adaptation of the "Brown Model" [Brown 81] and defined both model numbers and safe numbers. The Ada 95 model is closer to a one-level, classical Brown Model that defines only model numbers, although it innovates slightly in the treatment of the overflow threshold.

The existence of both model numbers and safe numbers in Ada 83 caused confusion which hopefully will not apply to Ada 95. Note however, that the model numbers in Ada 95 are conceptually closer to the safe numbers rather than the model numbers of Ada 83 in terms of their role in the accuracy requirements. Other problems with the Ada 83 model centered around inherent compromises in the way the Brown Model was adapted to Ada 83. These compromises are eliminated in Ada 95, and other improvements are made, by

- freeing the model numbers to have a mantissa length that depends only on the implementation's satisfaction of the accuracy requirements, rather than a quantized mantissa length;

- defining the model numbers to have the hardware radix, rather than a fixed radix of two;

- defining the model numbers to form an infinite set, and basing overflow considerations on the concept of a type's "safe range" rather than on the largest model number;

- separating range and precision considerations, rather than tying them together intimately via the infamous "4B Rule" [RM83 3.5.7]; and

- freeing the minimum exponent of the model numbers from a connection to the overflow threshold, allowing it to reflect underflow considerations only.

We will now consider these in detail.

Mantissa Length

The Ada 83 safe numbers have mantissa lengths that are a function of the `Digits` attribute of the underlying predefined type, giving them a quantized length chosen from the list (5, 8, 11, 15, 18, 21, 25, ...). Thus, on binary hardware having `T'Machine_Mantissa` equal to 24, which is a common mantissa length for the single-precision floating point hardware type, the last three bits of the machine representation exceed the precision of the safe numbers. As a consequence, even when the machine arithmetic is fully accurate (at the machine-number level), one cannot deduce that Ada arithmetic operations deliver full machine-number accuracy. By freeing the mantissa length from quantization, tighter accuracy claims will be provable on many machines. As an additional consequence of this change, in Ada 95 the two types declared as follows

```
type T1 is digits D;
type T2 is digits T1'Digits range T1'First .. T1'Last;
```

can be represented identically. This matches one's intuition, since the declaration of `T2` requests neither more precision nor more range than that of `T1`. In Ada 83, the chosen representations almost always differ, with `T2'Base'Digits` being greater than `T1'Base'Digits`, for reasons having nothing to do with hardware considerations. (Note that this artificial example is not intended to illustrate how one should declare two different types with the same representation.)

Radix

Using the hardware radix rather than a binary radix has two effects:

- It permits practical implementations on decimal hardware (which, though not currently of commercial significance for mainstream computers, is permitted by the radix-independent IEEE floating point arithmetic standard [IEEE 87]; is appealing for embedded computers in consumer electronics; and is used in at least one such application, a Hewlett-Packard calculator);

- On hexadecimal hardware, it allows more machine numbers to be classed as model numbers (and therefore to be proven to possess special properties, such as being exactly representable, contributing no error in certain arithmetic operations, and so on).

As an example of the latter effect, note that `T'Last` will become a model number on most hexadecimal machines. Also, on hexadecimal hardware, a 64-bit double-precision type having 14 hexadecimal (or 56 binary) digits in the hardware mantissa, as on many IBM machines, has safe numbers with a mantissa length of 51 binary bits in Ada 83, and thus no machine number of this type with more than 51 bits of significance is a safe number. In Ada 95, such a type would have a mantissa length of 14 hexadecimal digits, with the consequence that every machine number with 53 bits of significance is now a model number, as are some with even more.

Note that the type under discussion does not have Ada 83 safe numbers with 55 bits in the mantissa, even though that is the next possible quantized length and one which is less than that of the machine mantissa. This is because some machine numbers with 54 or 55 bits of significance do not yield exact results when divided by two and cannot therefore be safe numbers. This is a consequence of their hexadecimal normalization, and it gives rise to the phenomenon known as "wobbling precision": the hexadecimal exponent remains unchanged by the division, while the mantissa is shifted right, losing a bit at the low-order end.

Safe Range

Extending the model numbers to an infinite set is intended to fill a gap in Ada 83 wherein the results of arithmetic operations are not formally defined when they are outside the range of the safe numbers but an exception is not raised. Some of the reasons why this can happen are as follows:

•   the quantization of mantissa lengths may force the bounds of the range of safe numbers to lie inside the actual hardware overflow threshold;

•   arithmetic anomalies of one operation may require the attributes of model and safe numbers to be conservative, with the result that other operations exceed the minimum guaranteed performance;

•   the provision and use of extended registers in some machines moves the overflow threshold of the registers used to hold arithmetic results well away from that of the storage representation;

•   the positive and negative actual overflow thresholds may be different, as on radix-complement machines.

The change means, of course, that one can no longer say that the model numbers of a type are a subset of the machine numbers of the type. As a consequence we have introduced the concept of the "safe range" of a type in Ada 95. This is the subrange of the type's base range that is guaranteed to be free of overflow; in Ada 83 terms, this subrange was the range of the type's safe numbers. Thus, in Ada 95 the the model numbers of a type within the type's safe range are indeed a subset of the machine numbers of the type.

By continuing the model numbers beyond the safe range of a type, we can say that an operation whose result interval (defined, as usual, in terms of model numbers) transcends the safe range of the result type either raises Constraint_Error, signalling overflow, or delivers a value from that result interval (provided the Machine_Overflows attribute is True for the type). In Ada 83, the result when an exception was not raised was completely implementation defined in this case. Of course, it continues to be implementation defined when the Machine_Overflows attribute is False for the type.

Incidentally, the safe range of a type has bounds characterized by two independent attributes, Safe_First and Safe_Last. In Ada 83, the range of safe numbers of a type was necessarily symmetric, with its upper bound being given by the value of the Safe_Large attribute. This was necessary, because Safe_Large was itself defined in terms of Safe_Emax, which gave the maximum exponent of the safe numbers. Because the model numbers no longer have a finite range, we no longer talk about the maximum exponent of the model numbers, and in fact there is no longer such an atttribute. Allowing the safe range to be asymmetric accommodates radix-complement machines better than Ada 83; in fact, it removes another impediment to the identical representation of the types T1 and T2 in the example given earlier.

The 4B Rule

Separating range and precision considerations is equivalent to dropping the "4B Rule" as it applies to the predefined types. There is however a "4D Rule" which affects the implementation's implicit selection of an underlying representation for a user-declared floating point type lacking a range specification, providing *in that case* a guaranteed range tied to the requested precision.

The change in the application of the 4B Rule allows all hardware representations to be accommodated as predefined types with attributes that accurately characterize their properties. Such types are available for implicit selection by the implementation when their properties are compatible with the precision and range requested by the user; but they remain *unavailable* for implicit selection, in the absence of an explicit range specification, exactly as in Ada 83.

The *4D* Rule says that the representation chosen for a floating point type declared with a decimal precision of *d*, but lacking a range specification, must provide a safe range of at least $-10.0^{4d} .. 10.0^{4d}$. If the type declaration includes a range specification, the safe range need only cover the specified range.

The *4B* Rule was introduced in Ada 83 in order to define the model numbers of a type entirely as a function of a single parameter (the requested decimal precision). By its nature, the rule potentially precludes the implementation of Ada in some (hypothetical) environments; in other (actual) environments, it artificially penalizes some hardware types so strongly that they have only marginal utility as predefined types available for implicit selection and may end up being ignored by the vendor. Such matters are best left to the judgment of the marketplace and not dictated by the language. The particular minimum range required in Ada 83 (as a function of precision) is furthermore about twice that deemed minimally necessary for numeric applications [Brown 81].

Among implementations of Ada 83, the only predefined types whose characteristics are affected by the relaxation of the *4B* Rule are DEC VAX D-format and IBM Extended Precision, both of which have a narrow exponent range in relation to their precision.

In the case of VAX D-format, even though the hardware type provides the equivalent of 16 decimal digits of precision, its narrow exponent range requires that the Digits attribute for this type be severely penalized and reported as 9 in Ada 83; the Mantissa attribute is similarly penalized and reported as 31, and the other model attributes follow suit. In Ada 95, in contrast, the Digits attribute of this predefined type would have a truthful value of 16, the Model_Mantissa attribute (corresponding to Ada 83's Mantissa attribute, but interpreted relative to the hardware radix rather than a fixed radix of two) would have a value of 56, and the other model-oriented attributes would accurately reflect the type's actual properties. A user-declared floating point type requesting more than 9 digits of precision does not select D-format as the underlying representation in Ada 83, but instead selects H-format; in Ada 95, it still cannot select D-format *if it lacks a range specification* (because of the effect of the new *4D* Rule), but it *can* select D-format if it includes an explicit range specification with sufficiently small bounds.

The IBM Extended Precision hardware type has an actual decimal precision of 32, but the *4B* Rule requires the value of its Digits attribute to be severely penalized and reported as 18 in Ada 83, only three more than that of the double-precision type. Supporting this type allows an Ada 83 implementation to increase System.Max_Digits from 15 to 18, a marginal gain and perhaps the reason why it is rarely supported. In Ada 95, on the other hand, such an implementation can support Extended Precision with a Digits attribute having a truthful value of 32, though System.Max_Digits must still be 18. Although a floating point type declaration lacking a range specification cannot request more than 18 digits on this machine, those including an explicit range specification with sufficiently small bounds can do so and can thereby select Extended Precision.

Note that the named number System.Max_Base_Digits has been added to Ada 95; it gives the maximum decimal precision that can be requested in a type declaration that includes a range specification. In IBM systems having the Extended Precision type, the value of this named number can be 32.

Minimum Exponent

Freeing the minimum exponent of the model numbers to reflect only underflow considerations removes another compromise made necessary in Ada 83 by defining the model numbers of a type in terms of a single parameter. The minimum exponent of the model or safe numbers of a type in Ada 83 is required to be the negation of the maximum exponent (thereby tying it implicitly both to the overflow threshold and, through the *4B* Rule, to the precision of the model numbers).

One consequence of this is that Ada 83's range of safe numbers may need to be reduced simply to avoid having the smallest positive safe number lie inside the implementation's actual underflow threshold. Such a reduction gives yet another way of obtaining values outside the range of safe numbers without raising an exception. Another consequnce is that the smallest positive safe number may, on the other hand, have a value unnecessarily greater than the actual underflow threshold.

This change therefore allows more of the machine numbers to be model numbers, allowing sharper accuracy claims to be proved.

Machine and Model Numbers

Consideration was given to eliminating the model numbers and retaining only the machine numbers. While this would further simplify the semantics of floating point arithmetic, it would not eliminate the interval orientation of the accuracy requirements if variations in rounding mode from one implementation to another and the use of extended registers are both to be tolerated. It would simply substitute the machine numbers and intervals for the model numbers and intervals in those requirements, but their qualitative form would remain the same. However, rephrasing the accuracy requirements in terms of machine numbers and intervals cannot be realistically considered, since many platforms on which Ada has been implemented and might be implemented in the future could not conform to such stringent requirements.

If an implementation has clean arithmetic, its model numbers in the safe range will in fact coincide with its machine numbers, and an analysis of a program's behavior in terms of the model numbers will not only have the same qualitative form as it would have if the accuracy requirements were expressed in terms of machine numbers, but it will have the same quantitative implications as well. On the other hand, if an implementation lacks guard digits or has genuine anomalies, its model numbers in the safe range will be a subset of its machine numbers having less precision, a narrower exponent range, or both, and accuracy requirements expressed in the same qualitative form, albeit in terms of the machine numbers, would be unsatisfiable.

The values of the model-oriented attributes of a subtype S of a floating point type T are defined in terms of the model numbers and safe range of the type T, when the Numerics Annex is implemented; this is true even in the relaxed mode. (Some of these attributes have partially implementation-defined values if the Numerics Annex is not implemented.)

Although these attributes generally have counterparts in Ada 83, their names are new in Ada 95. The reason is that their values may be different in Ada 95. Clearly, S'Model_Mantissa and S'Model_Emin will have very different values on a nonbinary machine, since they are interpreted relative to the hardware radix, rather than a radix of two. (On a hexadecimal machine, each will have roughly a quarter of the value of the corresponding attribute in Ada 83.) S'Model_Small and S'Model_Epsilon will only change slightly, if at all, because various effects will tend to cancel each other out. In any case, the new names convert what would be upward inconsistencies into upward incompatibilities. We have recommended that implementations continue to provide the old attributes, as implementation-defined attributes, during a transition period, with compiler warning messages when they are used. An Ada 83 program using the Safe_Small or Base'Epsilon attributes should be able to substitute the Model_Small and Model_Epsilon attributes for an equivalent (and logically consistent) effect, but substitutions for the other attributes may require more careful case by case analysis.

It is instructive to consider how the fundamental model-oriented attributes and the Digits attribute of a predefined floating point type P are determined in Ada 95, when the Numerics Annex is implemented. The algorithm is as follows.

- Initially set P'Model_Emin to P'Machine_Emin and P'Model_Mantissa to P'Machine_Mantissa. This tentatively defines an infinite set of model numbers.

- If the accuracy requirements, defined in terms of the model numbers, are satisfied by every predefined arithmetic operation that is required to satisfy them, *when overflow does not occur*, then these are the final values of those attributes. Otherwise, if the machine lacks guard digits or exhibits precision anomalies independent of the exponent, reduce

P'Model_Mantissa by one until the accuracy requirements are satisfied (when overflow does not occur); if underflow occurs prematurely, increase P'Model_Emin by one until the accuracy requirements are satisfied near the underflow threshold. The final set of model numbers has now been determined.

• Let P'Safe_First be the smallest model number that is greater than P'First and similarly let P'Safe_Last be the largest model number that is less than P'Last. These tentatively define the safe range.

• If overflow is avoided throughout the safe range by every predefined arithmetic operation, then this is the final safe range. Otherwise, i.e. if overflow occurs prematurely, increase P'Safe_First and/or decrease P'Safe_Last by one model number until overflow is correctly avoided in the resulting safe range. The final safe range has now been determined.

• Finally, let P'Digits be the maximum value of *d* for which

$$\lceil d*\log(10.0)/\log(\text{P'Machine\_Radix}) + 1\rceil \leq \text{P'Model\_Mantissa}.$$

This is relevant in the context of the selection of a representation for a user-declared floating point type, which must provide at least as many decimal digits of precision as are requested. If this condition is satisfied, the type's arithmetic operations will satisfy the accuracy requirements.

P'Model_Epsilon and P'Model_Small are defined in terms of other attributes by familiar formulae. The algorithm for Ada 83, which is not given here, is much more complex and subtle, with more couplings among the attributes.

G.4.2 Fixed Point Arithmetic and Attributes

The revision of the model of fixed point arithmetic focuses on two of the problems concerning fixed point types that have been identified in Ada 83:

• The model used to define the accuracy requirements for operations of fixed point types is much more complicated than it needs to be, and many of its freedoms have never been exploited. The accuracy achieved by operations of fixed point types in a given implementation is ultimately determined, in Ada 83, by the safe numbers of the type, just as for floating point types, and indeed the safe numbers can, and in some implementations do, have more precision than the model numbers. However, the model in Ada 83 allows the values of a real type (either fixed or float) to have arbitrarily greater precision than the safe numbers, and so to lie between safe numbers on the real number axis. Implementations of fixed point typically do not exploit this freedom. Thus, the opportunity to perturb an operand value within its operand interval, although allowed, does not arise in the case of fixed point, since the operands are safe numbers to begin with. In a similar way, the opportunity to select any result within the result interval is not exploited by current implementations, which we believe always produce a safe number; furthermore, in many cases (for some operations) the result interval contains just a single safe number anyway, given that the operands are safe numbers, and it ought to be more readily apparent that the result is exact in these cases.

• Support for fixed point types is patchy, due to the difficulty of dealing accurately with multiplications and divisions having "incompatible *smalls*" as well as fixed point multiplications, divisions, and conversions yielding a result of an integer or floating point type. Algorithms have been published in [Hilfinger 90], but these are somewhat complicated and do not quite cover all cases, leading to implementations that do not support representation clauses for Small and that, therefore, only support binary *smalls*.

The solution adopted in Ada 95 is to remove some of the freedoms of the interval-based accuracy requirements that have never been exploited and to relax the accuracy requirements so as to encourage wider support for fixed point. Applications that use binary scaling and/or carefully matched ("compatible") scale factors in multiplications and divisions, which is typical of sensor-based and other embedded applications, will see no loss of accuracy or efficiency.

A host of specialized requirements for information systems applications is addressed by the division of fixed point types into ordinary and decimal fixed point types. The facilities for the latter are to be found in the Information Systems Annex, see Chapter F.

The default *small* in Ada 95 is an implementation-defined power of two less than or equal to the *delta*, whereas in Ada 83 it was defined to be the largest power of two less than or equal to the delta. The purpose of this change is merely to allow implementations that previously used extra bits in the representation of a fixed point type for increased precision rather than for increased range, giving the safe numbers more precision than the model numbers, to continue to do so. An implementation that does so must, however, accept the minor incompatibility represented by the fact that the type's default *small* will differ from its value in Ada 83. Implementations that used extra bits for extra range have no reason to change their default choice of *small*, even though Ada 95 allows them to do so.

Note that the simplification of the accuracy requirements that apply in the strict mode, by expressing them directly in terms of integer multiples of the result type's *small* rather than in terms of model or safe intervals, removes the need for many of the attributes of fixed point types. However, it is recommended that implementations continue to provide these attributes as implementation-defined attributes during a transition period, with their Ada 83 values, and that implementations produce warning messages upon detecting their use.

The accuracy requirements for the adding operators and comparisons now simply say that the result is exact. This was always the case in Ada 83, assuming operands were always safe numbers, and yet it was not clear from the model-interval form of the accuracy requirements that comparison of fixed point quantities was, in practice, deterministic.

Other accuracy requirements are now expressed in terms of small sets of allowable results, called "perfect result sets" or "close result sets" depending on the amount of accuracy that it is practical to require. These sets comprise consecutive integer multiples of the result type's *small* (or of a "virtual" *small* of 1.0 in the case of multiplication or division giving an integer result type). In some cases, the sets contain a single such multiple or a pair of consecutive multiples; this translates into a requirement that the result be exact, if possible, but never off by more than one rounding error or truncation error. This occurs with fixed point multiplications and divisions in which the operand and result smalls are "compatible" meaning that the product or quotient of the operand *smalls* (depending on whether the operation is a multiplication or a division) is either an integer multiple of the result *small*, or vice versa.

These compatible cases cover much of the careful matching of types typically exhibited by sensor-based and other embedded applications, which are intended to produce exact results for multiplications and at-most-one-rounding-error results for divisions, with no extra code for scaling; they can produce the same results in Ada 95, and with the same efficient implementation. Our definition of "compatible" is more general than required just to cover those cases of careful matching of operand and result types, permitting some multiplications that require scaling of the result by at worst a single integer division, with an error no worse than one rounding error.

In cases where the *smalls* are incompatible, the accuracy requirements are relaxed, in support of Requirement R2.2-A(1); in fact, they are left implementation defined. Implementations need not go so far as to use the Hilfinger algorithms [Hilfinger 90], though they may of course do so. An Ada 95 implementation could, for instance, perform all necessary scaling on the result of a multiplication or division by a single integer multiplication or division (or shifting). That is, the efficiency for the cases of incompatible *smalls* need not be less than that for the cases of compatible *smalls*. This relaxation of the requirements is intended to encourage support for a wider range of *smalls*. Indeed, we considered making support for all *smalls* mandatory in the strict mode on the grounds that the weaker requirements removed all barriers to practical support for arbitrary *smalls*, but we rejected it because it would make many existing implementations (which could in all other respects satisfy the requirements of strict mode) instantly nonconforming.

Ada 95 allows an operand of fixed point multiplication or division to be a real literal, named number, or attribute. Since the value v of that operand can always be factored as an integer multiple of a compatible *small*, the operation must be performed with no more than one rounding error and will cost no more than one integer multiplication or division for scaling. That v can always be factored in this way follows from the fact that it, and the *smalls* of the other operand and the result, are necessarily all rational quantities.

The accuracy requirements for fixed point multiplication, division, and conversion to a floating point target are left implementation defined (except when the operands' *smalls* are powers of the target's machine radix) because the implementation techniques described in [Hilfinger 90] rely on the availability of several extra bits in typical floating point representations beyond those belonging to the Ada 83 safe numbers; with the revision of the floating point model, in particular the elimination of the quantization of the mantissa lengths of model numbers, those bits are now likely gone. Except when the operands' *smalls* are powers of the target's machine radix, requiring model-number accuracy for these operations would demand implementation techniques that are more exacting, expensive, and complicated than those in [Hilfinger 90], or it would result in penalizing the mantissa length of the model numbers of a floating point type just to recover those bits for this one relatively unimportant operation. An implementation may use the techniques in [Hilfinger 90] for fixed point multiplication, division, and conversion to a floating point target; the accuracy achieved will be exactly as in Ada 83, but will simply not be categorizable as model-number accuracy, unless the operands' *smalls* are powers of the target's hardware radix. Furthermore, in the latter case, even simpler algorithms are available.

G.4.3 Accuracy of the Numerics Packages

The Numerics Annex specifies the accuracy or other performance requirements that the mandatory elementary function and random number packages must satisfy in the strict mode. These are discussed in A.3 with the packages themselves.

G.5 Requirements Summary

The facilities of the Numerics Annex and the floating point attributes of the Predefined Language Environment Annex relate to the requirements in 11.1 (Floating Point).

The requirement

R11.1-A(1) — Standard Mathematics Packages

is met in part by the Complex types and related packages of the Numerics Annex and in part by the elementary functions and random numbers packages of the Predefined Language Environment Annex.

The study topic

S11.1-B(1) — Floating Point Facilities

is met by the numeric model presented in the Numerics Annex and by the floating point attributes provided in the Predefined Language Environment Annex.

H Safety and Security

For critical software, the key issue is *assurance of the application*, that is, gaining sufficient confidence in the application in order to authorize its use. The Ada 95 language contributes to this process by providing a language definition which minimizes potential insecurities and which thus facilitates independent program validation and verification. However, the size and richness of the language also raise some issues that need to be addressed if it is to be fully exploited for safety and security applications.

*   As a high-level language, Ada 95 tries to leave implementation-oriented matters unspecified, but validation and verification of a system requires knowledge of these details.

*   Although software development takes place in Ada 95, validation logically needs to be performed at the object code level; understanding the correspondence between source and object is therefore essential for the most critical applications.

*   If the expressive power of the full language is not needed, there must be some way to ensure that a tailored version of the run-time system is used, without support for the unwanted features, thereby simplifying the process of validation and verification.

The Safety and Security Annex is designed to address these concerns. It should be noted that the prospective users of this annex form a small, specialized community who historically have been served by special contracts between large user organizations and specific vendors. However, such an approach can only satisfy the requirements of enterprises with significant resources. Since the Annex is part of the Ada 95 standard, "off-the-shelf" products should be able to satisfy the same requirements at substantially reduced costs. This will allow Ada 95 to be used with assurance by different application areas, including those outside the military sector such as medical electronics or electronic funds transfer. Over the period that the Ada 95 standard can be expected to be operative, the number of applications in such areas could rise quite steeply.

Relationship to Current Approaches

The UK Ministry of Defence standard for the procurement of safety-critical software [MoD 91] is based upon the use of mathematical specifications and formal proofs or rigorous arguments for showing compliance and has been effectively used in some environments. However, the complete application of this standard is often not feasible and hence other methods must be used, even within the defense context. Whatever approach is taken, the final form of the program is vital, since it is an analysis of the program itself which must provide the basis of most of the assurance procedures. This implies that the programming language used for the application is likely to have a key role. The Annex aids but does not require the application of mathematical specification techniques.

A mature standard in the safety-critical area which takes a different view to formal methods is the international avionics standard [DO-178B]. Here the emphasis is on design, analysis and test. Although there is little stated about programming languages, it is clear that any analysis will either depend upon the programming language or upon a corresponding analysis of the object code generated by the compiler. Quite rightly, the standard requires isolation from the correctness of the compiler for the most critical software, implying that one must either reason from the object code or else show that the object and source code are equivalent. The Annex provides facilities to aid in the analysis of the object code, including access to data values during testing, in order to ease validation.

In the context of safety, the requirements surrounding the application of computers to nuclear shut-down systems has been well documented [Archinoff 90]. In the same application area, the need to show that compiler errors can be detected is given in [Pavey 93].

In the security area, the general requirements are well documented in [DoD 85, ITSEC 91]. Although the latter document does imply some requirements on the programming language in use, they are at a level that is not really relevant to this Annex.

Dealing with Language Insecurities

To reason about a program requires that the structures used within the program be well-defined and properly implemented. However, almost all existing programming languages standardized by ISO are not defined in a mathematically precise form. Hence substantial care must be taken to ensure that the features of the language used are well-defined and that the program accords with the intention of the programmer.

Since programmers are fallible, languages which require checks for some forms of error are an advantage, especially if the design can allow the software to request the system to return to a safe state. Ada 83 is the only widely used language suitable for critical applications which requires such checking (and Ada 95 of course continues in this tradition). Many critical applications do not exploit this checking but demonstrate (perhaps by mathematical proof) that the checks could not fail. Undertaking this form of static checking is very expensive in staff time, and hence is not practical for less critical applications. A brief summary of the securities and insecurities of standard languages is shown in Figure H-1.

Standard Language	Security Features	Insecurities
Ada 83	Runtime checks required Pointer initialization Type-secure across packages Can recover from check failures	Access to unset scalars
Modula-2 (not yet an ISO standard)	Type-secure across modules Limited recovery from failures	Unset pointers (& scalars)
Pascal	Strongly typed	Runtime checks optional Unset pointers (& scalars)
C	(Additional tools: make and lint)	150 undefined "features" Runtime checking often not done
Fortran 77	Type checking No pointers	Default declarations No checking across routines

Figure H-1: Securities and Insecurities in Standard Languages

A comparison of programming languages for safety and security applications showed that a subset of Ada 83 was a good choice [Cullyer 91]. The subsequent maturity of Ada compilers, the better understanding of the language, and the provision of Ada-specific tools, makes the language the first choice for many applications. In contrast, the C language is deprecated in the IEC draft standard on safety software [IEC/SC65A 91] since it is very difficult to demonstrate that C code is restricted to the subset which is well-defined. Ada 95 fills a number of the insecurities noted in Ada 83 [Wichmann 89], and hence it provides the smallest area of uncertainty to the developer.

The C++ language is not listed in Figure H-1, since it is not yet standardized by ISO. There are substantial problems in the validation of C++ code, some of which arise due to the lack of an agreed standard. Moreover, since almost all C programs can be compiled by a C++ compiler, the inherent problems of the validation of C code are transferred to C++. In addition, compiler vendors are at a disadvantage compared to Ada in not having an internationally agreed and comprehensive validation suite for the language.

The insecurities may be avoided by suitably chosen subsets of Ada, such as that provided by SPARK [Carré 88]. The same subset could be used for Ada 83 and Ada 95, and may be exploited by the compiler through the pragma Restrictions described below. Note that the use of such subsets is not in conflict with Ada's traditional "no subsets, no supersets" policy, since for compiler validation purposes there must be a complete implementation of the language, and not simply a subset. The point is that any particular program will not use the full language, and if there are a set of features whose exclusion can result in software for which validation and verification is facilitated, then the implementation can enforce such exclusions in one mode of operation and can link in reduced versions of the run-time system.

Until now, language standards have not addressed the problem of the validation of the object code generated by a compiler. This is troublesome unless information is provided linking the source code to the object code. Such checking will be required for many years to come while there is a possibility of errors being introduced by a compiler. The alternative of having "trusted compilers" does not yet seem viable for the major languages.

The user can indicate exclusion of particular features in a partition by means of pragma Restrictions. For instance, the user can indicate that tasking is not needed, thus allowing the run-time system to be very much smaller and simpler. Similarly, the user can ensure that other language features are avoided. Through this facility, the language used on a particular system can be reduced to a quite small subset of Ada 95. This can facilitate the analysis of the source code, since not only can language features be avoided for which verification and validation are impractical, but one can be assured that these restrictions are enforced by the compiler.

One might argue in favor of a smaller language than Ada 95 for safety-critical systems, rather than a mechanism for indicating features to be excluded. However, past experience has shown that there is no consensus on what should be in such a language; applications differ, and agreement on a suitable subset is difficult since specific applications do require most features of Ada for convenient and maintainable coding.

After agreeing to the Ada 95 standard, WG9 discussed the problems in the validation and verification of Ada programs. Such activities could be substantially cheaper if tools could effectively analyze Ada source code to verify safety or security requirements. In practice, this is likely to require that the code conforms to some conventions, suh as being within a subset. These issues are to be investigated by the WG9 Verification Rapporteur Group (VRG).

H.1 Understanding Program Execution

A key issue for the language in critical applications is that of *understandable execution*. Ada 95 addresses this issue in several ways:

- Eliminating certain cases of Ada 83 erroneous execution, and replacing them by bounded errors;

- Adding an attribute to check for scalar data validity;

- Adding a pragma to cause otherwise uninitialized scalars to be set to values outside their nominal subtypes;

- Requiring documentation of implementation decisions.

H.1.1 The Valid Attribute

Although this feature is in the core language [RM95 13.9.2], it is discussed here since it is relevant to the safety and security applications. The Valid attribute allows the user to check whether the bit-pattern for a scalar object is valid with respect to the object's nominal subtype. A reason for including such a facility is that the other language-defined operations that could conceivably undertake the same function might not have the intended effect. The following example illustrates the issue.

```
declare
    I : Integer range 1 .. 10;   -- Uninitialized
    A : array (1 .. 10) of Float;
begin
    ...
    A(I) := 1.0;
    ...
end;
```

In Ada 83, users are sometimes surprised to learn that a compiler is permitted to remove the index check for A(I). The reason that such an optimization is allowed is that a reference to an uninitialized scalar object in Ada 83 yields an *erroneous execution*, and therefore unspecified effects. Thus the compiler may apply the following logic:

- If the value of I happens to be within 1 .. 10, then the check is unnecessary.

- On the other hand, if the value is not within 1 .. 10, then since execution is erroneous any effect is allowed including using the out of range value as an index.

Perhaps even more surprising, the programmer cannot count on the following style to ensure that a check is carried out:

```
declare
    I : Integer range 1 .. 10;   -- Uninitialized
    A : array (1 .. 10) of Float;
begin
    ...
    if I in 1 .. 10 then
        A(I) := 1.0;
    else
        raise Bad_Index;
    end if;
end;
```

In this example the compiler may optimize the test

```
I in 1 .. 10
```

to true, using the same logic that led to the suppression of the index check in A(I), namely that if the program's execution is not erroneous then the value of I will be within its declared subtype and hence the membership test can be omitted, and if the program's execution is erroneous then the effect is unspecified and thus again the test can be omitted.

Ironically, if the programmer had declared the variable I without a range constraint, then it is likely that the check would be performed (unless data flow analysis can show otherwise). The fact that including a range constraint with a scalar declaration might reduce the security of the code (by failing to raise a run-time exception) is against the Ada design philosophy.

This problem is addressed in several ways in Ada 95. First, a reference to an uninitialized scalar variable is no longer erroneous but rather a *bounded error*: the permitted effects are to yield a valid value (i.e., one within the variable's nominal subtype), to yield an invalid value (one within the variable's type but outside its nominal subtype), or to raise the exception Program_Error. This rule prevents the compiler from "reasoning from erroneousness". In the first example, unless the compiler has by default set the initial value of I to be within the range 1 .. 10 (which is not recommended, since it would mask errors), it will need either to raise Program_Error (because of the reference to an uninitialized object) or to generate a range check.

The second example will not have the problem of the **in** membership test being optimized away, but there is still the possibility that the reference to the uninitialized value of I will raise Program_Error, which is presumably not what the programmer intended. Moreover, to allow membership tests to be implemented simply and efficiently, the membership test only performs a range check and thus might not work as desired for enumeration types with "holes" in the representation.

These remaining issues have motivated the introduction of a simple, intuitive facility for checking that the value of a scalar object is within the object's nominal subtype. That is the purpose of the Valid attribute, which applies to any scalar object. As illustration, an alternative version of the second example, using Valid rather than the membership test, is as follows

```
declare
    I : Integer range 1 .. 10;   -- Uninitialized
    A : array (1 .. 10) of Float;
begin
    ...
    if I'Valid then
        A(I) := 1.0;
    else
        raise Bad_Index;
    end if;
end;
```

The purpose of the Valid attribute is to check the contents of a scalar object without formally reading its value. Using this attribute on an uninitialized object is not an error of any sort, and is guaranteed to either return True or False (it will never raise Program_Error), based on the actual contents of the object, rather than on what the optimizer might have assumed about the contents of the object based on some declaration.

Although the use of the Valid attribute for checking the validity of uninitialized data is somewhat contrived, other examples are more realistic, such as checking data from:

•   An unchecked conversion;

•   Calling procedure Read from Sequential_IO or Direct_IO;

•   An object for which pragma Import has been specified;

•   An object that has been assigned a value where checks have been suppressed.

The Valid attribute could potentially be applied to a wider range of types than that of scalars. Unfortunately, this extension is not easy to define with the rigor that should be expected. For instance, what action should an implementation perform to attempt to determine if a bit-pattern of an access type is a valid value? If the attribute *did* have a larger scope but with unspecified semantics, then its use on critical systems would require an implementation-defined specification, checked by analysis of the object code produce by the compiler. This complexity did not seem justified.

If the attribute is to be used on a record read from a file that was written by a COBOL program, it is important that the Ada program can check that the value is meaningful rather than execute code based upon the premise that the value is legal. In the context of safety-critical applications, such alien data is likely to be provided by some external device. Such data could well be a composite value, in which case the attribute must be applied to the scalar components. Checking on non-scalar components or for potential gaps between components cannot be undertaken with Valid.

It is not necessarily logically sound to apply Valid to a composite type, due to the presence of components which are undefined, as in the following example

```
type Stack_Data is array (1 .. 100) of Character range 'A' .. 'Z';

type Stack is
   record
      Index : Integer range 0 .. 100;
      Data  : Stack_Data;
   end record;
```

Only those elements of the array up to the position of Index need to be checked for validity, but there is no way for a general definition to capture such semantics.

In formulating the design of the Valid attribute, we considered several alternatives. One was to have it as a scalar subtype attribute function, applied to the object of that subtype whose validity was to be checked; for example,

```
declare
   subtype S is Integer range 1 .. 10;
   I : S;
begin
   . . .
   if S'Valid(I) then ... else ... end if;
   . . .
end;
```

However, this would present semantic difficulties since calling a function causes evaluation of the actual parameters; the main idea behind the Valid attribute, however, is that it should not read the value of the object, since this might raise an exception.

Another approach we considered was to have the attribute as a function associated with a "target" scalar subtype (either as an attribute or through generic instantiation) applied to a value of any (other) "source" scalar subtype. The idea is to check a source bit pattern (say an Integer value) to see if it is a valid value for the target subtype. As an example, if Enum is an enumeration type with "holes" (that is, it has a representation clause with non-contiguous integer values), and v is an Integer value, then Enum'Valid(V) would return True if V has one of the identified values, and False otherwise. The idea is to check validity *before* the source bits are copied to the target object.

One problem with such an approach, however, is that it raises some semantic and implementation questions with respect to the expected sizes of both the source value and the target subtype; this issue does not arise with the notation X'Valid since the object X is not itself evaluated. Another problem is that it is rather unwieldy in the common case where validity needs to be checked for data that is being read from an external device into a record, and where the record fields have scalar subtypes. In such a case it is simplest and most efficient to read the data into the record first, and then to check validity. This works conveniently using the `Valid` attribute applied to a scalar object

```
declare
   type Rec is
      record
         A : Character range 'A' .. 'Z';
         B : Integer range 1 .. 10;
      end record;
   R : Rec;
begin
   Read(R);
   if not R.A'Valid then ... end if;
   if not R.B'Valid then ... end if;
   ...
end;
```

With the alternative style, it would be necessary to have a record type with fields corresponding to the full types (`Character` and `Integer`), to read the data into an object of this record type, check validity of the fields, and then copy it into R so that constraint checks can be enforced on subsequent assignments to these fields.

As a result of analysis of these design alternatives, we decided on the approach where validity is realized through an attribute that is applicable to a scalar object, rather than an attribute function associated with a target scalar subtype.

H.1.2 Abnormal Values

A value can be *abnormal* instead of having an invalid representation [RM95 13.9.1]. From the point of view of safety and security, such abnormal values are a potential disaster, since they can give rise to erroneous execution — the opposite of predictable execution which the Annex strives to provide.

In general, it is not possible for a scalar value to be abnormal, and in any case, the user can take precautions against scalar values with an invalid representation by suitable use of the `Valid` attribute. It might be possible for an implementation to obtain an abnormal floating point value if a signalling NaN was produced in which no trap-handler was provided, since access to the value would produce unpredictable results.

(A signalling NaN is a bit pattern used in place of a floating point number in systems that support IEC 559; see [IEC 89]. Access to such a bit pattern will cause an interrupt, if the processor state is set correctly. If the interrupt is not then handled, disaster could ensue. In fact, signalling NaNs could be used to detect unset floating point values with very little overhead on some machines, although existing Ada systems do not appear to do this.)

Abnormal values can arise from an abort statement interrupting an assignment operation, or interactions with the environment external to the Ada program. Typically, the data type would be composite with a complex internal structure which can be placed in a state that the Ada system cannot subsequently handle. Task objects and types with discriminants are potential candidates for types which can have abnormal values. Vendors providing support for this Annex should be able to indicate if and how such value can arise (unless they require the use of the `Restrictions` pragma to effectively exclude such values).

Abnormal values can also arise if a language defined check would fail but the check has been suppressed. Suppressing checks can obviously lead to problems, since any storage could be overwritten making it generally impossible for the Ada run-time system to retain control.

H.1.3 The Pragma Normalize_Scalars

The use of an undefined scalar is a very common programming error which must be detected in critical systems (see [Wichmann 92] for a discussion of some of the subtleties of this issue in connection with an earlier draft of the Ada 9X mapping). As observed above, the Ada 95 rule treating this as a bounded error rather than an erroneous execution will inhibit certain compiler optimizations that would make this kind of error difficult to detect. However, it does not prevent the compiler from giving an in-range "default" initial value to otherwise uninitialized scalars, which would also make it difficult to find errors.

In the light of these considerations, Ada 95 supplies the configuration pragma Normalize_Scalars, which serves to ensure that elaboration of the declaration of an otherwise uninitialized scalar, sets the object to an invalid value if such a value exists. If no such invalid value exists for a scalar object, then the implementation needs to identify this (for example on the program listing) so that the programmer is alerted to ensure that the object is assigned before it is referenced. In such cases, the program will have a predictable (but not necessarily portable) value and the implementation needs to document the in-range value taken.

The name Normalize_Scalars reflects the intent of the pragma. A "normal" value for a scalar object is either valid (if within the object's nominal subtype) or invalid (if outside). Since scalar initializations induced by the pragma might or might not be invalid, "normalize" is an appropriate description. In general, an invalid value will be outside the object's nominal subtype, but there are also cases where it is possible for the implementation to produce an invalid value even when the nominal subtype has the same range as the type. For example, suppose that an implementation of the type Boolean reserves 8 bits for objects that are not in packed arrays or in records with representation clauses, with 16#00# corresponding to False and 16#01# to True. In the presence of pragma Normalize_Scalars, an otherwise uninitialized Boolean variable will be set to an invalid value, which is neither 0 nor 1.

Some interactions with other pragmas need to be understood by prospective users. First, if a scalar object is the argument to pragma Import, then its (probable lack of) initialization is not affected by pragma Normalize_Scalars. This is reasonable, since an imported data item is under the control of foreign language code that is not subject to Ada semantics. Note that if an Ada scalar variable corresponds to a memory-mapped I/O location, then any implicit initialization could have an unwanted effect. This can be avoided by importing the scalar variable.

Another interaction is with pragma Restrictions. If a system is being developed in which exception handling is absent, then the use of pragma Normalize_Scalars is inappropriate, and even dangerous. With the pragma Restrictions(No_Exceptions) in effect, there is no object code generated to perform constraint checks. Clearly, referencing an out-of-range scalar would then result in an unpredictable effect.

H.1.4 Documentation of Implementation Decisions

One aspect of predictability is to understand the behavior of a program in situations identified by the language rules as either bounded errors or unspecified effects. Thus the implementation needs to document these behaviors, either as part of a listing or tool-processable output, or (if a general rule) as independent documentation. Some specific requirements are now discussed.

Parameter Passing Mechanism

Some parameters can be passed by reference or by copy. A different mechanism could even be chosen for two calls of the same subprogram. Incorrect programs can be affected by the choice and hence safety and security applications need to check that either this error has not been made or that the effect will be acceptable. The simplest solution is for the compiler to indicate the choice made. If the choice is a simple static one (say, always by reference, except for entry parameters which are always by copy), then this could be stated once in the compiler documentation, otherwise the object code listing (or appropriate tool) should indicate the choice. In fact, some compilers have a complex algorithm which varies from call to call, especially for slices. The complexity of this algorithm is not relevant to the issue, merely that the choices made should be clear.

Storage Management

Many safety critical applications are in the form of an infinite loop. It is important that this loop should not permanently consume storage. Therefore it must be possible, by reviewing the object code, to ensure that this does not happen. In the security context, it is important that storage used to contain classified information does not leak via the storage allocation system. It is possible that this requirement can be met by proposals for a user-defined allocation and de-allocation of storage — in which case the run-time system may be less critical. There is a parameter to the Restrictions pragma to avoid storage leaks.

Of course, even if there is no net consumption of storage within a program, and if the storage is not allocated and de-allocated via a stack, it will be necessary to show that storage fragmentation does not undermine the system. For this reason, the algorithm used by the run-time system is important and must be fully documented.

For time-critical applications, additional constraints could be required on the run-time routines, such as having a tight upper bound in execution time. This requirement is not specified here, since it will be application specific and many systems avoid the use of the heap and hence are unlikely to have a problem.

Evaluation of Numeric Expressions

Problems can arise if the evaluation of numeric expressions involves extended range or extra precision. Counter-intuitive results can be produced with floating point expressions when combined with equality tests, which is quite common on IEEE systems. Hence the vendor should document the approach taken, independent of any annotation of the object code, so that any potential confusion can be avoided. This implies that for any specific expression, the range and precision with which it is computed should be clear from the documentation (see [RM95 H.2(2)]).

The evaluation of the exponentiate operator is not defined exactly in [RM95 4.5.6(11..12)]. Apart from the association of the multiplications (which only makes a marginal difference to the result), performing the division (for negative exponents) at the end or initially make a significant difference to the occurrence of overflow.

Adherence of an Ada implementation to the Language Independent Arithmetic standard [ISO 93] would be appropriate in the context of this annex, since that standard requires that the numeric operations used are precisely defined.

H.2 Reviewable Object Code

The relevant features supplied by the Annex are the pragmas Reviewable and Inspection_Point.

H.2.1 The Pragma Reviewable

Due to the well-known fact that all compilers have bugs, it is the conventional wisdom of the safety critical community to avoid assuming that the generated object code is automatically correct. For instance, the approach taken in the avionics standard DO-178B is one of Design,

Review and Test [DO-178B]. As far as practical, the review and test activities are undertaken at the object code level. Indeed, if the reliability requirements of Class 1 flight critical software (the most critical) are to be attained, every attempt must be made to detect errors induced by a compiler. This is expensive, but unavoidable given current technology.

The pragma Reviewable applies to a partition so that the compiler can generate code to match special documentation thus permitting independent review of the object code. The following specific requirements apply.

Elaboration Order for Library Units

Since the elaboration order may have a visible effect, it is essential that the chosen ordering be indicated by the implementation in forms convenient both for human readers (such as in a program listing) and for processing by automated tools. An example of such a tool is a static analyzer that determines the absence of accesses to undefined variables.

Object Code

It cannot be assumed that the vendor will provide every tool needed for validation and verification. In any case, complete reliance upon such tools may not be acceptable. Hence it should be possible to extract the object code in a form that can be easily machine processed. An example of a tool is one which provides maximal times for instruction sequences so that time-critical software can be shown to meet deadlines.

The wording in the Annex on the requirement of producing output suitable for tools uses the word "should" rather than the conventional (and stronger) "shall". This is because it may not be possible to check compliance with the requirement objectively. Since there are no standard data interchange formats for such information, there is no means of giving a precise description of what is "suitable".

Object Lifetime Analysis

The implementation needs to allow the user to determine which objects are assigned to which registers, and the lifetimes of those assignments.

An important aspect of code generation is the assignment of registers. The most general register assignment algorithm is known to be NP complete and hence it is quite unreasonable for compiler documentation to detail such an algorithm (especially since it may be proprietary). However, the result of the algorithm for the specific safety/security application is to be provided. The area allocated to any object is to be specified so that an object can be accessed, either via the register or via main memory for the entire lifetime of the object. Compilers typically produce code to address internal information as well as the information directly related to objects declared by the program. This issue is not specified in the Annex, since it is unclear how it can be specified in a testable form.

Initialization Analysis

For each reference to a scalar object, the implementation needs to identify whether the object is either "known to be initialized" or "possibly uninitialized". Note that pragma Normalize_Scalars does not affect this analysis.

Since the access to unset scalars can lead to severe errors, and compilers already perform some of the analysis required, the purpose of this requirement is to provide the information to aid validation and verification. In the case of "possibly uninitialized", the information would depend upon the strength of the analysis performed by the compiler, and hence different compilers (or even the same compiler under different options) could not be expected to give identical information.

Machine Instructions Used

For the most critical applications, it is necessary to check that the machine instructions required by an application are correctly handled by the processor hardware. Microcode faults in processor chips are not uncommon and therefore such checking may be needed [Wichmann 93]. A list of the used instructions aids the checking since unused instructions need not be checked. It would be helpful to identify instructions only used in the run-time system, but this is not essential.

For checking timing constraints, a user needs to consider only the instructions listed.

Relationship between Source and Object Code

Code sequences derived entirely from one Ada statement (or declaration) must be indicated as such. In those cases in which a code sequence is derived from a single Ada statement, this statement should be identified. Due to some optimizations, it could be that this identification is difficult. In such cases, some optimizations could be disabled when the pragma Reviewable is in force, rather than enhancing the compiler to meet the requirements with full optimization. In this area, a tool could be much more useful for independent validation and verification rather than an annotated listing.

Some compilers provide information based upon line numbers rather than Ada statements. For the purposes of this annex, it can be assumed that there is only one statement per line. For a single statement, several code sequences could be involved, especially if instruction scheduling merges the code from more than one statement. Addressing instructions derived from more than one statement would not have to be identified as such.

If an Ada statement results in no object code, then a positive indication of removal is required, rather than a mere absence of object code from a statement.

The user may need to compute the storage requirements for a program so that the absence of the Storage_Error exception can be checked. For subprograms containing only statically sized objects, an implementation should indicate the size of the stack frame required.

Exception Analysis

The implementation must indicate where compiler-generated run-time checks occur in the object code, and must also provide a method of determining which exceptions can be raised by any statement.

The handling of the predefined exceptions is problematic. Exception sites need not be in the same compilation unit as the handlers that service them. Some method is needed to indicate, explicitly in the object code, the actual locations at which exceptions are raised and handled. Some mechanism should be available, either through source or object code analysis, that permits the analysis of the program to determine which handler is used for each site that can raise an exception and to identify sites for which no handler is supplied. It would probably be most useful if this was in the form of a tool, rather than tables which required detailed analysis of each case. An example of a tool to undertake exception analysis is given by [Schaefer 93].

Since exceptions raised by predefined operations are not explicitly indicated in the source, and since the implementation is allowed some freedom in choosing actual execution order, this facility is best supported at the object code level. Even if a vendor does not choose to perform such an analysis, the information necessary to perform it should be made available to the user. For a detailed analysis of the issues involved, see Chapter 2 of the report on Formal Studies of Ada 9X [DoD 92].

Analysis of Run-Time System Components

Clearly, the fact that a compiler generates a call to an out-of-line routine does not obviate the need for reviewing the object code of the called routine. Hence the same requirements for reviewing the object code must apply to the run-time system components.

H.2.2 The Pragma Inspection_Point

A point in the program text can be marked as an *inspection point* through a pragma of the same name, optionally identifying a set of objects whose values are to be available. At the corresponding point(s) in the object code, the vendor is required to provide a means of determining the values of the specified objects, or, if none was specified, then a means of determining the values of all live objects. This implies that the object code can be analyzed with special tools so that properties of the code and object values can be verified, independently of the source code. In theory, full mathematical verification could be undertaken, although this implies that the specification of the application is available in a suitable form.

This proposal arose out of the discussion from the special meeting held in April 1993 [Brosgol 93] attended by experts associated with producing safety critical systems. The idea is to break down a program into code sections separated by inspection points to facilitate validation of the code. This idea is new, although the concept of "break-points" in assembly language debugging is clearly similar.

Note that a single occurrence of pragma Inspection_Point in the source text may correspond to several inspection points in the object code; for example, if the pragma appears in an inlined subprogram, a generic unit, or a loop that has been "unrolled" by the optimizer.

There are, not surprisingly, some interactions between the pragma and optimizations. Since a user will in general examine the values of inspectable objects when execution is suspended at an inspection point, it is essential that compilers not perform "dead code elimination" on prior assignments to such objects. On the other hand, disabling all optimization is too extreme and in fact is unnecessary. Thus the compiler is allowed to store inspectable objects in registers; the implementation needs to provide sufficient information to make this mapping known to the user. The compiler is also allowed to move expressions (including those which could raise predefined exceptions) over inspection points.

The main design decision in connection with inspection points was whether to provide a single pragma, or to separate it into two: one that identifies the inspectable objects, and the other that identifies the points in program execution where currently live inspectable objects could be inspected. An advantage of the two-pragma approach is separation of concerns, and the ability to specify that, say, a variable declared in a package body is inspectable outside the package without needing to have all live objects inspectable. (Note that, with the single pragma approach the name of a variable declared in a package body is inaccessible outside the package and hence cannot be used as an argument to pragma Inspection_Point. Thus in the single-pragma approach, if the user needs to be able to inspect such a variable, pragma Inspection_Point with no arguments needs to be provided, which makes all objects inspectable and thus may inhibit some optimizations.)

In the end, the choice of a single-pragma approach was based on anticipated usage of the functionality provided, and in particular on the desire to avoid tedious source code changes and recompilations during software development. That is, the exact set of objects that need to be inspected might not be apparent at the outset. With the two-pragma approach, a decision to identify an additional variable will require a source code modification and may induce significant recompilation costs depending on where the variable is declared. With the single-pragma approach, the default is to have all variables inspectable and hence this is not a problem.

In some respects the issue is similar to the decision taken in Ada that when a package is *with*ed, by default all entities declared in the package's visible part are available in the *with*ing unit. An alternative approach would have the latter specify exactly those entities that are needed. Although seemingly producing a narrower and more specific interface, this would in practice yield long lists of needed entities that no one would read, and programmers would end up using a notation that made all visible entities available. In the case of inspection points, the anticipated typical usage is to have all objects inspectable; in those contexts where the programmer knows that only a limited set is of interest, a specific list can be provided as argument to pragma `Inspection_Point`.

Pragma `Inspection_Point` with a specific list of names provides some of the capabilities of an assertion facility without the need of an additional language feature. For example, if one writes

pragma Inspection_Point(Alpha, Beta);

then, when the program is executed under the control of an appropriate monitor / debugger, it may be suspended at the corresponding point in the object code. Information is available at that point to examine `Alpha` and `Beta`. Therefore an assertion, say that `Alpha < Beta`, can be checked at that point. Note that no change to the generated code is required, which would be an issue if the assert capability were to be provided via an alternative mechanism. Variables such as `Alpha` and `Beta` must be in scope. Also, if such `Inspection_Point` pragmas are added at several points in a program, it may be possible to formally verify that the object code between the pragmas performs the operations in the source code.

H.3 Safety and Security Restrictions

A key technique that those developing critical software adopt is that of restricting the language constructs used. For instance, if tasking is not used, then the validation process is much simpler, since certain kinds of programming errors specific to tasking (such as deadlock, race conditions, and so on) cannot arise, and, moreover, the run-time system does not need to include any tasking support.

Although the term "subset" often has negative connotations, since in the past uncontrolled subsets for other languages have led to major portability problems, in the context of safety and security applications the use of subsets is essential. The issue is then how to satisfy these requirements without sacrificing the obvious significant advantages that Ada has enjoyed as a single-language standard. Interestingly, the current revision to the COBOL standard is going to a single-language model, in contrast to the language modules approach of the past, partly because of the success that Ada 83 has had with program portability.

The approach adopted is for the user to indicate excluded features as arguments to pragma `Restrictions`. The default behavior is for a compilation unit (or more generally a partition) to be rejected if it uses a feature identified in the pragma. Hence an Ada 95 compiler may enforce usage subsets in the manner required by [MoD 91], thus avoiding the potential risk of manual checking for adherence to restrictions. Moreover, an implementation is permitted to "bundle" restrictions, since otherwise compiler vendors would need to support 2^N versions of the run-time system, where N is the number of possible arguments to the pragma. Thus the pragma should not be seen as a way for precisely defining a subset, but as a framework which a vendor can exploit. As an example, consider the safety critical system produced by Alsys and described in [Brygier 93]. Here, an Ada 83 subset is defined which has a zero-byte run-time system, called CSMART. This subset is vendor-specific since it is oriented around the structure of the Alsys run-time system. An Ada 95 version of this system could be developed which is based on language-defined parameters to the `Restrictions` pragma.

The set of restrictions identified in the Safety and Security Annex is a representative set, but a compiler implementation may extend it. For example, in the SPARK system [Carré 88] the requirement is to use only those language features to which formal proof tools can be applied. Hence features such as generics are excluded, even though the implementation issues are straightforward.

Other analysis tools [Rex 88] impose similar restrictions on the source language. A vendor intending to support Ada 95 in those environments may thus add further restrictions to those defined in the Annex.

Although the default behavior in the presence of pragma Restrictions is to reject a compilation unit (or partition) if a restricted feature is used, the implementation may have a "full language" mode of operation where the use of a restricted feature elicits a warning message versus a fatal error. This could be useful in some environments, and it helps address the compiler validation concerns that might otherwise surround an implementation of a subset.

Possible scenarios showing uses of the Restrictions pragma are given in the following two examples.

Application to a Safety System

Vendor A produces a compiler and an implementation of the Safety and Security Annex, targeted to safety applications which use a standard similar to [DO-178B]. To simplify the production of the compiler and ensure the documentation aspects of reviewable object code are met, they *require* the use of the arguments No_Protected_Types, No_Allocators, No_Dispatch, No_Delay, No_Exceptions and Max_Tasks = 0 when the pragma Reviewable is applied to a partition.

The user of this system has chosen this compiler because of the option above, knowing that the object code produced has a very simple structure, and that therefore the source code and object code are easily related. The user understands that since checking code does not appear in the object code, it is essential for this application to ensure that the code is indeed exception-free. To this end, a program analysis tool is being used. The pragma Normalize_Scalars is not used.

To ensure that some language features are not used which would cause problems for the program analysis tool, additional parameters are specified by the user to the Restrictions pragma as follows: No_Floating_Point, No_Fixed_Point, No_Access_Subprograms. In other words, the design requirements of not using these features are enforced by the compiler by means of the pragma.

In fact, the program analysis tool cannot handle Unchecked_Conversion. However, this restriction cannot be imposed by use of the Restrictions pragma since the application does require its use. In consequence, the use of Unchecked_Conversion is confined to one package which is not analyzed by the tool. This package uses the attribute Valid to ensure that the raw data will not subsequently cause an unbounded error.

Application to a Security System

Vendor B produces a compiler specifically for the security community who produce systems complying with the Orange Book and ITSEC [DoD 85, ITSEC 91]. Here, the full language is supported by the vendor when pragma Reviewable is enforced, since some applications require almost all of the language.

The user chooses this compiler since the Annex is supported with the full language. Tested packages which have formed part of other systems are being imported into their applications, and therefore the imposition of the restrictions is not usually feasible.

Again, the user has tools to analyze the Ada source code to validate both the security kernel and the main application code for adherence to the security policy. Since the kernel and the application code are all in one partition, it is only possible to use the pragma Restrictions for those features not used in any part of the system. For instance, Unchecked_Conversion is used in the kernel but should not appear in the application code, and hence this rule cannot be enforced by the `Restrictions` pragma. On the other hand, the declaration of access-to-subprogram types is not required at all, and hence this restriction is checked by the pragma.

Since the full language is supported by the vendor, the documentation provided to adhere to the pragma `Reviewable` is quite complex. To aid the review of the object code, the vendor provides a special tool, based upon the debugger, to ease the process of independent validation and verification. In particular, the tool can be used to locate the object code arising from a specific statement or declaration. This facility depends on the removal of optimizations that would be applied in the absence of pragma `Reviewable`. The user decides to employ the pragma `Normalize_Scalars` to reduce the risk of a covert channel and also to aid the detection of programming errors. (In principle, program components could communicate information via unset scalar values, thus establishing a secret or covert communication channel.)

Hence, in this example, the pragma `Restrictions` has a modest effect upon the compiler and its method of use.

Other Applications

The `Restrictions` pragma could clearly be used in other contexts apart from safety and security. For instance, in the context of teaching Ada, it might be convenient to ensure students are using just those features which would be allowed when developing high integrity software. Since the pragma is a configuration pragma, it should be simple to set up an Ada compilation system so that the student does not need to use pragma `Restrictions` explicitly.

Some high performance applications could also use the pragma to ensure an appropriately tailored run-time system is used.

H.4 Validation against the Annex

The majority of the Ada 95 standard consists of specific features for which the conventional validation process works well. Corresponding to each feature, a number of Ada test programs can be written for which the outcome can be stated and checked, usually within the test program itself. In contrast, the essence of the Safety and Security Annex is not language features but high assurance for the application program. Thus it is clear that validation of implementations to this Annex is different from both the other Annexes and also from Ada 83. The problem of devising objective tests needs to be considered carefully in the context of the high assurance required, not just adherence to the standard.

H.5 Issues outside the Scope of the Standard

The Safety and Security community have concerns which cannot be addressed by the Ada 95 standard itself. These issues are recorded here for completeness and to demonstrate that the standard was not the correct place to have them resolved.

The general requirement is for a "high assurance" compiler and run-time system. However, it is not possible to characterize this by means of requirements which are consistent with a language standard. The philosophy adopted by the Annex is to require information so that a user can judge whether a specific compiler meets the (subjective) requirements of an application.

Some of the issues which arise here are as follows:

- Version control for compilers and run-time;

Each version of the compiler and/or run-time system must be distinguished by a version number. It is convenient if it is easy to trace back from the binary to the corresponding source code.

- Validation of compiler in non-standard modes;

  The compiler may well be used in a mode of operation which does not support the full language. In such a case, documentation is required (specified in the Annex). However, it is often convenient to provide information on the processing of the validation suite in this mode (not required by the Annex). There is a significant change from Ada 83 here, since a mode of operation in which some language features are not supported can be provided by means of the Restrictions pragma.

- Security of compiler against Orange book or ITSEC;

  If a compiler is being used in a security context, it would be necessary to know that it conformed to the relevant requirements [DoD 85, ITSEC 91].

- Compiler support;

  Critical projects are likely to require support from the vendor over an extended period.

- Evaluation;

  The Ada Compiler Evaluation Service provides additional tests to measure aspects such as processing speed which cannot be specified in the standard. Special tools are also available to stress test compilers in order to give further confidence in their quality; see [Austin 91] and [Elsom 91].

- Certification of a specific system;

  It would be convenient if a specific Ada run-time system could be formally certified. This would give additional confidence in a system, and would allow a vendor to provide an identical platform for several market areas. However, it is unclear how such a service would operate.

In short, the requirements for critical systems go beyond those aspects which are covered by a conventional standard, and hence those which can be satisfied by the ordinary validation process.

H.6 Requirements Summary

The facilities of the Safety and Security Annex relate generally to the requirements in 9.1 (Predictability of Execution), 9.2 (Certifiability), and 9.3 (Enforcement of Safety-Critical Programming Practices).
    More specifically, the study topic

S9.1-A(1) — Determining Implementation Choices

is met by the Normalize_Scalars pragma and by the requirements for documentation of implementation decisions.
    The requirement

R9.1-A(2) — Ensuring Canonical Application of Operations

is met by the pragma `Inspection_Point` and by the provision of `Off` as an argument to the pragma `Optimize`.
   The requirement

   R9.2-A(1) — Generating Easily Checked Code

is met by the `Reviewable` and `Inspection_Point` pragmas.
   The requirement

   R9.3-A(1) — Allow Additional Compile-Time Restrictions

is met by the pragma `Restrictions`.

Part Four

The Appendices

This fourth part comprises three appendices which summarize various aspects of the relationship between Ada 83 and Ada 95. Appendix X covers the incompatabilities of which there are few of real significance. Appendix Y gives the main changes betwen the Committee Draft, the Draft International Standard and the final International Standard; it shows that these changes are few and hence that the final language has had the benefit of considerable stability throughout the review periods. Appendix Z is a brief summary of the mapping between the original Requirements and the sections of this rationale where they are addressed; it concludes that Ada 95 meets the Requirements.

Appendix X   Upward Compatibility

A major design goal of Ada 95 was to avoid or at least minimize the need for modifying the existing base of Ada 83 software to make it compatible with Ada 95. This involves not only pursuing upward compatibility but also preserving implementation-dependent behavior that can currently be relied upon. In common with the experience of revising other language standards, it is infeasible to guarantee 100% compatibility.

Other languages have been more or less successful in meeting this goal. For example, COBOL 83 has been very successful in achieving upward compatibility with COBOL 74. Nevertheless some minor incompatibilities were introduced which affect existing programs. For example, IS_ALPHABETIC, accepts upper and lower case in the new COBOL standard. The transition from C to ANSI C and from there to C++ has also caused incompatibilities, for example C++ requires all procedure definitions in old-style C to be modified.

In the design of Ada 95, a very conservative approach has been adopted. The few incompatibilities that exist can be dealt with in a simple mechanical way. For example, the introduction of a small number of reserved words requires their replacement in any program using them as identifiers. Extensive surveys of existing code show few programs to be affected. Most of the other incompatibilities involve obscure or pathological programming styles which are expected to appear very infrequently in existing code.

The great majority of programs will not be significantly affected by these changes — the most likely incompatibilities being automatically detected at compilation time. Moreover, tools are being developed to aid in the reliable detection of any problems and thereby smooth the process of transition.

Only three incompatibilities are considered likely to occur in normal programs. They are as follows:

New reserved words — In Ada 95, six new reserved words have been added to the language.

Type `Character` has 256 positions — In Ada 95, the type `Character` has 256 positions. In Ada 83, it had 128 positions.

Unconstrained generic parameters — In Ada 95, different syntax must be used in a generic formal parameter to allow unconstrained actual parameters.

The following further two incompatibilities might occur in normal programs but are less likely:

Library package bodies illegal if not required — In Ada 95, it is illegal to provide a body for a library package that does not require one.

`Numeric_Error` renames `Constraint_Error` — In Ada 95, the declaration for `Numeric_Error` has been changed to a renaming of `Constraint_Error`.

These incompatibilities usually cause a legal Ada 83 program to be an illegal Ada 95 program and hence are detected at compile time. They are described in more detail in the ensuing sections. In each case we give an example of the incompatibility, an indication of how it can be avoided in existing Ada 83 programs and the possibility of its automatic detection and removal.

The remaining incompatibilities which are considered very unlikely to occur in normal programs are briefly considered in X.6.

The reader should note that we say that an incompatibility is consistent if the worst that can happen is that a legal Ada 83 program becomes illegal in Ada 95 and thus fails to compile. An incompatibility is said to be inconsistent if the program can remain legal but have a different meaning.

X.1 Reserved Words

Six new reserved words are introduced in Ada 95: **abstract**, **aliased**, **protected**, **requeue**, **tagged**, and **until**.

Two alternatives to new reserved words were considered: a new concept of unreserved keywords or the use of combinations of existing reserved words. Neither of these options was considered preferable to the transitory inconvenience caused by the introduction of the new reserved words.

An Ada 83 program that uses any of these words as identifiers is an illegal Ada 95 program. For example, the following fragment of Ada 83 will fail to compile in Ada 95 because it uses two of the new reserved words

```
Protected: Boolean := False;

procedure Requeue(The_Activity: Activity; On_Queue: Queue);
```

Avoidance is clearly straightforward — avoid use of these six words as identifiers. Detection of the incompatibility is also straightforward. Automatic correction is problematic — to ensure that a name change is valid requires significant analysis especially if the identifier is the name of a library unit, or occurs in a package specification for which use clauses occur.

X.2 Type Character

In Ada 95, the type Character has 256 positions. In Ada 83, it had 128 positions.

Although suitable for English-speaking nations, a character type based on ASCII is inappropriate for most of Europe. ISO has defined a number of 256 character standards such as Latin-1 and Latin-2. This change to the language thus accommodates non-English speaking nations.

An Ada 83 program could be an illegal Ada 95 program if it has a case statement or an array indexed by Character, but it could be a legal Ada 95 program with different semantics if it relies on the position number or value of Character'Last. For example

```
type Char_Kind is (Numeric, Alphabetic, Other);

Kind_Array: array (Character) of Char_Kind :=          -- (1)
                ('0' .. '9' => Numeric,
                 'A' .. 'Z' | 'a' .. 'z' => Alphabetic,
                 others => Other);

case Char is                                           -- (2)
    when Character'Val(0) .. Character'Val(63) => ...
    when Character'Val(64) .. Character'Val(127) => ...
end case;

I: Integer := Character'Pos(Character'Last);           -- (3)
```

Declaration (1) is legal in Ada 95 but probably does not achieve the desired effect. Statement (2) is illegal in Ada 95 and will be detected at compilation. Statement (3) illustrates a situation where the program will still execute but have a different effect in Ada 95 (it is inconsistent).

As it is likely that allowing for 256 characters is outside the scope of the original requirement for the program concerned, avoidance is not really the issue — a review of the requirements is necessary.

The inconsistency illustrated by the third example can be avoided by not depending on the position or value of Character'Last. Avoiding the other incompatibilities avoids the real issue of how the extra 128 characters are to be handled. Unless uniform behavior is acceptable for these extra characters, use of an others choice, whilst ensuring a legal (but bad style) Ada 95 program might cause unacceptable behavior.

Detection of the consistent incompatibilities is straightforward; detection that an inconsistency may arise is possible. Manual correction is necessary to determine whether the required semantics of the program are those defined by Ada 95.

Finally, it should be noted that the ISO Working Group with responsibility for maintaining the Ada standard, has decreed that this change can be introduced into Ada 83 compilers, so this will increasingly become an Ada 83 portability issue as more implementations support 256 characters.

X.3 Library Package Bodies

In Ada 95, library unit packages are allowed to have a body only if required by language rules. This avoids a nasty and not so rare error.

In Ada 83, a body need only be provided for a package that really needed one, such as where the specification contains subprogram or task declarations. If a body was provided for a library package that did not need a body (for performing initializations for example), then if the package specification was subsequently changed, the body became obsolete. However, since it was optional, subsequent builds incorporating the package would not incorporate the body, unless it was manually recompiled. This obviously affects packages, for example, that only declare types, constants and/or exceptions, a very common occurrence. As a trivial example in Ada 83 consider

```
package Optional_Body is
   Global_Variable: Integer;
end Optional_Body;

-----------------------------------------

with Integer_Function;
package body Optional_Body is
begin
   Global_Variable := Integer_Function;
end Optional_Body;
```

The solution adopted in Ada 95 is to allow a body for a library unit package only when one is required by some language rule; the above example is therefore illegal in Ada 95. However, the pragma Elaborate_Body can be used to cause a body to be required.

Given the non-uniform functionality of program libraries and sublibraries, it is probably wise not to try to automatically detect, let alone correct, this incompatibility.

X.4 Indefinite Generic Parameters

Ada 95 provides new syntax for a generic formal private type to indicate that the actual subtype is allowed to be indefinite. The old syntax is retained, but the meaning is changed to require definite actual parameters.

In Ada 83, no indication was given in a generic formal type declaration as to whether the actual needed to be definite, for example because the body declared an uninitialized variable for the type. It was thus possible for a legal instantiation to become illegal if the body was changed.

An Ada 83 program, where an indefinite type is used as a generic actual parameter is an illegal Ada 95 program. For example the following legal Ada 83 program is illegal in Ada 95

```
generic
    type Element_Type is private;
package Stack is ...
```

```
-----------------------------------------------------
```

```
with Stack;
package String_Stack is new Stack(Element_Type => String);
```

There is no way to avoid this incompatibility but an Ada 83 program can be annotated with an appropriate comment, thus

```
generic
    type Element_Type is private;   -- !! (<>) in Ada 95
package Stack ...
```

Detection of the incompatibility is straightforward. Manual correction is necessary to determine whether restricting the actual to being definite is acceptable.

It is interesting to note that some predefined library units in Ada 83 used this feature and so are changed. Examples are Unchecked_Conversion and Unchecked_Deallocation and also Sequential_IO.

Finally, it should be noted that the ISO Working Group has recommended that Ada 83 compilers be allowed to accept the new syntax in order to simplify transition.

X.5 Numeric Error

In Ada 95, the exception Numeric_Error is declared in the package Standard as a renaming of Constraint_Error.

The checks that could cause Numeric_Error to be raised in Ada 83 have all been reworded to cause Constraint_Error to be raised instead. Indeed, this change has been sanctioned by the Ada Rapporteur Group and encouraged in existing Ada 83 implementations.

However, the alternative of completely removing Numeric_Error was rejected because it would naturally have caused an incompatibility in programs using the construction

```
when Numeric_Error | Constraint_Error => Some_Action;
```

which is the currently recommended way of avoiding the confusion between Numeric_Error and Constraint_Error in Ada 83.

This construction is still allowed in Ada 95 because of an additional rule that permits an exception to be mentioned more than once in the same handler.

Programs which do have distinct separate handlers for Numeric_Error and Constraint_Error such as

```
exception
    when Constraint_Error => Action_1;
    when Numeric_Error => Action_2;
end;
```

are illegal in Ada 95. Moreover, an inconsistency will arise if a frame has an explicit handler for `Numeric_Error` or `Constraint_Error` but not both as in the following

```
exception
   when Constraint_Error => Action_1;
   when others => Action_2;
end;
```

since `Numeric_Error` will be caught by the first handler in Ada 95 but by the second in Ada 83.

Detection of the incompatibility is straightforward but manual correction will be necessary in cases where `Numeric_Error` is treated differently.

X.6 Other Incompatibilities

It is considered that other incompatibilities will be unlikely to occur in normal programs — the Ada 83 semantics being known only to the most erudite of Ada programmers — and so only a brief description seems appropriate in this document. In the following summary, they are grouped according to whether they result in a legal Ada 95 program but with different semantics; whether they would be detectable by an Ada 95 compiler and so on.

X.6.1 Unlikely Inconsistencies

These incompatibilities might cause a change in the runtime behavior, but they are not thought likely to occur in normal programs.

Derived type inherits all operations of parent — In Ada 95 a derived type inherits all its parent's primitive operations previously declared in the same declarative part. In Ada 83, it did not.

Floating point types may have less precision — the chosen representation for a floating point type may have less precision in Ada 95 for hardware with a non-binary radix.

Fixed point types may have less precision — the chosen representation for a fixed point type may have less precision in Ada 95. This is related to the next item.

Default *Small* for fixed point types — In Ada 83, the default value of *Small* was defined to be the largest power of two not exceeding `S'Delta`. In Ada 95, it is allowed to be a smaller power of two.

Rounding from real to integer is deterministic — Rounding is defined in Ada 95 as away from zero if the real number is midway between two integers.

Evaluation order of defaulted generic actual parameters — The order of evaluation of defaulted generic actuals is arbitrary in Ada 95.

Static expressions evaluated exactly — Static expressions are always evaluated exactly in Ada 95. In Ada 83 this was only required in a static context.

X.6.2 Unlikely Incompatibilities

These incompatibilities cause a legal Ada 83 program to be an illegal Ada 95 program and hence are detectable at compile time. They are considered to be unlikely in normal programs.

Bad pragmas illegal — In Ada 95, a pragma with an error in its arguments makes the compilation illegal. In Ada 83, it was ignored.

S'Base not defined for composite subtypes — In Ada 95, S'Base is not defined for a composite subtype S.

Wide_Character shares all character literals — As a result of adding types Wide_Character and Wide_String to package Standard, Ada 95 character literals are always overloaded and Ada 95 string literals are always overloaded.

Definition of freezing tightened — In Ada 95, range constraints on a type after its declaration and in occurrences in pragmas freeze the representation (are treated as forcing occurrences). In Ada 83 they were not treated as forcing occurrences.

Static matching of subtypes — In Ada 95, matching of subtypes is now performed statically instead of at runtime (as in Ada 83) in array conversions and generic instantiations.

Illegal to use value of deferred constant — In Ada 95 it is illegal to use the value of a deferred constant before it is set. In Ada 83 it was erroneous.

Explicit constraints in uninitialized allocators designating access types — in Ada 95 such constraints are illegal; in Ada 83 they were ignord.

Exceptions in static expressions illegal — in Ada 95, it is illegal to raise an exception in a static expression; in Ada 83 it made the expression non-static.

Preference for universal numeric operators — In Ada 95, the overload resolution rules have been changed to simplify them. As a consequence certain pathological Ada 83 programs become illegal.

Assume worst when checking generic bodies — Ada 83 generic contract model violations have been overcome in Ada 95 by assuming the worst case in a generic body.

New identifiers added to package System — New identifiers in package System may introduce illegalities into a unit having a use clause for System.

Append_Mode added to File_Mode enumeration — In Ada 95, subtype File_Mode in packages Sequential_IO and Text_IO has an extra literal, Append_Mode.

New identifiers added to package Text_IO — New identifiers in package Ada.Text_IO may introduce illegalities into a unit having a use clause for Text_IO.

New identifiers added to package Standard — New identifiers in package Standard may clash with existing use-visible identifiers.

Functions returning local variables containing tasks — In Ada 95 it is illegal or raises Program_Error if a function with a result type with a task subcomponent returns a local variable. In Ada 83 it was erroneous to return a variable containing a local task.

Illegal to change representation of types containing tasks — In Ada 95, it is illegal to give a representation item for a derived type containing a task.

Character literals always visible — In Ada 95, character literals are visible everywhere. In Ada 83 they followed the usual rules of visibility.

X.6.3 Implementation Dependent Incompatibilities

These incompatibilities only arise with some implementations. They occur either as a result of tightening up Ada semantics or where an Ada 83 implementation has used an identifier now predefined in Ada 95. In the latter case, an inconsistency could occur if the Ada 83 use of the identifier is compatible with the Ada 95 use, though this is unlikely.

Real attributes replaced — The Ada 83 attributes for a real subtype S (such as S'Mantissa) have been replaced by Ada 95 attributes defined in the Numerics Annex.

Certain pragmas removed — Some pragmas (including Interface and Shared) have been removed from the language and Priority has been moved to the Real-Time Systems annex.

New pragmas defined — The names of new pragmas may clash with implementation-defined pragmas.

New attributes defined — The names of new attributes may clash with implementation-defined attributes.

New library units defined — The names of new (language-defined) library units may clash with user-defined or implementation-defined library units.

X.6.4 Error Incompatibilities

These incompatibilities only occur in programs containing runtime errors, either detectable (an exception is raised) or undetectable (the execution is erroneous).

Exceeding 'First or 'Last of an unconstrained floating point type — In Ada 95, the 'First and 'Last of a floating point type declared without a range constraint are treated as minimum bounds and may be exceeded without causing Constraint_Error.

Dependent compatibility checks performed on object declaration — In Ada 95, dependent compatibility checks are performed on object declaration. In Ada 83, they were performed on subtype declaration.

Implicit array subtype conversion — Ada 95 allows sliding in more situations than did Ada 83, so Constraint_Error might not be raised as in Ada 83.

Lower bound of catenation changed for constrained array types — In Ada 95, the lower bound of the result of catenation for a constrained array type is defined to be 'First of the index subtype. In Ada 83, the lower bound of the result was 'First of the left operand.

Raising Time_Error deferred — In Ada 95, raising Time_Error can be deferred until Split or Year is called, or might not be raised at all. In Ada 83, it is raised on "+" or "-".

Data format for Get — In Ada 95, Get for real types accepts a wider range of formats which would raise Data_Error in Ada 83. Leading and trailing zeros and the radix point are not required.

X.7 Conclusion

This appendix has outlined the incompatibilities between Ada 83 and Ada 95. As we have seen, the small number that are likely to occur in practice are easily overcome. The remainder are unlikely to be encountered in normal programs but have been mentioned for completeness. For further details the reader should consult the comprehensive discussion in [Taylor 95] upon which this discussion has been based.

In conclusion, it is clear that there are unlikely to be significant transition issues for the vast majority of Ada 83 programs. Ada 95 has been carefully designed to minimize incompatibilities while meeting the overall goals of the requirements.

Appendix Y   Revisions To Drafts

The final International Standard for Ada 95 incorporates a number of changes to the Committee Draft [CD 93] of September 1993 (version 4.0 of RM9X) and the Draft International Standard [DIS 94] of June 1994 (version 5.0). These were made in response to formal comments made by the ISO members as part of the ballots on these drafts and to informal comments made by individual reviewers.

Although many of the changes are of an editorial nature several are of significance to the normal user. The more important changes are outlined in this appendix for the convenience of readers familiar with the drafts. Unless otherwise mentioned changes are with respect to the CD; if a change has occurred since the DIS then this is explicitly mentioned. A reference to that section of the rationale containing further discussion of the topic is given where appropriate.

The organization of the standard has been rearranged into a more logical order. The most significant to users familiar with Ada 83 is that chapter 14 on input-output has been moved into the annex on the predefined environment where it logically belongs. The annexes have themselves been reordered so that the mandatory annexes on the predefined environment and interfacing to other languages come first, followed by the six specialized needs annexes, the obsolescent features and then finally the non-normative annexes summarizing attributes and so on.

Y.1   Core Language

Trailing underlines

Trailing underlines are not allowed in identifiers whereas they were in the Committee Draft. Reversion to the Ada 83 rule was deemed appropriate because allowing just trailing underlines did not achieve the flexibility desired for wide compatibility with other languages such as C. Permitting leading underlines and multiple embedded underlines would have given greater compatibility but was considered unacceptable given the strength of concern for readability of program text. (2.1)

Modular types

Modular types are no longer described in terms of principal values and secondary values; they just have a value. A consequence is that conversion to and from integer types always preserves the numerical value or raises `Constraint_Error`. Wraparound on conversion no longer occurs. (3.3.2)

Extension aggregates

The ancestor part can now be a subtype name as an alternative to an expression. This enables an extension aggregate to be written even when the ancestor is abstract such as in the case of controlled types. (3.6.1, 7.4)

Controlled types

The package `Ada.Finalization` is restructured. The types `Controlled` and `Limited_Controlled` are no longer derived from types in the package `System.Implementation` (which no longer exists) but are simply abstract private types. The previous problem with writing aggregates for types derived from abstract types is now overcome by the new form of extension aggregate mentioned above.

The procedure `Split` is now called `Adjust`. The procedures `Adjust` and `Finalize` are no longer abstract but have null bodies like `Initialize`. (7.4)

Task storage size

The new pragma `Storage_Size` permits setting the storage size for individual tasks of a task type. This pragma is placed in the task specification and could thus depend on the value of a task discriminant. It replaces the use of an attribute definition clause for setting `Storage_Size` which gave the same attribute value to all tasks of the type. (9.6)

Children of generic units

It is no longer necessary for a child of a generic unit to be instantiated as a child of an instantiation of its parent. This requirement of the CD and DIS caused problems for many applications and a child can now be instantiated anywhere provided the generic child is visible. (10.1.3)

Exception occurrences

The package `Ada.Exceptions` is significantly restructured. The generic child `Ada.Exceptions.Messages` has been deleted. The ability to attach a user message to the raising of an exception can now be done more flexibly using the procedure `Raise_Occurrence` and the new attribute `Identity`. A major advantage is that exceptions so raised do not all have the same name `Exception_With_Message`.

The type `Exception_Occurrence` is now limited so that occurrences cannot be directly assigned. Exceptions can now be saved by a procedure and function `Save_Occurrence`. This approach overcomes implementation problems associated with the size of saved information. (11.2)

Access in generic bodies

The `Access` attribute can now be applied to objects in generic bodies when the access type is external. The associated accessibility check is dynamic and raises `Program_Error` if it fails. This gives greater flexibility in the use of generics. Note that the `Access` attribute still cannot be applied to subprograms in generic bodies when the access type is external. (12.3)

Alignment and Size attributes

The rules regarding these attributes have been somewhat changed. They can now only be applied to first subtypes (and objects) and not to all subtypes. Furthermore the `Address` must be a multiple of the `Alignment`. (13.1)

Y.2 Predefined Environment

Package Characters

This has been slightly restructured. The classification and conversion functions are now in a child package Characters.Handling and the package Characters is itself empty (other than the pragma Pure). The reason for this change is so that the child Characters.Latin_1 can be used without introducing any unnecessary executable code from its parent. A related change is that the package Standard.ASCII is now obsolescent; programmers are expected to use Characters.Latin_1 instead. (A.1)

Import and Export

The pragmas Import and Export now have a fourth parameter. The third parameter now gives the name of the entity in the other language and the fourth parameter gives the link name. (B.1)

Text_IO

A number of improvements have been made to Text_IO.

The concept of an error output stream has been added in line with facilities in many operating systems. Subprograms enable the error stream to be manipulated in a manner similar to the default output stream.

The functions Current_Input, Current_Output and Current_Error are overloaded with versions returning an access value. This enables the current stream to be preserved for later use in a more flexible manner.

The procedure Get_Immediate provides immediate non-buffered and non-blocking input; this is useful for interactive applications.

The procedure Look_Ahead returns the next character without removing it; this enables the user to write procedures which behave in a similar manner to the predefined procedures Get for integer and real types.

The procedure Get for real types will now accept a literal in more liberal formats; leading and trailing digits around the radix point are not required and indeed the point itself may be omitted. This enables data produced by programs written in languages such as Fortran to be processed directly.

The procedure Flush is added; this outputs the contents of the current buffer.

Nongeneric packages equivalent to instantiations of Integer_IO and Float_IO with the predefined types have been added since the DIS. These will be found of considerable benefit for teaching Ada since simple input-output of numbers can now be performed without the introduction of genericity. (A.4)

Command line

The package Ada.Command_Line enables a program to access the commands and parameters of the command line interpreter if any. It also enables a program to set its result status. (A.5)

Random number generator

The package `Ada.Numerics.Random_Numbers` has been considerably restructured and renamed as `Ada.Numerics.Float_Random`. The additional generic package `Ada.Numerics.-Discrete_Random` produces streams of random discrete values. (A.3)

Y.3 Specialized Needs Annexes

Edited output

The package `Ada.Text_IO.Pictures` is now called `Ada.Text_IO.Editing`. The description has been recast to avoid dependence on the COBOL standard. (F.2)

Appendix Z   Requirements

This appendix lists the various requirements and study topics discussed in the Requirements document [DoD 90] and generally indicates how they have been met (by refererence to other parts of this rationale) or else notes why they proved to be inappropriate.

Z.1 Analysis

The requirements are listed here in exactly the order of the requirements document; against each requirement is a list of the one or more Requirement Summary sections of this rationale containing an indication of how the requirement has been met.

Note that a detailed analysis of how the requirements themselves relate back to the original Revision Requests is contained in the Requirements Rationale [DoD 91].

General

R2.1-A(1) — Incorporate Approved Commentaries	1.5
R2.1-A(2) — Review Other Presentation Suggestions	1.5
R2.1-B(1) — Maintain Format of Existing Standard	1.5
R2.1-C(1) — Machine-Readable Version of the Standard	1.5
R2.2-A(1) — Reduce Deterrents to Efficiency	3.11, 8.5, 9.8
R2.2-B(1) — Understandability	1.5, 3.11, 8.5
R2.2-C(1) — Minimize Special-Case Restrictions	6.4, 8.5, 11.5
S2.3-A(1) — Improve Early Detection of Errors	1.5, 3.11
R2.3-A(2) — Limit Consequences of Erroneous Executions	1.5
R2.4-A(1) — Minimize Implementation Dependencies	3.11

International Users

R3.1-A(1) — Base Character Set	3.11
R3.1-A(2) — Extended Graphic Literals	3.11
R3.1-A(3) — Extended Character Set Support	3.11
R3.1-A(4) — Extended Comment Syntax	2.4

System Programming

Parallel Processing

No specific standard constructs for vector (SIMD) machines have been introduced; however the rules regarding exceptions have been changed so that vendors are able to provide optimizations through pragmas as discussed in 9.8.

Distributed Processing

Safety-Critical and Trusted

Information Systems

Scientific and Mathematical

Z.2 Conclusion

The above analysis shows that all the formal Requirements have been thoroughly met and it is only the Study Topics for parallel processing where compromises have been made.

We can therefore conclude that Ada 95 clearly meets the spirit of the Requirements as expressed in [DoD 90].

References

[1003.1 90]   The Institute of Electrical and Electronics Engineers. *Portable Operating System Interface (POSIX) — Part 1: System Application Program Interface (API) [C Language]*. The Institute of Electrical and Electronics Engineers, 1990.

[1003.4 93]   The Institute of Electrical and Electronics Engineers. *Portable Operating System Interface (POSIX) — Part 1: Amendment 1: Realtime Extensions [C Language]*. POSIX P1003.4/D14. March, 1993.

[1003.4a 93]   The Institute of Electrical and Electronics Engineers. *Portable Operating System Interface (POSIX) — Part 1: Amendment 2: Threads Extensions [C Language]*. POSIX P1003.4a/D7. April, 1993.

[1003.5 92]   The Institute of Electrical and Electronics Engineers. *POSIX Ada Language Interfaces, Part 1 Binding for System Application Program Interface (API)*. The Institute of Electrical and Electronics Engineers, 1992.

[AARM]   *Annotated Ada 95 Reference Manual, Version 6.0.* Intermetrics Inc, 1995.

[Abadi 91]   M. Abadi, L. Cardelli, B. Pierce, and G. Plotkin. "Dynamic Typing in a Statically Typed Language". *Transactions on Programming Languages and Systems* 13(2), April 1991.

[ANSI 83]   *Reference Manual for the Ada Programming Language.* ANSI/MIL-Std-1815a edition, 1983.

[Archinoff 90]   G. H. Archinoff, R. J. Hohendorf, A. Wassyng, B. Quigley and M. R. Borsch. "Verification of the Shutdown System Software at the Darlington Nuclear Generating Station". In *International Conference on Control & Instrumentation in Nuclear Installations*. May, 1990. Glasgow.

[Atkinson 88]   C. Atkinson, T. Moreton, and A. Natali (editors). *Ada for Distributed Systems*. The Ada Companion Series, Cambridge University Press, 1988.

[Austin 91]   S. M. Austin, D. R. Wilkins, and B. A. Wichmann. "An Ada Test Generator". In *Tri-Ada 1991 Proceedings*, ACM SIGAda, 1991.

[Baker 89]   T. Baker. "Time Issues Working Group". In *Proceedings of the First International Workshop on Real-Time Ada Issues,* pages 119-135. Software Engineering Institute and United States Office of Naval Research, Association for Computing Machinery, New York, NY, June, 1989. Appeared in ACM SIGAda *Ada Letters*, Vol. X, No..4.

[Baker 91]   T. Baker. "Stack-Based Scheduling of Realtime Processes". *The Real-Time Systems Journal* 3(1): 67-100, March, 1991.

[Bal 92]   H. E. Bal, M. F. Kaashoek, and A. S. Tanenbaum. "Orca: A Language for Parallel Programming of Distributed Systems". *IEEE Transactions on Software Engineering*, 18(3): 190-205, March 1992.

[Bardin 89]   B. M. Bardin and C. J. Thompson.   "Composable Ada Software Components and the Re-Export Paradigm". ACM SIGAda *Ada Letters* VIII(1), 1989.

[Barnes 76]   J. G. P. Barnes. *RTL/2 Design and Philosophy.* Heyden, 1976.

[Barnes 82]   J. G. P. Barnes. *Programming in Ada.* Addison-Wesley, London, 1982.

[Barnes 95]   J. G. P. Barnes. *Accessibility Rules OK!* Ada Letters XV(1), 1995.

[Birtwistle 73]   G. M. Birtwistle, O-J. Dahl, B. Myhrhaug, and K. Nygaard. *SIMULA Begin.* Auerbach, Philadelphia, PA, 1973.

[Blum 86]   L. Blum, M. Blum and M. Shub. "A Simple Unpredictable Pseudo-Random Number Generator". *SIAM Journal of Computing* 15(2):364-383, 1986.

[Booch 86]   G. E. Booch. "Object-Oriented Development".   *IEEE Transactions on Software Engineering* SE-12(2), February 1986.

[Booch 87]   G. E. Booch. *Software Components with Ada.*   Benjamin/Cummings, Menlo Park, CA, 1987.

[Brinch-Hansen 73] P. Brinch-Hansen.   *Concurrent Programming Concepts.*   Computing Surveys 5(4): 224-245, 1973.

[Brosgol 89]   B. Brosgol. "Is Ada Object-Oriented?" *ALSYS News.* Fall, 1989.

[Brosgol 92]   B. M. Brosgol, D. E. Emery and R. I. Eachus. "Decimal Arithmetic in Ada".   In *Proceedings of the Ada-Europe International Conference*, Amsterdam, June 1-5, 1992.

[Brosgol 93]   B. M. Brosgol. *Minutes of Special Meeting — Security & Safety Annex.* Unnumbered Ada 9X Project Document, 1993.

[Brown 81]   W. S. Brown. "A simple but realistic model of floating-point computation". *Transactions on Mathematical Software* 7(4): 445-480, December, 1981.

[Brygier 93]   J. Brygier and M. Richard-Foy. "Ada Run Time System Certification for Avionics Applications". In *Proceedings of the Ada-Europe International Conference.* June, 1993. Paris, France.

[Budd 91]   T. Budd. *An Introduction to Object-Oriented Programming.* Addison-Wesley, 1991.

[Burger 87]   T. M. Burger and K. W. Nielsen. "An Assessment of the Overhead Associated With Tasking Facilities and Tasking Paradigms in Ada". ACM SIGAda *Ada Letters* VII(1): 49-58, 1987.

[Burns 87]   A. Burns, A. M. Lister, and A. Wellings. *A Review of Ada Tasking.* Lecture Notes in Computer Science, Springer-Verlag, Berlin, 1987.

[Burns 89]   A. Burns and A. Wellings. *Real-Time Systems and their Programming Languages*. International Computer Science Series, Addison-Wesley, Reading, MA, 1989.

[Cardelli 85]   L. Cardelli and P. Wegner. "On Understanding Types, Data Abstraction, and Polymorphism". *ACM Computing Surveys* 17(4): 471-522, December 1985.

[Carré 88]   B. A. Carré and T. J. Jennings. *SPARK — The SPADE Ada Kernel*. Technical Report, University of Southampton, March, 1988.

[CD 93]   *Ada 9X Reference Manual, Version 4.0 (Committee Draft)*. Intermetrics Inc, 1993.

[Coffman 73]   Coffman and Denning. *Operating Systems Theory*. Prentice-Hall, Englewood Cliffs, New Jersey, 1973.

[Cohen 90]   S. Cohen. *Ada Support for Software Reuse*. Technical Report SEI-90-SR-16, Software Engineering Institute, October 1990.

[Cullyer 91]   W. J. Cullyer, S. J. Goodenough and B. A. Wichmann. "The Choice of Computer Languages in Safety-Critical Systems". *Software Engineering Journal* 6(2): 51-58, March, 1991.

[Dahl 72]   O-J. Dahl, E. W. Dijkstra, and C. A. R. Hoare. *Structured Programming*. Academic Press, London, 1972, p111.

[Dewar 90a]   R. B. K. Dewar. *Shared Variables and Ada 9X Issues*. Special Report SEI-90-SR-1, Software Engineering Institute, January 1990.

[Dewar 90b]   R. B. K. Dewar. *The Fixed-Point Facility in Ada*. Technical Report Special Report SEI-90-SR-2, Software Engineering Institute, Pittsburgh, PA, February, 1990.

[Dijkstra 72]   E. W. Dijkstra. "Notes on Structured Programming". In O-J. Dahl, E. W. Dijkstra, and C. A. R. Hoare. *Structured Programming*. Academic Press, London, 1972.

[DIS 94]   *Ada 9X Reference Manual, Version 5.0 (Draft International Standard)*. Intermetrics Inc, 1994.

[DO-178B]   Issued in the USA by the Requirements and Technical Concepts for Aviation (document RTCA SC167/D0-178B) and in Europe by the European Organization for Civil Aviation Electronics (EUROCAE document ED-12B).

[DoD 78]   Defense Advanced Research Projects Agency. *Department of Defense Requirements for High Order Computer Programming Languages — STEELMAN*. USDoD, Arlington, Virginia, 1978.

[DoD 85]   *Trusted Computer Systems Evaluation Criteria*. DOD 5200.28-STD edition, Department of Defense, 1985. [DoD 92] Formal Studies of Ada 9X, Formal Definition Report Ada 9X Project Report edition, Department of Defense, 1992.

[DoD 88]   *Ada Board's Recommended Ada 9X Strategy*. Office of the Under Secretary of Defense for Acquisition, Washington, D.C., 1988.

[DoD 89a]   *Ada 9X Project Plan*. Office of the Under Secretary of Defense for Acquisition, Washington, D.C., 1989.

[DoD 89b]   *Common Ada Programming Support Environment (APSE) Interface Set (CAIS) (Revision A) edition*. MIL-STD-1838A. United States Department of Defense, 1989.

[DoD 90]   *Ada 9X Requirements*. Office of the Under Secretary of Defense for Acquisition, Washington, D.C., 1990.

[DoD 91]   *Ada 9X Requirements Rationale*. Office of the Under Secretary of Defense for Acquisition, Washington, D.C., 1991.

[DoD 92]   *Formal Studies of Ada 9X*, Formal Definition Report. Ada 9X Project Report edition, Department of Defense, 1992.

[Dritz 91a]   K. W. Dritz. "Rationale for the Proposed Standard for a Generic Package of Elementary Functions for Ada". ACM SIGAda *Ada Letters* XI(7): 47-65, Fall, 1991.

[Dritz 91b]   K. W. Dritz. "Rationale for the Proposed Standard for a Generic Package of Primitive Functions for Ada". ACM SIGAda *Ada Letters* XI(7): 82-90, Fall, 1991.

[Eachus 92]   Personal communication from Robert Eachus, 1992.

[Ellis 90]   M. A. Ellis and B. Stroustrup. *The Annotated C++ Reference Manual*. Addison-Wesley, Reading, MA, 1990.

[Elrad 88]   T. Elrad. "Comprehensive Scheduling Controls for Ada Tasking". In *Proceedings of the Second International Workshop on Real-Time Ada Issues*, pages 12-19. Ada UK and United States Air Force Office of Scientific Research, Association for Computing Machinery, New York, NY, June 1988. Appeared in ACM SIGAda *Ada Letters*, VIII(7).

[Elsom 91]   K. C. Elsom. *Grow: an APSE Stress Tensor*. DRA Maritime Division, Portsmouth, 1991.

[Emery 91]   Personal communication from David Emery, 1991.

[Fowler 89]   K. J. Fowler. *A Study of Implementation-Dependent Pragmas and Attributes in Ada*. Technical Report Ada 9X Project Report, Software Engineering Institute, November 1989.

[Goldberg 83]   A. Goldberg and D. Robson. *Smalltalk-80: The Language and its Implementation*. Addison-Wesley, Reading, MA, 1983.

[Guimaraes 91] N. Guimaraes. "Building Generic User Interface Tools: An Experience with Multiple Inheritance". In *Proceedings of the Conference on Object-Oriented Programming Systems, Languages, and Applications*, 1991.

[Guttag 77]   J. Guttag. "Abstract Data Types and the Development of Data Structures". *Communications of the ACM* 20(6): 396-404, June 1977.

[Hilfinger 90]   P. N. Hilfinger. *Implementing Ada Fixed-point Types Having Arbitrary Scales.* Technical Report Report No. UCB/CSD 90/#582, University of California, Berkeley, CA, June, 1990.

[Hilzer 92]   R. C. Hilzer. "Synchronization of the Producer/Consumer Problem using Semaphores, Monitors, and the Ada Rendezvous". *ACM Operating Systems Review,* 26(3), July 1992.

[Hoare 73]   C. A. R. Hoare. "Towards a Theory of Parallel Programming". In C.A.R. Hoare and R.H. Perrott (editor), *Operating Systems Techniques.* Academic Press, New York, 1973.

[Hoare 74]   C. A. R. Hoare. "Monitors — An Operating Systems Structuring Concept". *Communications of the ACM* 17(10), pp 549-557, October 1974.

[Hoare 78]   C. A. R. Hoare. "Communicating Sequential Processes". *Communications of the ACM* 21(8): 666-677, August 1978.

[IBFW 86]   J. D. Ichbiah, J. G. P. Barnes, R. J. Firth, and M. Woodger. *Rationale for the Design of the Ada Programming Language.* Reprinted by Cambridge University Press, 1991.

[IEC 89]   *Binary Floating-Point Arithmetic for Microprocessor Systems.* IEC 559:1989 edition, IEC, 1989.

[IEC/SC65A 91]   *Software for Computers in the Application of Industrial Safety-Related Systems (Draft).* IEC/SC65A/(Secretariat 122), 1991.

[IEEE 87]   *Standard for Radix-Independent Floating-Point Arithmetic.* ANSI/IEEE Std. 854-1987 edition, 1987.

[IEEE 92]   *POSIX Ada Language Interfaces — Part 1: Binding for System Application Program Interface.* Std 1003.5, IEEE, New York, 1992.

[Ingalls 86]   D. H. H. Ingalls. "A Simple Technique for Handling Multiple Polymorphism". In *ACM OOPSLA'86 Conference Proceedings,* 1986.

[ISO 87]   International Standards Organization. *Reference Manual for the Ada Programming Language.* ISO/8652-1987, 1987.

[ISO 90]   International Standards Organization. *Memorandum of Understanding between the Ada 9X Project Office and ISO-IEC/JTC 1/SC 22/WG 9 Ada.* ISO-IEC/JTC 1/SC 22 N844, 1990.

[ISO 91]   International Standards Organization. *Generic Package of Elementary Functions for Ada.* ISO/JTC 1 DIS 11430.

[ISO 92]   *Database Language SQL.* Document ISO/IEC 9075:1992 edition, International Organization for Standardization (ISO), 1992.

[ISO 93]   *Information Technology—Language Independent Arithmetic— Part 1:*
                  Integer and Floating Point Arithmetic. DIS 10967-1:1993 edition,
                  ISO/IEC, 1993.

[ISO 94a]   International Standards Organization. *Generic Package of Elementary*
                  Functions for Ada. ISO-IEC/JTC 1 11430:1994.

[ISO 94b]   International Standards Organization. *Generic Package of Primitive*
                  Functions for Ada. ISO-IEC/JTC 1 11729:1994.

[ISO 95]   International Standards Organization. *Reference Manual for the Ada*
                  Programming Language. ISO/8652-1995, 1995.

[ISO WG9 93]   AI 00866/03, *The Latin-1 character set is used in source code and literals.*
                  ISO/IEC JTC1/SC22 WG9 Ada, June, 1993.

[ITSEC 91]   *Information Technology Security Evaluation Criteria.* Version 1.2 edition,
                  Provisional Harmonised Criteria, 1991. UK contact point: CESG Room
                  2/0805, Fiddlers Green Lane, Cheltenham, Glos, GL52 5AJ.

[Kahan 87]   W. Kahan. "Branch Cuts for Complex Elementary Functions, or Much Ado
                  About Nothing's Sign Bit". In *The State of the Art in Numerical Analysis.*
                  Clarendon Press, 1987, Chapter 7.

[Kahan 91]   W. Kahan and J. W. Thomas. *Augmenting a Programming Language with*
                  Complex Arithmetic. Technical Report UCB/CSD 91/667, Univ. of Calif. at
                  Berkeley, December, 1991.

[Klein 93]   M. H. Klein, T. Ralya, B. Pollak, R. Obenza, and M. G. Harbour. *A*
                  Practitioner's Handbook for Real-Time Analysis: Guide to Rate Monotonic
                  Analysis for Real-Time Systems. Klewer Academic Publishers, 1993.

[Knuth 81]   D. E. Knuth. *The Art of Computer Programming. Volume 2: Semi-*
                  numerical Algorithms. Addison-Wesley, 1981.

[LaLonde 89]   W. R. LaLonde. "Designing Families of Data Types using Exemplars".
                  ACM Transactions on Programming Languages and Systems 11(2), April
                  1989.

[L'Ecuyer 88]   P. L'Ecuyer. "Efficient and Portable Combined Random Number
                  Generators". *Communications of the ACM* 31(6):742-749, 774; 1988.

[Lehoczky 86]   J. P. Lehoczky and L. Sha. "Performance of Real-Time Bus Scheduling
                  Algorithms". *ACM Performance Evaluation Review*, Special Issue 14(1):
                  44-53, May, 1986.

[Lewis 69]   P. A. Lewis, A. S. Goodman, and J. M. Miller. " Pseudo-Random Number
                  Generator for the System/360" *IBM System Journal* 8(2):136-146, 1969.

[Liskov 77]   B. Liskov, A. Snyder, R. Atkinson, and C. Schaffert. "Abstraction
                  Mechanisms in CLU". *Communications of the ACM* 20(8): 564-576,
                  August 1977.

[Marsaglia 91]   G. Marsaglia and A. Zaman. "A New Class of Random Number Gener-
                        ators". *Annals of Applied Probability* 1(3):462-480, 1991.

[Meyer 88]   B. Meyer.   *Object-Oriented Software Construction*.   Prentice Hall,
                        Englewood Cliffs, NJ, 1988.

[MoD 91]   *The Procurement of Safety Critical Software in Defence Equipment (Part 1:
                        Requirements; Part 2: Guidance)*. Interim Defence Standard 00-55 edition,
                        Ministry of Defence, 1991.

[Nelson 91]   G. Nelson (ed). *Systems Programming with Modula-3*. Prentice Hall,
                        Englewood Cliffs, NJ, 1991.

[Pavey 93]   D. J. Pavey and L. A. Winsborrow. "Demonstrating Equivalence of Source
                        Code and PROM Contents". *Computer Journal* 36(7): 654-667, 1993.

[Plauger 92]   P. J. Plauger. *The Standard C Library*. Prentice Hall, Englewood Cliffs NJ,
                        1992.

[Rex 88]   *MALPAS User Guide* Release 4.1, RTP/4009/UG, Issue 3 edition, Rex,
                        Thompson and Partners Ltd., 1988.

[RM83]   See [ANSI 83].

[RM95]   See [ISO 95].

[Sales 92]   R. Sales. *Currency Sign Enhancements*. Technical Report X3J4/WR-684,
                        ANSI X3J4, 1992. COBOL Full Revision Working Paper.

[Schaeffer 93]   C. F. Schaeffer and G. N. Bundy. "Static Analysis of Exception Handling
                        in Ada". *Software Practice & Experience* 23(10):1157-1174, 1993.

[Schaffert 86]   C. Schaffert, T. Cooper, B. Bullis, M. Kilian, and C. Wilpolt.   *An*
                        "Introduction to Trellis/Owl". In *ACM OOPSLA'86 Proceedings*. Portland,
                        OR, 1986.

[Seidewitz 91]   E. Seidewitz. "Object-Oriented Programming Through Type Extension in
                        Ada 9X". ACM SIGAda *Ada Letters* XI(2), March/April 1991.

[Sha 90a]   L. Sha, and J. B. Goodenough. "Real-Time Scheduling Theory and Ada".
                        IEEE Computer 23(4): 53-62, April, 1990.

[Sha 90b]   L. Sha, R. Rajkumar, and J. P. Lehoczky. "Priority Inheritance Protocols —
                        An Approach to Real-Time Synchronization". *IEEE Transactions on
                        Computers* C-39(9), September, 1990.

[Stroustrup 91]   B. Stroustrup. *The C++ Programming Language, 2nd Ed*. Addison-
                        Wesley, Reading, MA, 1991.

[Taft 93]   S. Tucker Taft. "Ada 9X: From Abstraction-Oriented to Object-Oriented".
                        In *ACM OOPSLA'93 Conference Proceedings*, 1993.

[Tang 91]   P. T. P. Tang. "A Portable Generic Elementary Function Package in Ada
                 and an Accurate Test Suite". ACM SIGAda *Ada Letters* XI(7): 180-216,
                 Fall, 1991.

[Taylor 95]   W. J. Taylor. *Ada 95 Compatibility Guide, Version 6.0.* Transition
                 Technology, January 1995.

[Wellings 84]   A. J. Wellings, D. Keeffe, and G. M. Tomlinson. "A Problem with Ada and
                 Resource Allocation". ACM SIGAda *Ada Letters* III(4): 112-123, 1984.

[Wichmann 82]   B. A. Wichmann and I. D. Hill. "An Efficient and Portable Pseudo-Random
                 Number Generator". *Applied Statistics* 31:188-190, 1982.

[Wichmann 89]   B. A. Wichmann. *Insecurities in the Ada programming language.*
                 Technical Report DITC 137/89, NPL, January, 1989.

[Wichmann 92]   B. A. Wichmann. *Undefined scalars in Ada 9X.* March, 1992.

[Wichmann 93]   B. A. Wichmann. "Microprocessor design faults". *Microprocessors and
                 Microsystems* 17(7):399-401, 1993.

[Wirth 77]   N. Wirth. "Modula: A Language for Modular Multiprogramming".
                 Software Practice & Experience, January 1977, pp 3-35.

[Wirth 88]   N. Wirth. "Type Extensions". *ACM Transactions on Programming
                 Languages and Systems* 10(2): 204-214, April 1988.

Index

The entries in this index refer to the section and not to the page number. In identifying an appropriate entry the reader is reminded that references into Chapter II (of part One) are likely to give a general introduction to a new feature, those into Chapter III (of part One) are likely to briefly summarize a feature in the context of the whole language, whereas those in Parts Two and Three (identified by chapters 1 to 13 and A to H respectively) will give further detail of specific aspects of a feature. Furthermore Appendix X concerns incompatibilities with Ada 83 and Appendix Y concerns changes since the Committee Draft and the Draft International Standard.

Springer
and the
environment

At Springer we firmly believe that an international science publisher has a special obligation to the environment, and our corporate policies consistently reflect this conviction.

We also expect our business partners – paper mills, printers, packaging manufacturers, etc. – to commit themselves to using materials and production processes that do not harm the environment. The paper in this book is made from low- or no-chlorine pulp and is acid free, in conformance with international standards for paper permanency.

Springer

Lecture Notes in Computer Science

For information about Vols. 1–1170

please contact your bookseller or Springer-Verlag

Lecture Notes in Computer Science

Ada 95 Rationale

Ada 95, the enhanced version of the Ada programming language, is now in place and has attracted much attention in the community since the International Standard ISO/IEC 8652:1995(E) for the language was approved in 1995. The new language standard is publicly available and also published in the Ada 95 Reference Manual. This Ada 95 Rationale is the companion to the reference manual and language standard; it introduces Ada 95 and its attractive new features and explains the rationale behind them.

The Ada 95 Rationale comes in four parts. The introductory part is a general discussion of the scope and objectives of Ada 95 and its major technical features. The second part contains a more detailed step by step account of the core language. The third part consists of several annexes addressing the predefined environment and specialized application areas. Finally, the three appendices of the fourth part are devoted to the upward compatibility with Ada 83, a few changes since the drafts of the standard were made public, and a summary of requirements.

The Ada 95 Rationale should be studied in parallel with the Ada 95 Reference Manual or the language standard document. It will be of special value for anybody dealing seriously with Ada in a professional, academic, or educational environment.